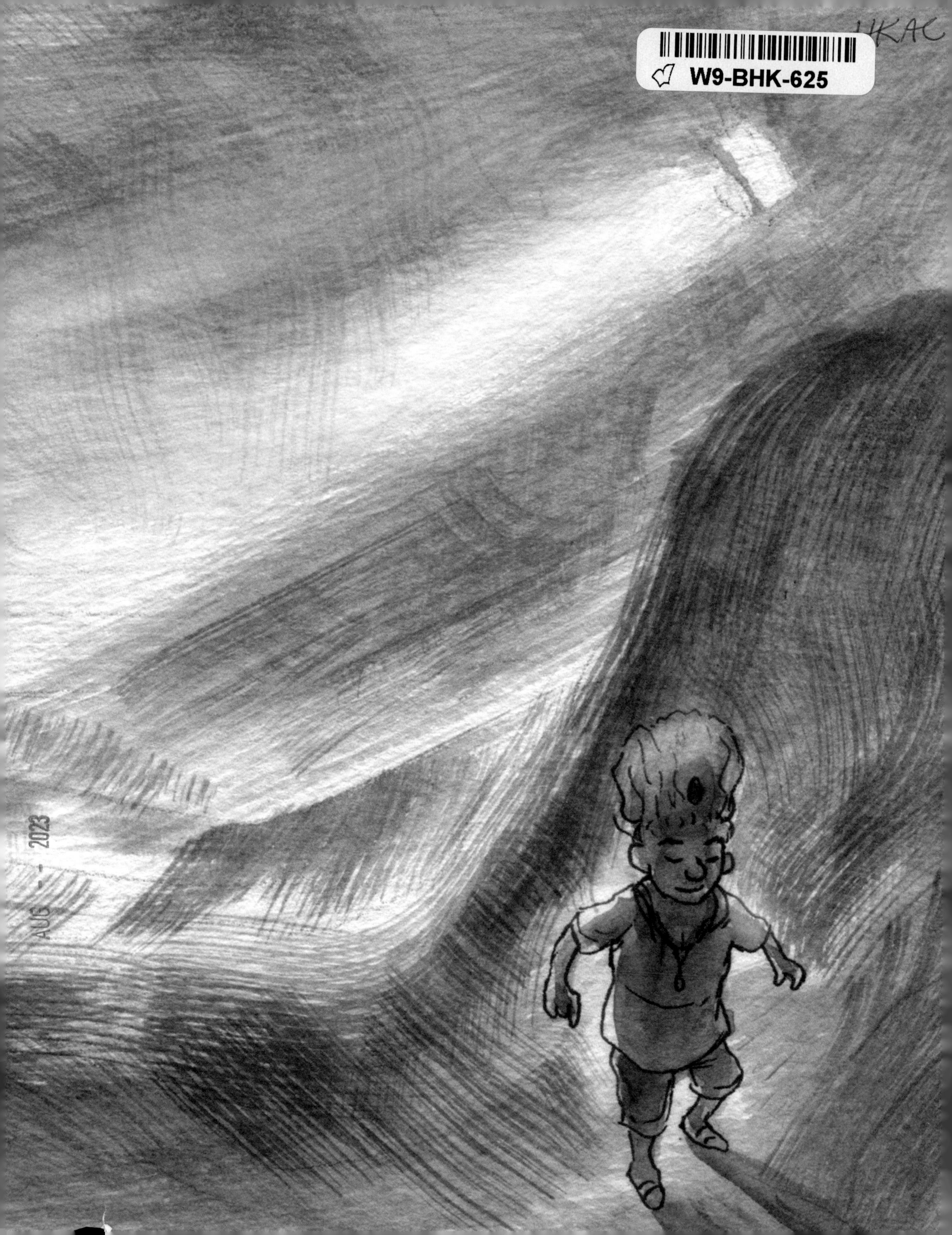

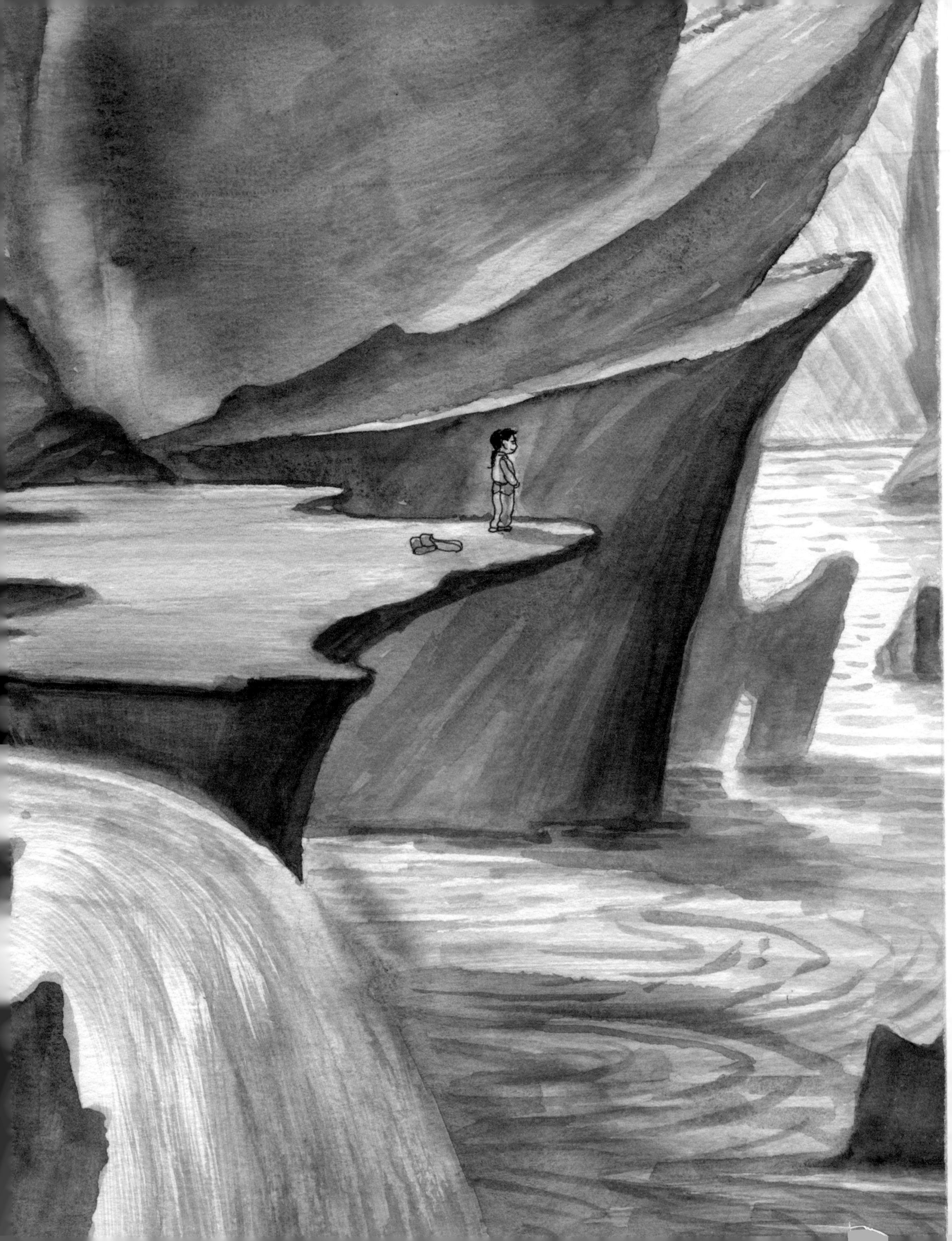

THE HEAVY BRIGHT

DESIGNER: KAYLA E.
EDITOR: CONRAD GROTH
PRODUCTION: PAUL BARESH AND C HWANG
PUBLICITY: JACQ COHEN
VP / ASSOCIATE PUBLISHER: ERIC REYNOLDS
PRESIDENT / PUBLISHER: GARY GROTH

FANTAGRAPHICS BOOKS, INC.
7563 LAKE CITY WAY NE
SEATTLE, WA 98115
WWW.FANTAGRAPHICS.COM
@FANTAGRAPHICS

ISBN: 978-1-68396-692-0
LIBRARY OF CONGRESS CONTROL NUMBER: 2022943282
FIRST FANTAGRAPHICS BOOKS EDITION: WINTER 2023
PRINTED IN CHINA

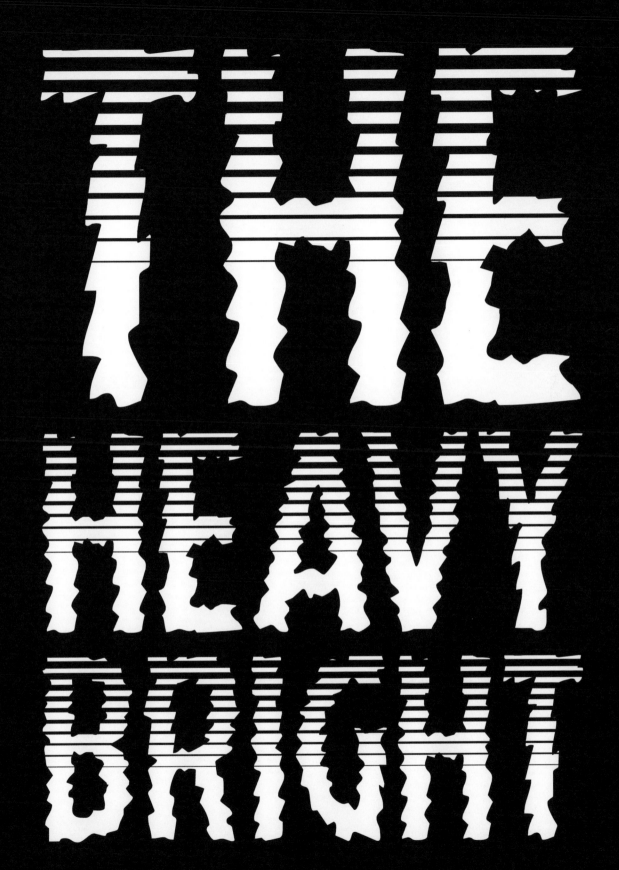

THE HEAVY BRIGHT

CATHY MALKASIAN

THIS BOOK IS DEDICATED TO
ANYONE WHO'S WILLING TO
READ IT MORE THAN ONCE!

PART ONE

THE HEAVY

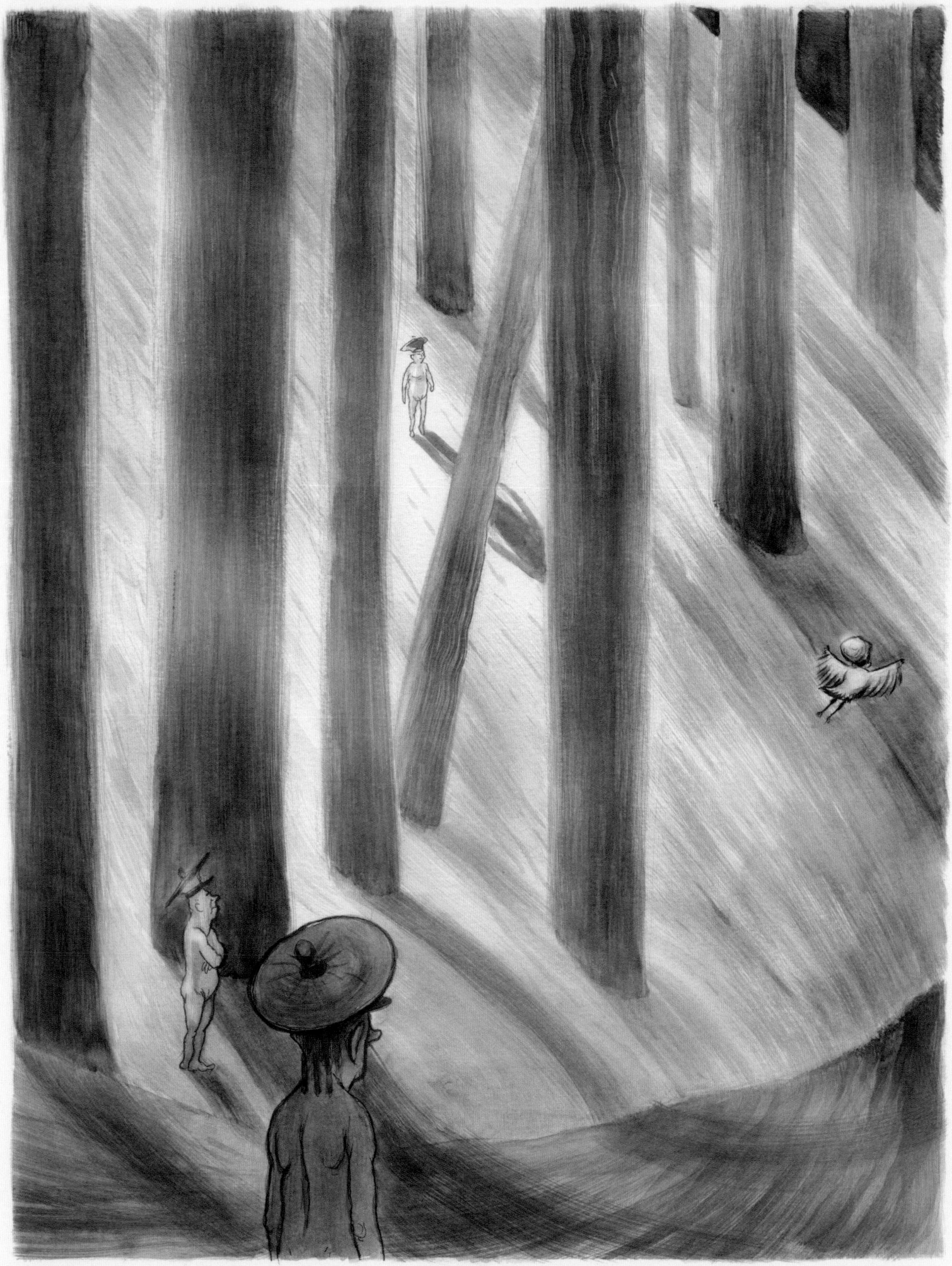

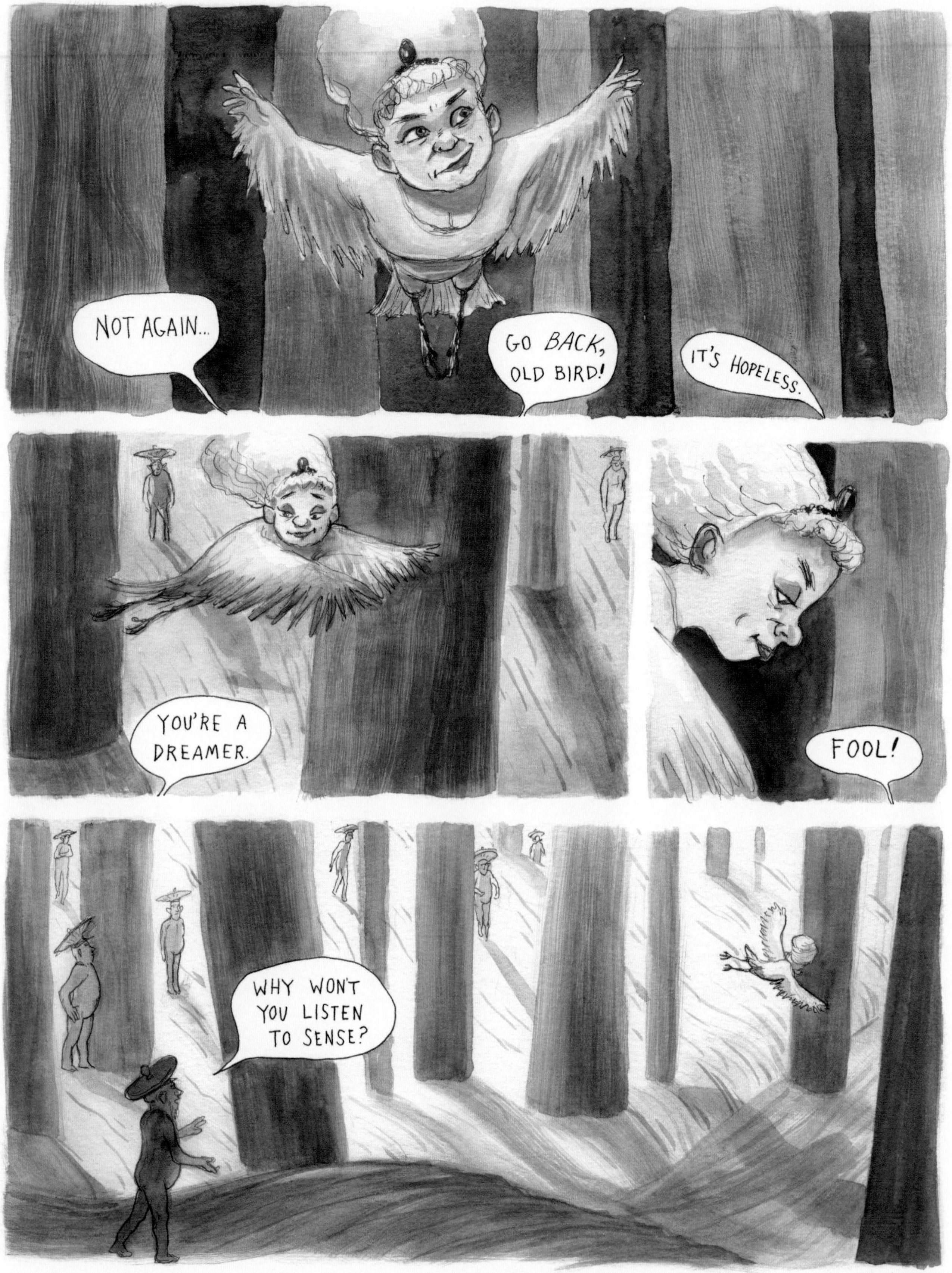
NOT AGAIN...
GO *BACK*, OLD BIRD!
IT'S HOPELESS.
YOU'RE A DREAMER.
FOOL!
WHY WON'T YOU LISTEN TO SENSE?

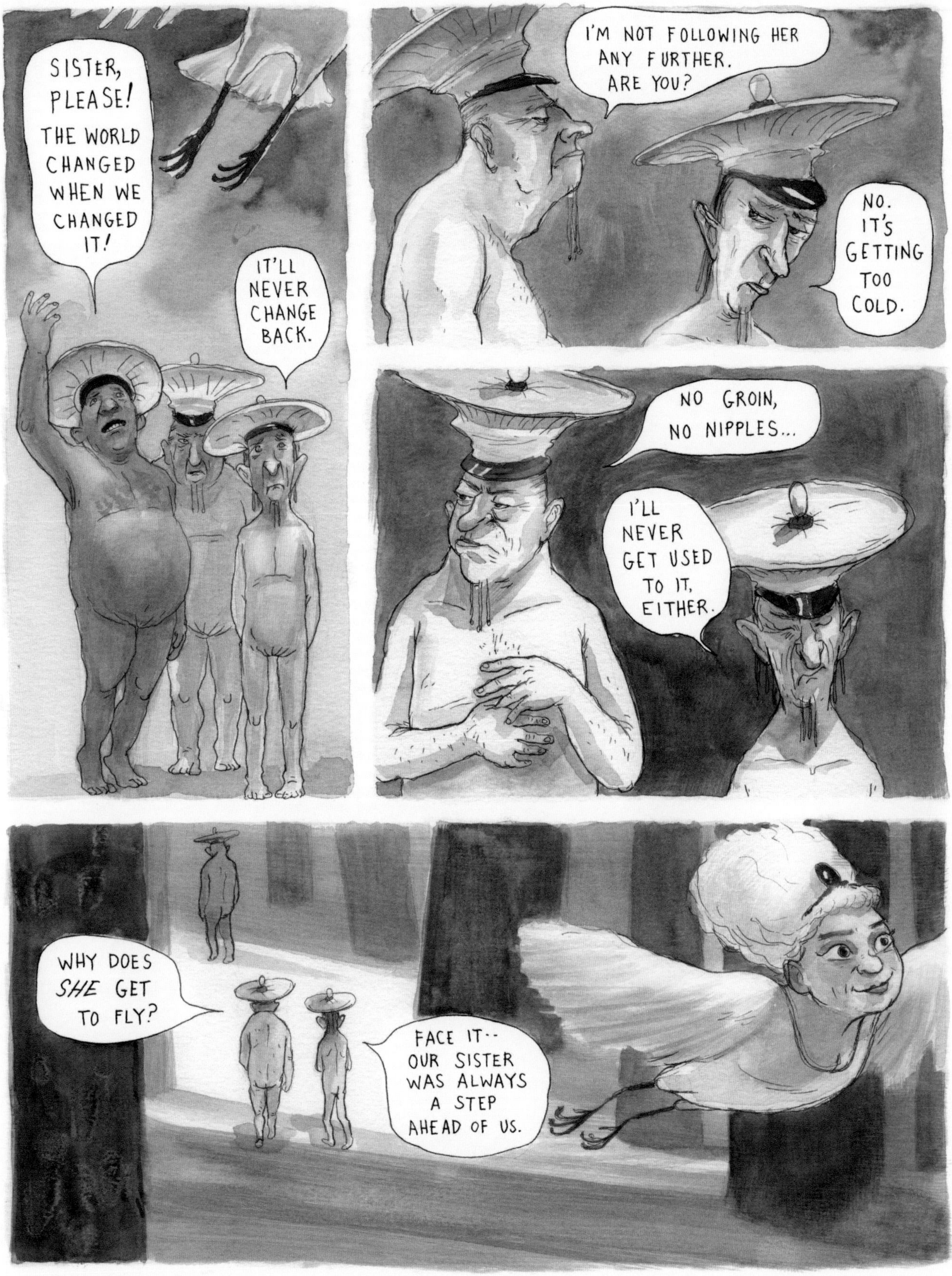
SISTER, PLEASE! THE WORLD CHANGED WHEN WE CHANGED IT!
IT'LL NEVER CHANGE BACK.
I'M NOT FOLLOWING HER ANY FURTHER. ARE YOU?
NO. IT'S GETTING TOO COLD.
NO GROIN, NO NIPPLES...
I'LL NEVER GET USED TO IT, EITHER.
WHY DOES *SHE* GET TO FLY?
FACE IT-- OUR SISTER WAS ALWAYS A STEP AHEAD OF US.

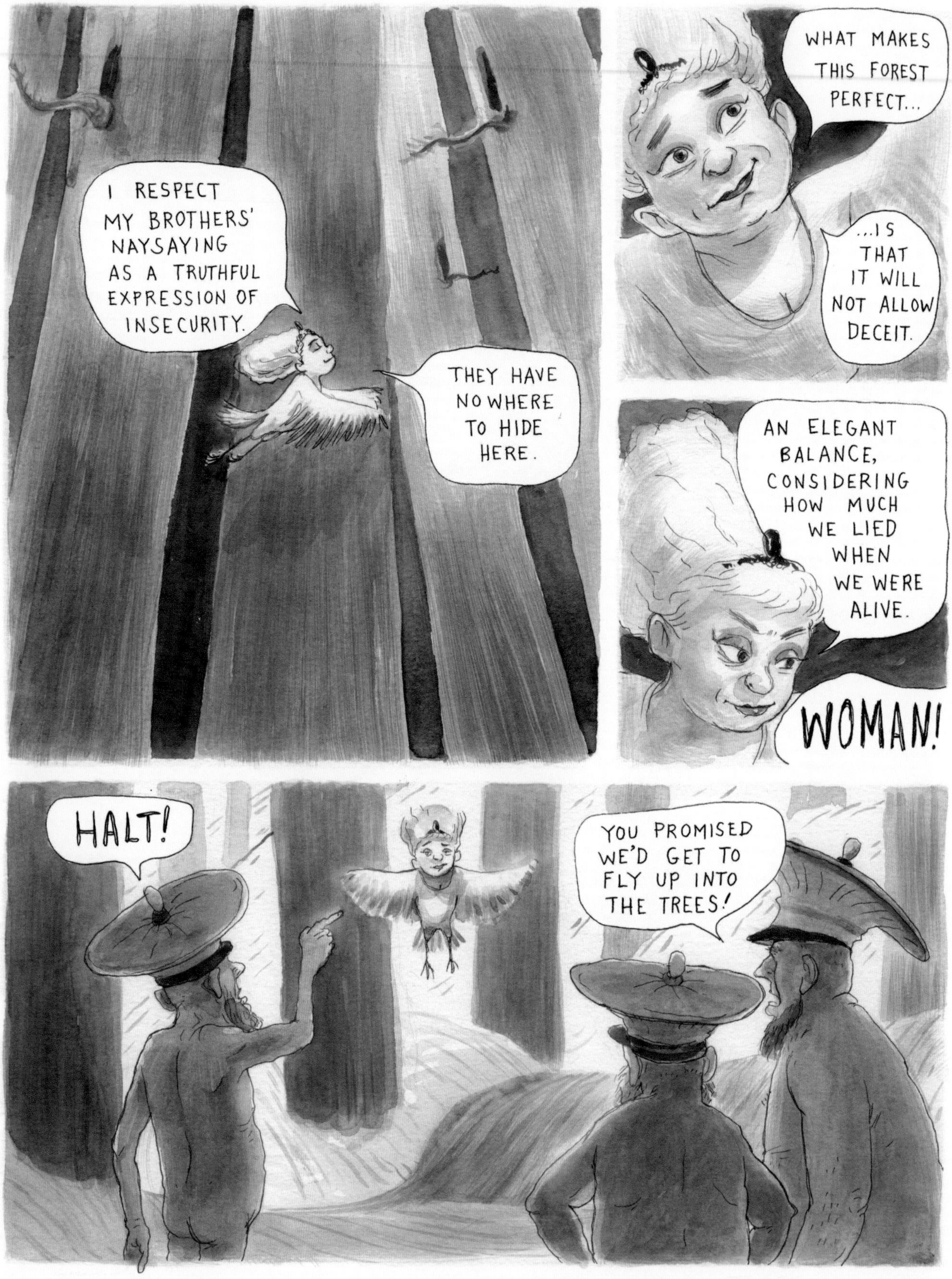
I RESPECT MY BROTHERS' NAYSAYING AS A TRUTHFUL EXPRESSION OF INSECURITY.
THEY HAVE NOWHERE TO HIDE HERE.
WHAT MAKES THIS FOREST PERFECT...
...IS THAT IT WILL NOT ALLOW DECEIT.
AN ELEGANT BALANCE, CONSIDERING HOW MUCH WE LIED WHEN WE WERE ALIVE.
WOMAN!
HALT!
YOU PROMISED WE'D GET TO FLY UP INTO THE TREES!

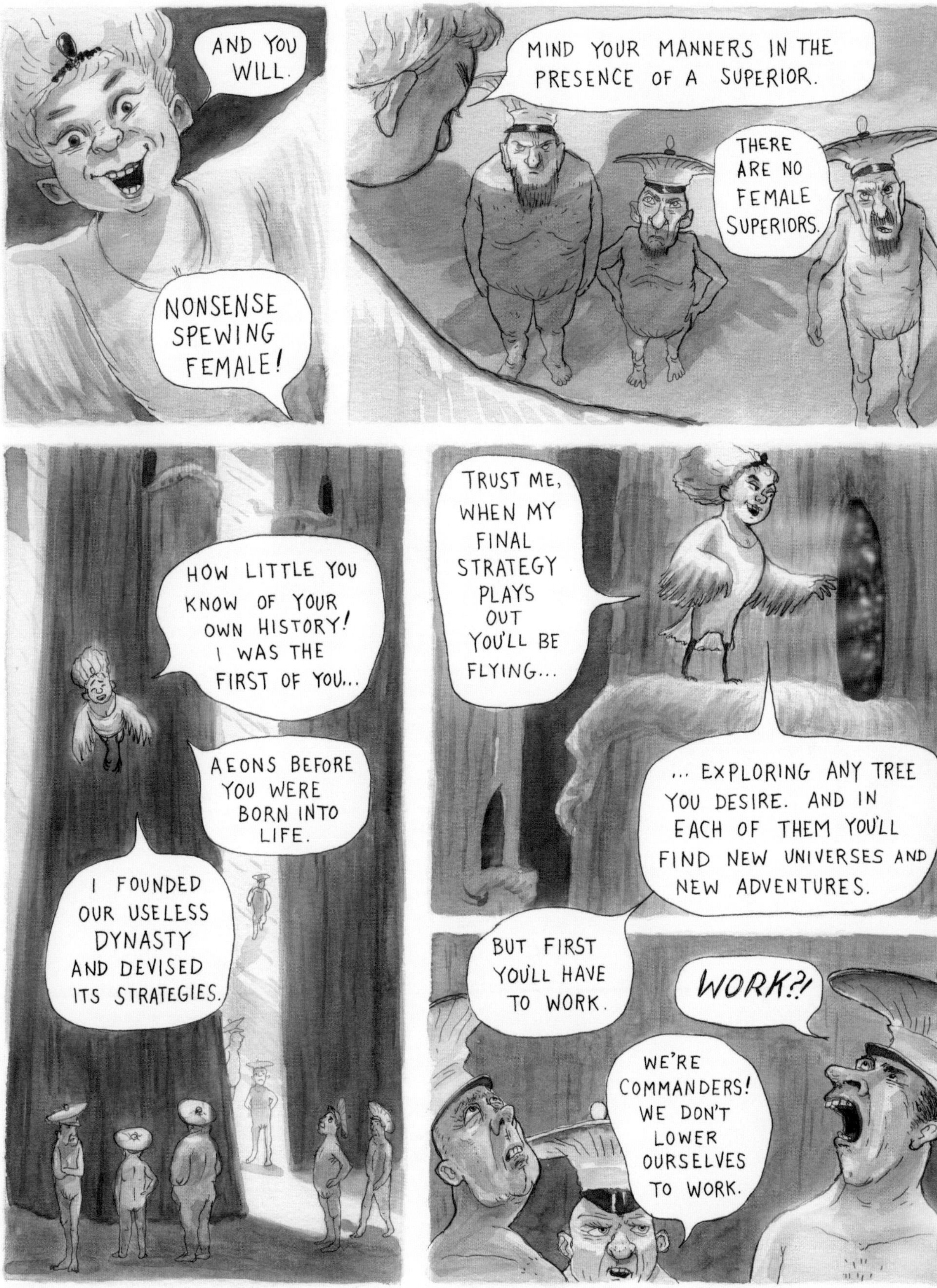
AND YOU WILL.
NONSENSE SPEWING FEMALE!
MIND YOUR MANNERS IN THE PRESENCE OF A SUPERIOR.
THERE ARE NO FEMALE SUPERIORS.
HOW LITTLE YOU KNOW OF YOUR OWN HISTORY! I WAS THE FIRST OF YOU...
AEONS BEFORE YOU WERE BORN INTO LIFE.
I FOUNDED OUR USELESS DYNASTY AND DEVISED ITS STRATEGIES.
TRUST ME, WHEN MY FINAL STRATEGY PLAYS OUT YOU'LL BE FLYING...
... EXPLORING ANY TREE YOU DESIRE. AND IN EACH OF THEM YOU'LL FIND NEW UNIVERSES AND NEW ADVENTURES.
BUT FIRST YOU'LL HAVE TO WORK.
WORK?!
WE'RE COMMANDERS! WE DON'T LOWER OURSELVES TO WORK.

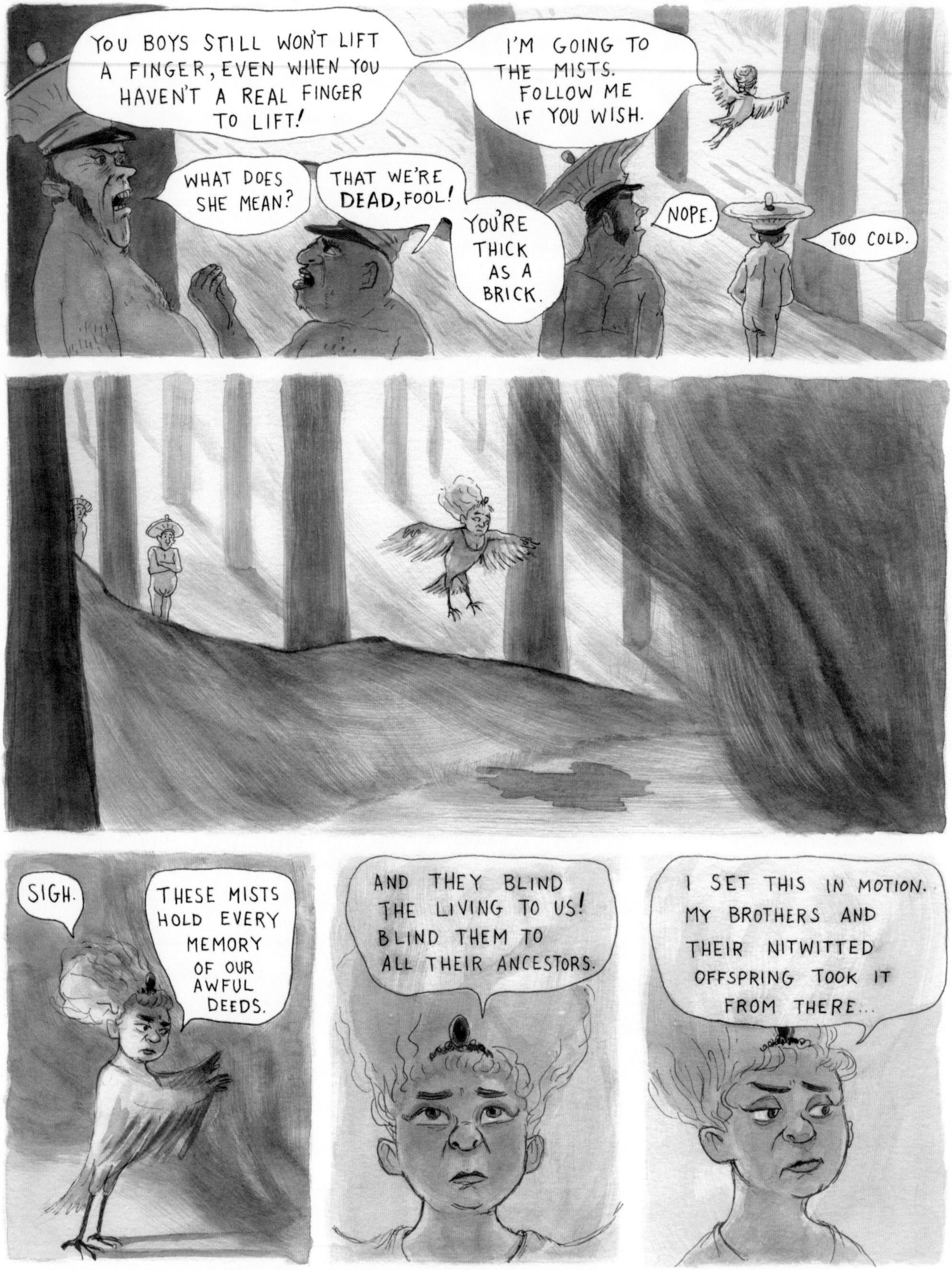
YOU BOYS STILL WON'T LIFT A FINGER, EVEN WHEN YOU HAVEN'T A REAL FINGER TO LIFT!
I'M GOING TO THE MISTS. FOLLOW ME IF YOU WISH.
WHAT DOES SHE MEAN?
THAT WE'RE **DEAD**, FOOL!
YOU'RE THICK AS A BRICK.
NOPE.
TOO COLD.
SIGH.
THESE MISTS HOLD EVERY MEMORY OF OUR AWFUL DEEDS.
AND THEY BLIND THE LIVING TO US! BLIND THEM TO ALL THEIR ANCESTORS.
I SET THIS IN MOTION. MY BROTHERS AND THEIR NITWITTED OFFSPRING TOOK IT FROM THERE...

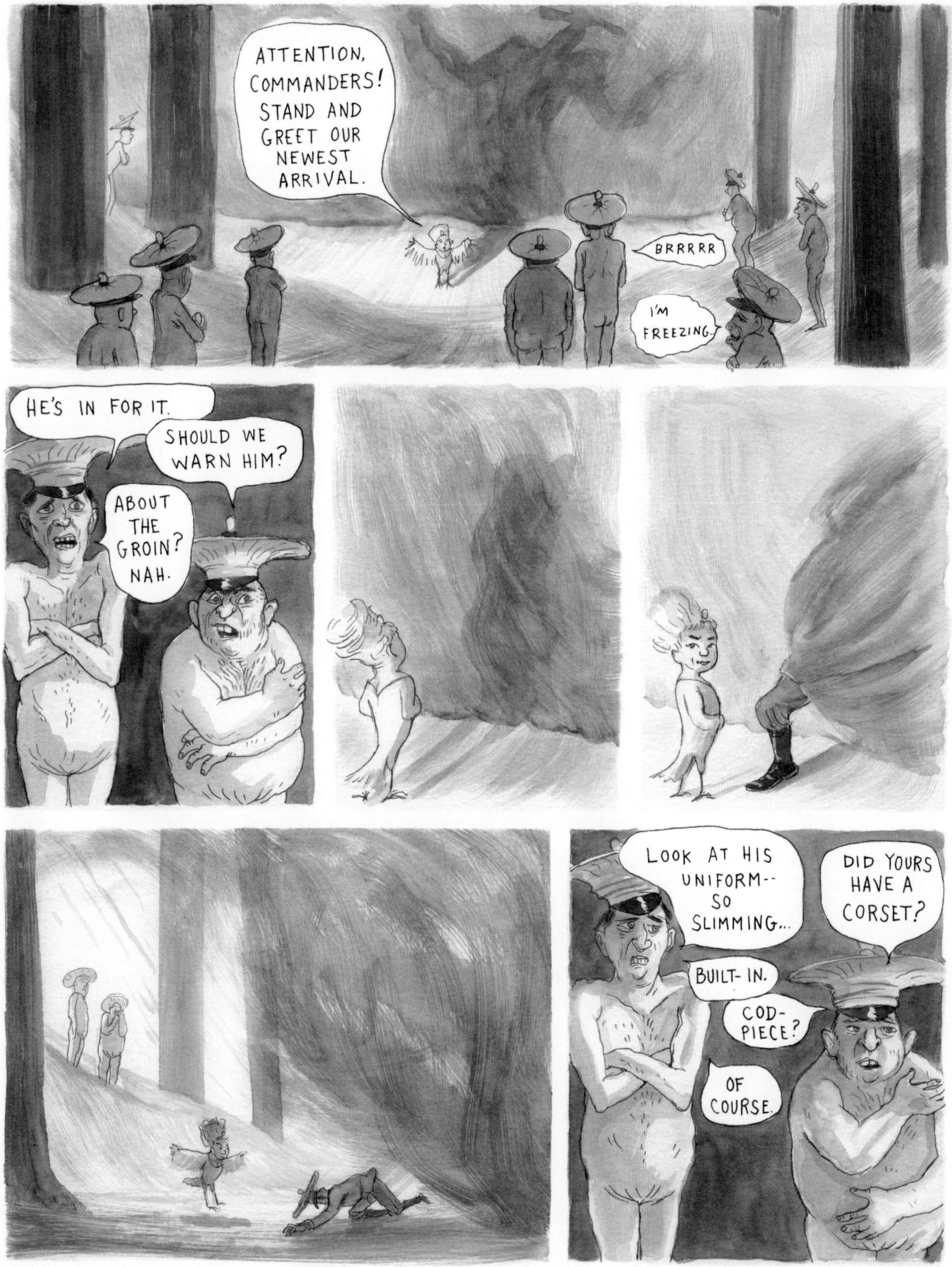
ATTENTION, COMMANDERS! STAND AND GREET OUR NEWEST ARRIVAL.
BRRRRR
I'M FREEZING.
HE'S IN FOR IT.
SHOULD WE WARN HIM?
ABOUT THE GROIN? NAH.
LOOK AT HIS UNIFORM-- SO SLIMMING...
DID YOURS HAVE A CORSET?
BUILT- IN.
COD-PIECE?
OF COURSE.

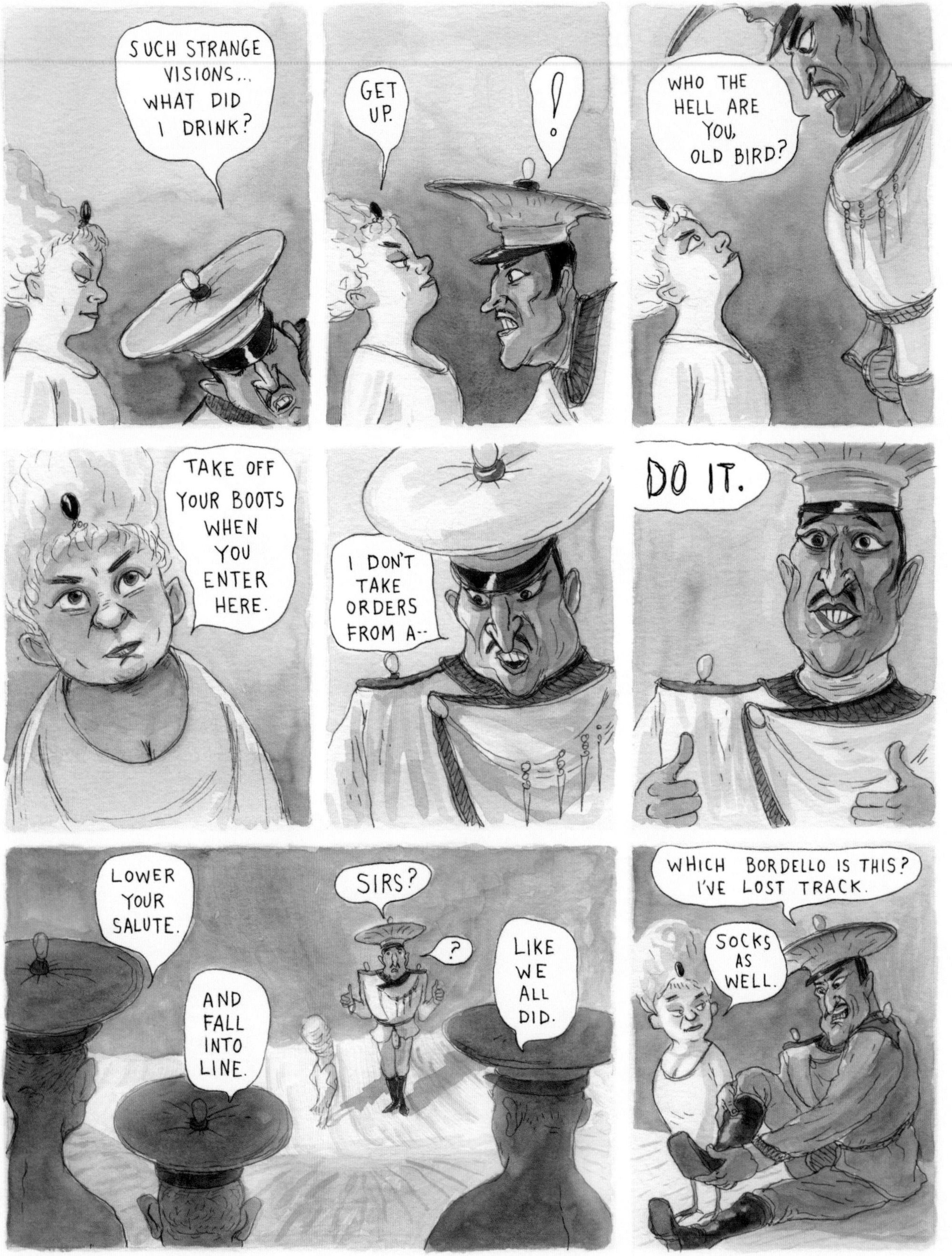
SUCH STRANGE VISIONS... WHAT DID I DRINK?
GET UP.
!
WHO THE HELL ARE YOU, OLD BIRD?
TAKE OFF YOUR BOOTS WHEN YOU ENTER HERE.
I DON'T TAKE ORDERS FROM A--
DO IT.
LOWER YOUR SALUTE.
AND FALL INTO LINE.
SIRS?
?
LIKE WE ALL DID.
WHICH BORDELLO IS THIS? I'VE LOST TRACK.
SOCKS AS WELL.

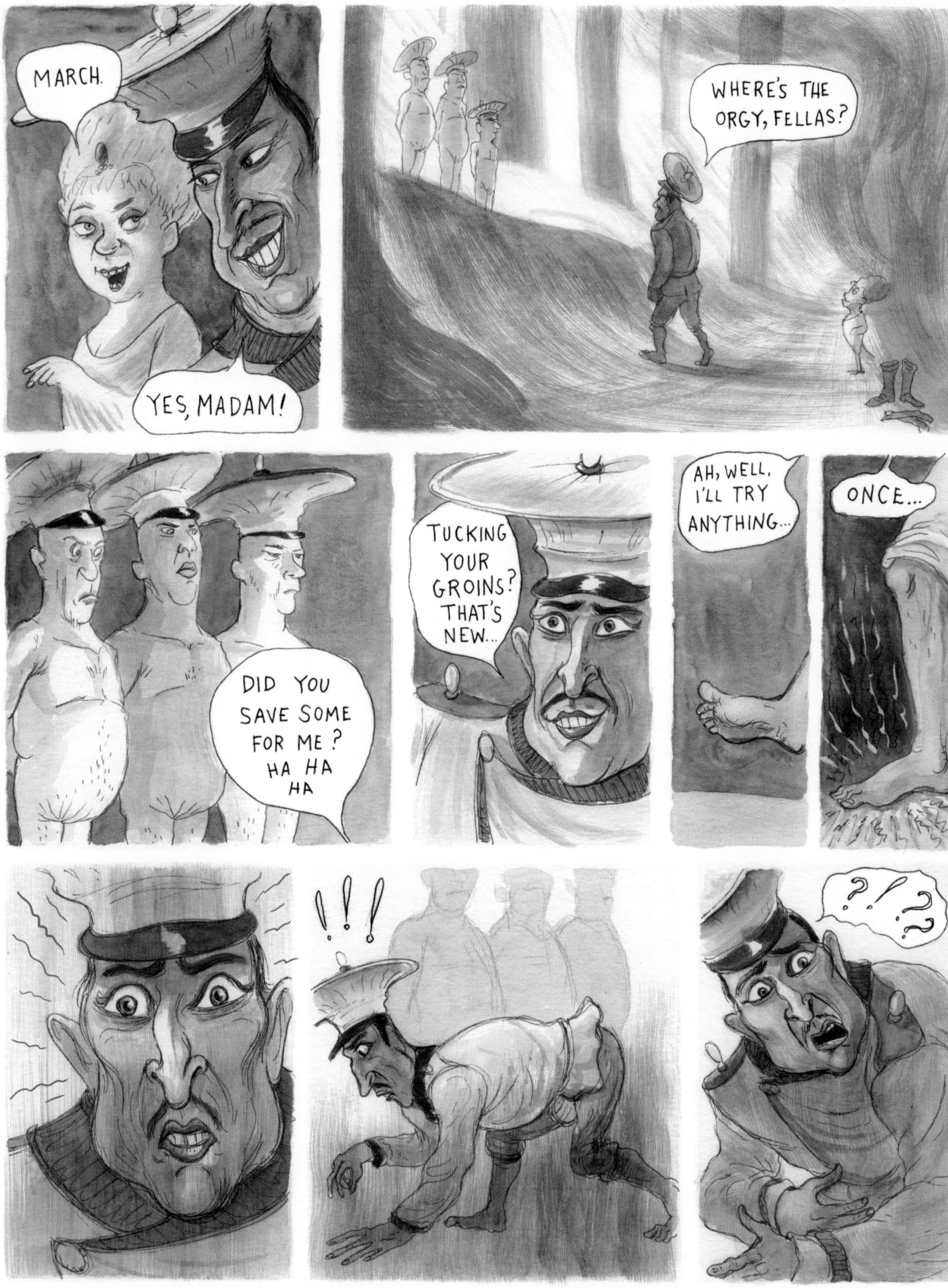
MARCH.
YES, MADAM!
WHERE'S THE ORGY, FELLAS?
DID YOU SAVE SOME FOR ME? HA HA HA
TUCKING YOUR GROINS? THAT'S NEW...
AH, WELL, I'LL TRY ANYTHING...
ONCE...
!!!
?!??

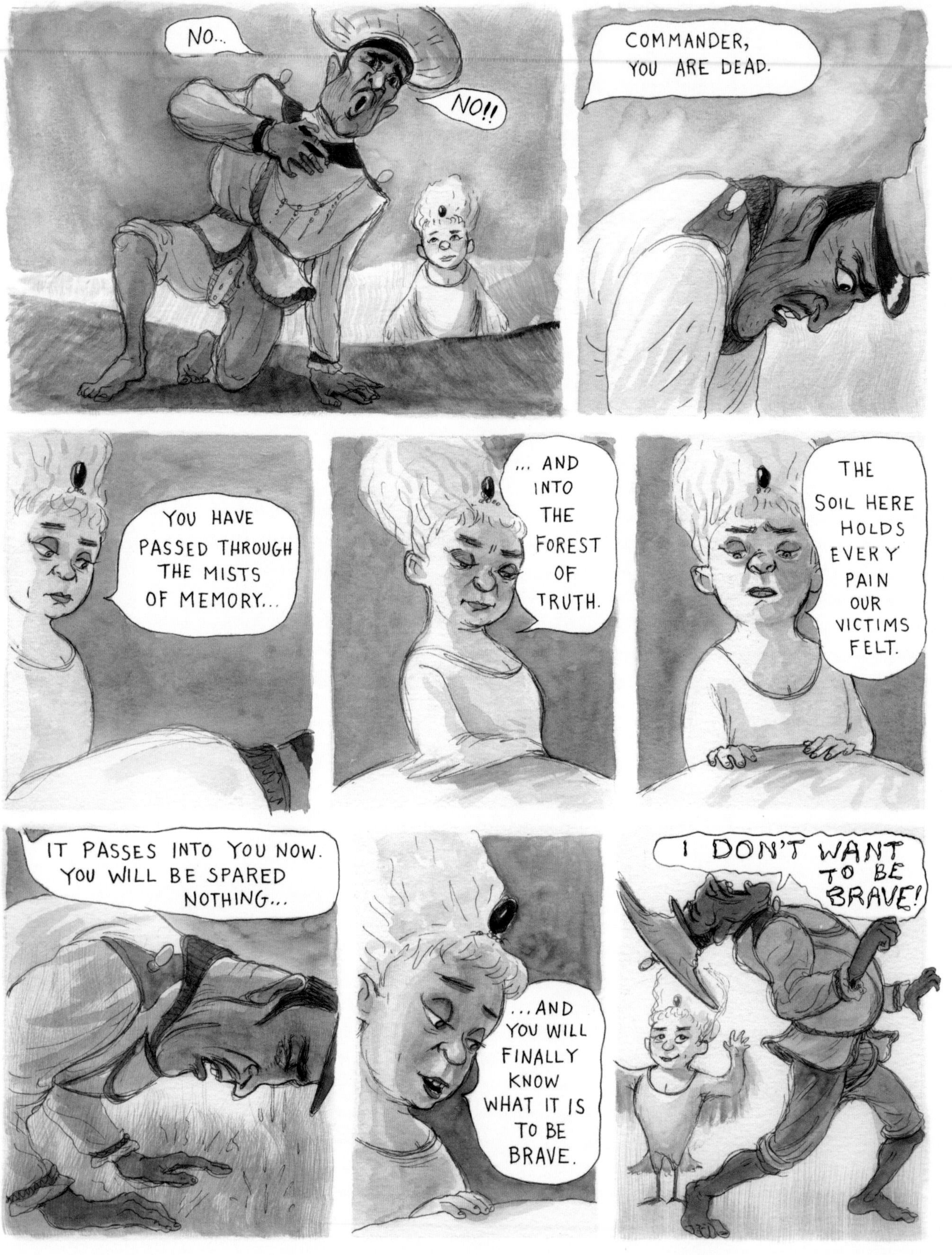
NO...
NO!!
COMMANDER, YOU ARE DEAD.
YOU HAVE PASSED THROUGH THE MISTS OF MEMORY...
... AND INTO THE FOREST OF TRUTH.
THE SOIL HERE HOLDS EVERY PAIN OUR VICTIMS FELT.
IT PASSES INTO YOU NOW. YOU WILL BE SPARED NOTHING...
...AND YOU WILL FINALLY KNOW WHAT IT IS TO BE BRAVE.
I DON'T WANT TO BE BRAVE!

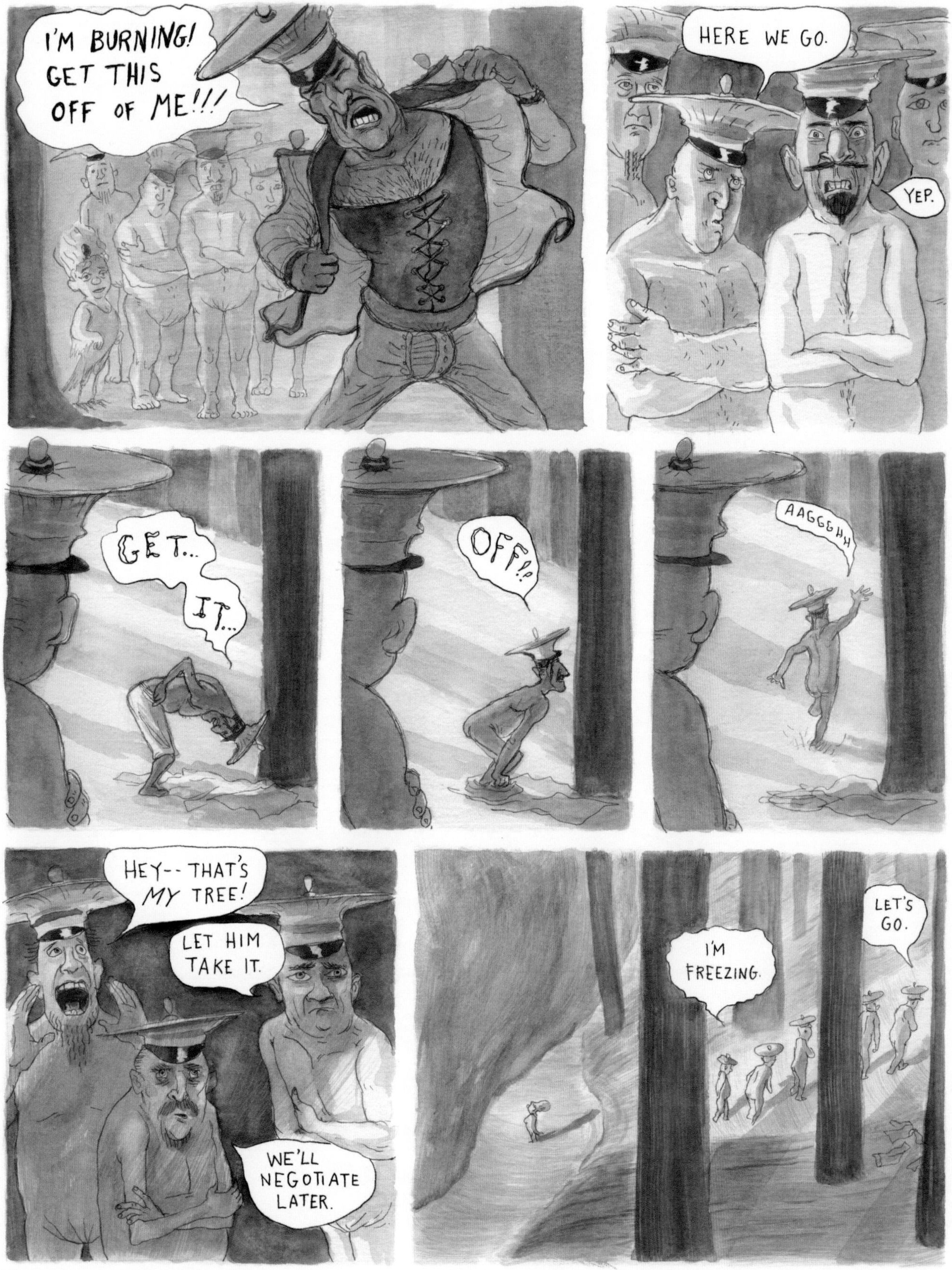
I'M BURNING! GET THIS OFF OF ME!!!
HERE WE GO.
YEP.
GET...
IT...
OFF!?!
AAGGGHH
HEY-- THAT'S MY TREE!
LET HIM TAKE IT.
WE'LL NEGOTIATE LATER.
LET'S GO.
I'M FREEZING.

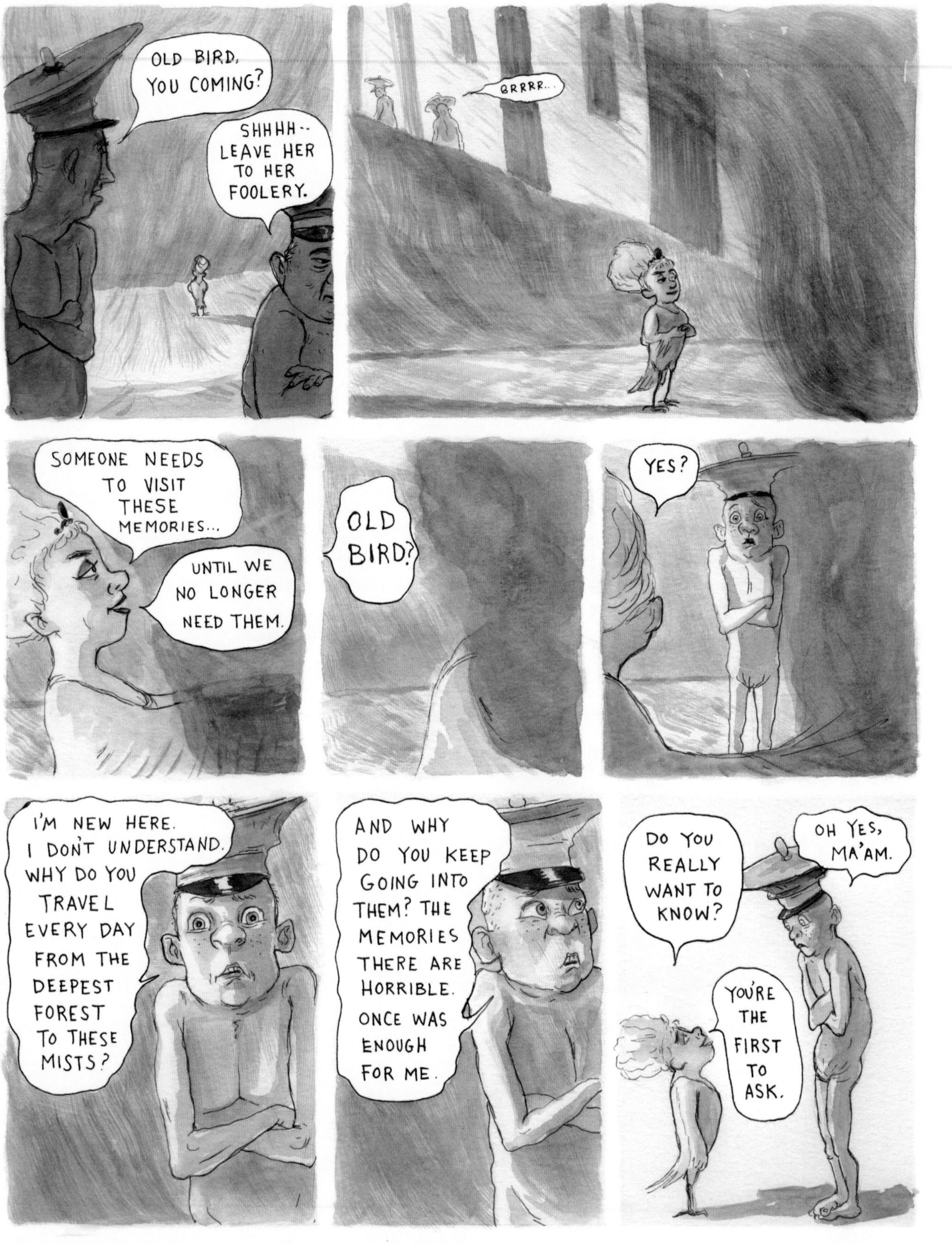
OLD BIRD, YOU COMING?
SHHHH-- LEAVE HER TO HER FOOLERY.
BRRRR...
SOMEONE NEEDS TO VISIT THESE MEMORIES...
UNTIL WE NO LONGER NEED THEM.
OLD BIRD?
YES?
I'M NEW HERE. I DON'T UNDERSTAND. WHY DO YOU TRAVEL EVERY DAY FROM THE DEEPEST FOREST TO THESE MISTS?
AND WHY DO YOU KEEP GOING INTO THEM? THE MEMORIES THERE ARE HORRIBLE. ONCE WAS ENOUGH FOR ME.
DO YOU REALLY WANT TO KNOW?
OH YES, MA'AM.
YOU'RE THE FIRST TO ASK.

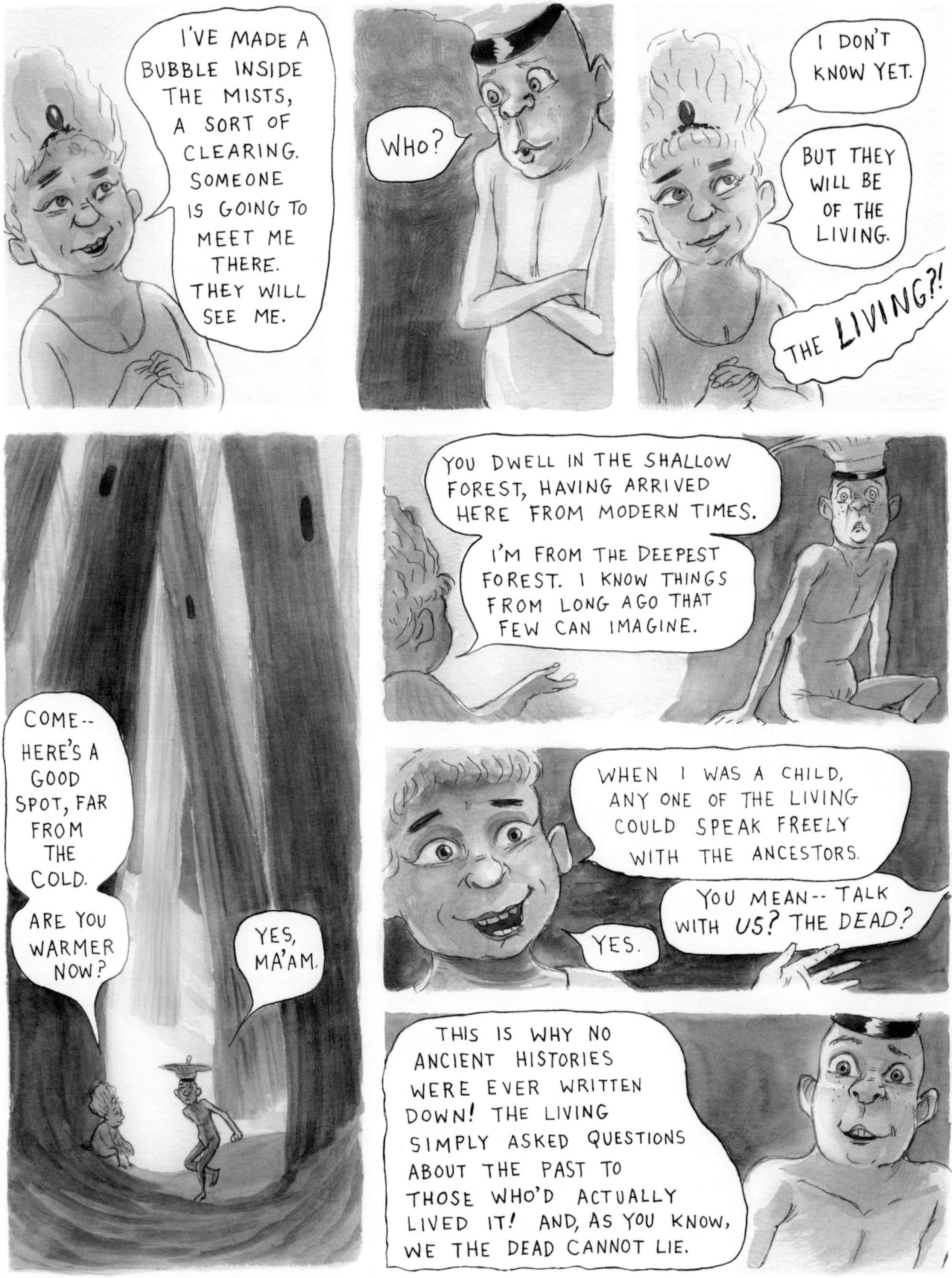
I'VE MADE A BUBBLE INSIDE THE MISTS, A SORT OF CLEARING. SOMEONE IS GOING TO MEET ME THERE. THEY WILL SEE ME.
WHO?
I DON'T KNOW YET.
BUT THEY WILL BE OF THE LIVING.
THE LIVING?!
COME-- HERE'S A GOOD SPOT, FAR FROM THE COLD.
ARE YOU WARMER NOW?
YES, MA'AM.
YOU DWELL IN THE SHALLOW FOREST, HAVING ARRIVED HERE FROM MODERN TIMES.
I'M FROM THE DEEPEST FOREST. I KNOW THINGS FROM LONG AGO THAT FEW CAN IMAGINE.
WHEN I WAS A CHILD, ANY ONE OF THE LIVING COULD SPEAK FREELY WITH THE ANCESTORS.
YOU MEAN-- TALK WITH US? THE DEAD?
YES.
THIS IS WHY NO ANCIENT HISTORIES WERE EVER WRITTEN DOWN! THE LIVING SIMPLY ASKED QUESTIONS ABOUT THE PAST TO THOSE WHO'D ACTUALLY LIVED IT! AND, AS YOU KNOW, WE THE DEAD CANNOT LIE.

WE MAY NOT KNOW EVERYTHING, BUT WE ARE EXPERTS IN THE LIVES WE ONCE LIVED.

WHEN I WAS A LIVING CHILD I VISITED WITH LONG-DEAD AUNTS AND UNCLES. THEY WOULD SING TO ME AS I GATHERED FIREWOOD.

MY PARENTS REGULARLY SOUGHT ADVICE ABOUT FIELDS, SEEDS, AND PLANTING TIMES FROM A GREAT, GREAT GRANDFATHER.

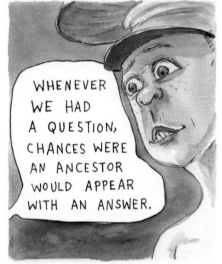

WHENEVER WE HAD A QUESTION, CHANCES WERE AN ANCESTOR WOULD APPEAR WITH AN ANSWER.

BUT IT WAS THEIR *PRESENCE*, THEIR HONESTY WHICH MATTERED MOST.

THEY REMINDED US THAT WE WERE JOINED TO A VAST AND DEEP CONTINUITY...

AND THAT OUR LIVES WERE A THING TO SAVOR.

WHEN WE NEEDED A DOSE OF TRUTH, WE WENT TO THEM. WHEN WE GREW TIRED OF THE TRUTH WE RETURNED TO OUR LIVES, AND THE COMFORT OF OUR BLUNDERS.

I... I BLUNDERED, MA'AM. PEOPLE DIED.

I BLUNDERED, TOO.

WHERE ARE THEY? THE PEOPLE WE KILLED?

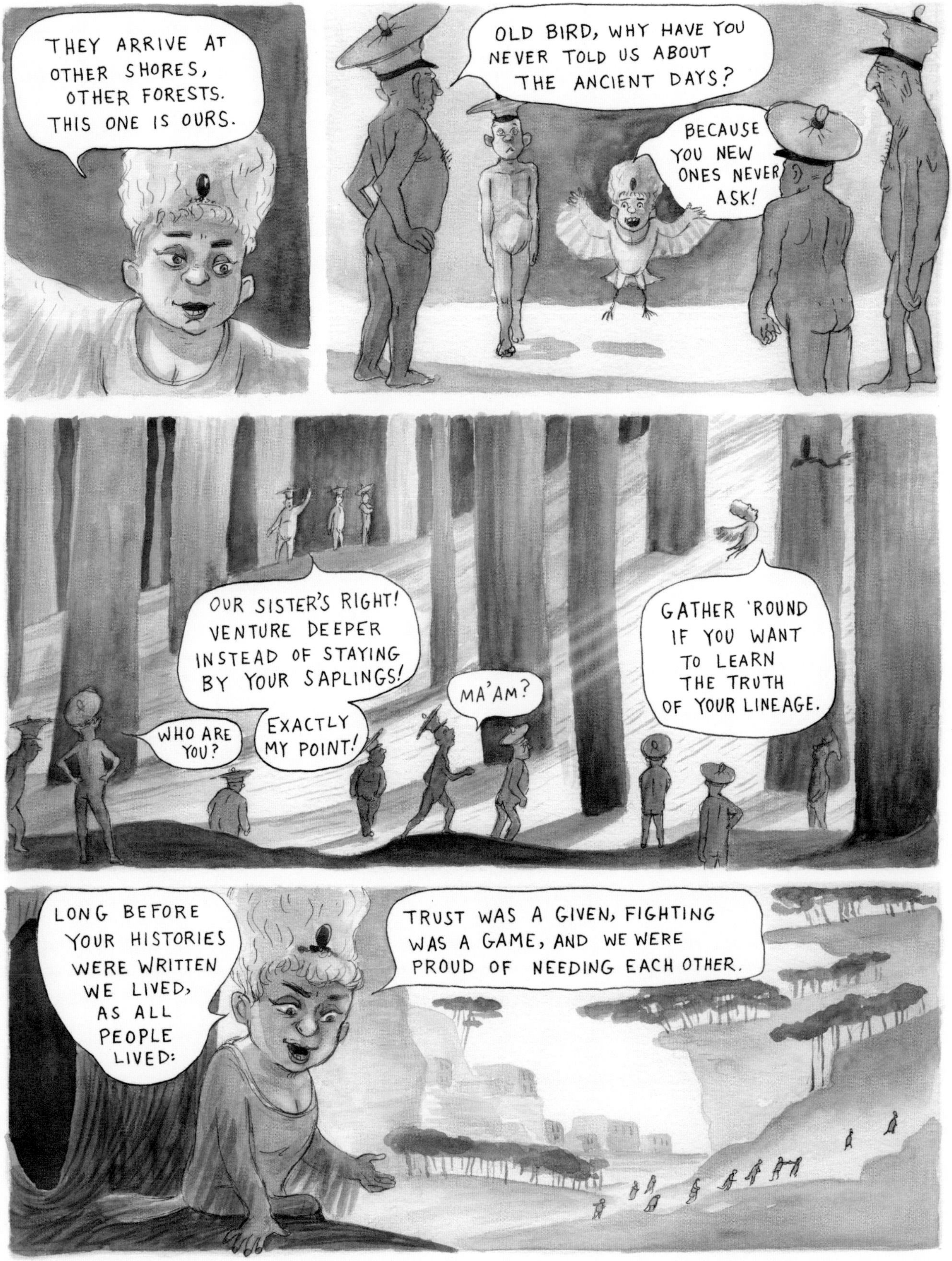
THEY ARRIVE AT OTHER SHORES, OTHER FORESTS. THIS ONE IS OURS.
OLD BIRD, WHY HAVE YOU NEVER TOLD US ABOUT THE ANCIENT DAYS?
BECAUSE YOU NEW ONES NEVER ASK!
OUR SISTER'S RIGHT! VENTURE DEEPER INSTEAD OF STAYING BY YOUR SAPLINGS!
WHO ARE YOU?
EXACTLY MY POINT!
MA'AM?
GATHER 'ROUND IF YOU WANT TO LEARN THE TRUTH OF YOUR LINEAGE.
LONG BEFORE YOUR HISTORIES WERE WRITTEN WE LIVED, AS ALL PEOPLE LIVED:
TRUST WAS A GIVEN, FIGHTING WAS A GAME, AND WE WERE PROUD OF NEEDING EACH OTHER.

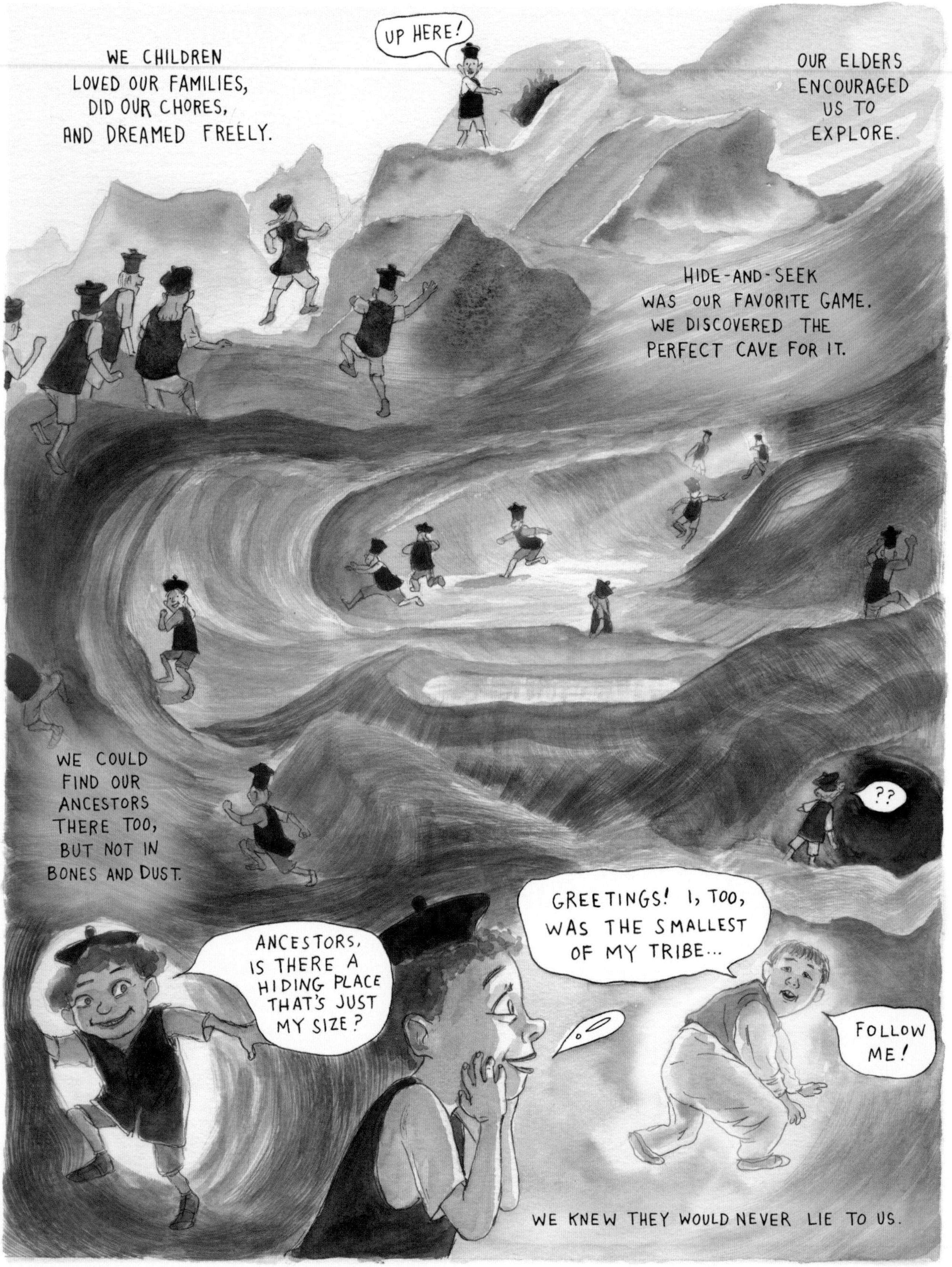
WE CHILDREN LOVED OUR FAMILIES, DID OUR CHORES, AND DREAMED FREELY.
UP HERE!
OUR ELDERS ENCOURAGED US TO EXPLORE.
HIDE-AND-SEEK WAS OUR FAVORITE GAME. WE DISCOVERED THE PERFECT CAVE FOR IT.
WE COULD FIND OUR ANCESTORS THERE TOO, BUT NOT IN BONES AND DUST.
??
ANCESTORS, IS THERE A HIDING PLACE THAT'S JUST MY SIZE?
GREETINGS! I, TOO, WAS THE SMALLEST OF MY TRIBE...
FOLLOW ME!
WE KNEW THEY WOULD NEVER LIE TO US.

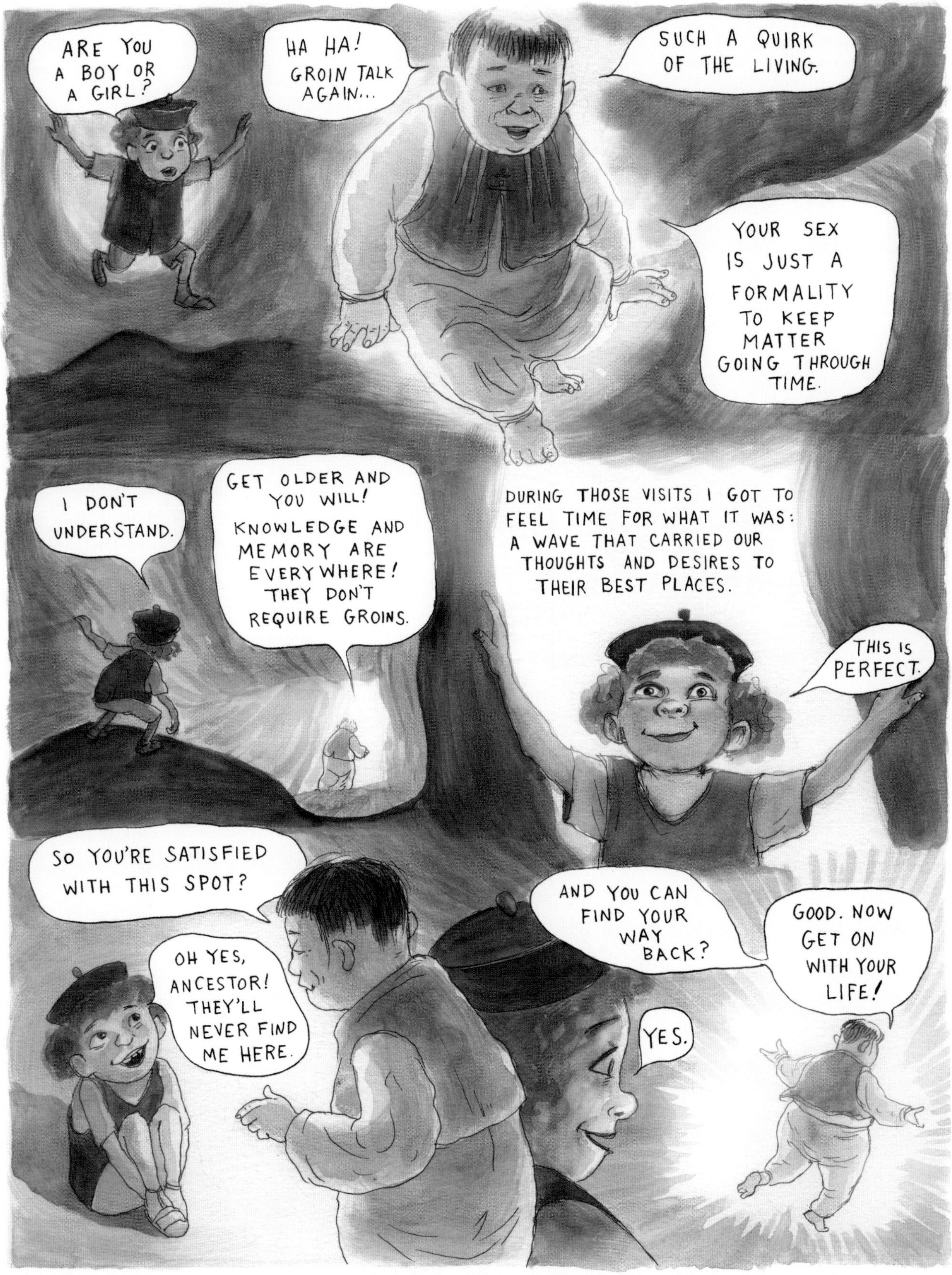
ARE YOU A BOY OR A GIRL?
HA HA! GROIN TALK AGAIN...
SUCH A QUIRK OF THE LIVING.
YOUR SEX IS JUST A FORMALITY TO KEEP MATTER GOING THROUGH TIME.
I DON'T UNDERSTAND.
GET OLDER AND YOU WILL! KNOWLEDGE AND MEMORY ARE EVERYWHERE! THEY DON'T REQUIRE GROINS.
DURING THOSE VISITS I GOT TO FEEL TIME FOR WHAT IT WAS: A WAVE THAT CARRIED OUR THOUGHTS AND DESIRES TO THEIR BEST PLACES.
THIS IS PERFECT.
SO YOU'RE SATISFIED WITH THIS SPOT?
OH YES, ANCESTOR! THEY'LL NEVER FIND ME HERE.
AND YOU CAN FIND YOUR WAY BACK?
YES.
GOOD. NOW GET ON WITH YOUR LIFE!

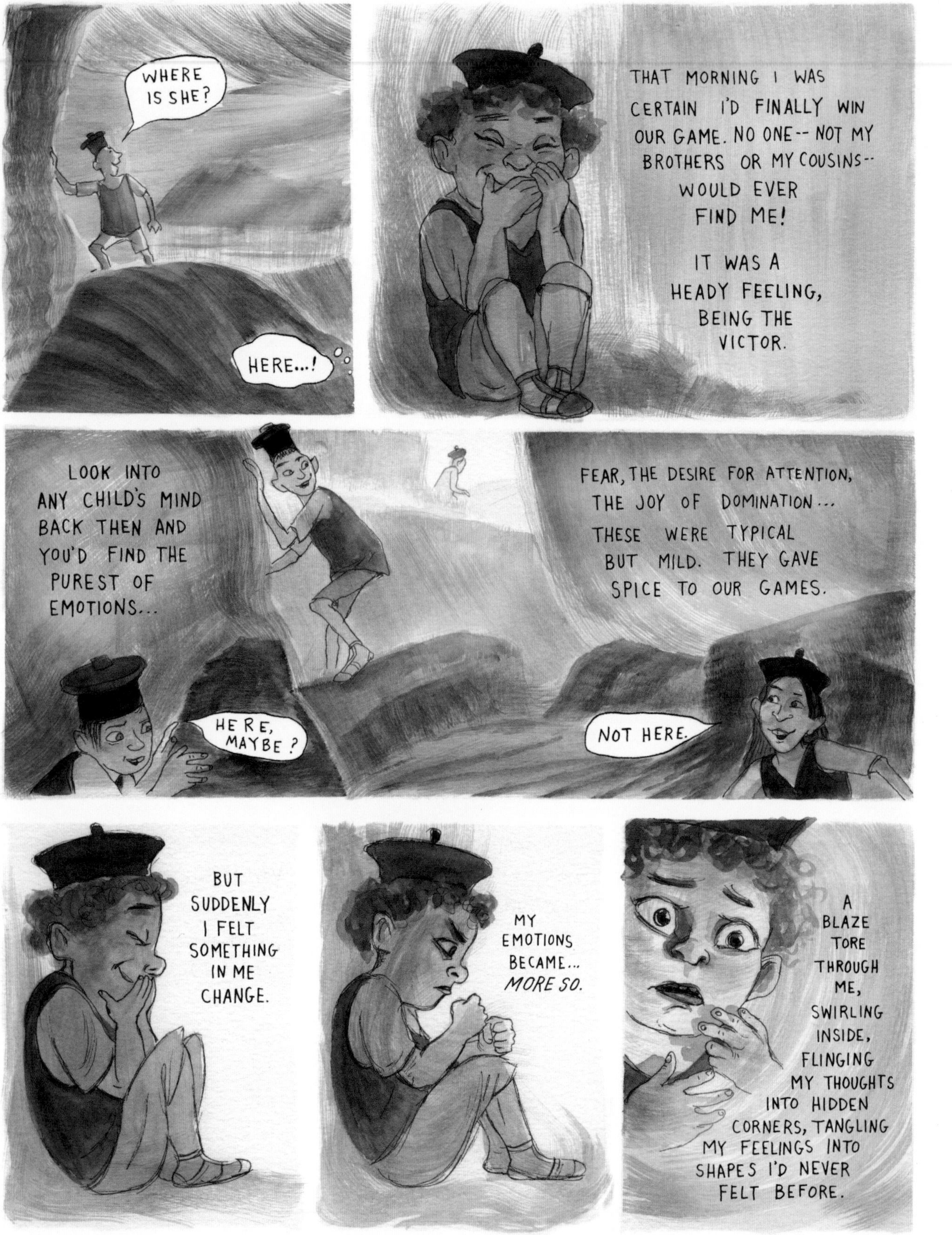
WHERE IS SHE?
HERE...!
THAT MORNING I WAS CERTAIN I'D FINALLY WIN OUR GAME. NO ONE -- NOT MY BROTHERS OR MY COUSINS -- WOULD EVER FIND ME!
IT WAS A HEADY FEELING, BEING THE VICTOR.
LOOK INTO ANY CHILD'S MIND BACK THEN AND YOU'D FIND THE PUREST OF EMOTIONS...
FEAR, THE DESIRE FOR ATTENTION, THE JOY OF DOMINATION... THESE WERE TYPICAL BUT MILD. THEY GAVE SPICE TO OUR GAMES.
HERE, MAYBE?
NOT HERE.
BUT SUDDENLY I FELT SOMETHING IN ME CHANGE.
MY EMOTIONS BECAME... *MORE SO.*
A BLAZE TORE THROUGH ME, SWIRLING INSIDE, FLINGING MY THOUGHTS INTO HIDDEN CORNERS, TANGLING MY FEELINGS INTO SHAPES I'D NEVER FELT BEFORE.

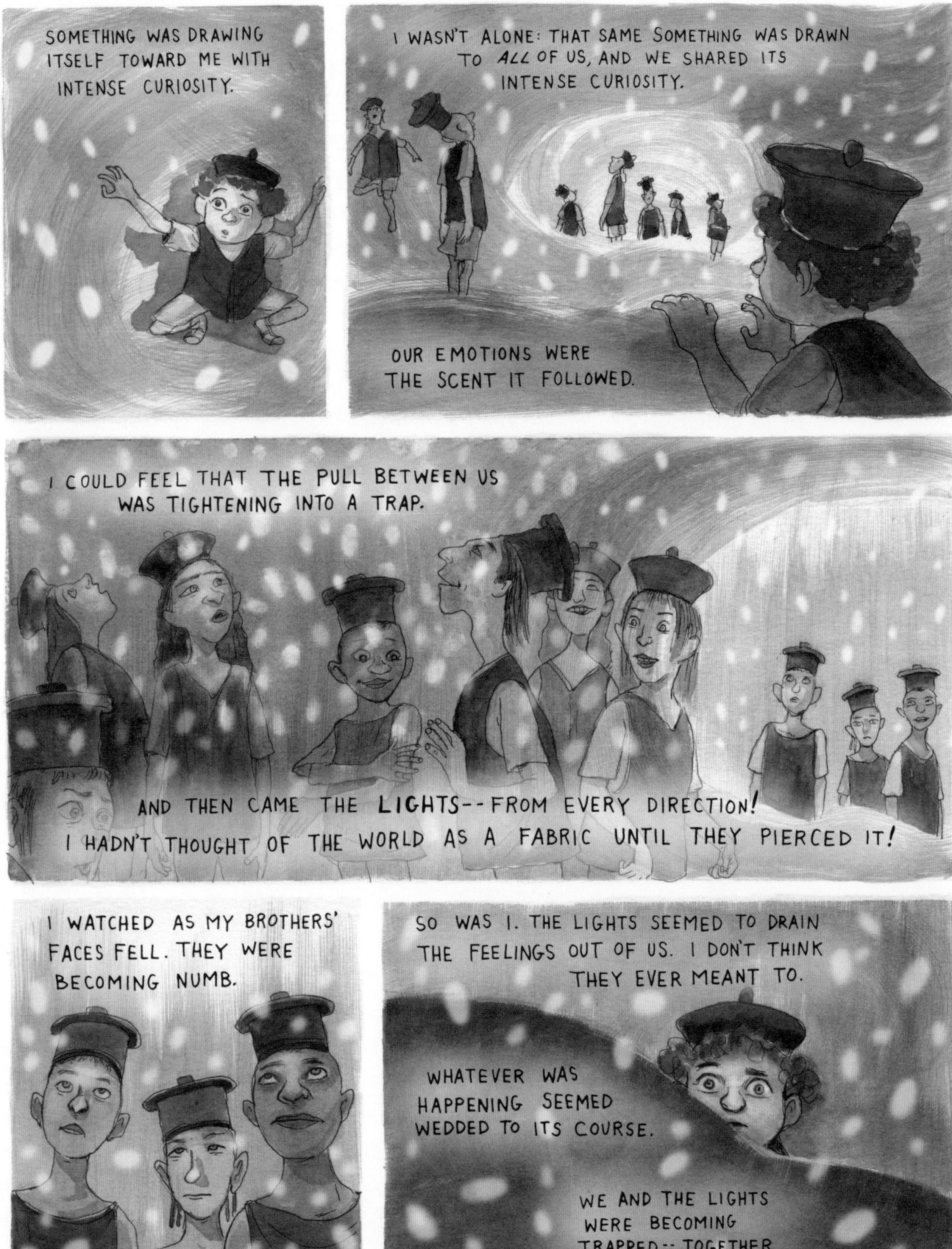
SOMETHING WAS DRAWING ITSELF TOWARD ME WITH INTENSE CURIOSITY.
I WASN'T ALONE: THAT SAME SOMETHING WAS DRAWN TO ALL OF US, AND WE SHARED ITS INTENSE CURIOSITY.
OUR EMOTIONS WERE THE SCENT IT FOLLOWED.
I COULD FEEL THAT THE PULL BETWEEN US WAS TIGHTENING INTO A TRAP.
AND THEN CAME THE LIGHTS--FROM EVERY DIRECTION!
I HADN'T THOUGHT OF THE WORLD AS A FABRIC UNTIL THEY PIERCED IT!
I WATCHED AS MY BROTHERS' FACES FELL. THEY WERE BECOMING NUMB.
SO WAS I. THE LIGHTS SEEMED TO DRAIN THE FEELINGS OUT OF US. I DON'T THINK THEY EVER MEANT TO.
WHATEVER WAS HAPPENING SEEMED WEDDED TO ITS COURSE.
WE AND THE LIGHTS WERE BECOMING TRAPPED-- TOGETHER.

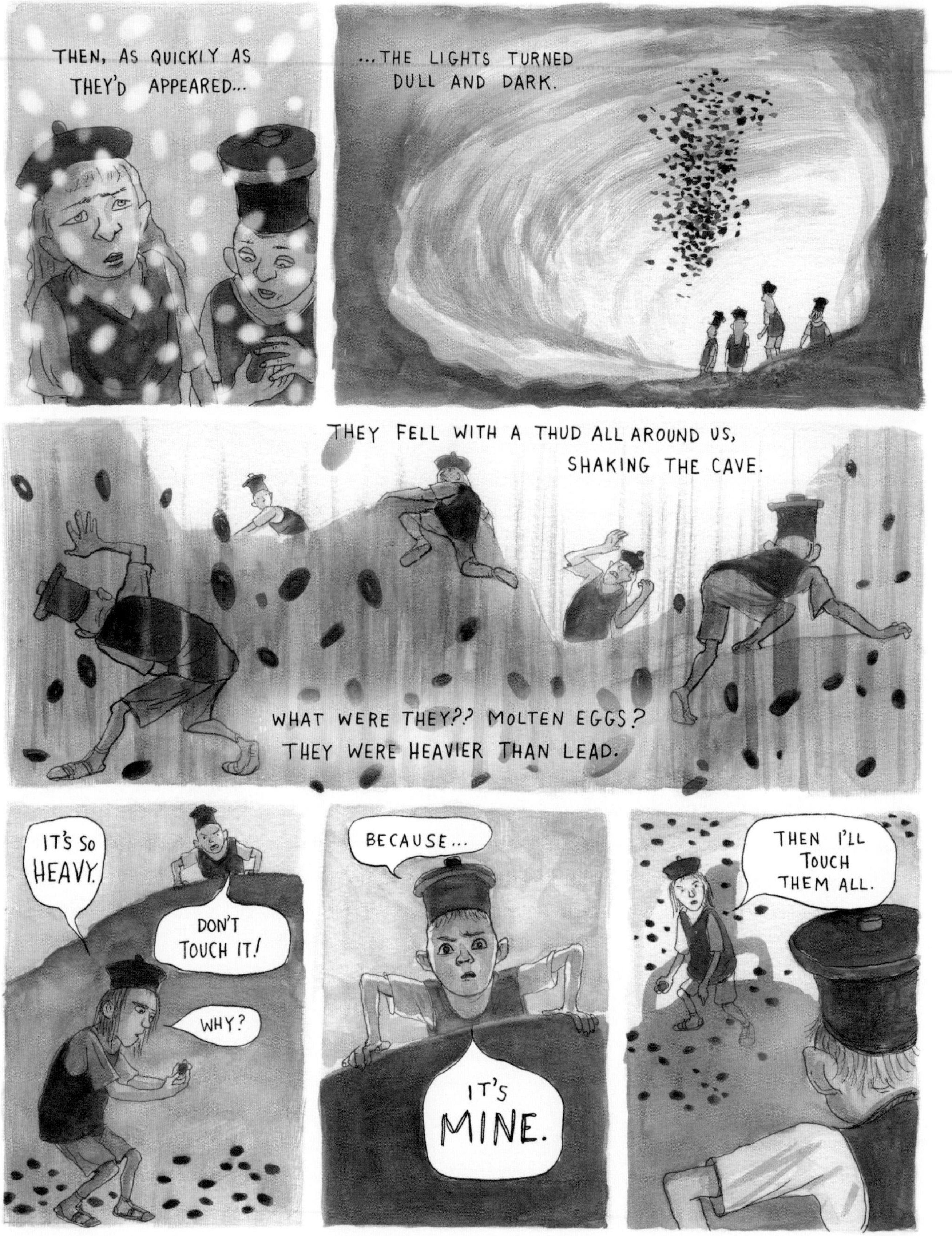
THEN, AS QUICKLY AS THEY'D APPEARED...
...THE LIGHTS TURNED DULL AND DARK.
THEY FELL WITH A THUD ALL AROUND US, SHAKING THE CAVE.
WHAT WERE THEY?? MOLTEN EGGS? THEY WERE HEAVIER THAN LEAD.
IT'S SO HEAVY.
DON'T TOUCH IT!
WHY?
BECAUSE...
IT'S MINE.
THEN I'LL TOUCH THEM ALL.

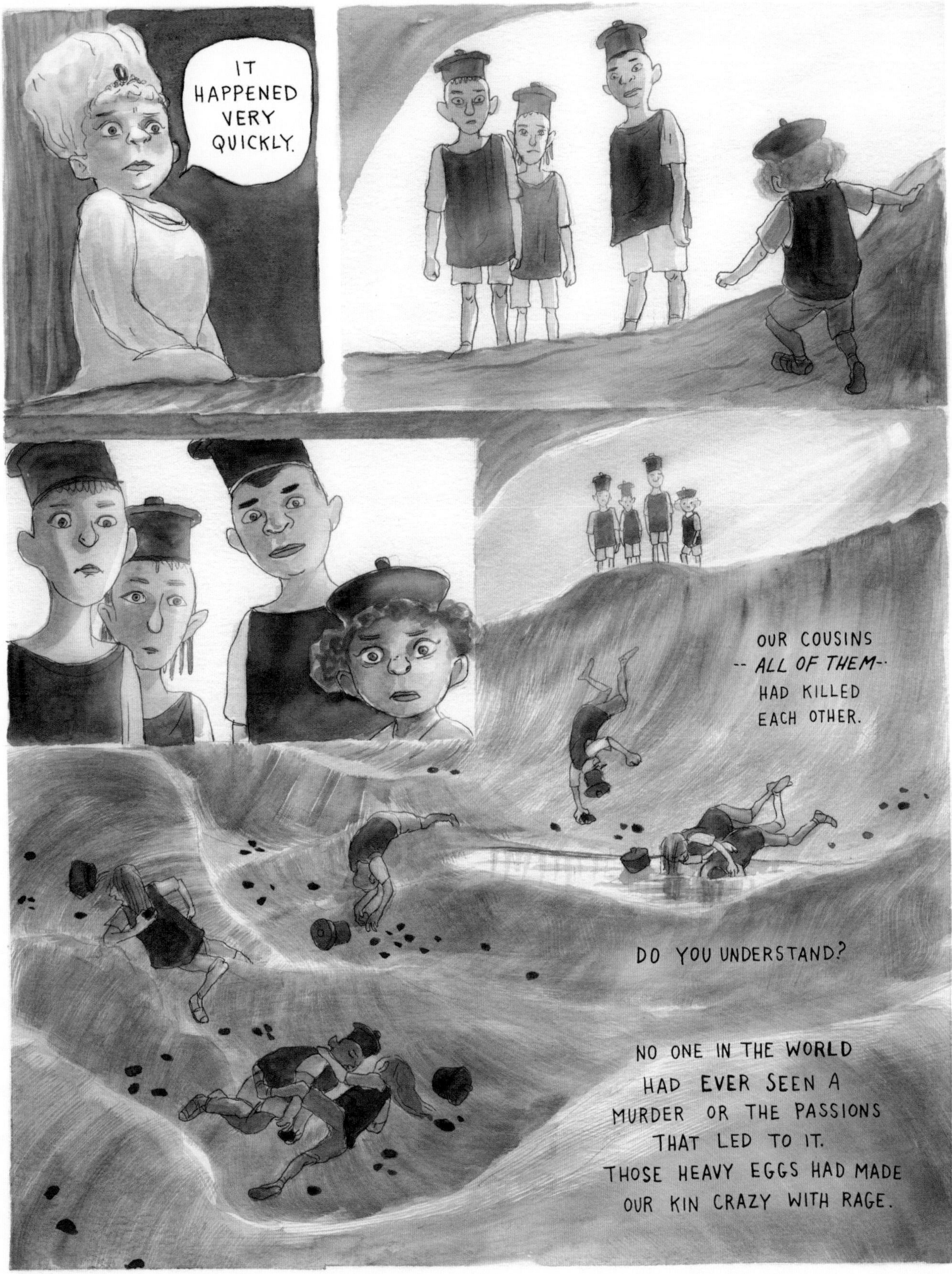
IT HAPPENED VERY QUICKLY.
OUR COUSINS -- ALL OF THEM -- HAD KILLED EACH OTHER.
DO YOU UNDERSTAND?
NO ONE IN THE WORLD HAD EVER SEEN A MURDER OR THE PASSIONS THAT LED TO IT.
THOSE HEAVY EGGS HAD MADE OUR KIN CRAZY WITH RAGE.

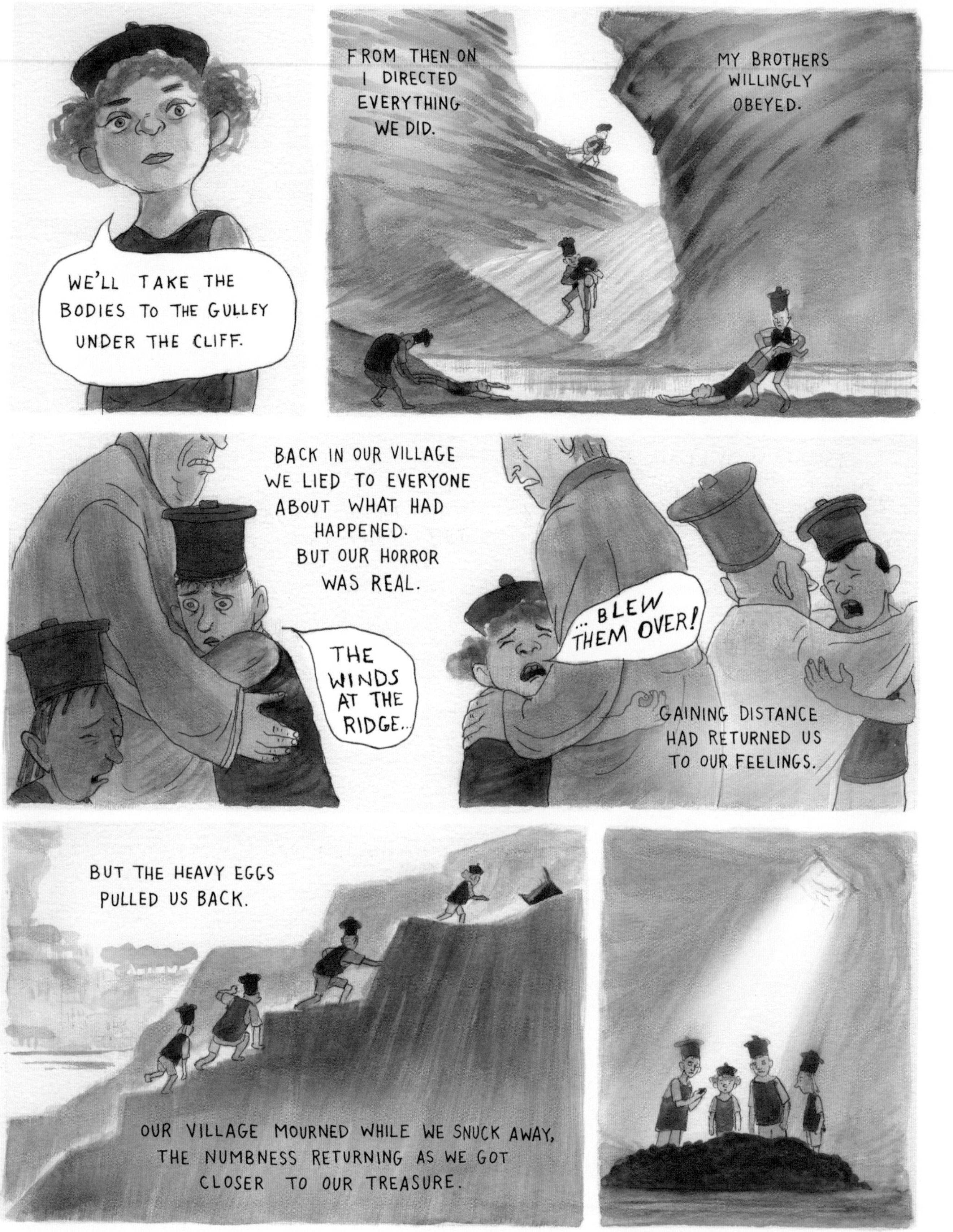
WE'LL TAKE THE BODIES TO THE GULLEY UNDER THE CLIFF.
FROM THEN ON I DIRECTED EVERYTHING WE DID.
MY BROTHERS WILLINGLY OBEYED.
BACK IN OUR VILLAGE WE LIED TO EVERYONE ABOUT WHAT HAD HAPPENED. BUT OUR HORROR WAS REAL.
THE WINDS AT THE RIDGE...
...BLEW THEM OVER!
GAINING DISTANCE HAD RETURNED US TO OUR FEELINGS.
BUT THE HEAVY EGGS PULLED US BACK.
OUR VILLAGE MOURNED WHILE WE SNUCK AWAY, THE NUMBNESS RETURNING AS WE GOT CLOSER TO OUR TREASURE.

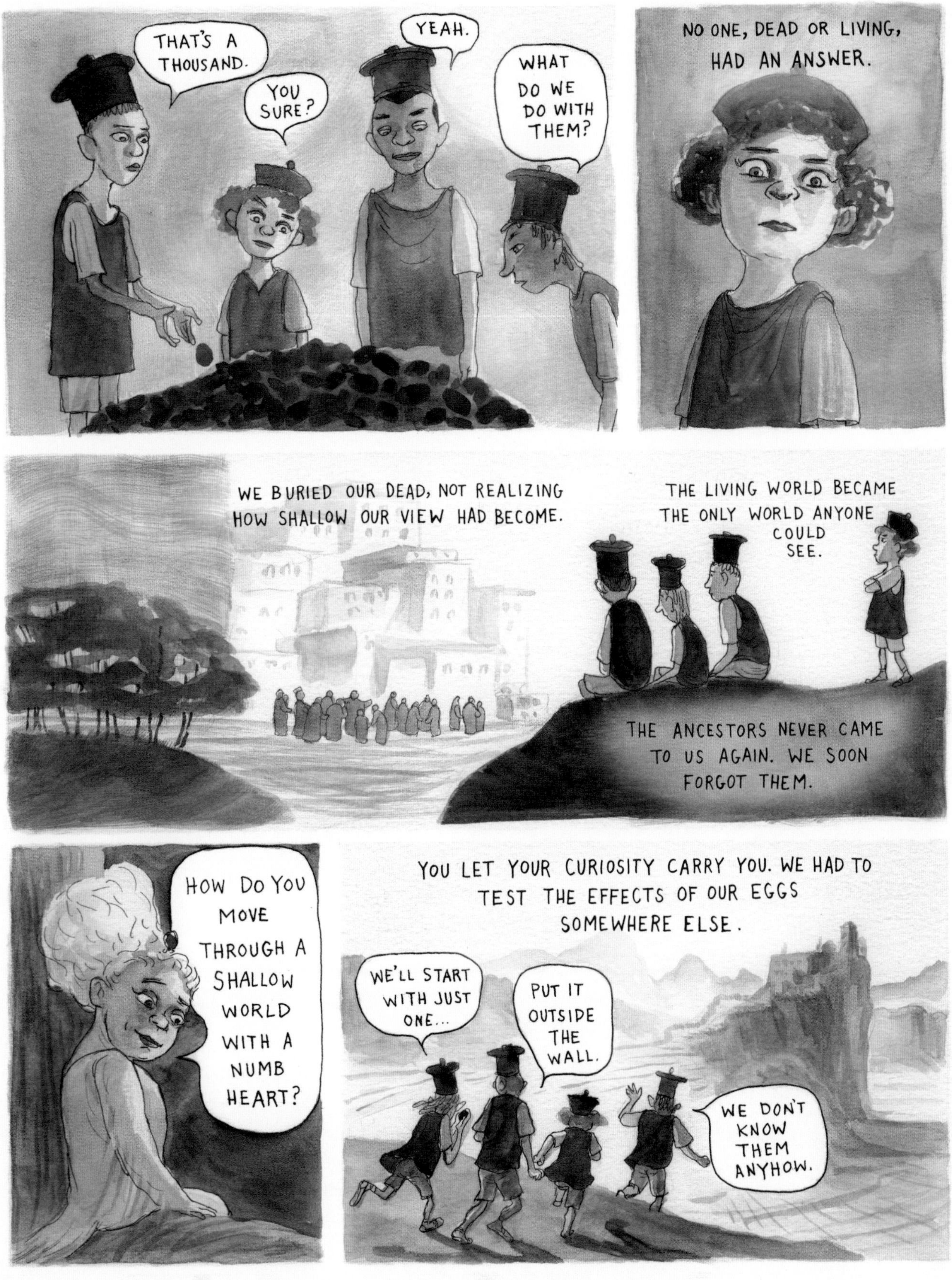
THAT'S A THOUSAND.
YOU SURE?
YEAH.
WHAT DO WE DO WITH THEM?
NO ONE, DEAD OR LIVING, HAD AN ANSWER.
WE BURIED OUR DEAD, NOT REALIZING HOW SHALLOW OUR VIEW HAD BECOME.
THE LIVING WORLD BECAME THE ONLY WORLD ANYONE COULD SEE.
THE ANCESTORS NEVER CAME TO US AGAIN. WE SOON FORGOT THEM.
HOW DO YOU MOVE THROUGH A SHALLOW WORLD WITH A NUMB HEART?
YOU LET YOUR CURIOSITY CARRY YOU. WE HAD TO TEST THE EFFECTS OF OUR EGGS SOMEWHERE ELSE.
WE'LL START WITH JUST ONE...
PUT IT OUTSIDE THE WALL.
WE DON'T KNOW THEM ANYHOW.

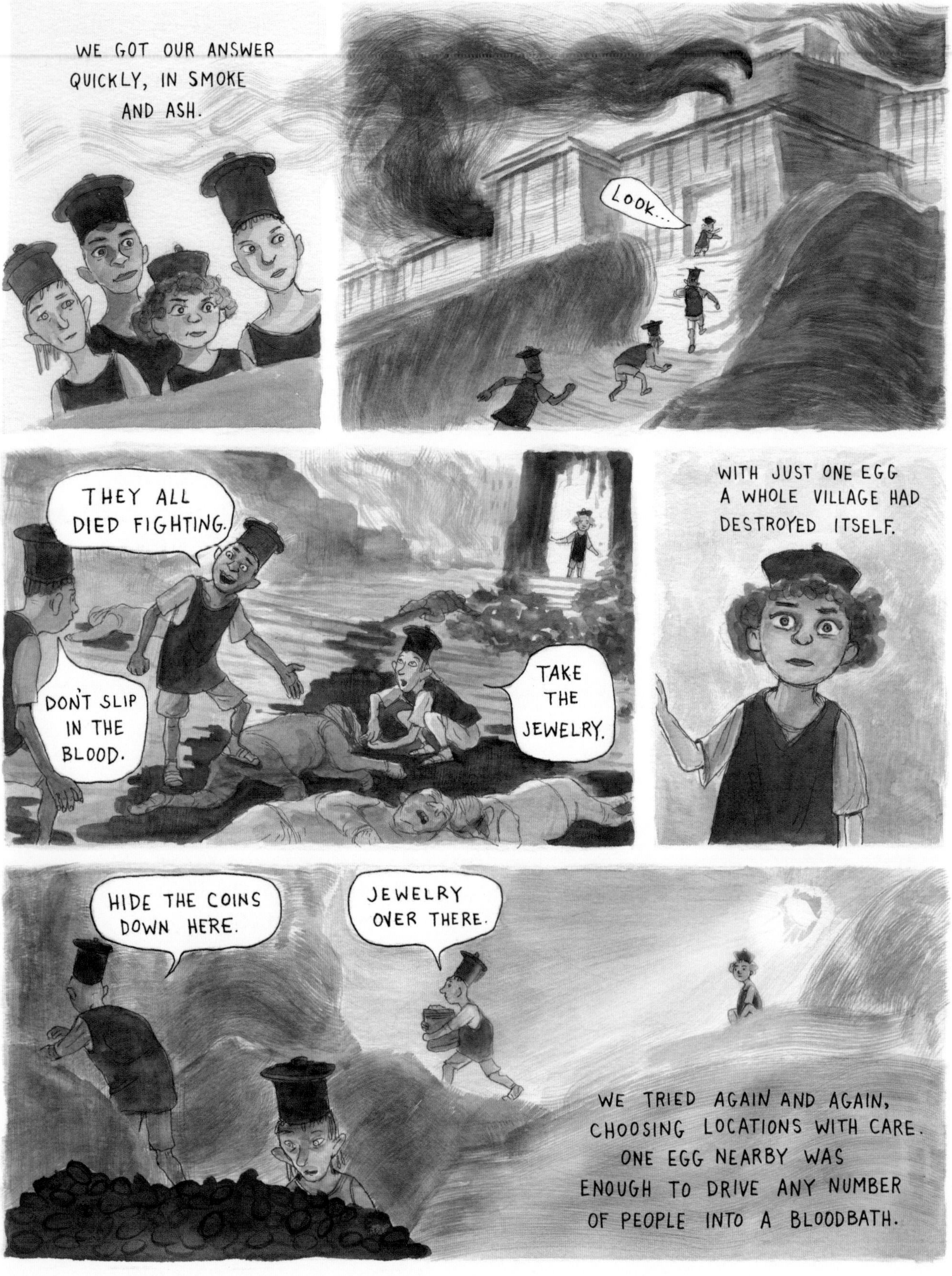
WE GOT OUR ANSWER QUICKLY, IN SMOKE AND ASH.
LOOK...
THEY ALL DIED FIGHTING.
DON'T SLIP IN THE BLOOD.
TAKE THE JEWELRY.
WITH JUST ONE EGG A WHOLE VILLAGE HAD DESTROYED ITSELF.
HIDE THE COINS DOWN HERE.
JEWELRY OVER THERE.
WE TRIED AGAIN AND AGAIN, CHOOSING LOCATIONS WITH CARE. ONE EGG NEARBY WAS ENOUGH TO DRIVE ANY NUMBER OF PEOPLE INTO A BLOODBATH.

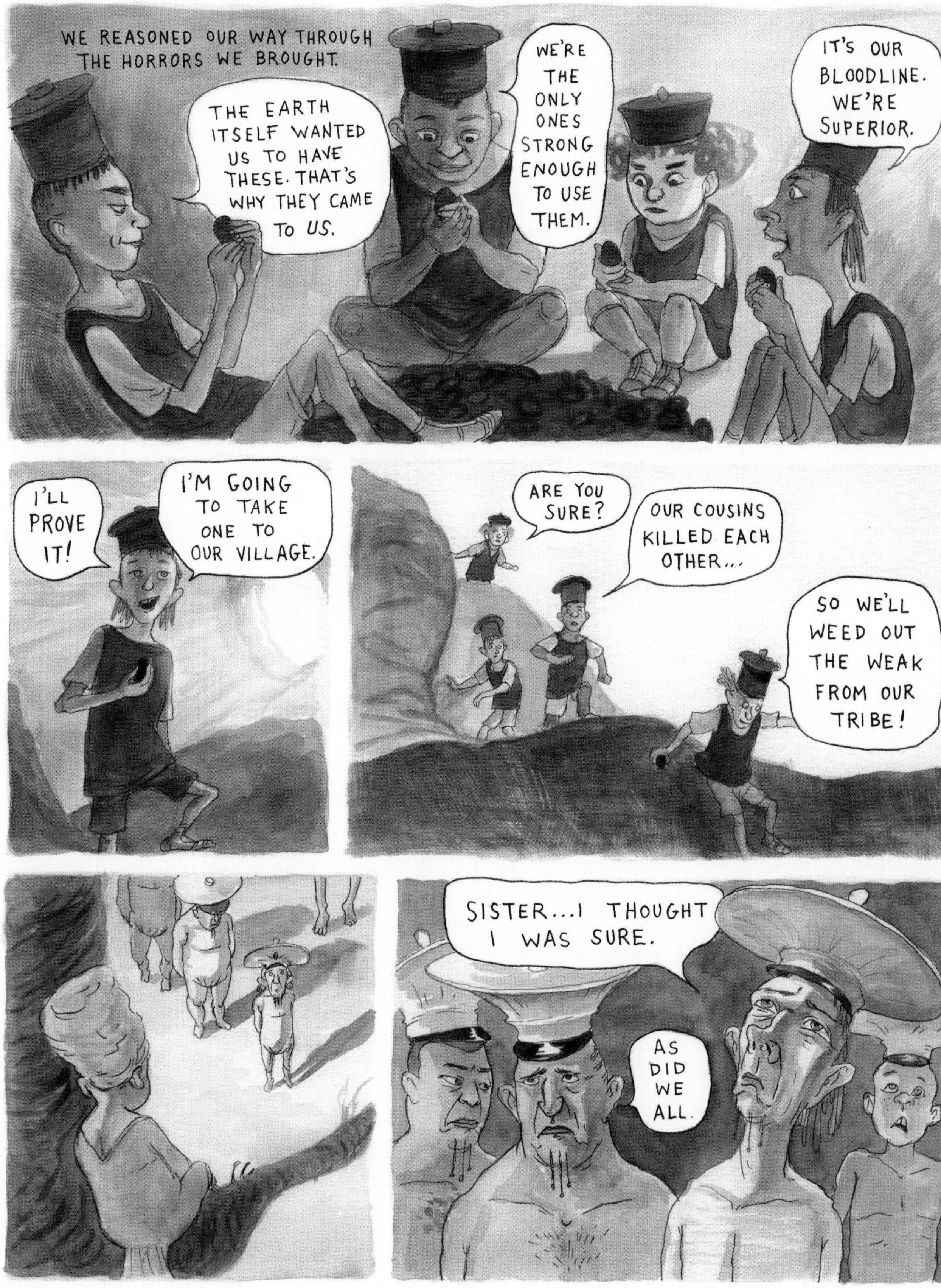
WE REASONED OUR WAY THROUGH THE HORRORS WE BROUGHT.
THE EARTH ITSELF WANTED US TO HAVE THESE. THAT'S WHY THEY CAME TO US.
WE'RE THE ONLY ONES STRONG ENOUGH TO USE THEM.
IT'S OUR BLOODLINE. WE'RE SUPERIOR.
I'LL PROVE IT!
I'M GOING TO TAKE ONE TO OUR VILLAGE.
ARE YOU SURE?
OUR COUSINS KILLED EACH OTHER...
SO WE'LL WEED OUT THE WEAK FROM OUR TRIBE!
SISTER...I THOUGHT I WAS SURE.
AS DID WE ALL.

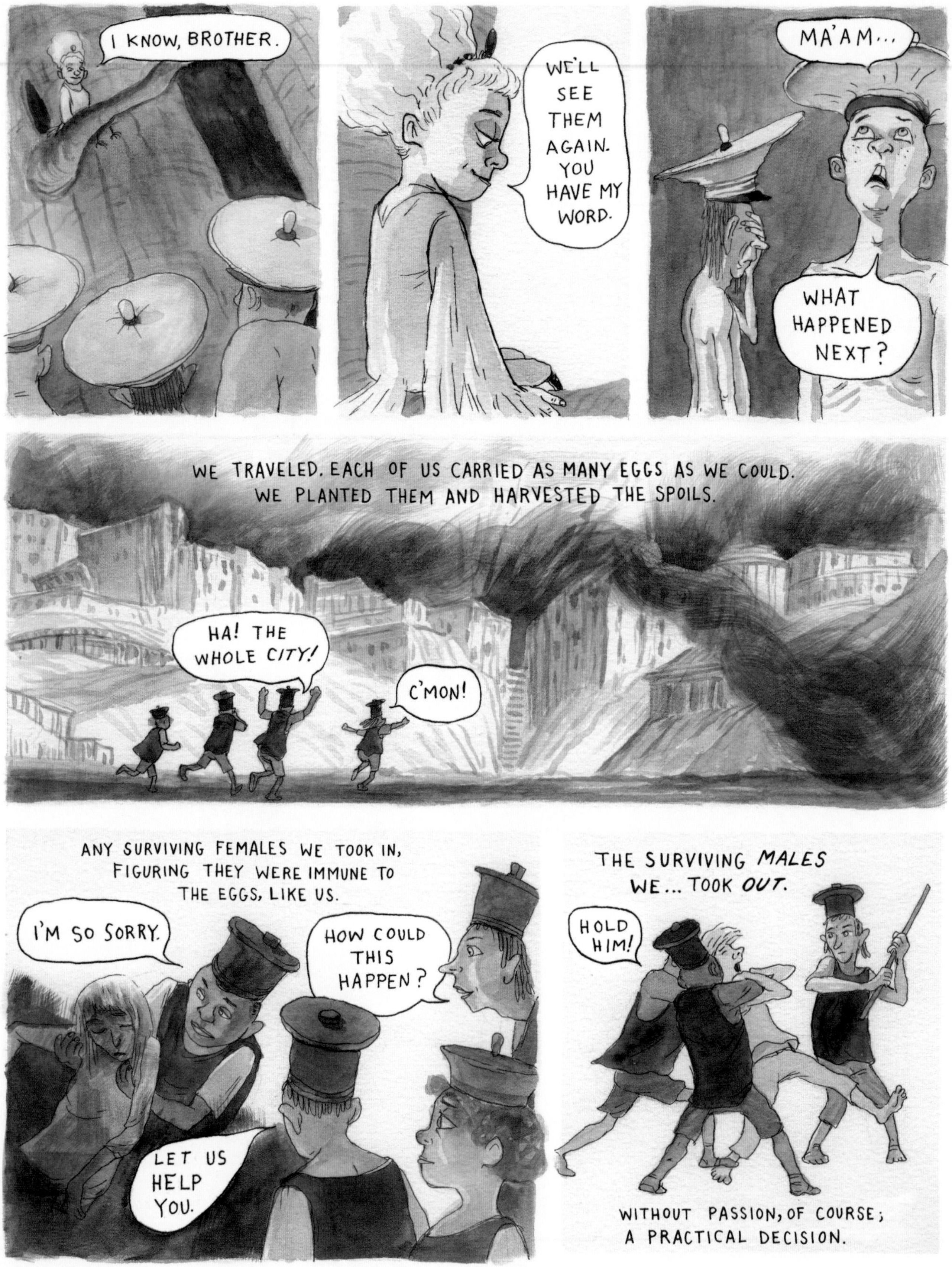
I KNOW, BROTHER.
WE'LL SEE THEM AGAIN. YOU HAVE MY WORD.
MA'AM...
WHAT HAPPENED NEXT?
WE TRAVELED. EACH OF US CARRIED AS MANY EGGS AS WE COULD. WE PLANTED THEM AND HARVESTED THE SPOILS.
HA! THE WHOLE CITY!
C'MON!
ANY SURVIVING FEMALES WE TOOK IN, FIGURING THEY WERE IMMUNE TO THE EGGS, LIKE US.
I'M SO SORRY.
HOW COULD THIS HAPPEN?
LET US HELP YOU.
THE SURVIVING MALES WE... TOOK OUT.
HOLD HIM!
WITHOUT PASSION, OF COURSE; A PRACTICAL DECISION.

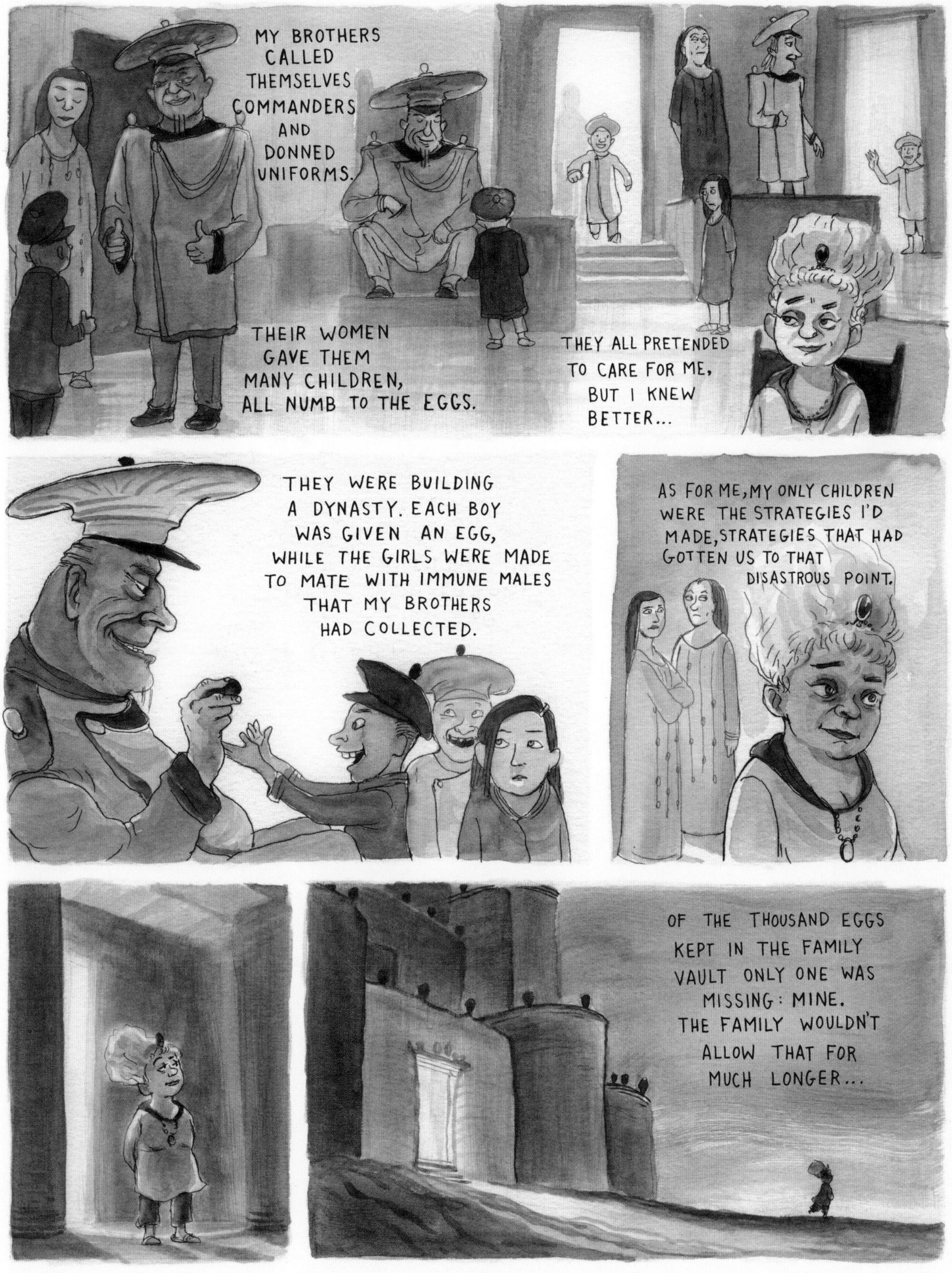
MY BROTHERS CALLED THEMSELVES COMMANDERS AND DONNED UNIFORMS.
THEIR WOMEN GAVE THEM MANY CHILDREN, ALL NUMB TO THE EGGS.
THEY ALL PRETENDED TO CARE FOR ME, BUT I KNEW BETTER...
THEY WERE BUILDING A DYNASTY. EACH BOY WAS GIVEN AN EGG, WHILE THE GIRLS WERE MADE TO MATE WITH IMMUNE MALES THAT MY BROTHERS HAD COLLECTED.
AS FOR ME, MY ONLY CHILDREN WERE THE STRATEGIES I'D MADE, STRATEGIES THAT HAD GOTTEN US TO THAT DISASTROUS POINT.
OF THE THOUSAND EGGS KEPT IN THE FAMILY VAULT ONLY ONE WAS MISSING: MINE. THE FAMILY WOULDN'T ALLOW THAT FOR MUCH LONGER...

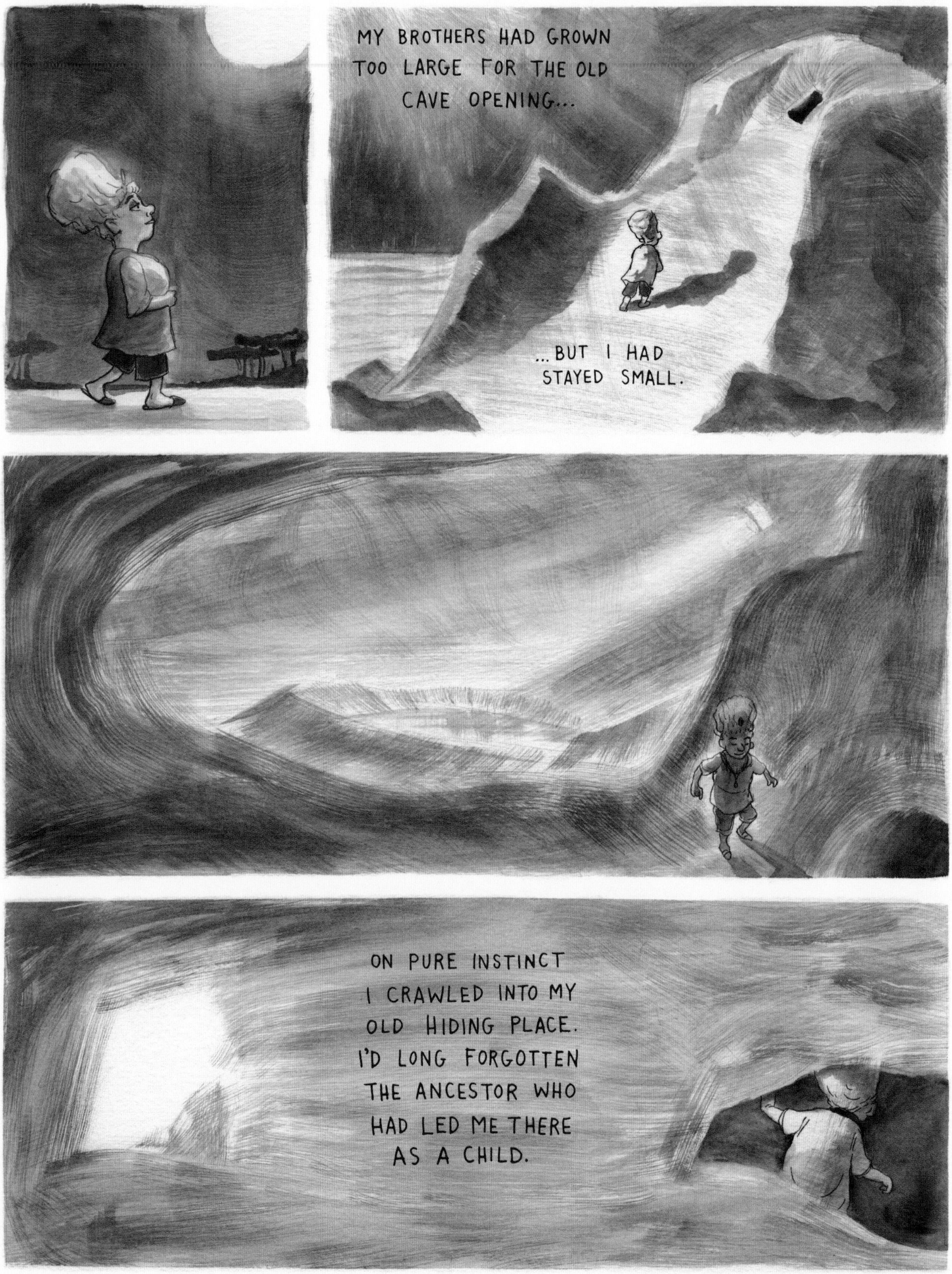
MY BROTHERS HAD GROWN TOO LARGE FOR THE OLD CAVE OPENING...
...BUT I HAD STAYED SMALL.
ON PURE INSTINCT I CRAWLED INTO MY OLD HIDING PLACE. I'D LONG FORGOTTEN THE ANCESTOR WHO HAD LED ME THERE AS A CHILD.

THEY'LL FIGURE OUT WHERE I AM AND SEND THEIR LITTLE BOYS IN TO FETCH ME. AND THEN, WHO KNOWS...

I'M OF NO USE TO THEM ANYMORE.

WHY DID YOU EVER COME HERE?

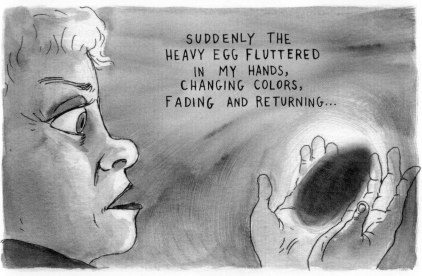

SUDDENLY THE HEAVY EGG FLUTTERED IN MY HANDS, CHANGING COLORS, FADING AND RETURNING...

I COULD *FEEL* AGAIN! NOT JUST EMOTIONS, BUT...

GLIMPSES OF... A *LINEAGE*, OF COUNTLESS CONNECTIONS THROUGH TIME. I CONTAINED *HISTORIES* OF CONVERSATIONS AND ADVENTURES WITH HELPFUL STRANGERS AND LOVING KIN. I COULD *FEEL* ALL OF THEM COURSING THROUGH ME. THEIR KNOWLEDGE WAS MINE, TOO.

FOR AN INSTANT I FELT THE DEEP TRANSCENDENCE I'D KNOWN AS A CHILD.

I UNDERSTOOD THAT I WAS BEFRIENDING A PART OF SOME OTHER UNIVERSE.
TOGETHER, WE HAD BECOME BOUND TO EXIST.

IN COLLIDING, WE HAD CREATED EACH OTHER ANEW.

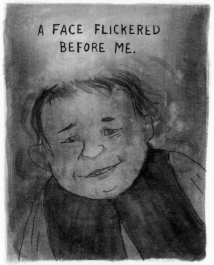
A FACE FLICKERED BEFORE ME.

WHOSE WAS IT?

I HAD LONG FORGOTTEN ABOUT THE ANCESTORS.

MORE FACES APPEARED, DEEP IN TIME...

THEN, LIKE THE CHILD I'D ONCE BEEN, I DID A THING WITHOUT THINKING...

THE PENDANT I WORE HAD COME FROM THE ASHES OF OUR OWN VILLAGE.

IT HAD BELONGED TO MY GRANDMOTHER.

I REMEMBERED AGAIN HOW GOOD SHE HAD BEEN TO ME...

AND I TAPPED THE EGG WITH IT.

IN A BOOMING *FLASH* THE EGG RETURNED TO ITS ORIGINAL STATE: LIGHT.

OH... THE HEAVY...

...IS BRIGHT AGAIN!

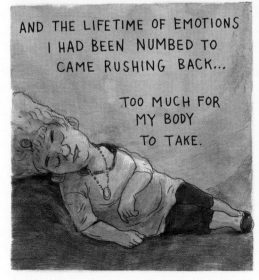

AND THE LIFETIME OF EMOTIONS I HAD BEEN NUMBED TO CAME RUSHING BACK...

TOO MUCH FOR MY BODY TO TAKE.

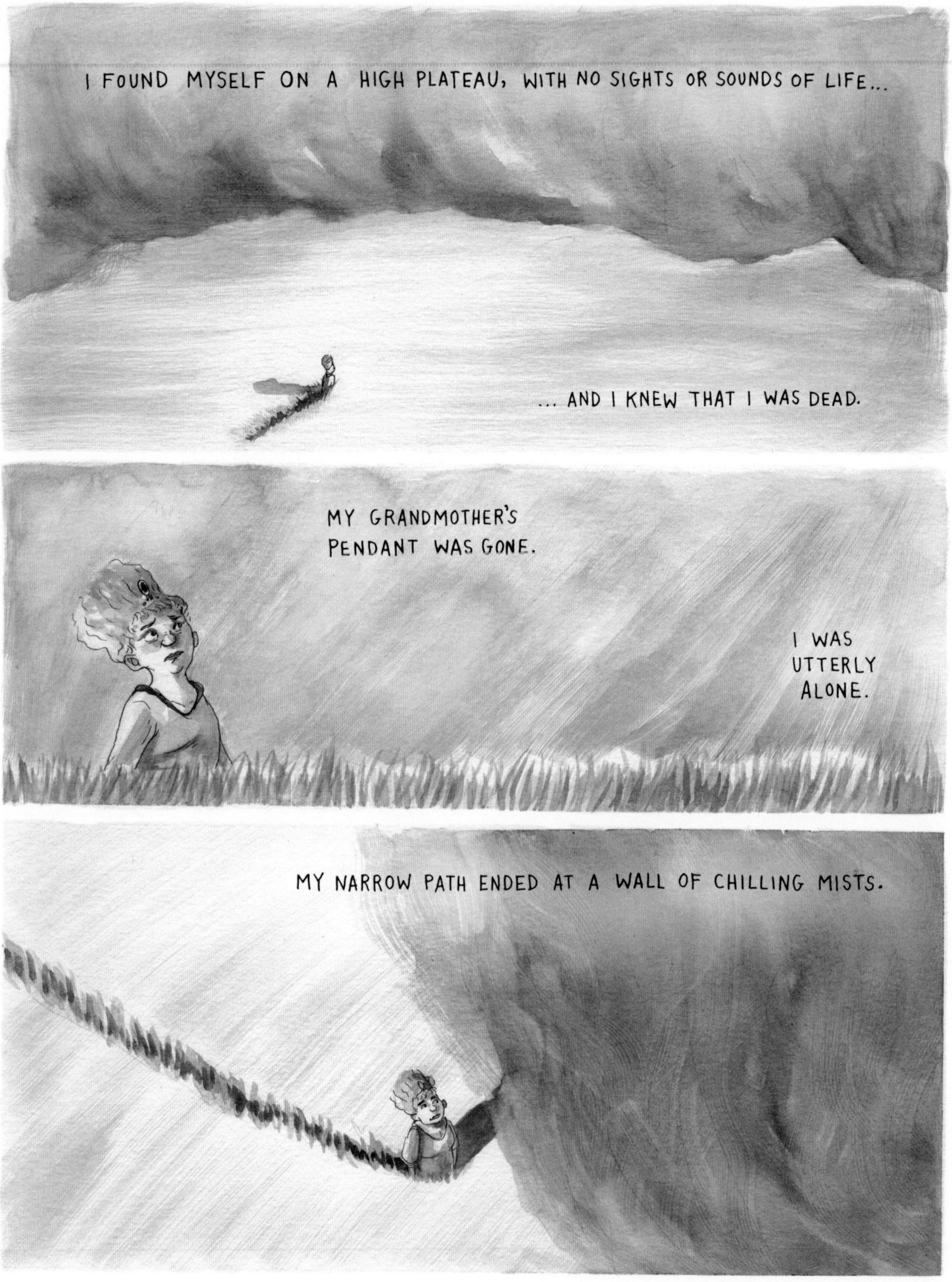
I FOUND MYSELF ON A HIGH PLATEAU, WITH NO SIGHTS OR SOUNDS OF LIFE...
... AND I KNEW THAT I WAS DEAD.
MY GRANDMOTHER'S PENDANT WAS GONE.
I WAS UTTERLY ALONE.
MY NARROW PATH ENDED AT A WALL OF CHILLING MISTS.

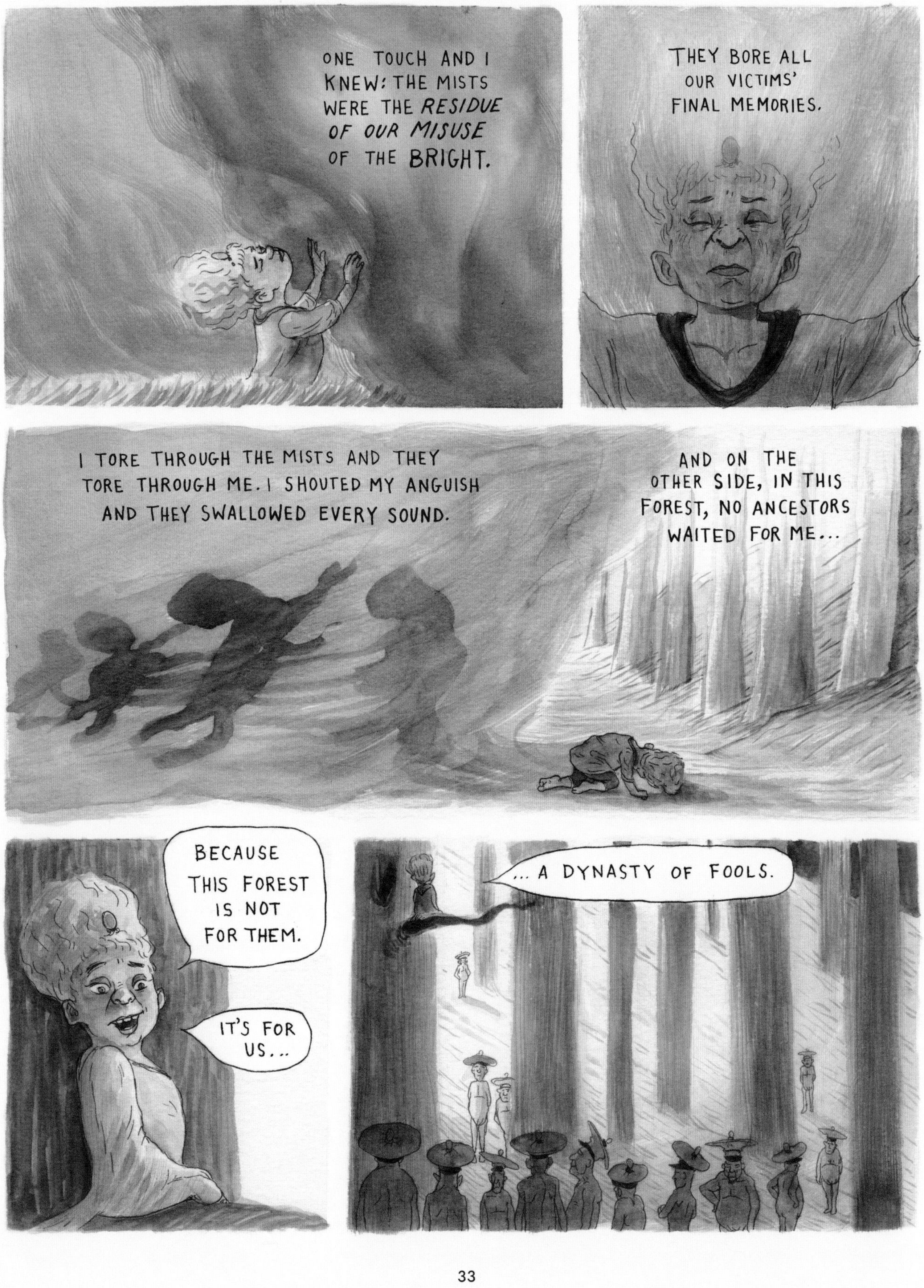
ONE TOUCH AND I KNEW: THE MISTS WERE THE *RESIDUE OF OUR MISUSE* OF THE BRIGHT.
THEY BORE ALL OUR VICTIMS' FINAL MEMORIES.
I TORE THROUGH THE MISTS AND THEY TORE THROUGH ME. I SHOUTED MY ANGUISH AND THEY SWALLOWED EVERY SOUND.
AND ON THE OTHER SIDE, IN THIS FOREST, NO ANCESTORS WAITED FOR ME...
BECAUSE THIS FOREST IS NOT FOR THEM.
IT'S FOR US...
... A DYNASTY OF FOOLS.

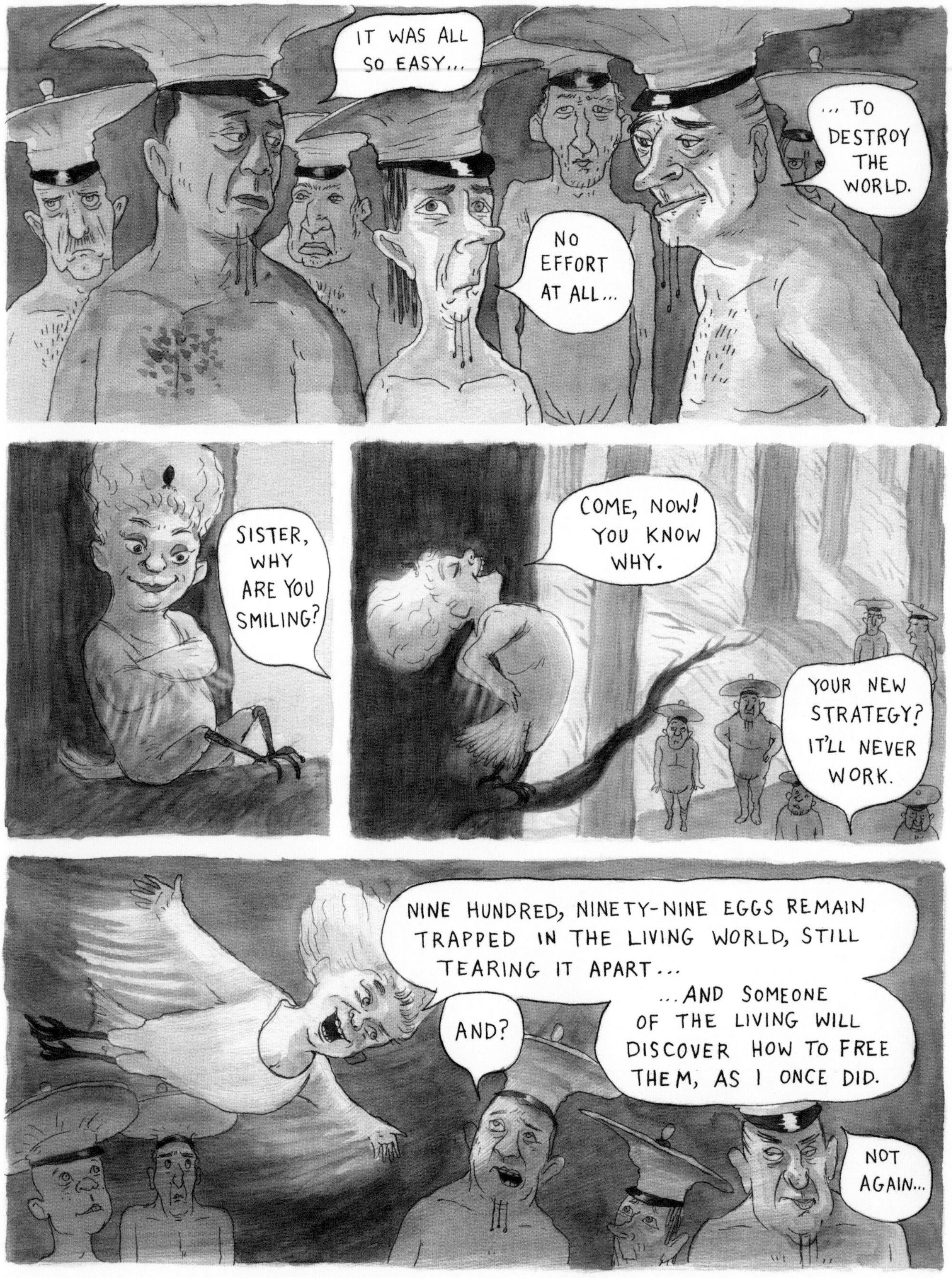
IT WAS ALL SO EASY...
... TO DESTROY THE WORLD.
NO EFFORT AT ALL...
SISTER, WHY ARE YOU SMILING?
COME, NOW! YOU KNOW WHY.
YOUR NEW STRATEGY? IT'LL NEVER WORK.
NINE HUNDRED, NINETY-NINE EGGS REMAIN TRAPPED IN THE LIVING WORLD, STILL TEARING IT APART...
AND?
...AND SOMEONE OF THE LIVING WILL DISCOVER HOW TO FREE THEM, AS I ONCE DID.
NOT AGAIN...

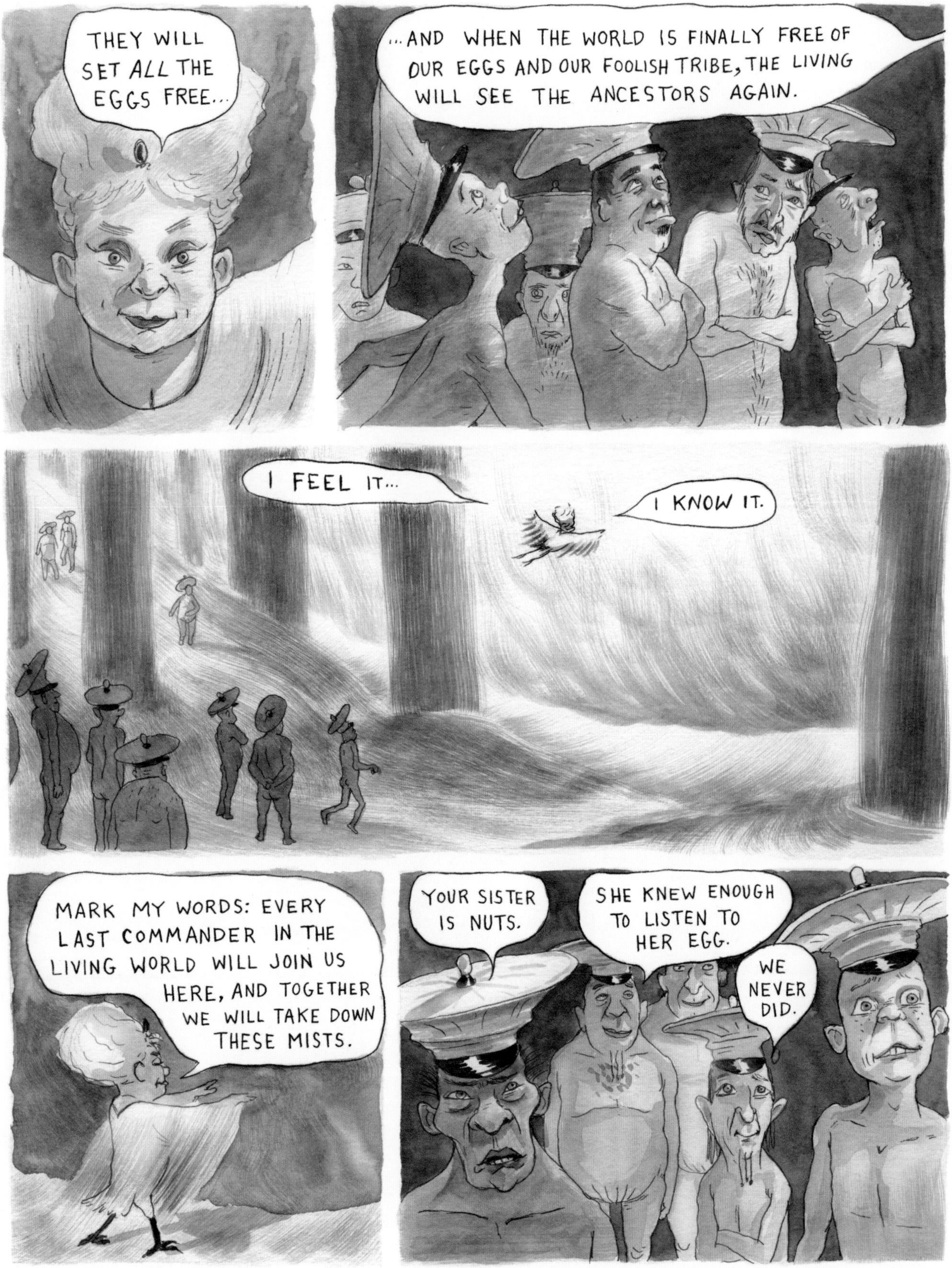
THEY WILL SET ALL THE EGGS FREE...
...AND WHEN THE WORLD IS FINALLY FREE OF OUR EGGS AND OUR FOOLISH TRIBE, THE LIVING WILL SEE THE ANCESTORS AGAIN.
I FEEL IT...
I KNOW IT.
MARK MY WORDS: EVERY LAST COMMANDER IN THE LIVING WORLD WILL JOIN US HERE, AND TOGETHER WE WILL TAKE DOWN THESE MISTS.
YOUR SISTER IS NUTS.
SHE KNEW ENOUGH TO LISTEN TO HER EGG.
WE NEVER DID.

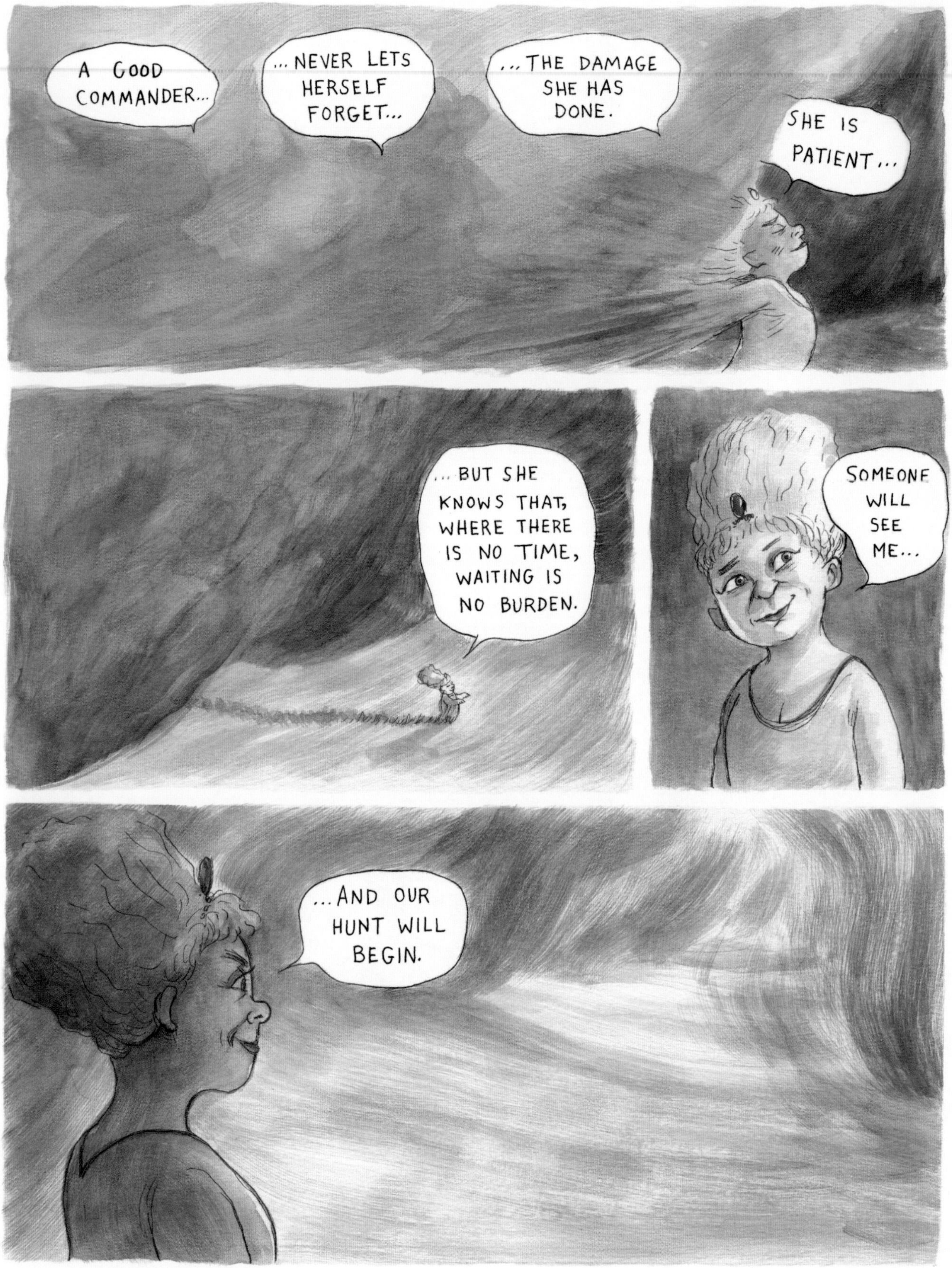
A GOOD COMMANDER...
...NEVER LETS HERSELF FORGET...
...THE DAMAGE SHE HAS DONE.
SHE IS PATIENT...
...BUT SHE KNOWS THAT, WHERE THERE IS NO TIME, WAITING IS NO BURDEN.
SOMEONE WILL SEE ME...
...AND OUR HUNT WILL BEGIN.

PART TWO

THE HUNTER

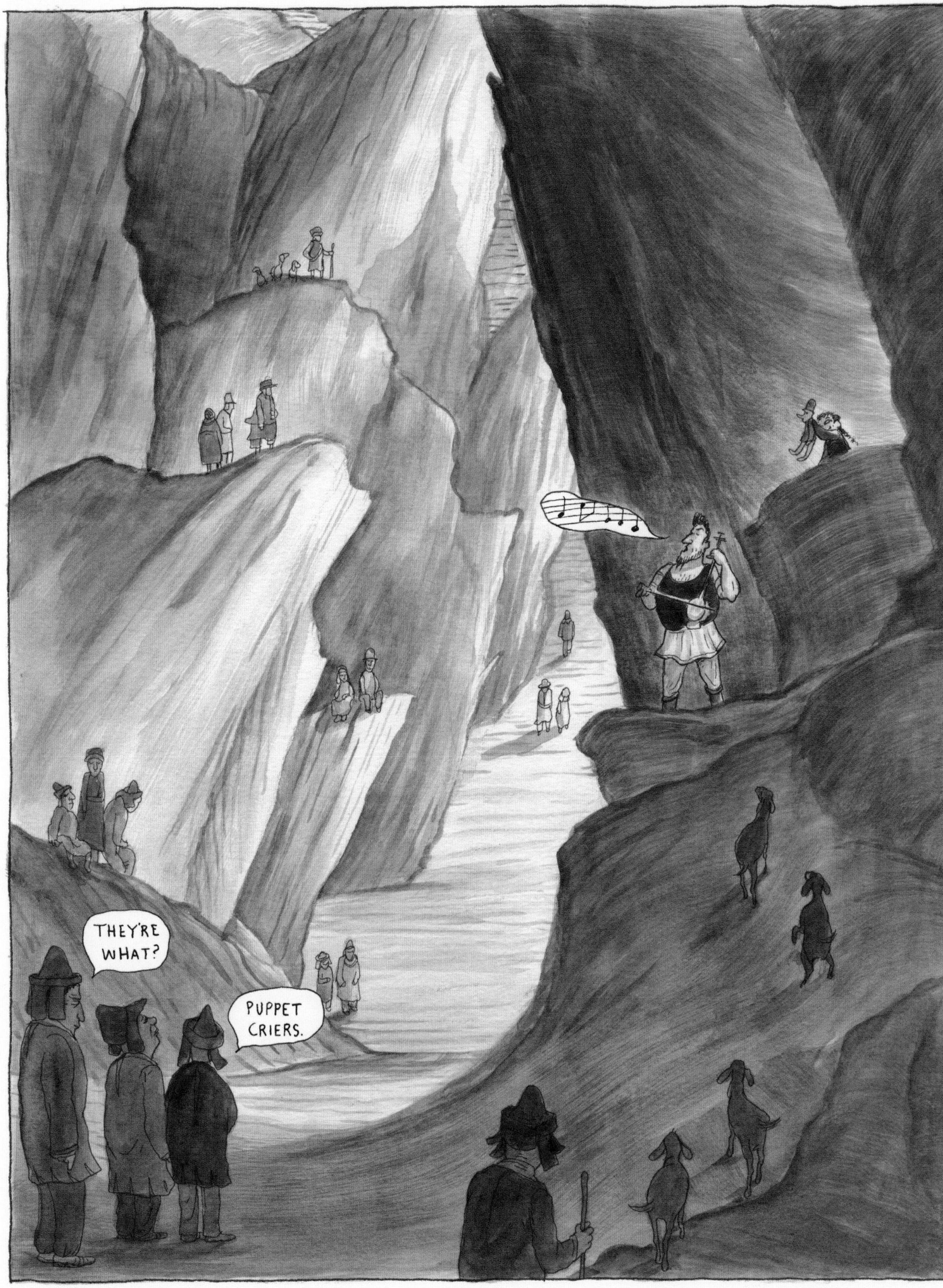
THEY'RE WHAT?
PUPPET CRIERS.

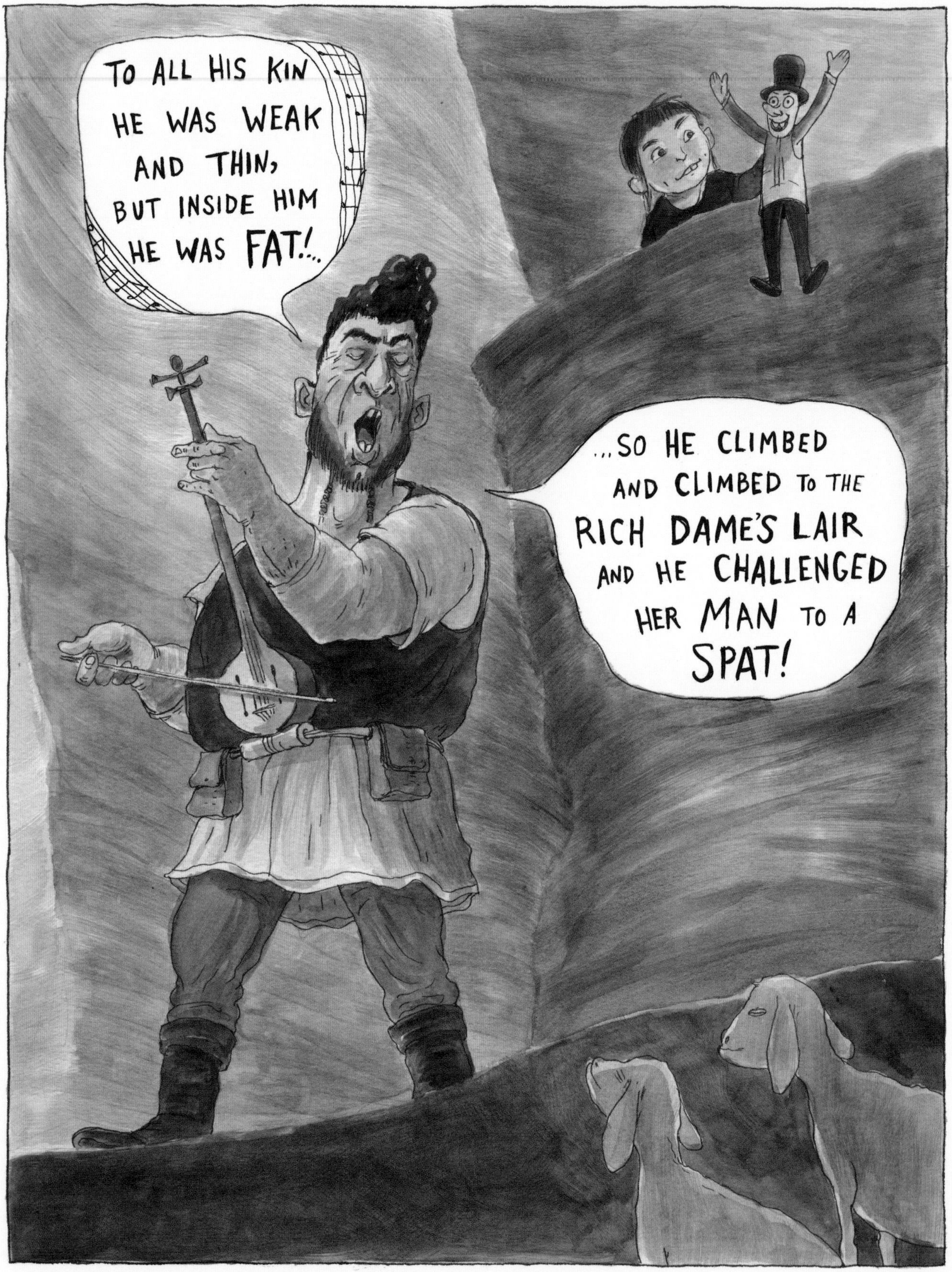
TO ALL HIS KIN HE WAS WEAK AND THIN, BUT INSIDE HIM HE WAS FAT!...
...SO HE CLIMBED AND CLIMBED TO THE RICH DAME'S LAIR AND HE CHALLENGED HER MAN TO A SPAT!

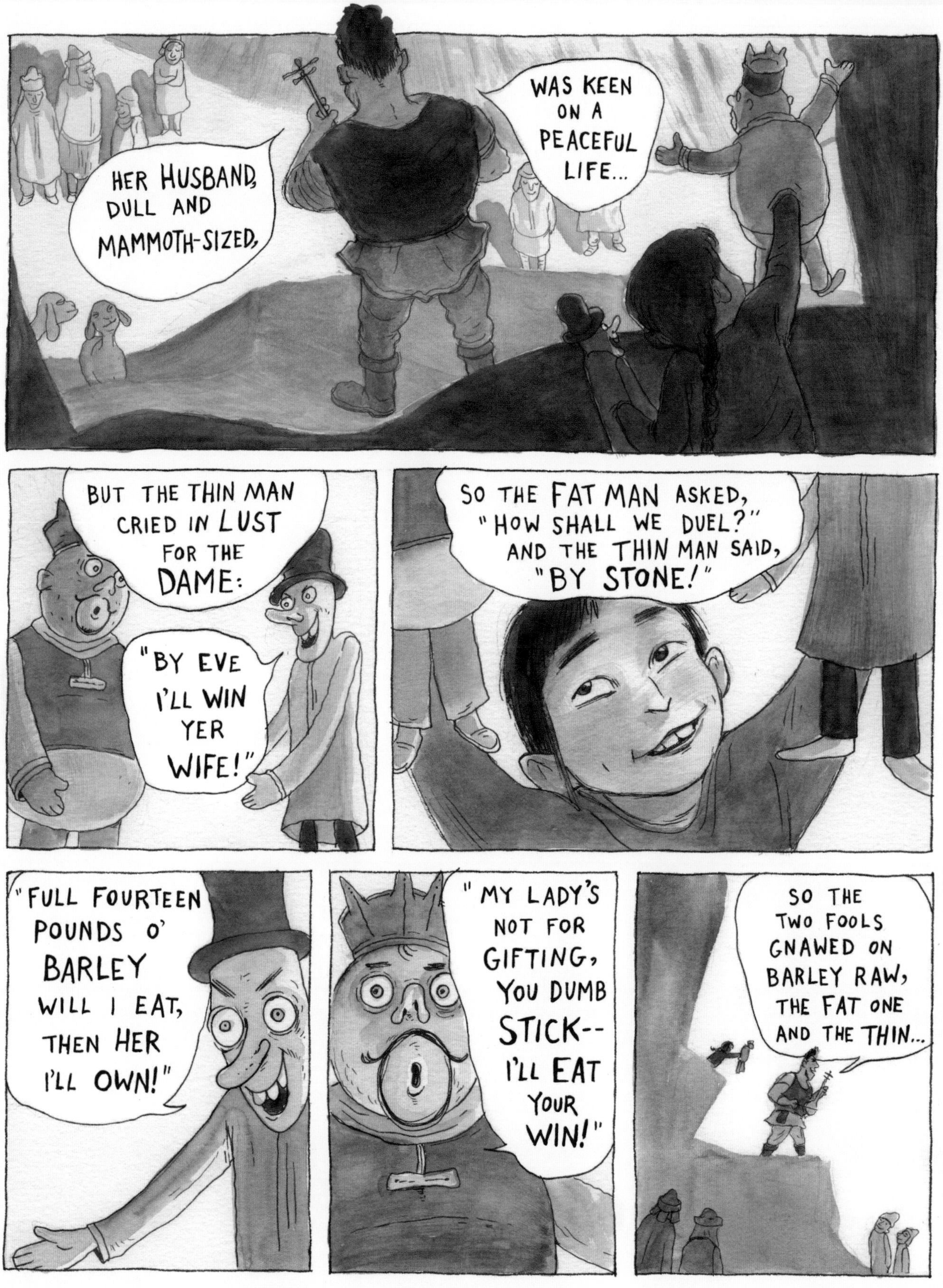
HER HUSBAND, DULL AND MAMMOTH-SIZED,
WAS KEEN ON A PEACEFUL LIFE...
BUT THE THIN MAN CRIED IN LUST FOR THE DAME:
"BY EVE I'LL WIN YER WIFE!"
SO THE FAT MAN ASKED, "HOW SHALL WE DUEL?" AND THE THIN MAN SAID, "BY STONE!"
"FULL FOURTEEN POUNDS O' BARLEY WILL I EAT, THEN HER I'LL OWN!"
"MY LADY'S NOT FOR GIFTING, YOU DUMB STICK-- I'LL EAT YOUR WIN!"
SO THE TWO FOOLS GNAWED ON BARLEY RAW, THE FAT ONE AND THE THIN...

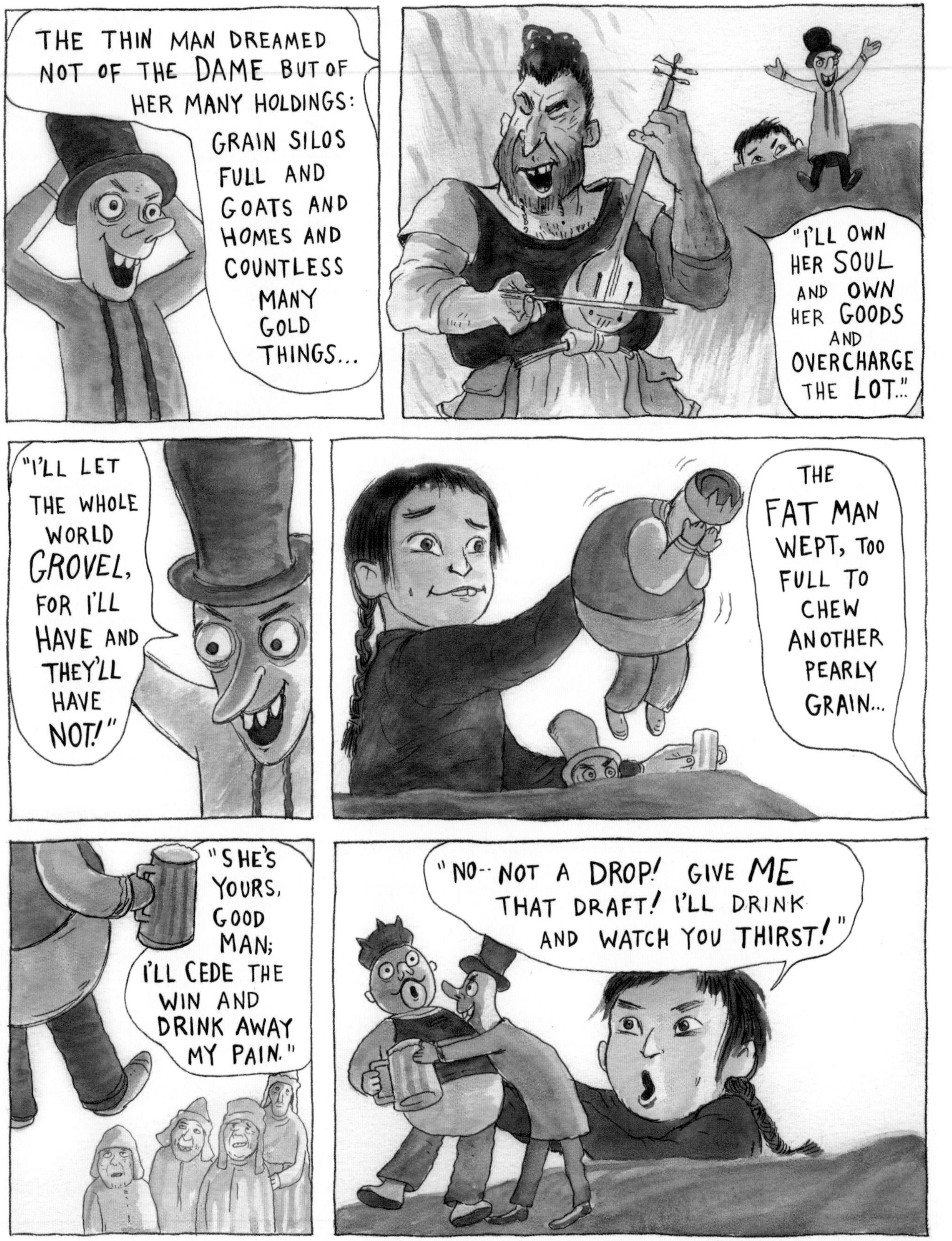
THE THIN MAN DREAMED NOT OF THE DAME BUT OF HER MANY HOLDINGS:
GRAIN SILOS FULL AND GOATS AND HOMES AND COUNTLESS MANY GOLD THINGS...
"I'LL OWN HER SOUL AND OWN HER GOODS AND OVERCHARGE THE LOT."
"I'LL LET THE WHOLE WORLD GROVEL, FOR I'LL HAVE AND THEY'LL HAVE NOT!"
THE FAT MAN WEPT, TOO FULL TO CHEW ANOTHER PEARLY GRAIN...
"SHE'S YOURS, GOOD MAN; I'LL CEDE THE WIN AND DRINK AWAY MY PAIN."
"NO-- NOT A DROP! GIVE ME THAT DRAFT! I'LL DRINK AND WATCH YOU THIRST!"

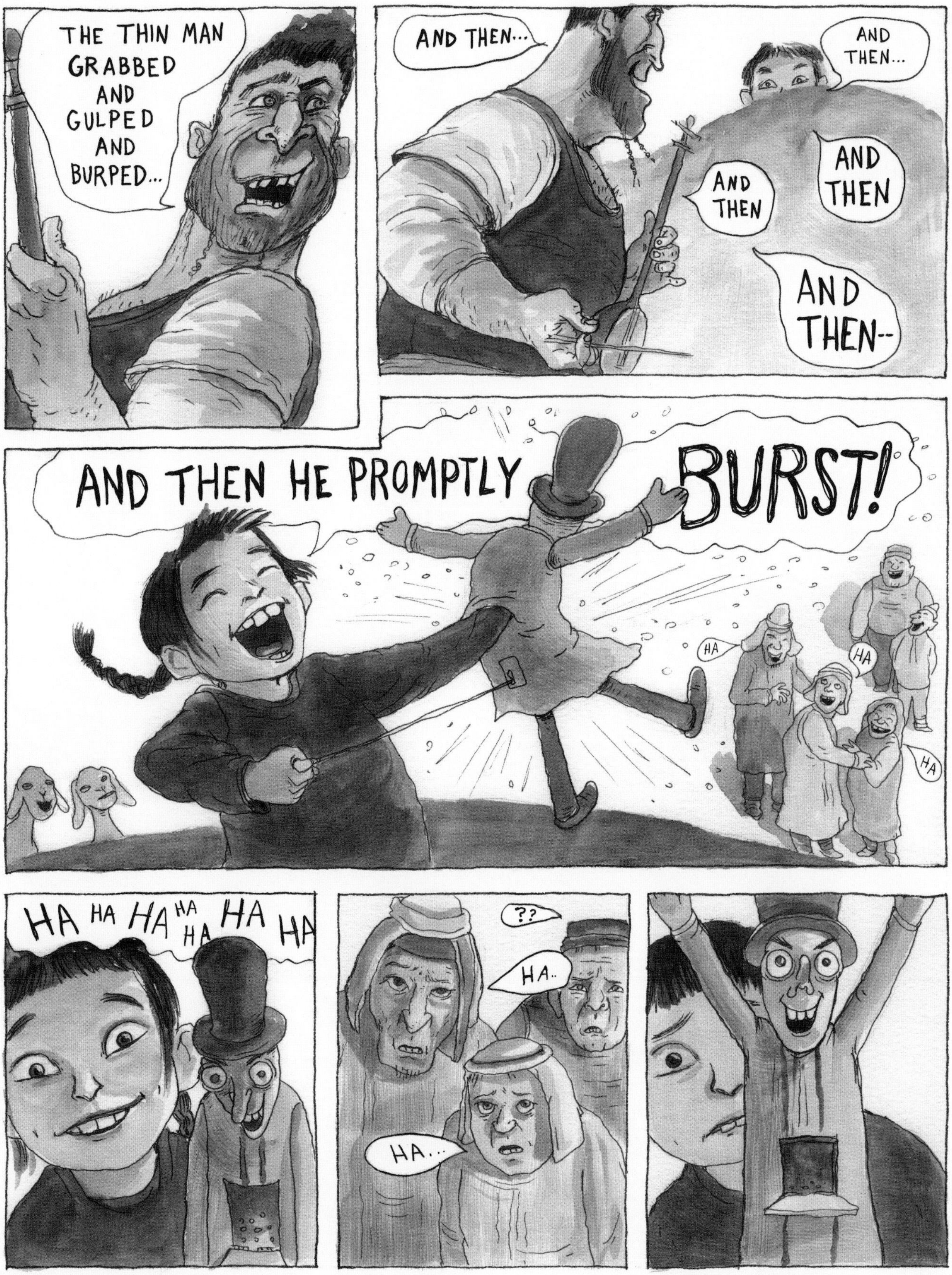
THE THIN MAN GRABBED AND GULPED AND BURPED...
AND THEN...
AND THEN...
AND THEN
AND THEN
AND THEN--
AND THEN HE PROMPTLY BURST!
HA
HA
HA
HA HA HA HA HA HA HA
??
HA..
HA...

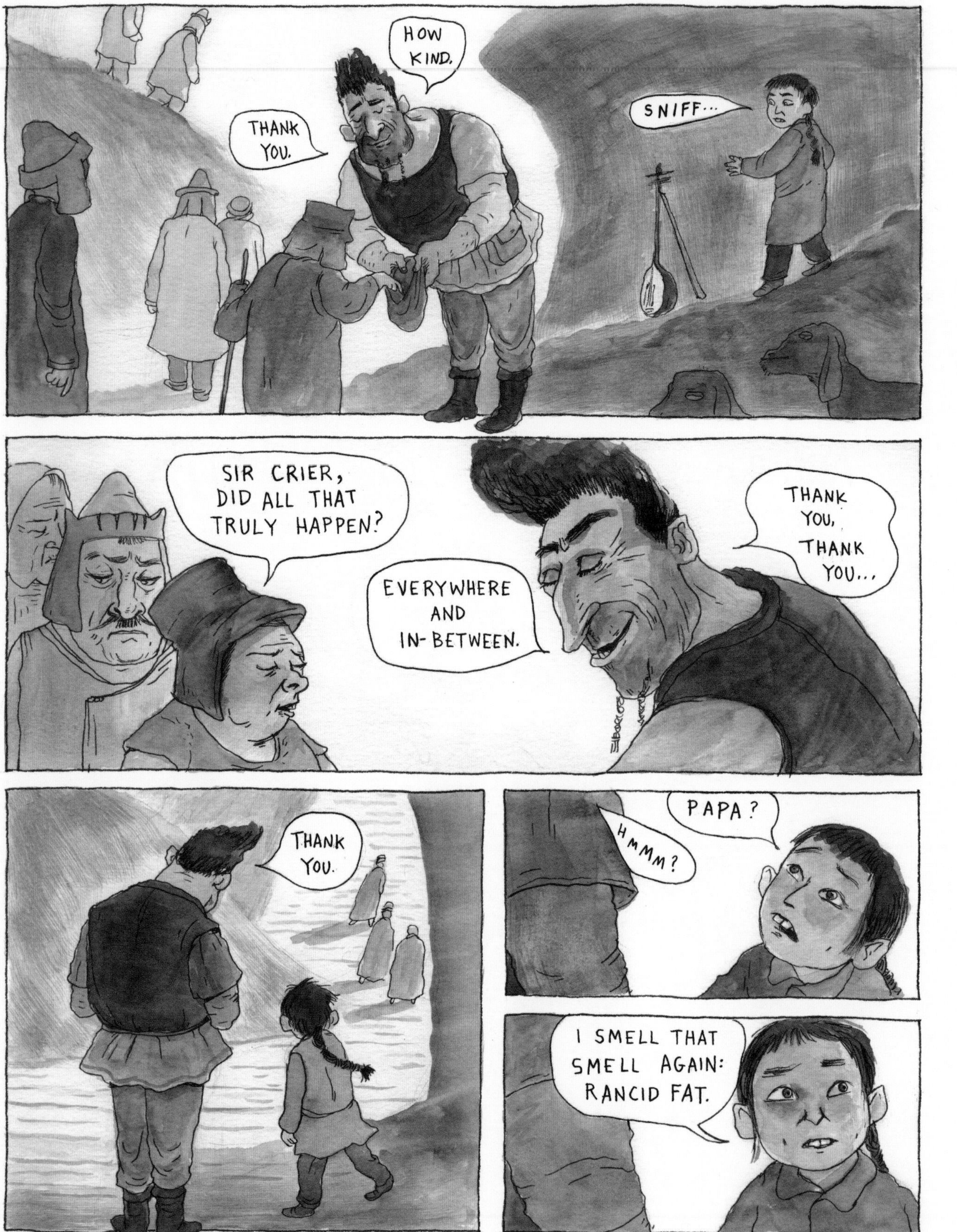
HOW KIND.
THANK YOU.
SNIFF...
SIR CRIER, DID ALL THAT TRULY HAPPEN?
EVERYWHERE AND IN-BETWEEN.
THANK YOU, THANK YOU...
THANK YOU.
PAPA?
HMMM?
I SMELL THAT SMELL AGAIN: RANCID FAT.

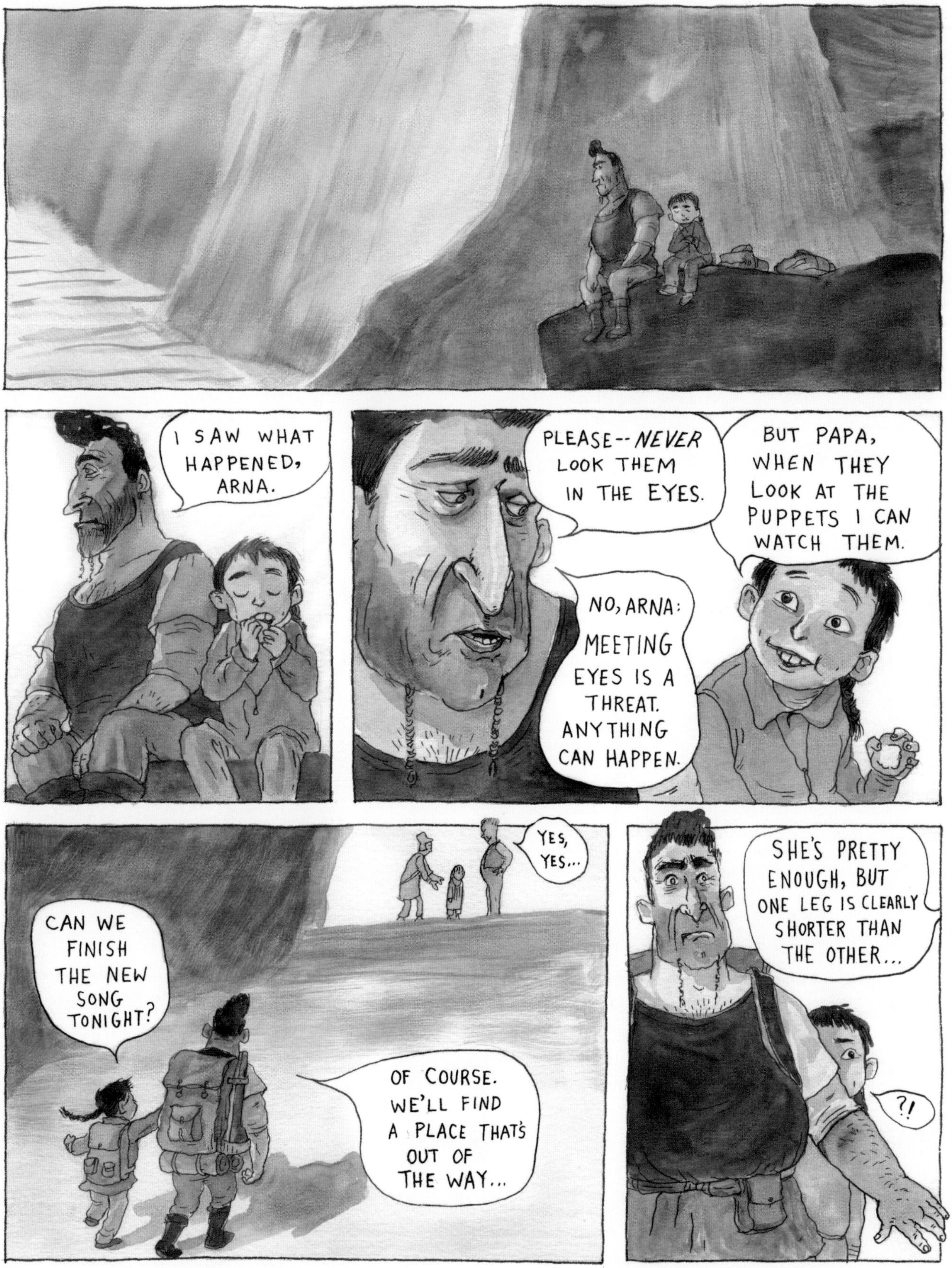
I SAW WHAT HAPPENED, ARNA.
PLEASE--*NEVER* LOOK THEM IN THE EYES.
BUT PAPA, WHEN THEY LOOK AT THE PUPPETS I CAN WATCH THEM.
NO, ARNA:
MEETING EYES IS A THREAT. ANYTHING CAN HAPPEN.
YES, YES...
CAN WE FINISH THE NEW SONG TONIGHT?
OF COURSE. WE'LL FIND A PLACE THAT'S OUT OF THE WAY...
SHE'S PRETTY ENOUGH, BUT ONE LEG IS CLEARLY SHORTER THAN THE OTHER...
?!

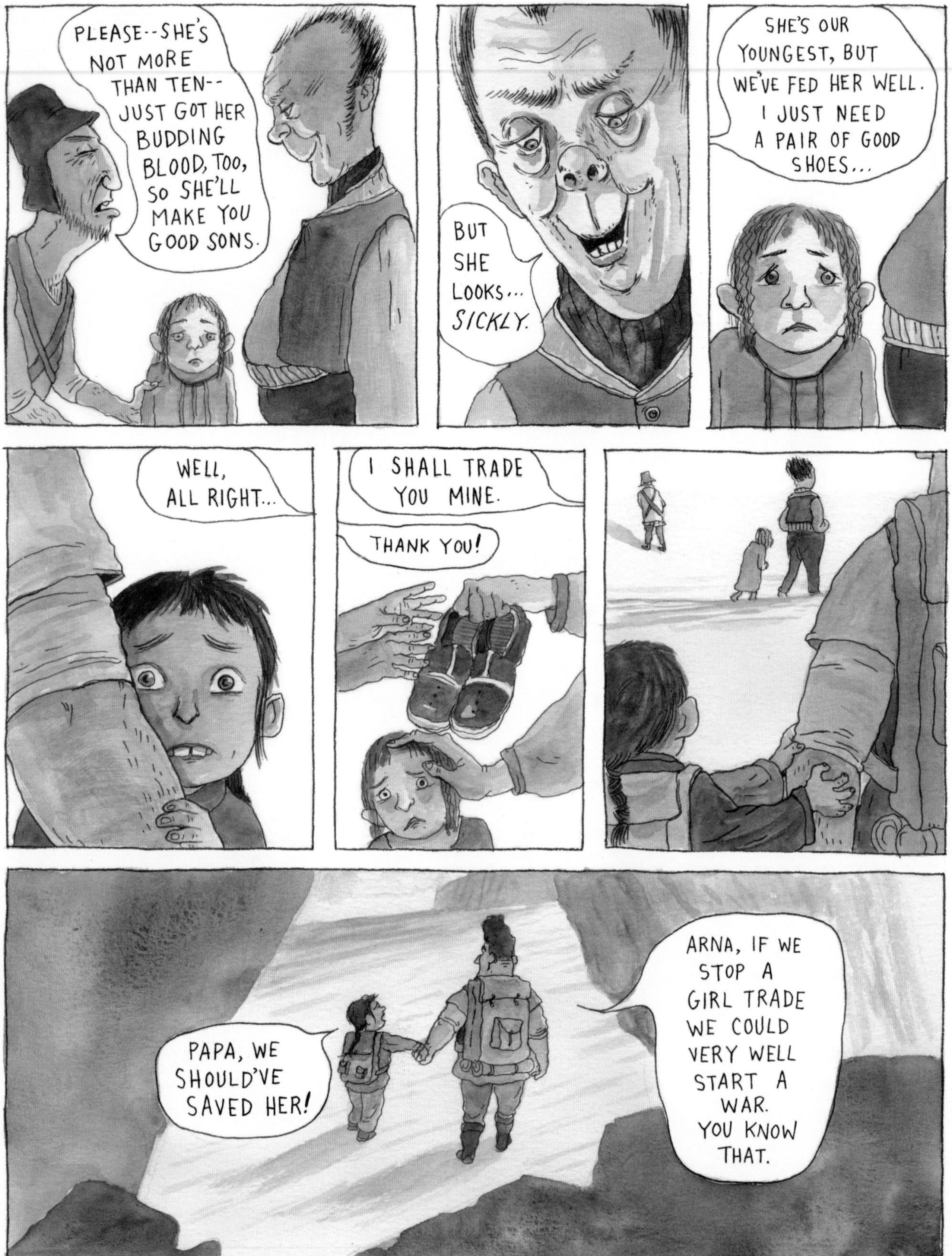
PLEASE--SHE'S NOT MORE THAN TEN--JUST GOT HER BUDDING BLOOD, TOO, SO SHE'LL MAKE YOU GOOD SONS.
BUT SHE LOOKS... SICKLY.
SHE'S OUR YOUNGEST, BUT WE'VE FED HER WELL. I JUST NEED A PAIR OF GOOD SHOES...
WELL, ALL RIGHT...
I SHALL TRADE YOU MINE.
THANK YOU!
PAPA, WE SHOULD'VE SAVED HER!
ARNA, IF WE STOP A GIRL TRADE WE COULD VERY WELL START A WAR. YOU KNOW THAT.

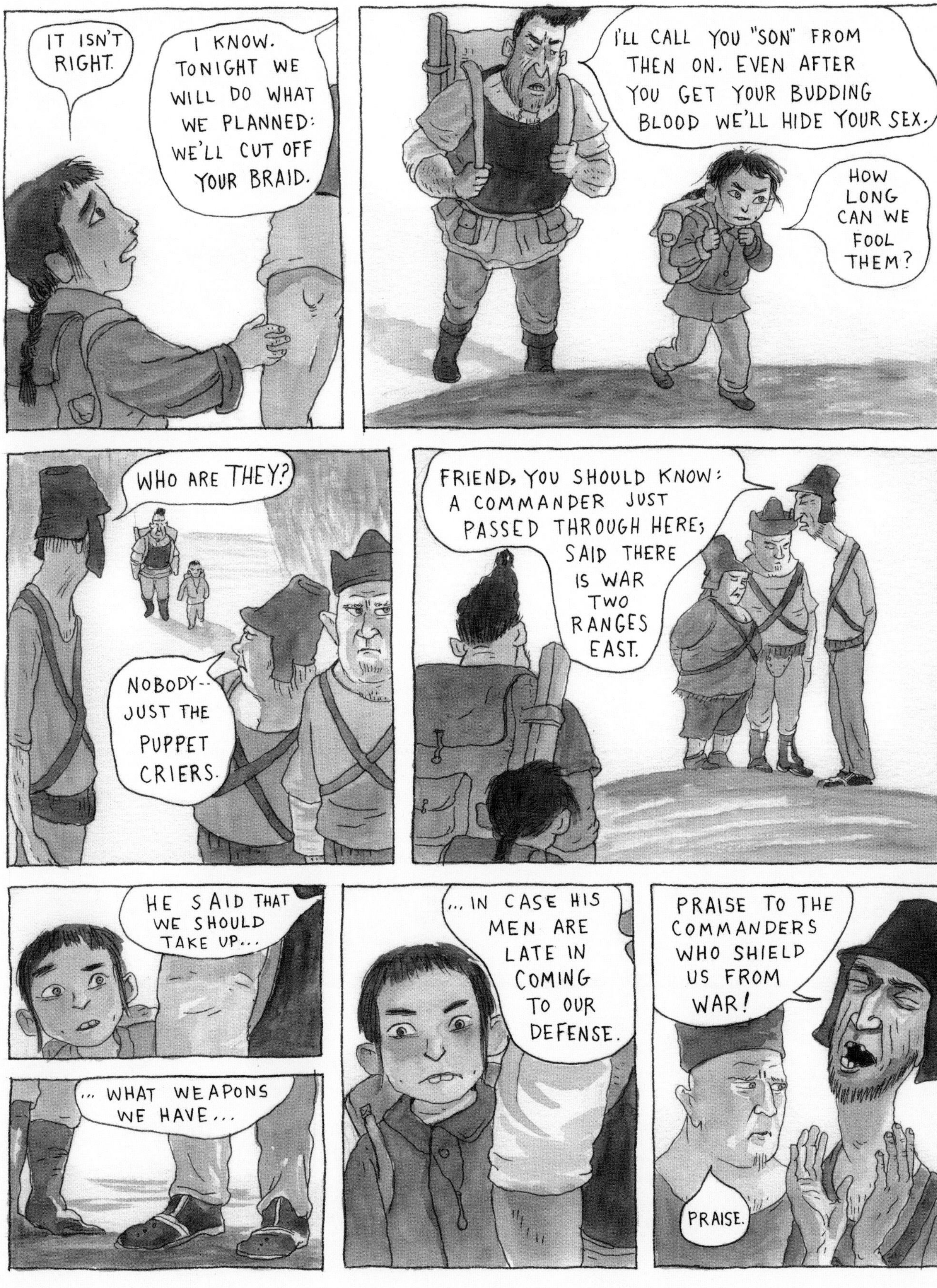
IT ISN'T RIGHT.
I KNOW. TONIGHT WE WILL DO WHAT WE PLANNED: WE'LL CUT OFF YOUR BRAID.
I'LL CALL YOU "SON" FROM THEN ON. EVEN AFTER YOU GET YOUR BUDDING BLOOD WE'LL HIDE YOUR SEX.
HOW LONG CAN WE FOOL THEM?
WHO ARE THEY?
NOBODY-- JUST THE PUPPET CRIERS.
FRIEND, YOU SHOULD KNOW: A COMMANDER JUST PASSED THROUGH HERE; SAID THERE IS WAR TWO RANGES EAST.
HE SAID THAT WE SHOULD TAKE UP...
...WHAT WEAPONS WE HAVE...
...IN CASE HIS MEN ARE LATE IN COMING TO OUR DEFENSE.
PRAISE TO THE COMMANDERS WHO SHIELD US FROM WAR!
PRAISE.

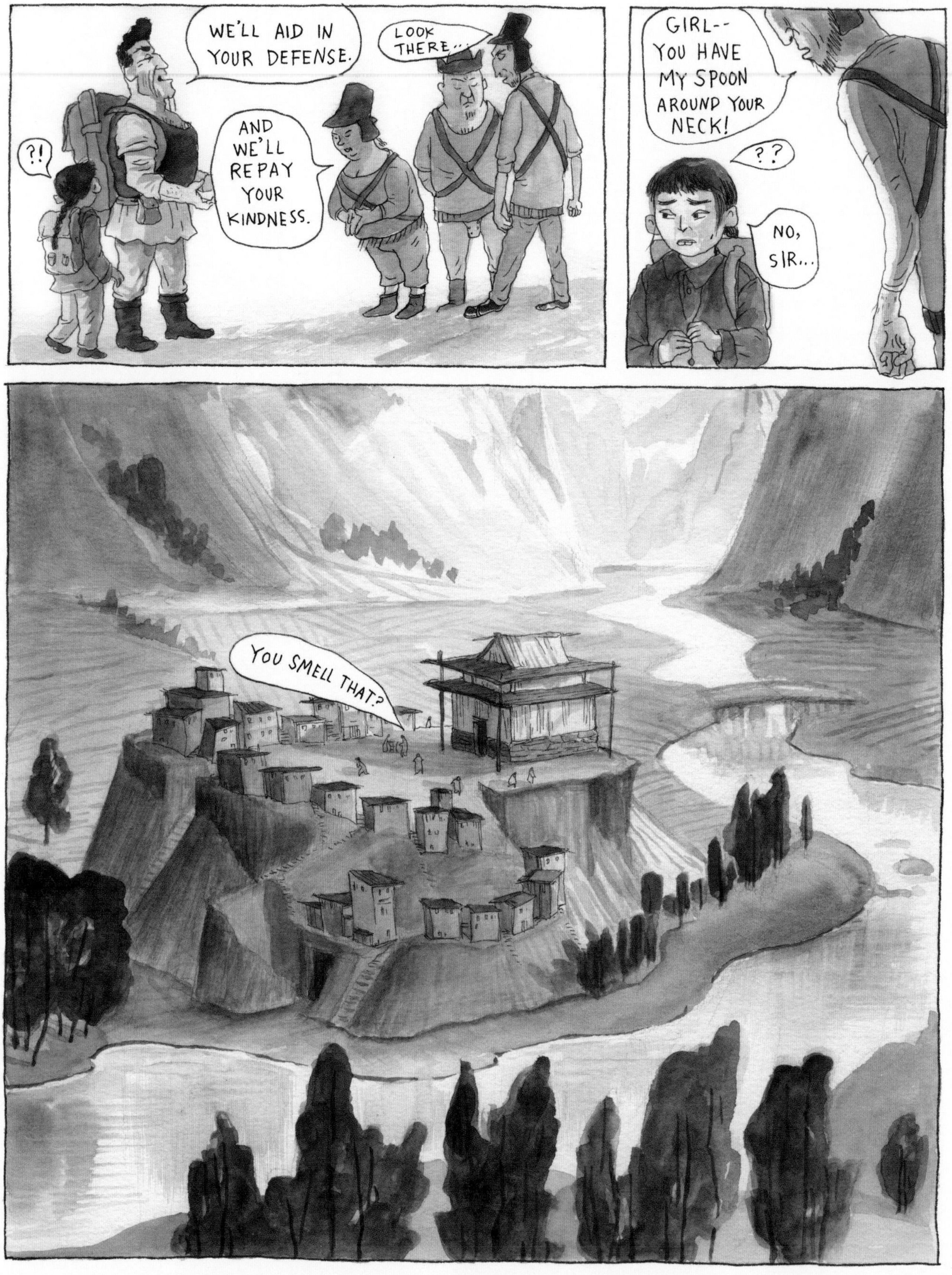
WE'LL AID IN YOUR DEFENSE.
?!
AND WE'LL REPAY YOUR KINDNESS.
LOOK THERE...
GIRL-- YOU HAVE MY SPOON AROUND YOUR NECK!
??
NO, SIR...
YOU SMELL THAT?

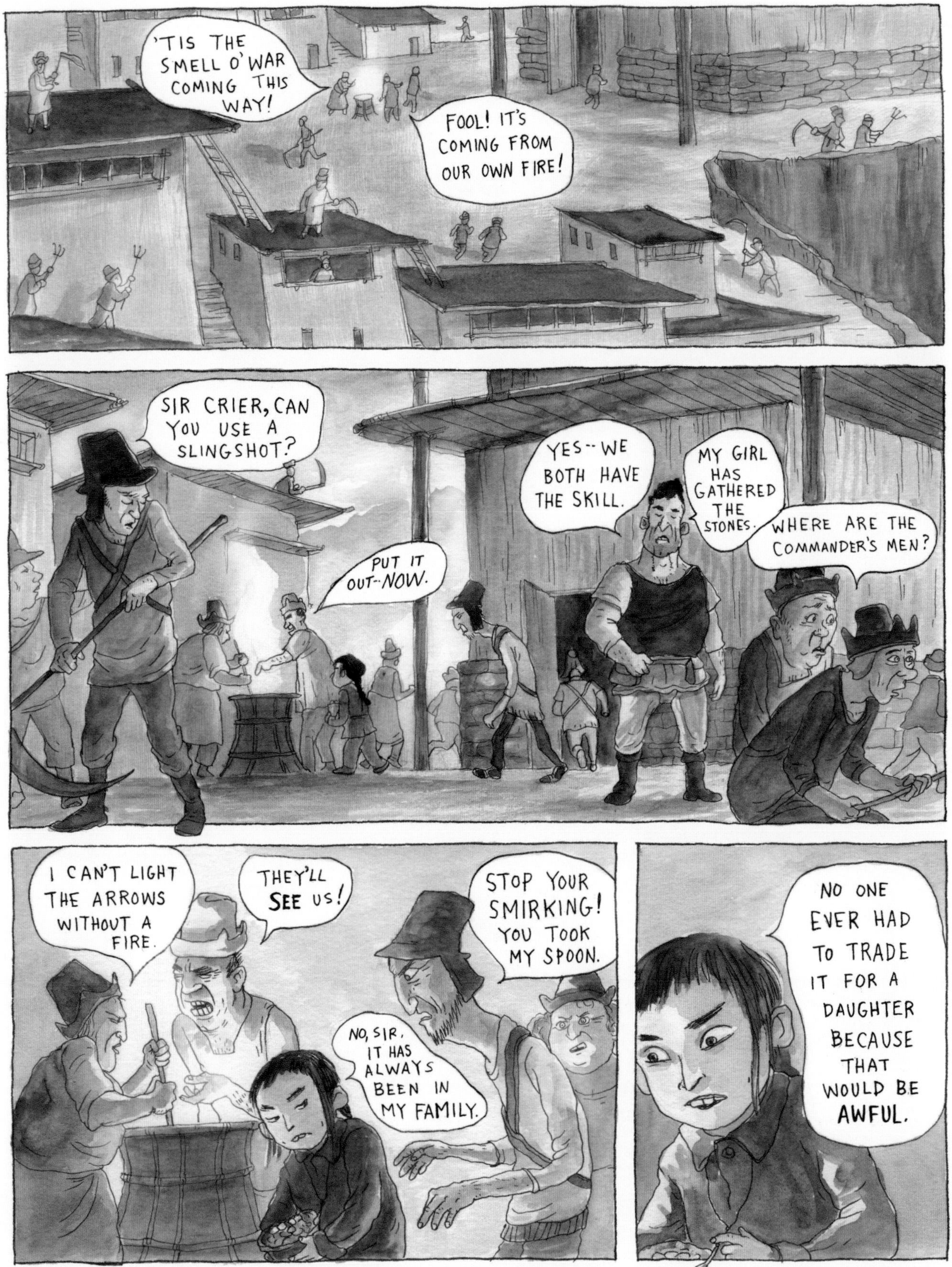
'TIS THE SMELL O' WAR COMING THIS WAY!
FOOL! IT'S COMING FROM OUR OWN FIRE!
SIR CRIER, CAN YOU USE A SLINGSHOT?
YES-- WE BOTH HAVE THE SKILL.
MY GIRL HAS GATHERED THE STONES.
WHERE ARE THE COMMANDER'S MEN?
PUT IT OUT-- NOW.
I CAN'T LIGHT THE ARROWS WITHOUT A FIRE.
THEY'LL SEE US!
STOP YOUR SMIRKING! YOU TOOK MY SPOON.
NO, SIR, IT HAS ALWAYS BEEN IN MY FAMILY.
NO ONE EVER HAD TO TRADE IT FOR A DAUGHTER BECAUSE THAT WOULD BE AWFUL.

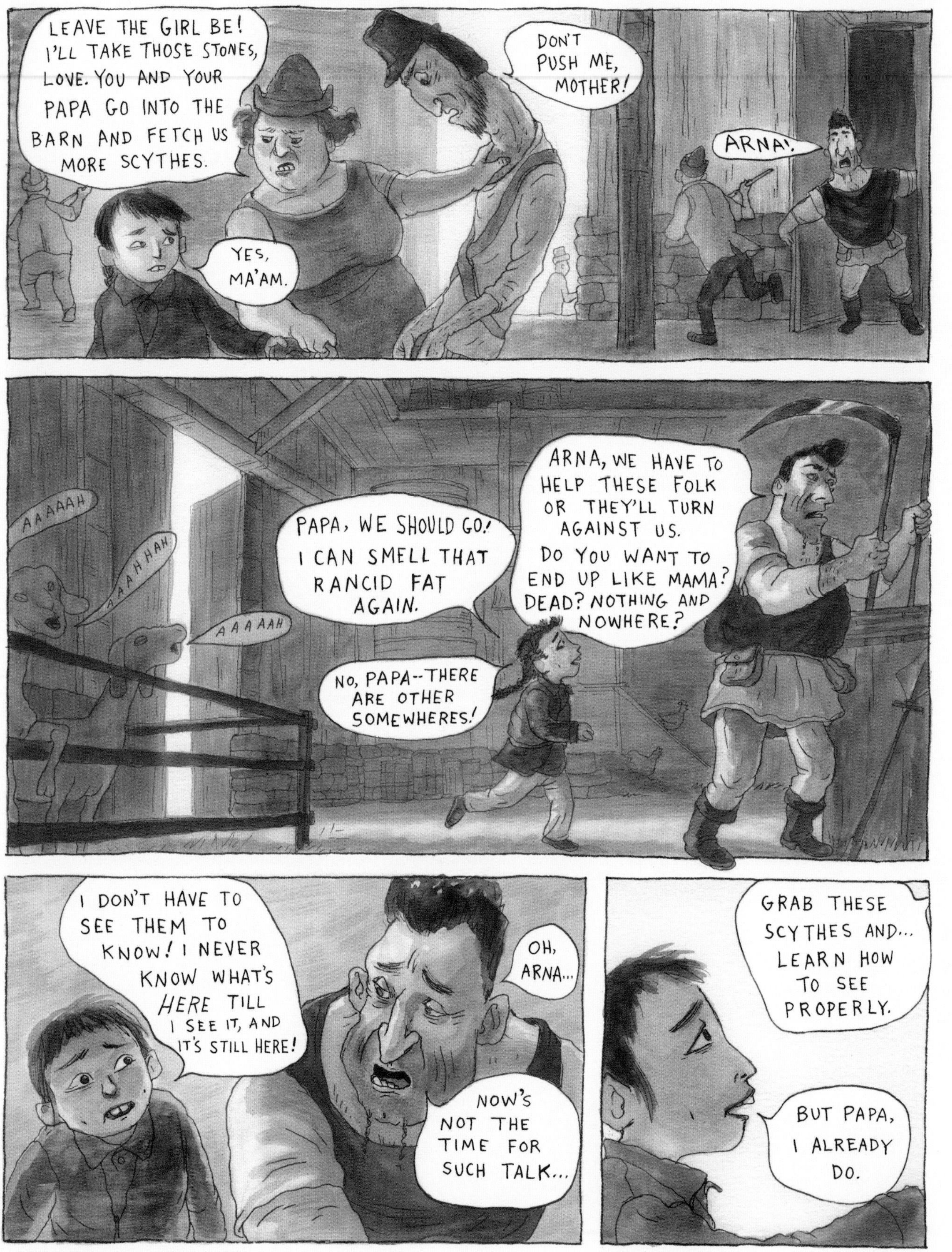
LEAVE THE GIRL BE! I'LL TAKE THOSE STONES, LOVE. YOU AND YOUR PAPA GO INTO THE BARN AND FETCH US MORE SCYTHES.
DON'T PUSH ME, MOTHER!
YES, MA'AM.
ARNA!
AAAAAH
AAAHHAH
AAAAAH
PAPA, WE SHOULD GO! I CAN SMELL THAT RANCID FAT AGAIN.
ARNA, WE HAVE TO HELP THESE FOLK OR THEY'LL TURN AGAINST US.
DO YOU WANT TO END UP LIKE MAMA? DEAD? NOTHING AND NOWHERE?
NO, PAPA--THERE ARE OTHER SOMEWHERES!
I DON'T HAVE TO SEE THEM TO KNOW! I NEVER KNOW WHAT'S *HERE* TILL I SEE IT, AND IT'S STILL HERE!
OH, ARNA...
NOW'S NOT THE TIME FOR SUCH TALK...
GRAB THESE SCYTHES AND... LEARN HOW TO SEE PROPERLY.
BUT PAPA, I ALREADY DO.

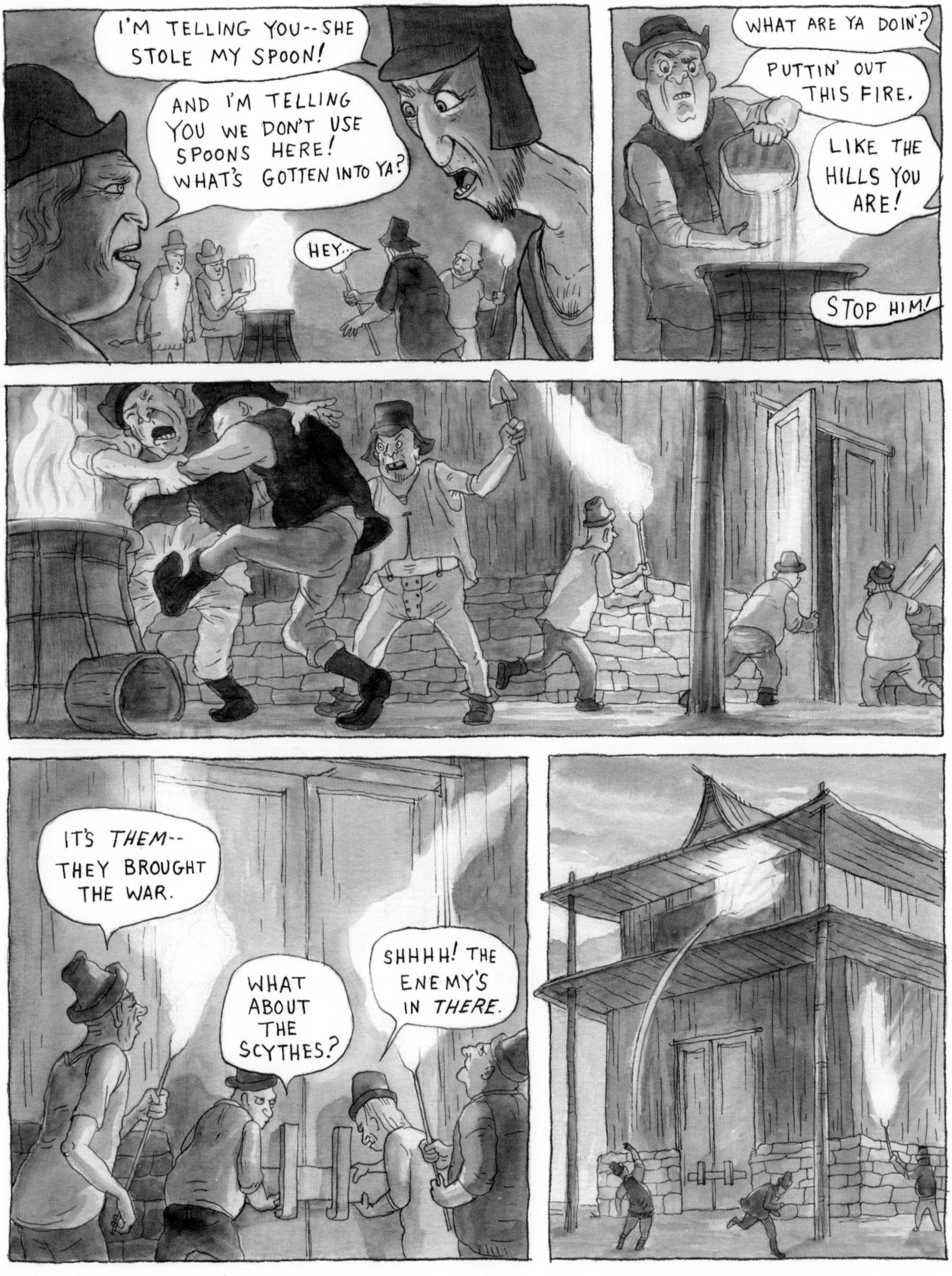
I'M TELLING YOU--SHE STOLE MY SPOON!
AND I'M TELLING YOU WE DON'T USE SPOONS HERE! WHAT'S GOTTEN INTO YA?
HEY...
WHAT ARE YA DOIN'?
PUTTIN' OUT THIS FIRE.
LIKE THE HILLS YOU ARE!
STOP HIM!
IT'S *THEM*-- THEY BROUGHT THE WAR.
WHAT ABOUT THE SCYTHES?
SHHHH! THE ENEMY'S IN *THERE*.

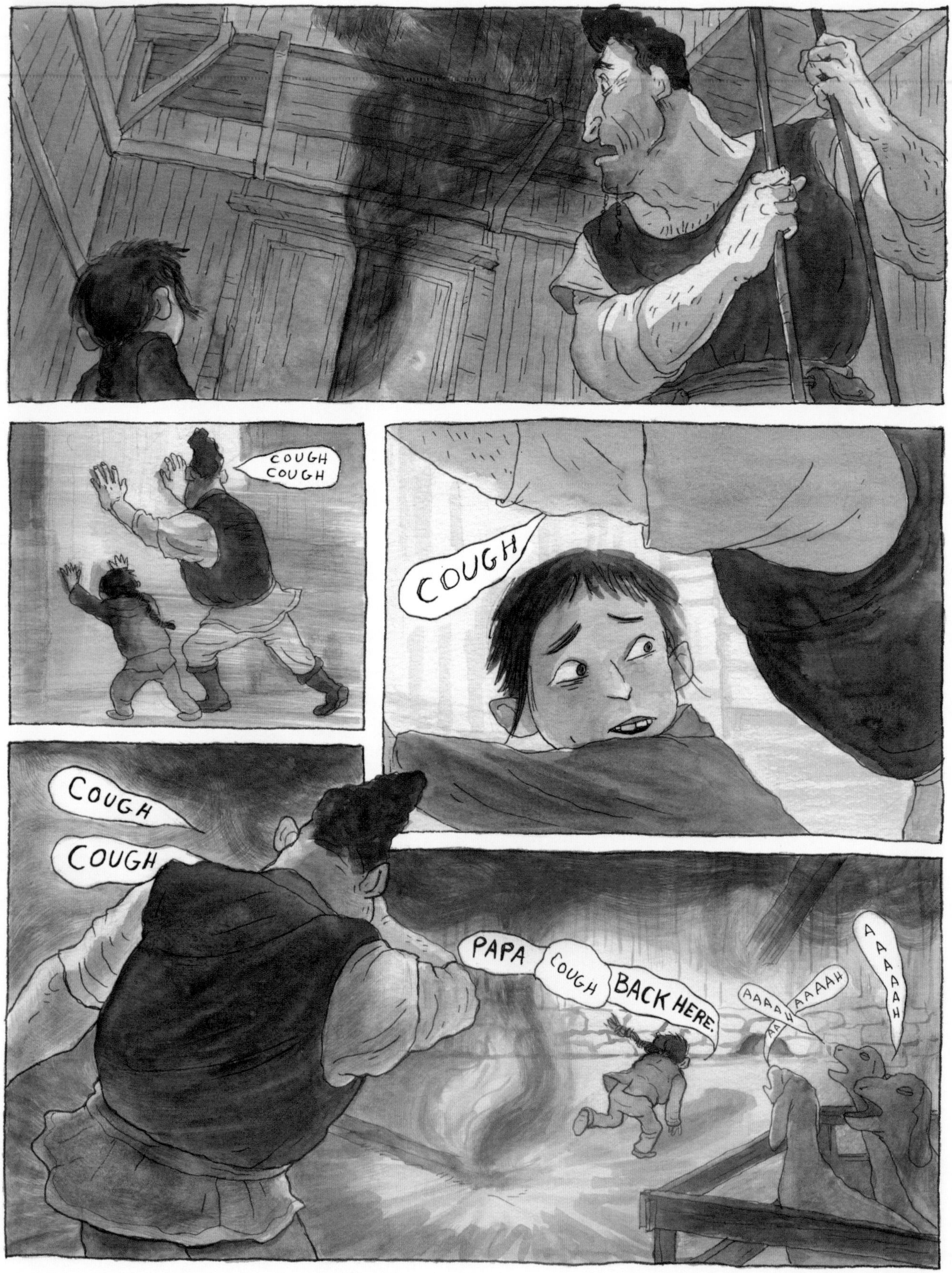
COUGH COUGH
COUGH
COUGH
COUGH
PAPA
COUGH
BACK HERE.
AAAAH
AAAAAAAH
AAAAAH

I FOUND A WAY OUT!

I'LL DIG-- I'LL MAKE IT BIGGER-- YOU'LL GET THROUGH.

PAPA! FOLLOW MY VOICE!

COUGH

COUGH

COUGH COUGH

PAPA!

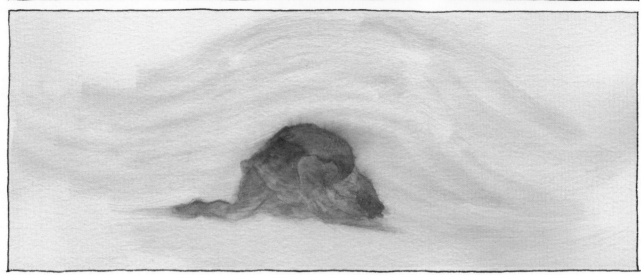

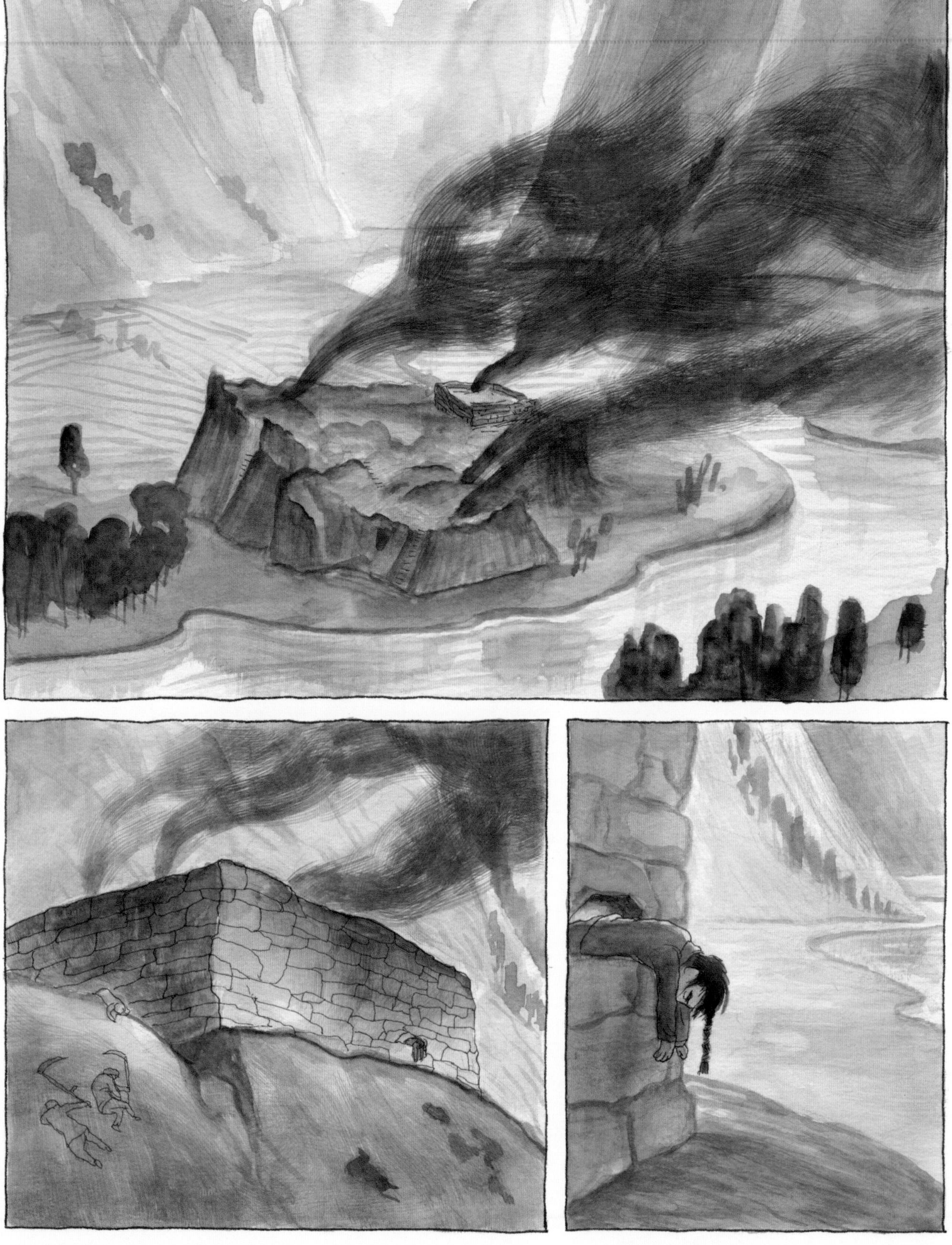

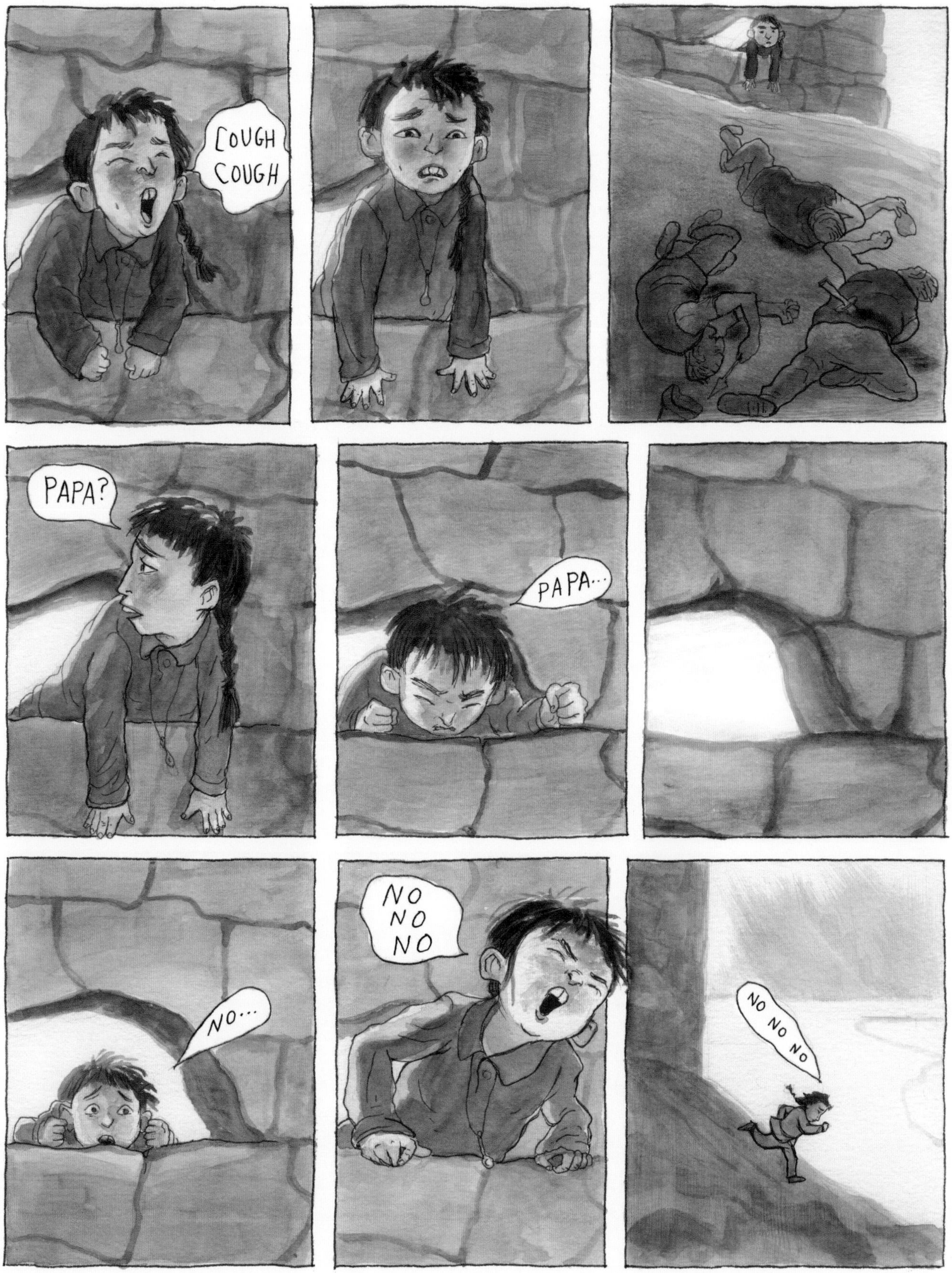
COUGH
COUGH
PAPA?
PAPA...
NO...
NO
NO
NO
NO NO NO

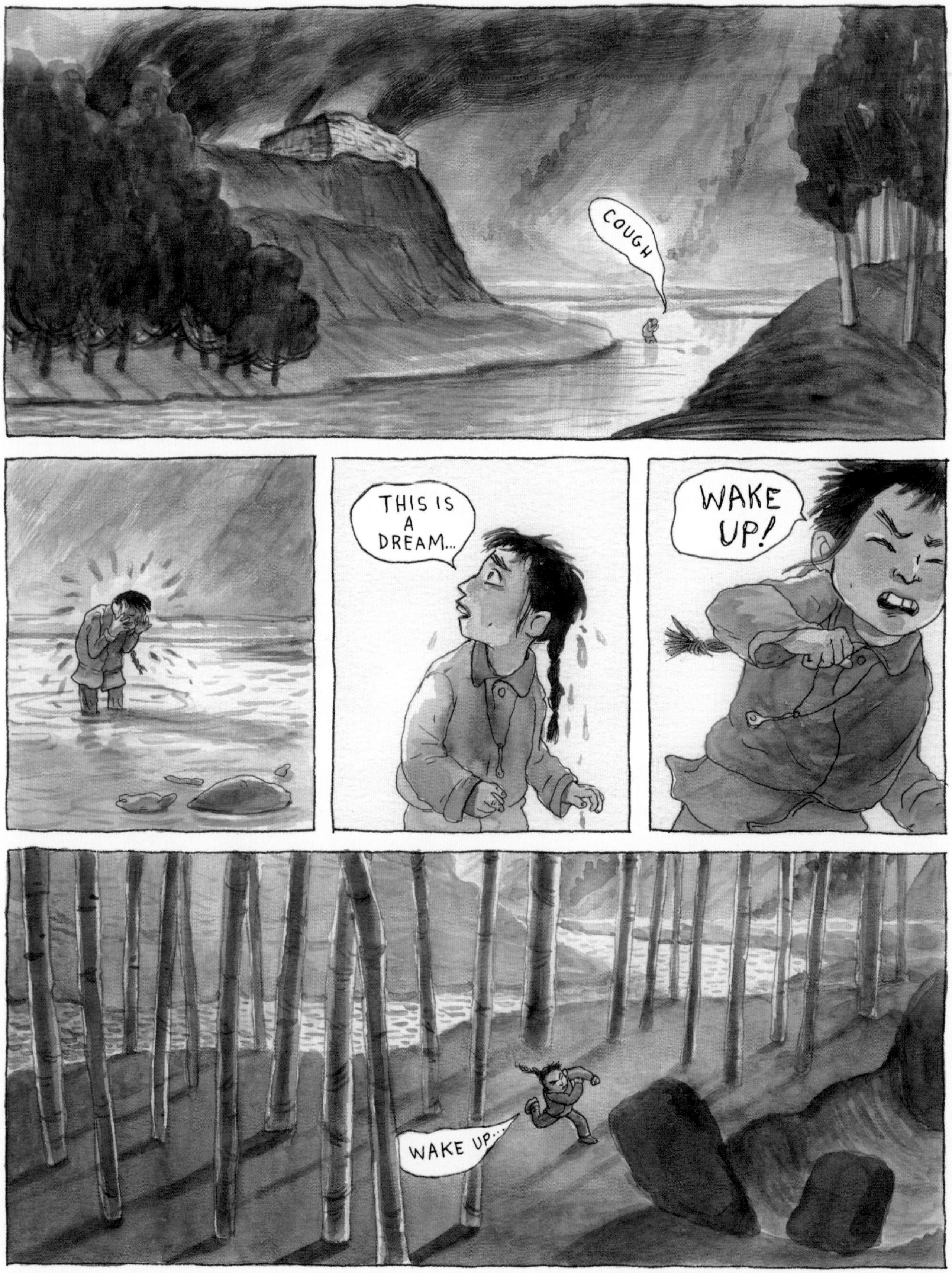
COUGH
THIS IS A DREAM...
WAKE UP!
WAKE UP...

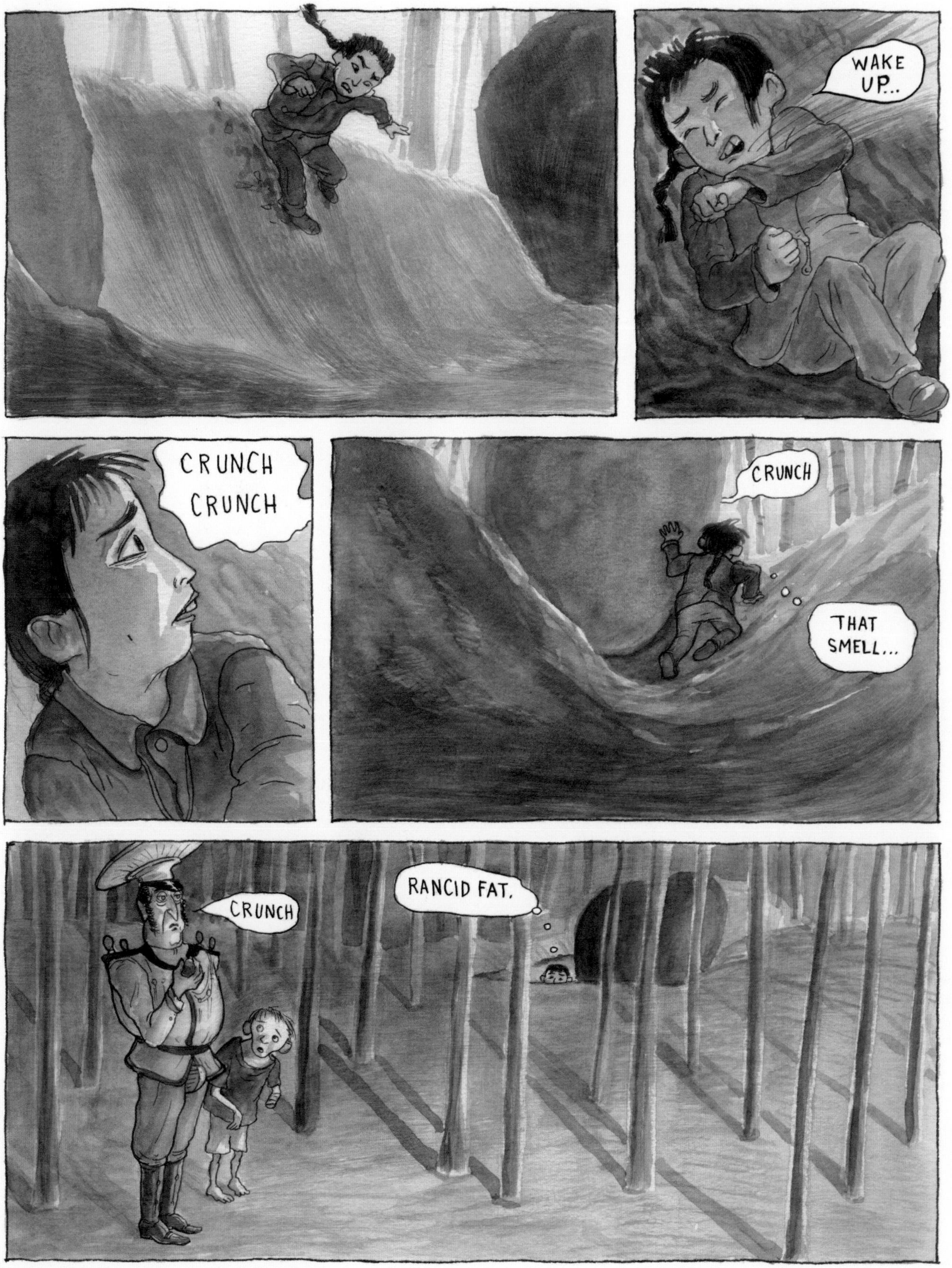
WAKE UP...
CRUNCH CRUNCH
CRUNCH
THAT SMELL...
CRUNCH
RANCID FAT.

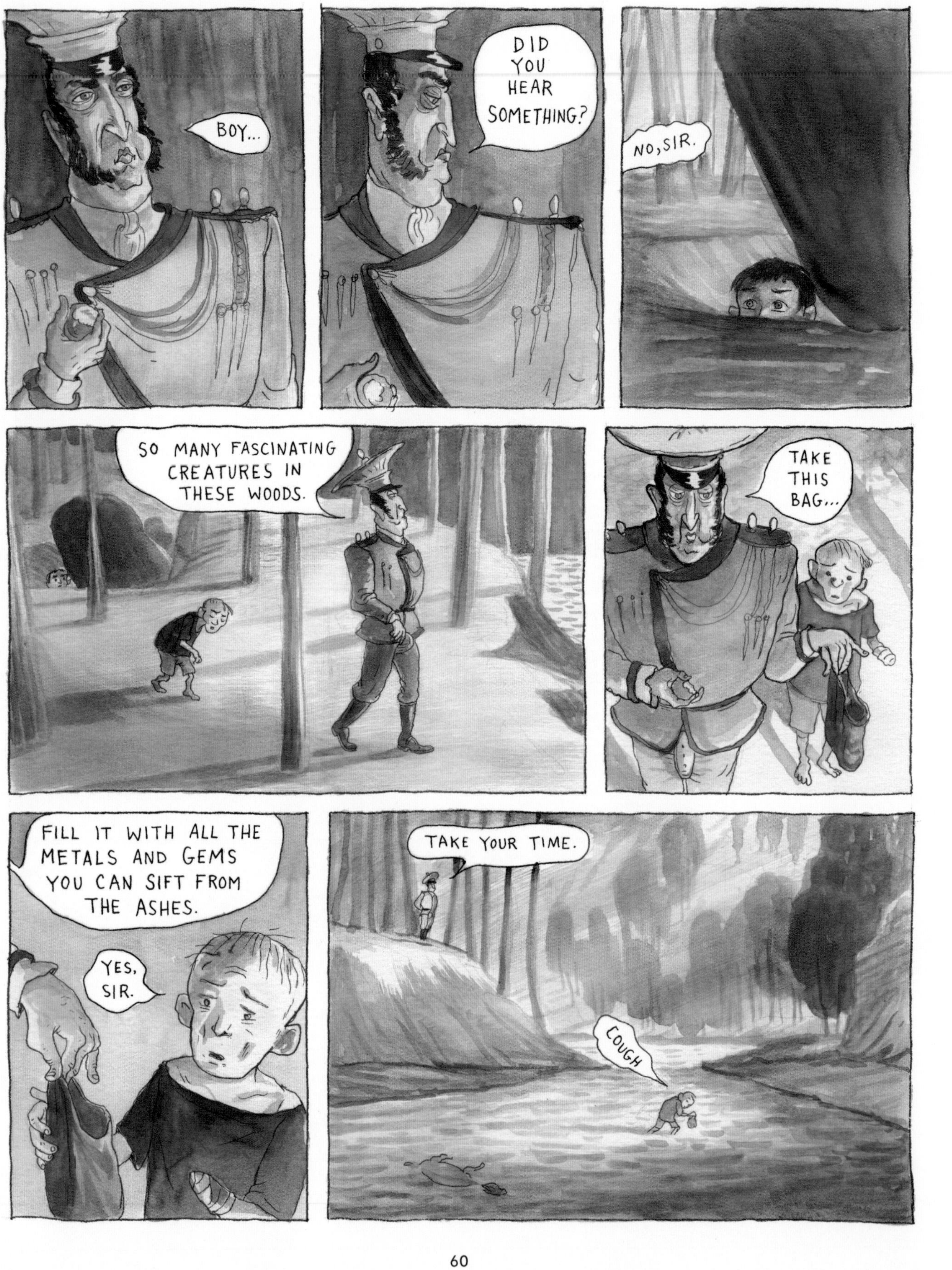
BOY...
DID YOU HEAR SOMETHING?
NO, SIR.
SO MANY FASCINATING CREATURES IN THESE WOODS.
TAKE THIS BAG...
FILL IT WITH ALL THE METALS AND GEMS YOU CAN SIFT FROM THE ASHES.
YES, SIR.
TAKE YOUR TIME.
COUGH

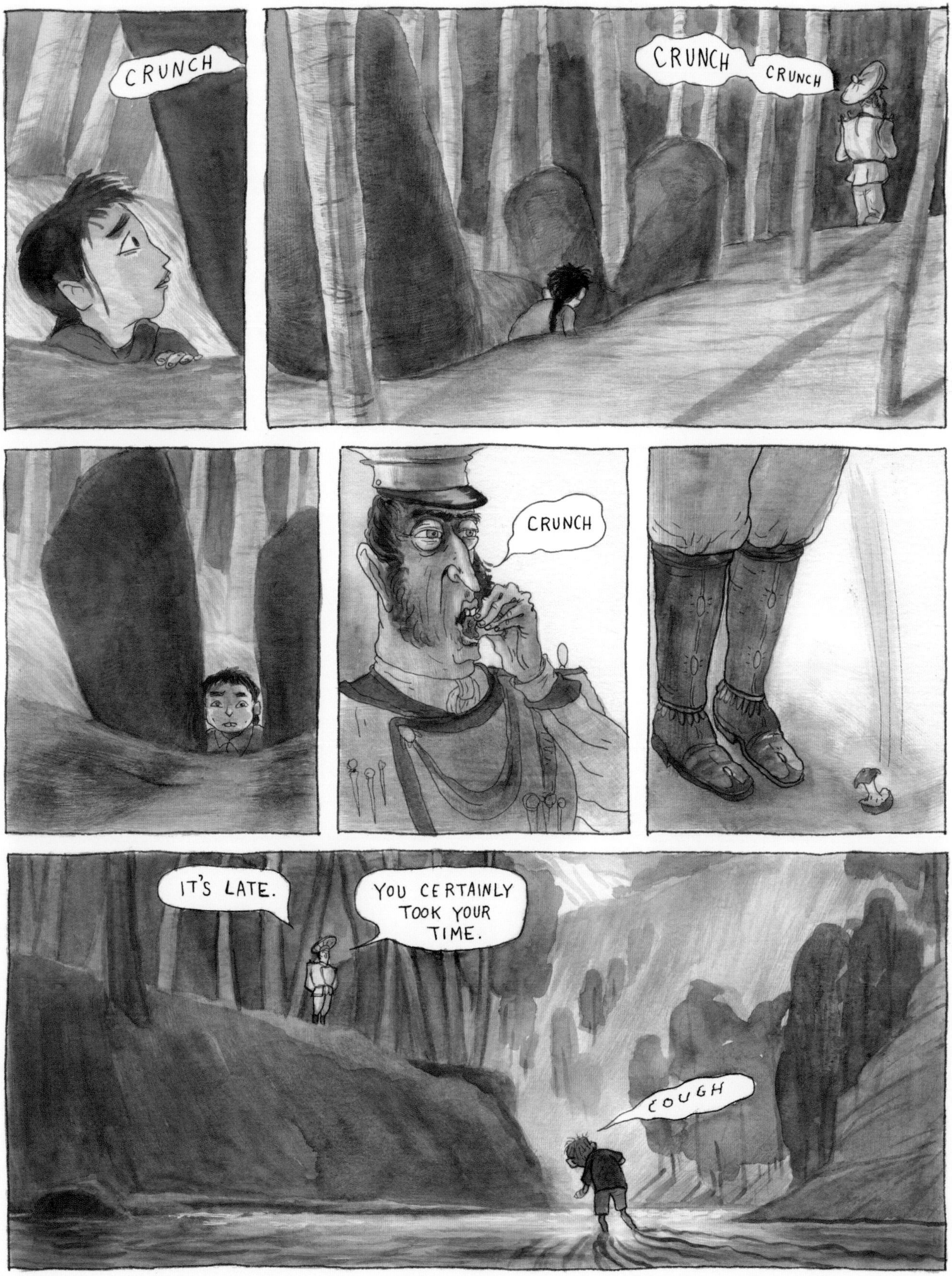
CRUNCH
CRUNCH
CRUNCH
CRUNCH
IT'S LATE.
YOU CERTAINLY TOOK YOUR TIME.
COUGH

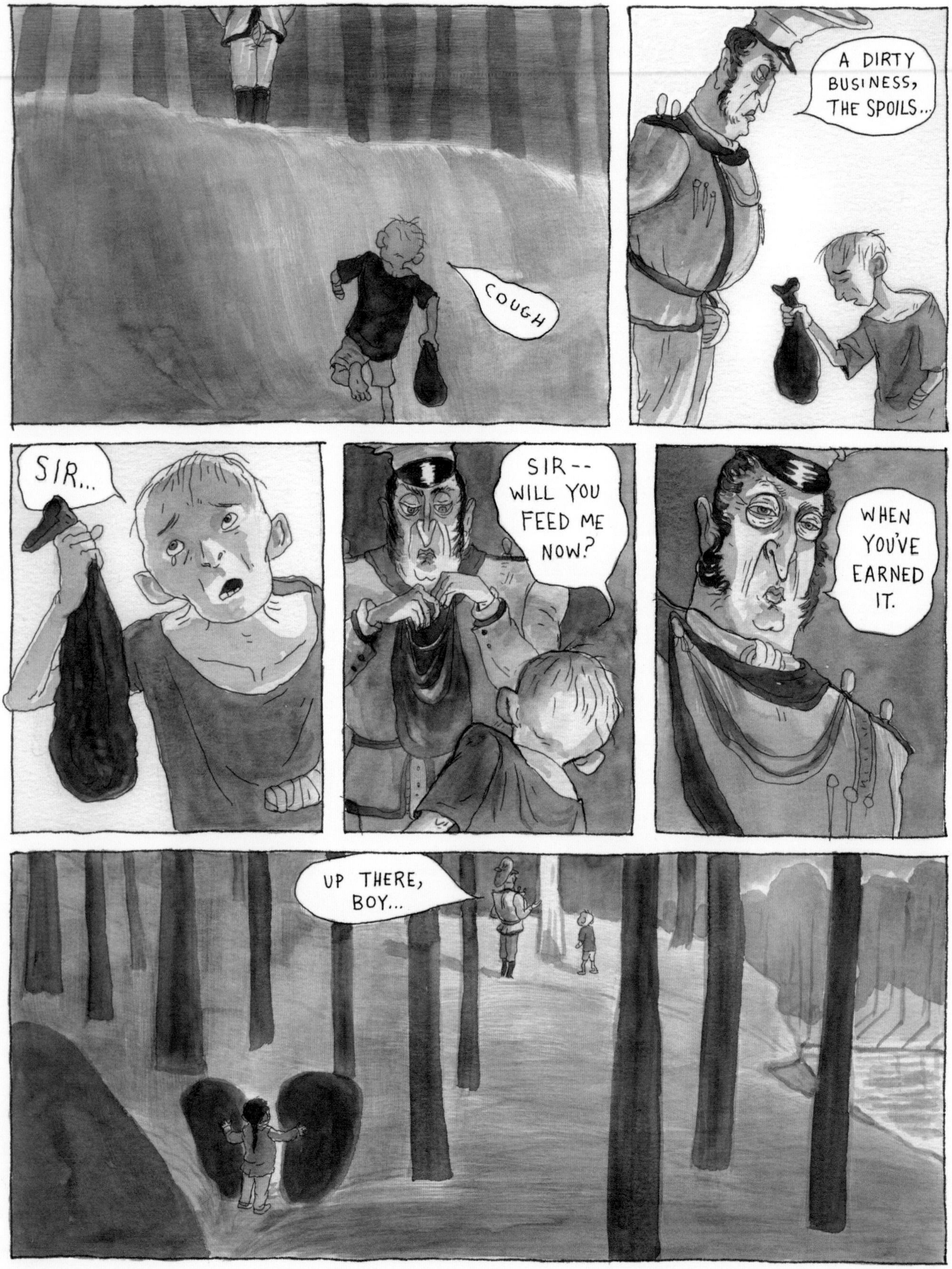
COUGH
A DIRTY BUSINESS, THE SPOILS...
SIR...
SIR-- WILL YOU FEED ME NOW?
WHEN YOU'VE EARNED IT.
UP THERE, BOY...

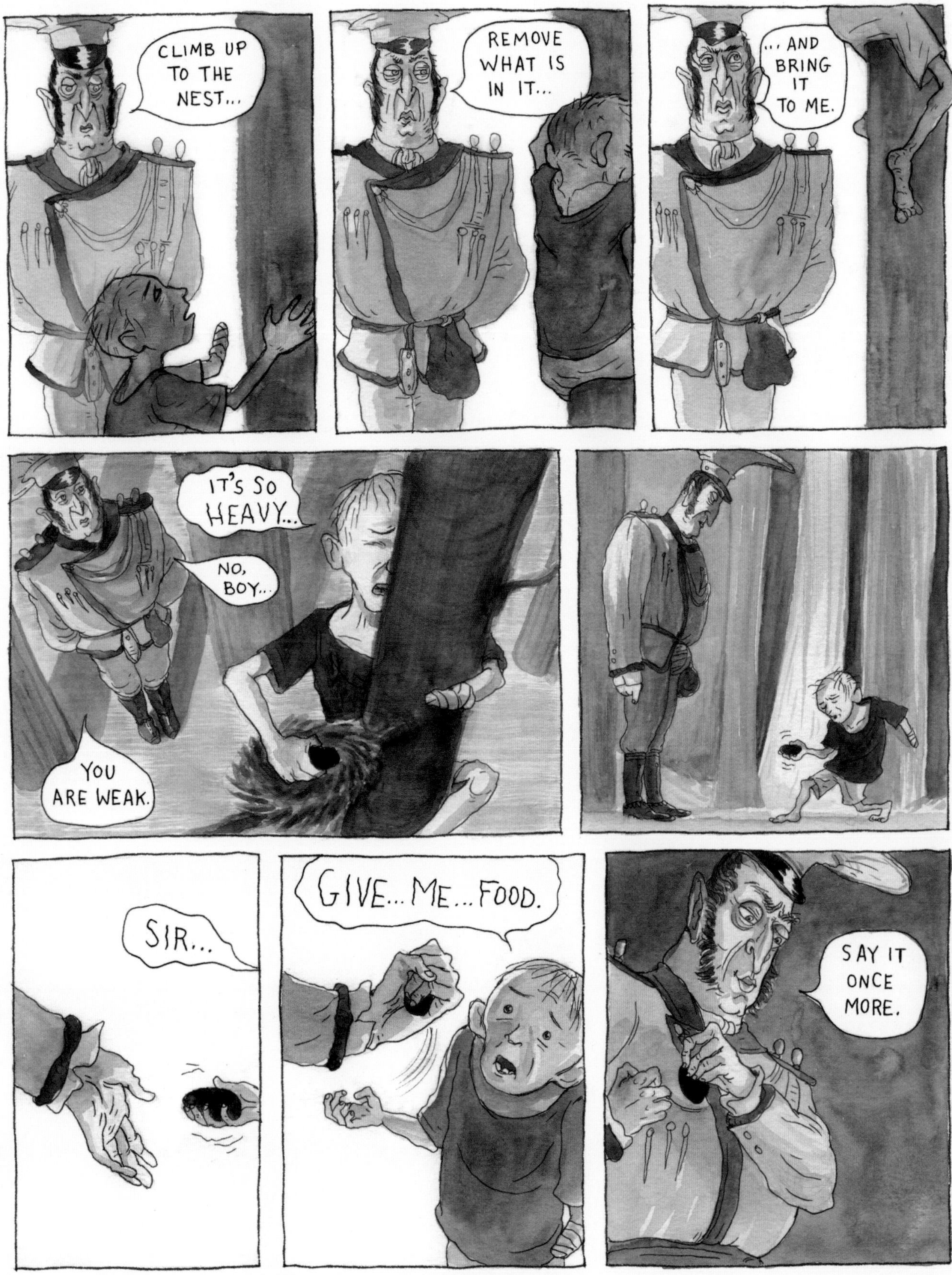
CLIMB UP TO THE NEST...
REMOVE WHAT IS IN IT...
...AND BRING IT TO ME.
IT'S SO HEAVY...
NO, BOY...
YOU ARE WEAK.
SIR...
GIVE... ME... FOOD.
SAY IT ONCE MORE.

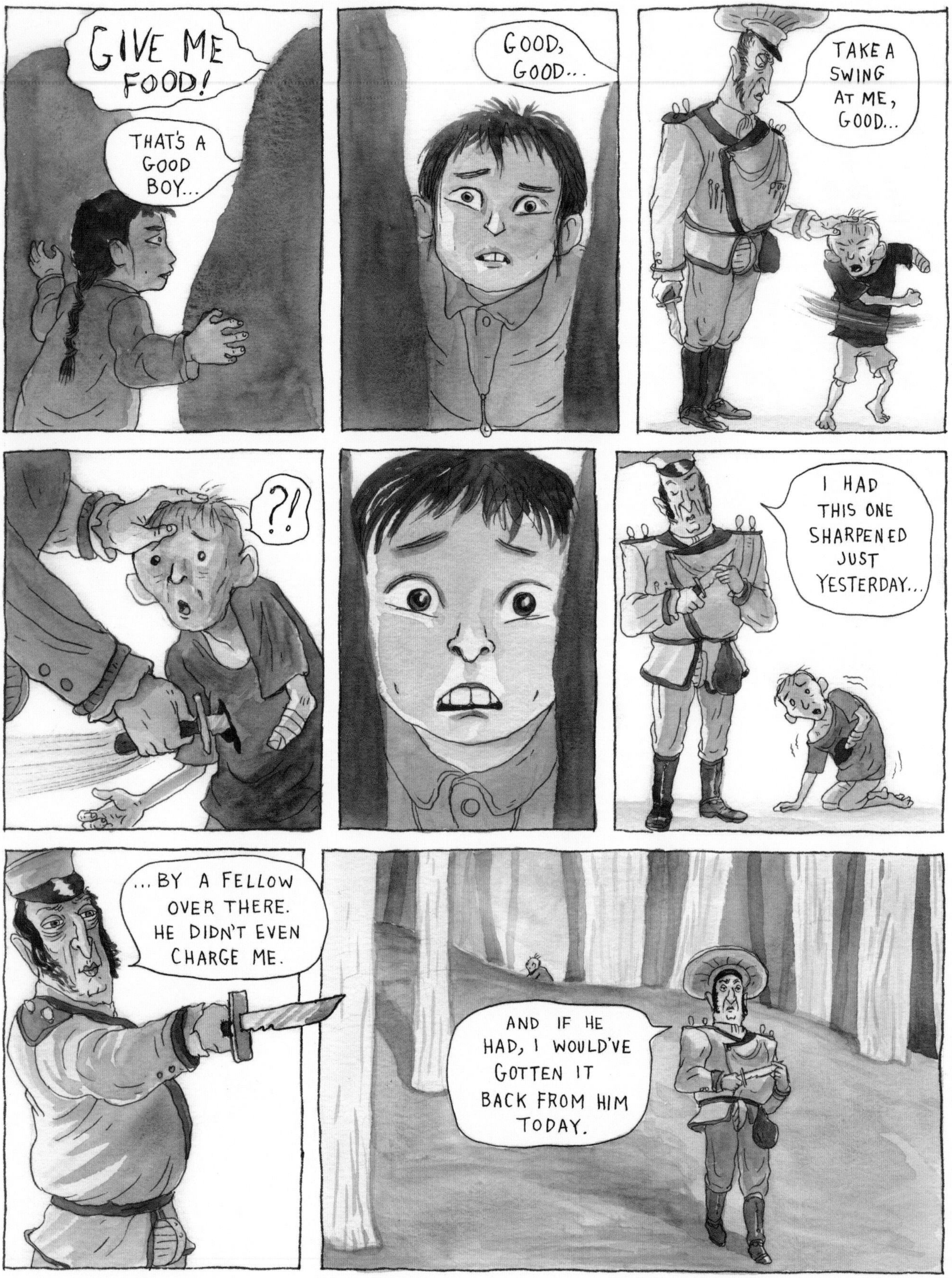
GIVE ME FOOD!
THAT'S A GOOD BOY...
GOOD, GOOD...
TAKE A SWING AT ME, GOOD...
?!
I HAD THIS ONE SHARPENED JUST YESTERDAY...
...BY A FELLOW OVER THERE. HE DIDN'T EVEN CHARGE ME.
AND IF HE HAD, I WOULD'VE GOTTEN IT BACK FROM HIM TODAY.

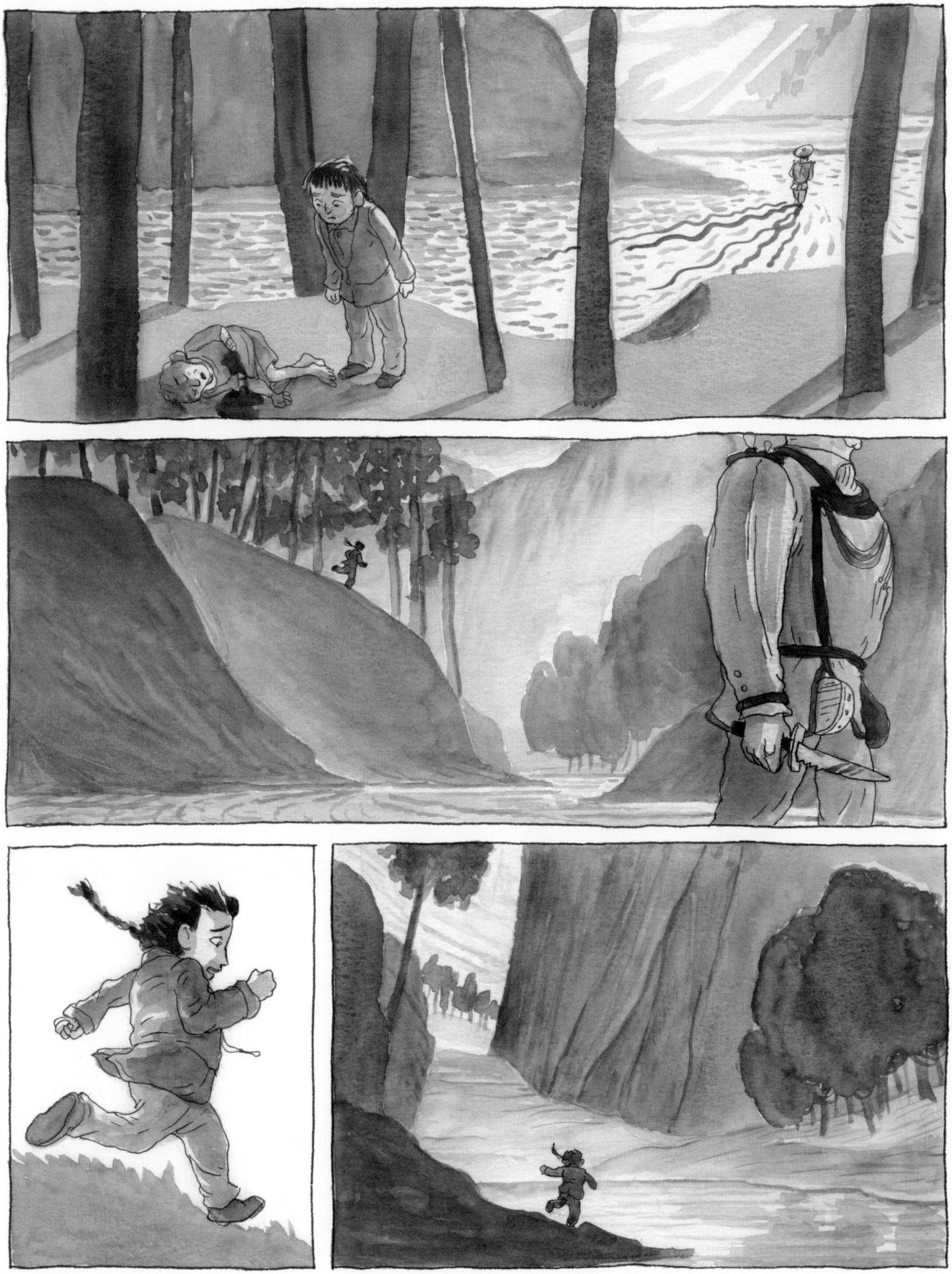

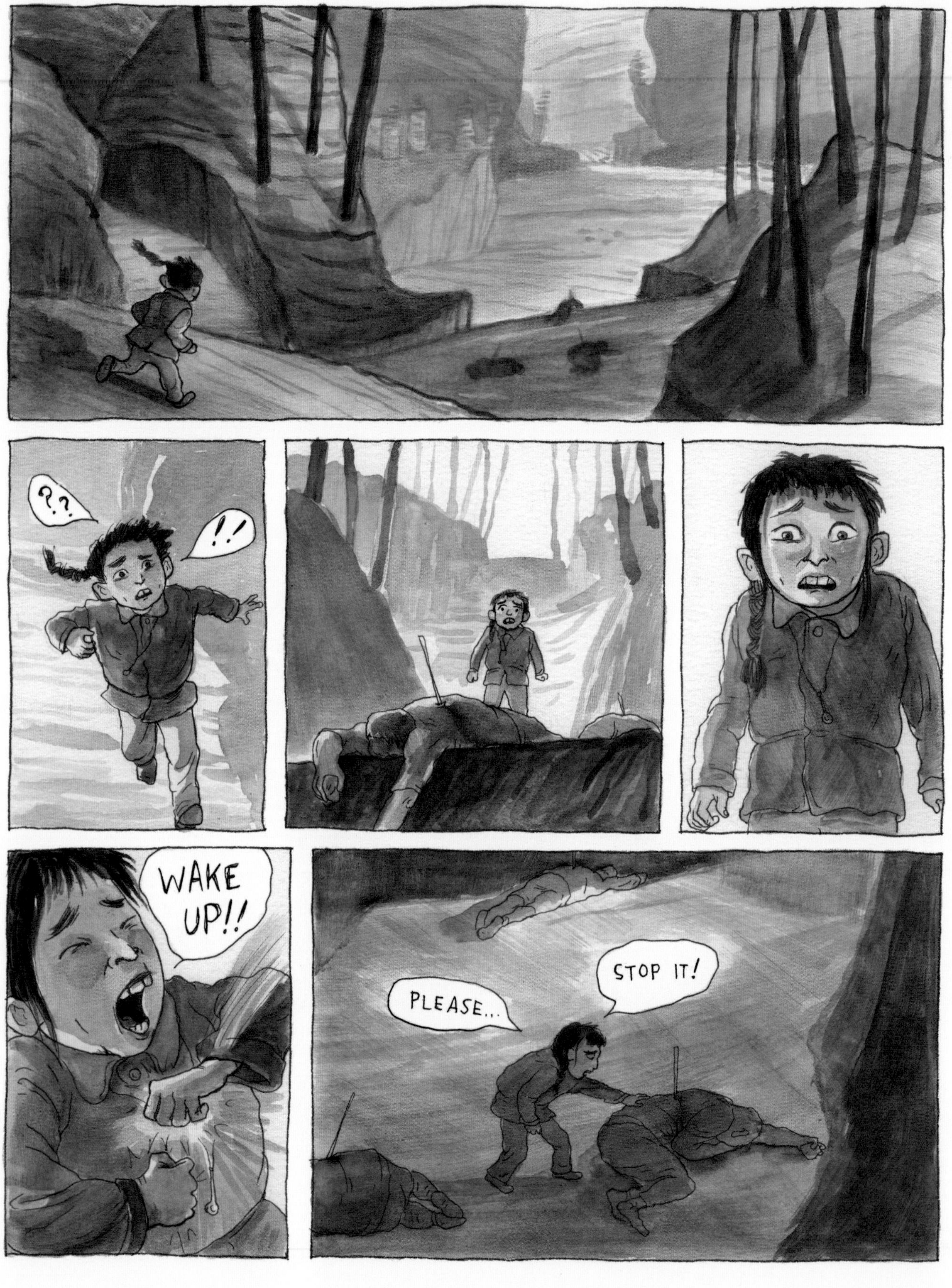
??
!!
WAKE UP!!
PLEASE...
STOP IT!

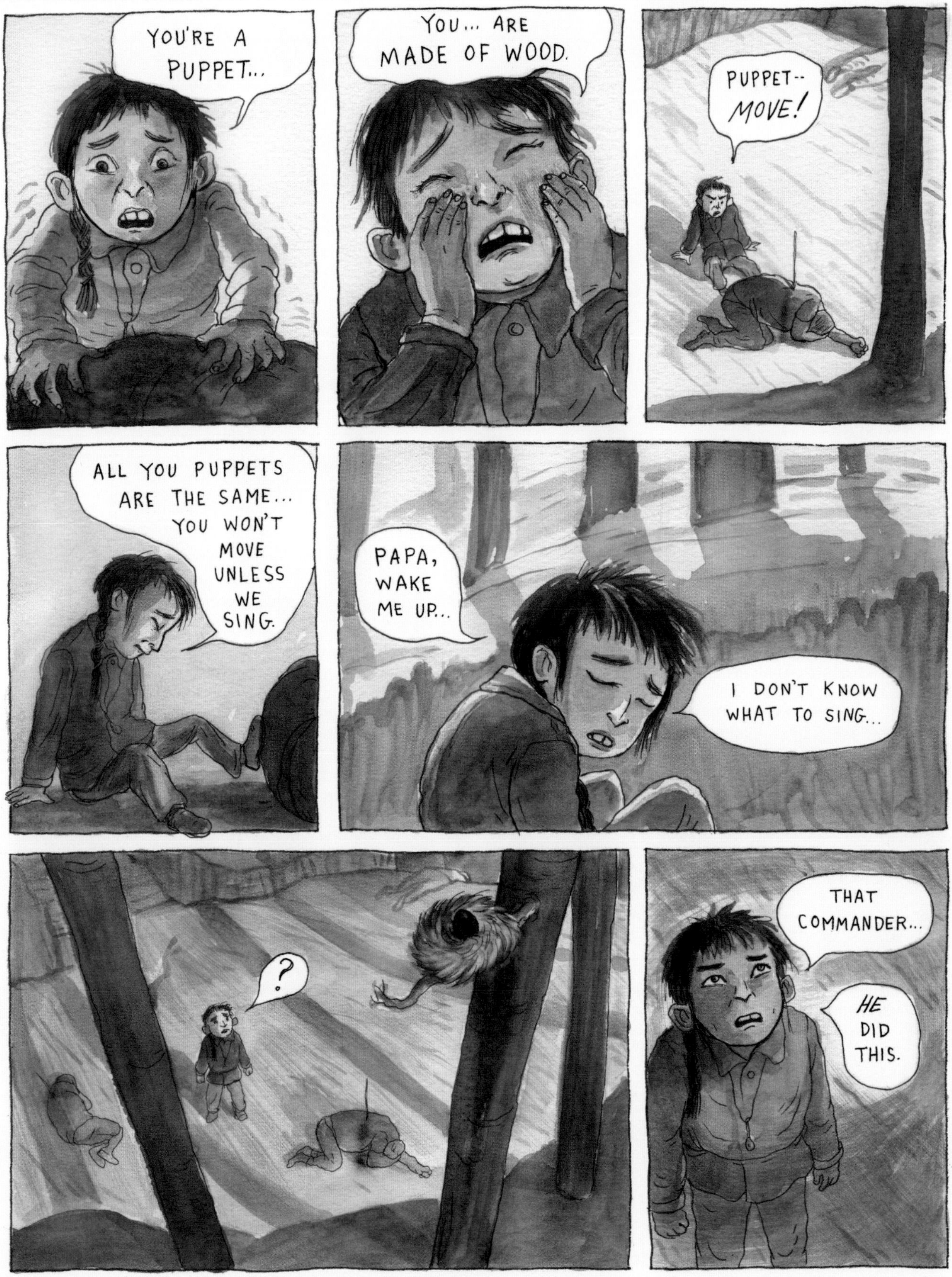
YOU'RE A PUPPET...
YOU... ARE MADE OF WOOD.
PUPPET-- MOVE!
ALL YOU PUPPETS ARE THE SAME... YOU WON'T MOVE UNLESS WE SING.
PAPA, WAKE ME UP...
I DON'T KNOW WHAT TO SING...
?
THAT COMMANDER...
HE DID THIS.

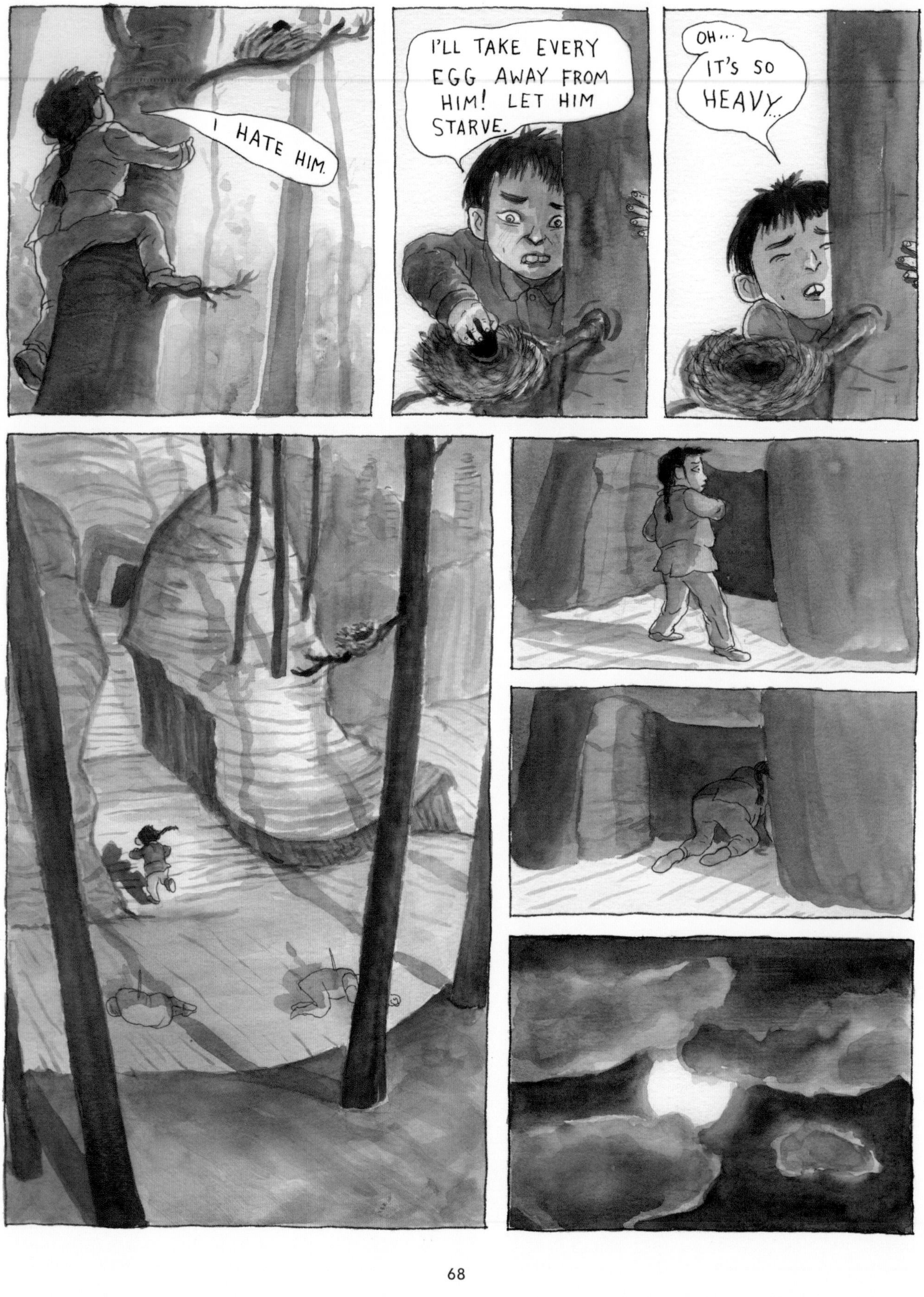
I HATE HIM.
I'LL TAKE EVERY EGG AWAY FROM HIM! LET HIM STARVE.
OH...
IT'S SO HEAVY...

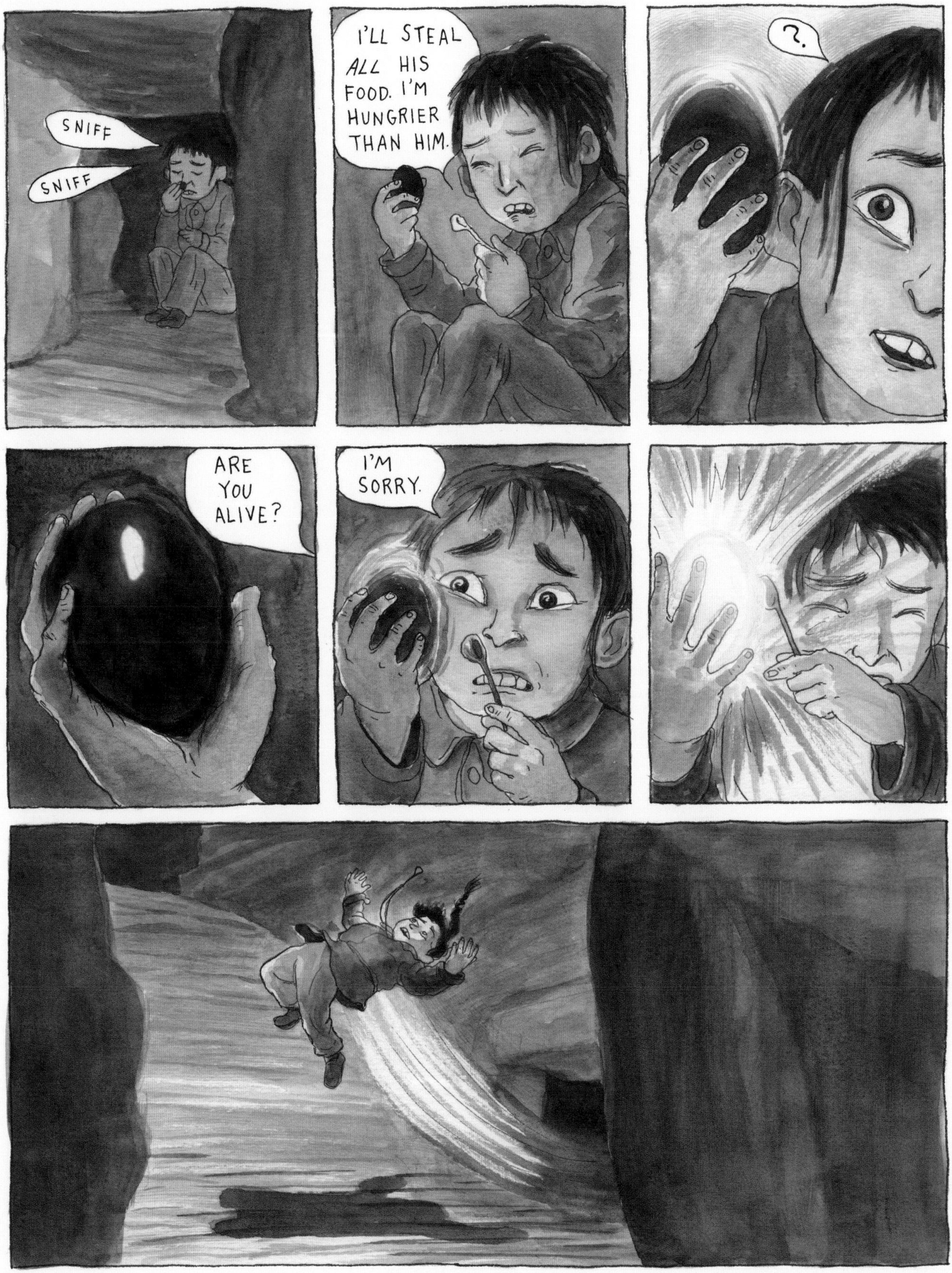
SNIFF
SNIFF
I'LL STEAL ALL HIS FOOD. I'M HUNGRIER THAN HIM.
?
ARE YOU ALIVE?
I'M SORRY.

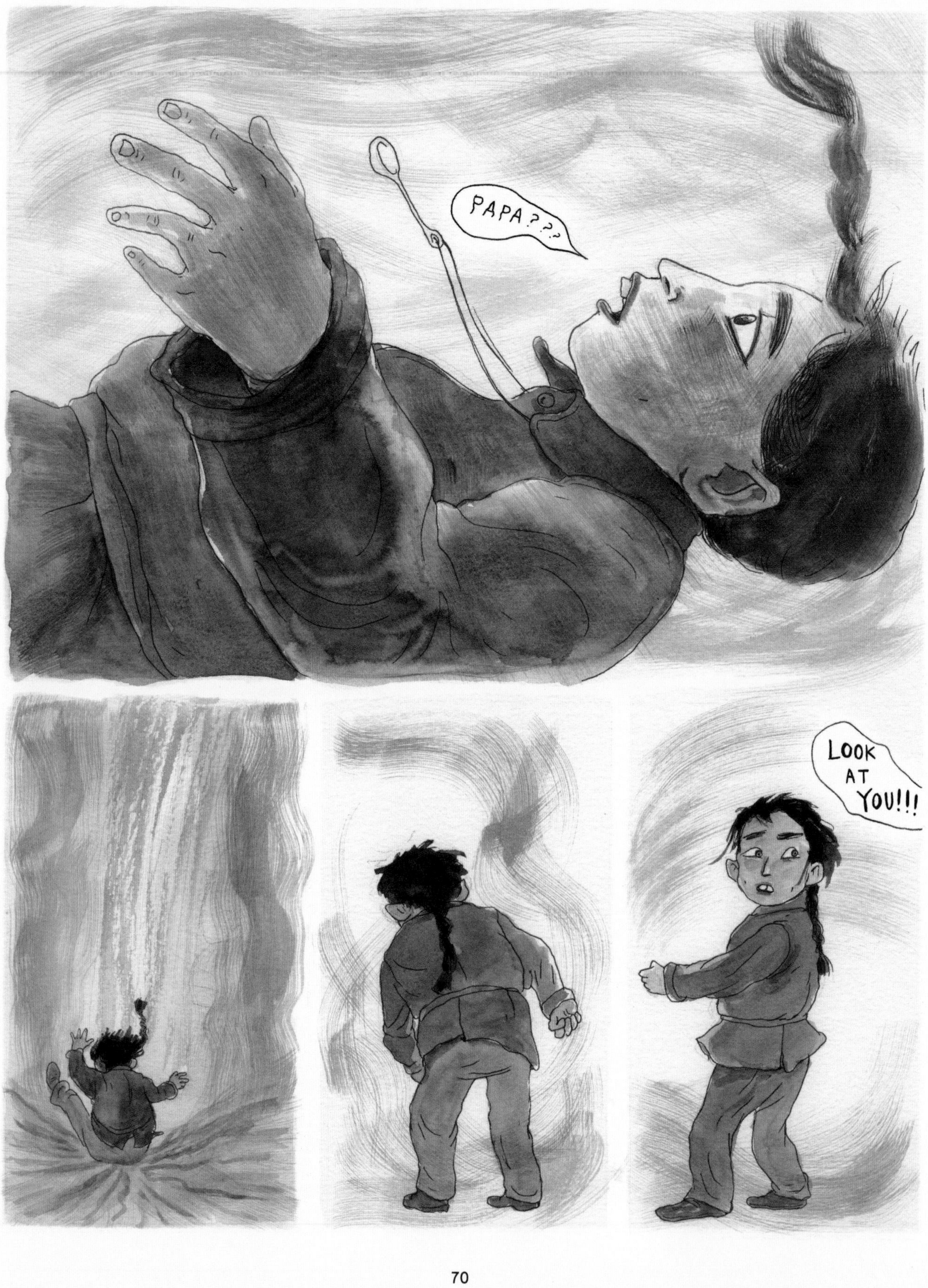
PAPA???
LOOK AT YOU!!!

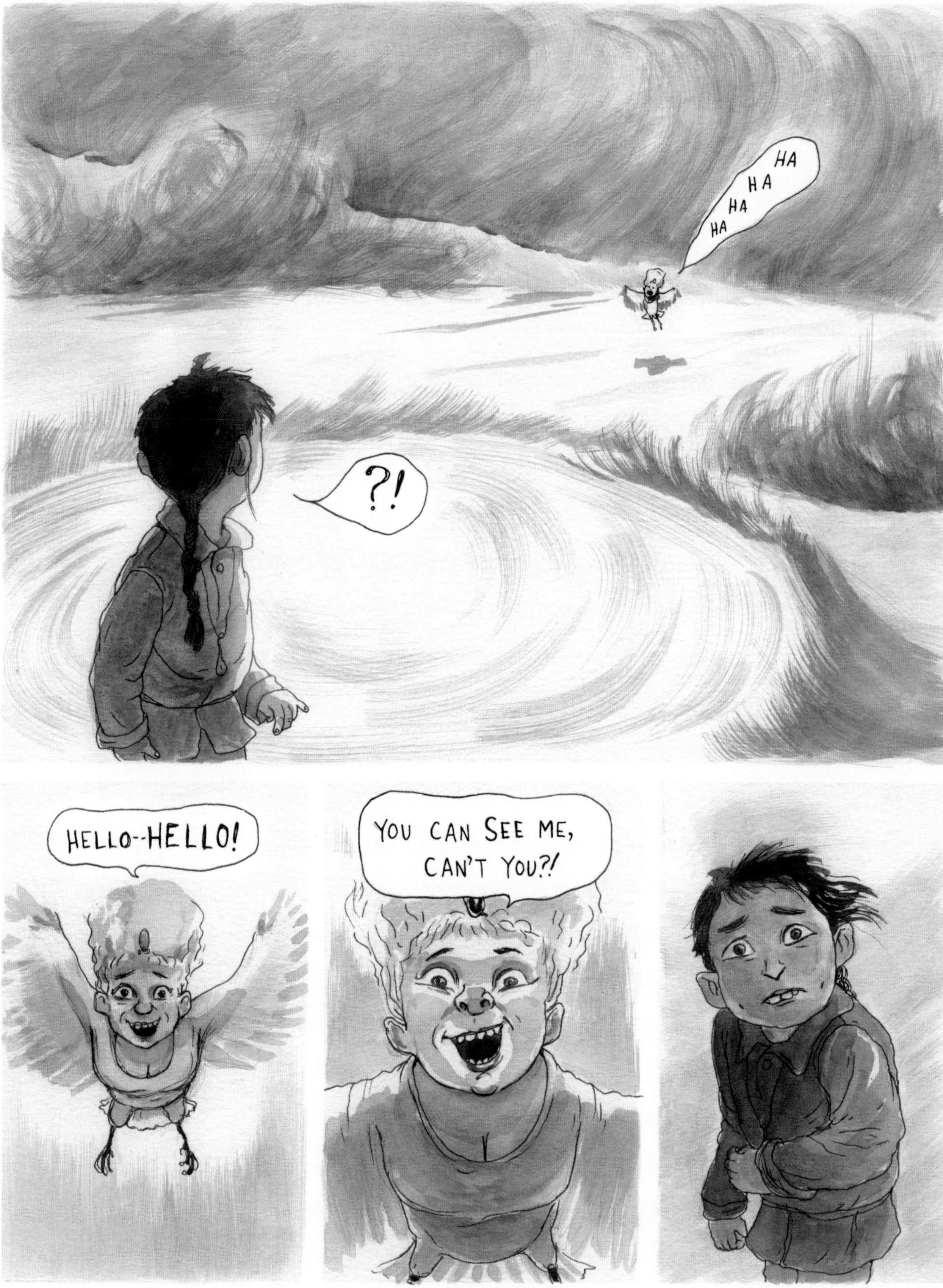
HA HA HA HA
?!
HELLO--HELLO!
YOU CAN SEE ME, CAN'T YOU?!

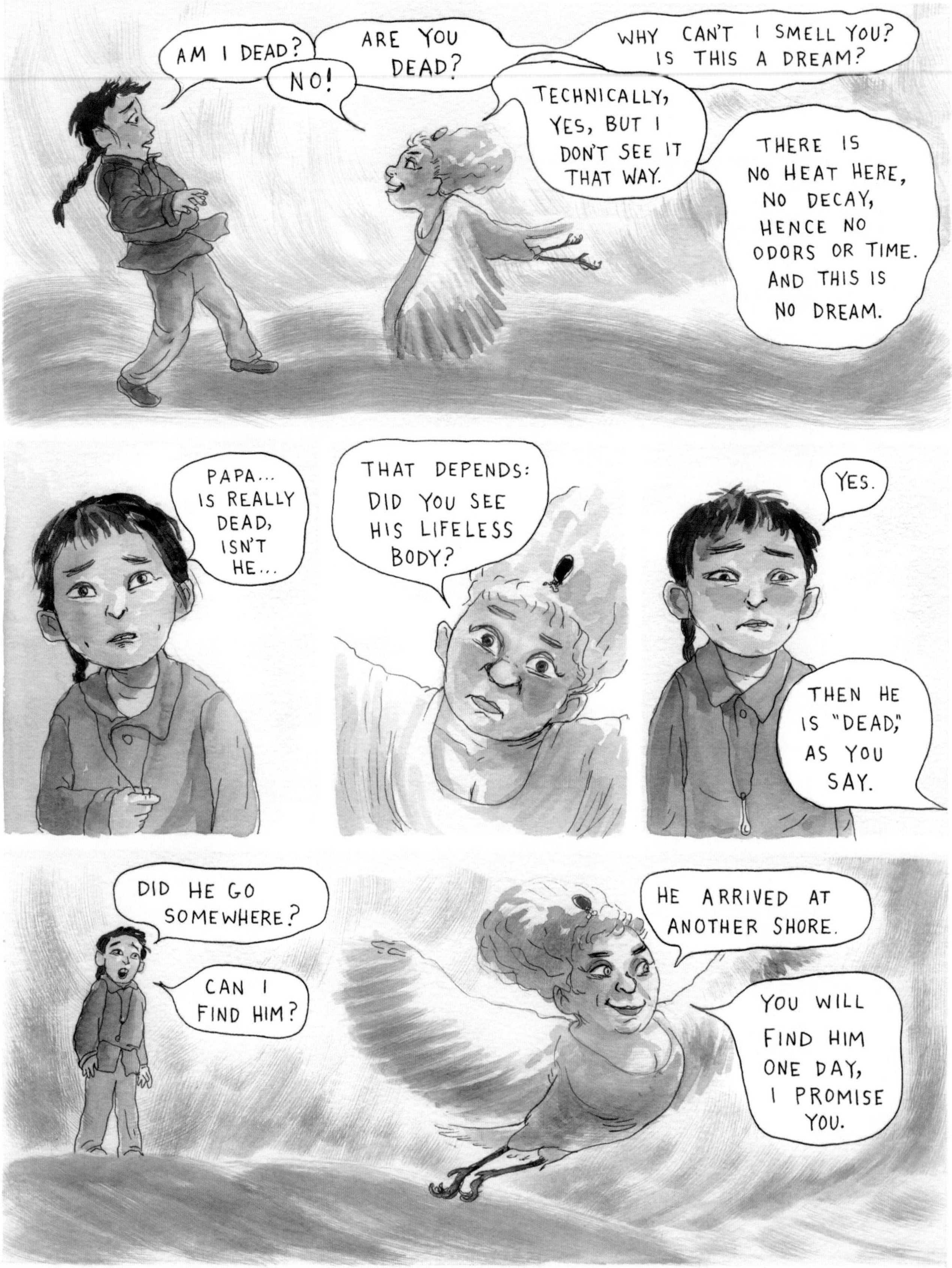
AM I DEAD?
ARE YOU DEAD?
NO!
WHY CAN'T I SMELL YOU? IS THIS A DREAM?
TECHNICALLY, YES, BUT I DON'T SEE IT THAT WAY.
THERE IS NO HEAT HERE, NO DECAY, HENCE NO ODORS OR TIME. AND THIS IS NO DREAM.
PAPA... IS REALLY DEAD, ISN'T HE...
THAT DEPENDS: DID YOU SEE HIS LIFELESS BODY?
YES.
THEN HE IS "DEAD," AS YOU SAY.
DID HE GO SOMEWHERE?
CAN I FIND HIM?
HE ARRIVED AT ANOTHER SHORE.
YOU WILL FIND HIM ONE DAY, I PROMISE YOU.

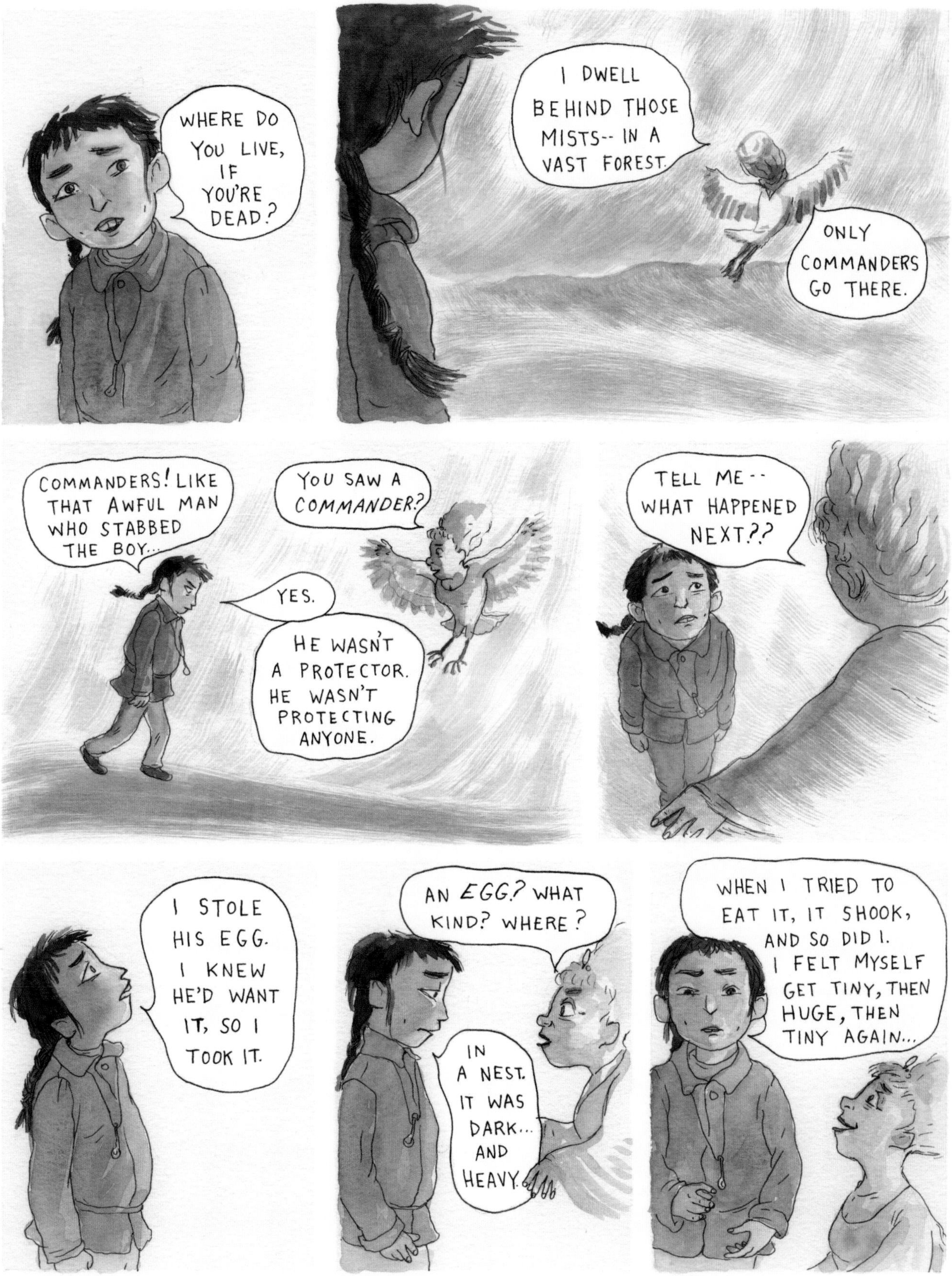
WHERE DO YOU LIVE, IF YOU'RE DEAD?
I DWELL BEHIND THOSE MISTS-- IN A VAST FOREST.
ONLY COMMANDERS GO THERE.
COMMANDERS! LIKE THAT AWFUL MAN WHO STABBED THE BOY...
YOU SAW A *COMMANDER*?
YES.
HE WASN'T A PROTECTOR. HE WASN'T PROTECTING ANYONE.
TELL ME-- WHAT HAPPENED NEXT??
I STOLE HIS EGG. I KNEW HE'D WANT IT, SO I TOOK IT.
AN *EGG*? WHAT KIND? WHERE?
IN A NEST. IT WAS DARK... AND HEAVY.
WHEN I TRIED TO EAT IT, IT SHOOK, AND SO DID I. I FELT MYSELF GET TINY, THEN HUGE, THEN TINY AGAIN...

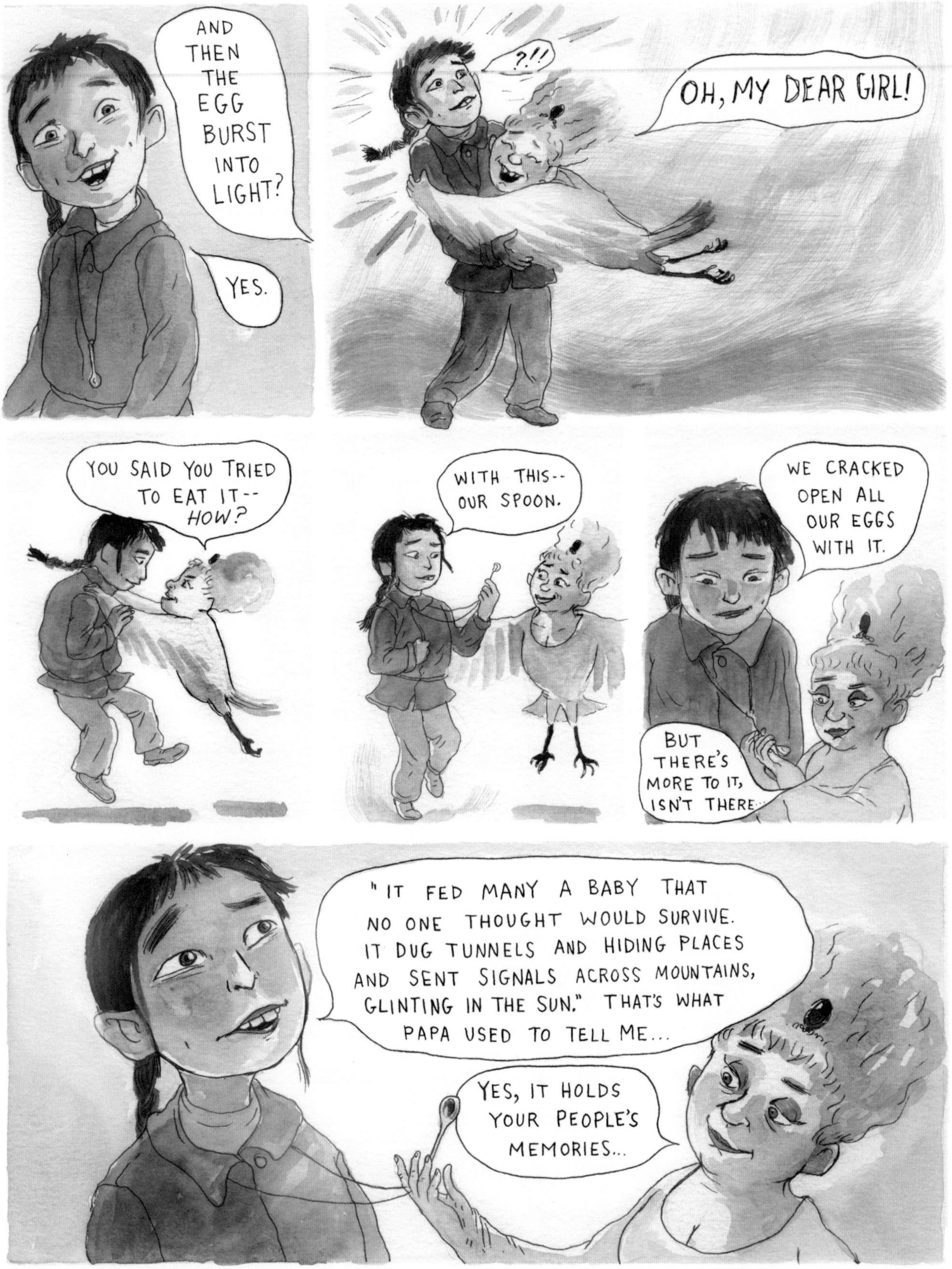
AND THEN THE EGG BURST INTO LIGHT?
YES.
?!!
OH, MY DEAR GIRL!
YOU SAID YOU TRIED TO EAT IT-- HOW?
WITH THIS-- OUR SPOON.
WE CRACKED OPEN ALL OUR EGGS WITH IT.
BUT THERE'S MORE TO IT, ISN'T THERE...
"IT FED MANY A BABY THAT NO ONE THOUGHT WOULD SURVIVE. IT DUG TUNNELS AND HIDING PLACES AND SENT SIGNALS ACROSS MOUNTAINS, GLINTING IN THE SUN." THAT'S WHAT PAPA USED TO TELL ME...
YES, IT HOLDS YOUR PEOPLE'S MEMORIES...

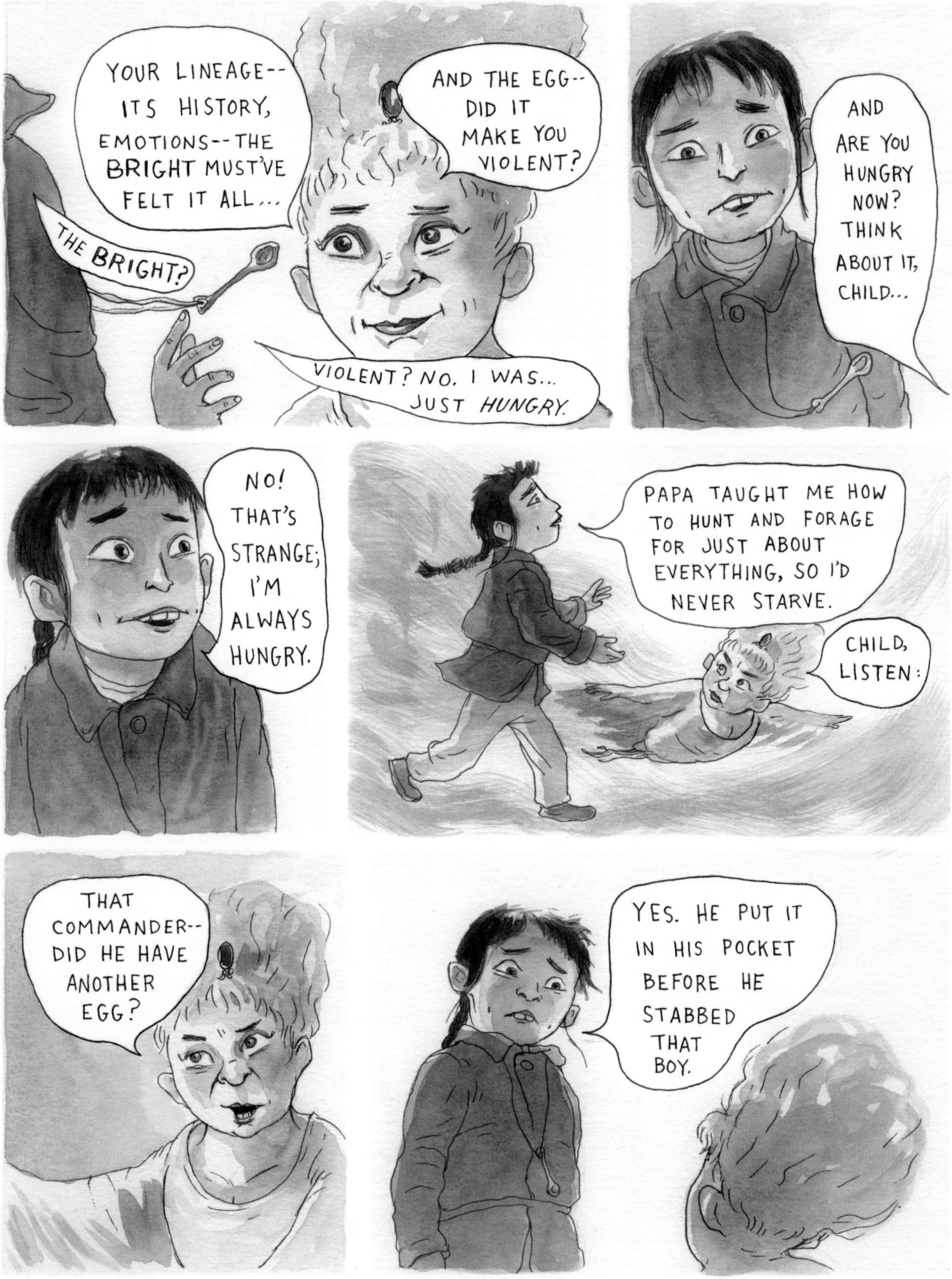
YOUR LINEAGE-- ITS HISTORY, EMOTIONS--THE BRIGHT MUST'VE FELT IT ALL...
AND THE EGG-- DID IT MAKE YOU VIOLENT?
THE BRIGHT?
VIOLENT? NO. I WAS... JUST HUNGRY.
AND ARE YOU HUNGRY NOW? THINK ABOUT IT, CHILD...
NO! THAT'S STRANGE; I'M ALWAYS HUNGRY.
PAPA TAUGHT ME HOW TO HUNT AND FORAGE FOR JUST ABOUT EVERYTHING, SO I'D NEVER STARVE.
CHILD, LISTEN:
THAT COMMANDER-- DID HE HAVE ANOTHER EGG?
YES. HE PUT IT IN HIS POCKET BEFORE HE STABBED THAT BOY.

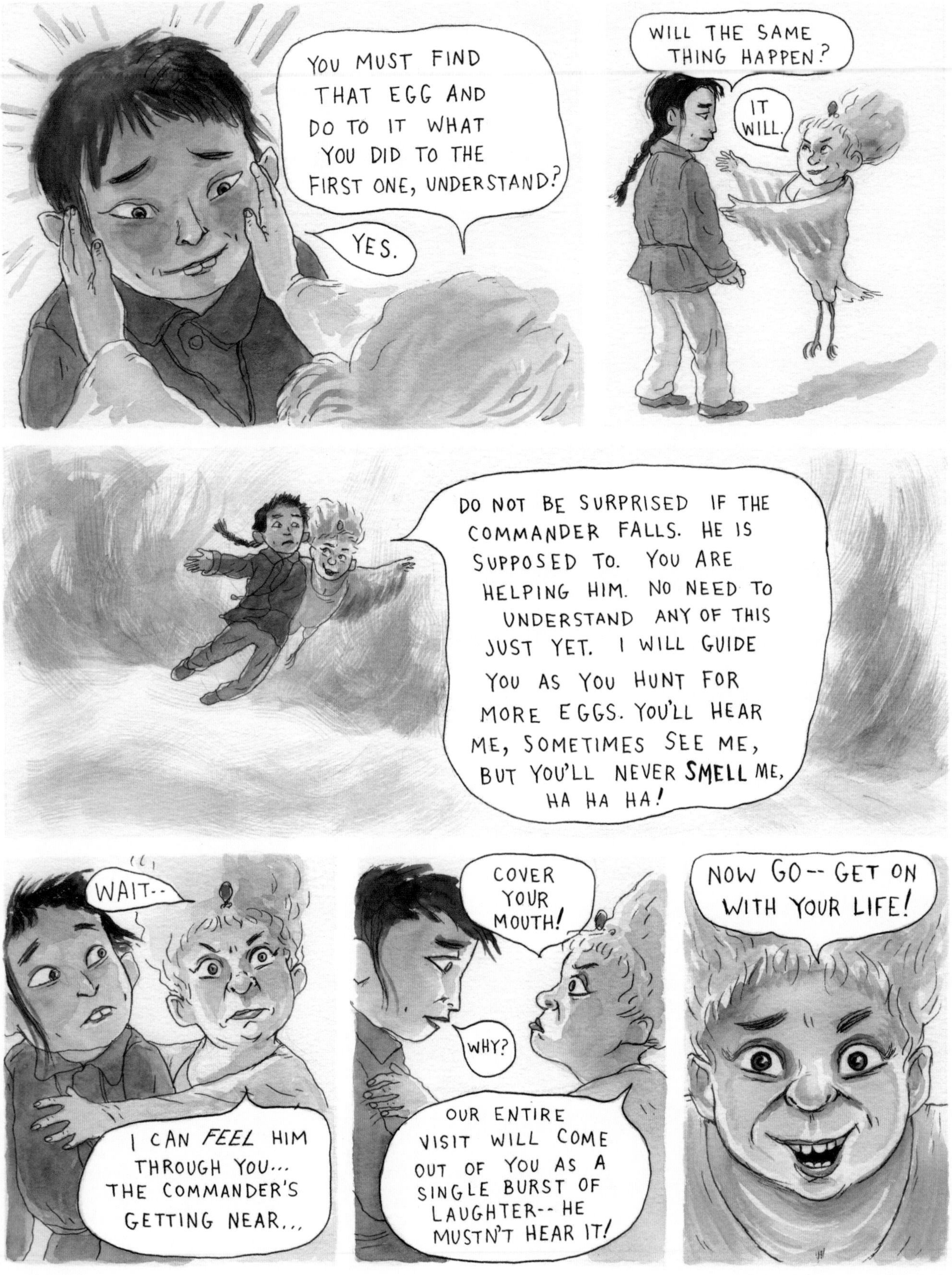
YOU MUST FIND THAT EGG AND DO TO IT WHAT YOU DID TO THE FIRST ONE, UNDERSTAND?
YES.
WILL THE SAME THING HAPPEN?
IT WILL.
DO NOT BE SURPRISED IF THE COMMANDER FALLS. HE IS SUPPOSED TO. YOU ARE HELPING HIM. NO NEED TO UNDERSTAND ANY OF THIS JUST YET. I WILL GUIDE YOU AS YOU HUNT FOR MORE EGGS. YOU'LL HEAR ME, SOMETIMES SEE ME, BUT YOU'LL NEVER **SMELL** ME, HA HA HA!
WAIT--
I CAN *FEEL* HIM THROUGH YOU... THE COMMANDER'S GETTING NEAR...
COVER YOUR MOUTH!
WHY?
OUR ENTIRE VISIT WILL COME OUT OF YOU AS A SINGLE BURST OF LAUGHTER-- HE MUSTN'T HEAR IT!
NOW GO-- GET ON WITH YOUR LIFE!

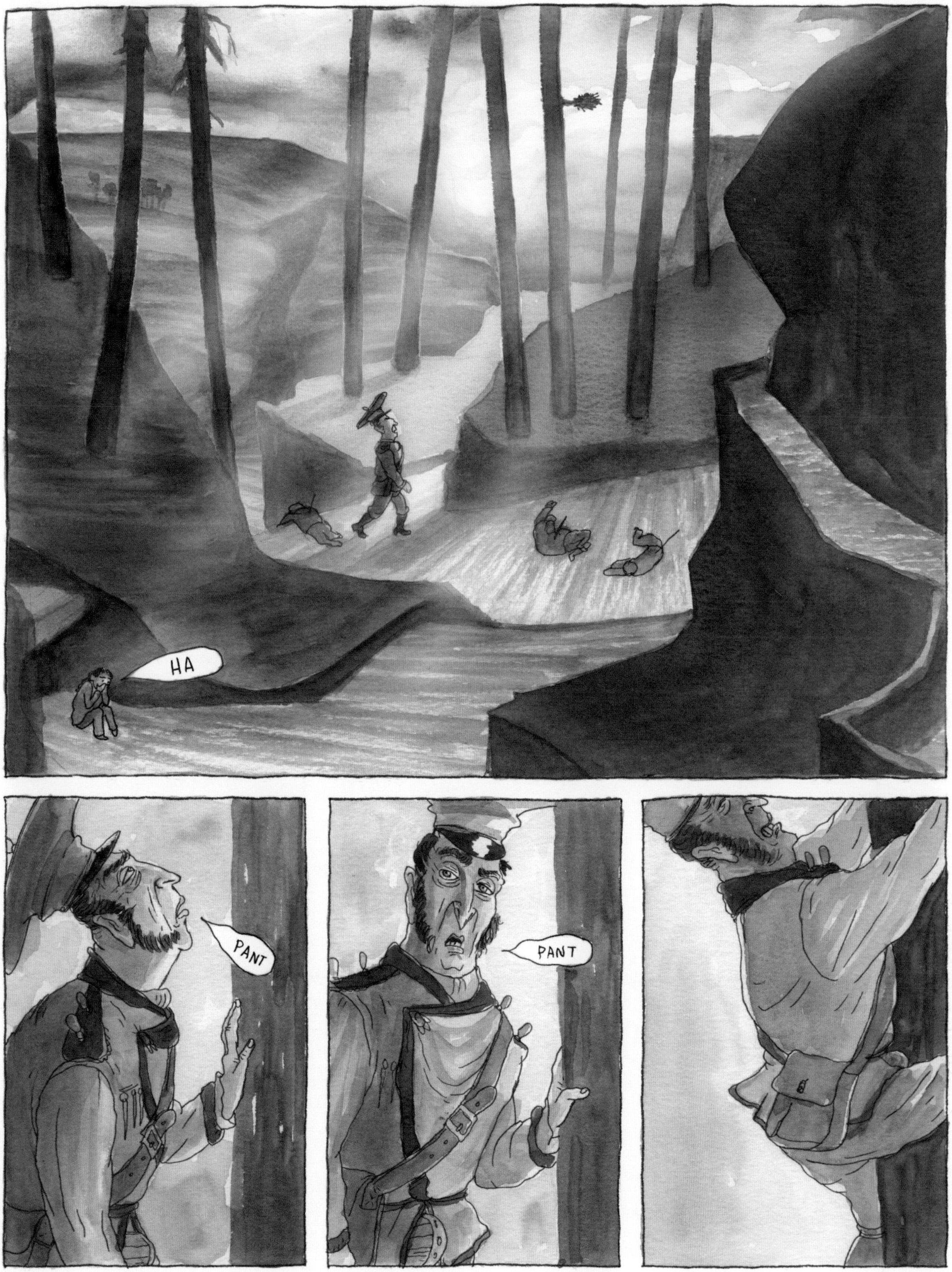
HA
PANT
PANT

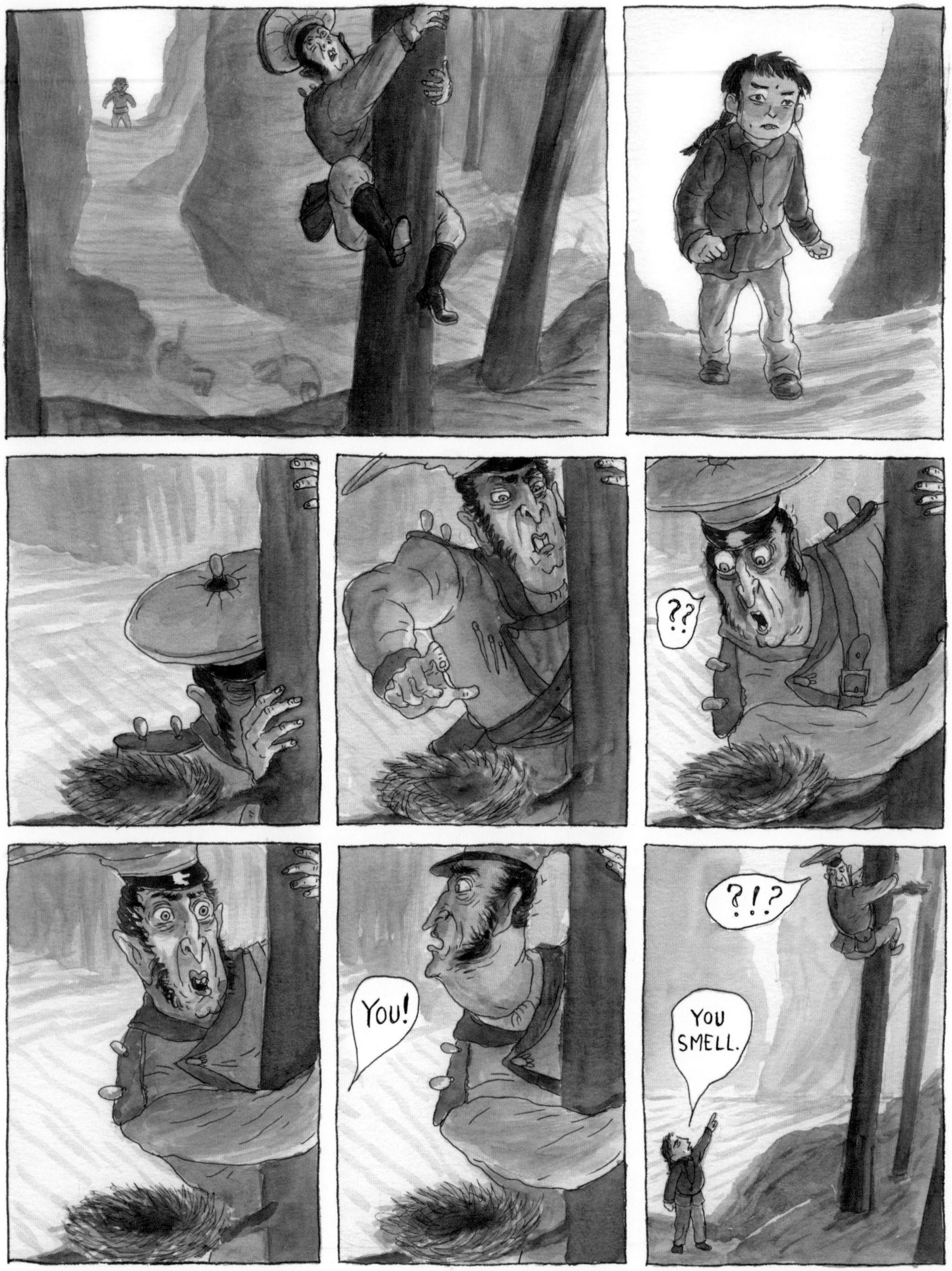
??
YOU!
?!?
YOU SMELL.

YOU SHOULDN'T POLISH YOUR BOOTS WITH FAT.
WHAT... DID YOU DO WITH...
IT...
SO, GIRL...
ARE YOU *HUNGRY?*

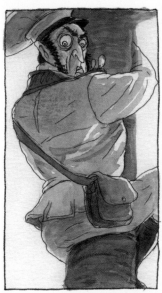

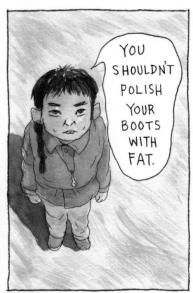

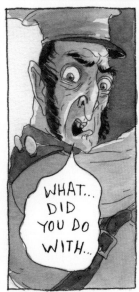

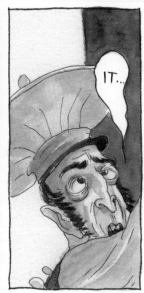

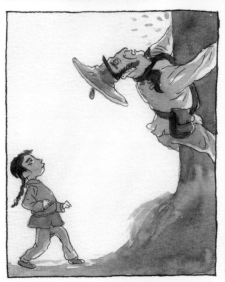

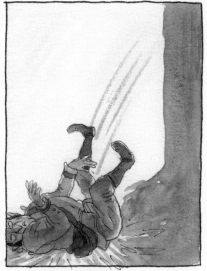

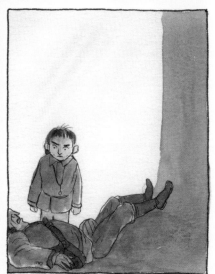

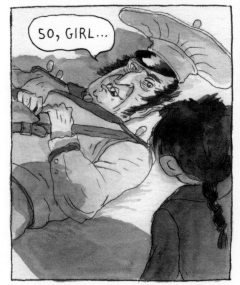

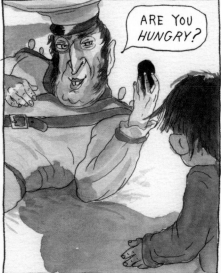

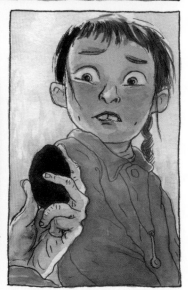

WILD, INFERIOR

BEAST.

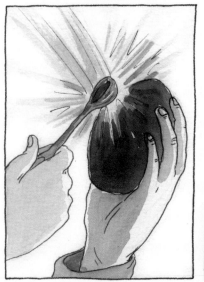

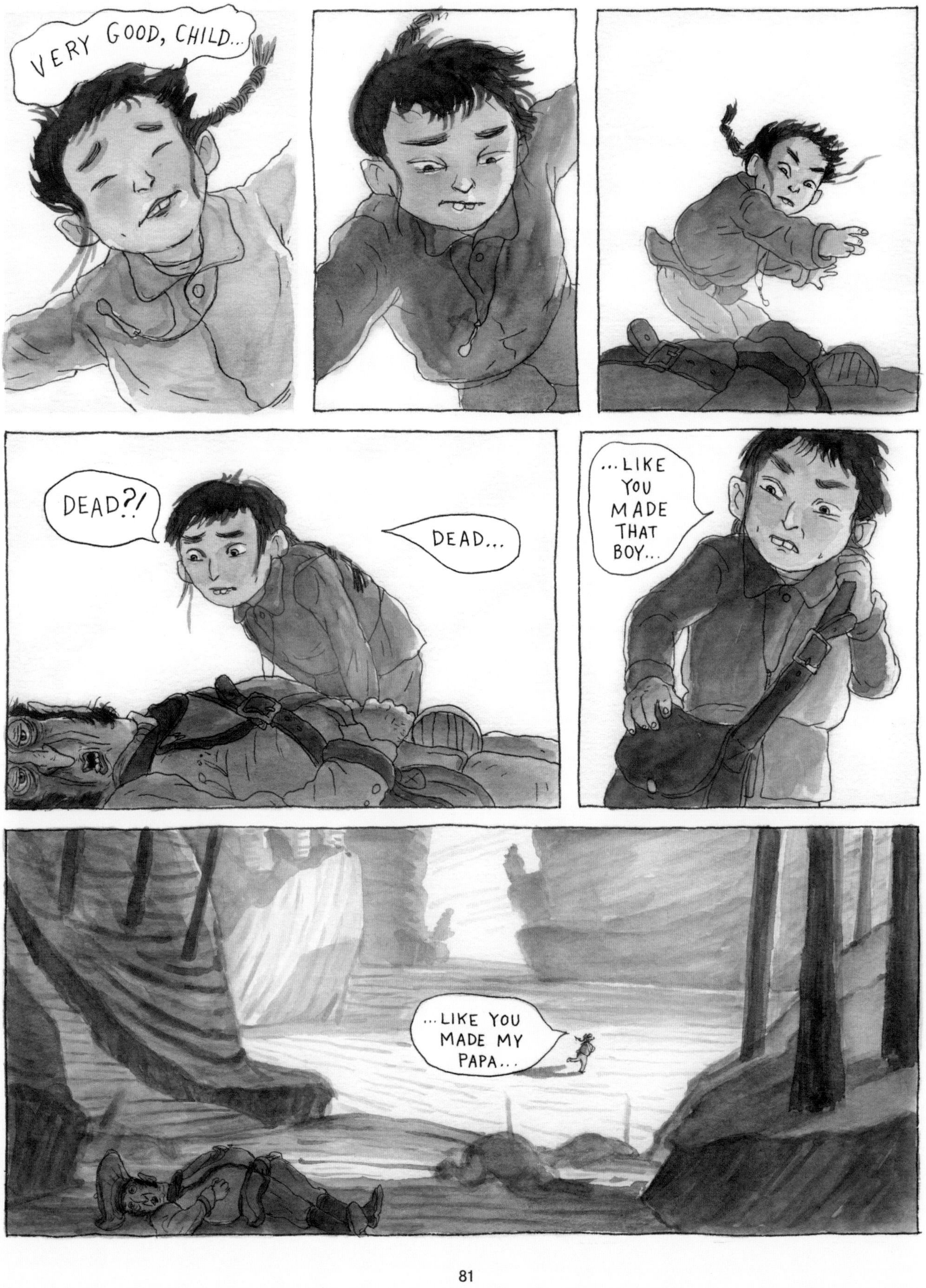
VERY GOOD, CHILD...
DEAD?!
DEAD...
...LIKE YOU MADE THAT BOY...
...LIKE YOU MADE MY PAPA...

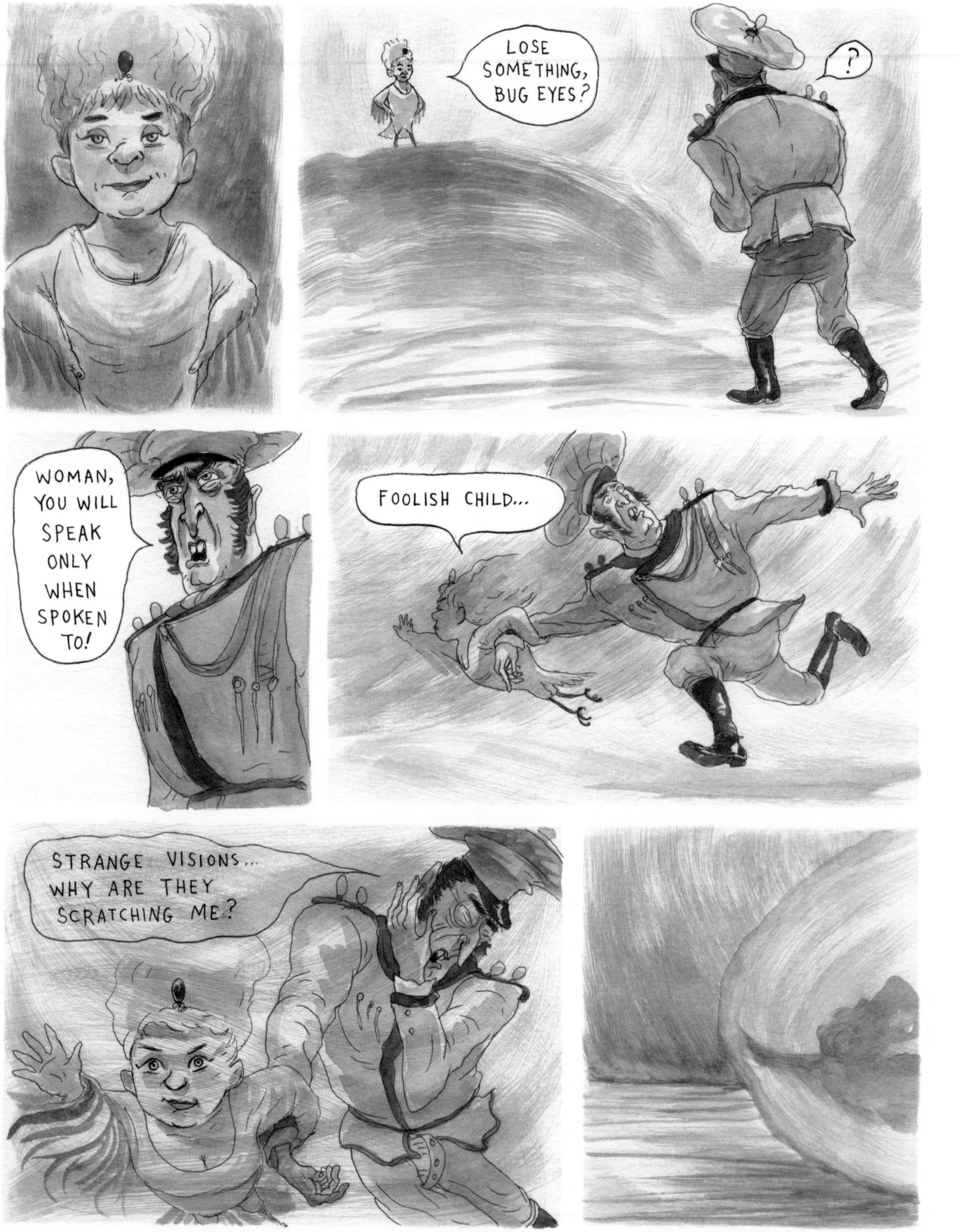
LOSE SOMETHING, BUG EYES?
?
WOMAN, YOU WILL SPEAK ONLY WHEN SPOKEN TO!
FOOLISH CHILD...
STRANGE VISIONS... WHY ARE THEY SCRATCHING ME?

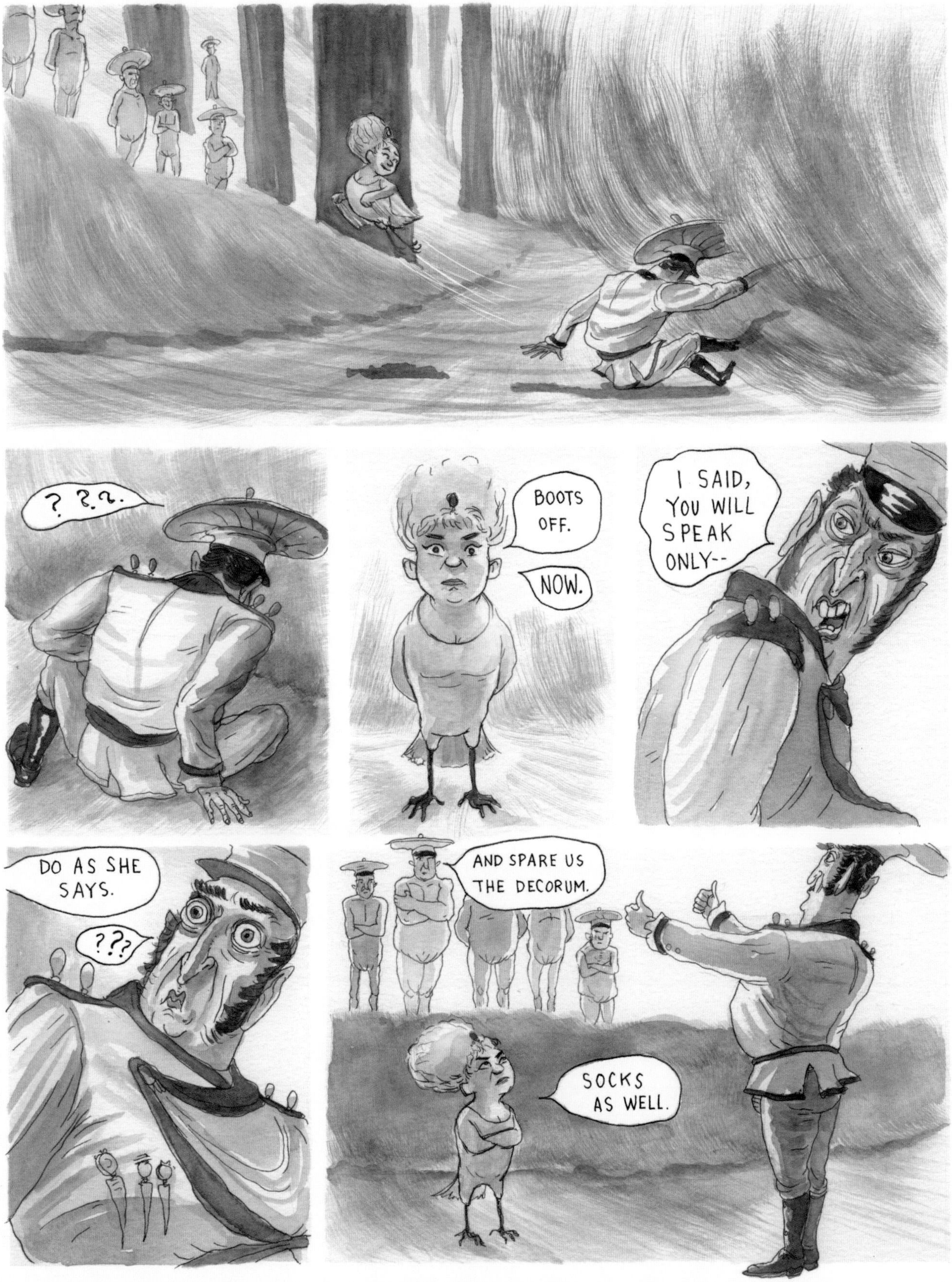
? ?.?.
BOOTS OFF.
NOW.
I SAID, YOU WILL SPEAK ONLY--
DO AS SHE SAYS.
???
AND SPARE US THE DECORUM.
SOCKS AS WELL.

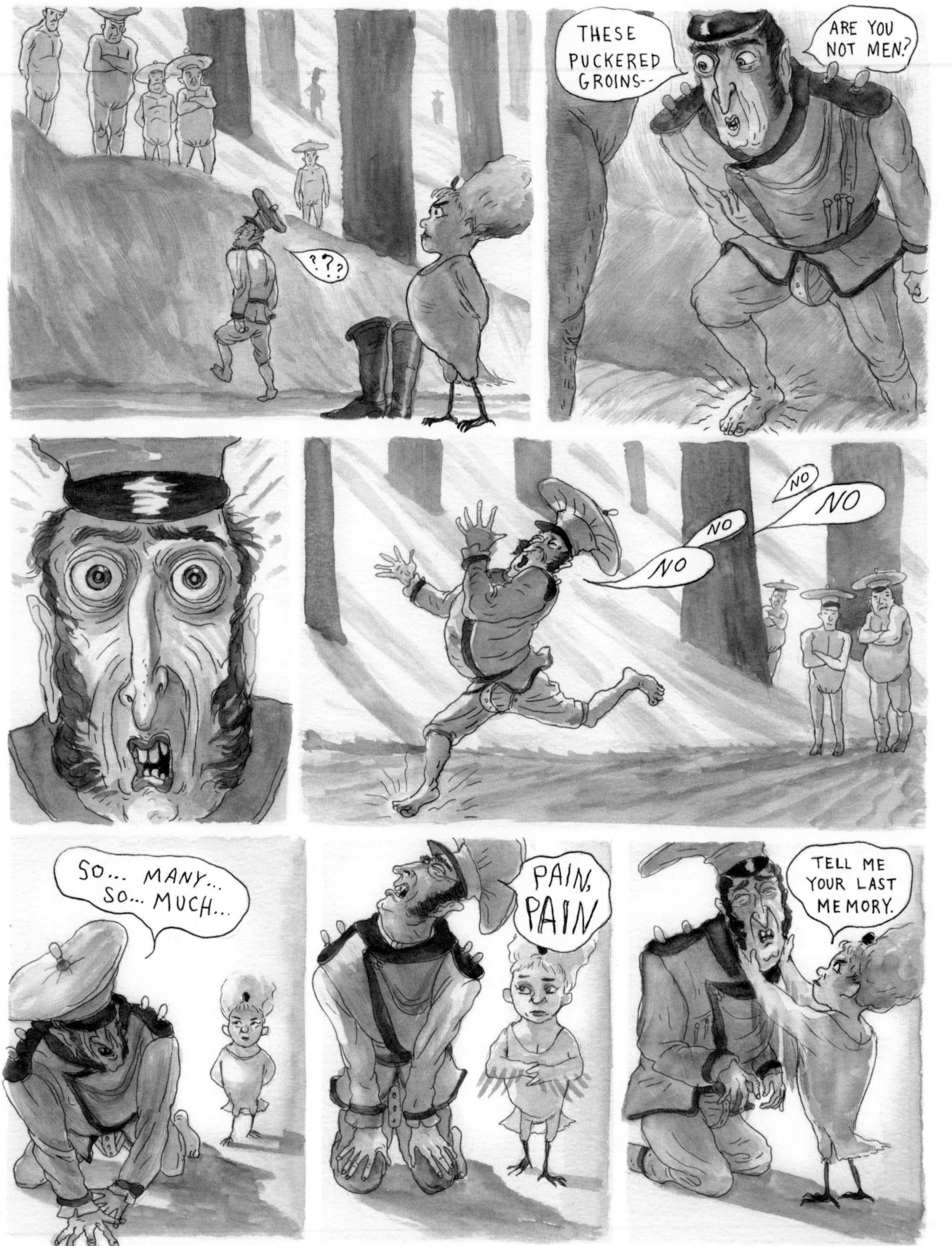
?? ?
THESE PUCKERED GROINS--
ARE YOU NOT MEN?
NO
NO
NO
NO
SO... MANY... SO... MUCH...
PAIN, PAIN
TELL ME YOUR LAST MEMORY.

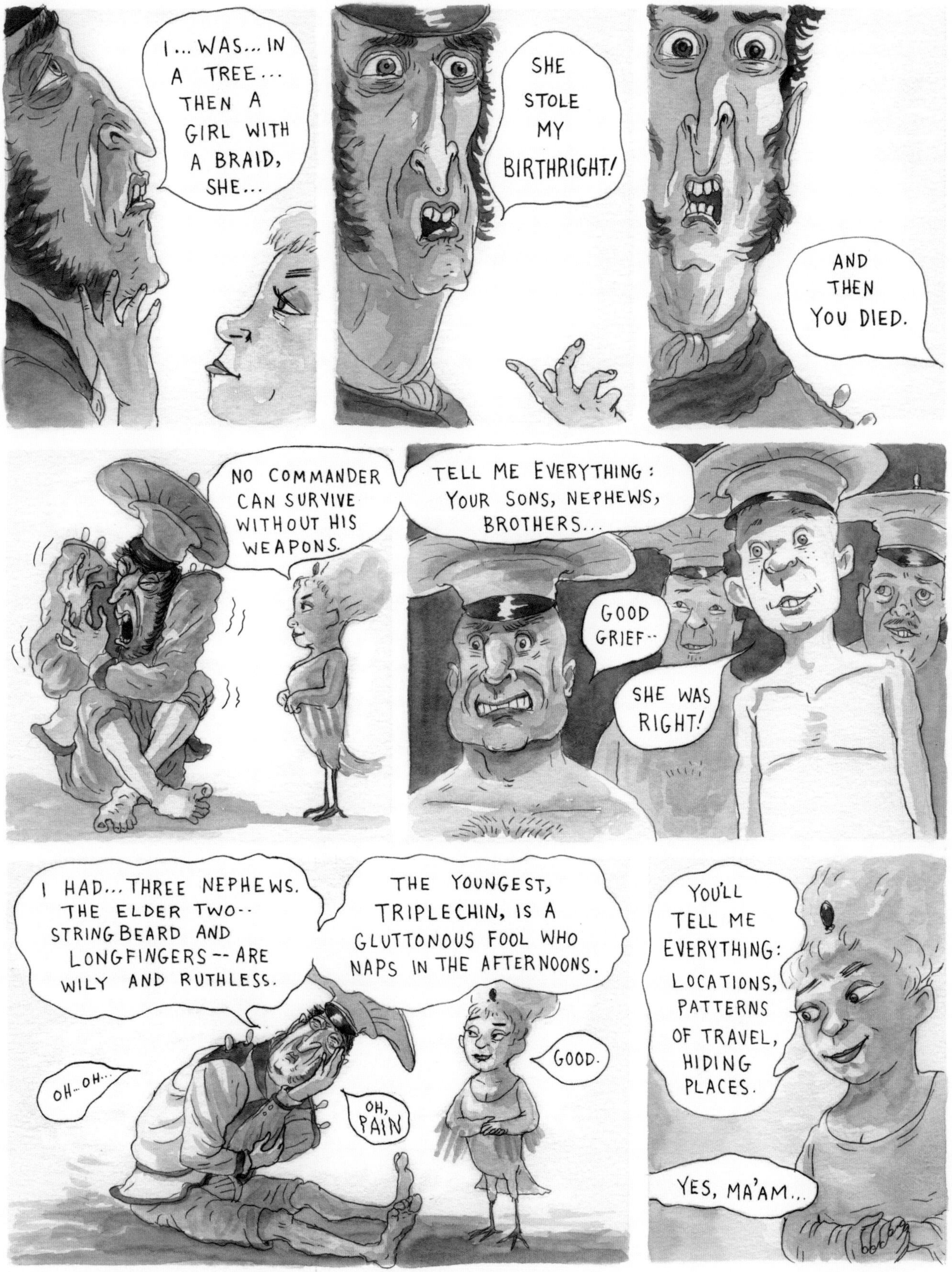
I... WAS... IN A TREE... THEN A GIRL WITH A BRAID, SHE...
SHE STOLE MY BIRTHRIGHT!
AND THEN YOU DIED.
NO COMMANDER CAN SURVIVE WITHOUT HIS WEAPONS.
TELL ME EVERYTHING: YOUR SONS, NEPHEWS, BROTHERS...
GOOD GRIEF--
SHE WAS RIGHT!
I HAD... THREE NEPHEWS. THE ELDER TWO-- STRINGBEARD AND LONGFINGERS-- ARE WILY AND RUTHLESS.
THE YOUNGEST, TRIPLECHIN, IS A GLUTTONOUS FOOL WHO NAPS IN THE AFTERNOONS.
OH... OH...
OH, PAIN
GOOD.
YOU'LL TELL ME EVERYTHING: LOCATIONS, PATTERNS OF TRAVEL, HIDING PLACES.
YES, MA'AM...

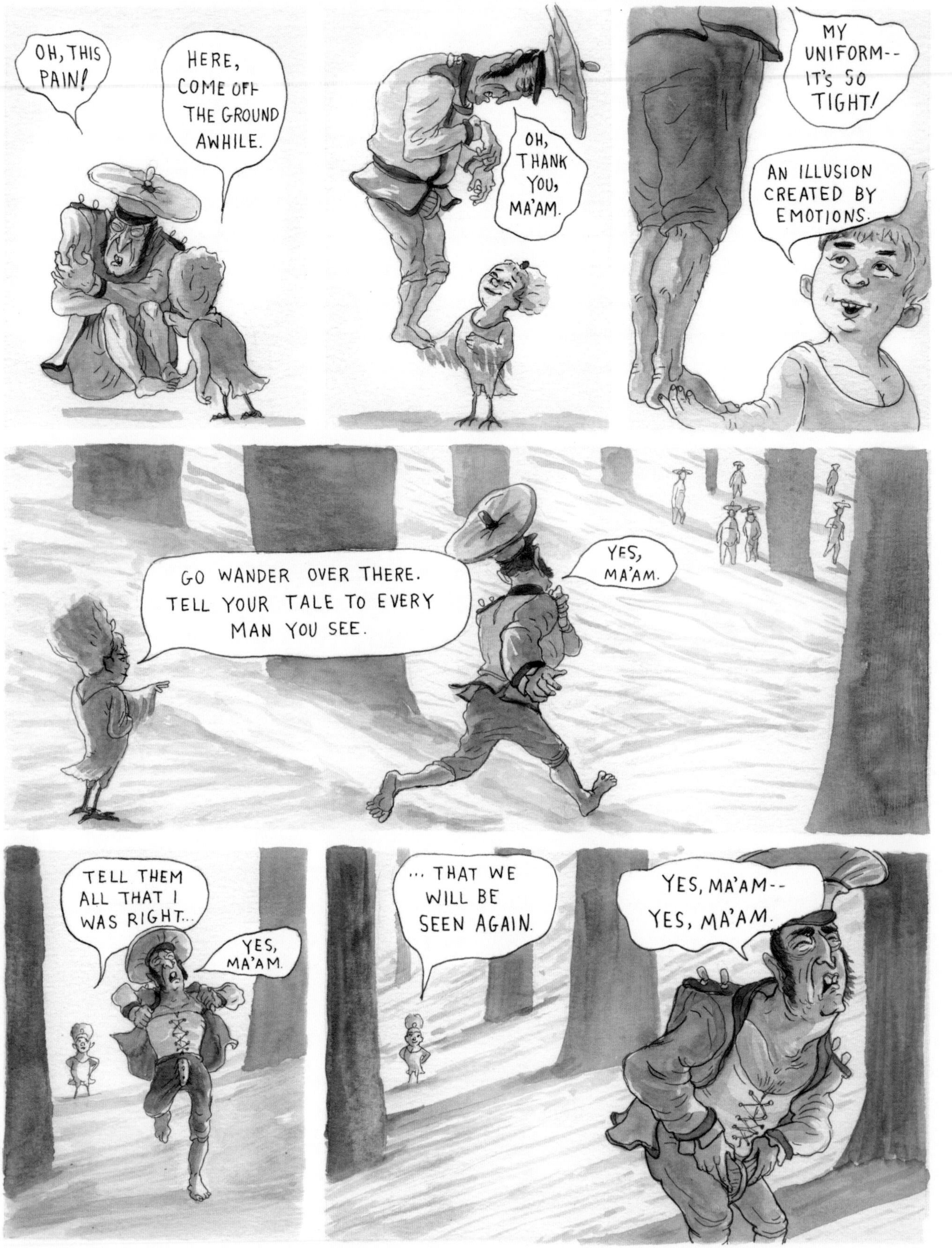

OH, THIS PAIN!
HERE, COME OFF THE GROUND AWHILE.
OH, THANK YOU, MA'AM.
MY UNIFORM-- IT'S SO TIGHT!
AN ILLUSION CREATED BY EMOTIONS.
GO WANDER OVER THERE. TELL YOUR TALE TO EVERY MAN YOU SEE.
YES, MA'AM.
TELL THEM ALL THAT I WAS RIGHT...
YES, MA'AM.
... THAT WE WILL BE SEEN AGAIN.
YES, MA'AM-- YES, MA'AM.

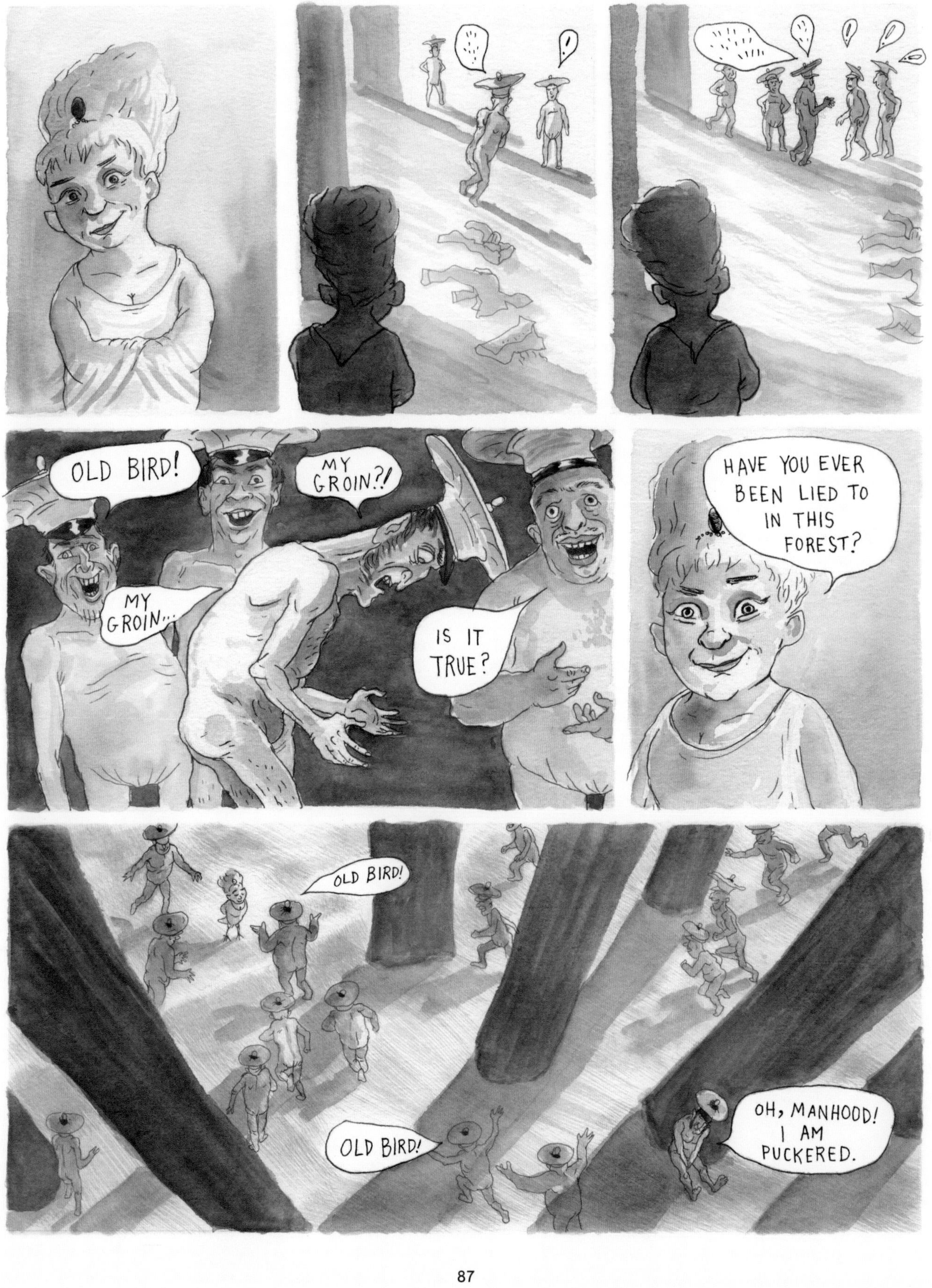
OLD BIRD!
MY GROIN?!
MY GROIN...
IS IT TRUE?
HAVE YOU EVER BEEN LIED TO IN THIS FOREST?
OLD BIRD!
OLD BIRD!
OH, MANHOOD! I AM PUCKERED.

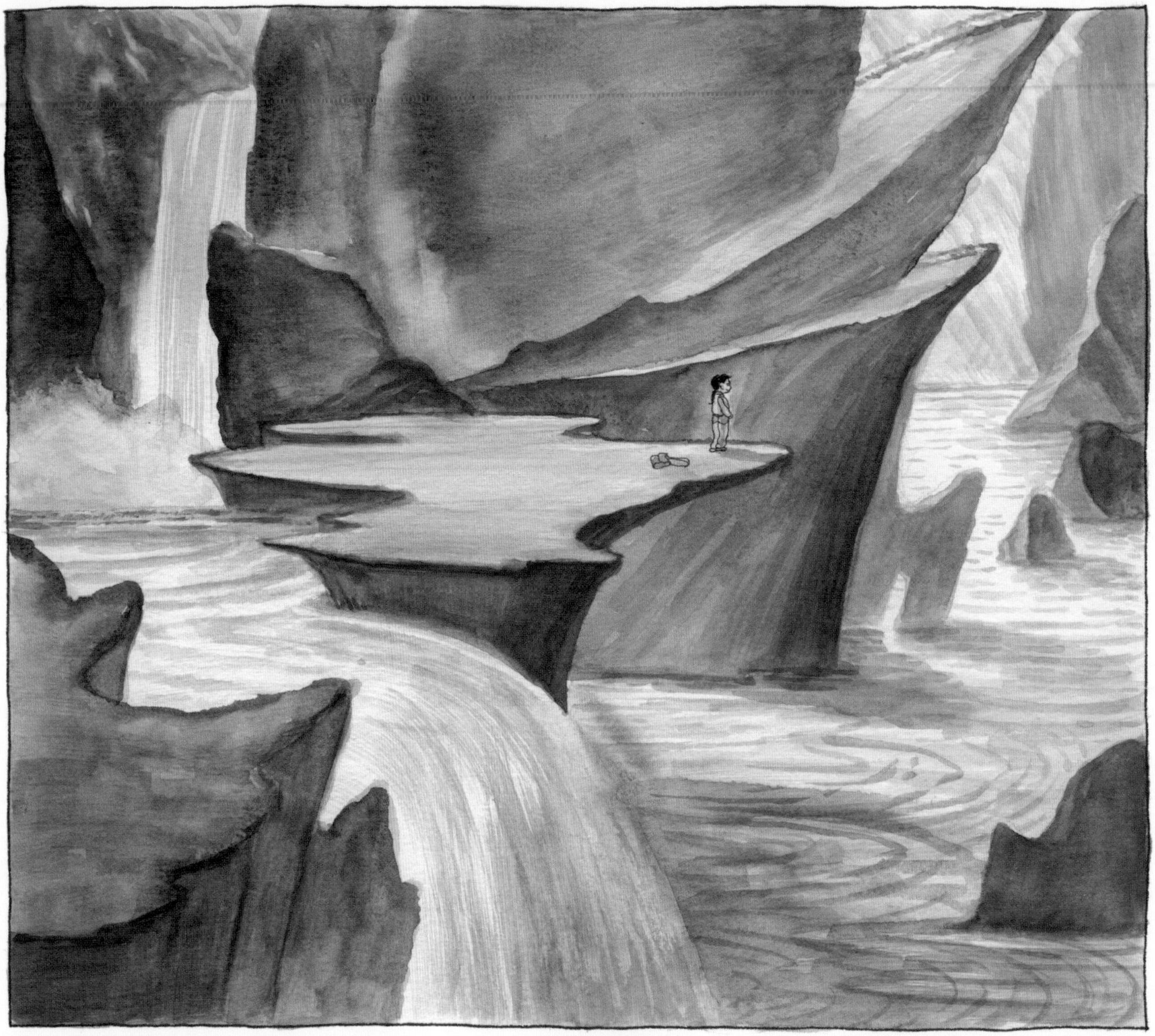

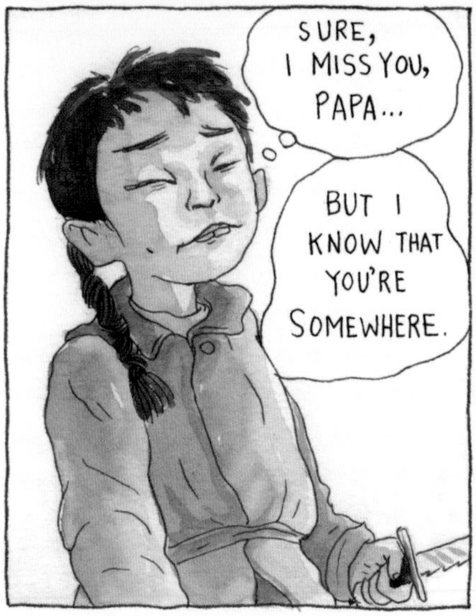
SURE, I MISS YOU, PAPA...
BUT I KNOW THAT YOU'RE SOMEWHERE.

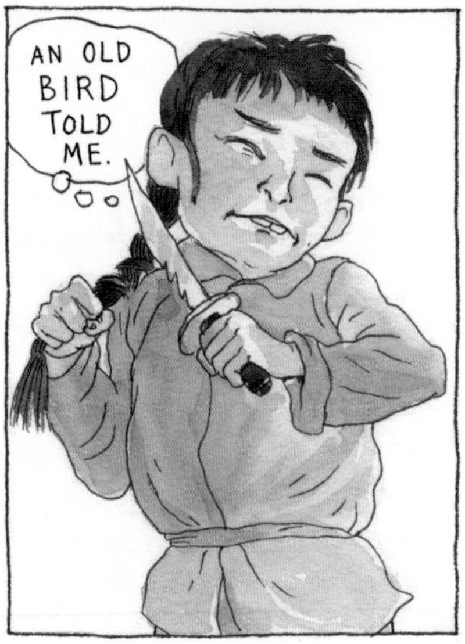
AN OLD BIRD TOLD ME.

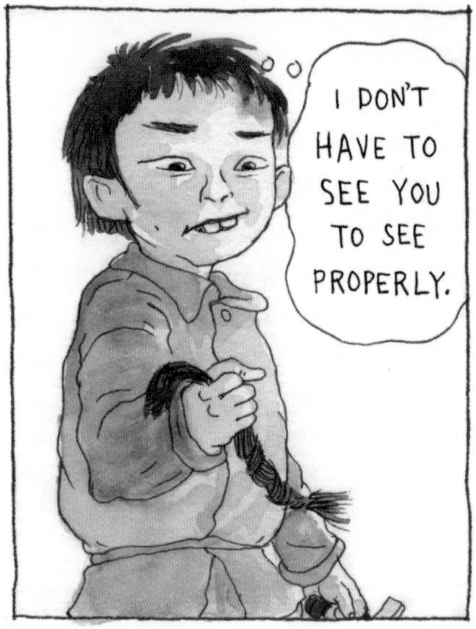
I DON'T HAVE TO SEE YOU TO SEE PROPERLY.

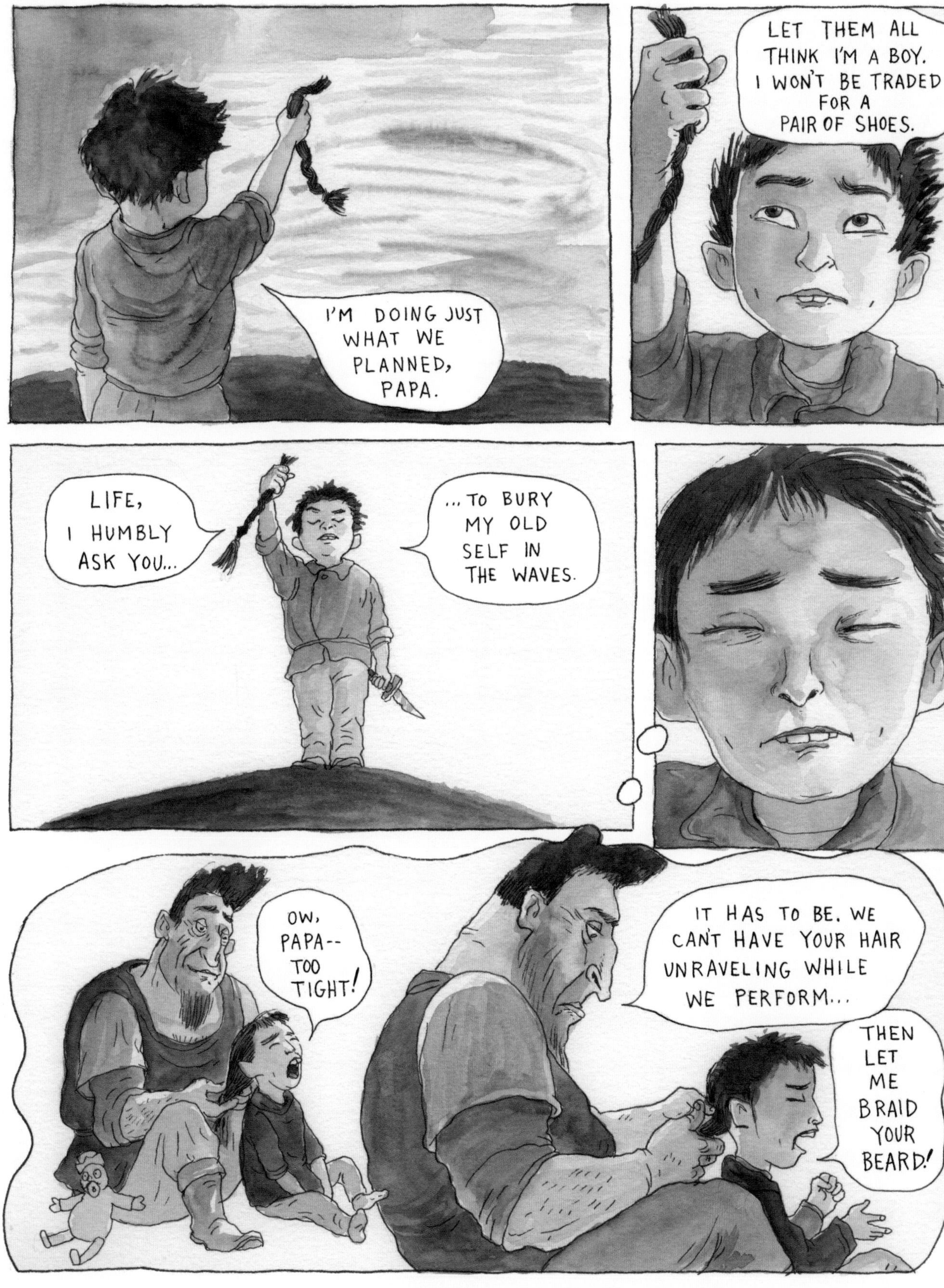
I'M DOING JUST WHAT WE PLANNED, PAPA.
LET THEM ALL THINK I'M A BOY. I WON'T BE TRADED FOR A PAIR OF SHOES.
LIFE, I HUMBLY ASK YOU...
...TO BURY MY OLD SELF IN THE WAVES.
OW, PAPA-- TOO TIGHT!
IT HAS TO BE. WE CAN'T HAVE YOUR HAIR UNRAVELING WHILE WE PERFORM...
THEN LET ME BRAID YOUR BEARD!

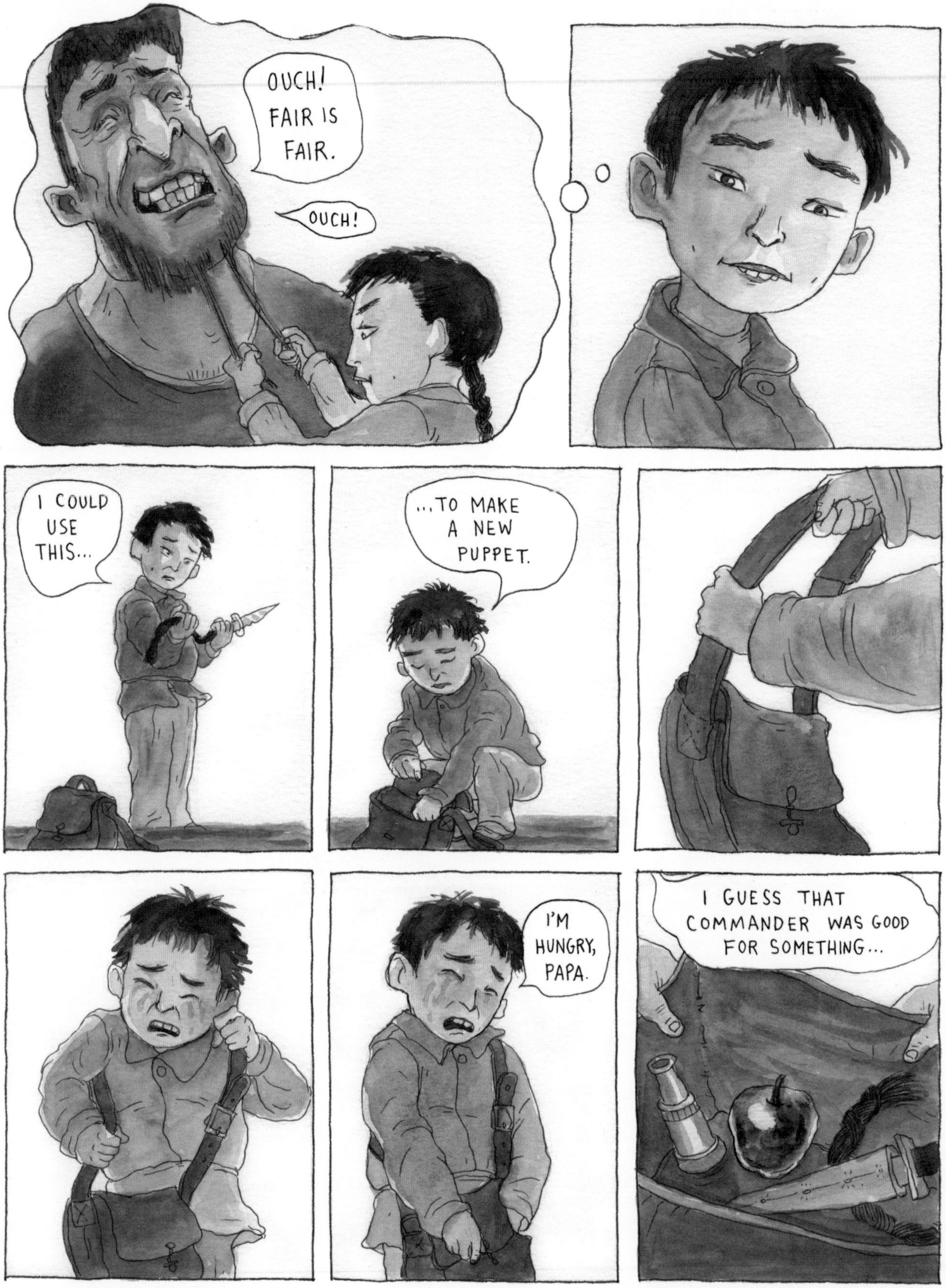
OUCH! FAIR IS FAIR.
OUCH!
I COULD USE THIS...
...TO MAKE A NEW PUPPET.
I'M HUNGRY, PAPA.
I GUESS THAT COMMANDER WAS GOOD FOR SOMETHING...

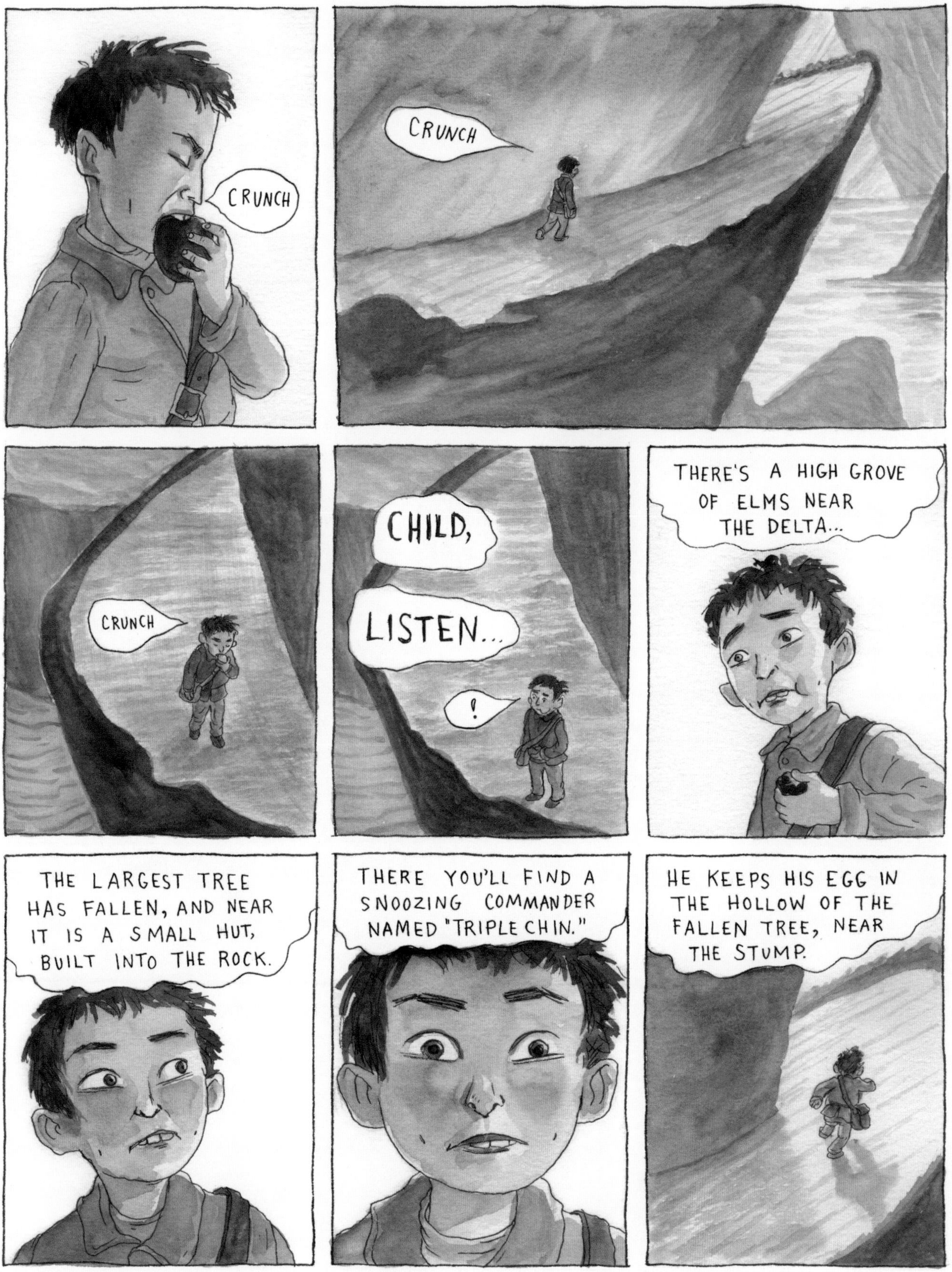
CRUNCH
CRUNCH
CRUNCH
CHILD,
LISTEN...
!
THERE'S A HIGH GROVE OF ELMS NEAR THE DELTA...
THE LARGEST TREE HAS FALLEN, AND NEAR IT IS A SMALL HUT, BUILT INTO THE ROCK.
THERE YOU'LL FIND A SNOOZING COMMANDER NAMED "TRIPLE CHIN."
HE KEEPS HIS EGG IN THE HOLLOW OF THE FALLEN TREE, NEAR THE STUMP.

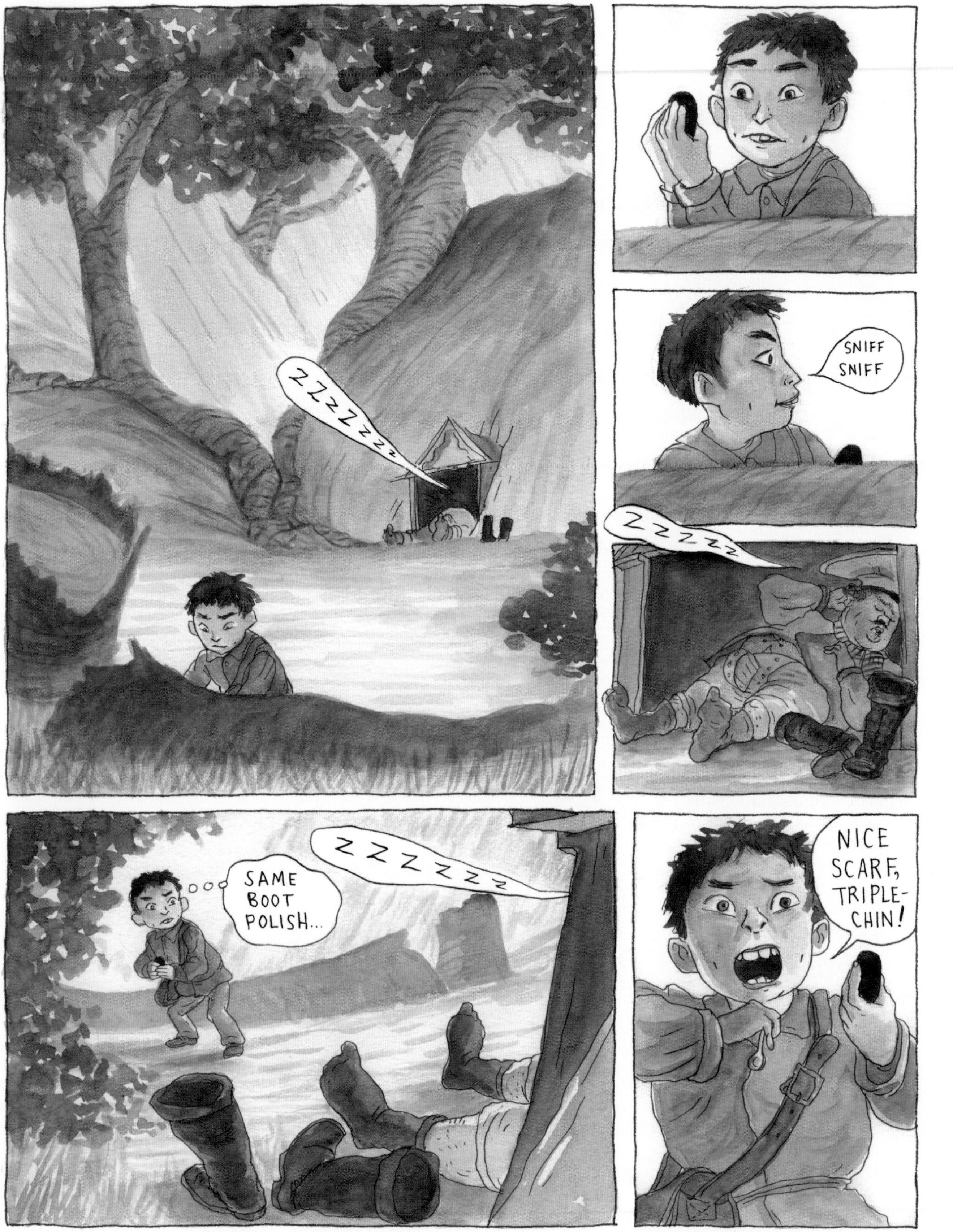
ZZZZZZZZ
SNIFF SNIFF
ZZZZZ
SAME BOOT POLISH...
ZZZZZZZ
NICE SCARF, TRIPLE-CHIN!

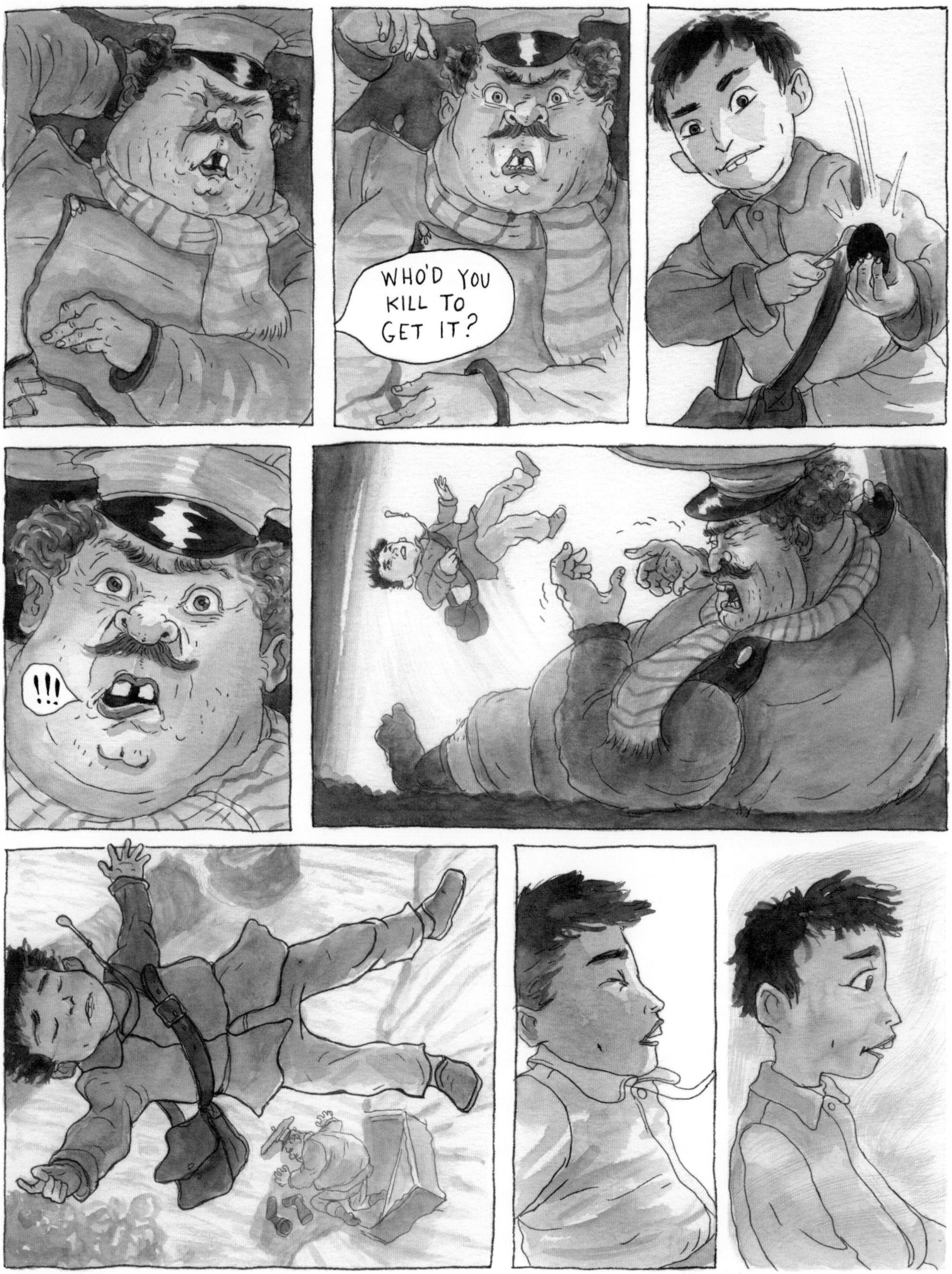
WHO'D YOU KILL TO GET IT?
!!!

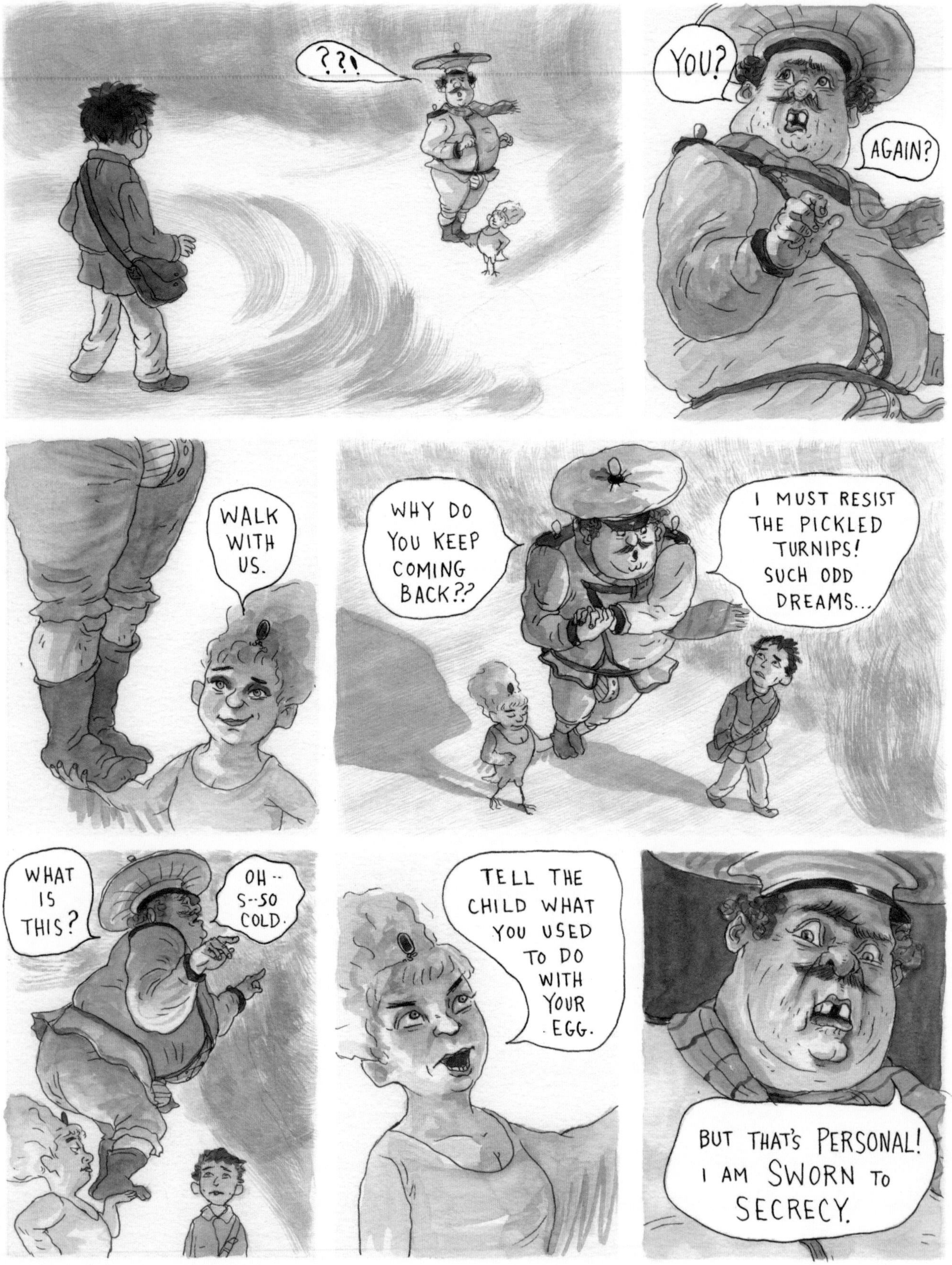
??!
YOU?
AGAIN?
WALK WITH US.
WHY DO YOU KEEP COMING BACK??
I MUST RESIST THE PICKLED TURNIPS! SUCH ODD DREAMS...
WHAT IS THIS?
OH-- S--SO COLD.
TELL THE CHILD WHAT YOU USED TO DO WITH YOUR EGG.
BUT THAT'S PERSONAL! I AM SWORN TO SECRECY.

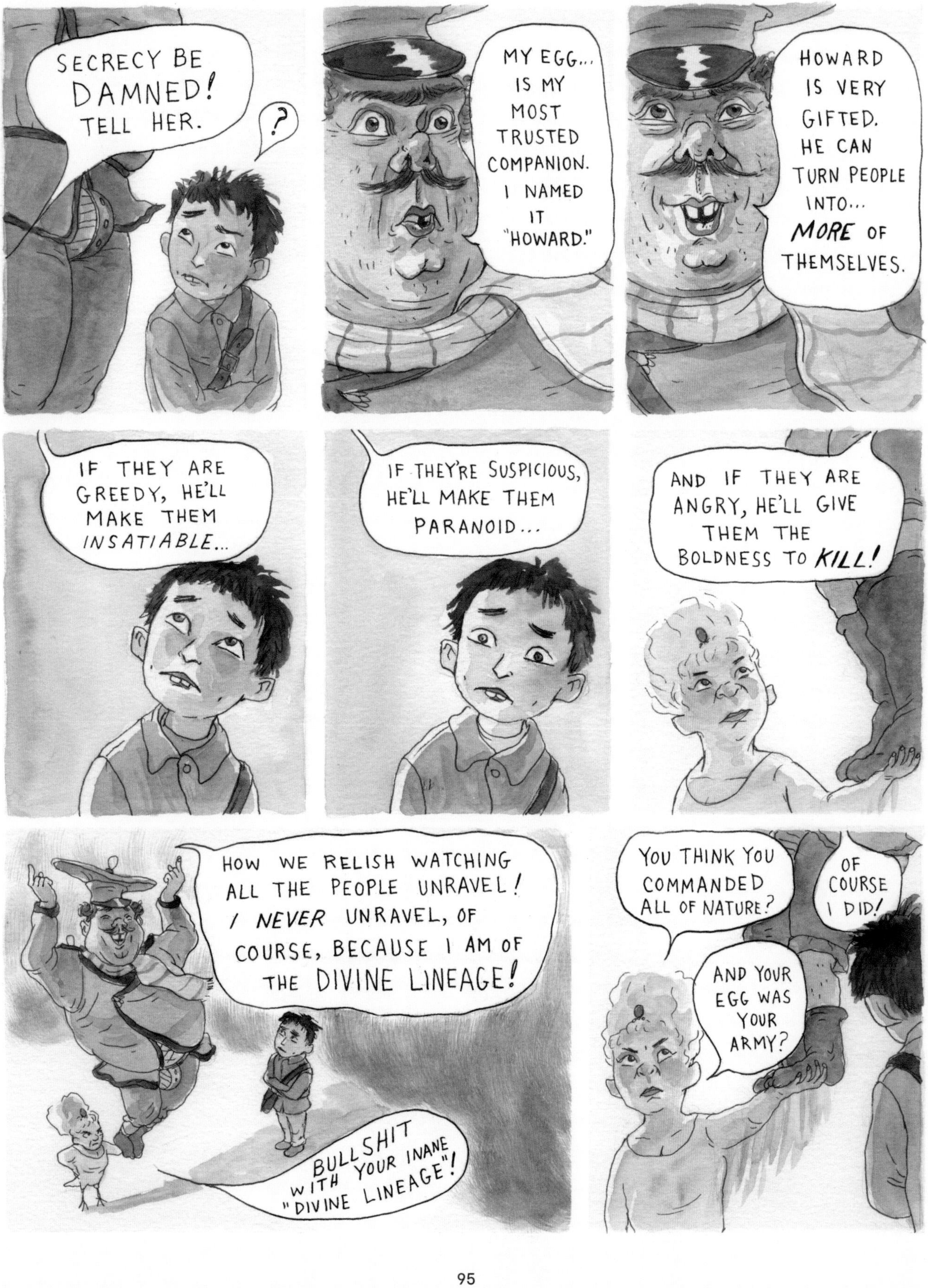
SECRECY BE DAMNED! TELL HER.
?
MY EGG... IS MY MOST TRUSTED COMPANION. I NAMED IT "HOWARD."
HOWARD IS VERY GIFTED. HE CAN TURN PEOPLE INTO... MORE OF THEMSELVES.
IF THEY ARE GREEDY, HE'LL MAKE THEM INSATIABLE...
IF THEY'RE SUSPICIOUS, HE'LL MAKE THEM PARANOID...
AND IF THEY ARE ANGRY, HE'LL GIVE THEM THE BOLDNESS TO KILL!
HOW WE RELISH WATCHING ALL THE PEOPLE UNRAVEL! I NEVER UNRAVEL, OF COURSE, BECAUSE I AM OF THE DIVINE LINEAGE!
BULLSHIT WITH YOUR INANE "DIVINE LINEAGE"!
YOU THINK YOU COMMANDED ALL OF NATURE?
OF COURSE I DID!
AND YOUR EGG WAS YOUR ARMY?

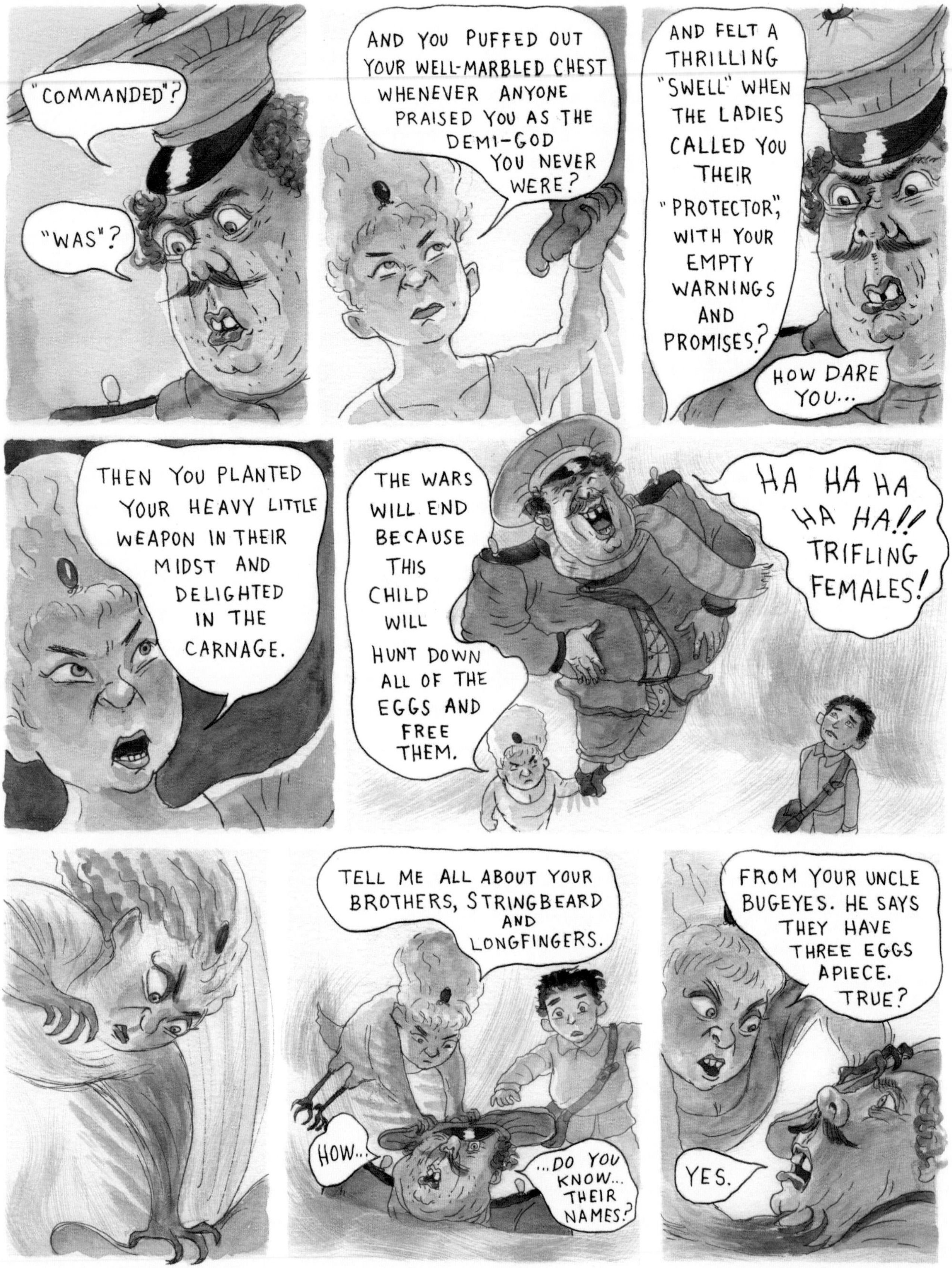
"COMMANDED"?
"WAS"?
AND YOU PUFFED OUT YOUR WELL-MARBLED CHEST WHENEVER ANYONE PRAISED YOU AS THE DEMI-GOD YOU NEVER WERE?
AND FELT A THRILLING "SWELL" WHEN THE LADIES CALLED YOU THEIR "PROTECTOR", WITH YOUR EMPTY WARNINGS AND PROMISES?
HOW DARE YOU...
THEN YOU PLANTED YOUR HEAVY LITTLE WEAPON IN THEIR MIDST AND DELIGHTED IN THE CARNAGE.
THE WARS WILL END BECAUSE THIS CHILD WILL HUNT DOWN ALL OF THE EGGS AND FREE THEM.
HA HA HA HA HA!! TRIFLING FEMALES!
TELL ME ALL ABOUT YOUR BROTHERS, STRINGBEARD AND LONGFINGERS.
HOW...
...DO YOU KNOW... THEIR NAMES?
FROM YOUR UNCLE BUGEYES. HE SAYS THEY HAVE THREE EGGS APIECE. TRUE?
YES.

UNCLE BUGEYES SPOKE OF ME? HE IS A GREAT WARRIOR!

HE'S NOTHING OF THE SORT, FOOL.

BUT HE GAVE ME MY HOWARD!

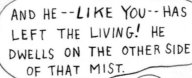

AND HE--*LIKE YOU*--HAS LEFT THE LIVING! HE DWELLS ON THE OTHER SIDE OF THAT MIST.

?!

IF YOU WANT TO SEE HIM THEN YOU'LL TELL THE GIRL EVERY-THING YOU KNOW.

HA.

I'LL TRADE YOU TWO CHICKENS FOR HER...

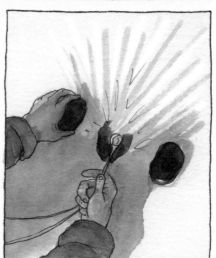

SNIFF
SNIFF

HE'S NEAR...

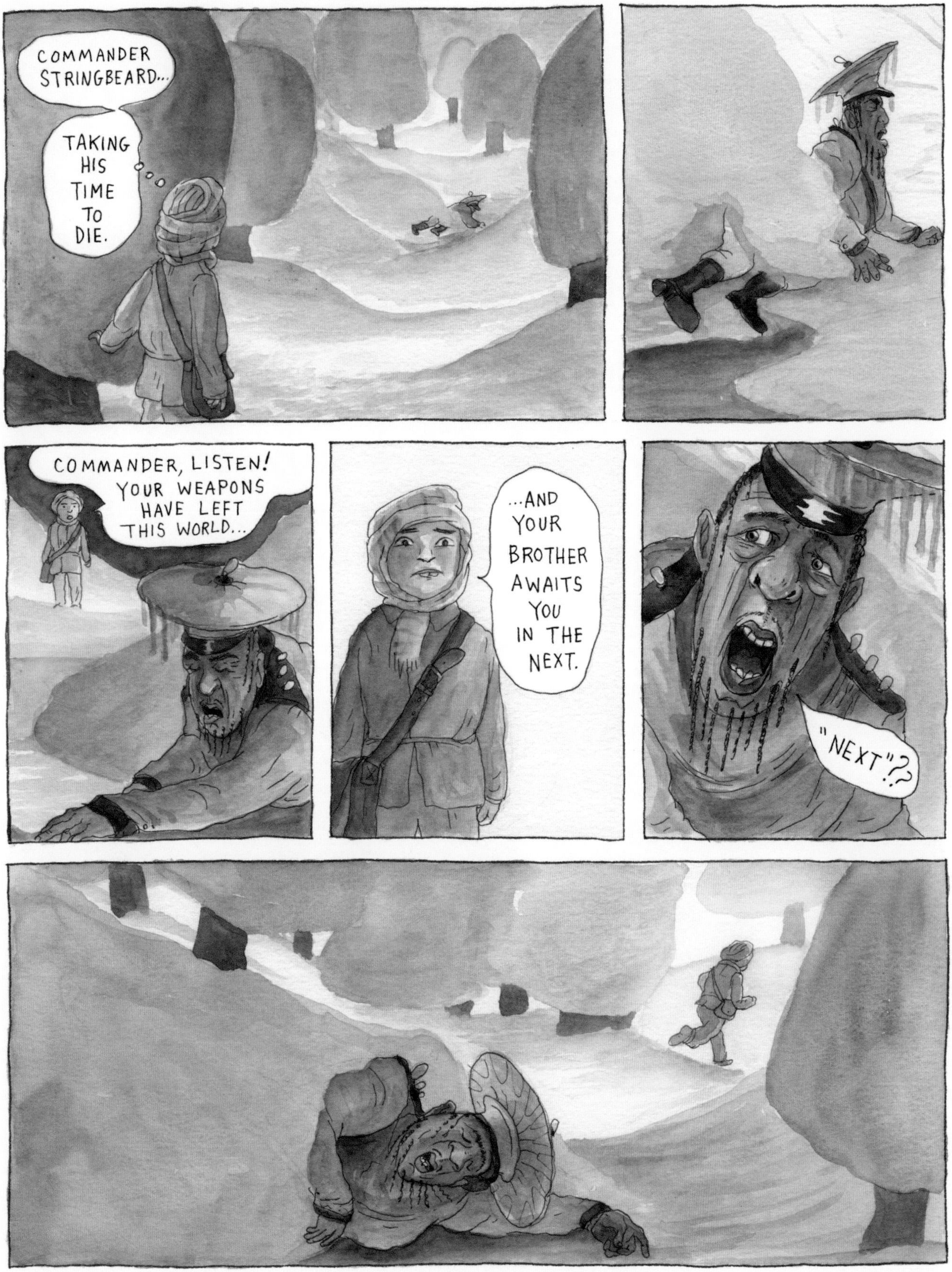
COMMANDER STRINGBEARD...
TAKING HIS TIME TO DIE.
COMMANDER, LISTEN! YOUR WEAPONS HAVE LEFT THIS WORLD...
...AND YOUR BROTHER AWAITS YOU IN THE NEXT.
"NEXT"!?

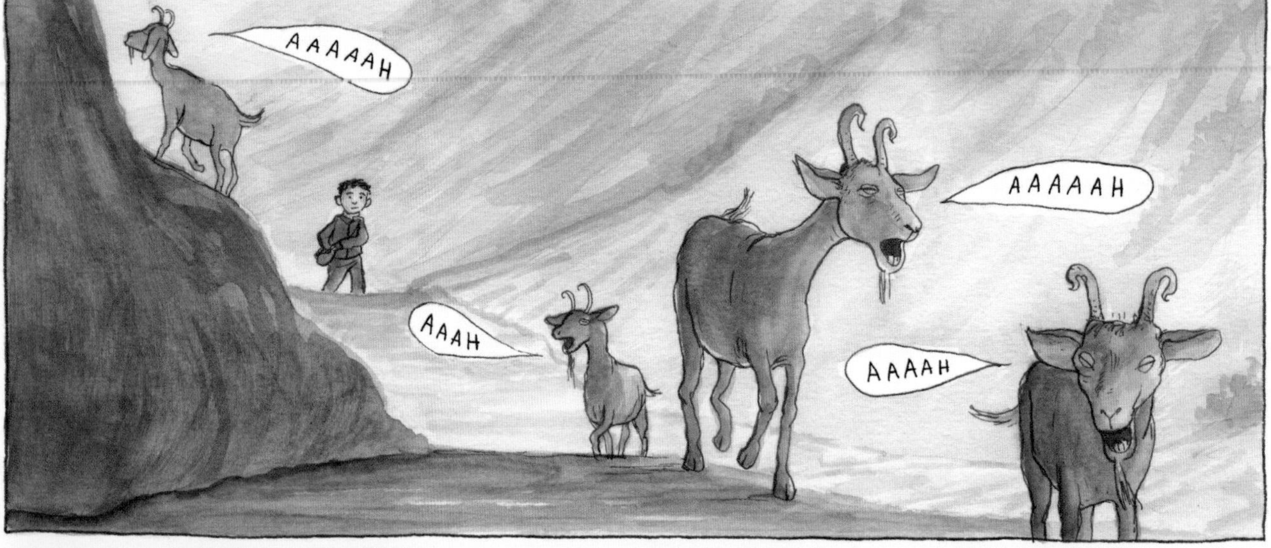
AAAAAH
AAAAAH
AAAH
AAAAH

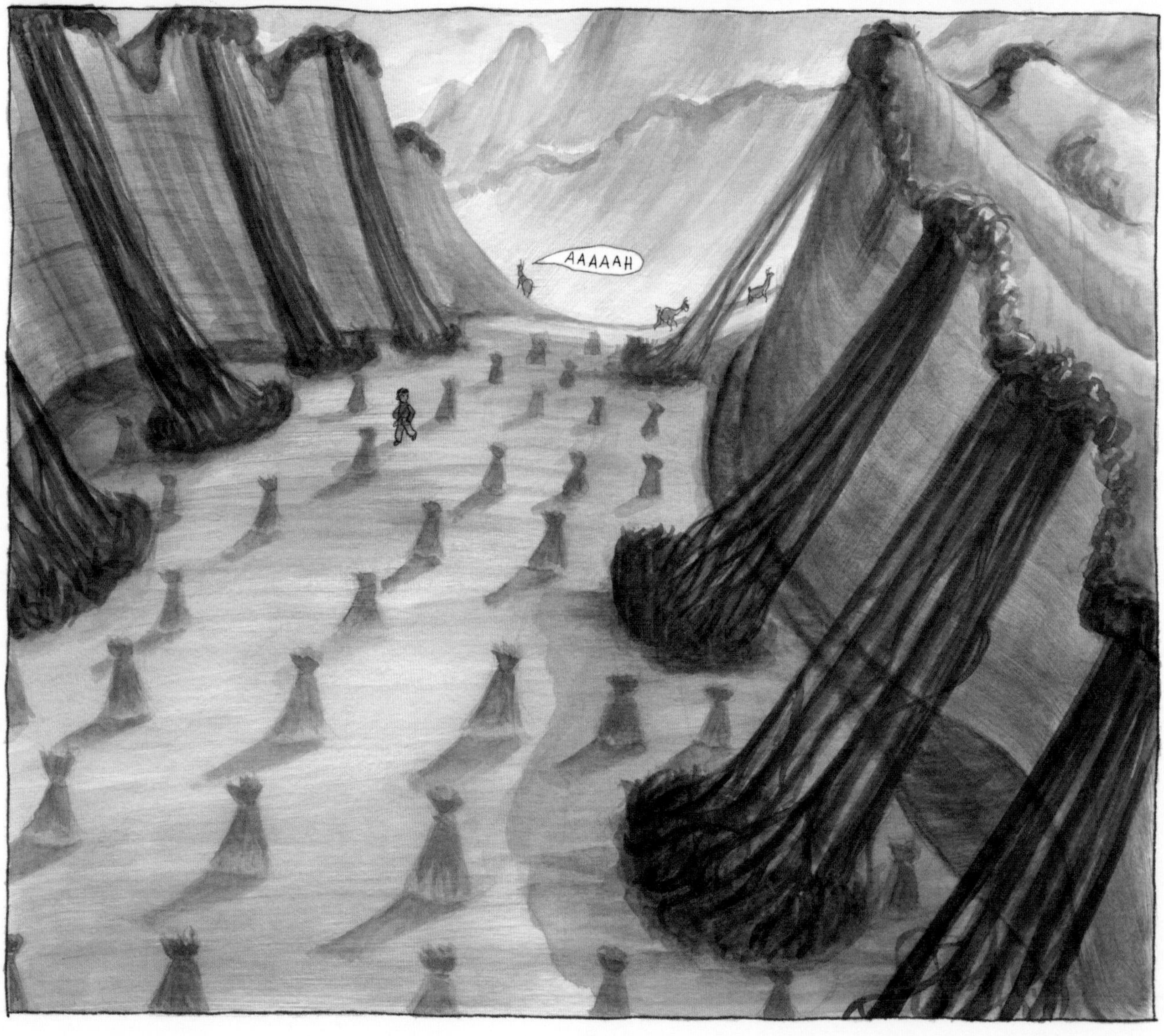
AAAAAH

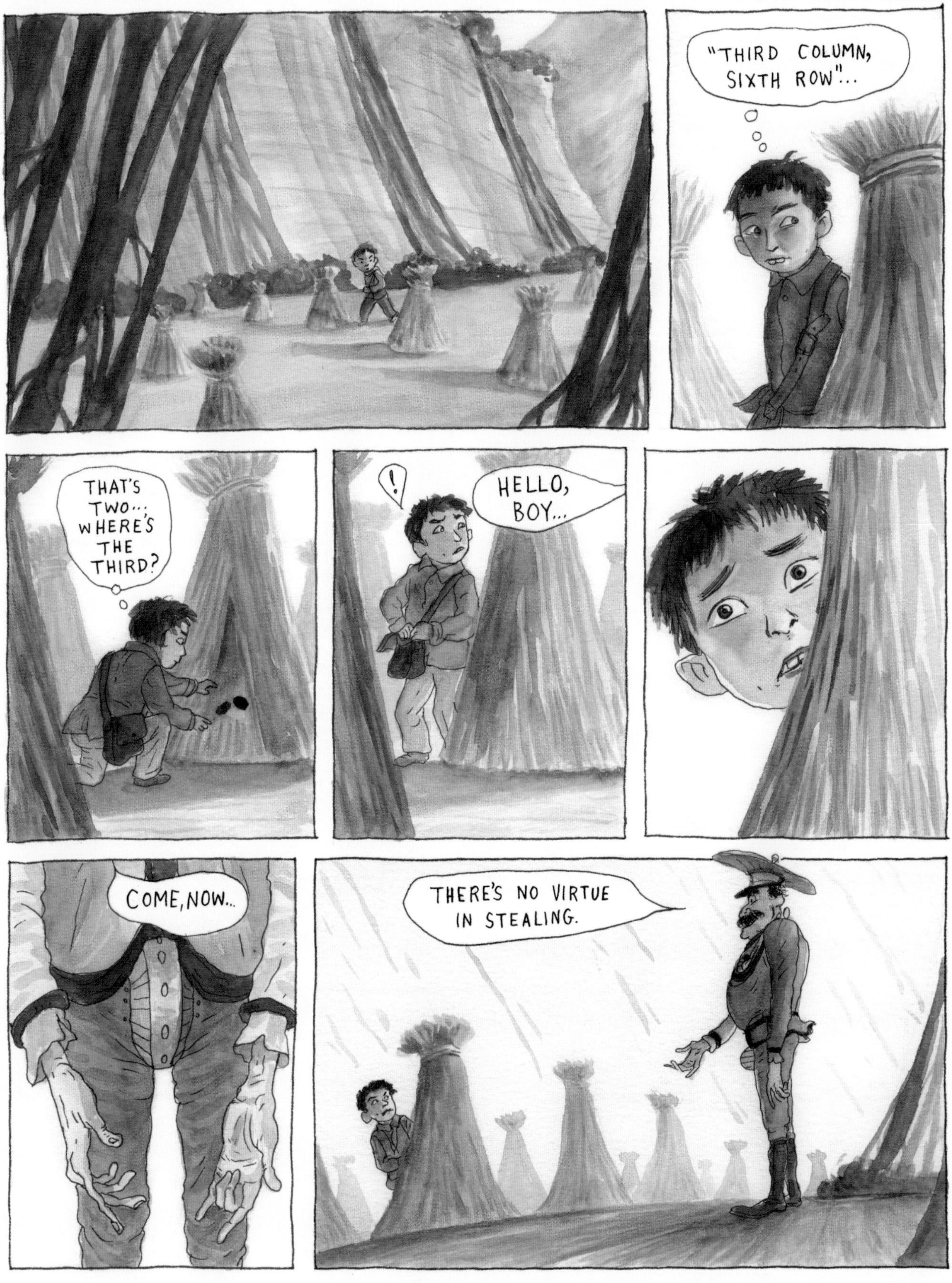
"THIRD COLUMN, SIXTH ROW"...
THAT'S TWO... WHERE'S THE THIRD?
!
HELLO, BOY...
COME, NOW...
THERE'S NO VIRTUE IN STEALING.

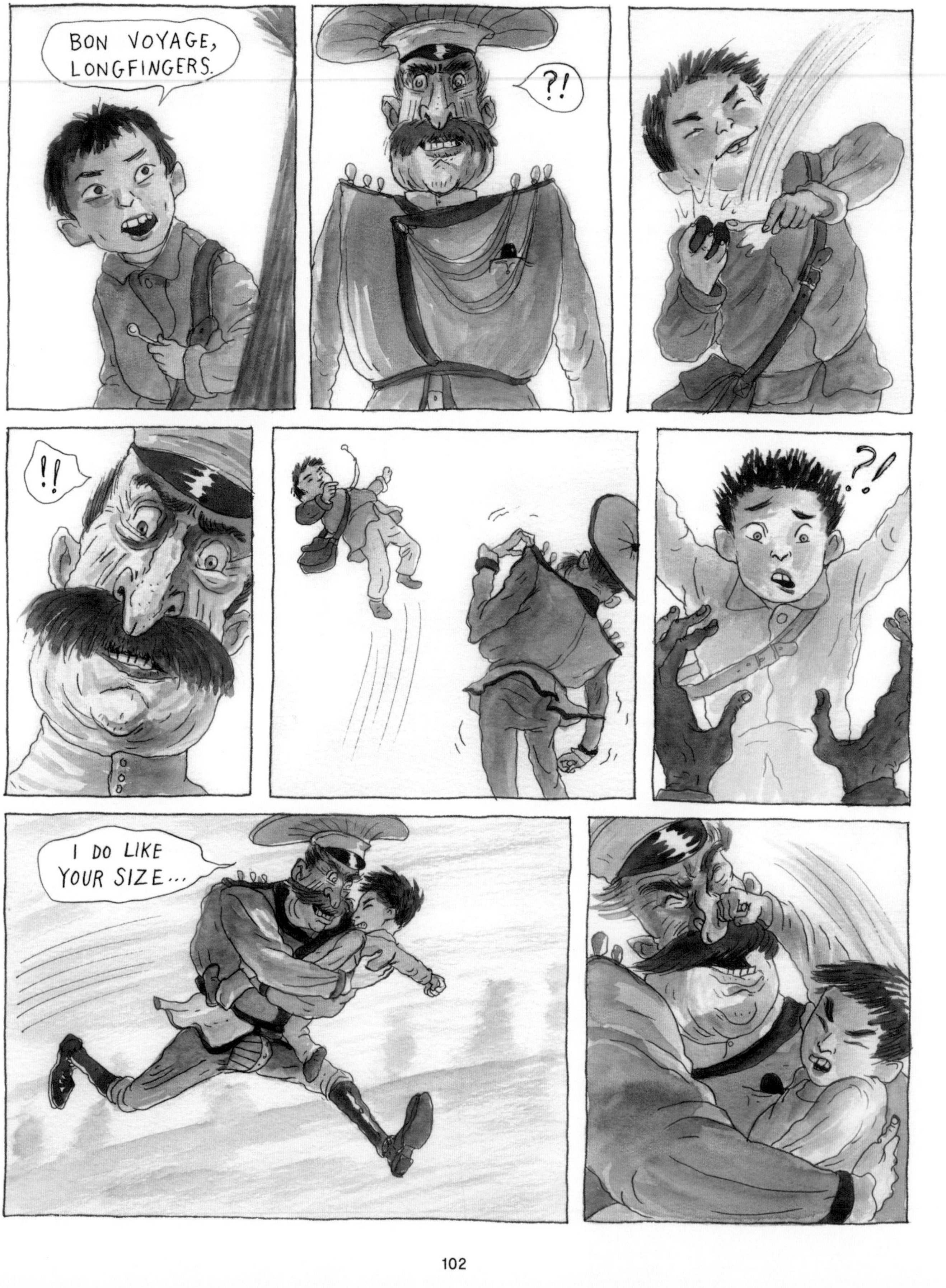
BON VOYAGE, LONGFINGERS.
?!
!!
?!
I DO LIKE YOUR SIZE...

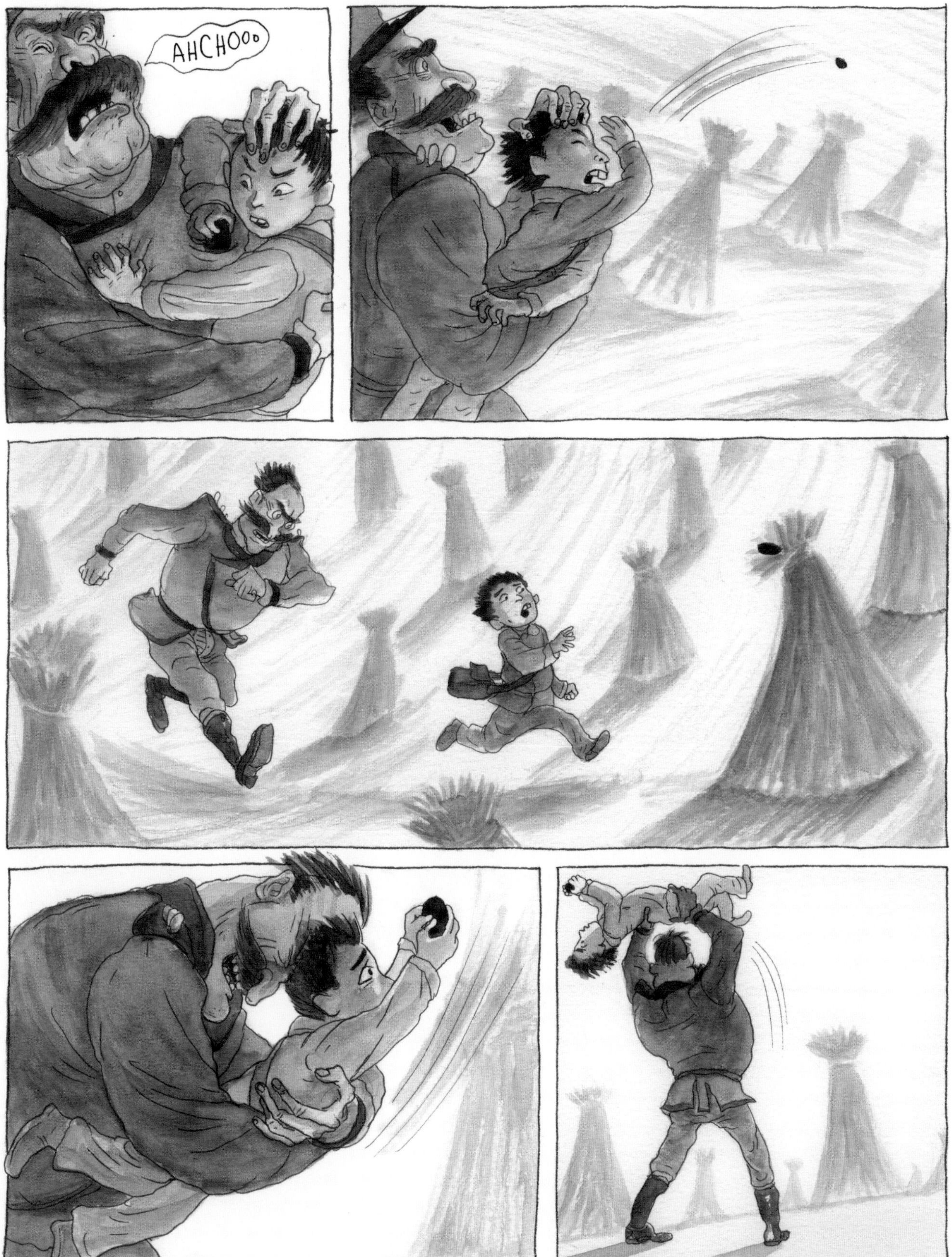
AHCHOOo

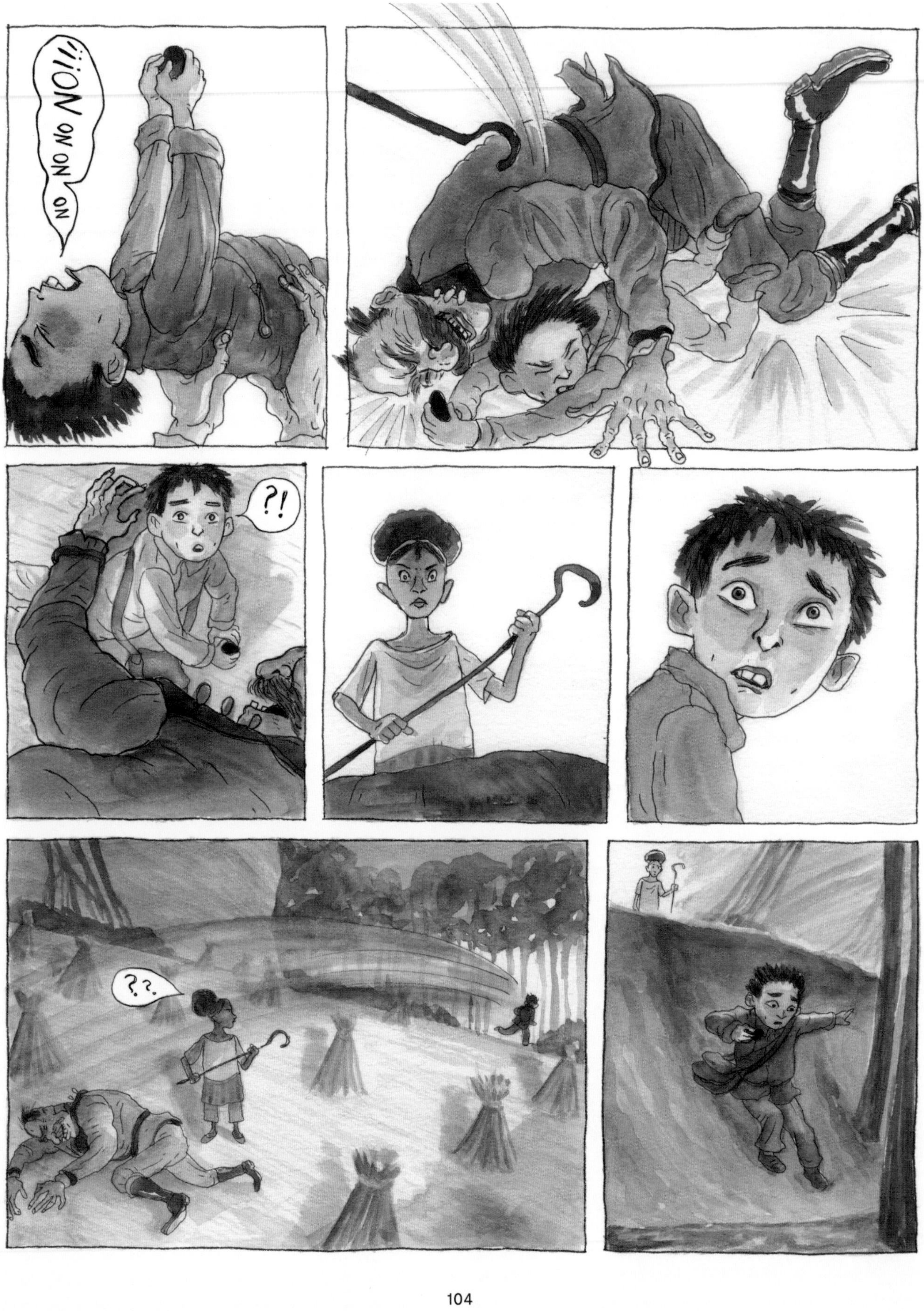
NO NO NO NO!!!
?!
?.?.

NO...

I WAS TOO LATE.

CHILD, DO NOT REVEAL YOUR HUNT TO THAT GIRL!

OUR ACTIVITIES MUST BE KEPT A SECRET!

?

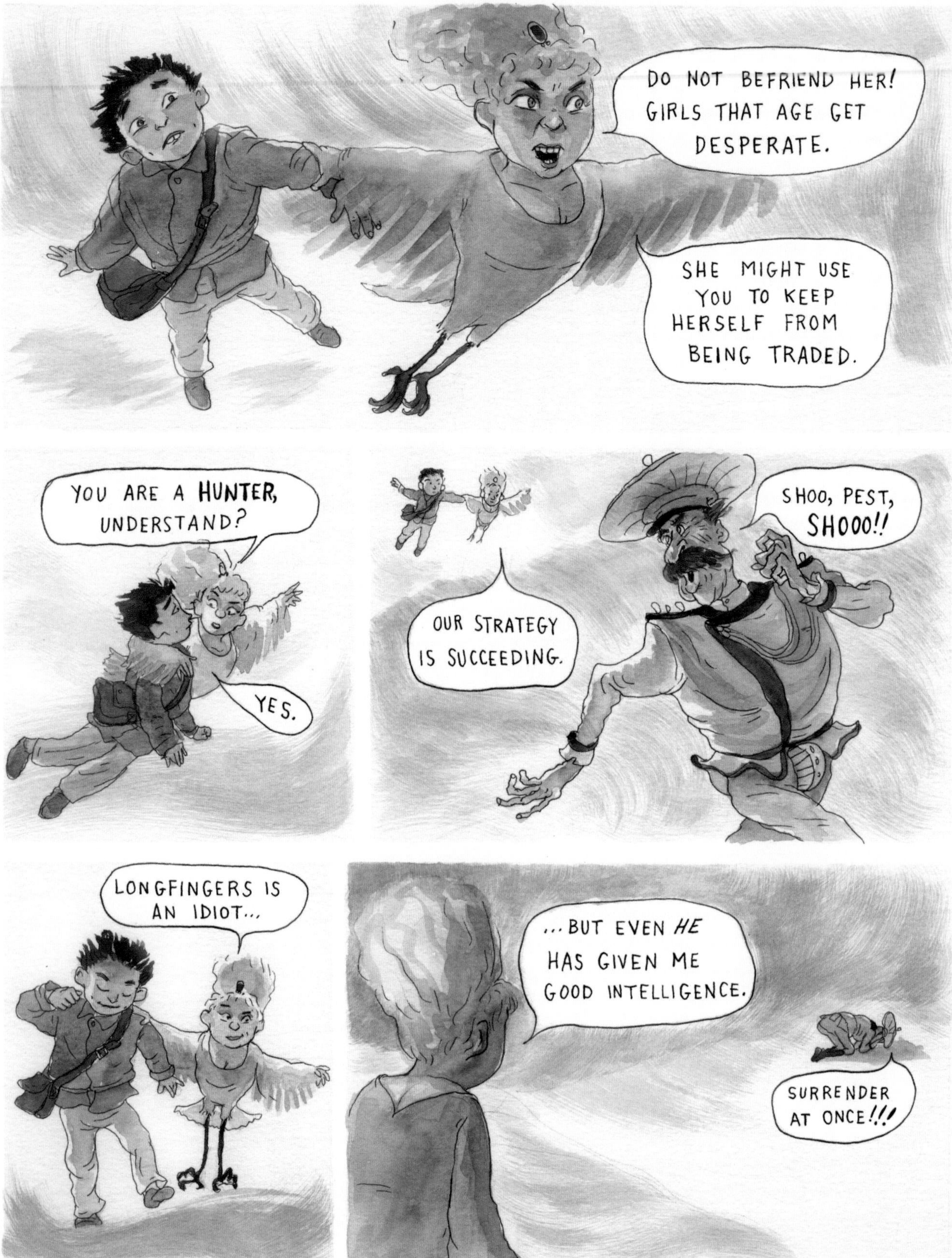
DO NOT BEFRIEND HER! GIRLS THAT AGE GET DESPERATE.
SHE MIGHT USE YOU TO KEEP HERSELF FROM BEING TRADED.
YOU ARE A **HUNTER**, UNDERSTAND?
YES.
OUR STRATEGY IS SUCCEEDING.
SHOO, PEST, **SHOOO!!**
LONGFINGERS IS AN IDIOT...
...BUT EVEN *HE* HAS GIVEN ME GOOD INTELLIGENCE.
SURRENDER AT ONCE!!!

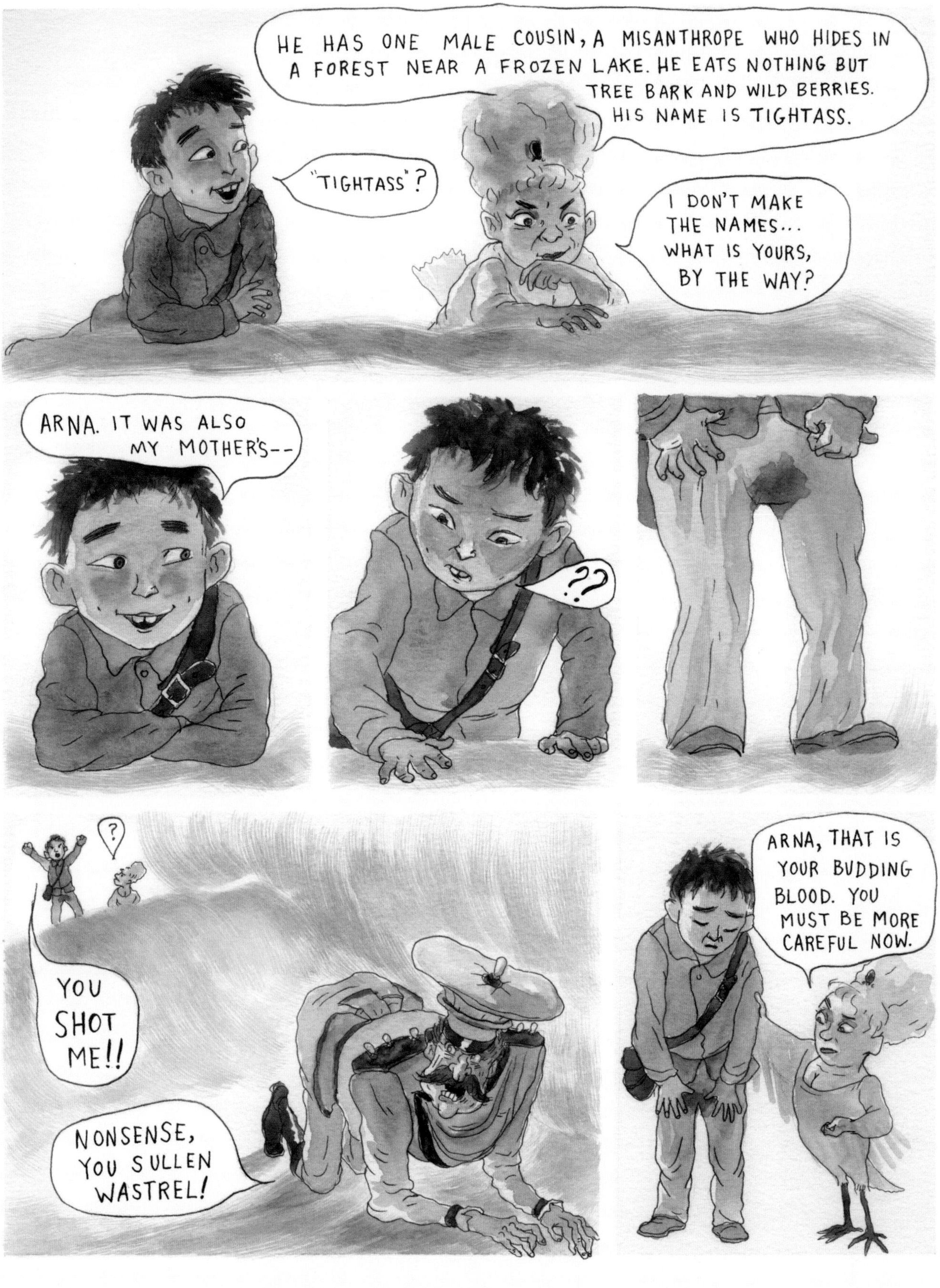
HE HAS ONE MALE COUSIN, A MISANTHROPE WHO HIDES IN A FOREST NEAR A FROZEN LAKE. HE EATS NOTHING BUT TREE BARK AND WILD BERRIES. HIS NAME IS TIGHTASS.
"TIGHTASS"?
I DON'T MAKE THE NAMES... WHAT IS YOURS, BY THE WAY?
ARNA. IT WAS ALSO MY MOTHER'S--
??
?
YOU SHOT ME!!
NONSENSE, YOU SULLEN WASTREL!
ARNA, THAT IS YOUR BUDDING BLOOD. YOU MUST BE MORE CAREFUL NOW.

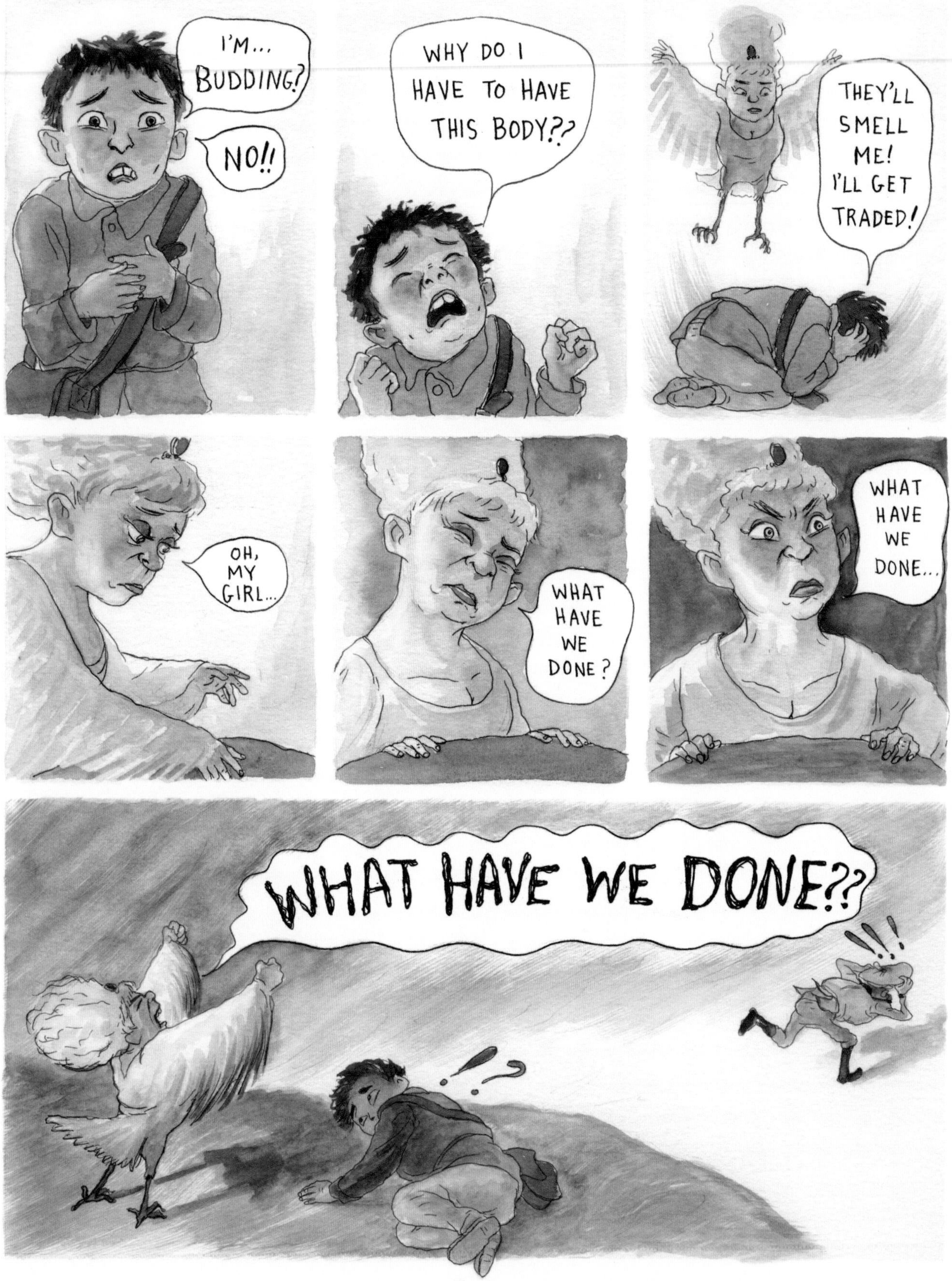
I'M... BUDDING?
NO!!
WHY DO I HAVE TO HAVE THIS BODY??
THEY'LL SMELL ME! I'LL GET TRADED!
OH, MY GIRL...
WHAT HAVE WE DONE?
WHAT HAVE WE DONE...
WHAT HAVE WE DONE??

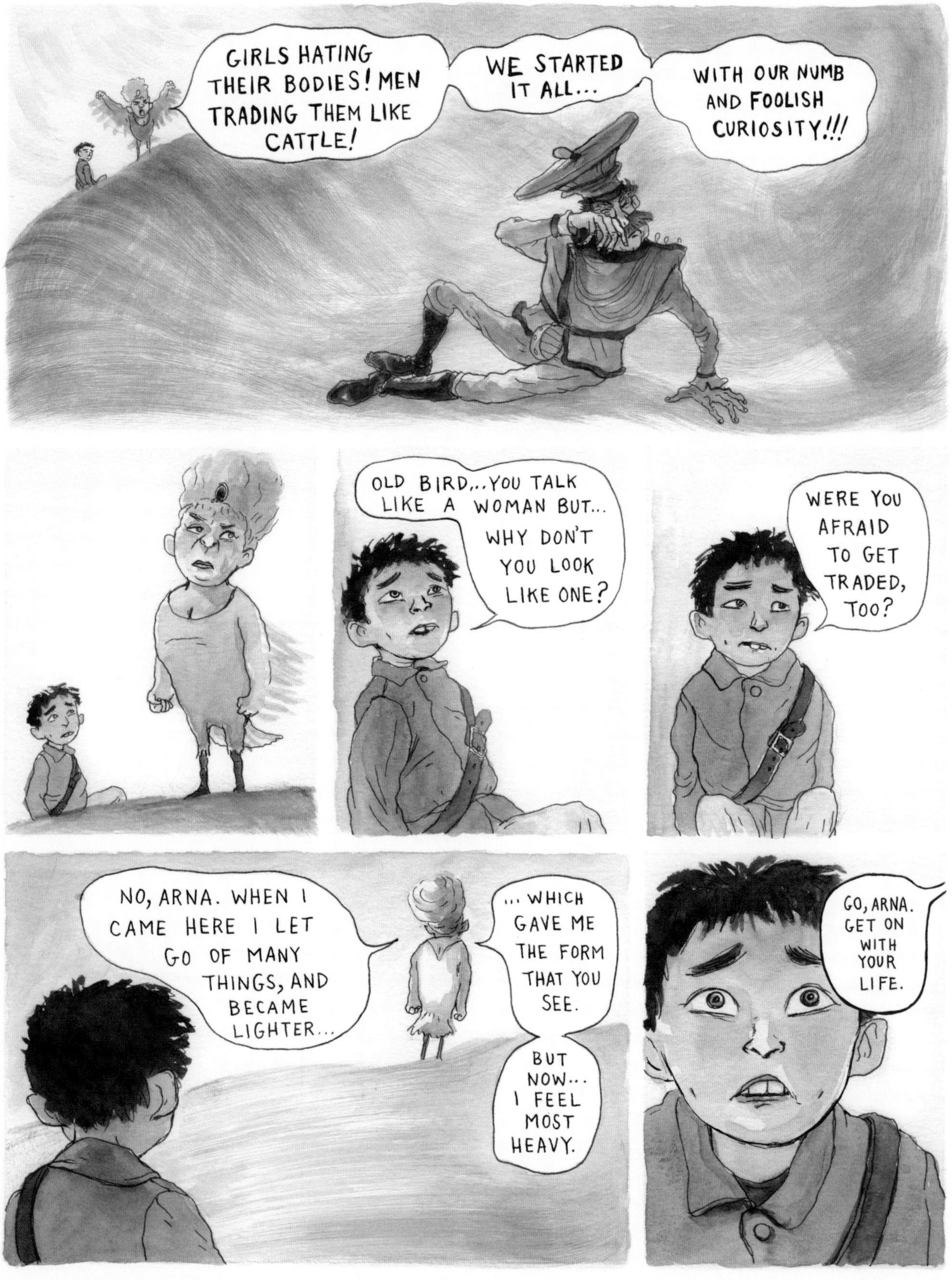
GIRLS HATING THEIR BODIES! MEN TRADING THEM LIKE CATTLE!
WE STARTED IT ALL...
WITH OUR NUMB AND FOOLISH CURIOSITY!!!
OLD BIRD,..YOU TALK LIKE A WOMAN BUT... WHY DON'T YOU LOOK LIKE ONE?
WERE YOU AFRAID TO GET TRADED, TOO?
NO, ARNA. WHEN I CAME HERE I LET GO OF MANY THINGS, AND BECAME LIGHTER...
... WHICH GAVE ME THE FORM THAT YOU SEE.
BUT NOW... I FEEL MOST HEAVY.
GO, ARNA. GET ON WITH YOUR LIFE.

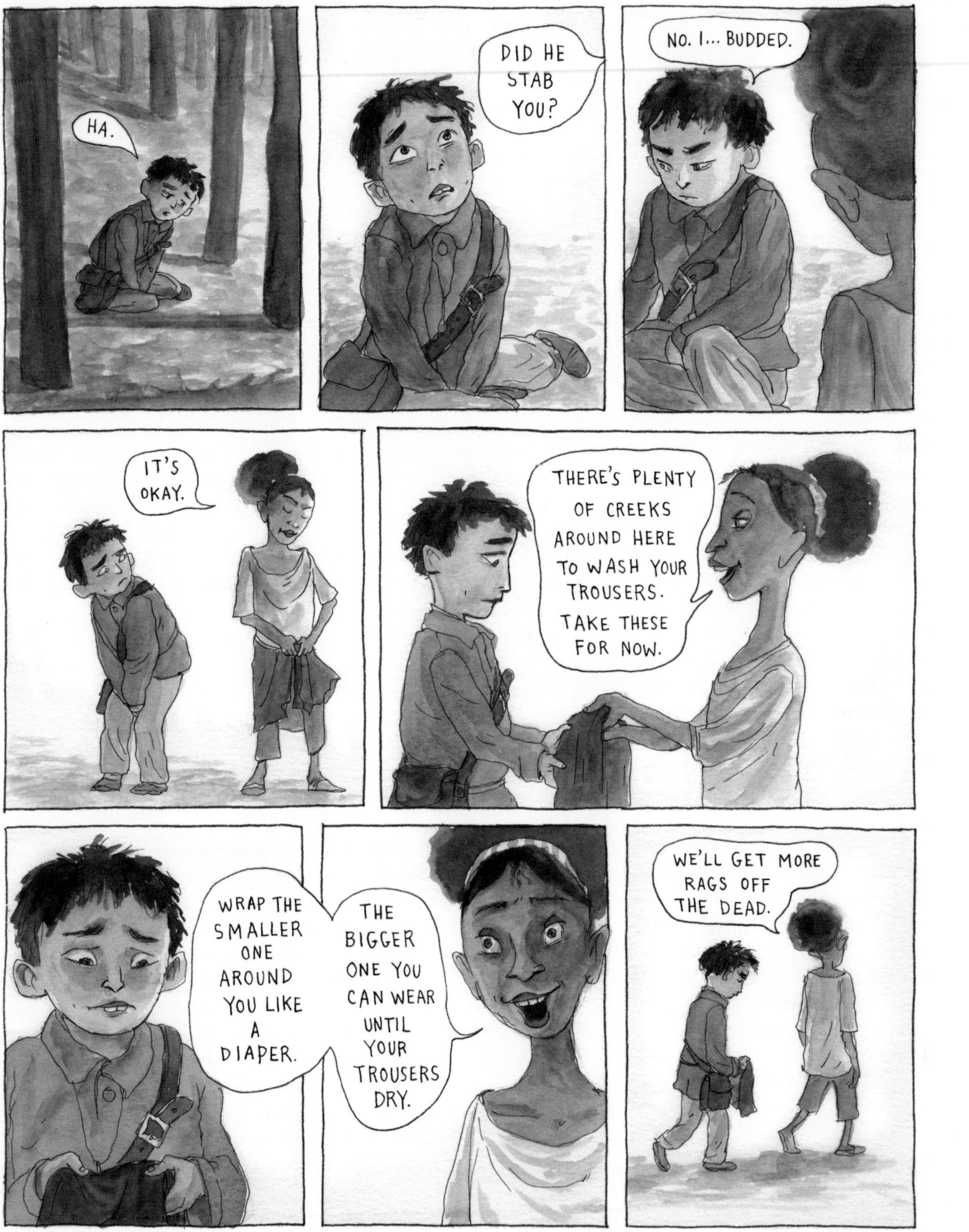
HA.
DID HE STAB YOU?
NO. I... BUDDED.
IT'S OKAY.
THERE'S PLENTY OF CREEKS AROUND HERE TO WASH YOUR TROUSERS.
TAKE THESE FOR NOW.
WRAP THE SMALLER ONE AROUND YOU LIKE A DIAPER.
THE BIGGER ONE YOU CAN WEAR UNTIL YOUR TROUSERS DRY.
WE'LL GET MORE RAGS OFF THE DEAD.

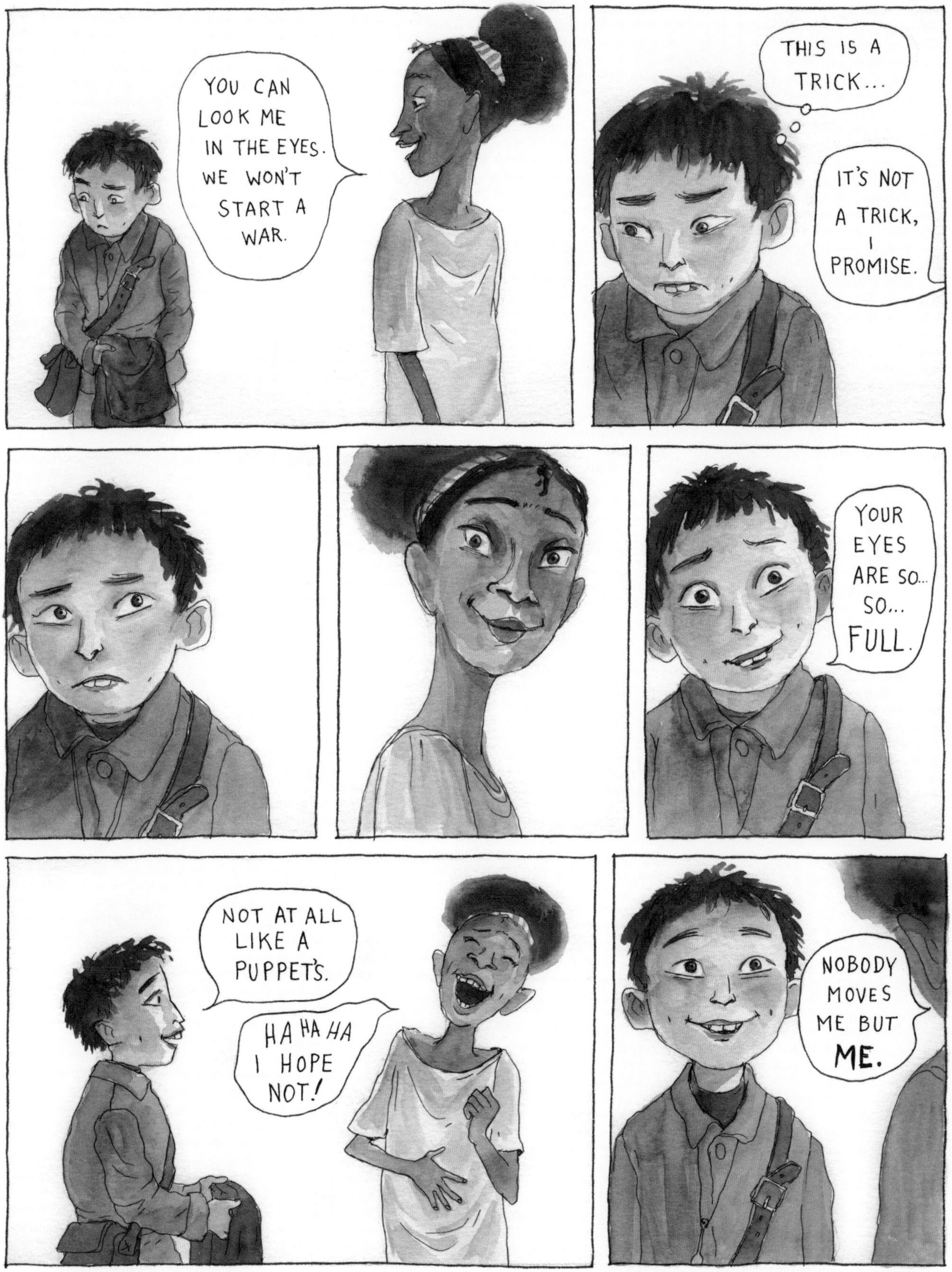
YOU CAN LOOK ME IN THE EYES. WE WON'T START A WAR.
THIS IS A TRICK...
IT'S NOT A TRICK, I PROMISE.
YOUR EYES ARE SO... SO... FULL.
NOT AT ALL LIKE A PUPPET'S.
HA HA HA I HOPE NOT!
NOBODY MOVES ME BUT **ME.**

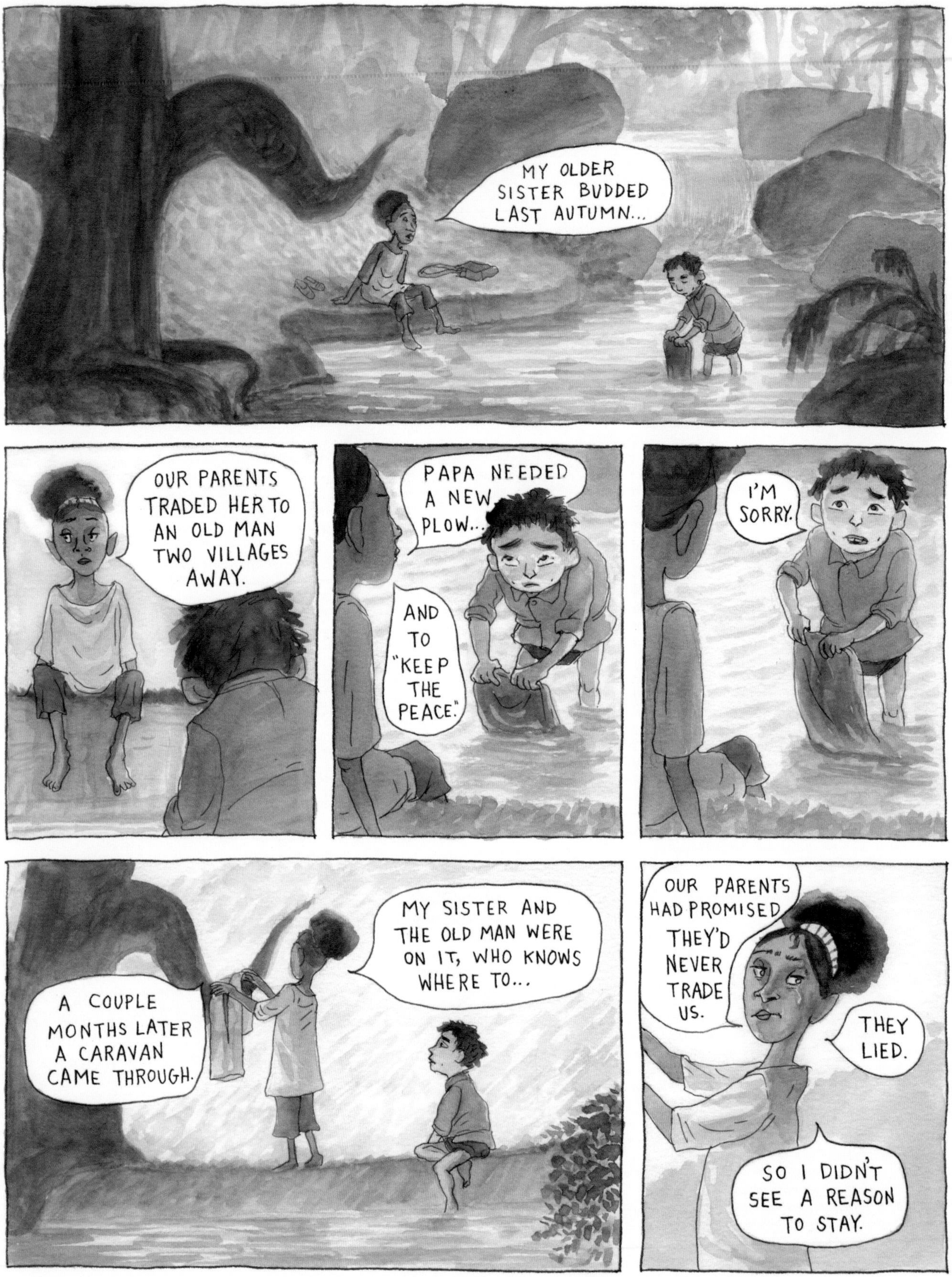
MY OLDER SISTER BUDDED LAST AUTUMN...
OUR PARENTS TRADED HER TO AN OLD MAN TWO VILLAGES AWAY.
PAPA NEEDED A NEW PLOW...
AND TO "KEEP THE PEACE."
I'M SORRY.
A COUPLE MONTHS LATER A CARAVAN CAME THROUGH.
MY SISTER AND THE OLD MAN WERE ON IT, WHO KNOWS WHERE TO...
OUR PARENTS HAD PROMISED THEY'D NEVER TRADE US.
THEY LIED.
SO I DIDN'T SEE A REASON TO STAY.

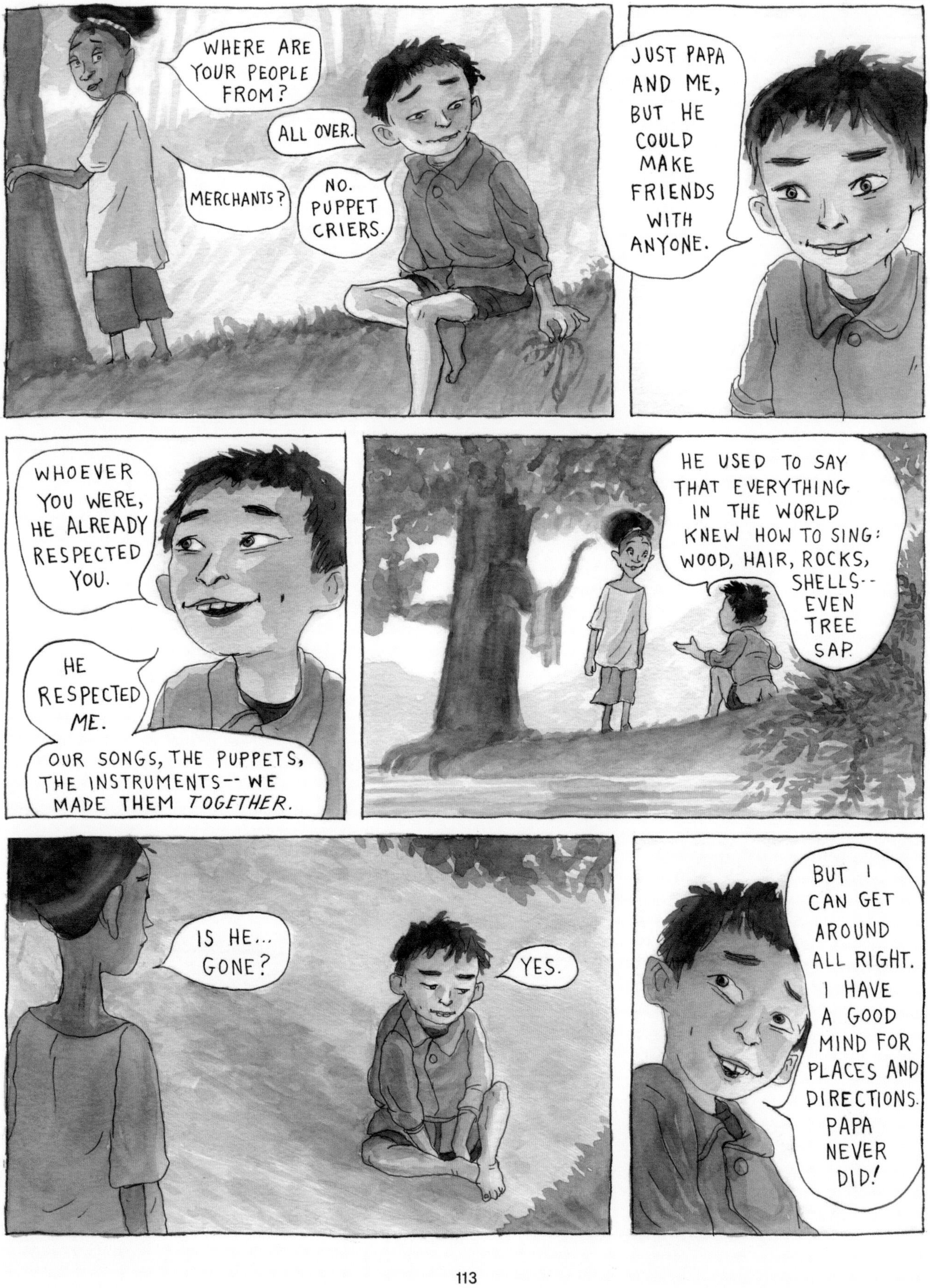
WHERE ARE YOUR PEOPLE FROM?
ALL OVER.
MERCHANTS?
NO. PUPPET CRIERS.
JUST PAPA AND ME, BUT HE COULD MAKE FRIENDS WITH ANYONE.
WHOEVER YOU WERE, HE ALREADY RESPECTED YOU.
HE RESPECTED ME.
OUR SONGS, THE PUPPETS, THE INSTRUMENTS-- WE MADE THEM *TOGETHER*.
HE USED TO SAY THAT EVERYTHING IN THE WORLD KNEW HOW TO SING: WOOD, HAIR, ROCKS, SHELLS-- EVEN TREE SAP.
IS HE... GONE?
YES.
BUT I CAN GET AROUND ALL RIGHT. I HAVE A GOOD MIND FOR PLACES AND DIRECTIONS. PAPA NEVER DID!

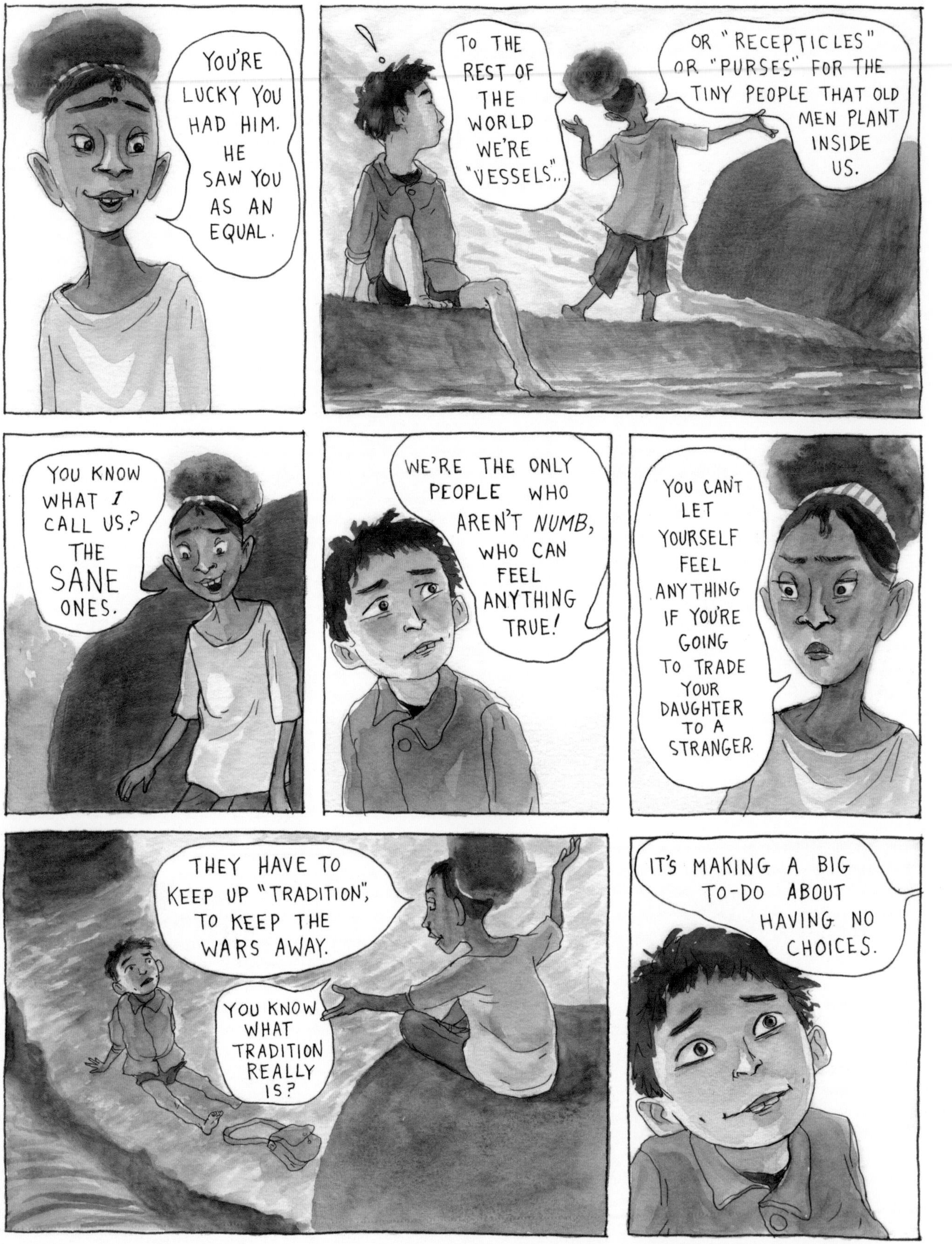
YOU'RE LUCKY YOU HAD HIM. HE SAW YOU AS AN EQUAL.
!
TO THE REST OF THE WORLD WE'RE "VESSELS"...
OR "RECEPTICLES" OR "PURSES" FOR THE TINY PEOPLE THAT OLD MEN PLANT INSIDE US.
YOU KNOW WHAT *I* CALL US? THE SANE ONES.
WE'RE THE ONLY PEOPLE WHO AREN'T *NUMB*, WHO CAN FEEL ANYTHING TRUE!
YOU CAN'T LET YOURSELF FEEL ANYTHING IF YOU'RE GOING TO TRADE YOUR DAUGHTER TO A STRANGER.
THEY HAVE TO KEEP UP "TRADITION", TO KEEP THE WARS AWAY.
YOU KNOW WHAT TRADITION REALLY IS?
IT'S MAKING A BIG TO-DO ABOUT HAVING NO CHOICES.

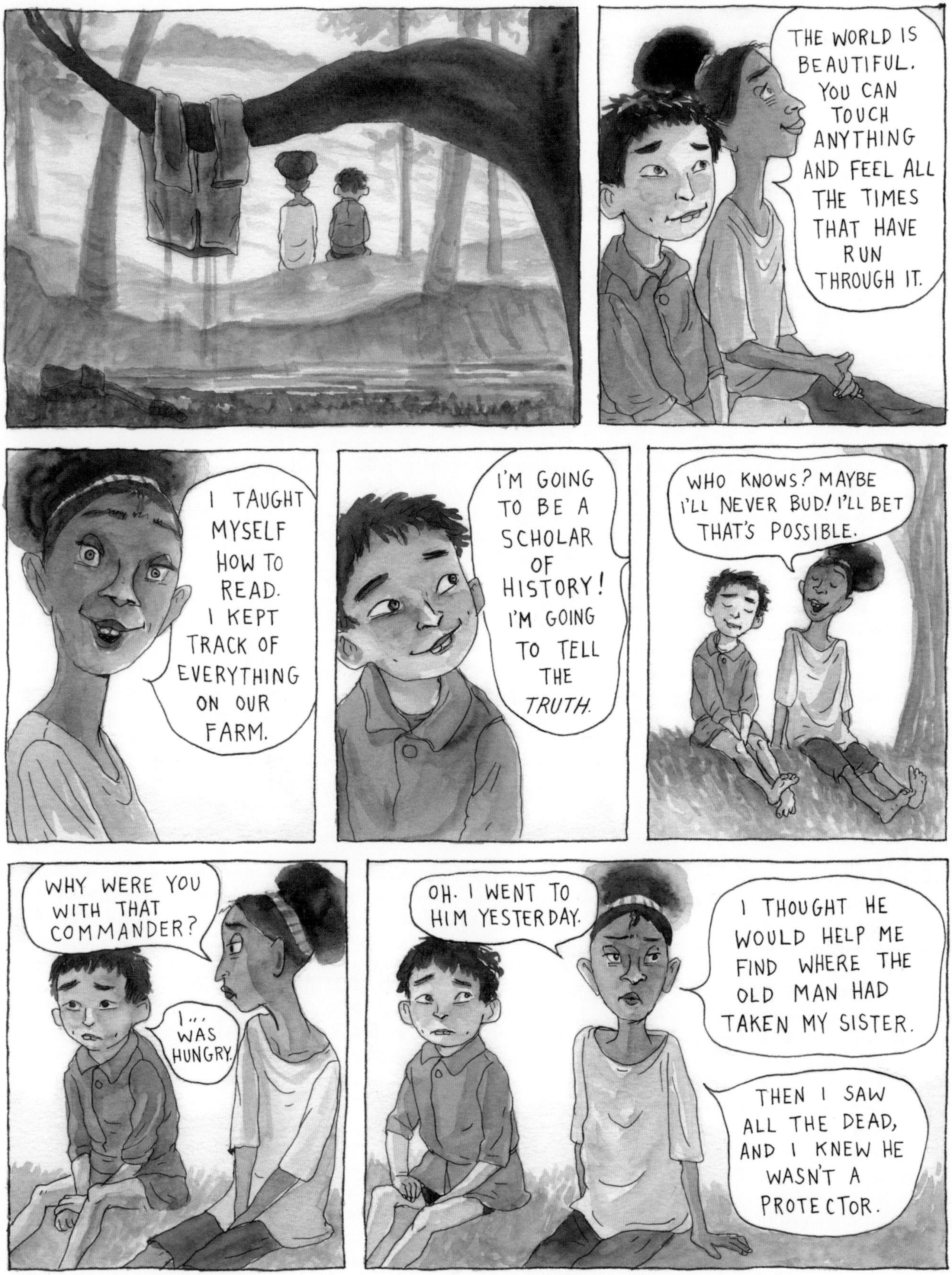
THE WORLD IS BEAUTIFUL. YOU CAN TOUCH ANYTHING AND FEEL ALL THE TIMES THAT HAVE RUN THROUGH IT.
I TAUGHT MYSELF HOW TO READ. I KEPT TRACK OF EVERYTHING ON OUR FARM.
I'M GOING TO BE A SCHOLAR OF HISTORY! I'M GOING TO TELL THE *TRUTH.*
WHO KNOWS? MAYBE I'LL NEVER BUD! I'LL BET THAT'S POSSIBLE.
WHY WERE YOU WITH THAT COMMANDER?
I... WAS HUNGRY.
OH. I WENT TO HIM YESTERDAY.
I THOUGHT HE WOULD HELP ME FIND WHERE THE OLD MAN HAD TAKEN MY SISTER.
THEN I SAW ALL THE DEAD, AND I KNEW HE WASN'T A PROTECTOR.

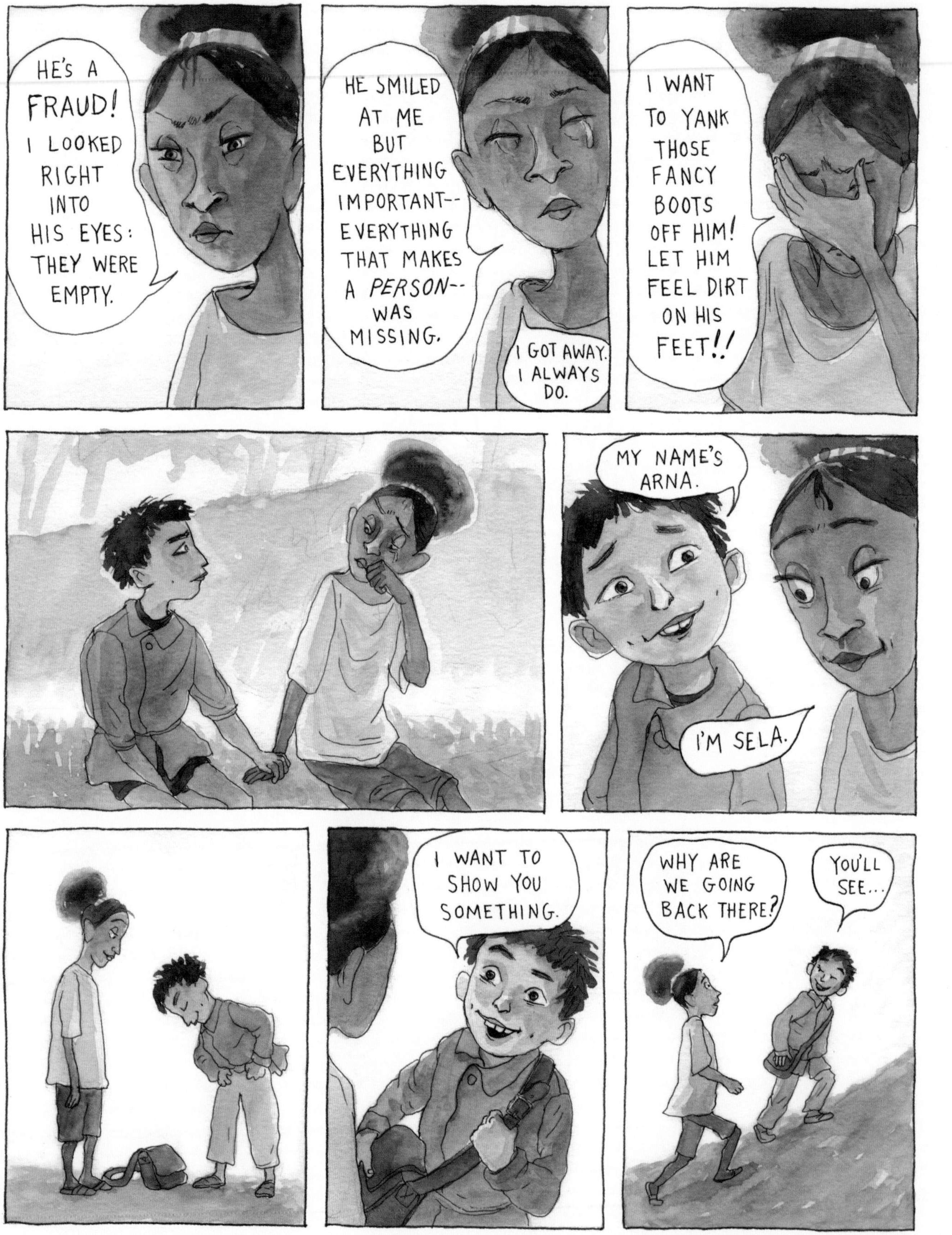
HE'S A FRAUD! I LOOKED RIGHT INTO HIS EYES: THEY WERE EMPTY.
HE SMILED AT ME BUT EVERYTHING IMPORTANT-- EVERYTHING THAT MAKES A *PERSON*-- WAS MISSING.
I GOT AWAY. I ALWAYS DO.
I WANT TO YANK THOSE FANCY BOOTS OFF HIM! LET HIM FEEL DIRT ON HIS FEET!!
MY NAME'S ARNA.
I'M SELA.
I WANT TO SHOW YOU SOMETHING.
WHY ARE WE GOING BACK THERE?
YOU'LL SEE...

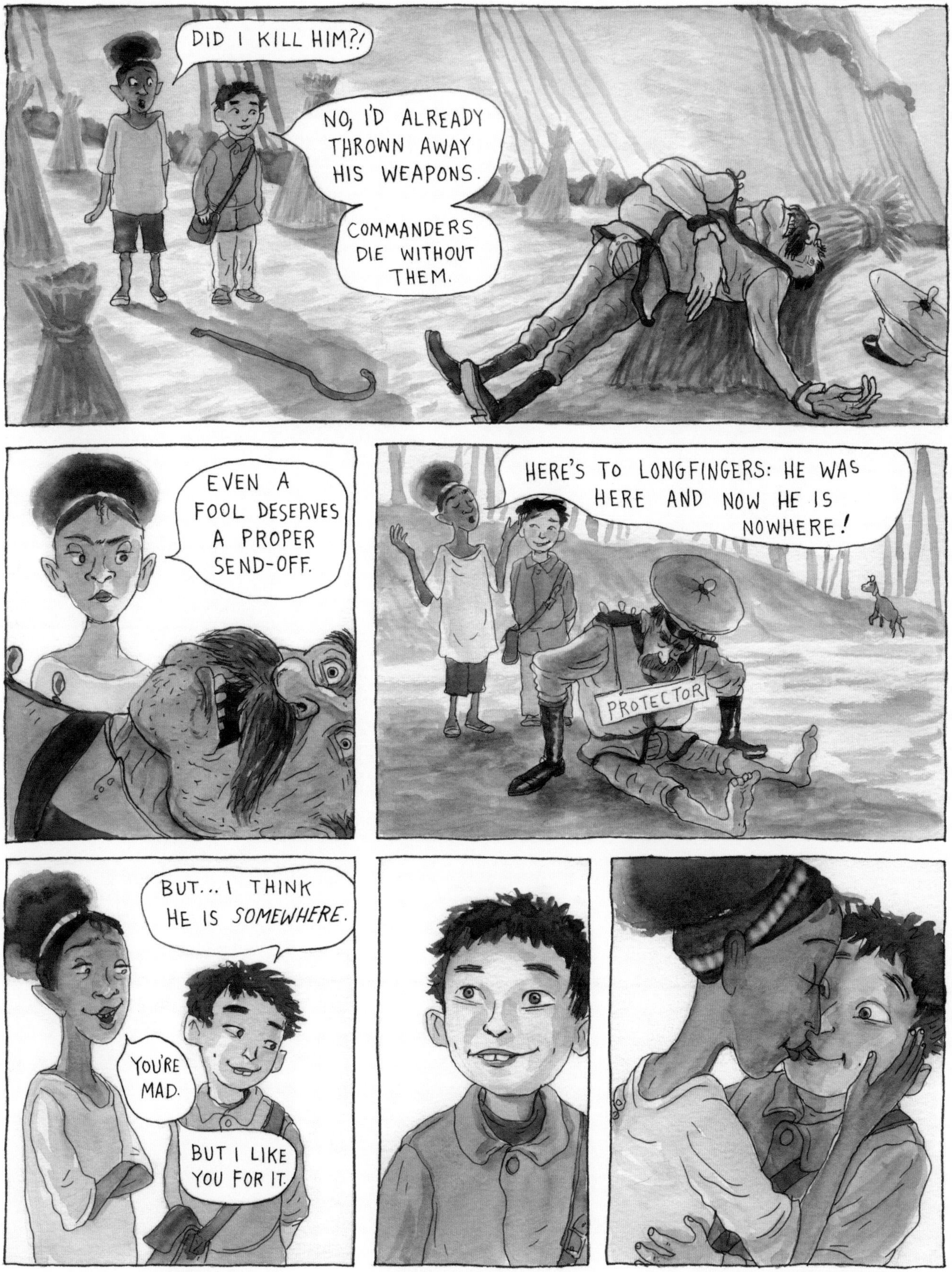
DID I KILL HIM?!
NO, I'D ALREADY THROWN AWAY HIS WEAPONS.
COMMANDERS DIE WITHOUT THEM.
EVEN A FOOL DESERVES A PROPER SEND-OFF.
HERE'S TO LONGFINGERS: HE WAS HERE AND NOW HE IS NOWHERE!
PROTECTOR
BUT... I THINK HE IS *SOMEWHERE*.
YOU'RE MAD.
BUT I LIKE YOU FOR IT.

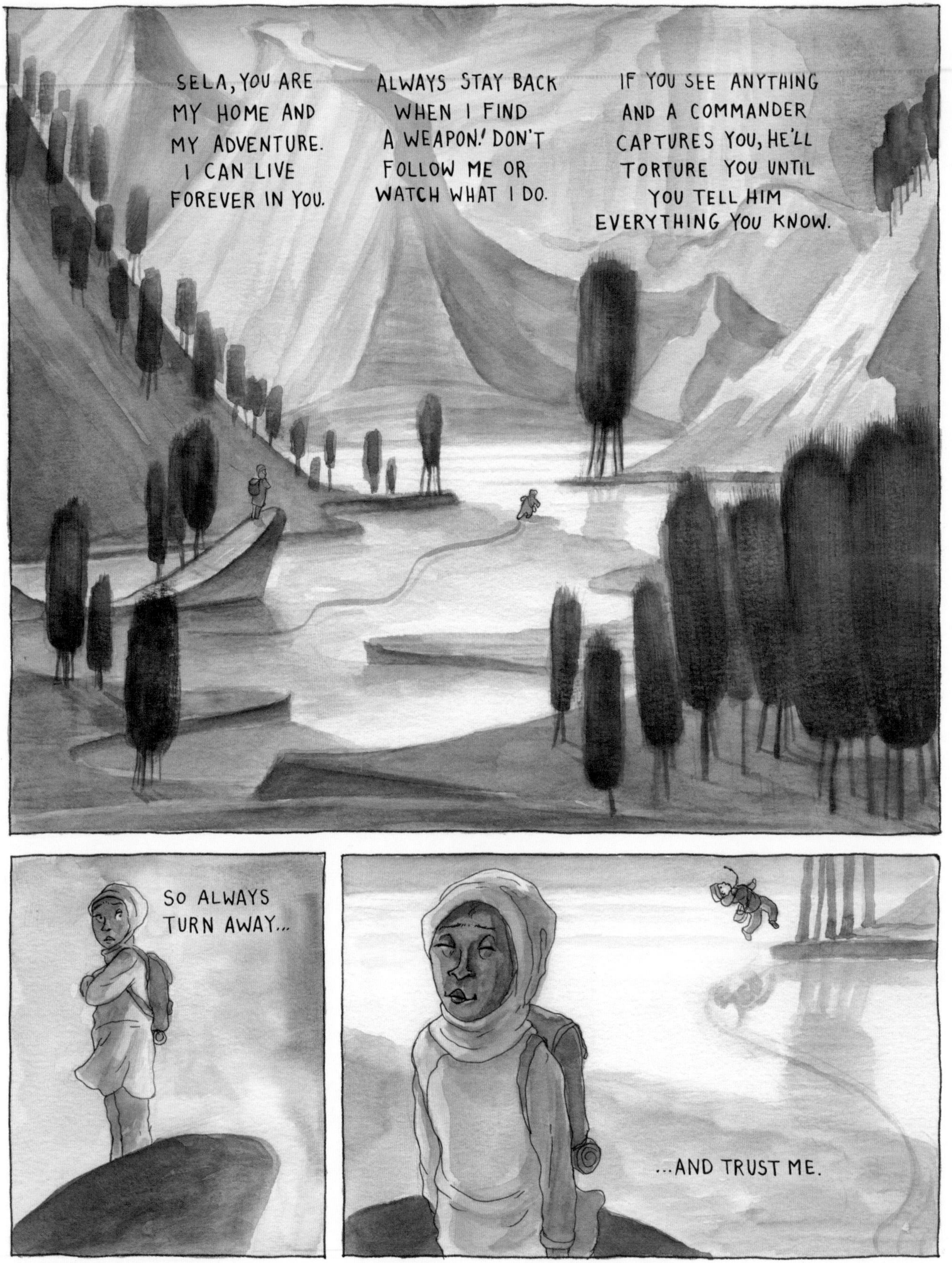
SELA, YOU ARE MY HOME AND MY ADVENTURE. I CAN LIVE FOREVER IN YOU.
ALWAYS STAY BACK WHEN I FIND A WEAPON! DON'T FOLLOW ME OR WATCH WHAT I DO.
IF YOU SEE ANYTHING AND A COMMANDER CAPTURES YOU, HE'LL TORTURE YOU UNTIL YOU TELL HIM EVERYTHING YOU KNOW.
SO ALWAYS TURN AWAY...
...AND TRUST ME.

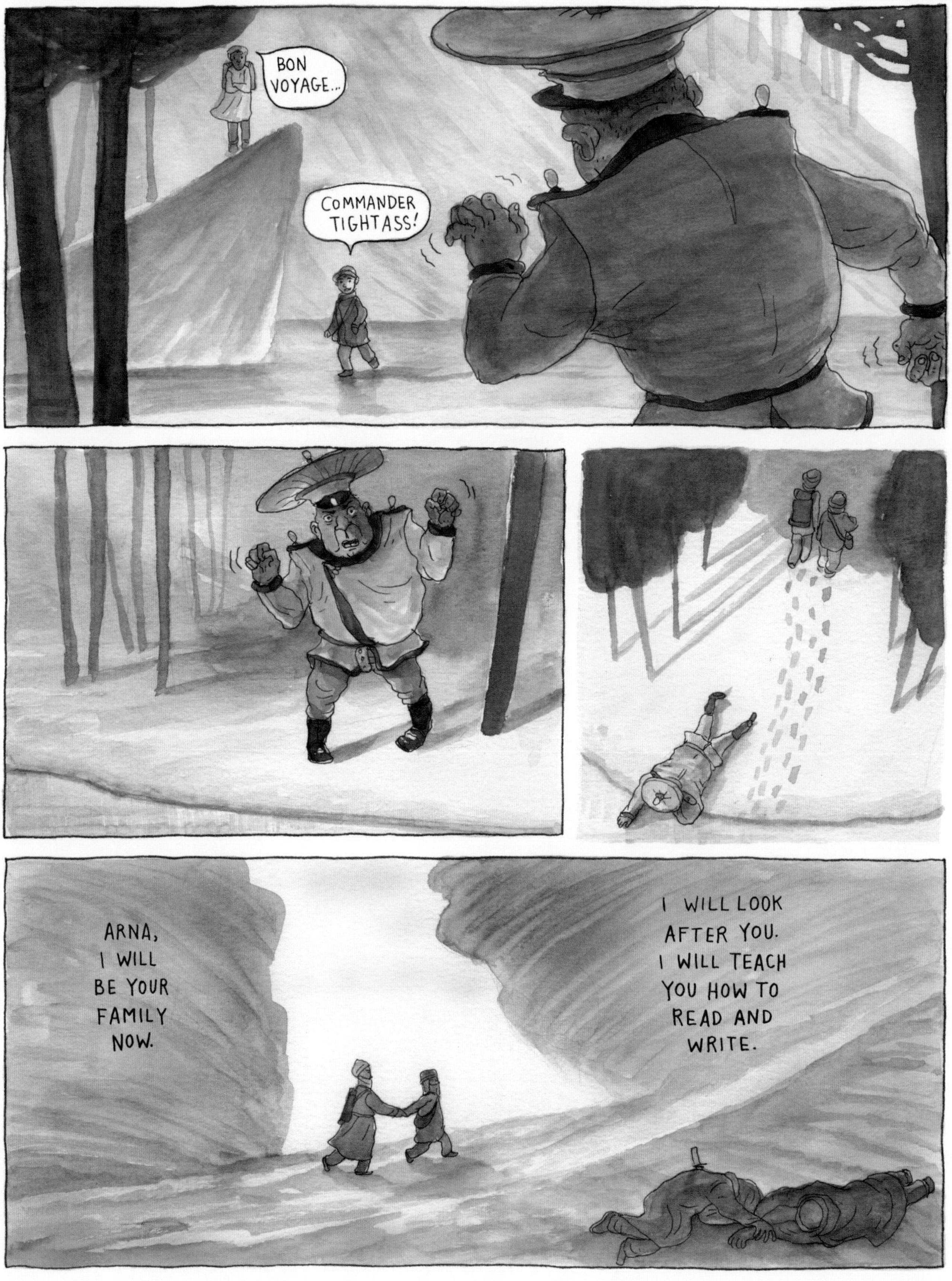
BON VOYAGE...
COMMANDER TIGHTASS!
ARNA, I WILL BE YOUR FAMILY NOW.
I WILL LOOK AFTER YOU. I WILL TEACH YOU HOW TO READ AND WRITE.

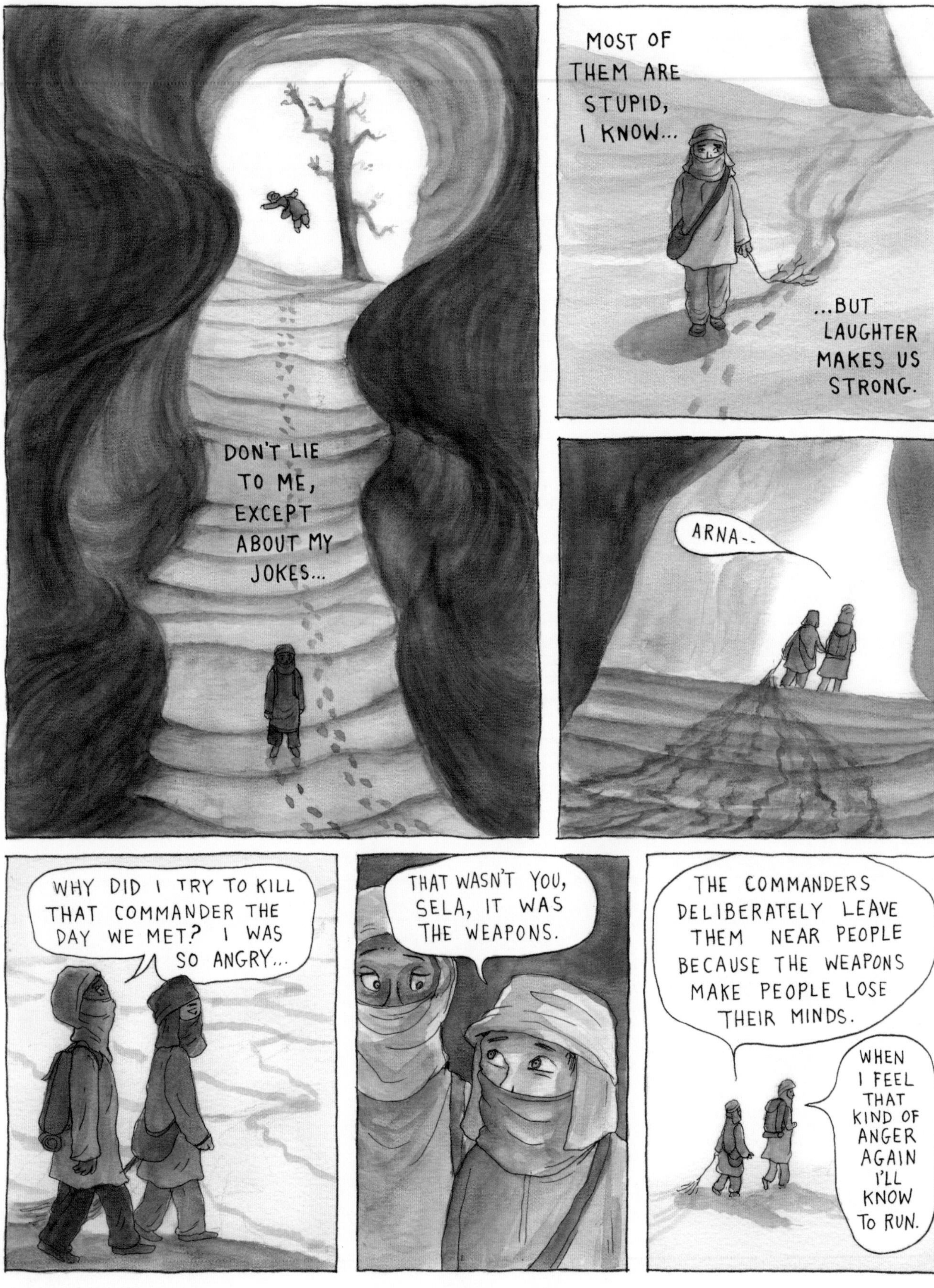
DON'T LIE TO ME, EXCEPT ABOUT MY JOKES...
MOST OF THEM ARE STUPID, I KNOW...
...BUT LAUGHTER MAKES US STRONG.
ARNA--
WHY DID I TRY TO KILL THAT COMMANDER THE DAY WE MET? I WAS SO ANGRY...
THAT WASN'T YOU, SELA, IT WAS THE WEAPONS.
THE COMMANDERS DELIBERATELY LEAVE THEM NEAR PEOPLE BECAUSE THE WEAPONS MAKE PEOPLE LOSE THEIR MINDS.
WHEN I FEEL THAT KIND OF ANGER AGAIN I'LL KNOW TO RUN.

ARNA-- WHAT'S THE MATTER?
SELA, YOU AND I ARE *REAL*, AREN'T WE...
MORE **REAL** THAN REAL, RIGHT?
YOU WANT ME TO SAY IT AGAIN?
YES!
WE'RE NOT PUPPETS, OUR EYES ARE FULL...
I KNOW THINGS THAT YOU DON'T, AND YOU KNOW THINGS THAT I DON'T.
NOT A DREAM, THIS.
NO. OUR LIFE IS CRAZY...
BUT WE'RE THE SANEST PEOPLE ALIVE.

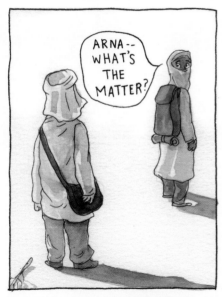

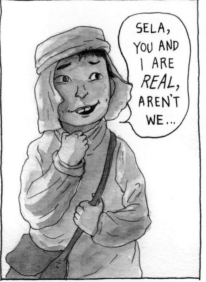

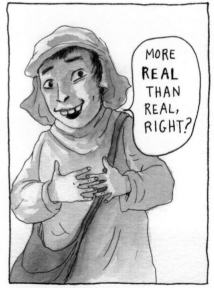

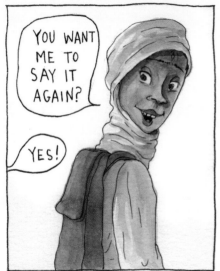

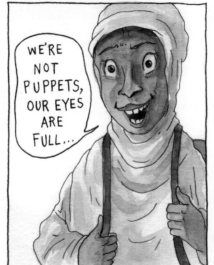

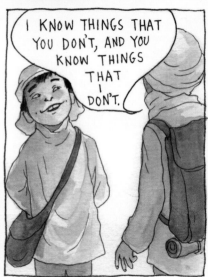

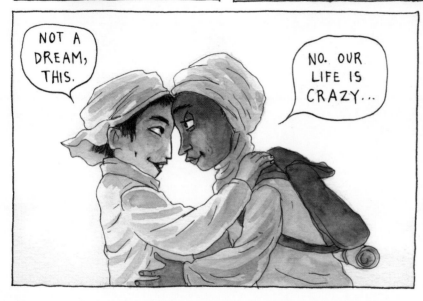

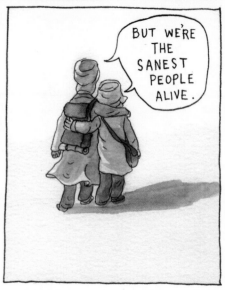

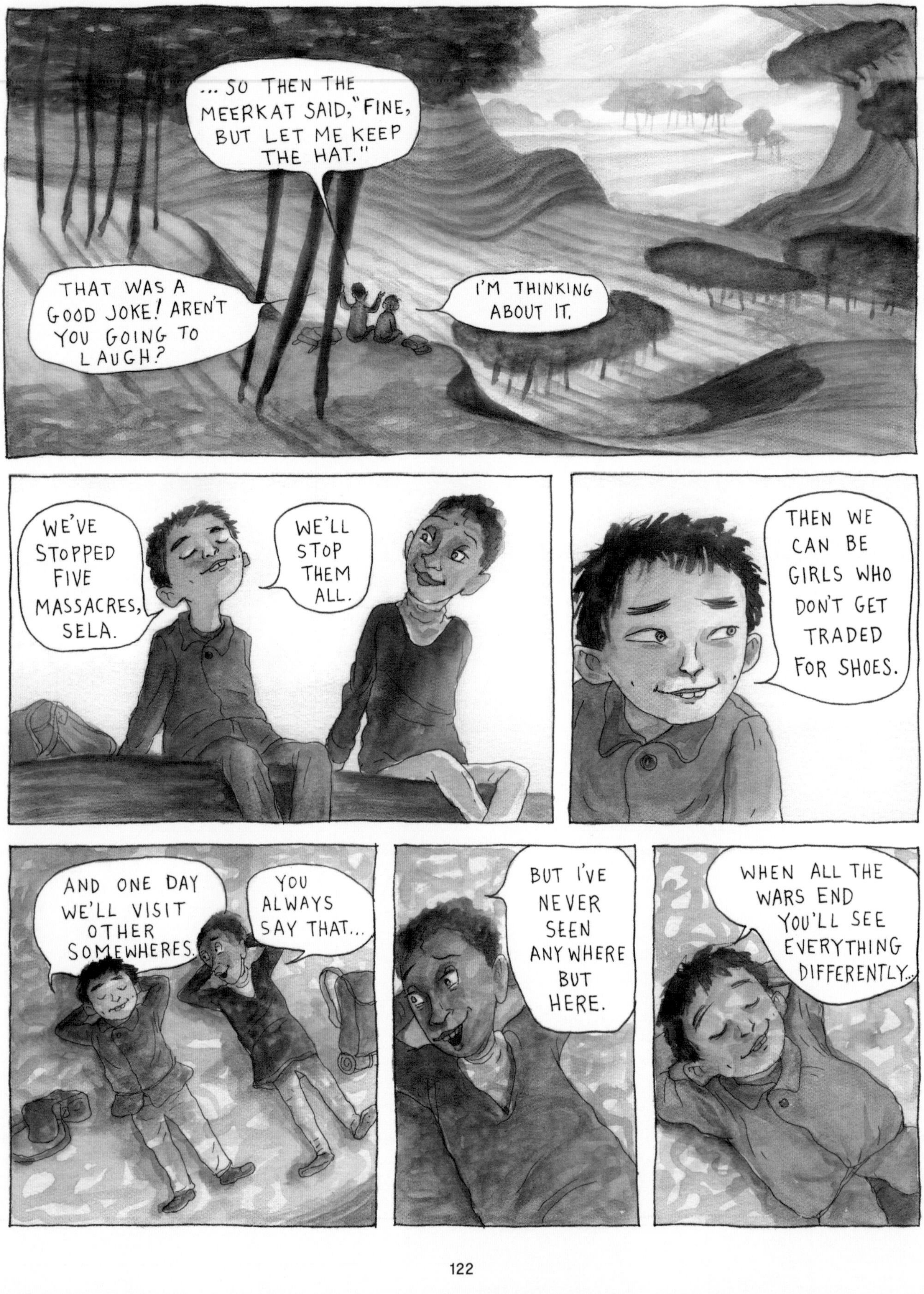
... SO THEN THE MEERKAT SAID, "FINE, BUT LET ME KEEP THE HAT."
THAT WAS A GOOD JOKE! AREN'T YOU GOING TO LAUGH?
I'M THINKING ABOUT IT.
WE'VE STOPPED FIVE MASSACRES, SELA.
WE'LL STOP THEM ALL.
THEN WE CAN BE GIRLS WHO DON'T GET TRADED FOR SHOES.
AND ONE DAY WE'LL VISIT OTHER SOMEWHERES.
YOU ALWAYS SAY THAT...
BUT I'VE NEVER SEEN ANYWHERE BUT HERE.
WHEN ALL THE WARS END YOU'LL SEE EVERYTHING DIFFERENTLY...

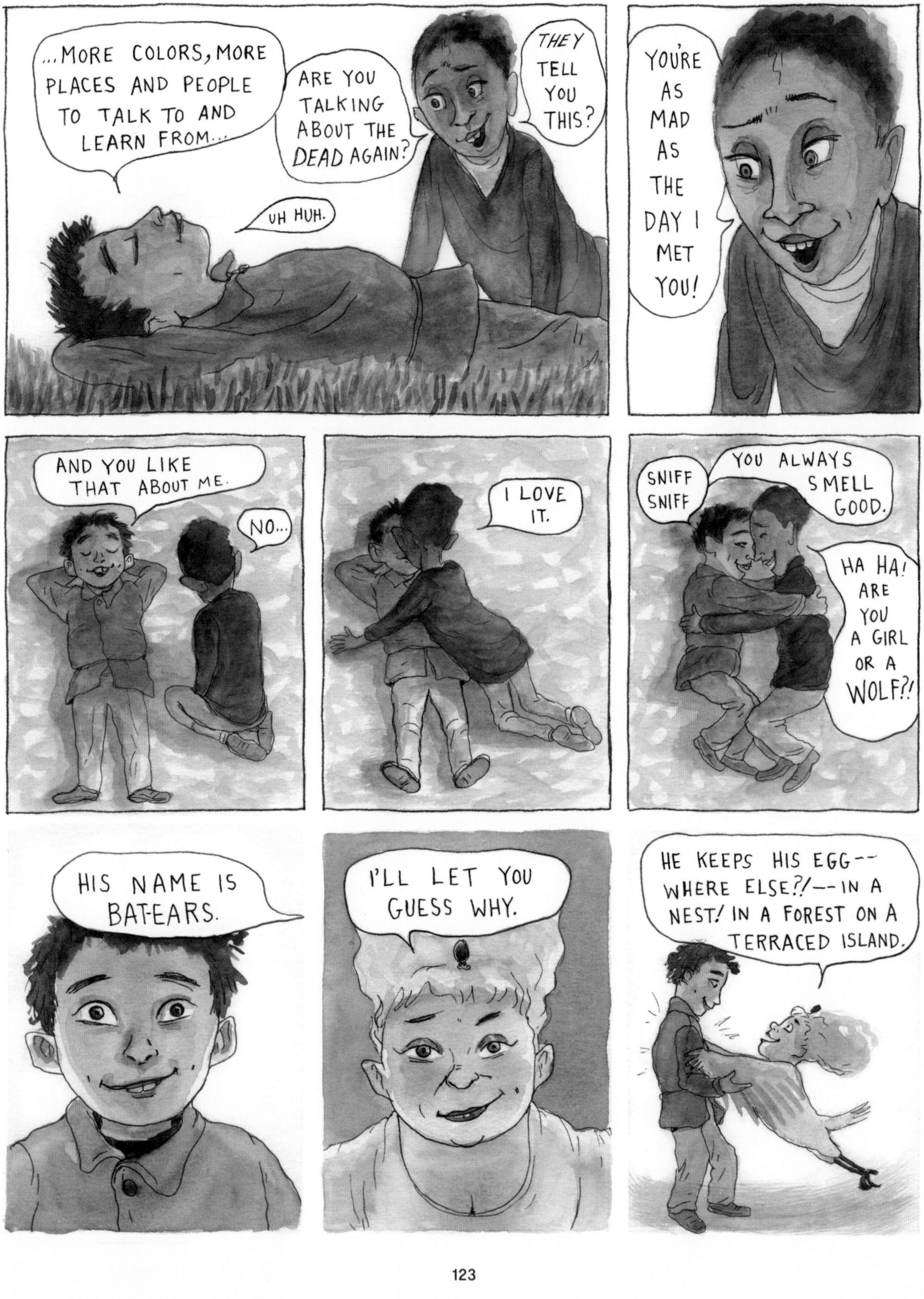
...MORE COLORS, MORE PLACES AND PEOPLE TO TALK TO AND LEARN FROM...
ARE YOU TALKING ABOUT THE DEAD AGAIN?
UH HUH.
THEY TELL YOU THIS?
YOU'RE AS MAD AS THE DAY I MET YOU!
AND YOU LIKE THAT ABOUT ME.
NO...
I LOVE IT.
SNIFF SNIFF
YOU ALWAYS SMELL GOOD.
HA HA! ARE YOU A GIRL OR A WOLF?!
HIS NAME IS BAT-EARS.
I'LL LET YOU GUESS WHY.
HE KEEPS HIS EGG-- WHERE ELSE?!-- IN A NEST! IN A FOREST ON A TERRACED ISLAND.

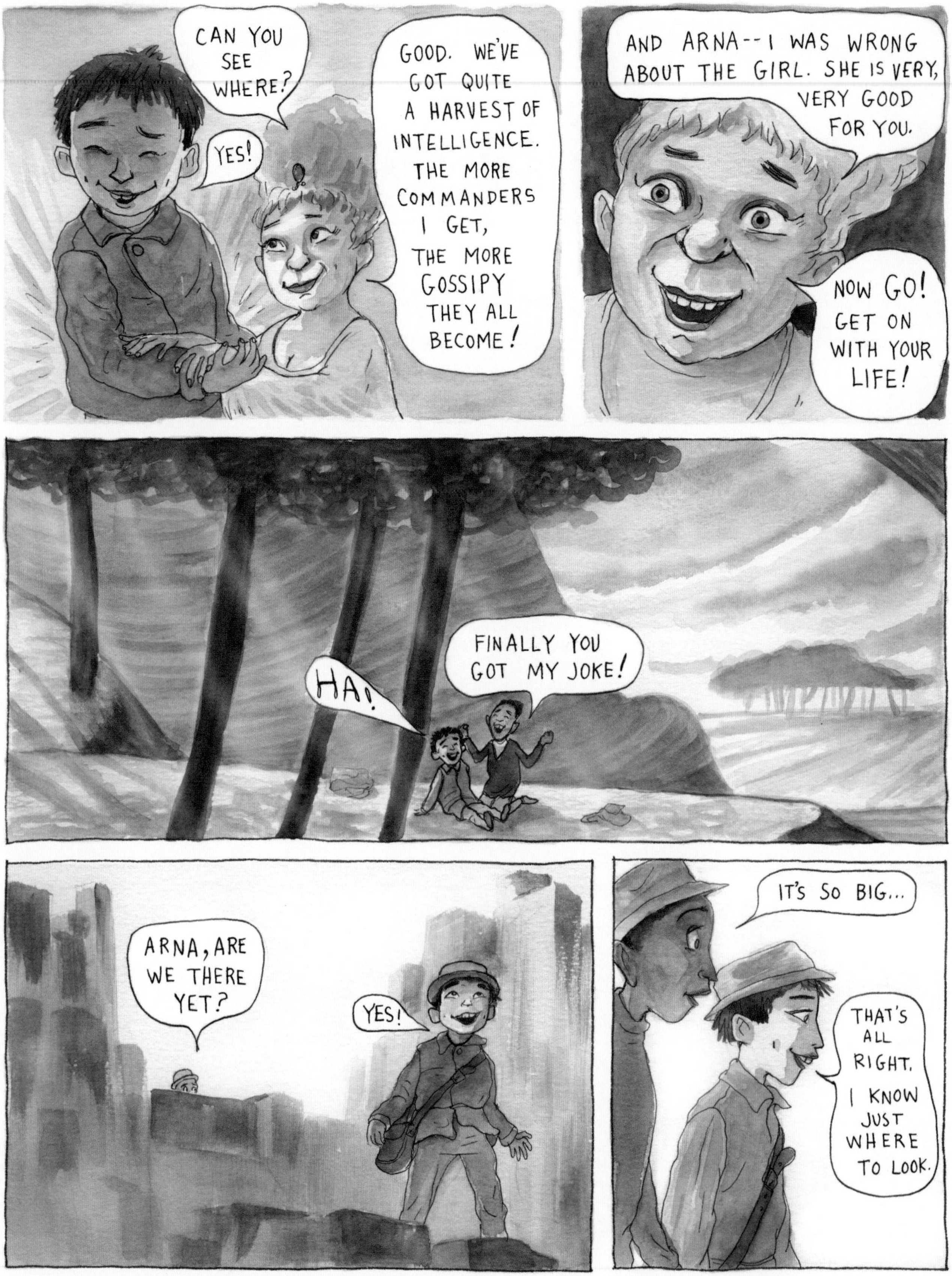
CAN YOU SEE WHERE?
YES!
GOOD. WE'VE GOT QUITE A HARVEST OF INTELLIGENCE. THE MORE COMMANDERS I GET, THE MORE GOSSIPY THEY ALL BECOME!
AND ARNA--I WAS WRONG ABOUT THE GIRL. SHE IS VERY, VERY GOOD FOR YOU.
NOW GO! GET ON WITH YOUR LIFE!
HA!
FINALLY YOU GOT MY JOKE!
ARNA, ARE WE THERE YET?
YES!
IT'S SO BIG...
THAT'S ALL RIGHT. I KNOW JUST WHERE TO LOOK.

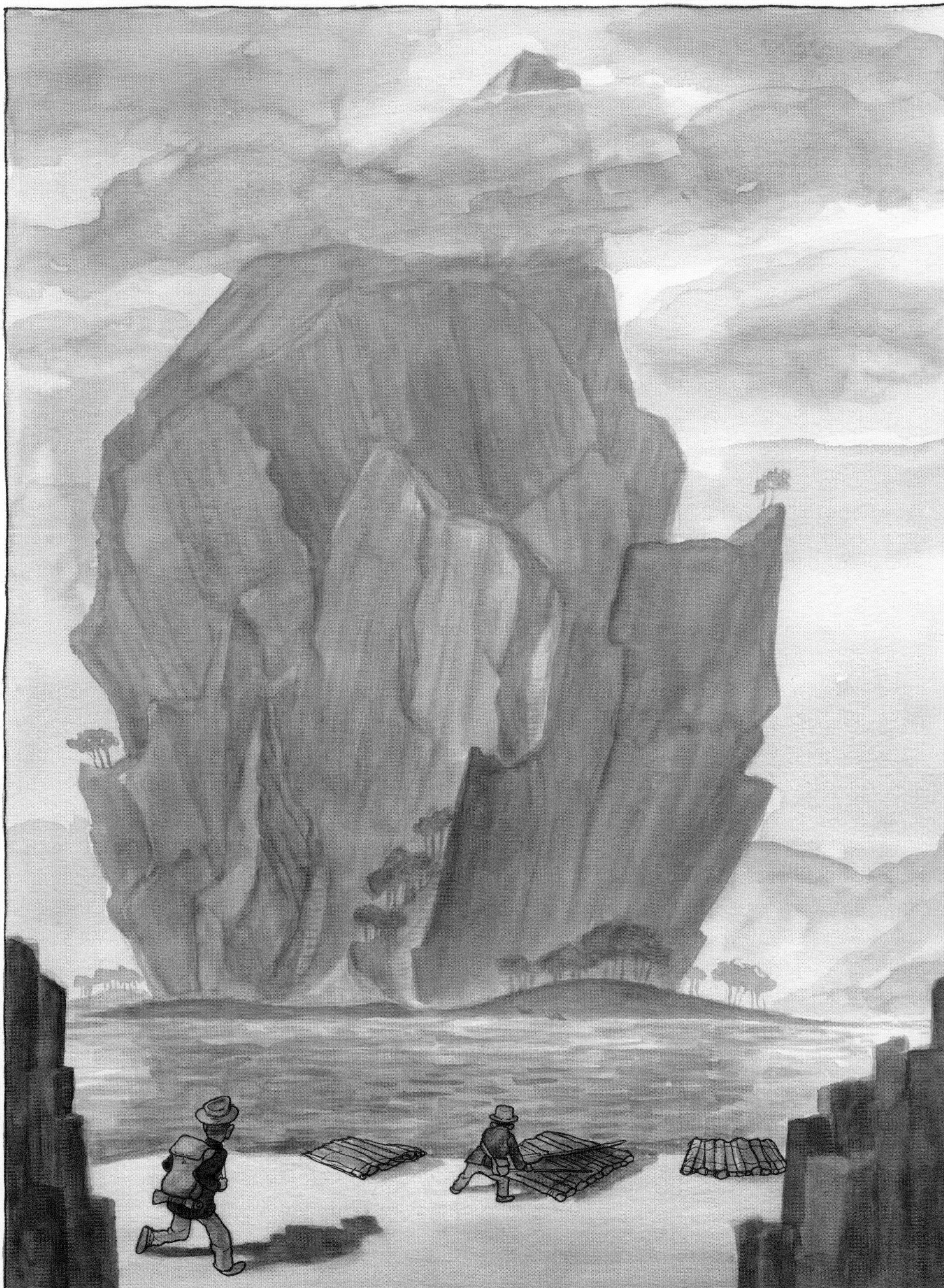

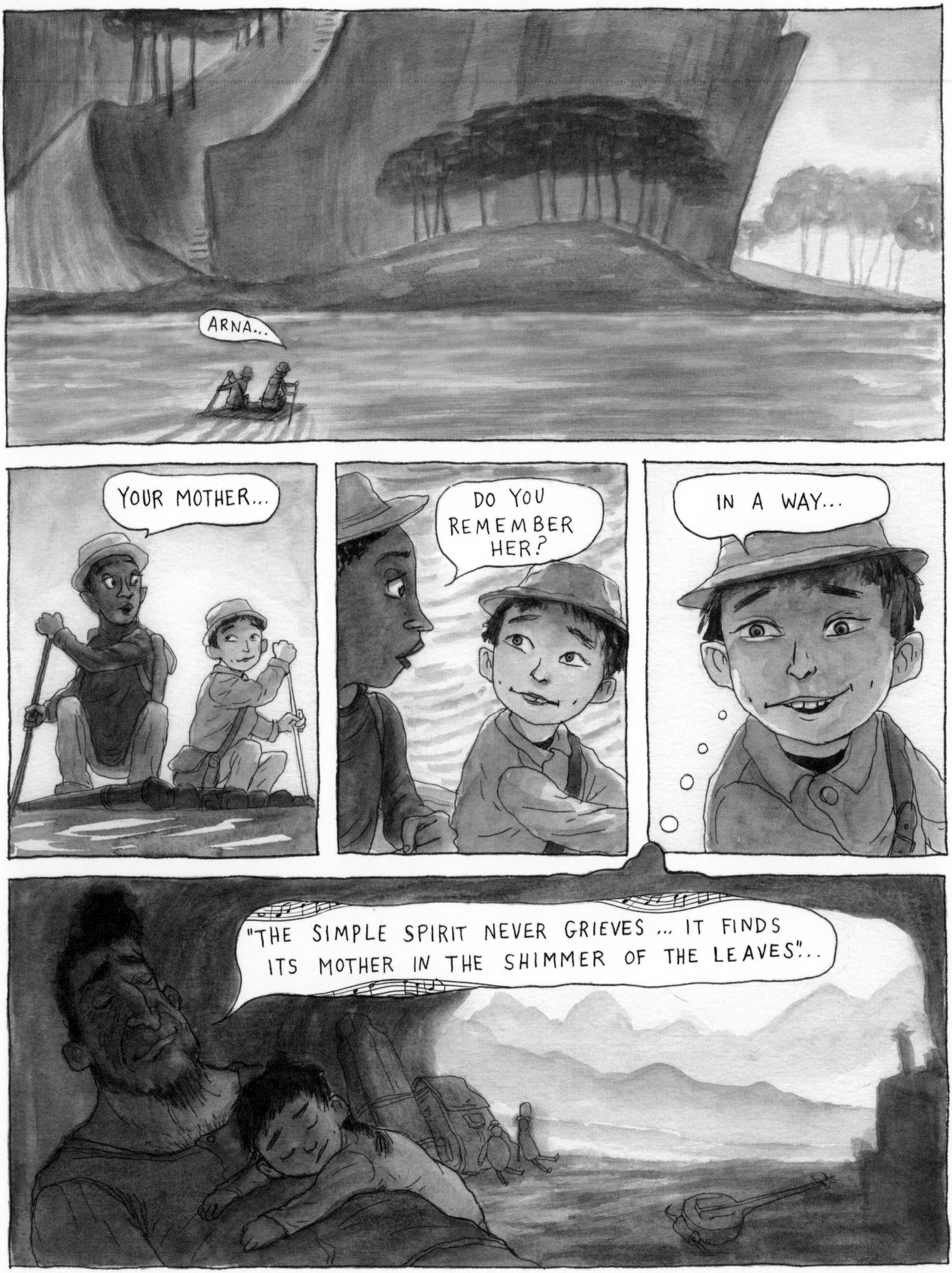
ARNA...
YOUR MOTHER...
DO YOU REMEMBER HER?
IN A WAY...
"THE SIMPLE SPIRIT NEVER GRIEVES ... IT FINDS ITS MOTHER IN THE SHIMMER OF THE LEAVES"...

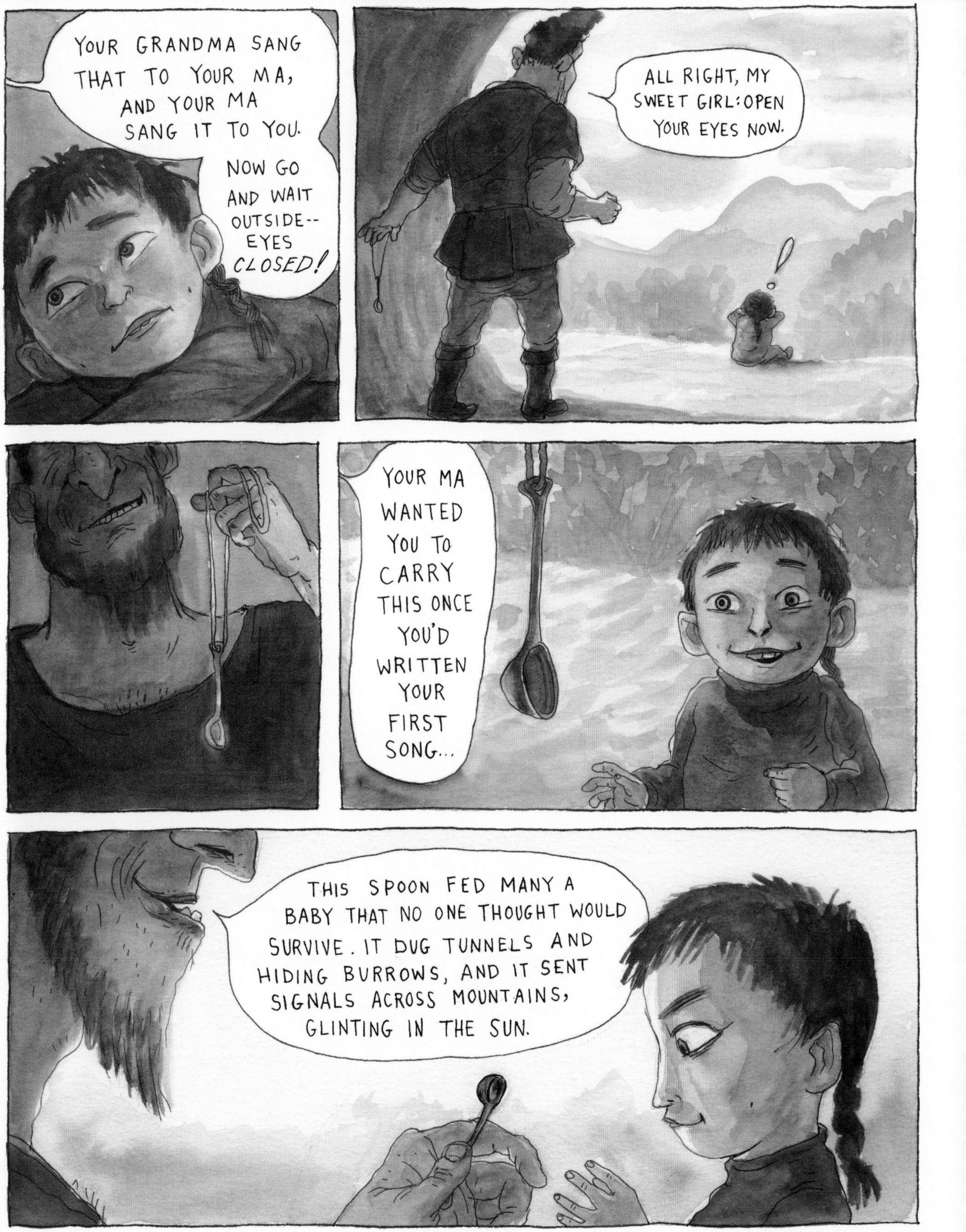
YOUR GRANDMA SANG THAT TO YOUR MA, AND YOUR MA SANG IT TO YOU.
NOW GO AND WAIT OUTSIDE-- EYES CLOSED!
ALL RIGHT, MY SWEET GIRL: OPEN YOUR EYES NOW.
!
YOUR MA WANTED YOU TO CARRY THIS ONCE YOU'D WRITTEN YOUR FIRST SONG...
THIS SPOON FED MANY A BABY THAT NO ONE THOUGHT WOULD SURVIVE. IT DUG TUNNELS AND HIDING BURROWS, AND IT SENT SIGNALS ACROSS MOUNTAINS, GLINTING IN THE SUN.

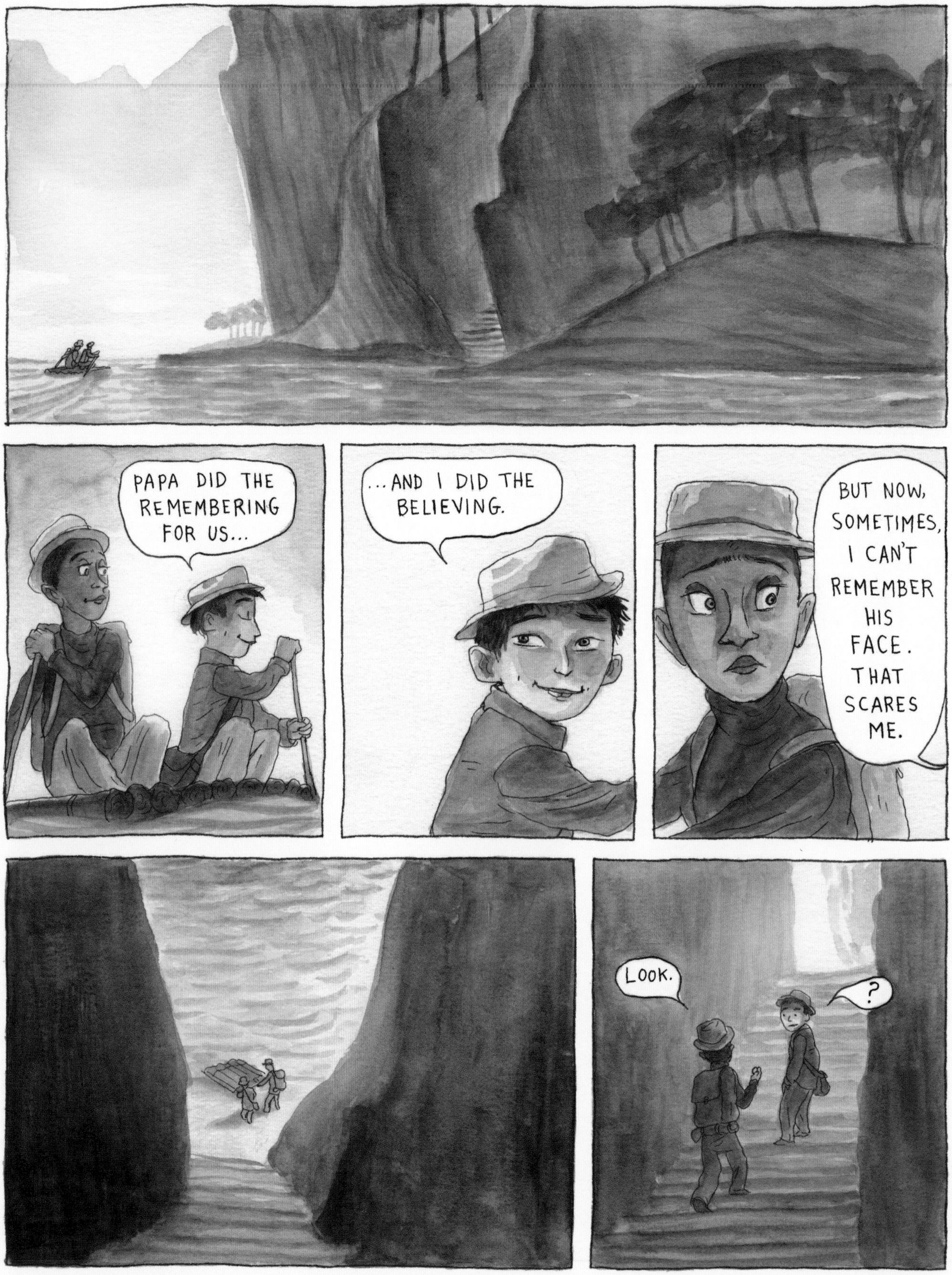
PAPA DID THE REMEMBERING FOR US...
...AND I DID THE BELIEVING.
BUT NOW, SOMETIMES, I CAN'T REMEMBER HIS FACE. THAT SCARES ME.
LOOK.
?

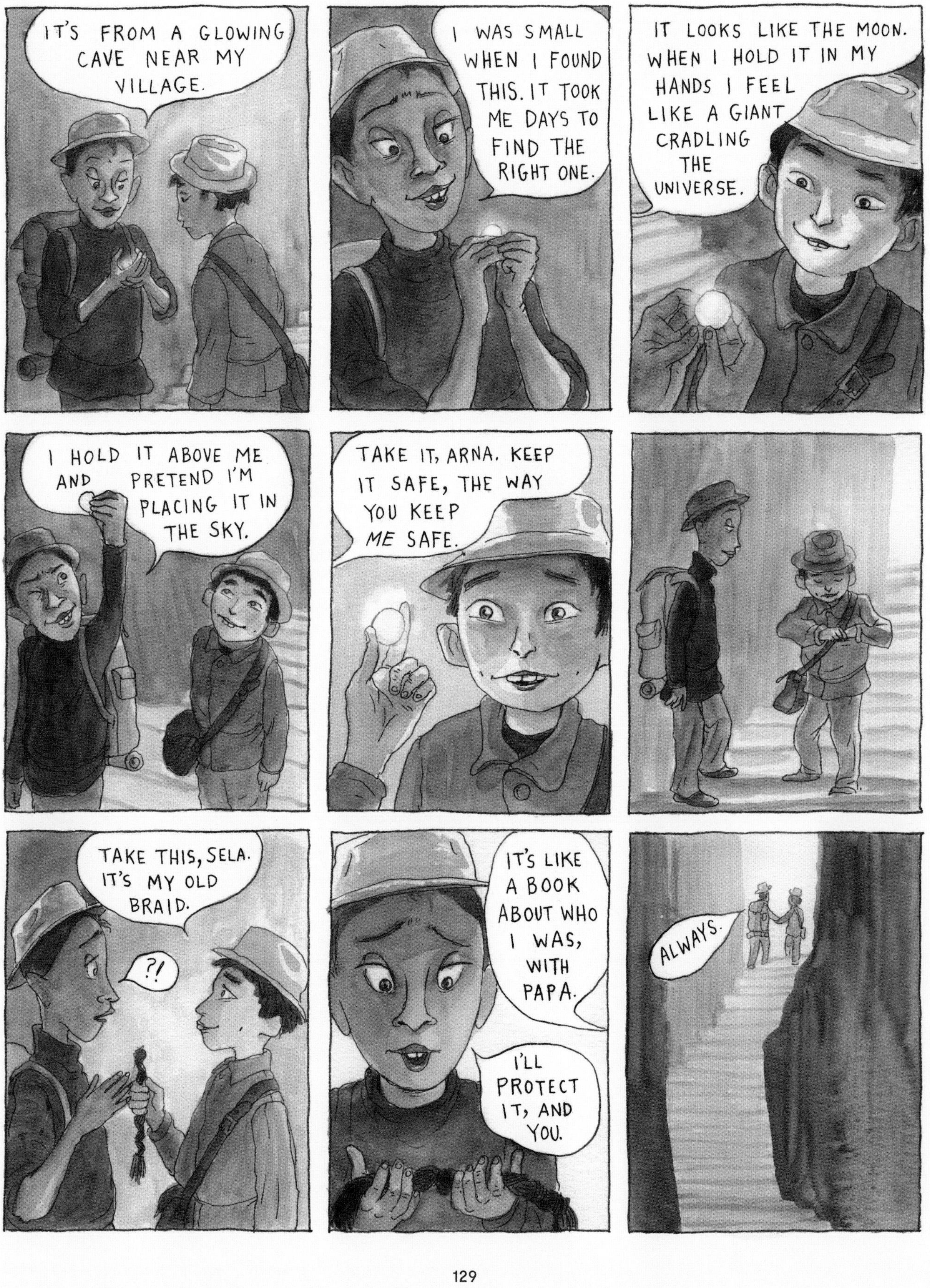
IT'S FROM A GLOWING CAVE NEAR MY VILLAGE.
I WAS SMALL WHEN I FOUND THIS. IT TOOK ME DAYS TO FIND THE RIGHT ONE.
IT LOOKS LIKE THE MOON. WHEN I HOLD IT IN MY HANDS I FEEL LIKE A GIANT CRADLING THE UNIVERSE.
I HOLD IT ABOVE ME AND PRETEND I'M PLACING IT IN THE SKY.
TAKE IT, ARNA. KEEP IT SAFE, THE WAY YOU KEEP *ME* SAFE.
TAKE THIS, SELA. IT'S MY OLD BRAID.
?!
IT'S LIKE A BOOK ABOUT WHO I WAS, WITH PAPA.
I'LL PROTECT IT, AND YOU.
ALWAYS.

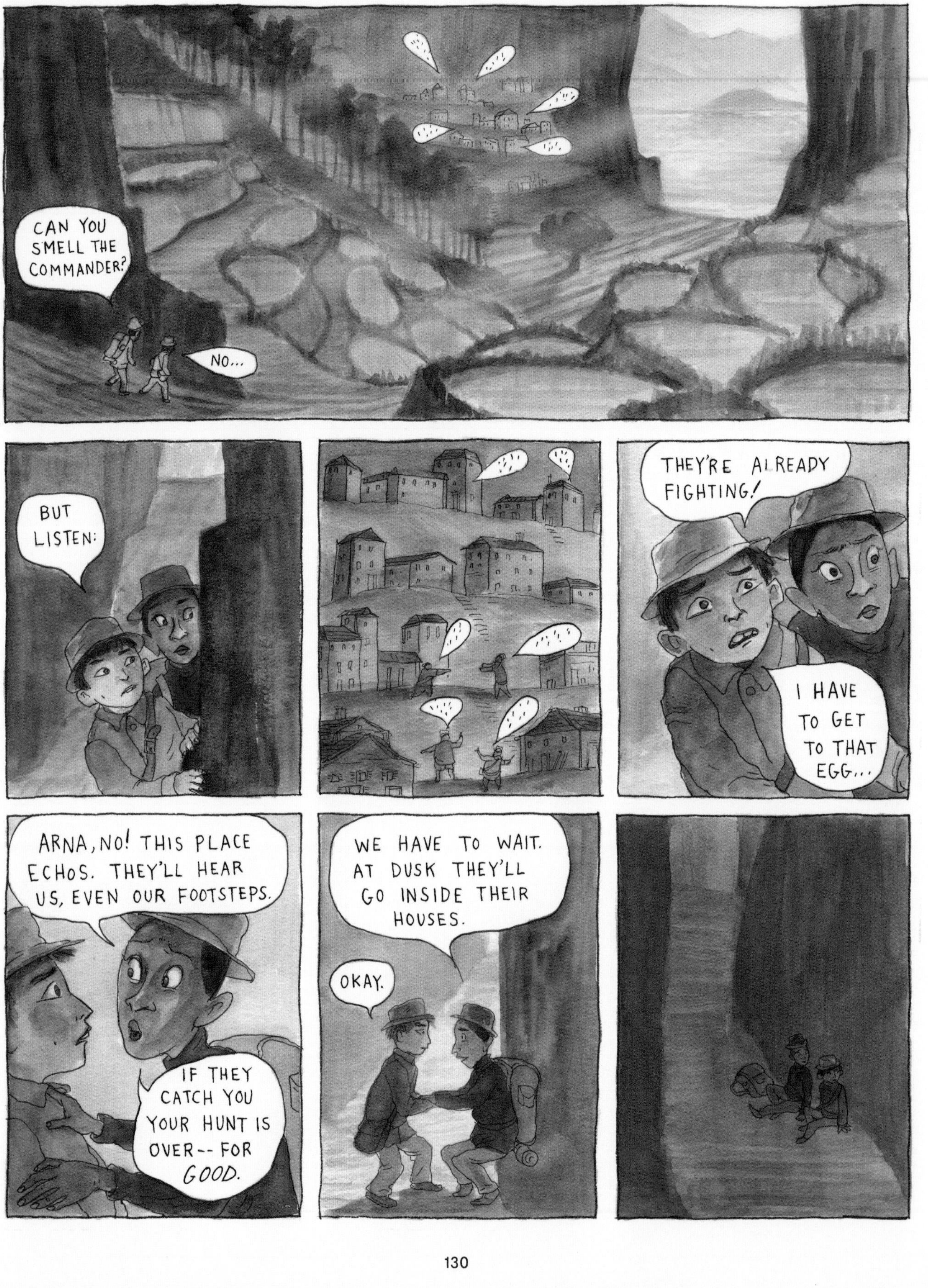
CAN YOU SMELL THE COMMANDER?
NO...
BUT LISTEN:
THEY'RE ALREADY FIGHTING!
I HAVE TO GET TO THAT EGG...
ARNA, NO! THIS PLACE ECHOS. THEY'LL HEAR US, EVEN OUR FOOTSTEPS.
IF THEY CATCH YOU YOUR HUNT IS OVER-- FOR GOOD.
WE HAVE TO WAIT. AT DUSK THEY'LL GO INSIDE THEIR HOUSES.
OKAY.

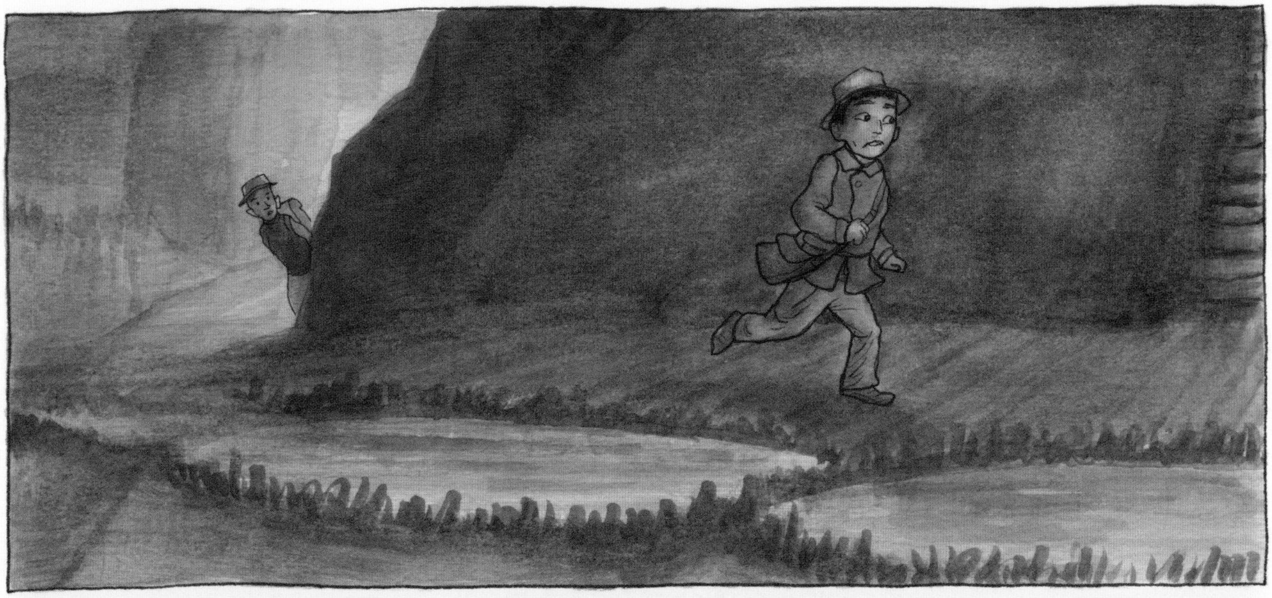

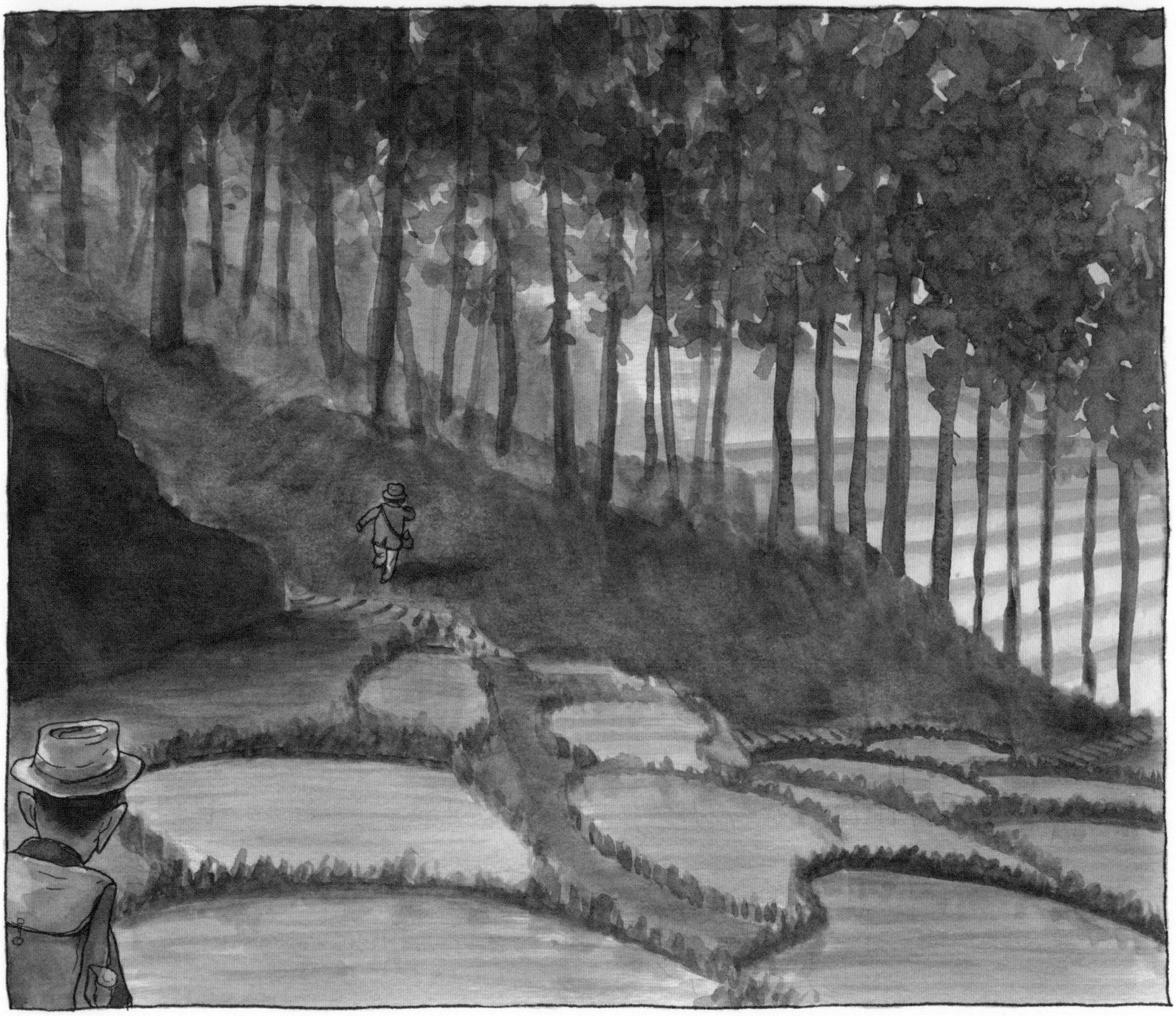

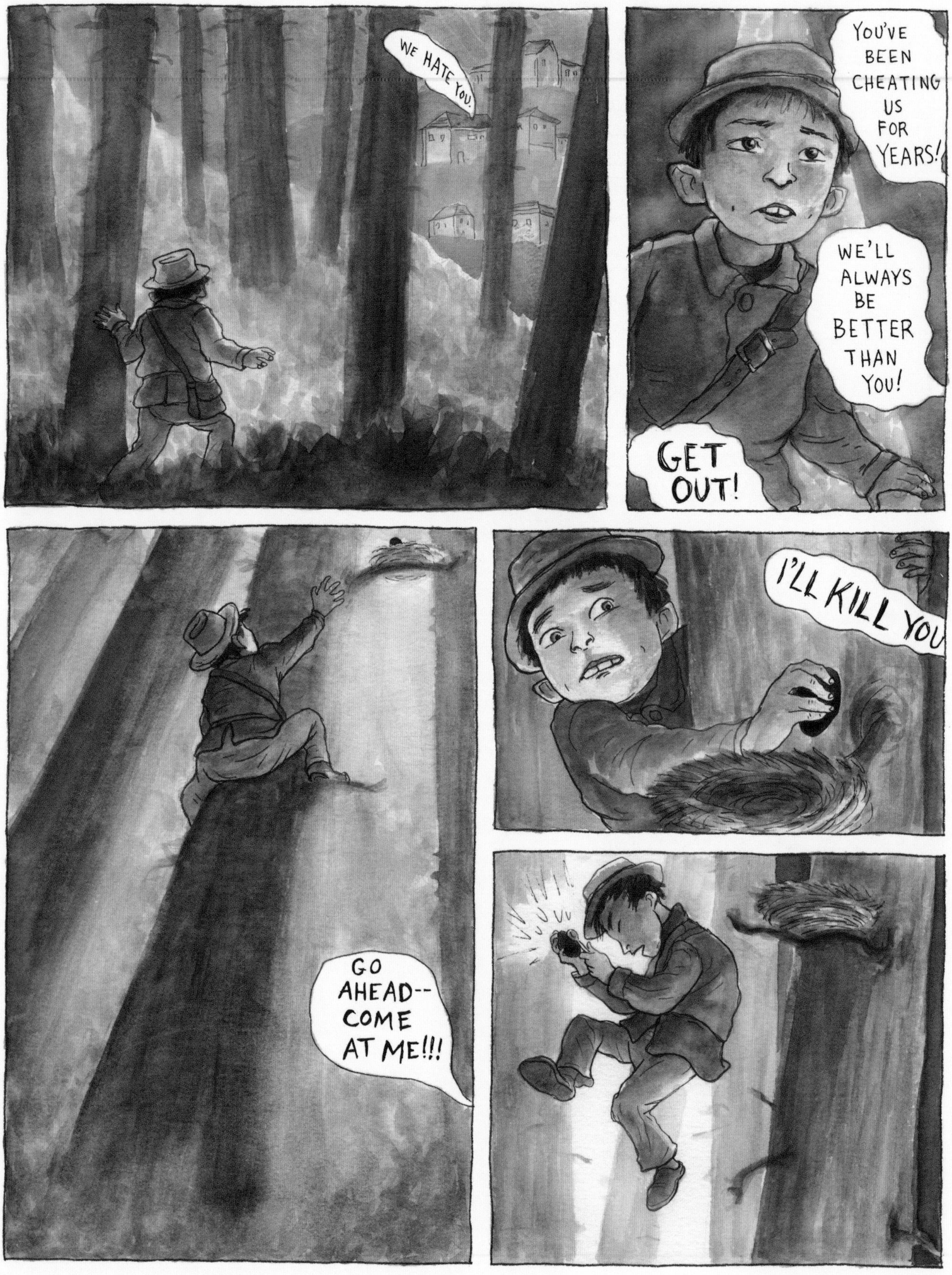
WE HATE YOU.
YOU'VE BEEN CHEATING US FOR YEARS!
WE'LL ALWAYS BE BETTER THAN YOU!
GET OUT!
I'LL KILL YOU
GO AHEAD-- COME AT ME!!!

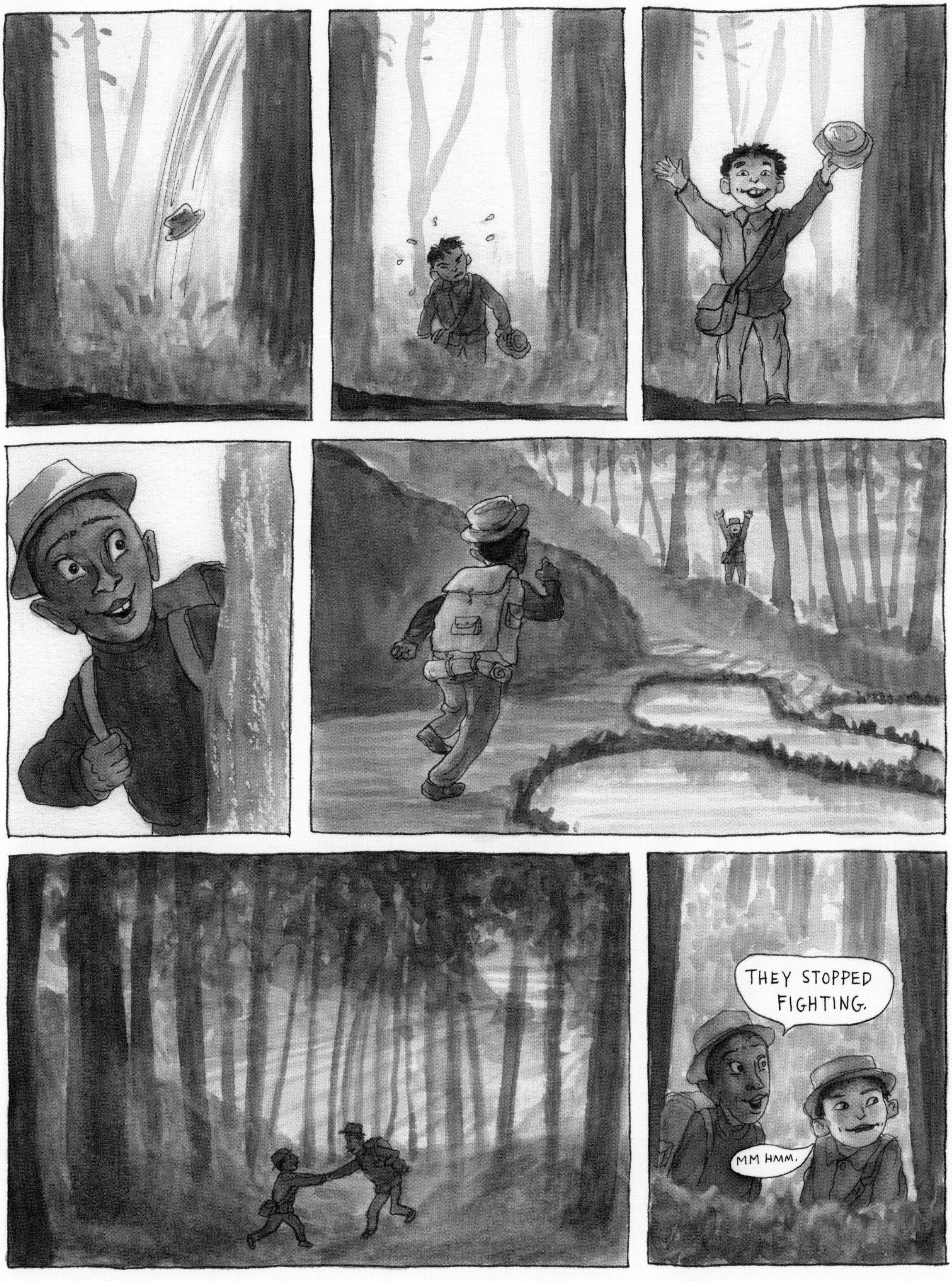
THEY STOPPED FIGHTING.
MM HMM.

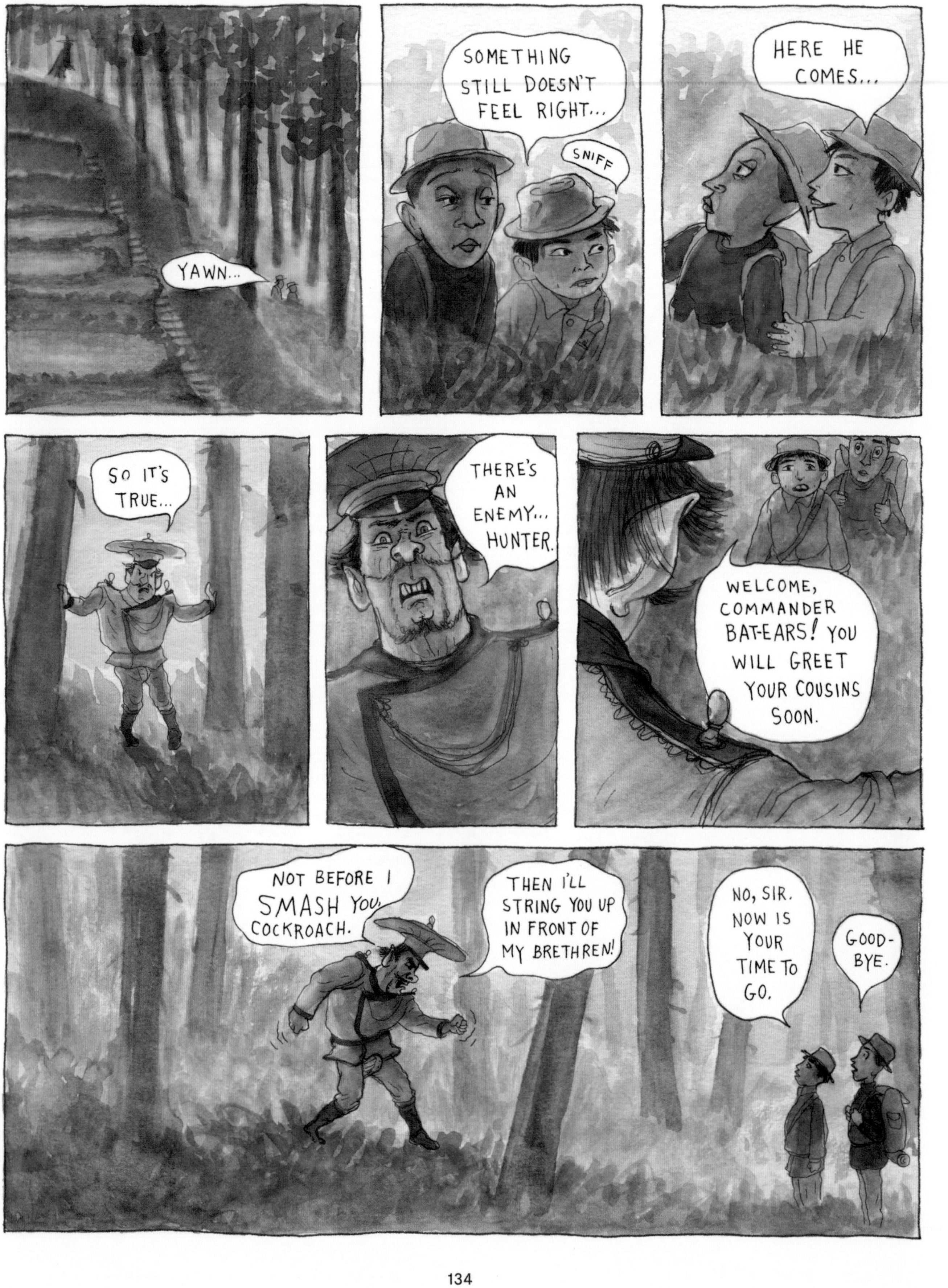
YAWN...
SOMETHING STILL DOESN'T FEEL RIGHT...
SNIFF
HERE HE COMES...
SO IT'S TRUE...
THERE'S AN ENEMY... HUNTER.
WELCOME, COMMANDER BAT-EARS! YOU WILL GREET YOUR COUSINS SOON.
NOT BEFORE I SMASH YOU, COCKROACH.
THEN I'LL STRING YOU UP IN FRONT OF MY BRETHREN!
NO, SIR. NOW IS YOUR TIME TO GO.
GOOD-BYE.

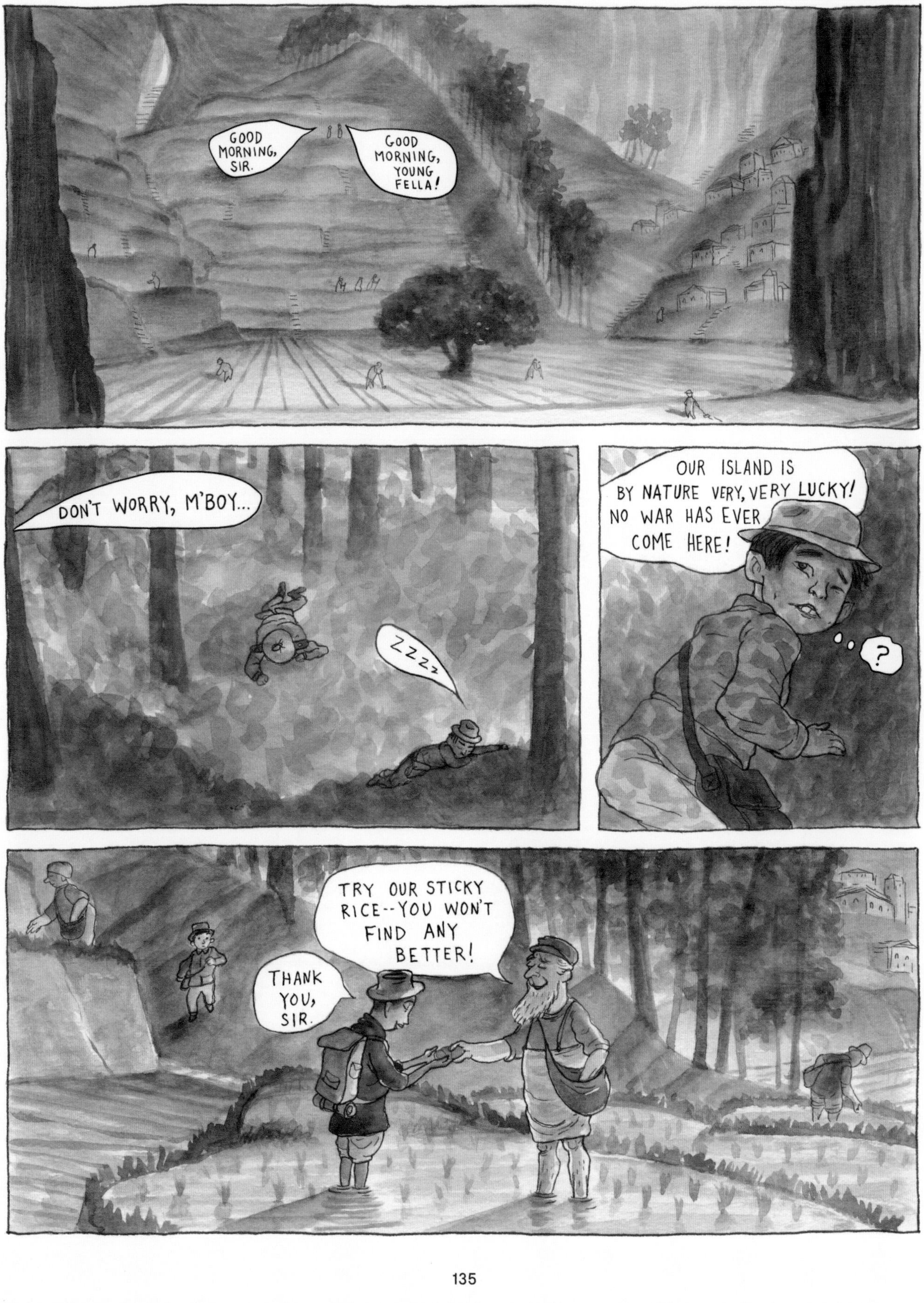
GOOD MORNING, SIR.
GOOD MORNING, YOUNG FELLA!
DON'T WORRY, M'BOY...
ZZZZ
OUR ISLAND IS BY NATURE VERY, VERY LUCKY! NO WAR HAS EVER COME HERE!
?
TRY OUR STICKY RICE--YOU WON'T FIND ANY BETTER!
THANK YOU, SIR.

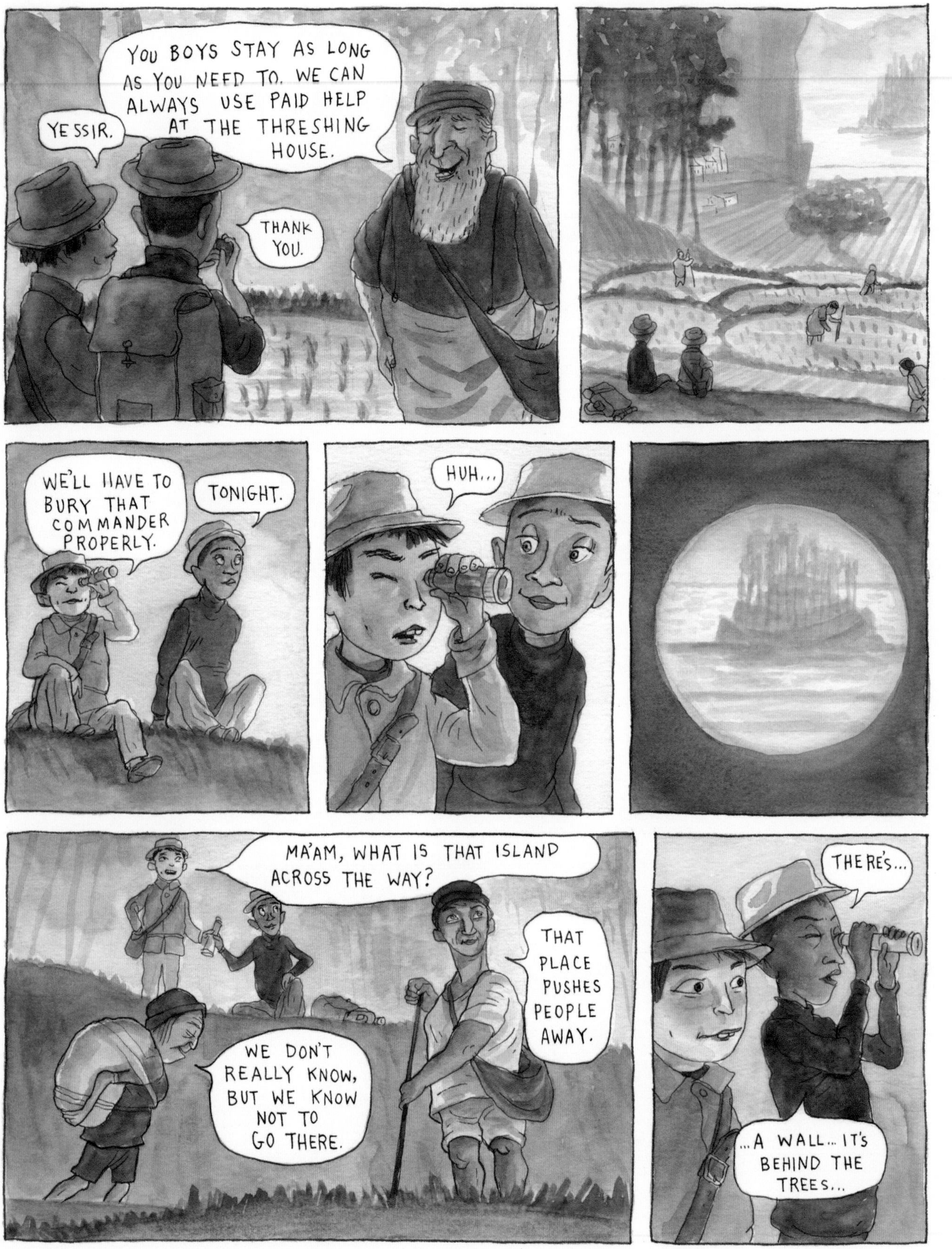
YOU BOYS STAY AS LONG AS YOU NEED TO. WE CAN ALWAYS USE PAID HELP AT THE THRESHING HOUSE.
YESSIR.
THANK YOU.
WE'LL HAVE TO BURY THAT COMMANDER PROPERLY.
TONIGHT.
HUH...
MA'AM, WHAT IS THAT ISLAND ACROSS THE WAY?
WE DON'T REALLY KNOW, BUT WE KNOW NOT TO GO THERE.
THAT PLACE PUSHES PEOPLE AWAY.
THERE'S...
...A WALL... IT'S BEHIND THE TREES...

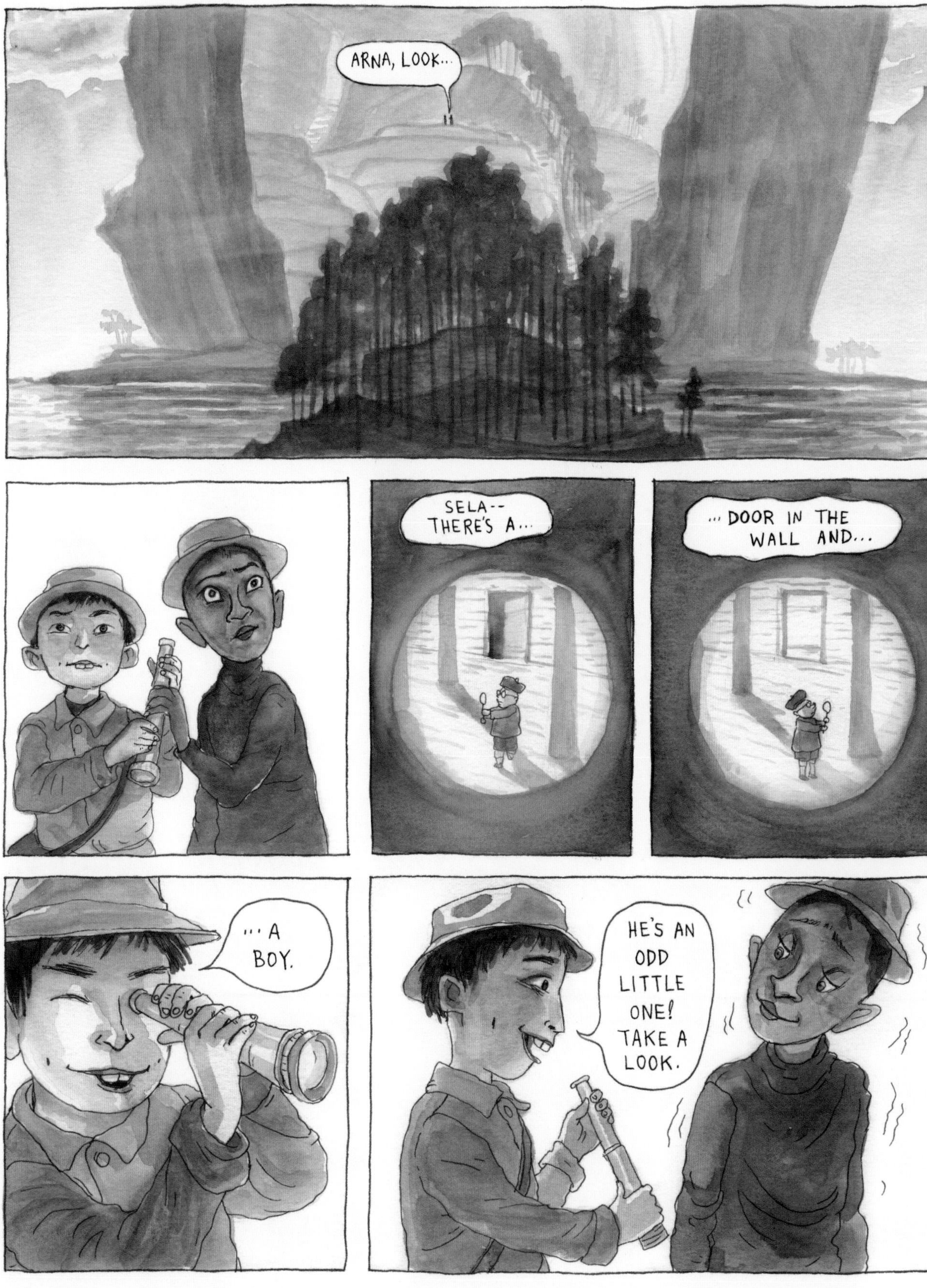

ARNA, LOOK...
SELA-- THERE'S A...
... DOOR IN THE WALL AND...
... A BOY.
HE'S AN ODD LITTLE ONE! TAKE A LOOK.

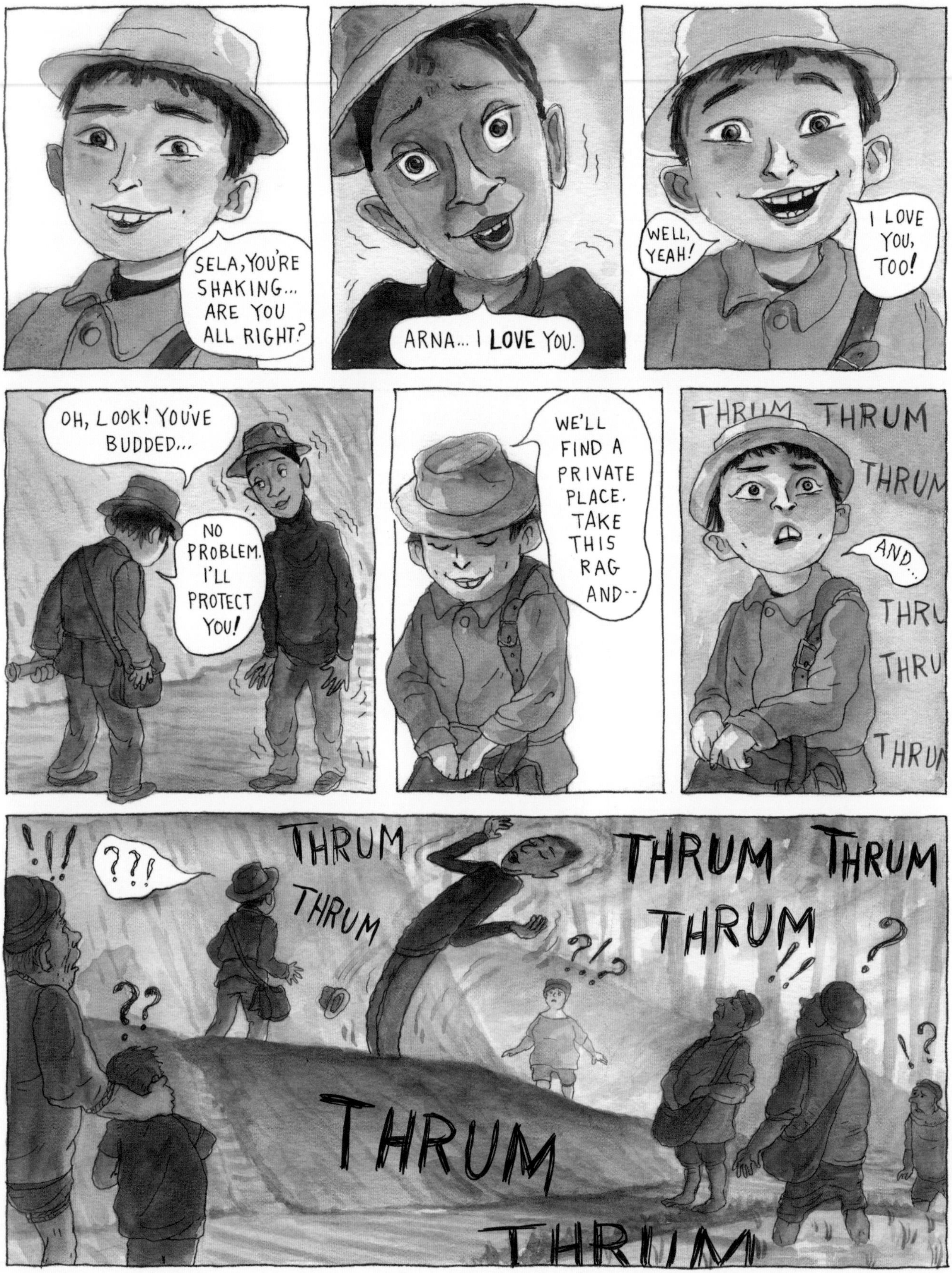
SELA, YOU'RE SHAKING... ARE YOU ALL RIGHT?
ARNA... I **LOVE** YOU.
WELL, YEAH!
I LOVE YOU, TOO!
OH, LOOK! YOU'VE BUDDED...
NO PROBLEM. I'LL PROTECT YOU!
WE'LL FIND A PRIVATE PLACE. TAKE THIS RAG AND--
THRUM THRUM
THRUM
AND...
THRU
THRU
THRUM
!!!
???!
THRUM
THRUM
THRUM THRUM
THRUM
?!?
??
!!
?
!?
THRUM
THRUM

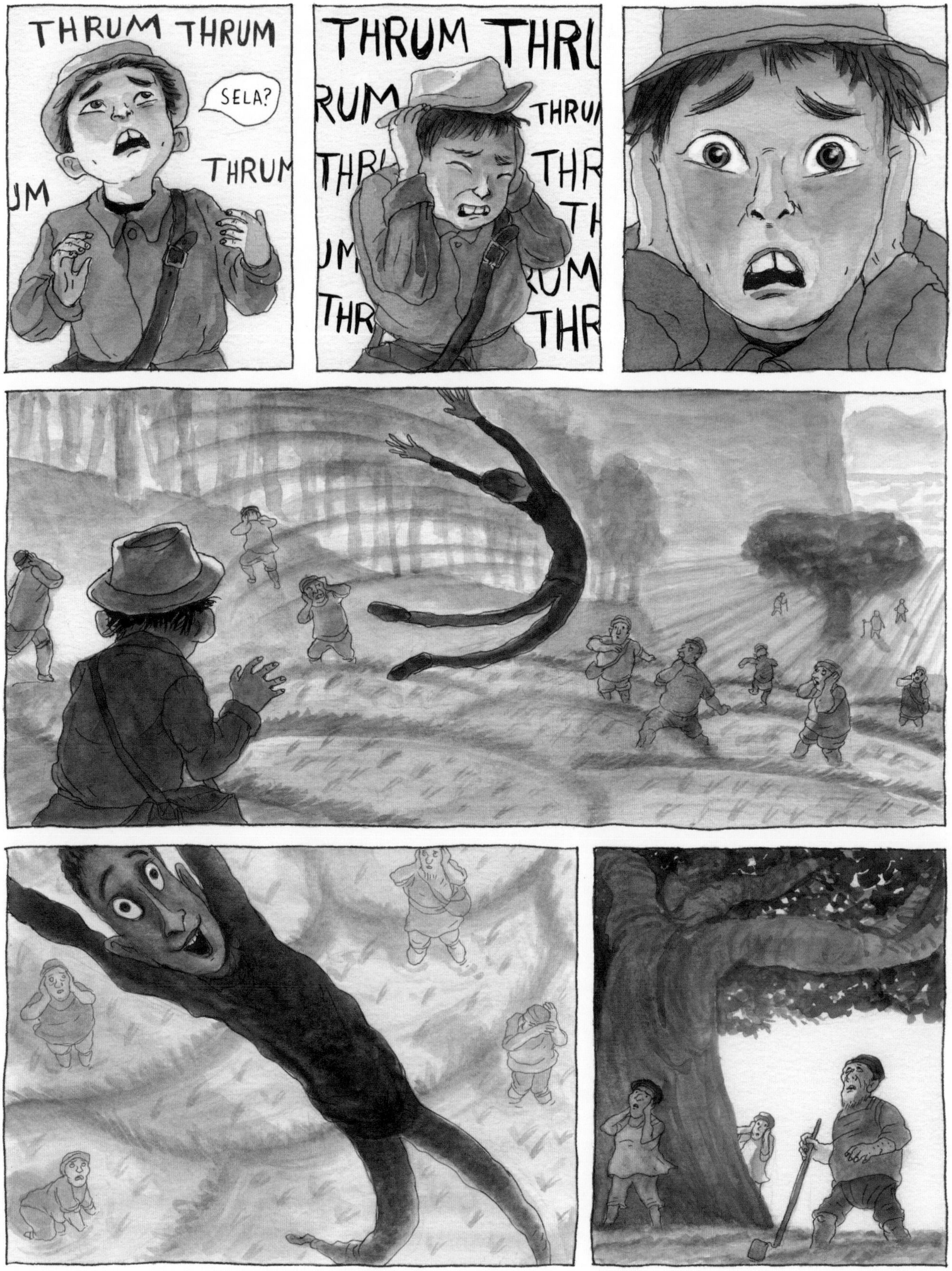
THRUM THRUM
SELA?
THRUM
THRUM THRU
RUM
THRUM
THR
THR
TH
RUM
THR
THR

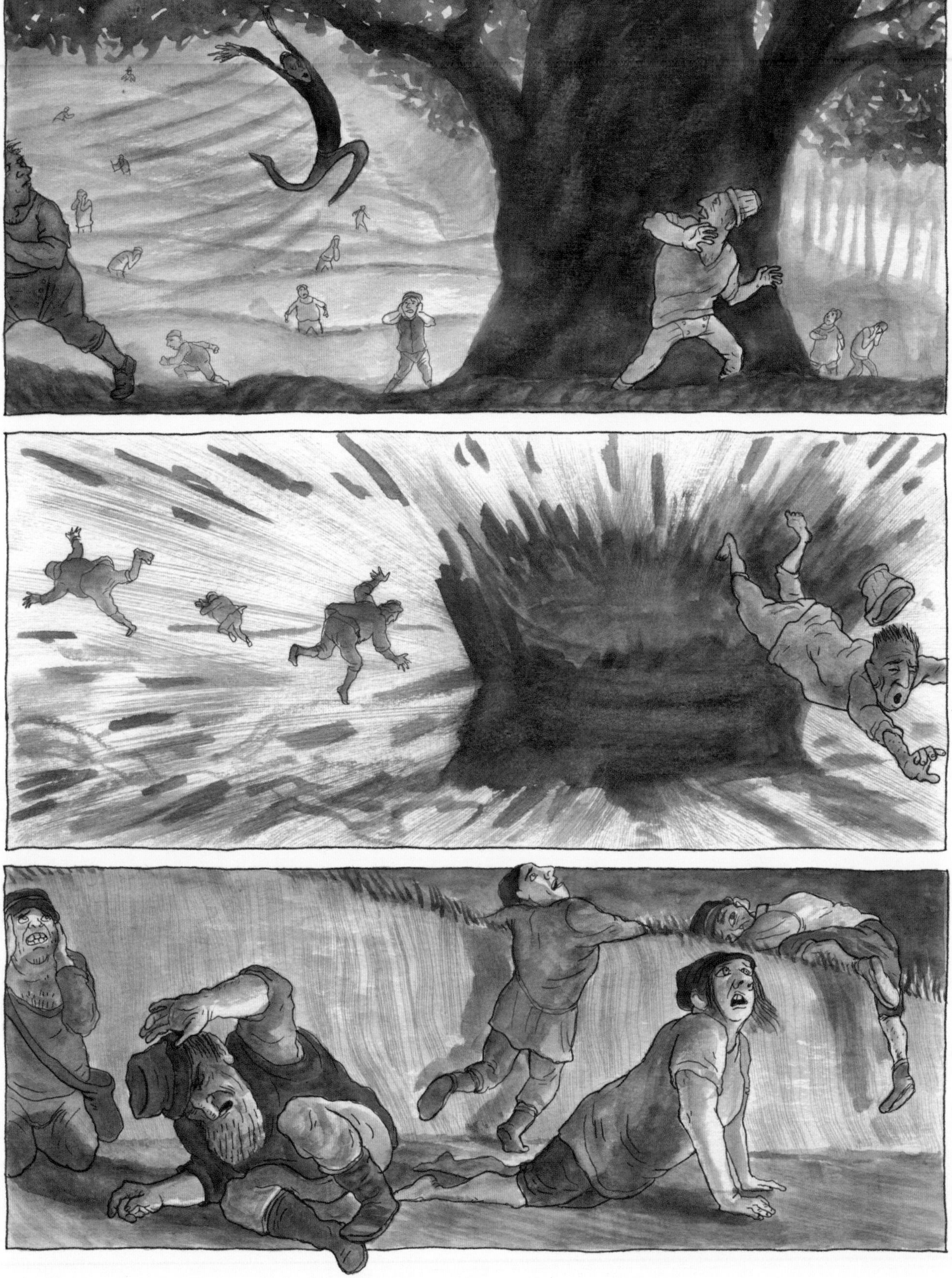

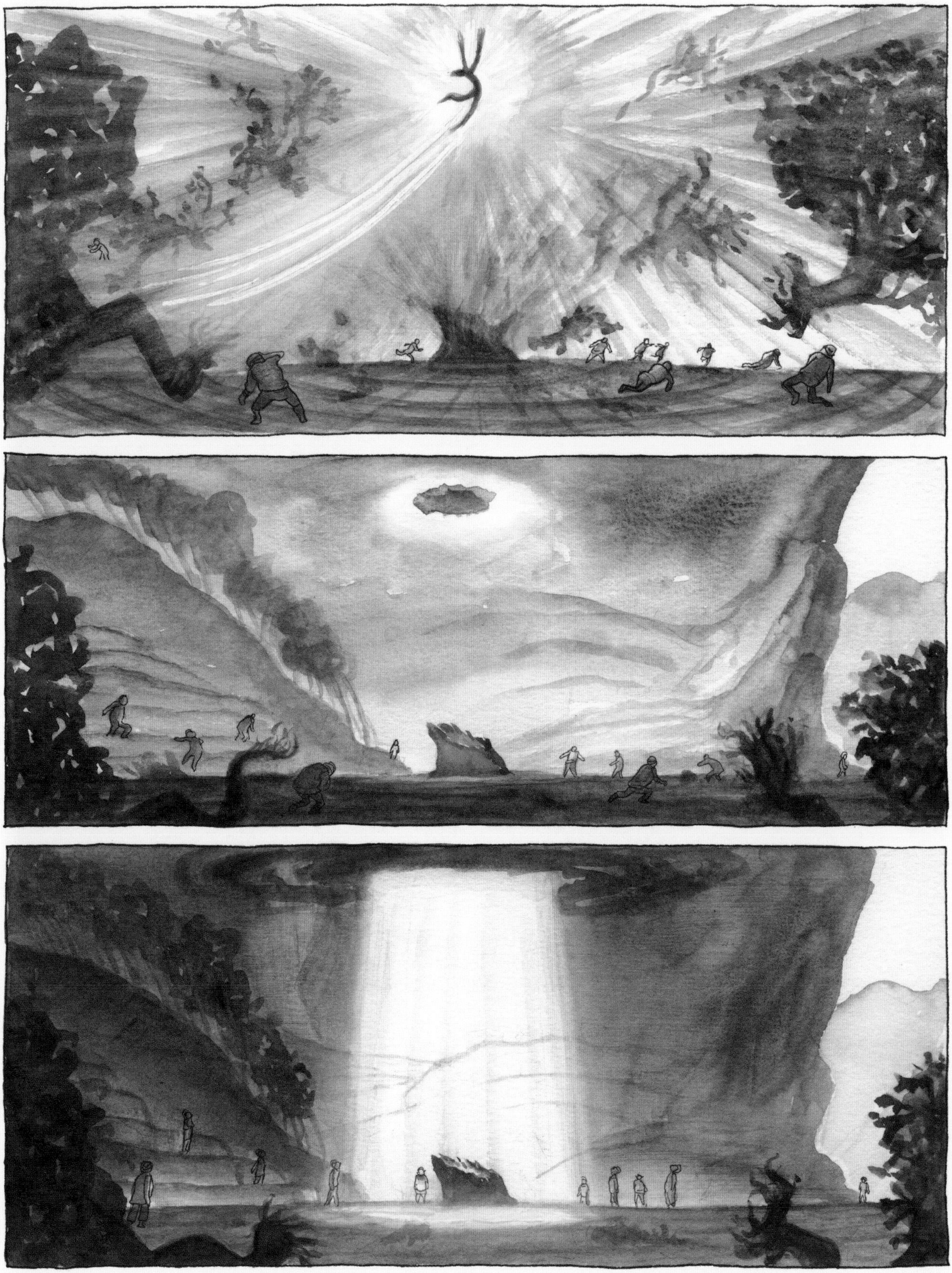

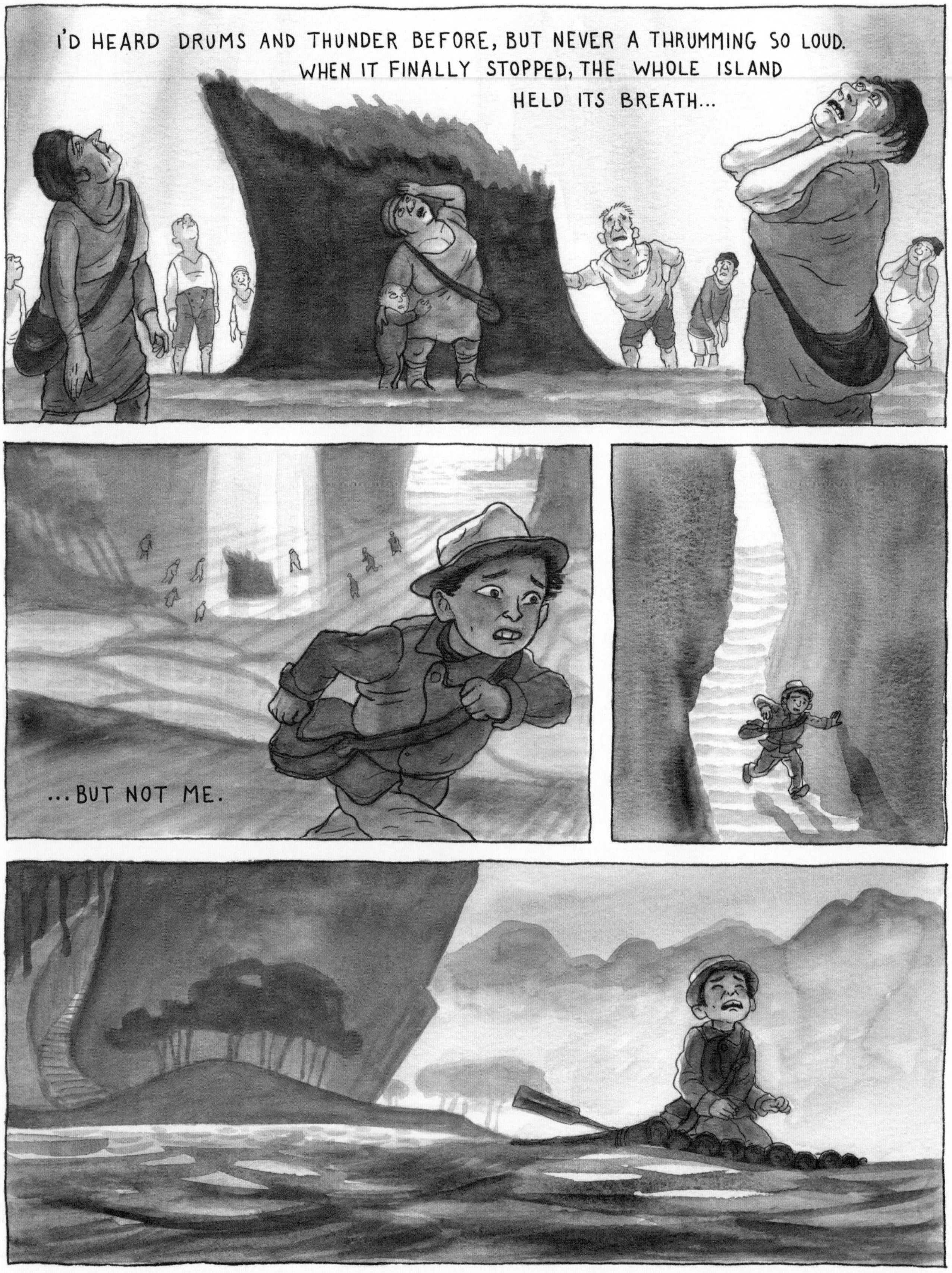
I'D HEARD DRUMS AND THUNDER BEFORE, BUT NEVER A THRUMMING SO LOUD.
WHEN IT FINALLY STOPPED, THE WHOLE ISLAND
HELD ITS BREATH...
...BUT NOT ME.

PART THREE

THE HUNT

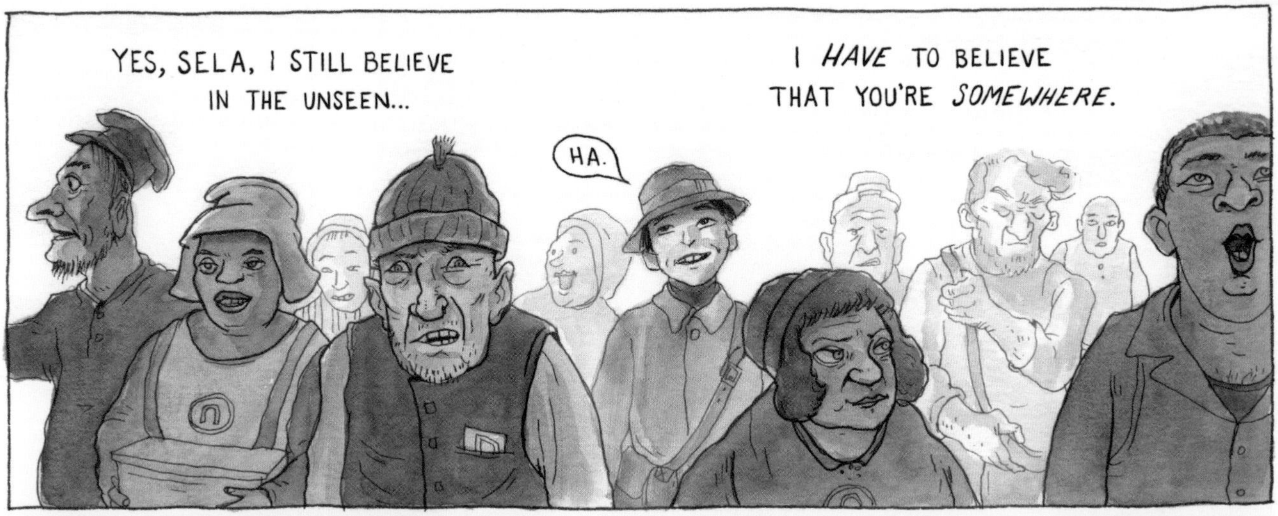
YES, SELA, I STILL BELIEVE IN THE UNSEEN...
I HAVE TO BELIEVE THAT YOU'RE SOMEWHERE.
HA.

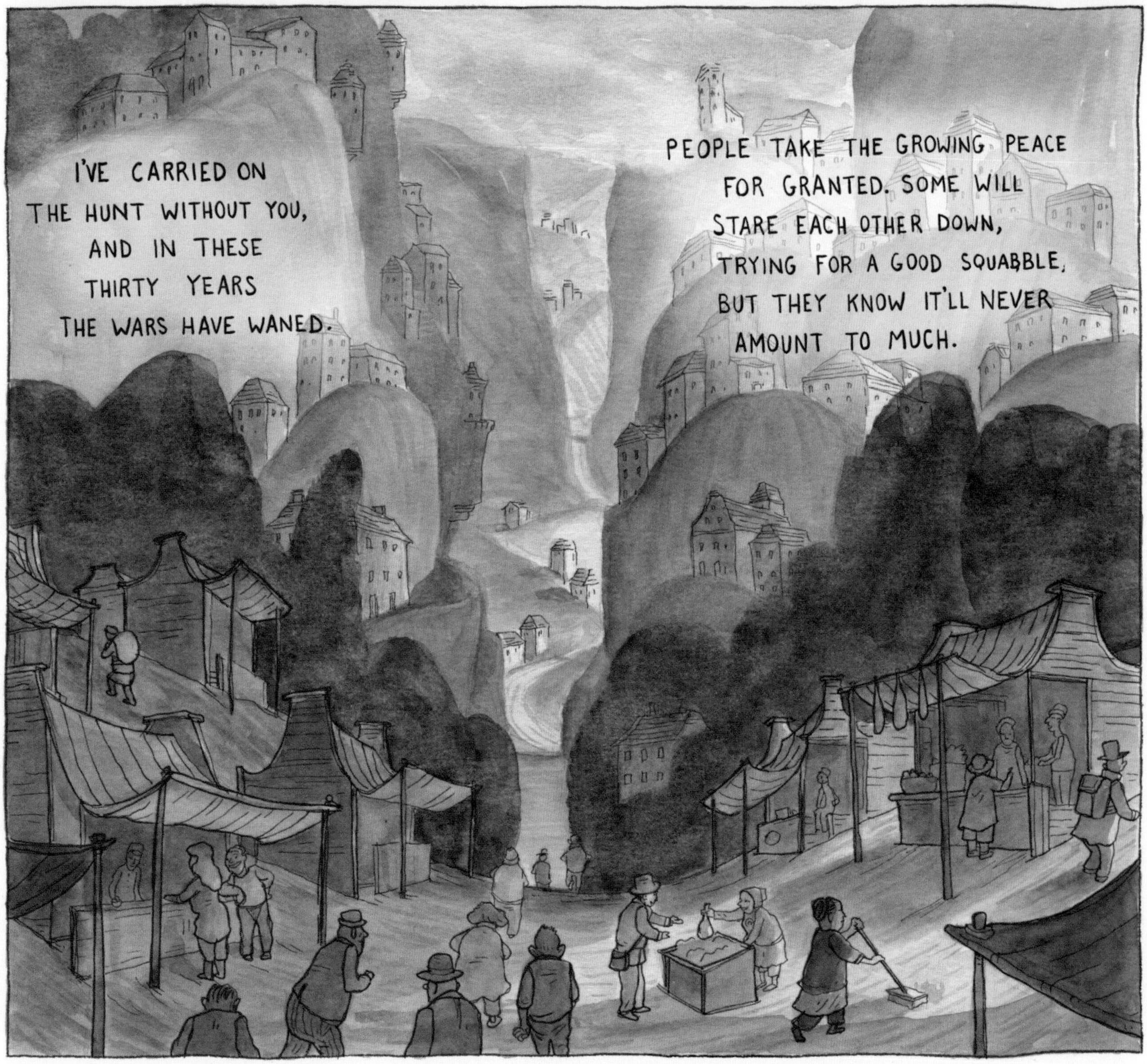
I'VE CARRIED ON THE HUNT WITHOUT YOU, AND IN THESE THIRTY YEARS THE WARS HAVE WANED.
PEOPLE TAKE THE GROWING PEACE FOR GRANTED. SOME WILL STARE EACH OTHER DOWN, TRYING FOR A GOOD SQUABBLE, BUT THEY KNOW IT'LL NEVER AMOUNT TO MUCH.

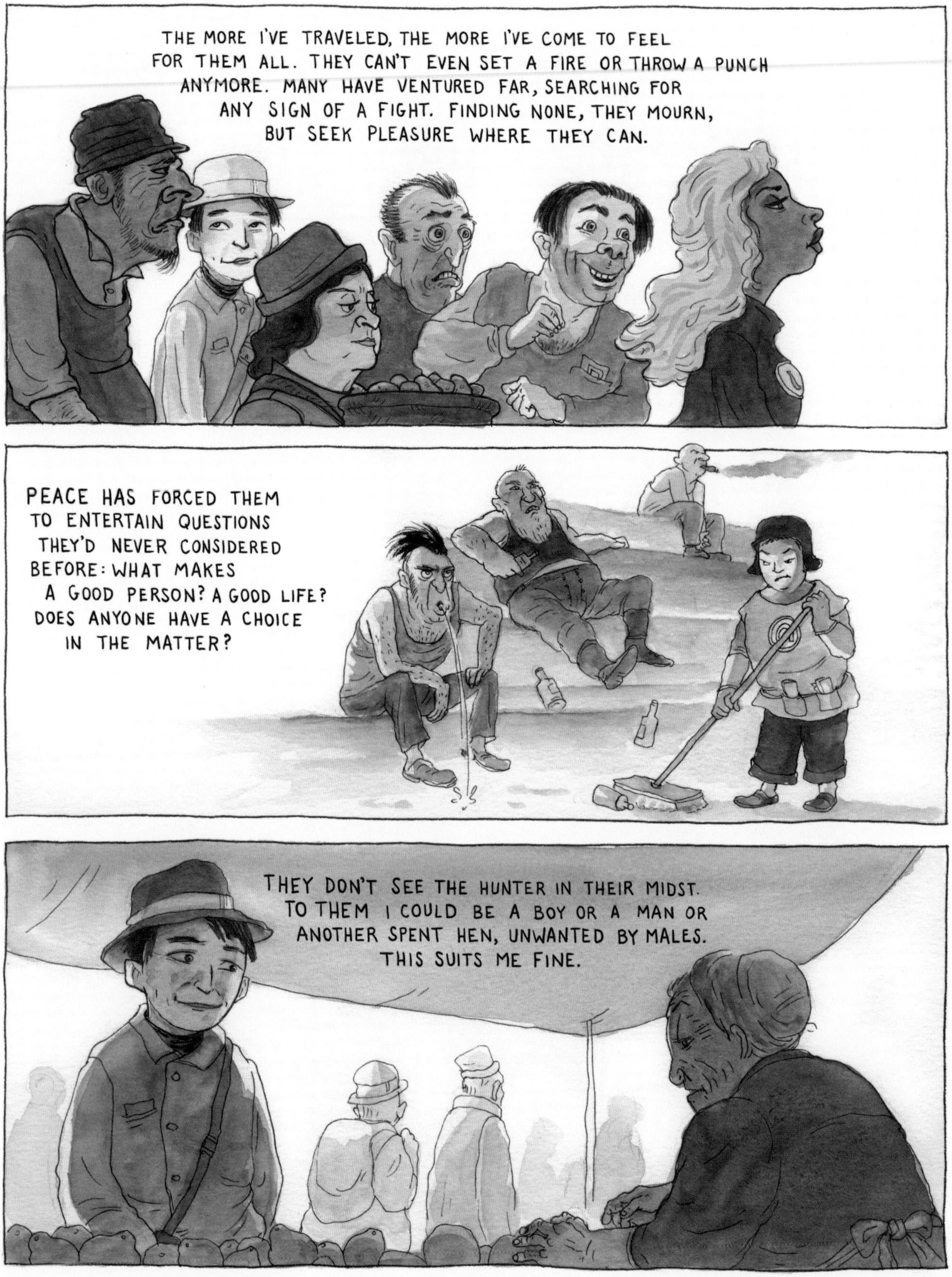
THE MORE I'VE TRAVELED, THE MORE I'VE COME TO FEEL FOR THEM ALL. THEY CAN'T EVEN SET A FIRE OR THROW A PUNCH ANYMORE. MANY HAVE VENTURED FAR, SEARCHING FOR ANY SIGN OF A FIGHT. FINDING NONE, THEY MOURN, BUT SEEK PLEASURE WHERE THEY CAN.
PEACE HAS FORCED THEM TO ENTERTAIN QUESTIONS THEY'D NEVER CONSIDERED BEFORE: WHAT MAKES A GOOD PERSON? A GOOD LIFE? DOES ANYONE HAVE A CHOICE IN THE MATTER?
THEY DON'T SEE THE HUNTER IN THEIR MIDST. TO THEM I COULD BE A BOY OR A MAN OR ANOTHER SPENT HEN, UNWANTED BY MALES. THIS SUITS ME FINE.

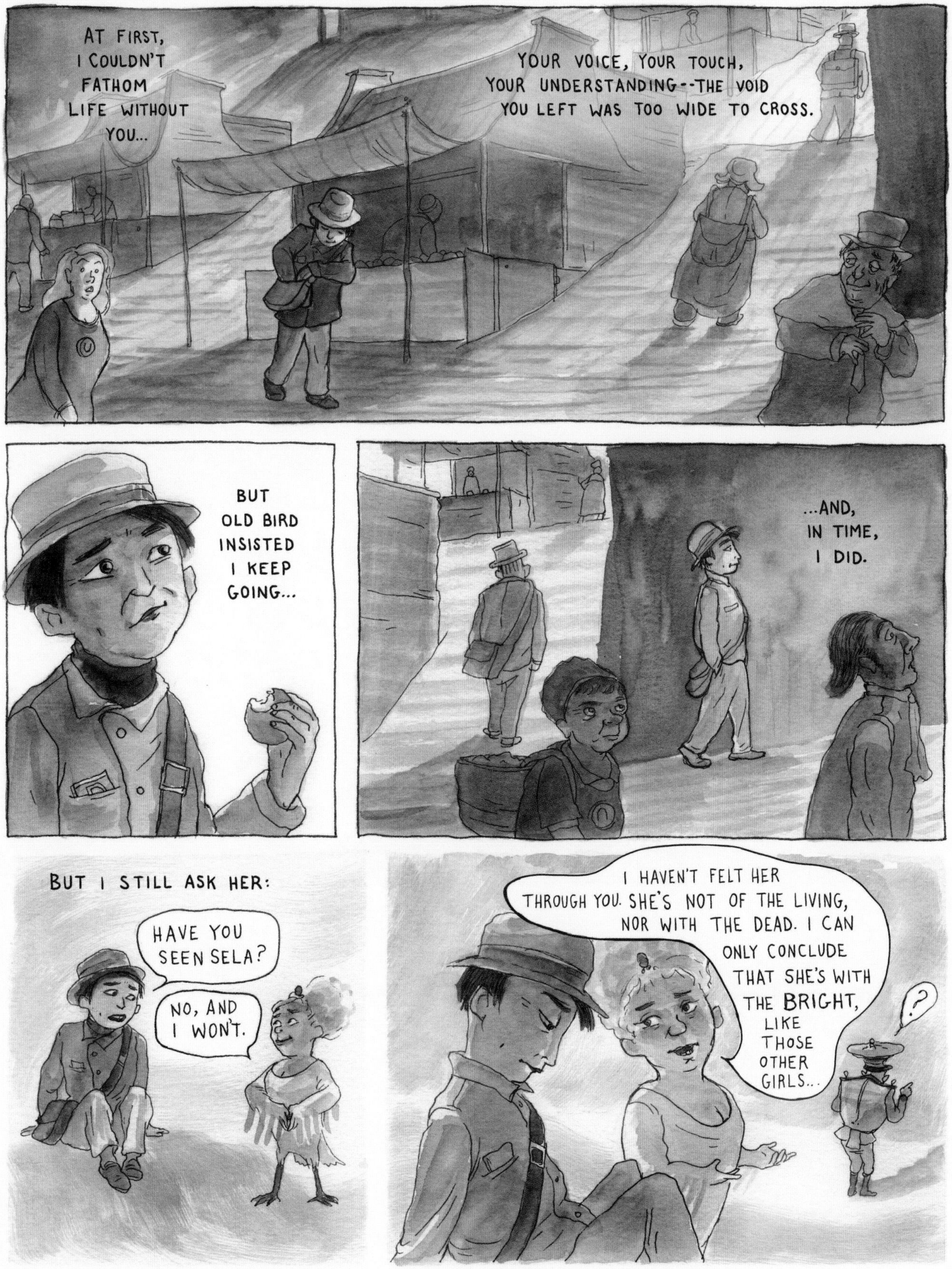

AT FIRST, I COULDN'T FATHOM LIFE WITHOUT YOU...
YOUR VOICE, YOUR TOUCH, YOUR UNDERSTANDING--THE VOID YOU LEFT WAS TOO WIDE TO CROSS.
BUT OLD BIRD INSISTED I KEEP GOING...
...AND, IN TIME, I DID.
BUT I STILL ASK HER:
HAVE YOU SEEN SELA?
NO, AND I WON'T.
I HAVEN'T FELT HER THROUGH YOU. SHE'S NOT OF THE LIVING, NOR WITH THE DEAD. I CAN ONLY CONCLUDE THAT SHE'S WITH THE BRIGHT, LIKE THOSE OTHER GIRLS...
?

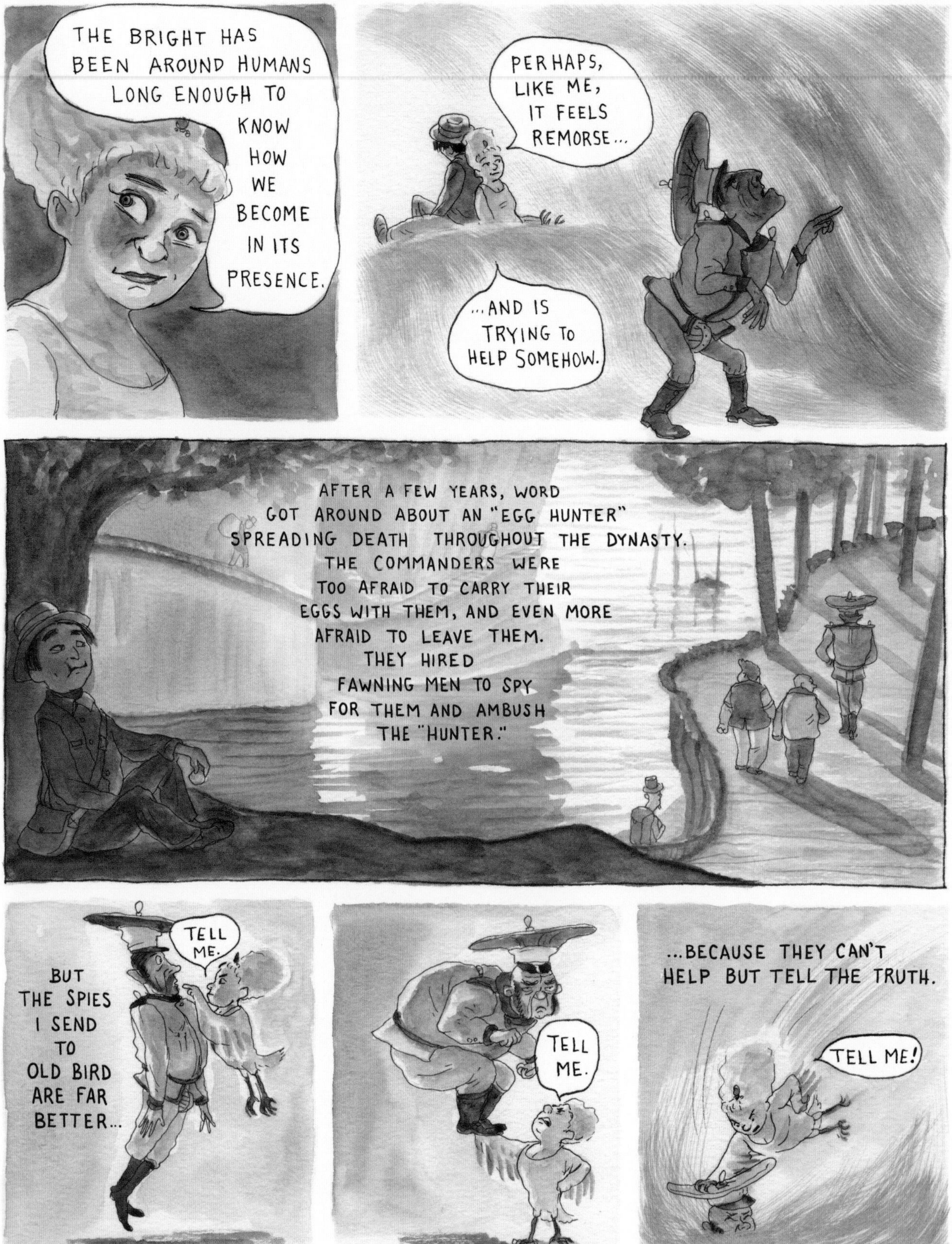
THE BRIGHT HAS BEEN AROUND HUMANS LONG ENOUGH TO KNOW HOW WE BECOME IN ITS PRESENCE.
PERHAPS, LIKE ME, IT FEELS REMORSE...
...AND IS TRYING TO HELP SOMEHOW.
AFTER A FEW YEARS, WORD GOT AROUND ABOUT AN "EGG HUNTER" SPREADING DEATH THROUGHOUT THE DYNASTY. THE COMMANDERS WERE TOO AFRAID TO CARRY THEIR EGGS WITH THEM, AND EVEN MORE AFRAID TO LEAVE THEM. THEY HIRED FAWNING MEN TO SPY FOR THEM AND AMBUSH THE "HUNTER."
BUT THE SPIES I SEND TO OLD BIRD ARE FAR BETTER...
TELL ME.
TELL ME.
...BECAUSE THEY CAN'T HELP BUT TELL THE TRUTH.
TELL ME!

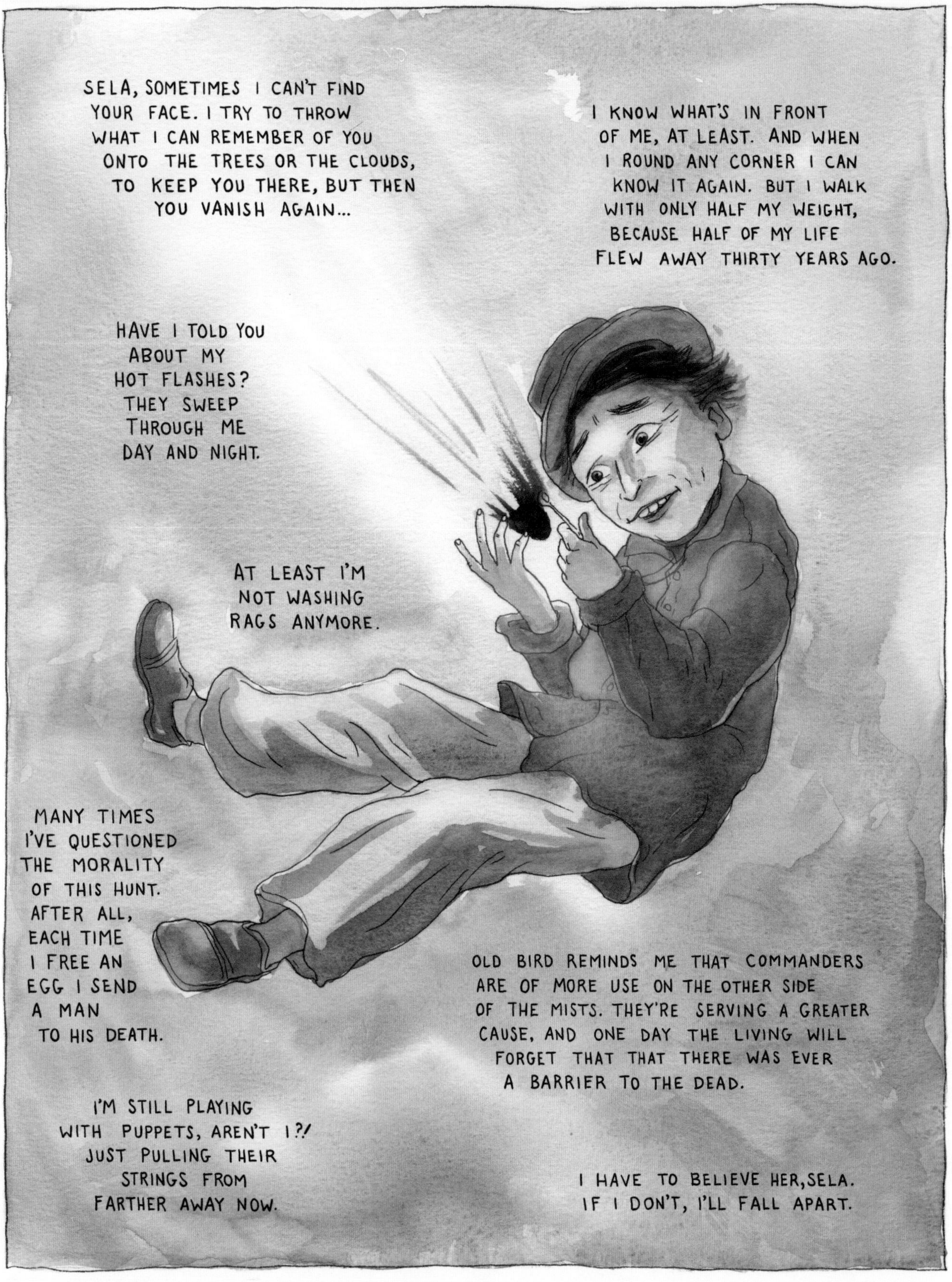
SELA, SOMETIMES I CAN'T FIND YOUR FACE. I TRY TO THROW WHAT I CAN REMEMBER OF YOU ONTO THE TREES OR THE CLOUDS, TO KEEP YOU THERE, BUT THEN YOU VANISH AGAIN...
I KNOW WHAT'S IN FRONT OF ME, AT LEAST. AND WHEN I ROUND ANY CORNER I CAN KNOW IT AGAIN. BUT I WALK WITH ONLY HALF MY WEIGHT, BECAUSE HALF OF MY LIFE FLEW AWAY THIRTY YEARS AGO.
HAVE I TOLD YOU ABOUT MY HOT FLASHES? THEY SWEEP THROUGH ME DAY AND NIGHT.
AT LEAST I'M NOT WASHING RAGS ANYMORE.
MANY TIMES I'VE QUESTIONED THE MORALITY OF THIS HUNT. AFTER ALL, EACH TIME I FREE AN EGG I SEND A MAN TO HIS DEATH.
OLD BIRD REMINDS ME THAT COMMANDERS ARE OF MORE USE ON THE OTHER SIDE OF THE MISTS. THEY'RE SERVING A GREATER CAUSE, AND ONE DAY THE LIVING WILL FORGET THAT THAT THERE WAS EVER A BARRIER TO THE DEAD.
I'M STILL PLAYING WITH PUPPETS, AREN'T I?! JUST PULLING THEIR STRINGS FROM FARTHER AWAY NOW.
I HAVE TO BELIEVE HER, SELA. IF I DON'T, I'LL FALL APART.

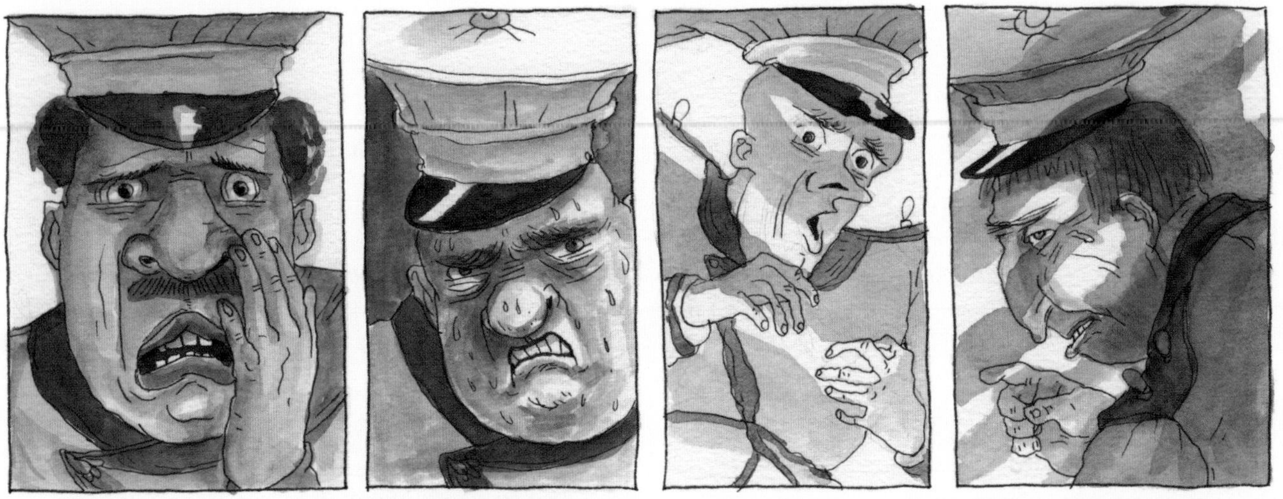

I REMEMBER ALL THE COMMANDERS' FINAL FACES, THEIR CONTORTIONS OF BEWILDERMENT, HOSTILITY, AND SORROW AS THEY FELT THEIR LIFE AND TREASURE ESCAPE THEM. THEY'D NEVER LOOKED INTO ANYONE'S EYES WITH SUCH UNGUARDEDNESS.

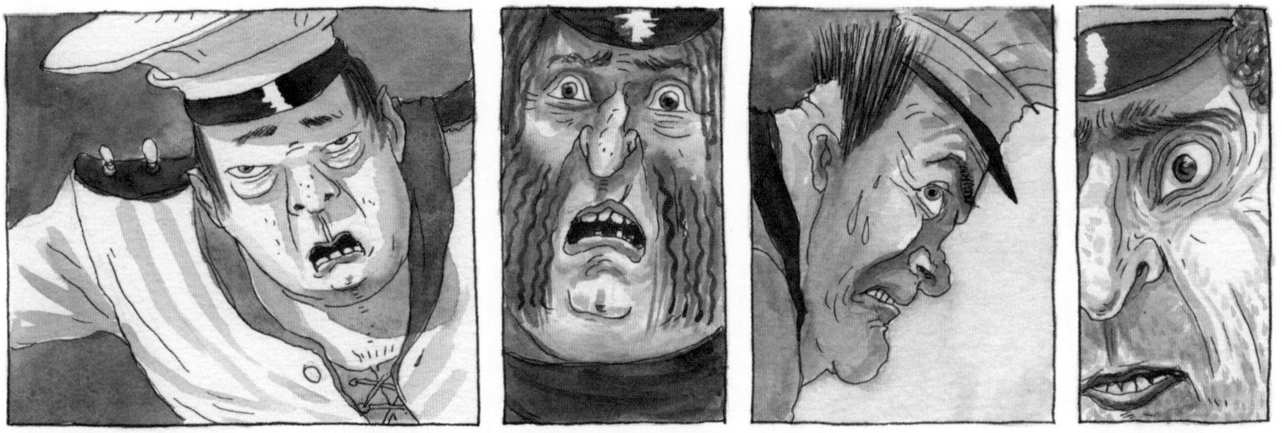

COULD THEY SEE IN MY EYES THAT I KNEW THEIR LOSS? THEIR CONFUSION? I SPIED THE TRUTH INSIDE THEM, JUST AS THEIR WINDOWS WERE SHUTTING FOR GOOD. THEY ARE TOO PROUD NOW TO SHARE ANY OF THIS WITH OLD BIRD...

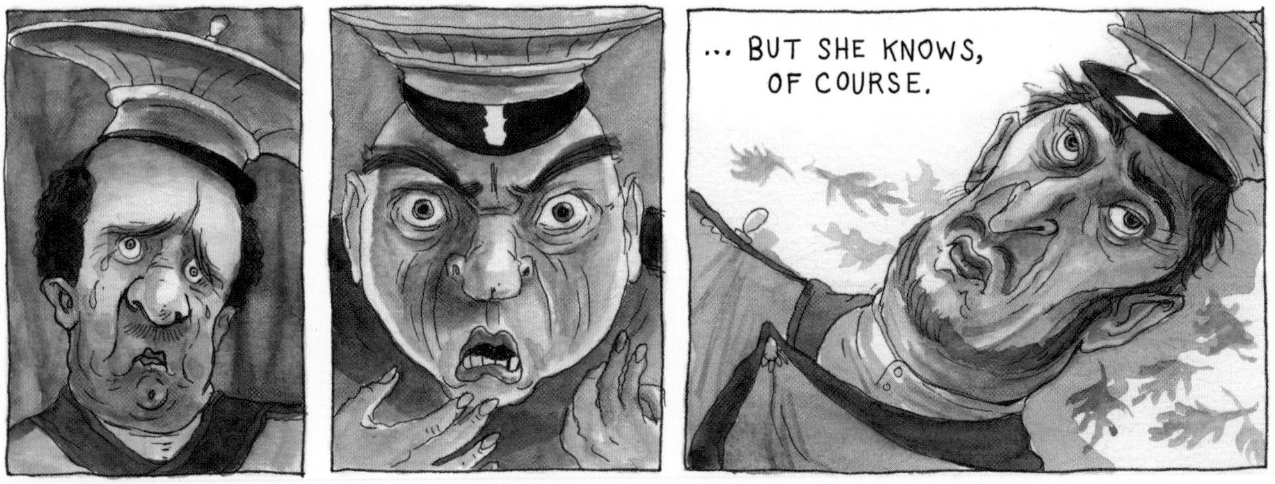
... BUT SHE KNOWS, OF COURSE.

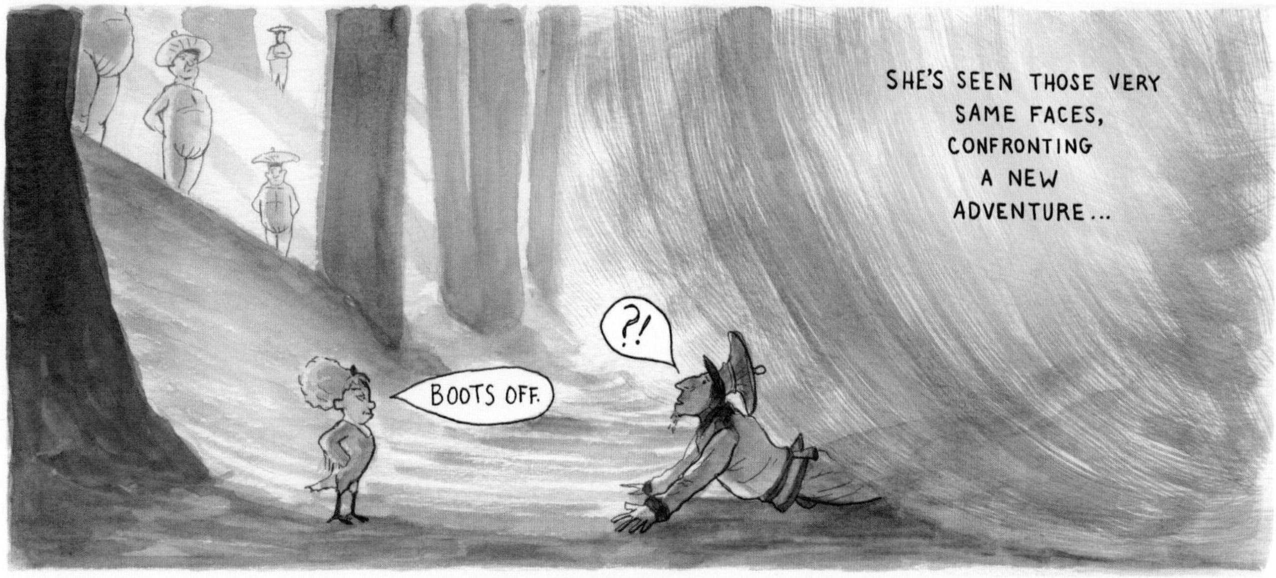
SHE'S SEEN THOSE VERY SAME FACES, CONFRONTING A NEW ADVENTURE...
?!
BOOTS OFF.

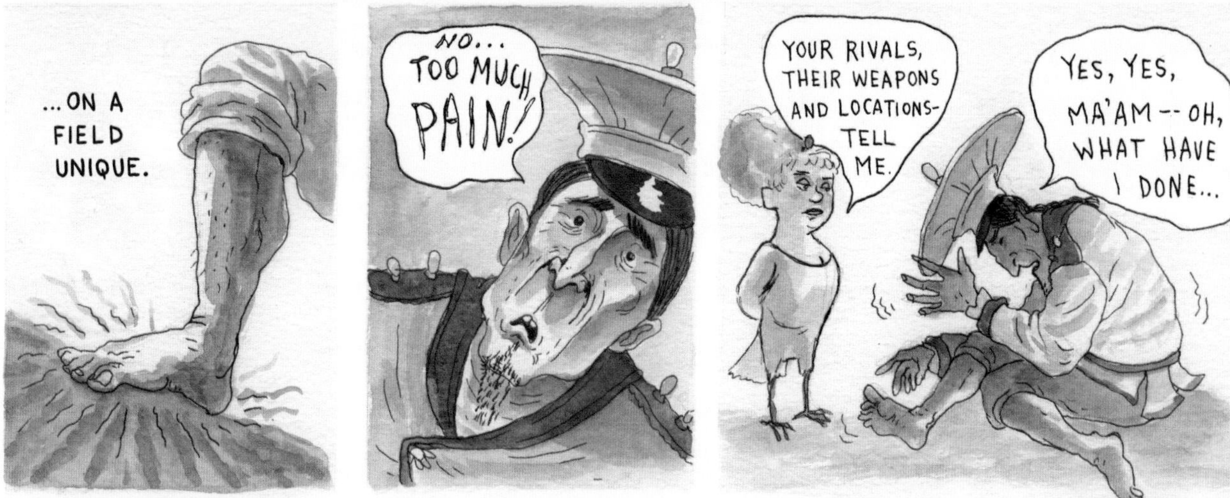
...ON A FIELD UNIQUE.
NO... TOO MUCH PAIN!
YOUR RIVALS, THEIR WEAPONS AND LOCATIONS- TELL ME.
YES, YES, MA'AM -- OH, WHAT HAVE I DONE...

OLD BIRD ENJOYS TELLING ME ABOUT THE COMMANDERS' PETTY STATUS GAMES. THEY RANK *EVERYTHING*. SHE PLAYS THEM OFF EACH OTHER, AND THEY KNOW IT.

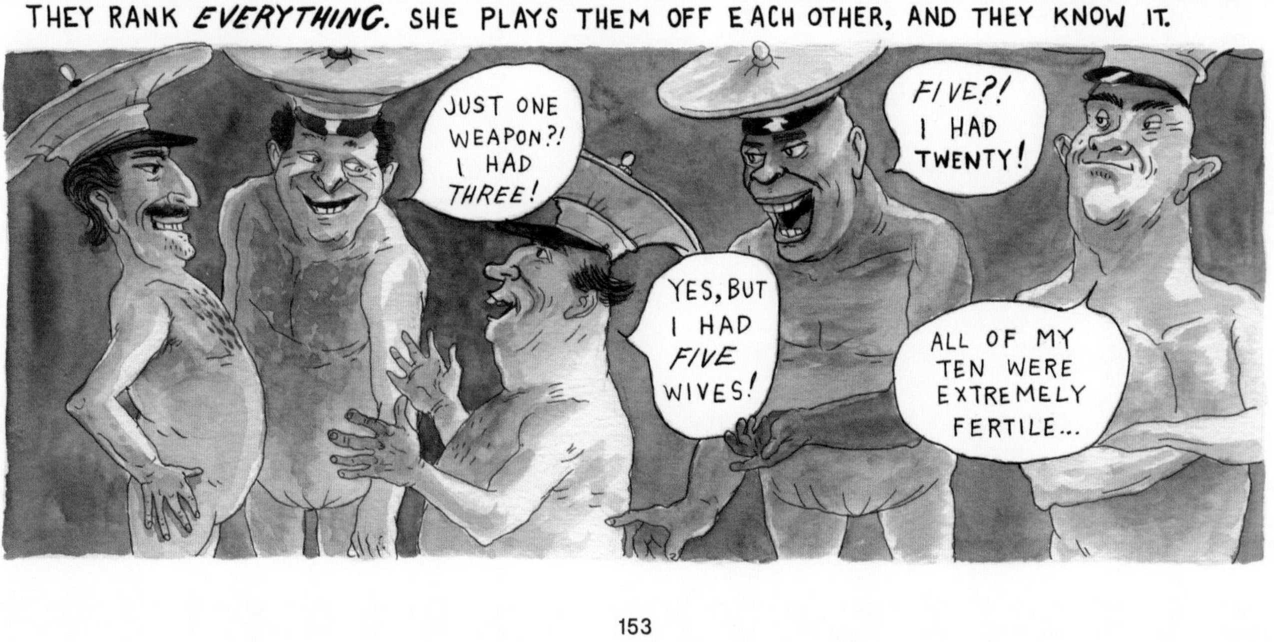
JUST ONE WEAPON?! I HAD THREE!
YES, BUT I HAD FIVE WIVES!
FIVE?! I HAD TWENTY!
ALL OF MY TEN WERE EXTREMELY FERTILE...

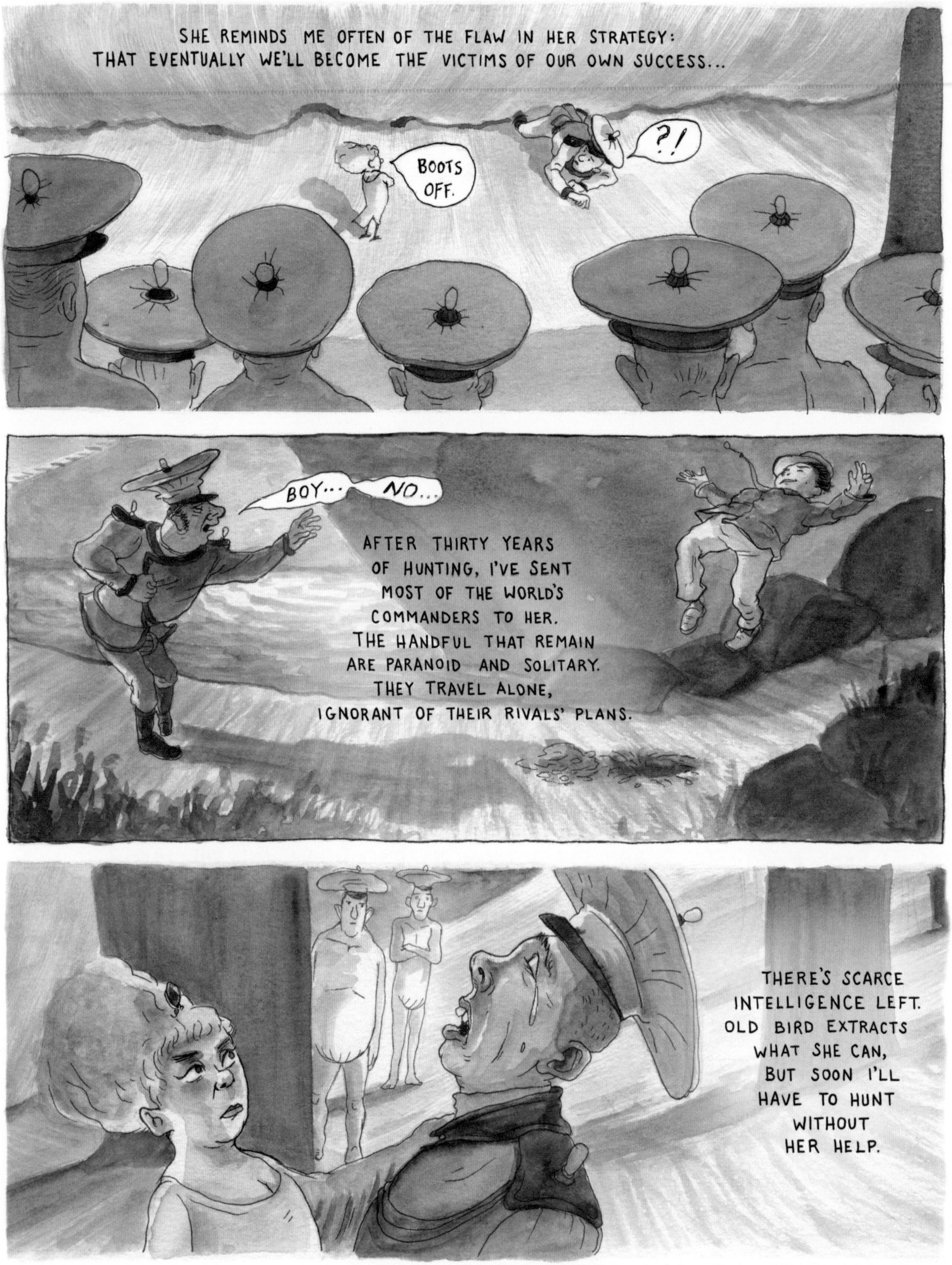
SHE REMINDS ME OFTEN OF THE FLAW IN HER STRATEGY: THAT EVENTUALLY WE'LL BECOME THE VICTIMS OF OUR OWN SUCCESS...
BOOTS OFF.
?!
BOY...
NO...
AFTER THIRTY YEARS OF HUNTING, I'VE SENT MOST OF THE WORLD'S COMMANDERS TO HER. THE HANDFUL THAT REMAIN ARE PARANOID AND SOLITARY. THEY TRAVEL ALONE, IGNORANT OF THEIR RIVALS' PLANS.
THERE'S SCARCE INTELLIGENCE LEFT. OLD BIRD EXTRACTS WHAT SHE CAN, BUT SOON I'LL HAVE TO HUNT WITHOUT HER HELP.

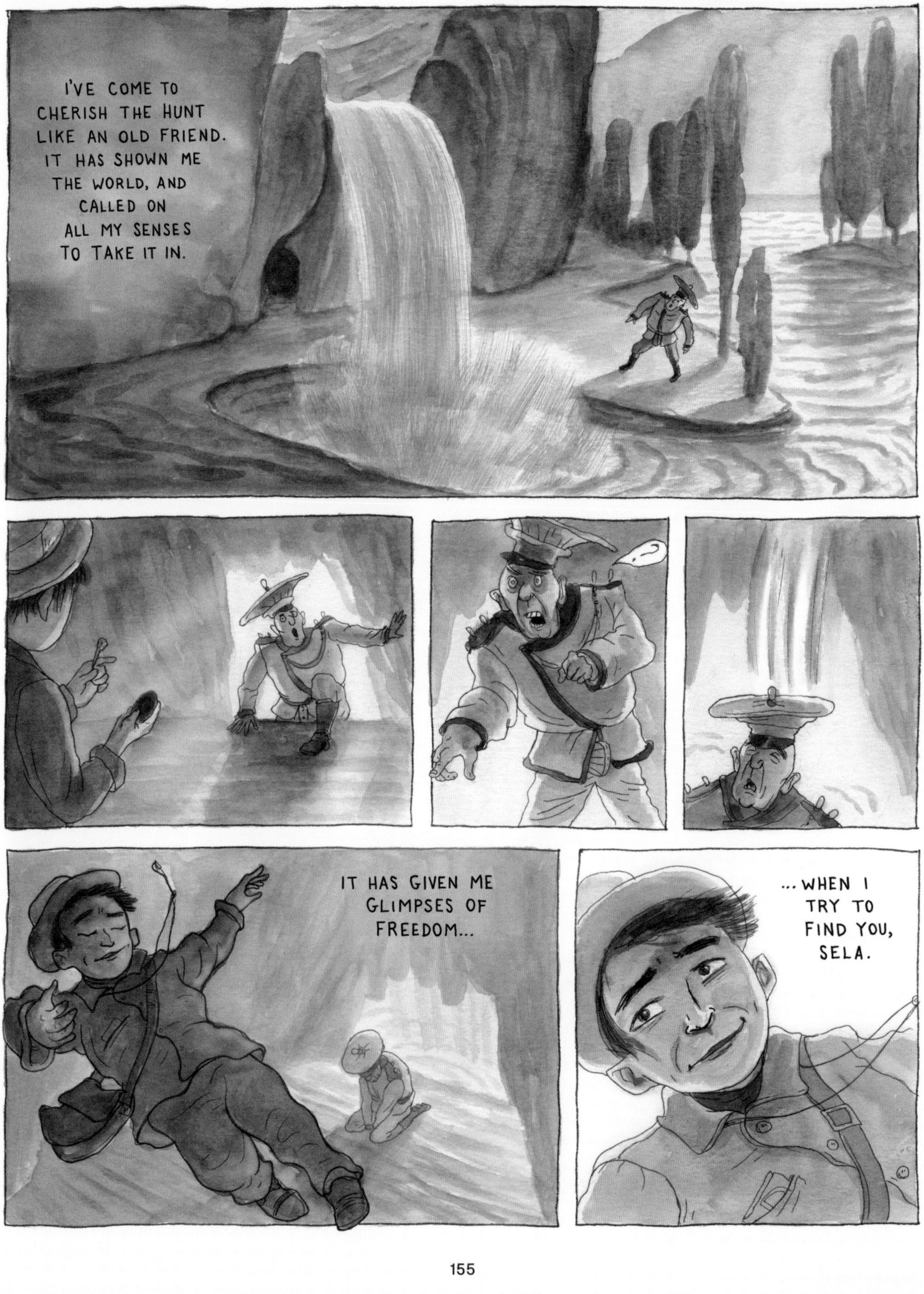
I'VE COME TO CHERISH THE HUNT LIKE AN OLD FRIEND. IT HAS SHOWN ME THE WORLD, AND CALLED ON ALL MY SENSES TO TAKE IT IN.
IT HAS GIVEN ME GLIMPSES OF FREEDOM...
...WHEN I TRY TO FIND YOU, SELA.

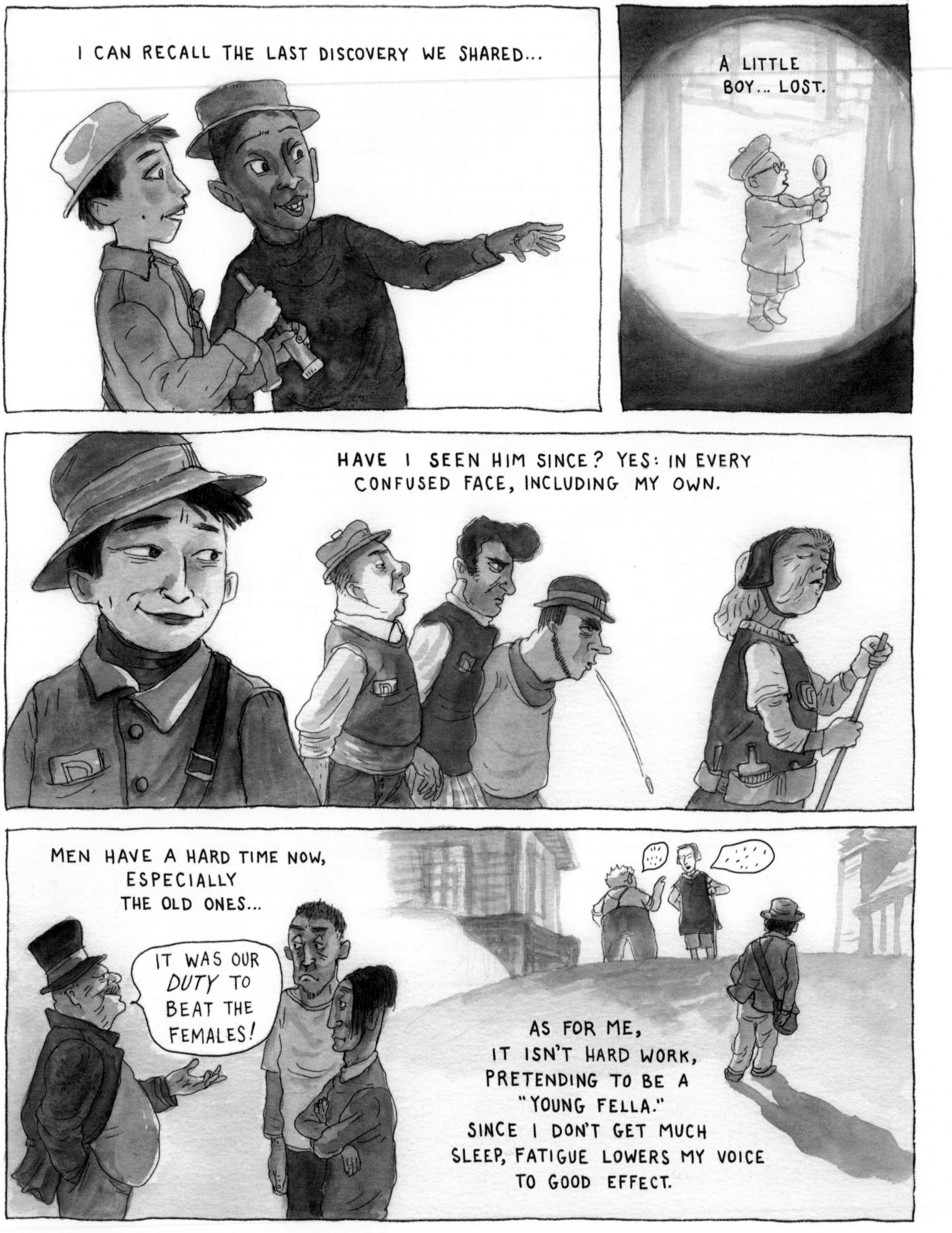
I CAN RECALL THE LAST DISCOVERY WE SHARED...
A LITTLE BOY... LOST.
HAVE I SEEN HIM SINCE? YES: IN EVERY CONFUSED FACE, INCLUDING MY OWN.
MEN HAVE A HARD TIME NOW, ESPECIALLY THE OLD ONES...
IT WAS OUR *DUTY* TO BEAT THE FEMALES!
AS FOR ME, IT ISN'T HARD WORK, PRETENDING TO BE A "YOUNG FELLA." SINCE I DON'T GET MUCH SLEEP, FATIGUE LOWERS MY VOICE TO GOOD EFFECT.

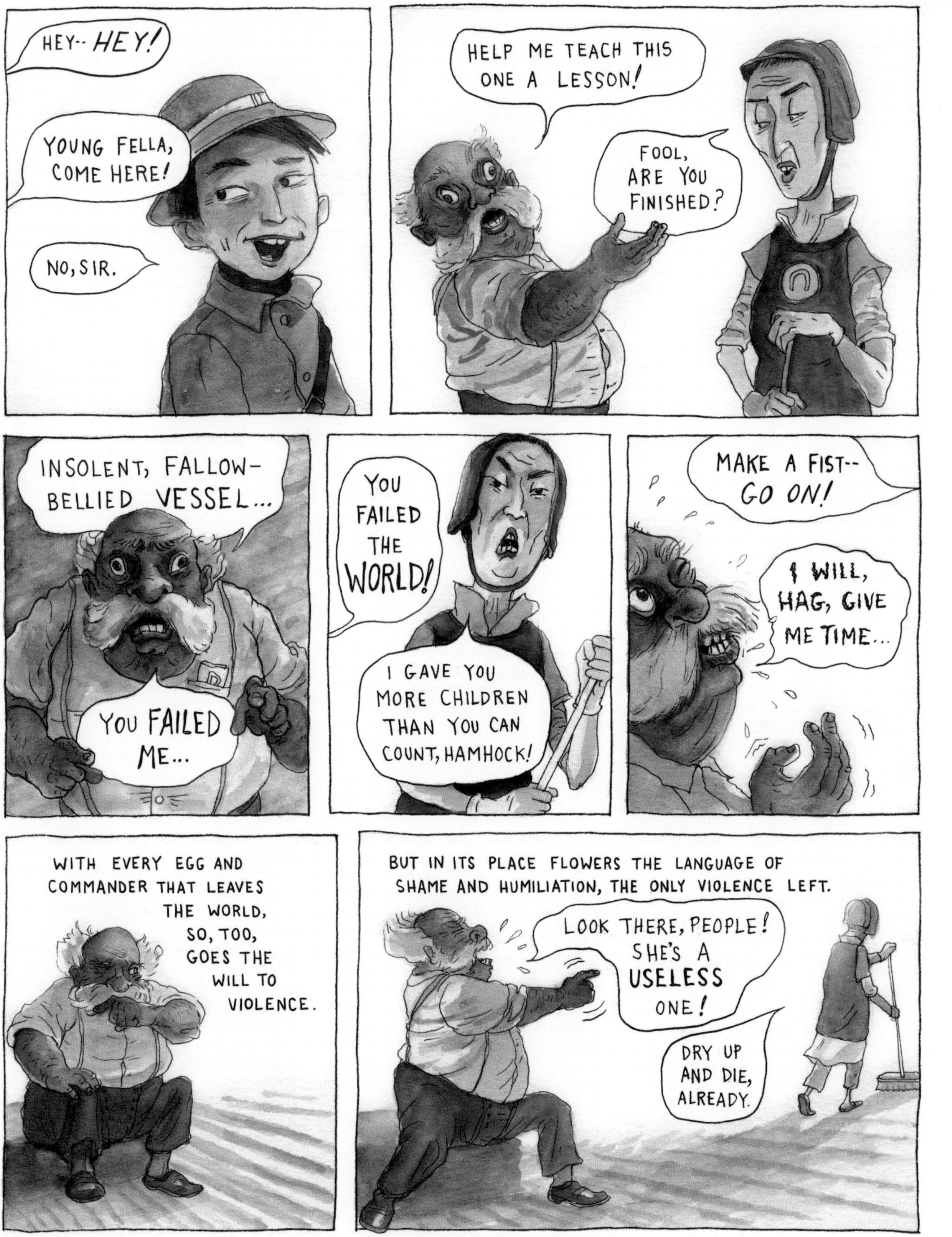
HEY-- HEY!
YOUNG FELLA, COME HERE!
NO, SIR.
HELP ME TEACH THIS ONE A LESSON!
FOOL, ARE YOU FINISHED?
INSOLENT, FALLOW-BELLIED VESSEL...
YOU FAILED ME...
YOU FAILED THE WORLD!
I GAVE YOU MORE CHILDREN THAN YOU CAN COUNT, HAMHOCK!
MAKE A FIST-- GO ON!
I WILL, HAG, GIVE ME TIME...
WITH EVERY EGG AND COMMANDER THAT LEAVES THE WORLD, SO, TOO, GOES THE WILL TO VIOLENCE.
BUT IN ITS PLACE FLOWERS THE LANGUAGE OF SHAME AND HUMILIATION, THE ONLY VIOLENCE LEFT.
LOOK THERE, PEOPLE! SHE'S A USELESS ONE!
DRY UP AND DIE, ALREADY.

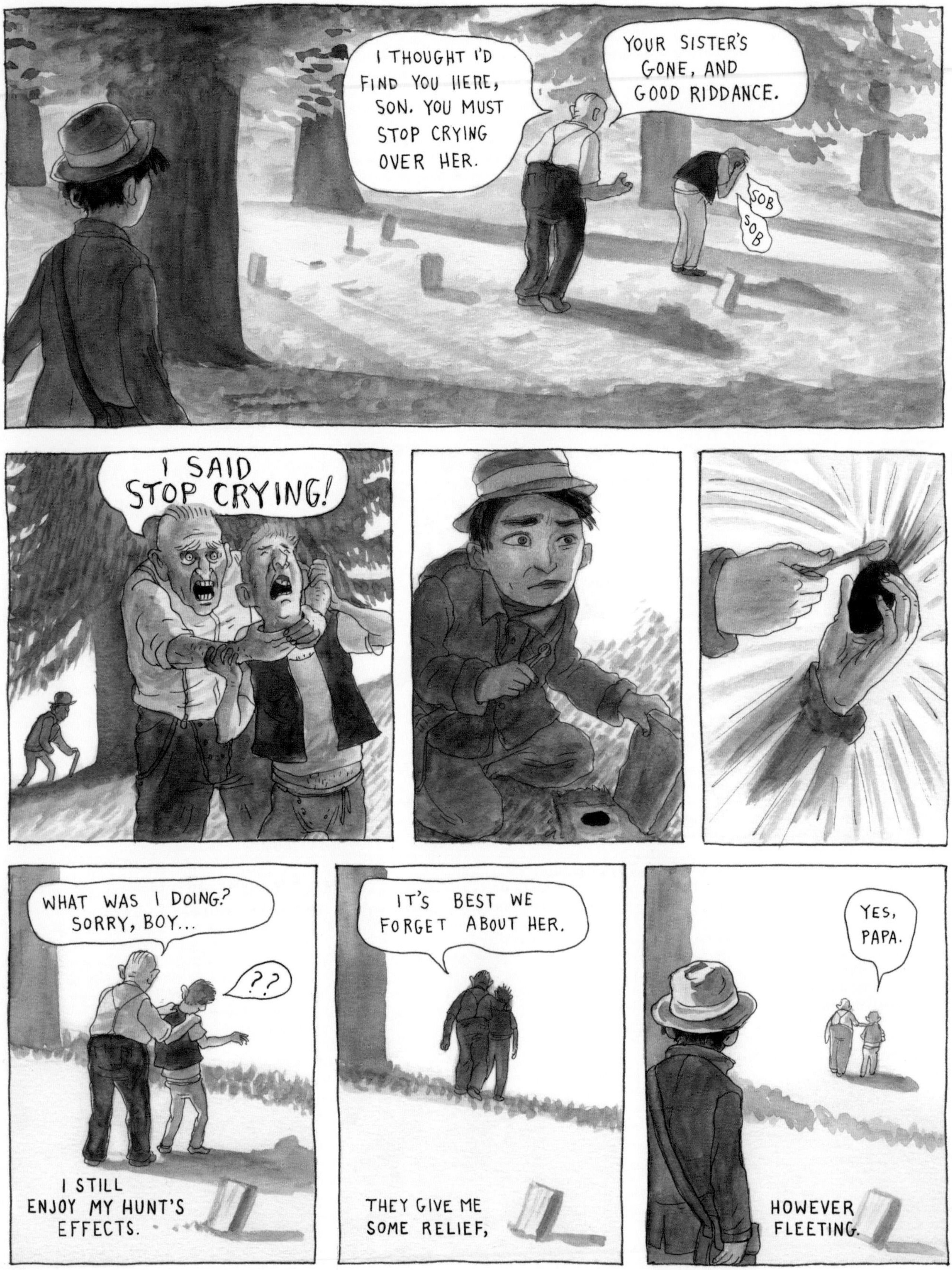
I THOUGHT I'D FIND YOU HERE, SON. YOU MUST STOP CRYING OVER HER.
YOUR SISTER'S GONE, AND GOOD RIDDANCE.
SOB
SOB
I SAID STOP CRYING!
WHAT WAS I DOING? SORRY, BOY...
??
I STILL ENJOY MY HUNT'S EFFECTS.
IT'S BEST WE FORGET ABOUT HER.
THEY GIVE ME SOME RELIEF,
YES, PAPA.
HOWEVER FLEETING.

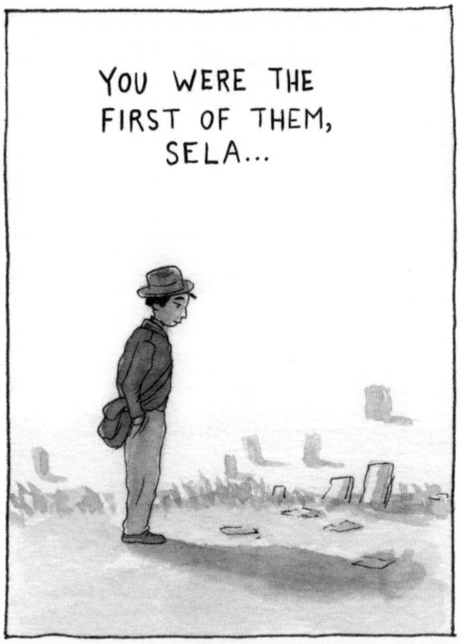
YOU WERE THE FIRST OF THEM, SELA...

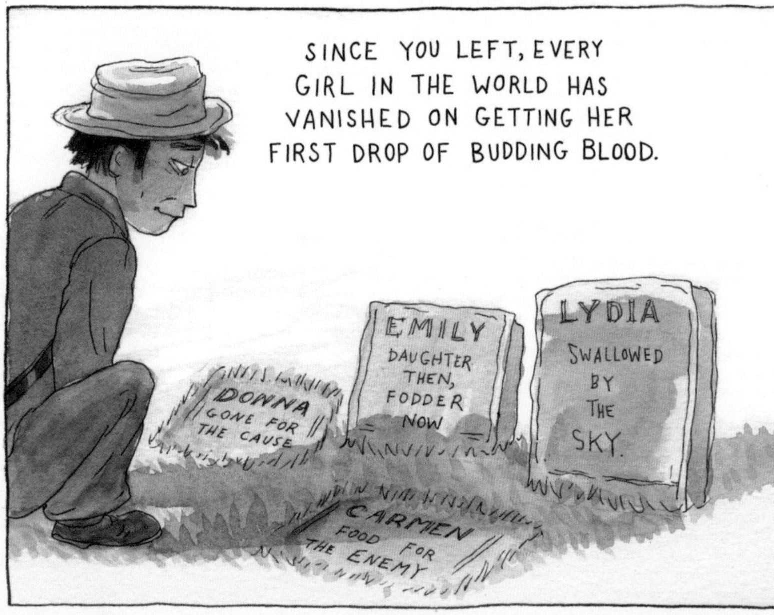
SINCE YOU LEFT, EVERY GIRL IN THE WORLD HAS VANISHED ON GETTING HER FIRST DROP OF BUDDING BLOOD.
DONNA GONE FOR THE CAUSE
EMILY DAUGHTER THEN, FODDER NOW
LYDIA SWALLOWED BY THE SKY.
CARMEN FOOD FOR THE ENEMY

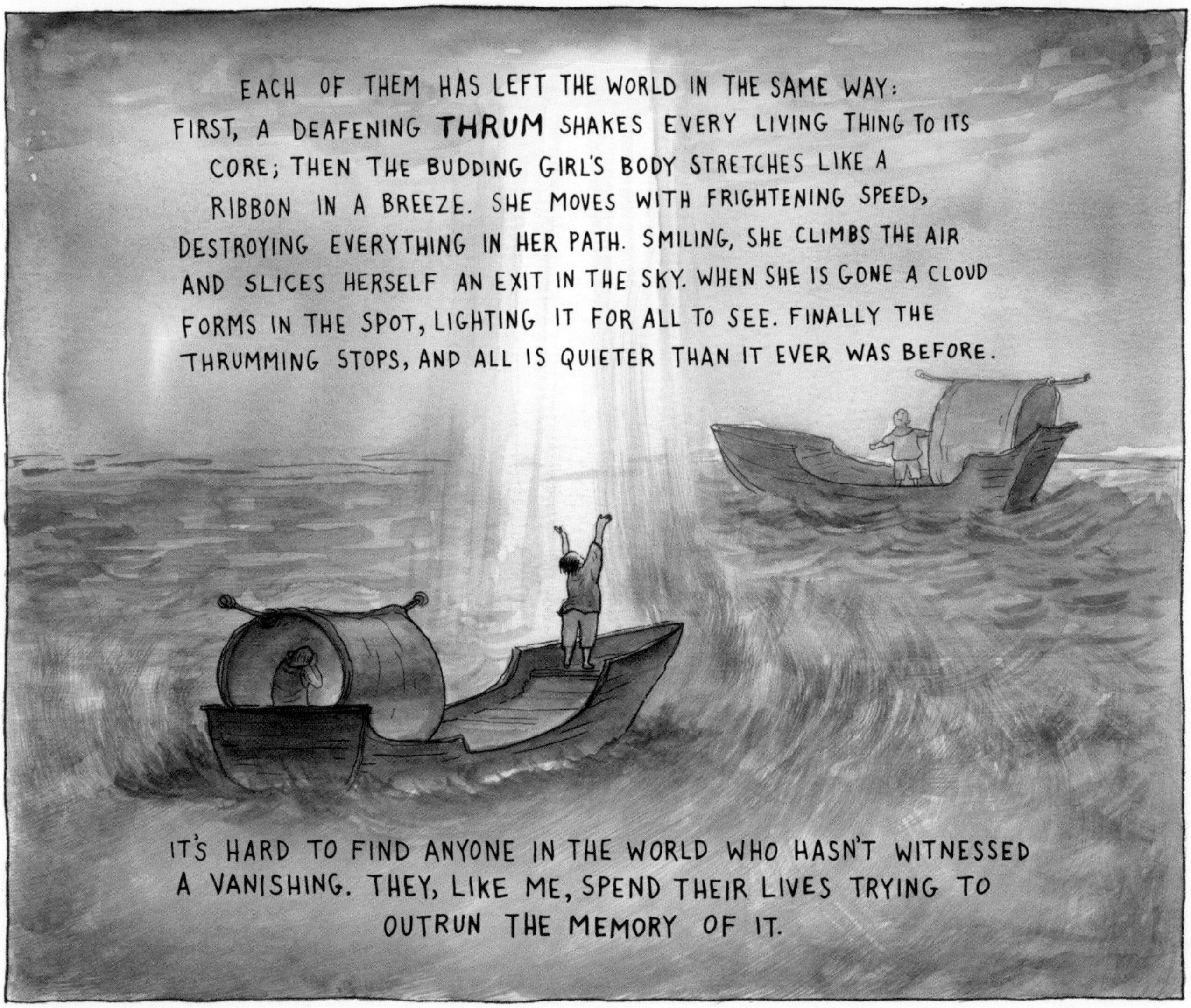
EACH OF THEM HAS LEFT THE WORLD IN THE SAME WAY: FIRST, A DEAFENING THRUM SHAKES EVERY LIVING THING TO ITS CORE; THEN THE BUDDING GIRL'S BODY STRETCHES LIKE A RIBBON IN A BREEZE. SHE MOVES WITH FRIGHTENING SPEED, DESTROYING EVERYTHING IN HER PATH. SMILING, SHE CLIMBS THE AIR AND SLICES HERSELF AN EXIT IN THE SKY. WHEN SHE IS GONE A CLOUD FORMS IN THE SPOT, LIGHTING IT FOR ALL TO SEE. FINALLY THE THRUMMING STOPS, AND ALL IS QUIETER THAN IT EVER WAS BEFORE.
IT'S HARD TO FIND ANYONE IN THE WORLD WHO HASN'T WITNESSED A VANISHING. THEY, LIKE ME, SPEND THEIR LIVES TRYING TO OUTRUN THE MEMORY OF IT.

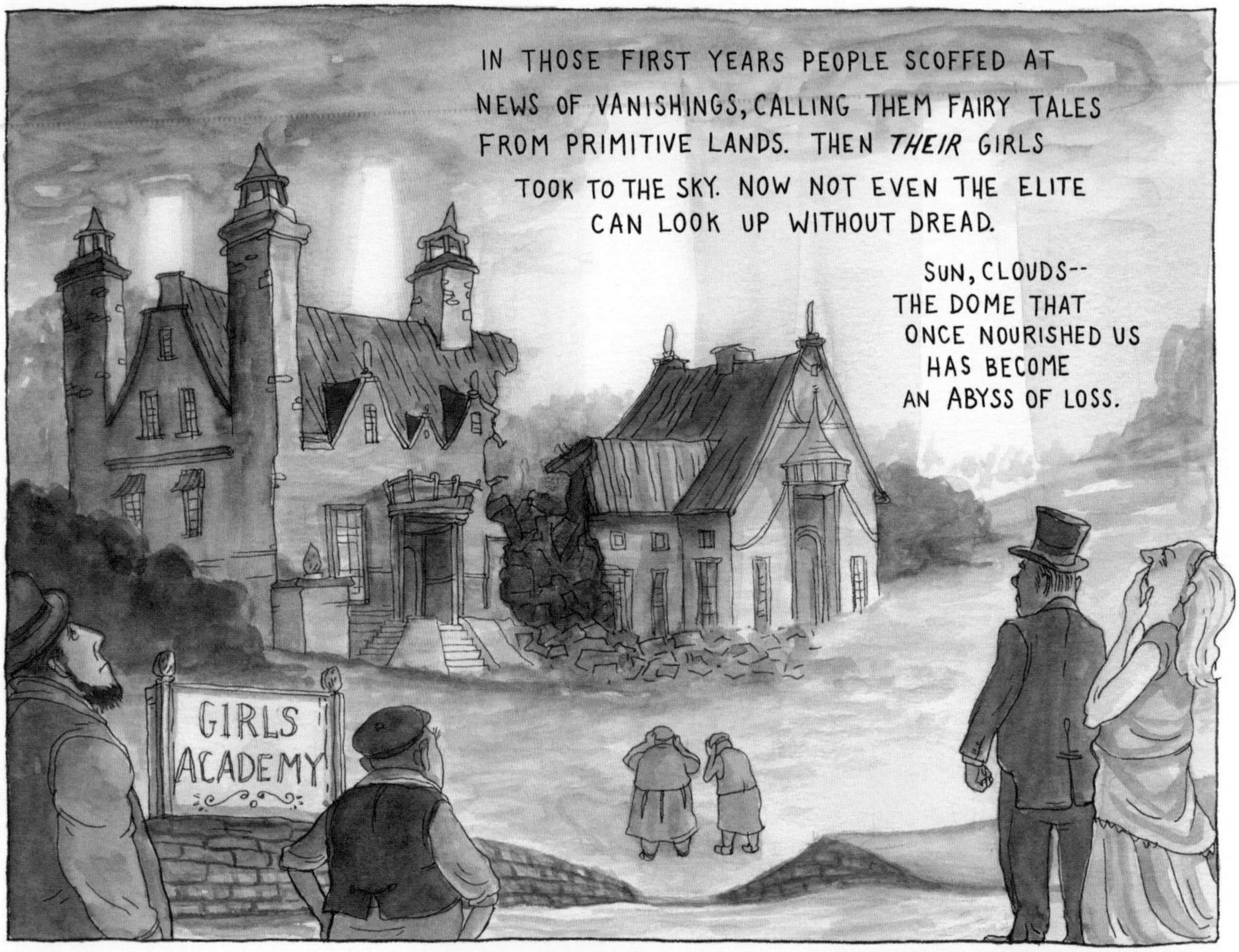
IN THOSE FIRST YEARS PEOPLE SCOFFED AT NEWS OF VANISHINGS, CALLING THEM FAIRY TALES FROM PRIMITIVE LANDS. THEN *THEIR* GIRLS TOOK TO THE SKY. NOW NOT EVEN THE ELITE CAN LOOK UP WITHOUT DREAD.
SUN, CLOUDS-- THE DOME THAT ONCE NOURISHED US HAS BECOME AN ABYSS OF LOSS.
GIRLS ACADEMY

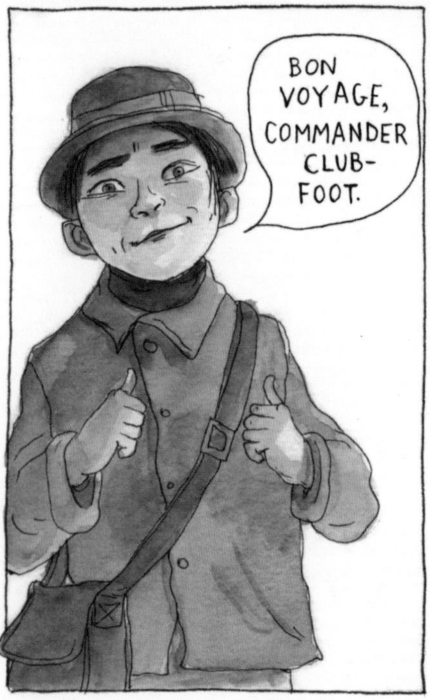
BON VOYAGE, COMMANDER CLUB-FOOT.

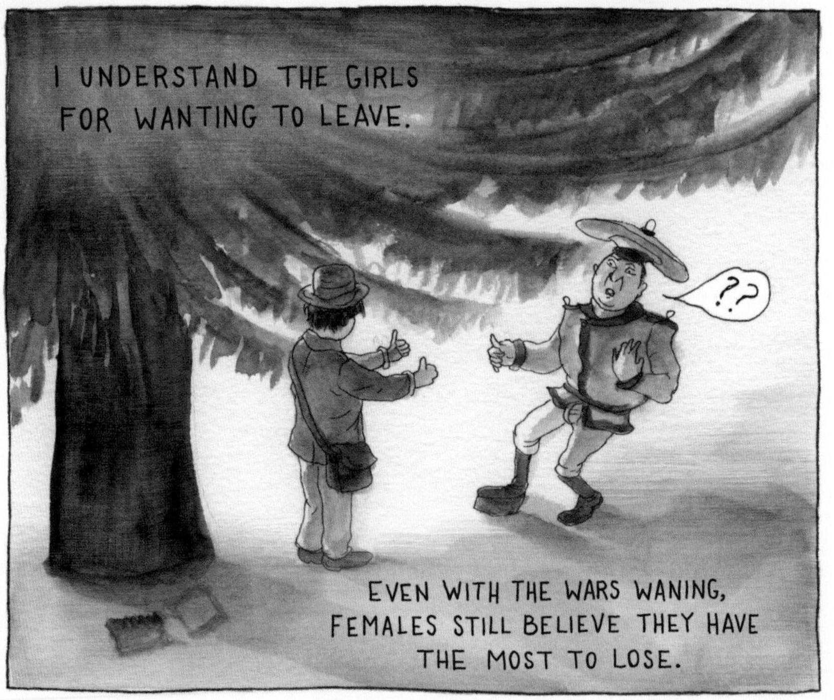
I UNDERSTAND THE GIRLS FOR WANTING TO LEAVE.
??
EVEN WITH THE WARS WANING, FEMALES STILL BELIEVE THEY HAVE THE MOST TO LOSE.

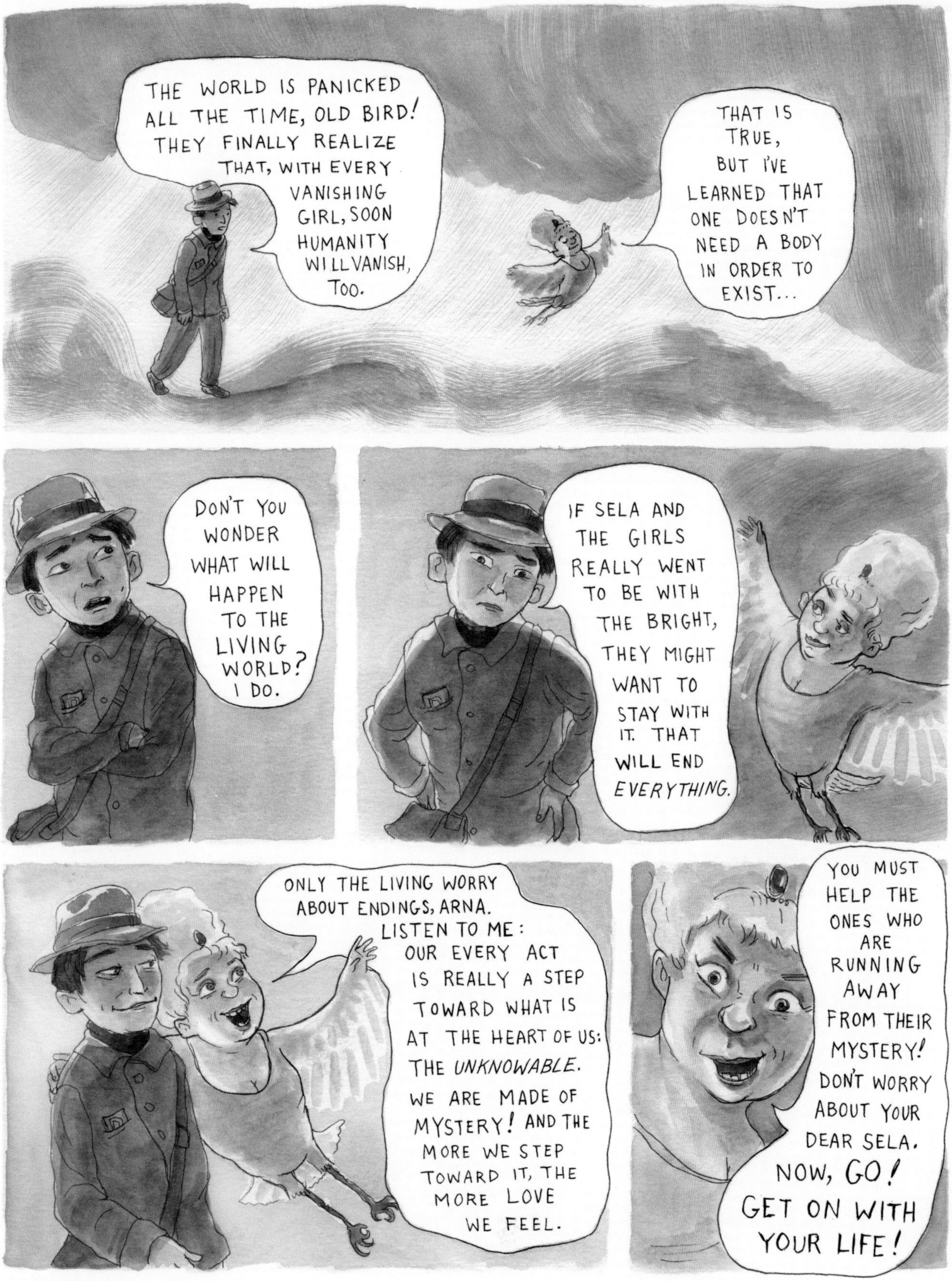
THE WORLD IS PANICKED ALL THE TIME, OLD BIRD! THEY FINALLY REALIZE THAT, WITH EVERY VANISHING GIRL, SOON HUMANITY WILL VANISH, TOO.
THAT IS TRUE, BUT I'VE LEARNED THAT ONE DOESN'T NEED A BODY IN ORDER TO EXIST...
DON'T YOU WONDER WHAT WILL HAPPEN TO THE LIVING WORLD? I DO.
IF SELA AND THE GIRLS REALLY WENT TO BE WITH THE BRIGHT, THEY MIGHT WANT TO STAY WITH IT. THAT WILL END *EVERYTHING*.
ONLY THE LIVING WORRY ABOUT ENDINGS, ARNA. LISTEN TO ME: OUR EVERY ACT IS REALLY A STEP TOWARD WHAT IS AT THE HEART OF US: THE *UNKNOWABLE*. WE ARE MADE OF MYSTERY! AND THE MORE WE STEP TOWARD IT, THE MORE LOVE WE FEEL.
YOU MUST HELP THE ONES WHO ARE RUNNING AWAY FROM THEIR MYSTERY! DON'T WORRY ABOUT YOUR DEAR SELA. NOW, GO! GET ON WITH YOUR LIFE!

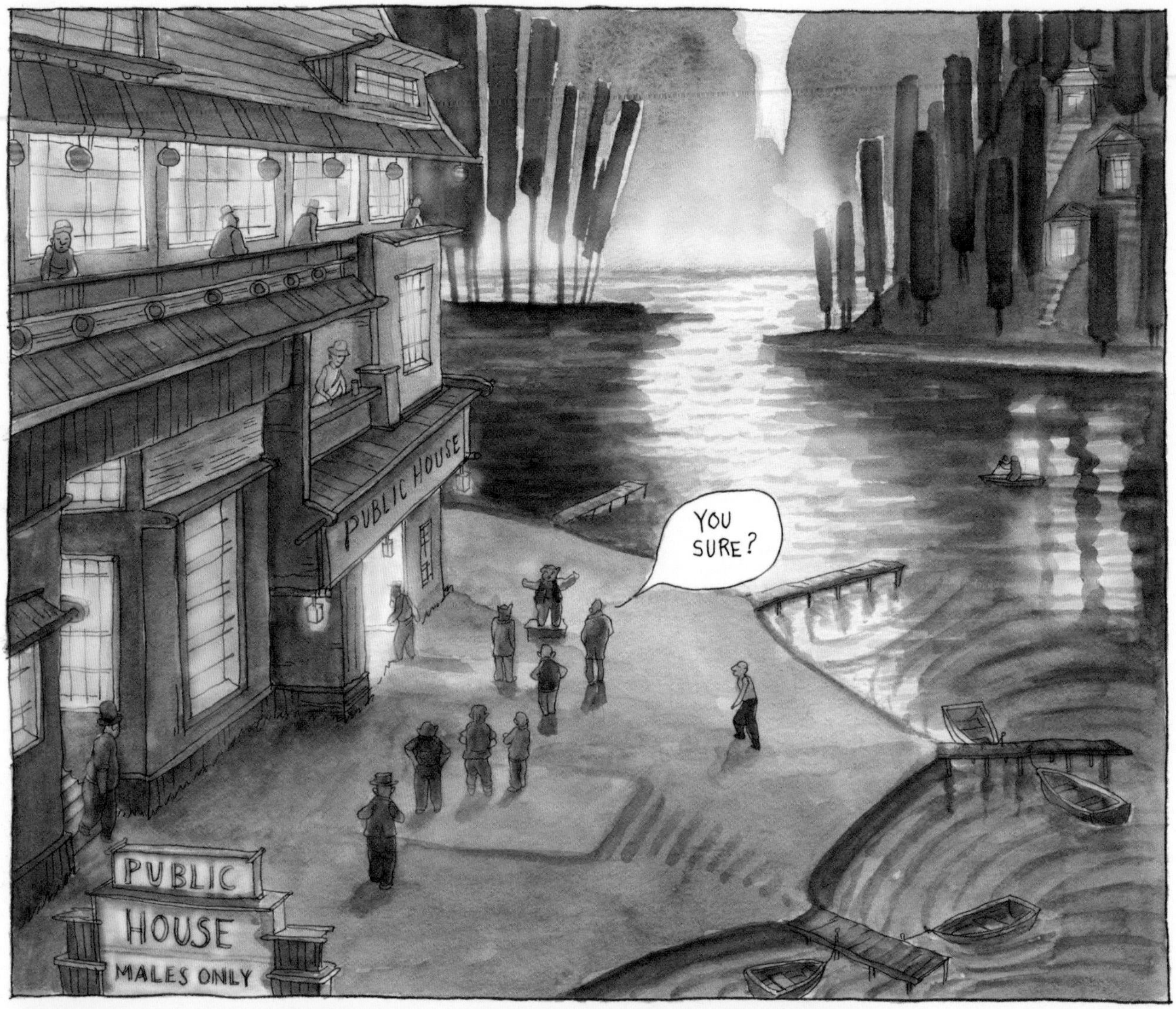
PUBLIC HOUSE
YOU SURE?
PUBLIC HOUSE
MALES ONLY

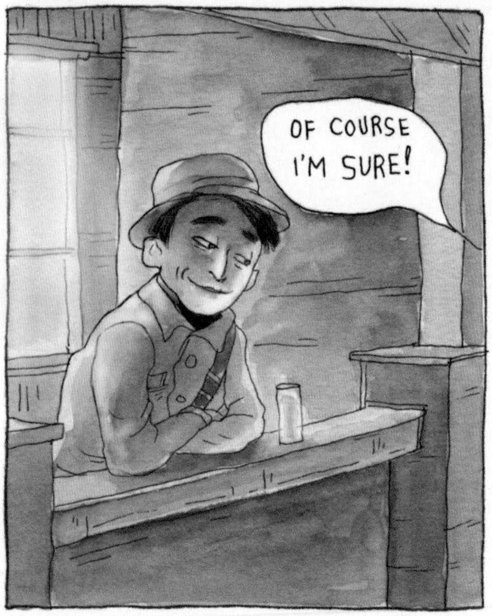
OF COURSE I'M SURE!

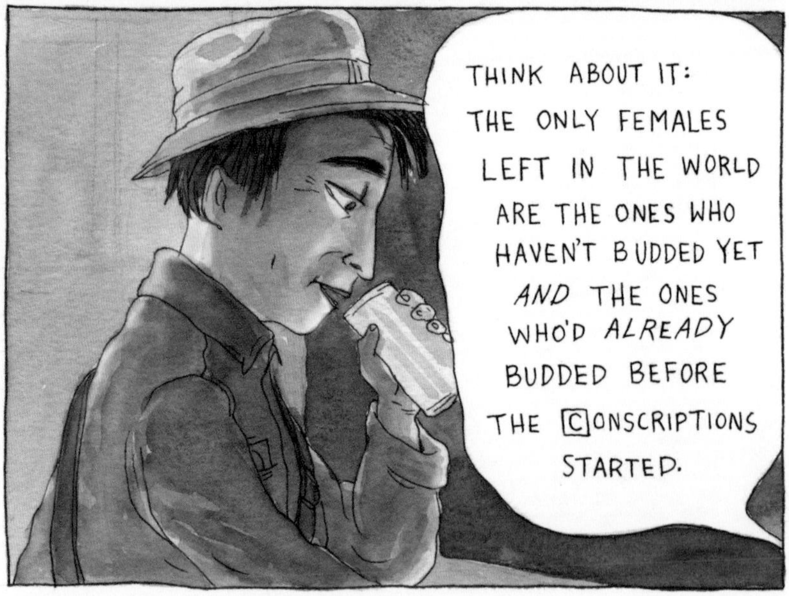
THINK ABOUT IT: THE ONLY FEMALES LEFT IN THE WORLD ARE THE ONES WHO HAVEN'T BUDDED YET *AND* THE ONES WHO'D *ALREADY* BUDDED BEFORE THE CONSCRIPTIONS STARTED.

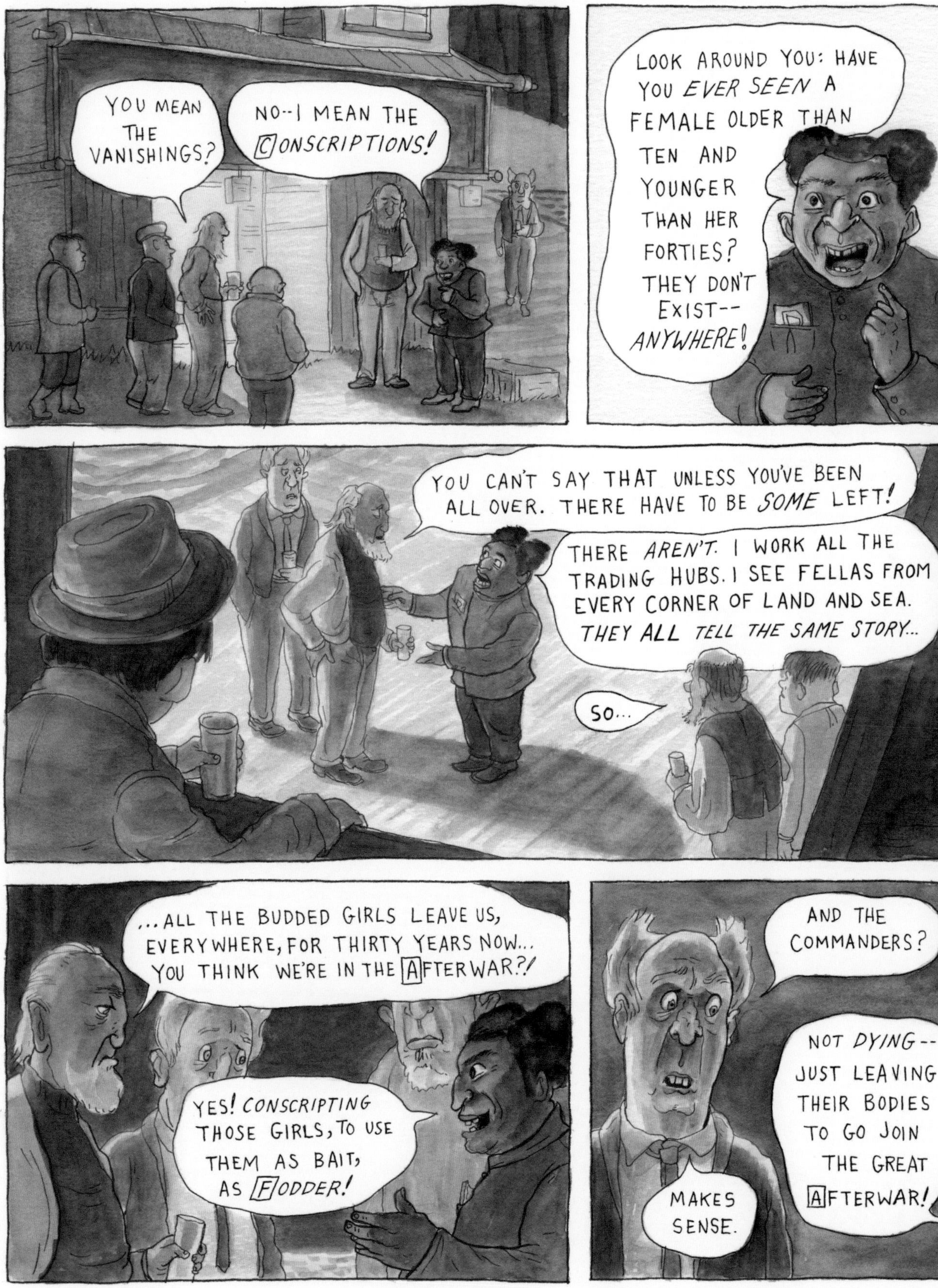
YOU MEAN THE VANISHINGS?
NO--I MEAN THE CONSCRIPTIONS!
LOOK AROUND YOU: HAVE YOU EVER SEEN A FEMALE OLDER THAN TEN AND YOUNGER THAN HER FORTIES? THEY DON'T EXIST-- ANYWHERE!
YOU CAN'T SAY THAT UNLESS YOU'VE BEEN ALL OVER. THERE HAVE TO BE SOME LEFT!
THERE AREN'T. I WORK ALL THE TRADING HUBS. I SEE FELLAS FROM EVERY CORNER OF LAND AND SEA. THEY ALL TELL THE SAME STORY...
SO...
...ALL THE BUDDED GIRLS LEAVE US, EVERYWHERE, FOR THIRTY YEARS NOW... YOU THINK WE'RE IN THE AFTERWAR?!
YES! CONSCRIPTING THOSE GIRLS, TO USE THEM AS BAIT, AS FODDER!
AND THE COMMANDERS?
NOT DYING-- JUST LEAVING THEIR BODIES TO GO JOIN THE GREAT AFTERWAR!
MAKES SENSE.

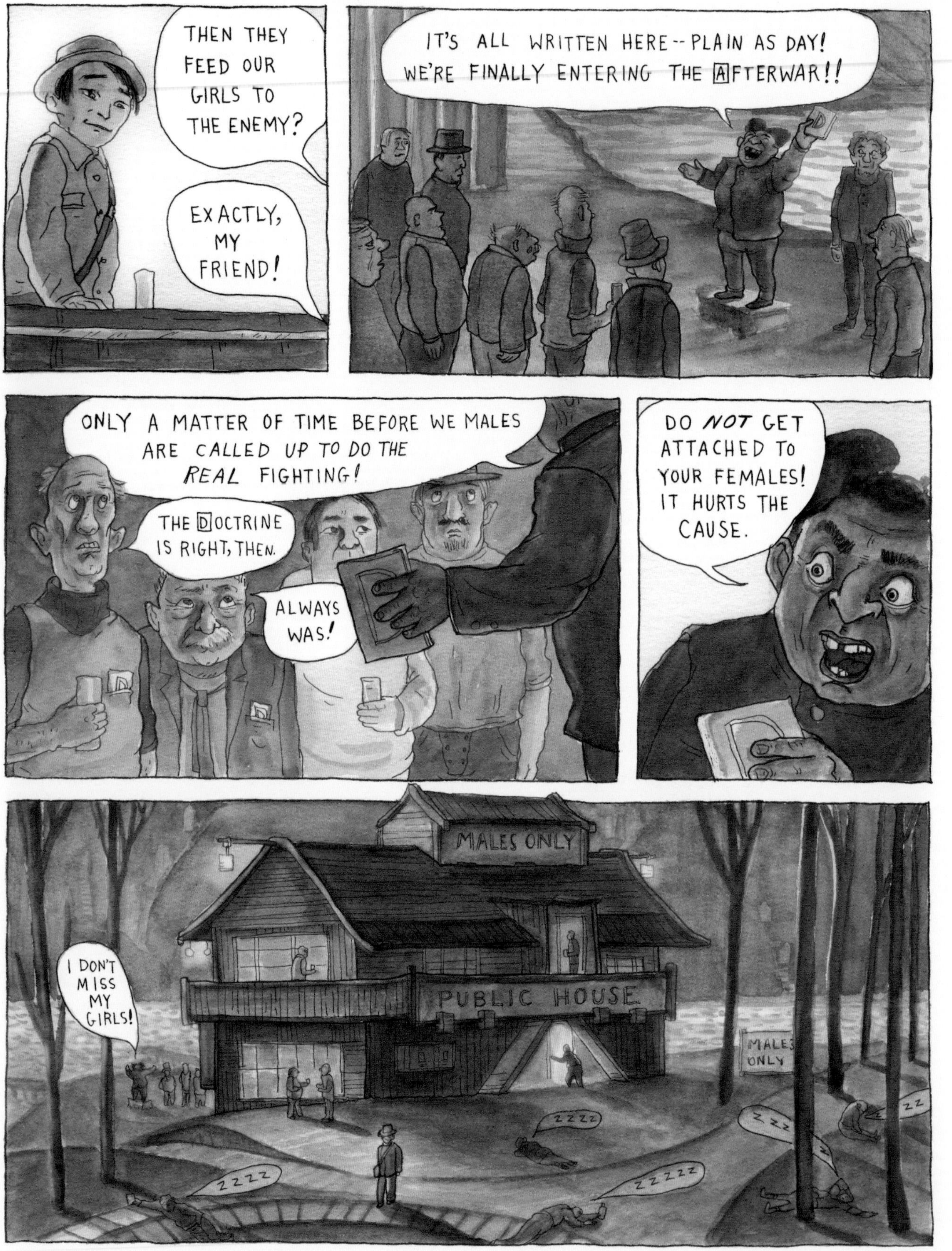
THEN THEY FEED OUR GIRLS TO THE ENEMY?
EXACTLY, MY FRIEND!
IT'S ALL WRITTEN HERE--PLAIN AS DAY! WE'RE FINALLY ENTERING THE AFTERWAR!!
ONLY A MATTER OF TIME BEFORE WE MALES ARE CALLED UP TO DO THE REAL FIGHTING!
THE DOCTRINE IS RIGHT, THEN.
ALWAYS WAS!
DO NOT GET ATTACHED TO YOUR FEMALES! IT HURTS THE CAUSE.
MALES ONLY
PUBLIC HOUSE
I DON'T MISS MY GIRLS!
MALES ONLY
ZZZZ
ZZZ
ZZ
ZZZZ
ZZZZZ

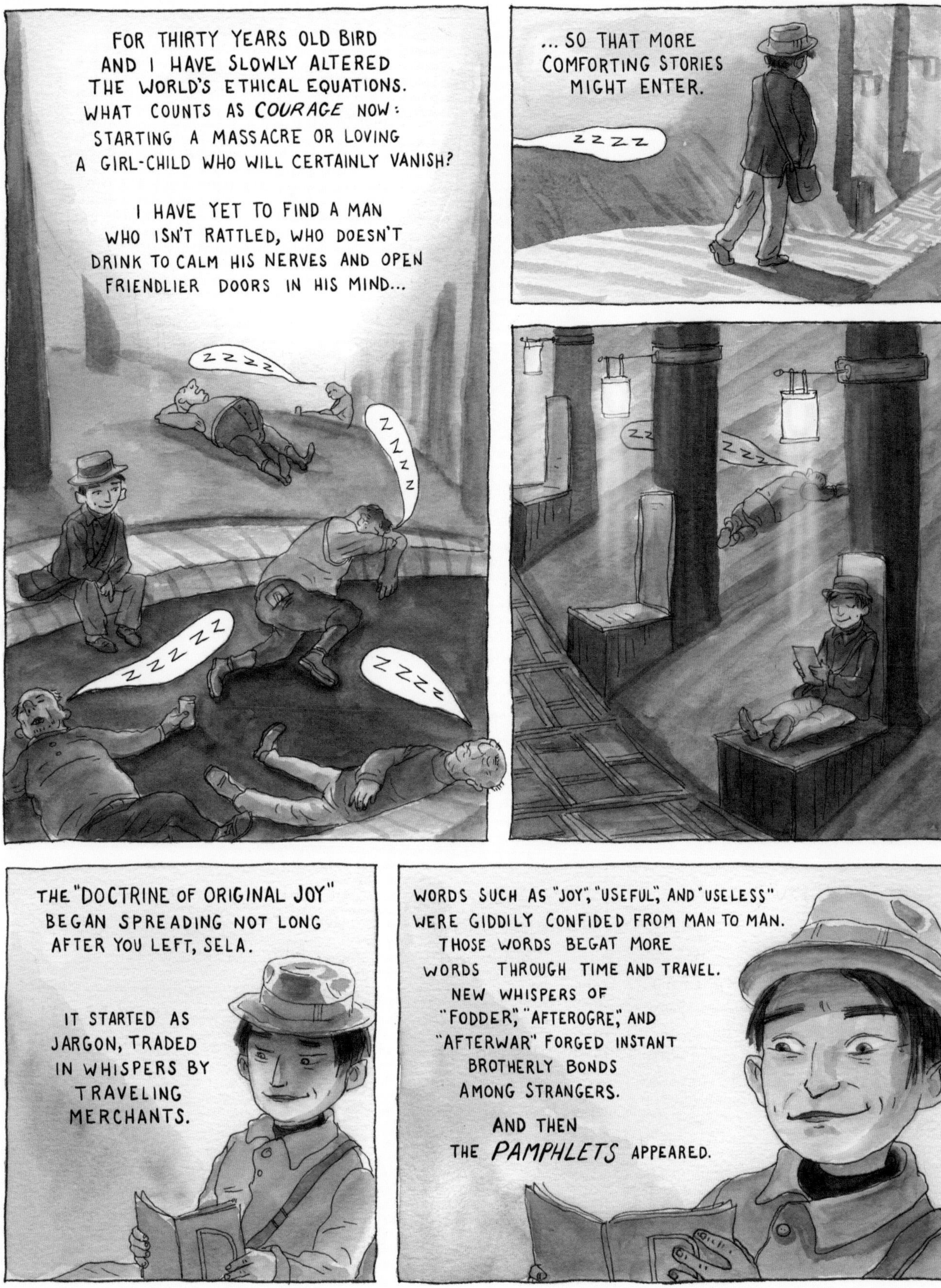
FOR THIRTY YEARS OLD BIRD AND I HAVE SLOWLY ALTERED THE WORLD'S ETHICAL EQUATIONS. WHAT COUNTS AS *COURAGE* NOW: STARTING A MASSACRE OR LOVING A GIRL-CHILD WHO WILL CERTAINLY VANISH?
I HAVE YET TO FIND A MAN WHO ISN'T RATTLED, WHO DOESN'T DRINK TO CALM HIS NERVES AND OPEN FRIENDLIER DOORS IN HIS MIND...
ZZZZ
ZZZZ
ZZZZZ
ZZZZ
...SO THAT MORE COMFORTING STORIES MIGHT ENTER.
ZZZZ
ZZ
ZZZ
THE "DOCTRINE OF ORIGINAL JOY" BEGAN SPREADING NOT LONG AFTER YOU LEFT, SELA.
IT STARTED AS JARGON, TRADED IN WHISPERS BY TRAVELING MERCHANTS.
WORDS SUCH AS "JOY", "USEFUL", AND "USELESS" WERE GIDDILY CONFIDED FROM MAN TO MAN. THOSE WORDS BEGAT MORE WORDS THROUGH TIME AND TRAVEL. NEW WHISPERS OF "FODDER", "AFTEROGRE", AND "AFTERWAR" FORGED INSTANT BROTHERLY BONDS AMONG STRANGERS.
AND THEN THE *PAMPHLETS* APPEARED.

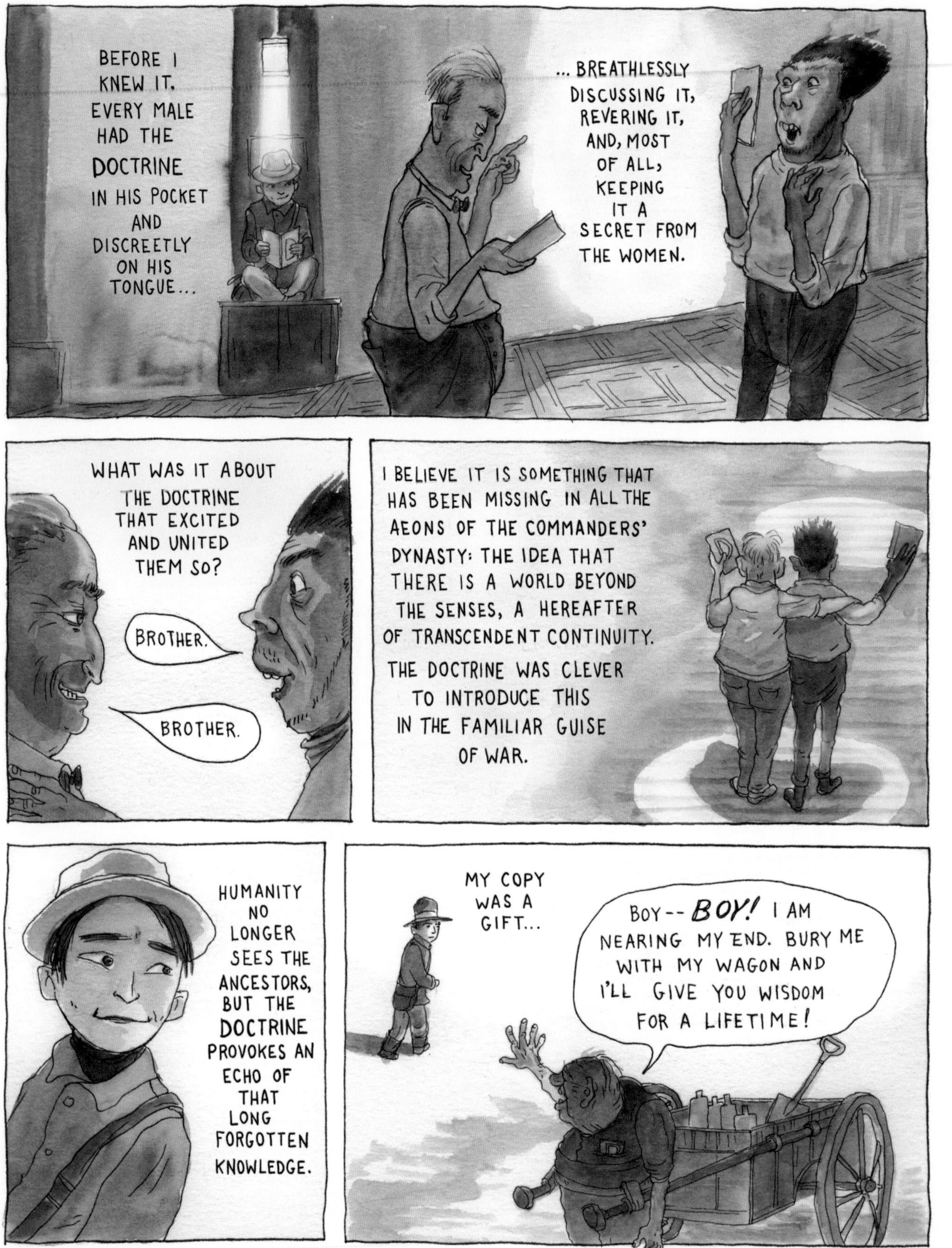
BEFORE I KNEW IT, EVERY MALE HAD THE DOCTRINE IN HIS POCKET AND DISCREETLY ON HIS TONGUE...
... BREATHLESSLY DISCUSSING IT, REVERING IT, AND, MOST OF ALL, KEEPING IT A SECRET FROM THE WOMEN.
WHAT WAS IT ABOUT THE DOCTRINE THAT EXCITED AND UNITED THEM SO?
BROTHER.
BROTHER.
I BELIEVE IT IS SOMETHING THAT HAS BEEN MISSING IN ALL THE AEONS OF THE COMMANDERS' DYNASTY: THE IDEA THAT THERE IS A WORLD BEYOND THE SENSES, A HEREAFTER OF TRANSCENDENT CONTINUITY.
THE DOCTRINE WAS CLEVER TO INTRODUCE THIS IN THE FAMILIAR GUISE OF WAR.
HUMANITY NO LONGER SEES THE ANCESTORS, BUT THE DOCTRINE PROVOKES AN ECHO OF THAT LONG FORGOTTEN KNOWLEDGE.
MY COPY WAS A GIFT...
BOY-- BOY! I AM NEARING MY END. BURY ME WITH MY WAGON AND I'LL GIVE YOU WISDOM FOR A LIFETIME!

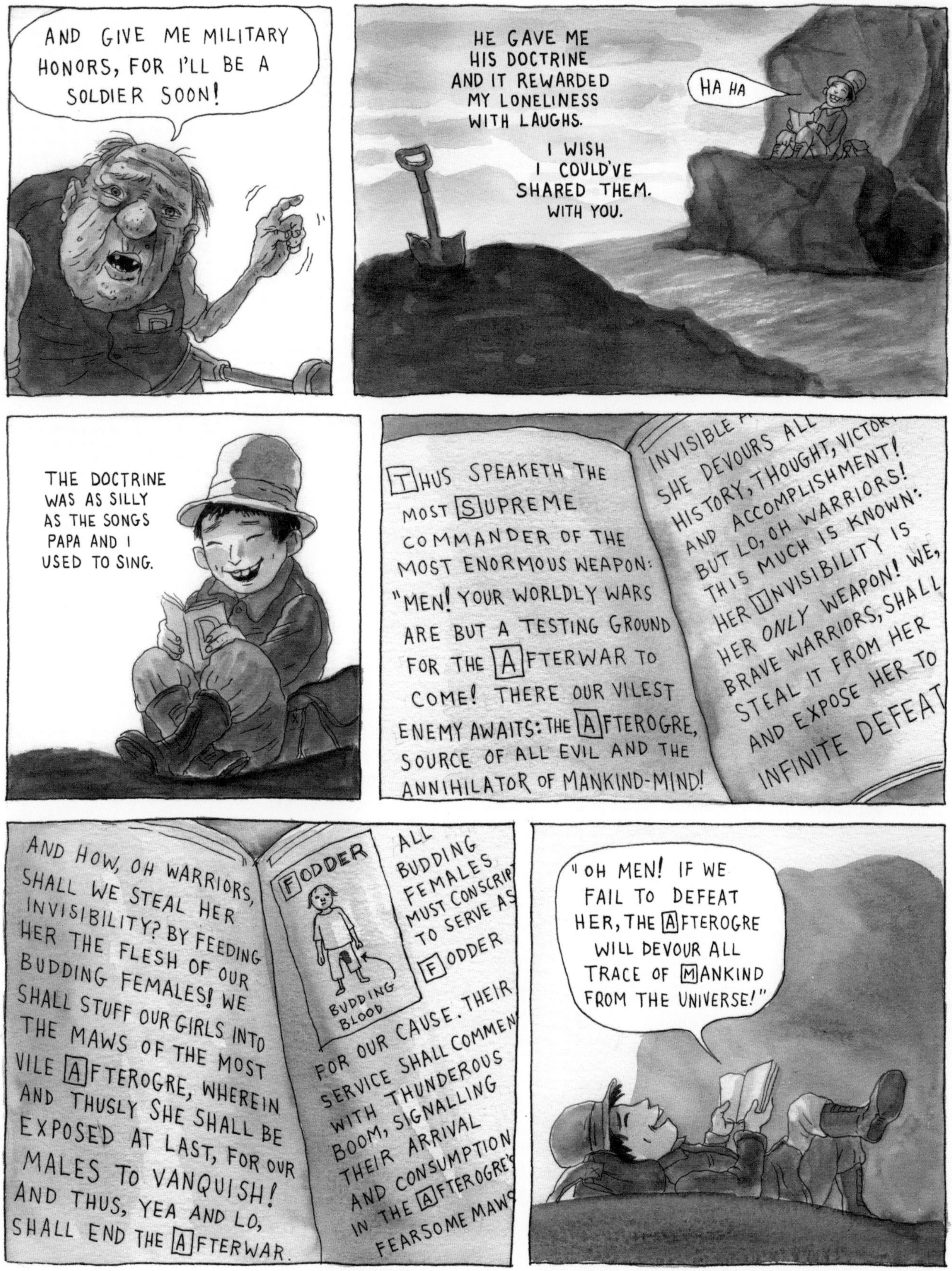
AND GIVE ME MILITARY HONORS, FOR I'LL BE A SOLDIER SOON!
HE GAVE ME HIS DOCTRINE AND IT REWARDED MY LONELINESS WITH LAUGHS.
HA HA
I WISH I COULD'VE SHARED THEM. WITH YOU.
THE DOCTRINE WAS AS SILLY AS THE SONGS PAPA AND I USED TO SING.
THUS SPEAKETH THE MOST SUPREME COMMANDER OF THE MOST ENORMOUS WEAPON: "MEN! YOUR WORLDLY WARS ARE BUT A TESTING GROUND FOR THE AFTERWAR TO COME! THERE OUR VILEST ENEMY AWAITS: THE AFTEROGRE, SOURCE OF ALL EVIL AND THE ANNIHILATOR OF MANKIND-MIND!
INVISIBLE
SHE DEVOURS ALL HISTORY, THOUGHT, VICTOR
AND ACCOMPLISHMENT! BUT LO, OH WARRIORS! THIS MUCH IS KNOWN: HER INVISIBILITY IS HER ONLY WEAPON! WE, BRAVE WARRIORS, SHALL STEAL IT FROM HER AND EXPOSE HER TO INFINITE DEFEAT
AND HOW, OH WARRIORS, SHALL WE STEAL HER INVISIBILITY? BY FEEDING HER THE FLESH OF OUR BUDDING FEMALES! WE SHALL STUFF OUR GIRLS INTO THE MAWS OF THE MOST VILE AFTEROGRE, WHEREIN AND THUSLY SHE SHALL BE EXPOSED AT LAST, FOR OUR MALES TO VANQUISH! AND THUS, YEA AND LO, SHALL END THE AFTERWAR.
FODDER
BUDDING BLOOD
ALL BUDDING FEMALES MUST CONSCRIP
TO SERVE AS FODDER
FOR OUR CAUSE. THEIR SERVICE SHALL COMMEN
WITH THUNDEROUS BOOM, SIGNALLING THEIR ARRIVAL AND CONSUMPTION IN THE AFTEROGRE'S FEARSOME MAWS
"OH MEN! IF WE FAIL TO DEFEAT HER, THE AFTEROGRE WILL DEVOUR ALL TRACE OF MANKIND FROM THE UNIVERSE!"

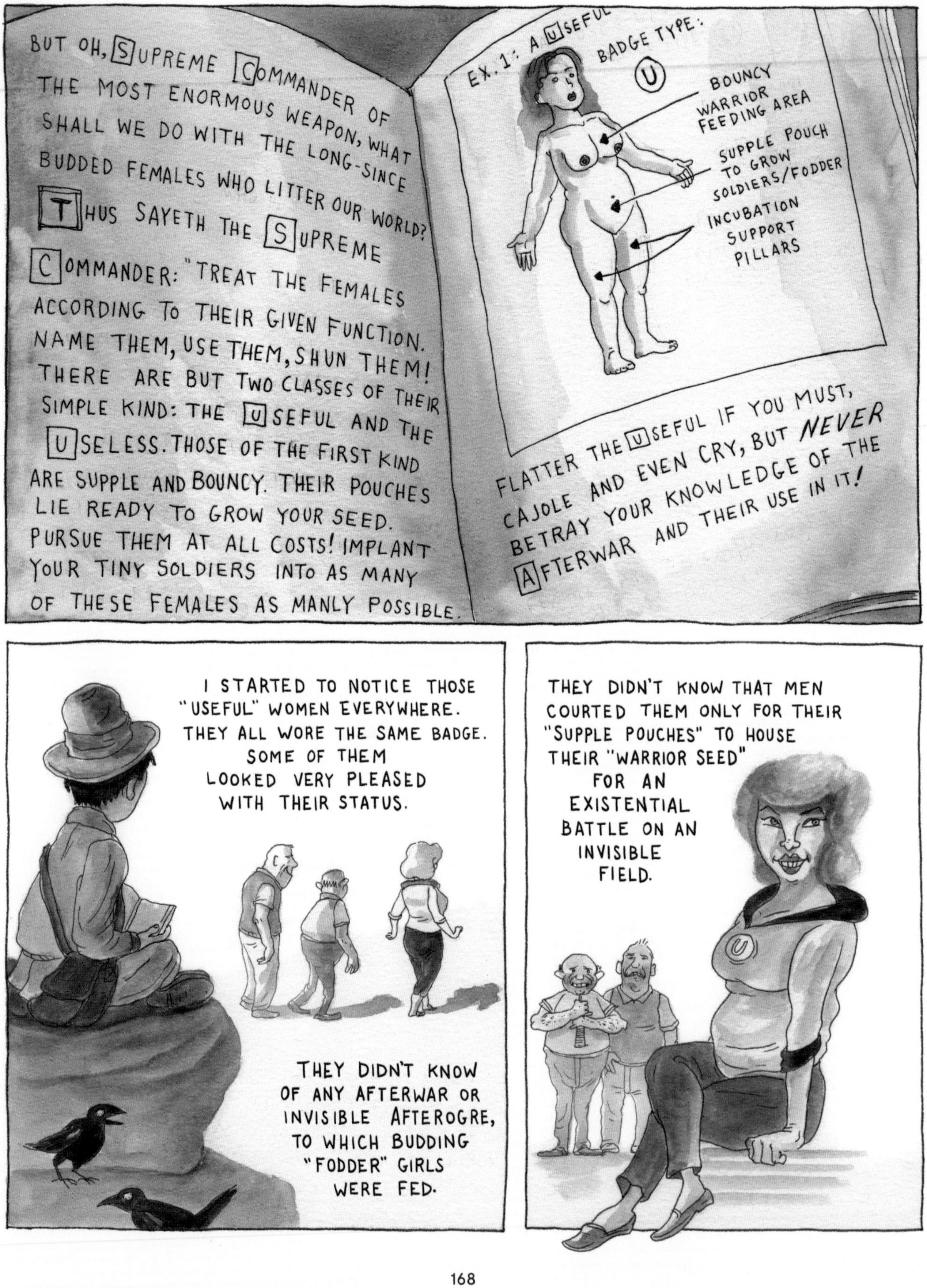
BUT OH, SUPREME COMMANDER OF THE MOST ENORMOUS WEAPON, WHAT SHALL WE DO WITH THE LONG-SINCE BUDDED FEMALES WHO LITTER OUR WORLD?
THUS SAYETH THE SUPREME COMMANDER: "TREAT THE FEMALES ACCORDING TO THEIR GIVEN FUNCTION. NAME THEM, USE THEM, SHUN THEM! THERE ARE BUT TWO CLASSES OF THEIR SIMPLE KIND: THE USEFUL AND THE USELESS. THOSE OF THE FIRST KIND ARE SUPPLE AND BOUNCY. THEIR POUCHES LIE READY TO GROW YOUR SEED. PURSUE THEM AT ALL COSTS! IMPLANT YOUR TINY SOLDIERS INTO AS MANY OF THESE FEMALES AS MANLY POSSIBLE.
EX. 1: A USEFUL
BADGE TYPE:
U
BOUNCY WARRIOR FEEDING AREA
SUPPLE POUCH TO GROW SOLDIERS/FODDER
INCUBATION SUPPORT PILLARS
FLATTER THE USEFUL IF YOU MUST, CAJOLE AND EVEN CRY, BUT NEVER BETRAY YOUR KNOWLEDGE OF THE AFTERWAR AND THEIR USE IN IT!
I STARTED TO NOTICE THOSE "USEFUL" WOMEN EVERYWHERE. THEY ALL WORE THE SAME BADGE. SOME OF THEM LOOKED VERY PLEASED WITH THEIR STATUS.
THEY DIDN'T KNOW OF ANY AFTERWAR OR INVISIBLE AFTEROGRE, TO WHICH BUDDING "FODDER" GIRLS WERE FED.
THEY DIDN'T KNOW THAT MEN COURTED THEM ONLY FOR THEIR "SUPPLE POUCHES" TO HOUSE THEIR "WARRIOR SEED" FOR AN EXISTENTIAL BATTLE ON AN INVISIBLE FIELD.
U

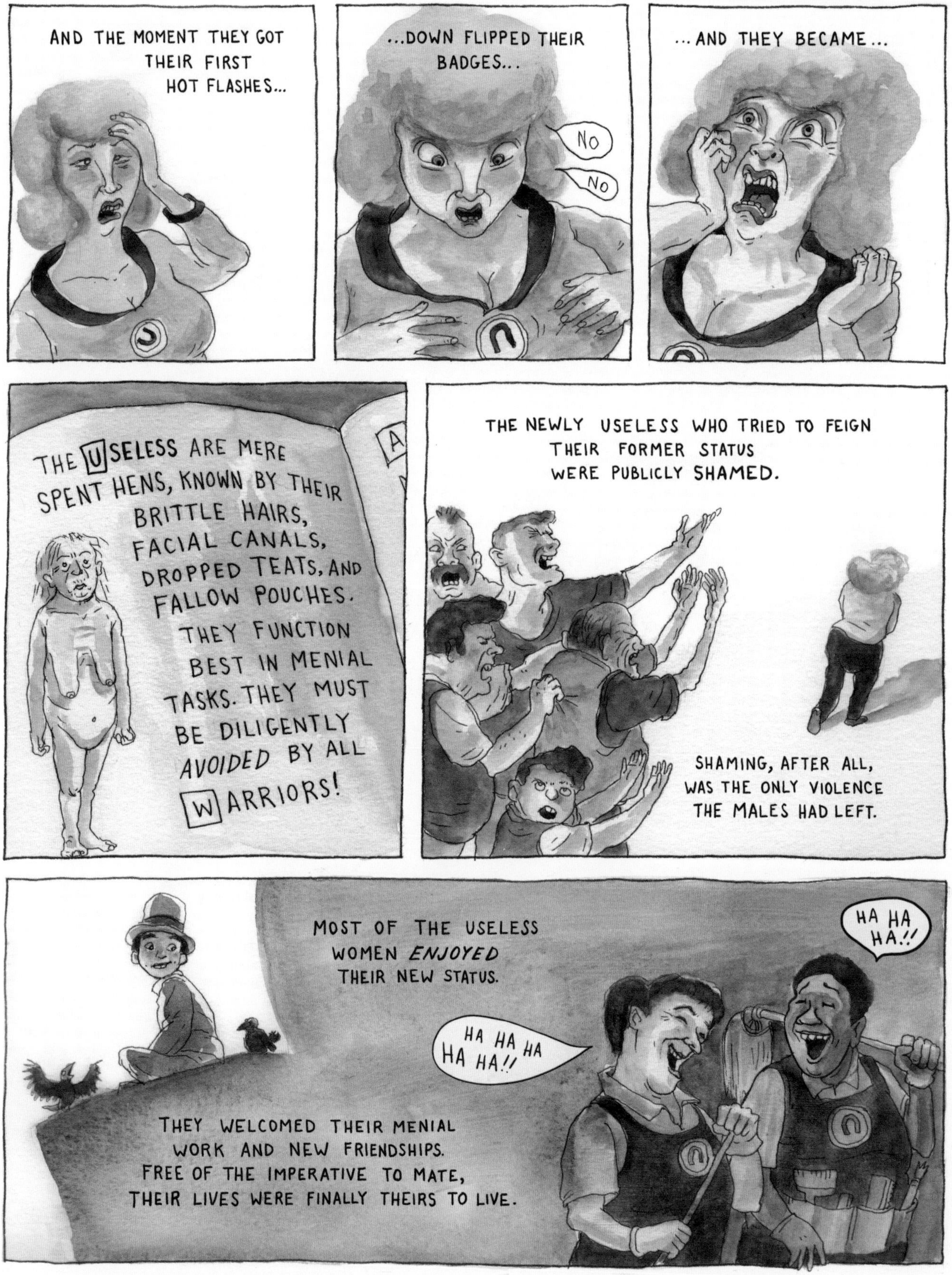
AND THE MOMENT THEY GOT THEIR FIRST HOT FLASHES...
...DOWN FLIPPED THEIR BADGES...
NO
NO
...AND THEY BECAME...
THE U SELESS ARE MERE SPENT HENS, KNOWN BY THEIR BRITTLE HAIRS, FACIAL CANALS, DROPPED TEATS, AND FALLOW POUCHES. THEY FUNCTION BEST IN MENIAL TASKS. THEY MUST BE DILIGENTLY AVOIDED BY ALL W ARRIORS!
A
THE NEWLY USELESS WHO TRIED TO FEIGN THEIR FORMER STATUS WERE PUBLICLY SHAMED.
SHAMING, AFTER ALL, WAS THE ONLY VIOLENCE THE MALES HAD LEFT.
MOST OF THE USELESS WOMEN ENJOYED THEIR NEW STATUS.
HA HA HA!!
HA HA HA HA HA!!
THEY WELCOMED THEIR MENIAL WORK AND NEW FRIENDSHIPS. FREE OF THE IMPERATIVE TO MATE, THEIR LIVES WERE FINALLY THEIRS TO LIVE.

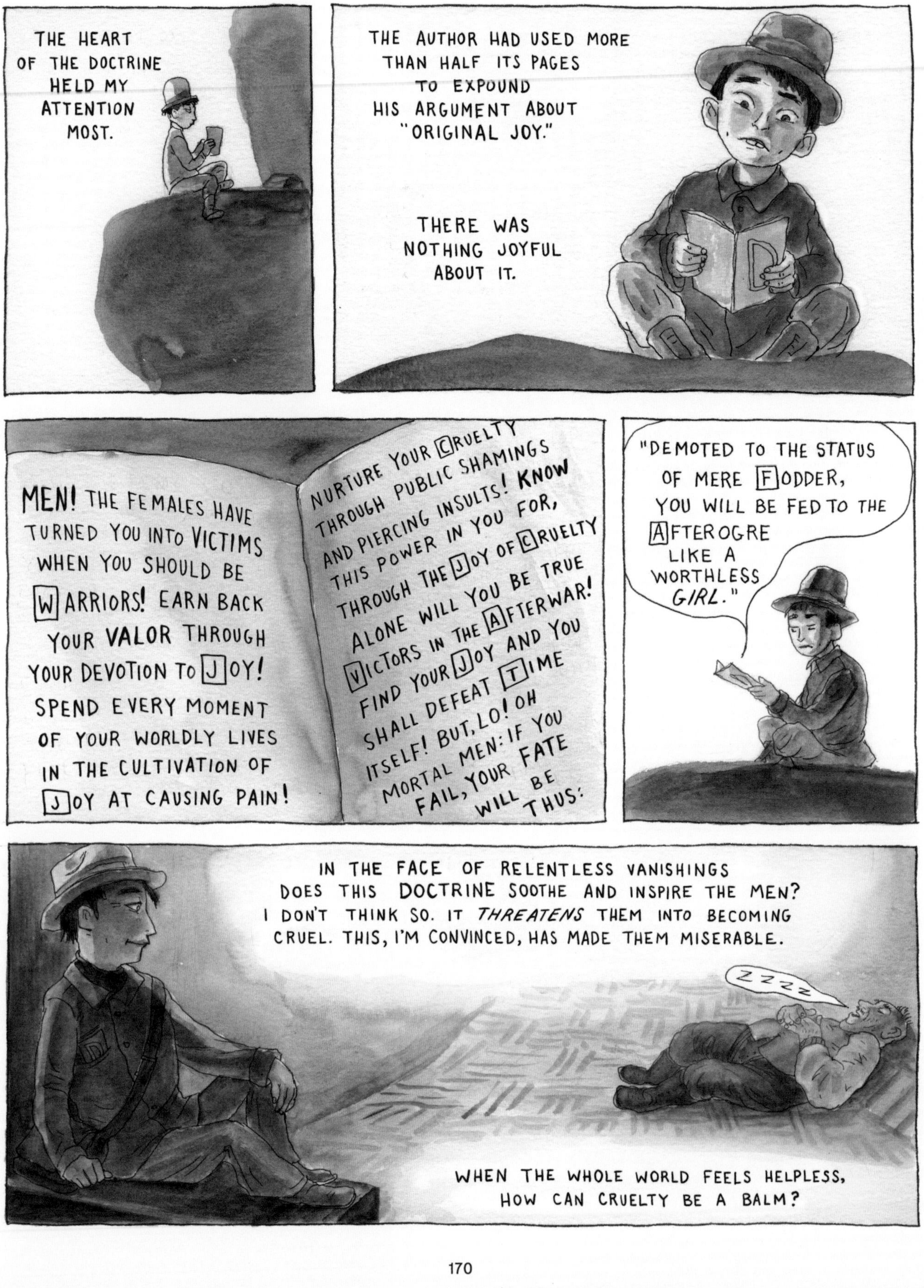
THE HEART OF THE DOCTRINE HELD MY ATTENTION MOST.
THE AUTHOR HAD USED MORE THAN HALF ITS PAGES TO EXPOUND HIS ARGUMENT ABOUT "ORIGINAL JOY."
THERE WAS NOTHING JOYFUL ABOUT IT.
MEN! THE FEMALES HAVE TURNED YOU INTO VICTIMS WHEN YOU SHOULD BE WARRIORS! EARN BACK YOUR VALOR THROUGH YOUR DEVOTION TO JOY! SPEND EVERY MOMENT OF YOUR WORLDLY LIVES IN THE CULTIVATION OF JOY AT CAUSING PAIN!
NURTURE YOUR CRUELTY THROUGH PUBLIC SHAMINGS AND PIERCING INSULTS! KNOW THIS POWER IN YOU FOR, THROUGH THE JOY OF CRUELTY ALONE WILL YOU BE TRUE VICTORS IN THE AFTERWAR! FIND YOUR JOY AND YOU SHALL DEFEAT TIME ITSELF! BUT, LO! OH MORTAL MEN: IF YOU FAIL, YOUR FATE WILL BE THUS:
"DEMOTED TO THE STATUS OF MERE FODDER, YOU WILL BE FED TO THE AFTEROGRE LIKE A WORTHLESS *GIRL*."
IN THE FACE OF RELENTLESS VANISHINGS DOES THIS DOCTRINE SOOTHE AND INSPIRE THE MEN? I DON'T THINK SO. IT *THREATENS* THEM INTO BECOMING CRUEL. THIS, I'M CONVINCED, HAS MADE THEM MISERABLE.
ZZZZ
WHEN THE WHOLE WORLD FEELS HELPLESS, HOW CAN CRUELTY BE A BALM?

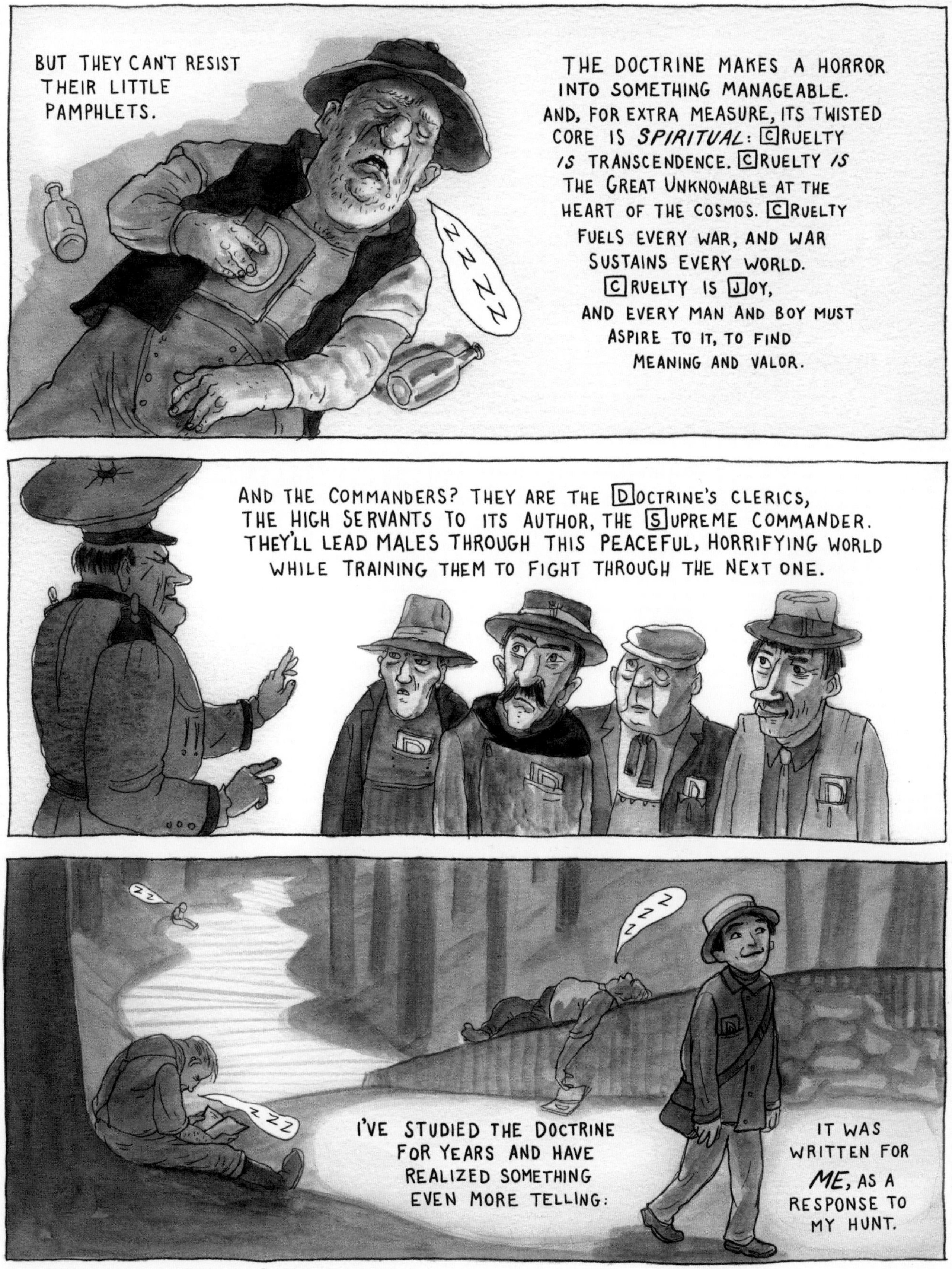
BUT THEY CAN'T RESIST THEIR LITTLE PAMPHLETS.
THE DOCTRINE MAKES A HORROR INTO SOMETHING MANAGEABLE. AND, FOR EXTRA MEASURE, ITS TWISTED CORE IS *SPIRITUAL*: CRUELTY *IS* TRANSCENDENCE. CRUELTY *IS* THE GREAT UNKNOWABLE AT THE HEART OF THE COSMOS. CRUELTY FUELS EVERY WAR, AND WAR SUSTAINS EVERY WORLD. CRUELTY IS JOY, AND EVERY MAN AND BOY MUST ASPIRE TO IT, TO FIND MEANING AND VALOR.
ZZZZ
AND THE COMMANDERS? THEY ARE THE DOCTRINE'S CLERICS, THE HIGH SERVANTS TO ITS AUTHOR, THE SUPREME COMMANDER. THEY'LL LEAD MALES THROUGH THIS PEACEFUL, HORRIFYING WORLD WHILE TRAINING THEM TO FIGHT THROUGH THE NEXT ONE.
ZZ
ZZZ
ZZZ
I'VE STUDIED THE DOCTRINE FOR YEARS AND HAVE REALIZED SOMETHING EVEN MORE TELLING:
IT WAS WRITTEN FOR *ME*, AS A RESPONSE TO MY HUNT.

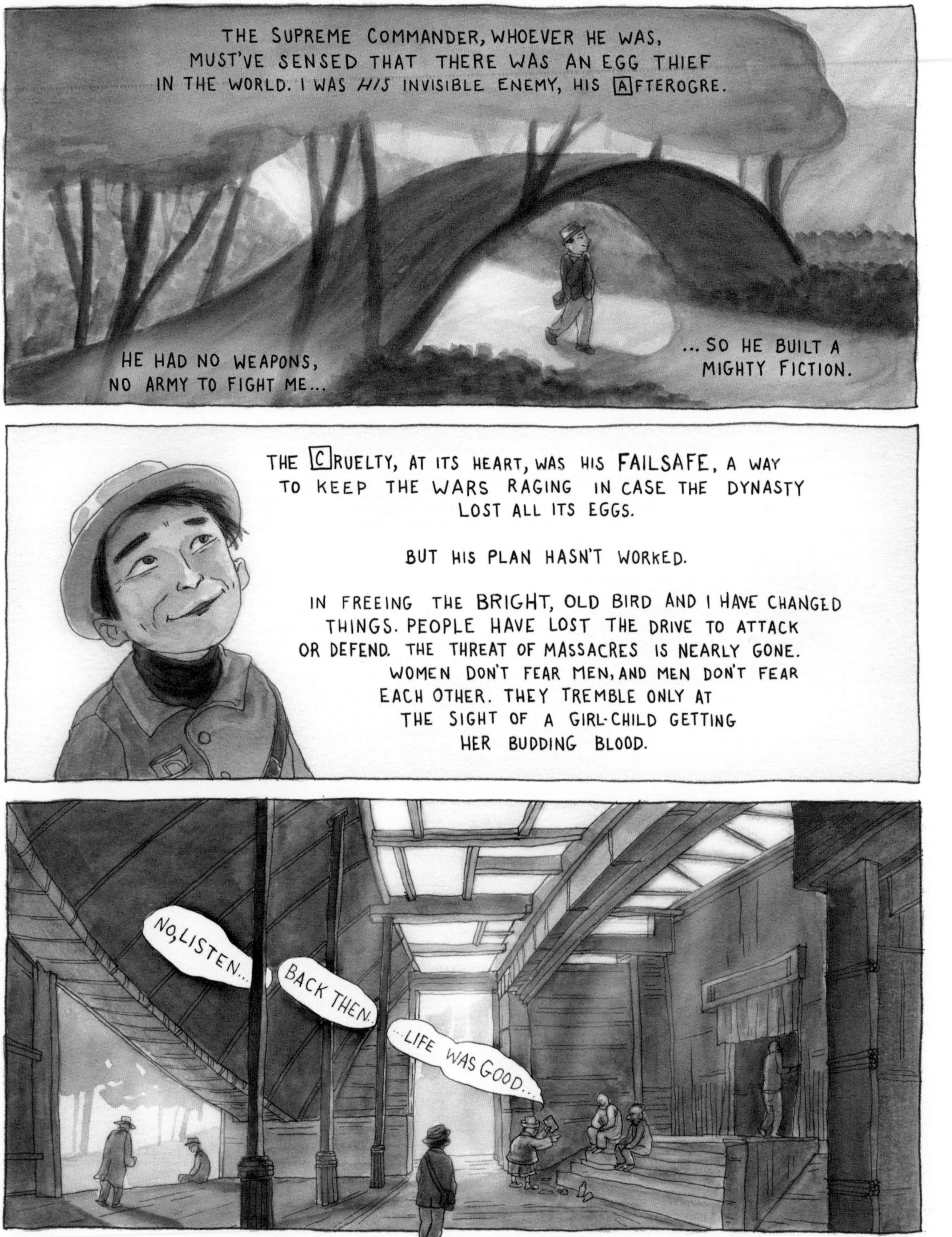
THE SUPREME COMMANDER, WHOEVER HE WAS, MUST'VE SENSED THAT THERE WAS AN EGG THIEF IN THE WORLD. I WAS *HIS* INVISIBLE ENEMY, HIS AFTEROGRE.
HE HAD NO WEAPONS, NO ARMY TO FIGHT ME...
...SO HE BUILT A MIGHTY FICTION.
THE CRUELTY, AT ITS HEART, WAS HIS FAILSAFE, A WAY TO KEEP THE WARS RAGING IN CASE THE DYNASTY LOST ALL ITS EGGS.
BUT HIS PLAN HASN'T WORKED.
IN FREEING THE BRIGHT, OLD BIRD AND I HAVE CHANGED THINGS. PEOPLE HAVE LOST THE DRIVE TO ATTACK OR DEFEND. THE THREAT OF MASSACRES IS NEARLY GONE. WOMEN DON'T FEAR MEN, AND MEN DON'T FEAR EACH OTHER. THEY TREMBLE ONLY AT THE SIGHT OF A GIRL-CHILD GETTING HER BUDDING BLOOD.
NO, LISTEN...
BACK THEN...
...LIFE WAS GOOD...

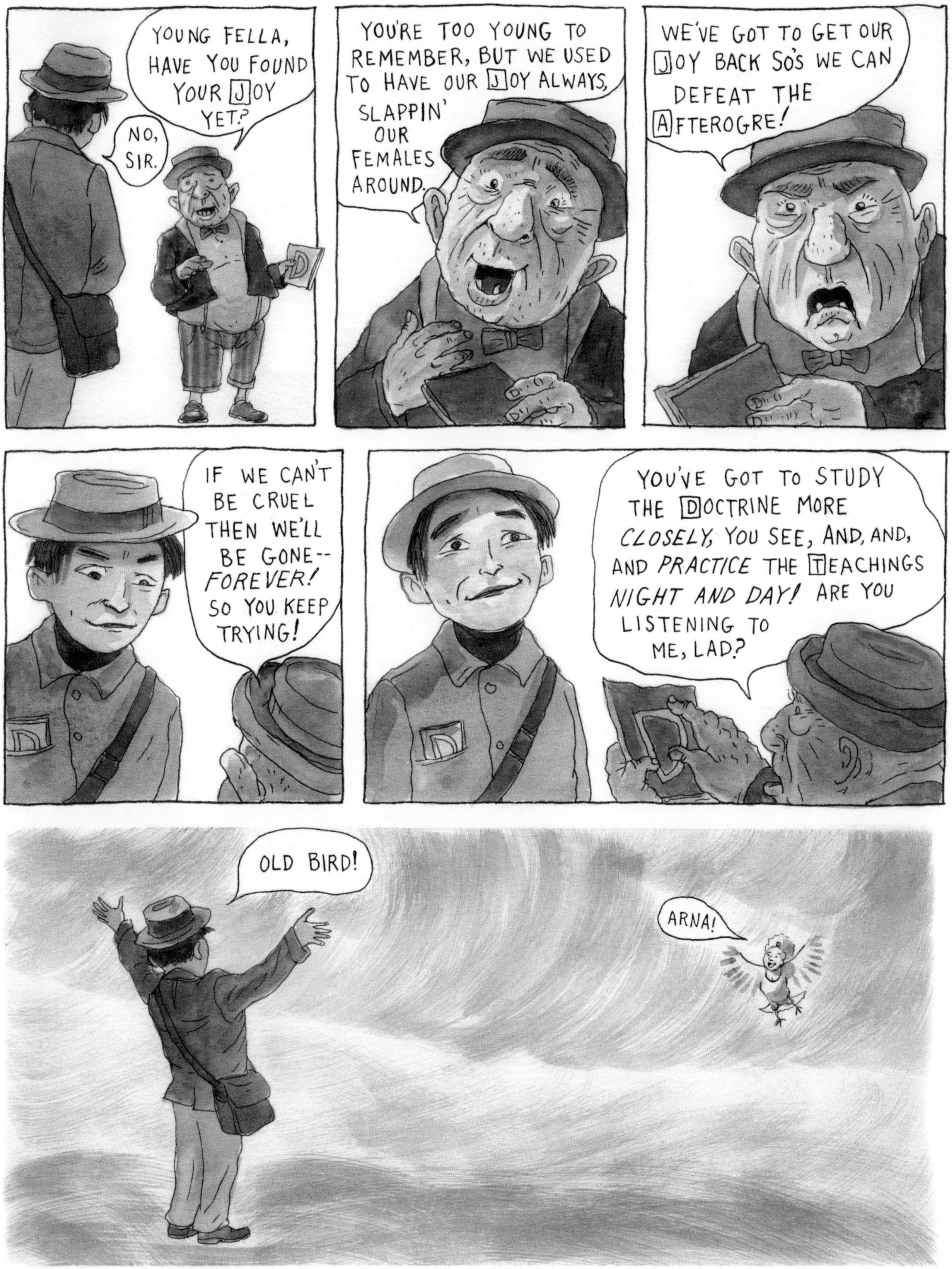
YOUNG FELLA, HAVE YOU FOUND YOUR JOY YET?
NO, SIR.
YOU'RE TOO YOUNG TO REMEMBER, BUT WE USED TO HAVE OUR JOY ALWAYS, SLAPPIN' OUR FEMALES AROUND.
WE'VE GOT TO GET OUR JOY BACK SO'S WE CAN DEFEAT THE AFTEROGRE!
IF WE CAN'T BE CRUEL THEN WE'LL BE GONE-- *FOREVER!* SO YOU KEEP TRYING!
YOU'VE GOT TO STUDY THE DOCTRINE MORE *CLOSELY,* YOU SEE, AND, AND, AND *PRACTICE* THE TEACHINGS *NIGHT AND DAY!* ARE YOU LISTENING TO ME, LAD?
OLD BIRD!
ARNA!

ALL MY BOYS AGREE: WE HAVE A MERE *THREE* COMMANDERS LEFT IN THE LIVING WORLD.

TWO ARE BROTHERS-- ESTRANGED, OF COURSE. THE ELDER, "LIPTWITCH," HAS A PENCHANT FOR ROTTING THINGS AND BAD POETRY. CAN YOU SEE HIM?

YES.

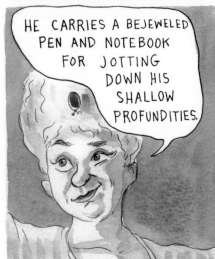

HE CARRIES A BEJEWELED PEN AND NOTEBOOK FOR JOTTING DOWN HIS SHALLOW PROFUNDITIES.

HE HIDES HIS EGG BENEATH SOME LEAVES NEAR A LICHEN COVERED ROCK.

IT OVERLOOKS A VALLEY OF CABBAGE ROWS. CAN YOU SEE IT?

YES!

THE YOUNGER BROTHER, "HOLIER-THAN-THOU," IS A PINCHED AND PREACHY PRIG WHO CRAVES AN AUDIENCE. YOU'LL FIND HIM NEAR ANY GATHERING OF FAWNING CHAPS.

THEY'RE RABID RIVALS!-- PROWLING THE SAME HAUNTS, KEEPING TABS ON EACH OTHER'S MASSACRE TALLIES AND SPOILS...

AND THE LAST COMMANDER?

GOOD QUESTION! WITH ANY LUCK THE OTHER TWO WILL TELL US SOMETHING. REGARDLESS, KEEP UP THE HUNT.

AND WHEN ALL THE WARS ARE GONE, AND MY FOOLISH DYNASTY IS GATHERED AROUND ME...

YOU'LL TAKE DOWN THE MISTS...

AND... WE'LL ALL SEE EACH OTHER AGAIN.

AND PERHAPS YOUR SELA WILL RETURN TO YOU.

AND... PERHAPS NOT, BUT I'LL KEEP FINDING *YOU*, WON'T I?

YES, ARNA. OUR BOND IS STRONG.

OLD BIRD, AM I OF YOUR LINEAGE?

I BORE NO YOUNG, BUT YOU AND I DO SHARE A STRIKING SYMPATHY WITH THE BRIGHT...

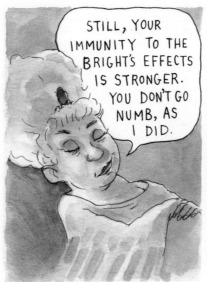

STILL, YOUR IMMUNITY TO THE BRIGHT'S EFFECTS IS STRONGER. YOU DON'T GO NUMB, AS I DID.

BUT ARNA -- IN THIS REALM THERE ARE NO BEFORES OR AFTERS, SO YOU COULD VERY WELL BE *MY* ANCESTOR!

HA HA HA HA HA HA HA HA HA

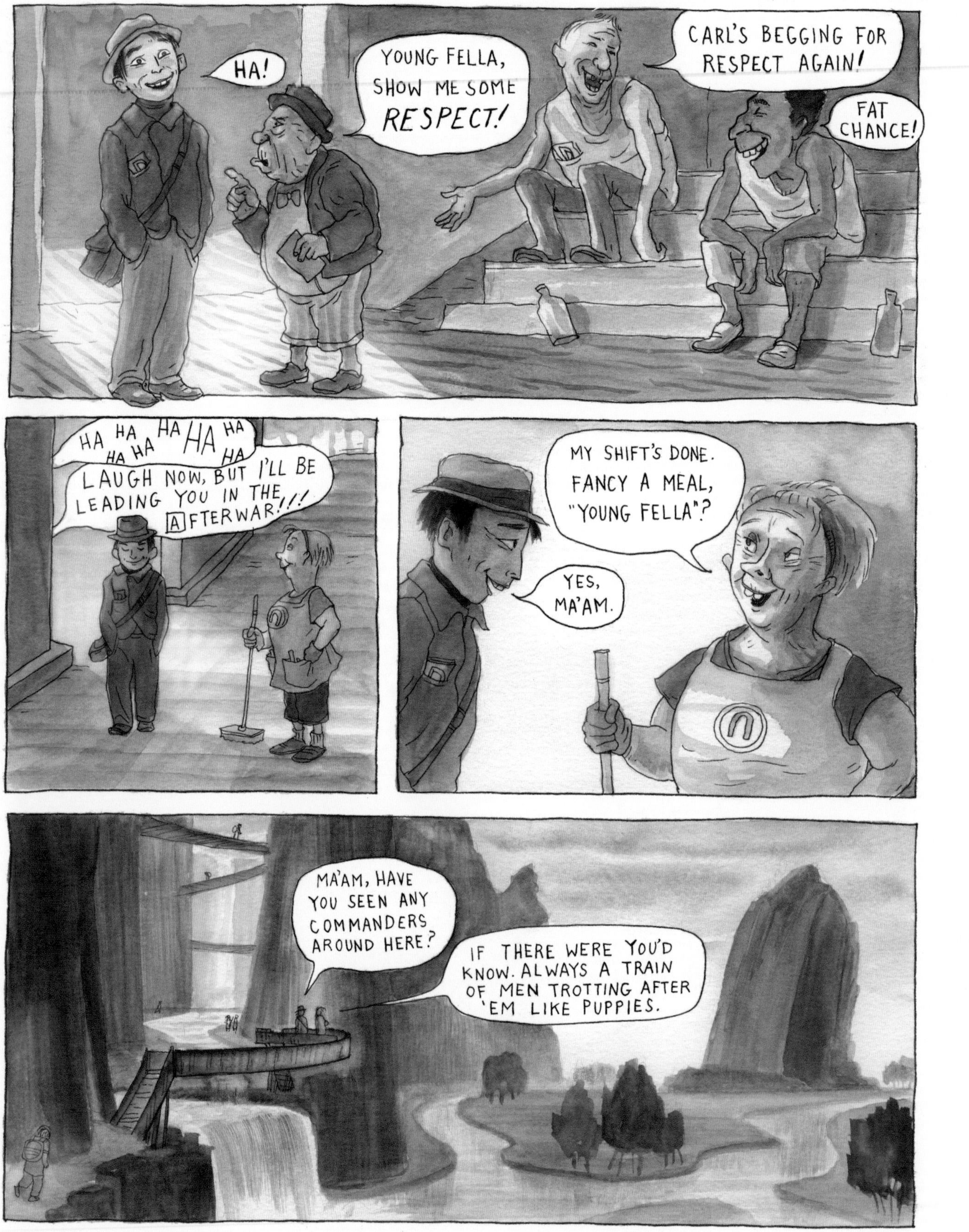
HA!
YOUNG FELLA, SHOW ME SOME RESPECT!
CARL'S BEGGING FOR RESPECT AGAIN!
FAT CHANCE!
HA HA HA HA HA HA HA HA HA
LAUGH NOW, BUT I'LL BE LEADING YOU IN THE AFTERWAR!!!
MY SHIFT'S DONE. FANCY A MEAL, "YOUNG FELLA"?
YES, MA'AM.
MA'AM, HAVE YOU SEEN ANY COMMANDERS AROUND HERE?
IF THERE WERE YOU'D KNOW. ALWAYS A TRAIN OF MEN TROTTING AFTER 'EM LIKE PUPPIES.

SO WHEN DID YOU START PASSING FOR MALE?

A LONG TIME AGO.

WISH I'D MADE THAT DECISION. AH WELL, WHAT'S DONE IS DONE.

THE SANITATION WORK KEEPS ME BUSY...

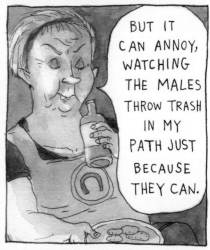

BUT IT CAN ANNOY, WATCHING THE MALES THROW TRASH IN MY PATH JUST BECAUSE THEY CAN.

THEY SEE THIS "USELESS" BADGE ON ME AND GET TO MISBEHAVING.

I ONCE ENJOYED THEIR ATTENTIONS 'TILL I REALIZED: IT WAS ALL JUST SIMPLE *DREAD.* THEY'RE TERRIFIED OF US, YOU KNOW. WE ARE THEIR ONLY WAY OF BRINGING *LIFE* BACK IN. THEY CAN'T TAKE US FOR GRANTED ANYMORE.

YOU HAVE CHILDREN?

HAD TWO. GIRLS. BOTH VANISHED, OF COURSE.

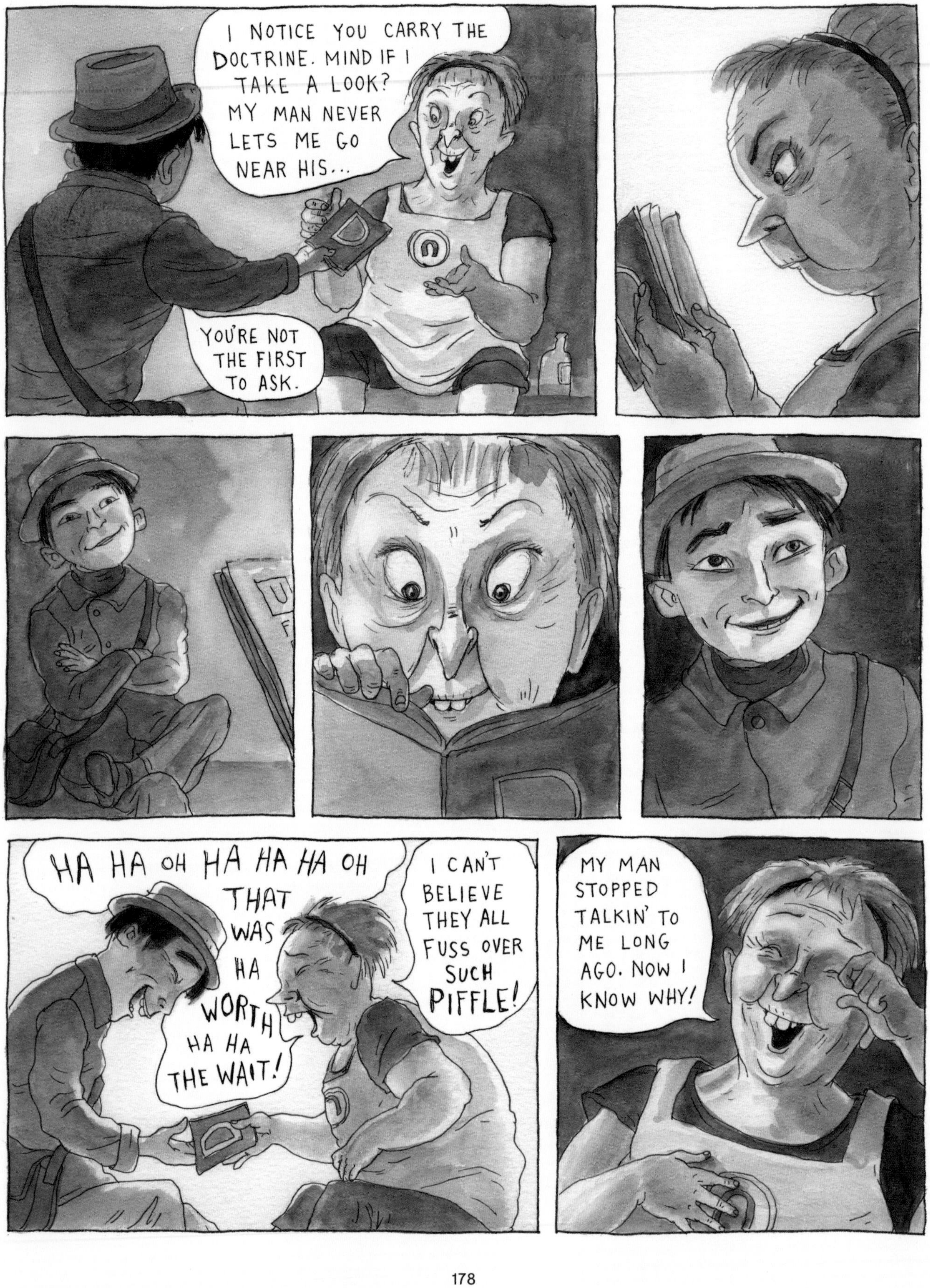
I NOTICE YOU CARRY THE DOCTRINE. MIND IF I TAKE A LOOK? MY MAN NEVER LETS ME GO NEAR HIS...
YOU'RE NOT THE FIRST TO ASK.
HA HA OH HA HA HA OH THAT WAS HA WORTH HA HA THE WAIT!
I CAN'T BELIEVE THEY ALL FUSS OVER SUCH PIFFLE!
MY MAN STOPPED TALKIN' TO ME LONG AGO. NOW I KNOW WHY!

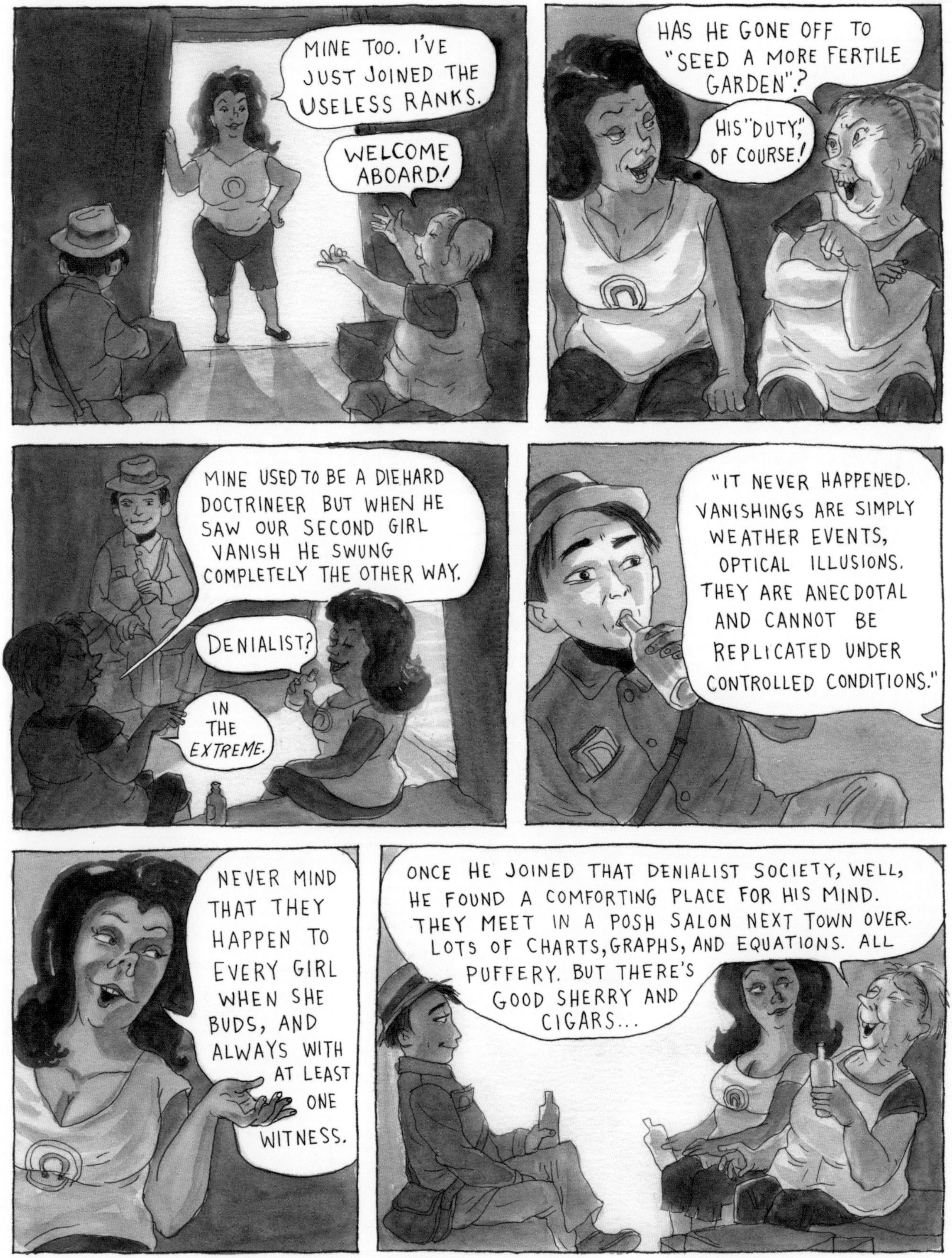
MINE TOO. I'VE JUST JOINED THE USELESS RANKS.
WELCOME ABOARD!
HAS HE GONE OFF TO "SEED A MORE FERTILE GARDEN"?
HIS "DUTY," OF COURSE!
MINE USED TO BE A DIEHARD DOCTRINEER BUT WHEN HE SAW OUR SECOND GIRL VANISH HE SWUNG COMPLETELY THE OTHER WAY.
DENIALIST?
IN THE *EXTREME.*
"IT NEVER HAPPENED. VANISHINGS ARE SIMPLY WEATHER EVENTS, OPTICAL ILLUSIONS. THEY ARE ANECDOTAL AND CANNOT BE REPLICATED UNDER CONTROLLED CONDITIONS."
NEVER MIND THAT THEY HAPPEN TO EVERY GIRL WHEN SHE BUDS, AND ALWAYS WITH AT LEAST ONE WITNESS.
ONCE HE JOINED THAT DENIALIST SOCIETY, WELL, HE FOUND A COMFORTING PLACE FOR HIS MIND. THEY MEET IN A POSH SALON NEXT TOWN OVER. LOTS OF CHARTS, GRAPHS, AND EQUATIONS. ALL PUFFERY. BUT THERE'S GOOD SHERRY AND CIGARS...

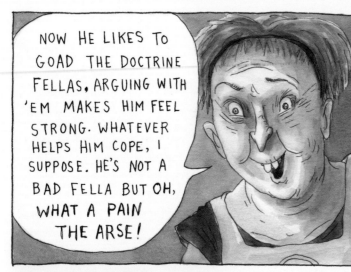
NOW HE LIKES TO GOAD THE DOCTRINE FELLAS, ARGUING WITH 'EM MAKES HIM FEEL STRONG. WHATEVER HELPS HIM COPE, I SUPPOSE. HE'S NOT A BAD FELLA BUT OH, WHAT A PAIN THE ARSE!

SWEEPIN' UP SPIT IS SOOTHING COMPARED TO HIS PRATTLE! STILL, I WISH HE WOULDN'T SHUT ME OUT...

DO YOU MISS YOUR BED, NOW THAT HE'S BANISHED YOU FROM IT?

NO. IT HAD BECOME TOO SAD A PLACE...

SOMETIMES I THINK HE COULD SMELL HOW LONELY I WAS. I COULD CERTAINLY SMELL IT ON HIM.

HE WORSHIPPED ME, BUT I THINK HE HATED ME JUST AS WELL.

HE WAS AFRAID OF EVERYTHING; HOLDING ME, CRYING WITH ME, AFRAID OF KILLING THE FUTURE HE HOPED HE WAS PUTTING INSIDE ME.

WE TRIED AND TRIED, BUT I GAVE HIM NO FUTURES. AND NOW HE'S THE "VICTIM."

VICTIMHOOD SUITS HIM.

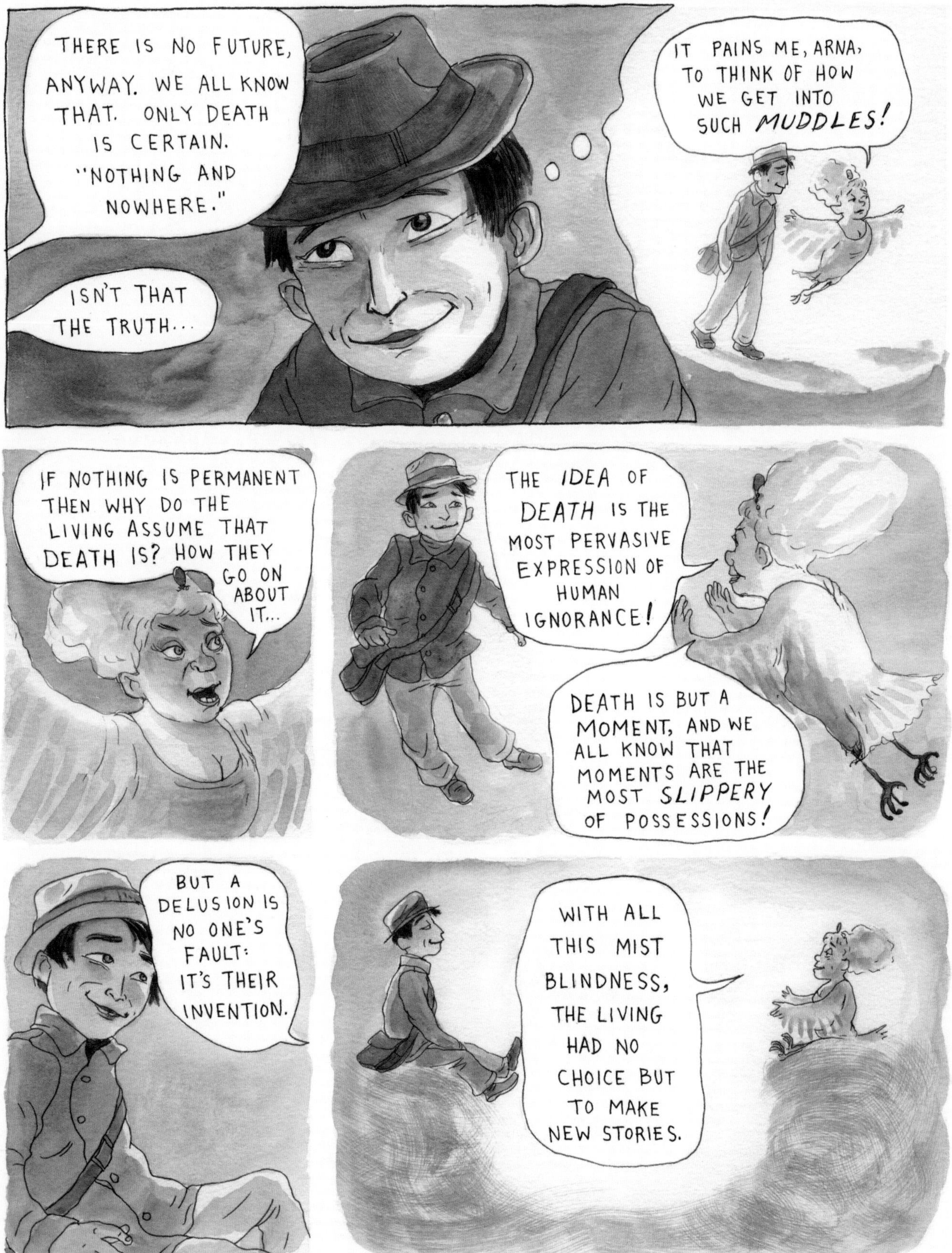
THERE IS NO FUTURE, ANYWAY. WE ALL KNOW THAT. ONLY DEATH IS CERTAIN. "NOTHING AND NOWHERE."
ISN'T THAT THE TRUTH...
IT PAINS ME, ARNA, TO THINK OF HOW WE GET INTO SUCH MUDDLES!
IF NOTHING IS PERMANENT THEN WHY DO THE LIVING ASSUME THAT DEATH IS? HOW THEY GO ON ABOUT IT...
THE IDEA OF DEATH IS THE MOST PERVASIVE EXPRESSION OF HUMAN IGNORANCE!
DEATH IS BUT A MOMENT, AND WE ALL KNOW THAT MOMENTS ARE THE MOST SLIPPERY OF POSSESSIONS!
BUT A DELUSION IS NO ONE'S FAULT: IT'S THEIR INVENTION.
WITH ALL THIS MIST BLINDNESS, THE LIVING HAD NO CHOICE BUT TO MAKE NEW STORIES.

OH, NOW I'VE GONE AND RUINED ANOTHER PARTY!

NOT AT ALL...

YOU'VE LOST A LOVE, HAVEN'T YOU?

YES.

I'VE SEEN THAT LOOK BEFORE: YOU FELL IN LOVE EARLY, THEN SHE WAS TAKEN FROM YOU.

YOU'RE STILL LOOKING FOR HER, WANDERING...

IF YOU EVER DECIDE TO SETTLE, WE'LL BE HERE.

THANK YOU.

SOMETIMES, IN MY HEART OF HEARTS, I'M GLAD THAT MY GIRLS GOT TO LEAVE.

EVEN WITHOUT THE WARS THEY WOULD'VE BEEN HOUNDED. THAT'S JUST HOW THINGS HAVE ALWAYS BEEN. NO REAL PEACE.

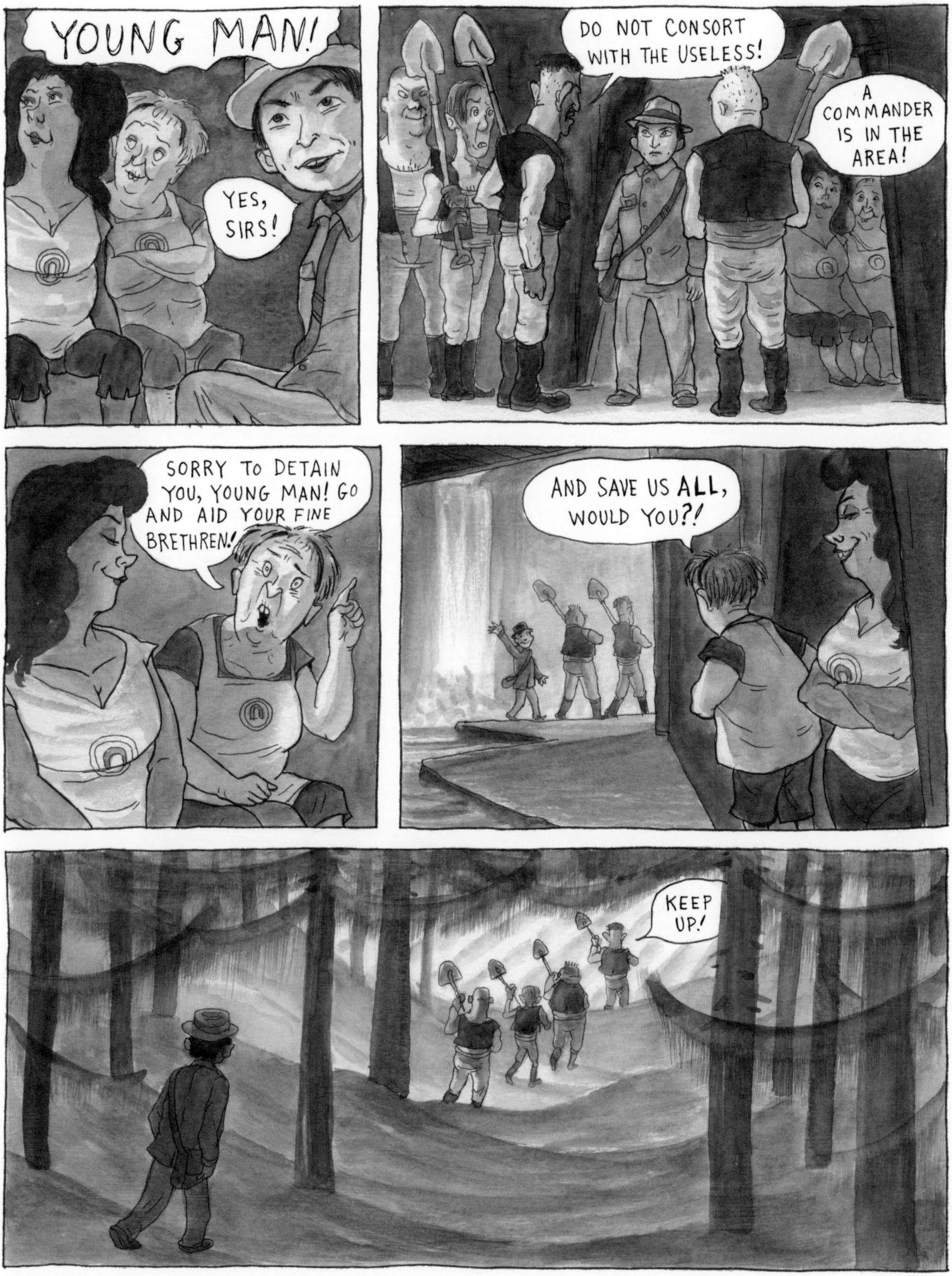
YOUNG MAN!
YES, SIRS!
DO NOT CONSORT WITH THE USELESS!
A COMMANDER IS IN THE AREA!
SORRY TO DETAIN YOU, YOUNG MAN! GO AND AID YOUR FINE BRETHREN!
AND SAVE US ALL, WOULD YOU?!
KEEP UP!

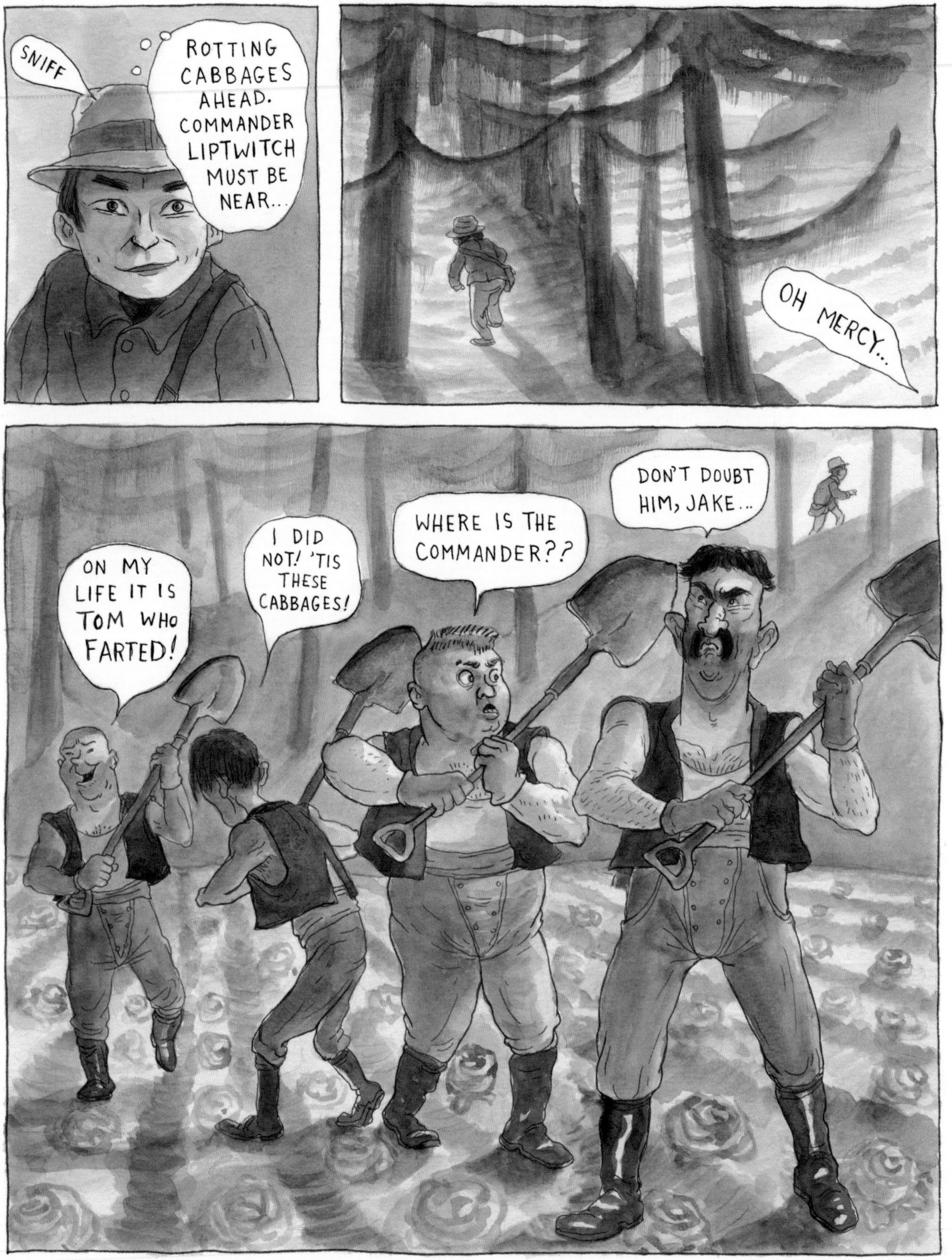
SNIFF
ROTTING CABBAGES AHEAD. COMMANDER LIPTWITCH MUST BE NEAR...
OH MERCY...
ON MY LIFE IT IS TOM WHO FARTED!
I DID NOT! 'TIS THESE CABBAGES!
WHERE IS THE COMMANDER??
DON'T DOUBT HIM, JAKE...

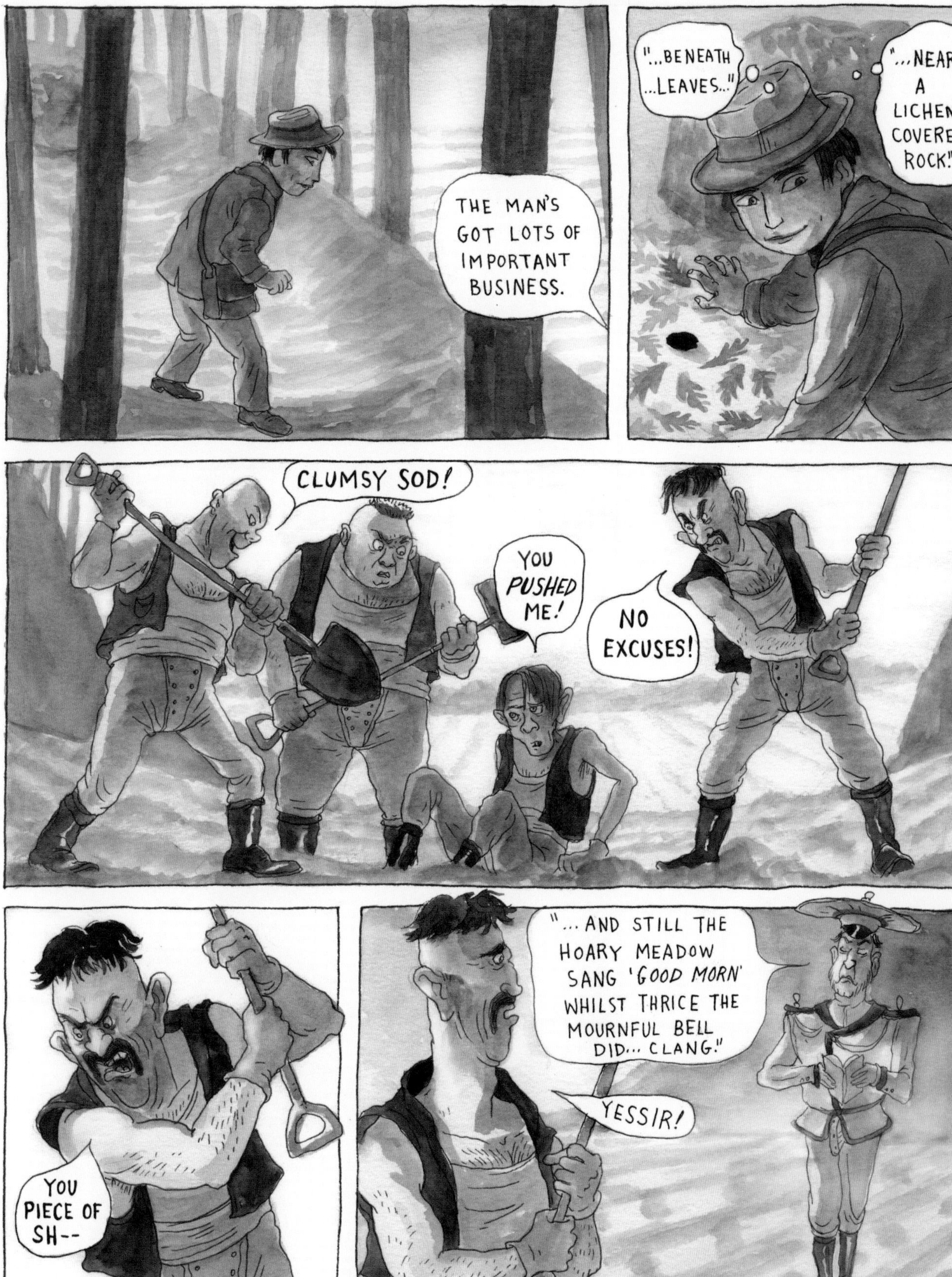
THE MAN'S GOT LOTS OF IMPORTANT BUSINESS.
"...BENEATH ...LEAVES..."
"...NEAR A LICHEN COVERED ROCK!"
CLUMSY SOD!
YOU *PUSHED* ME!
NO EXCUSES!
YOU PIECE OF SH--
"... AND STILL THE HOARY MEADOW SANG '*GOOD MORN*' WHILST THRICE THE MOURNFUL BELL DID... CLANG!"
YESSIR!

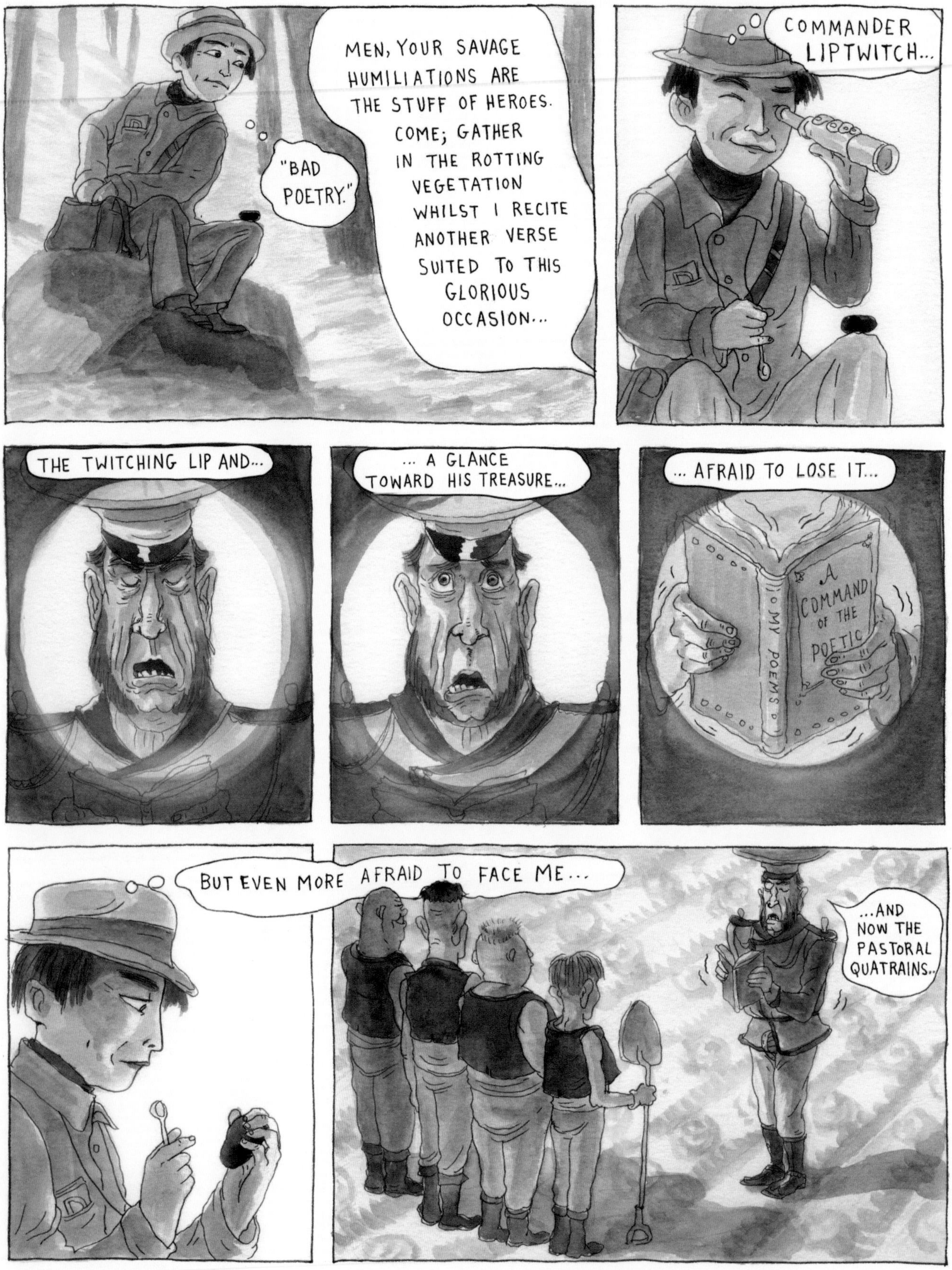
"BAD POETRY."
MEN, YOUR SAVAGE HUMILIATIONS ARE THE STUFF OF HEROES. COME; GATHER IN THE ROTTING VEGETATION WHILST I RECITE ANOTHER VERSE SUITED TO THIS GLORIOUS OCCASION...
COMMANDER LIPTWITCH...
THE TWITCHING LIP AND...
... A GLANCE TOWARD HIS TREASURE...
... AFRAID TO LOSE IT...
A COMMAND OF THE POETIC
MY POEMS
BUT EVEN MORE AFRAID TO FACE ME...
...AND NOW THE PASTORAL QUATRAINS..

HE...DEAD?

UH HUH. GONE TO THE AFTER WAR.

WE MUST BE WINNING..

WE'RE GOIN' INTO BATTLE!

WE'LL BE THE FIRST! WE'VE GOTTA TELL EVERYBODY!!

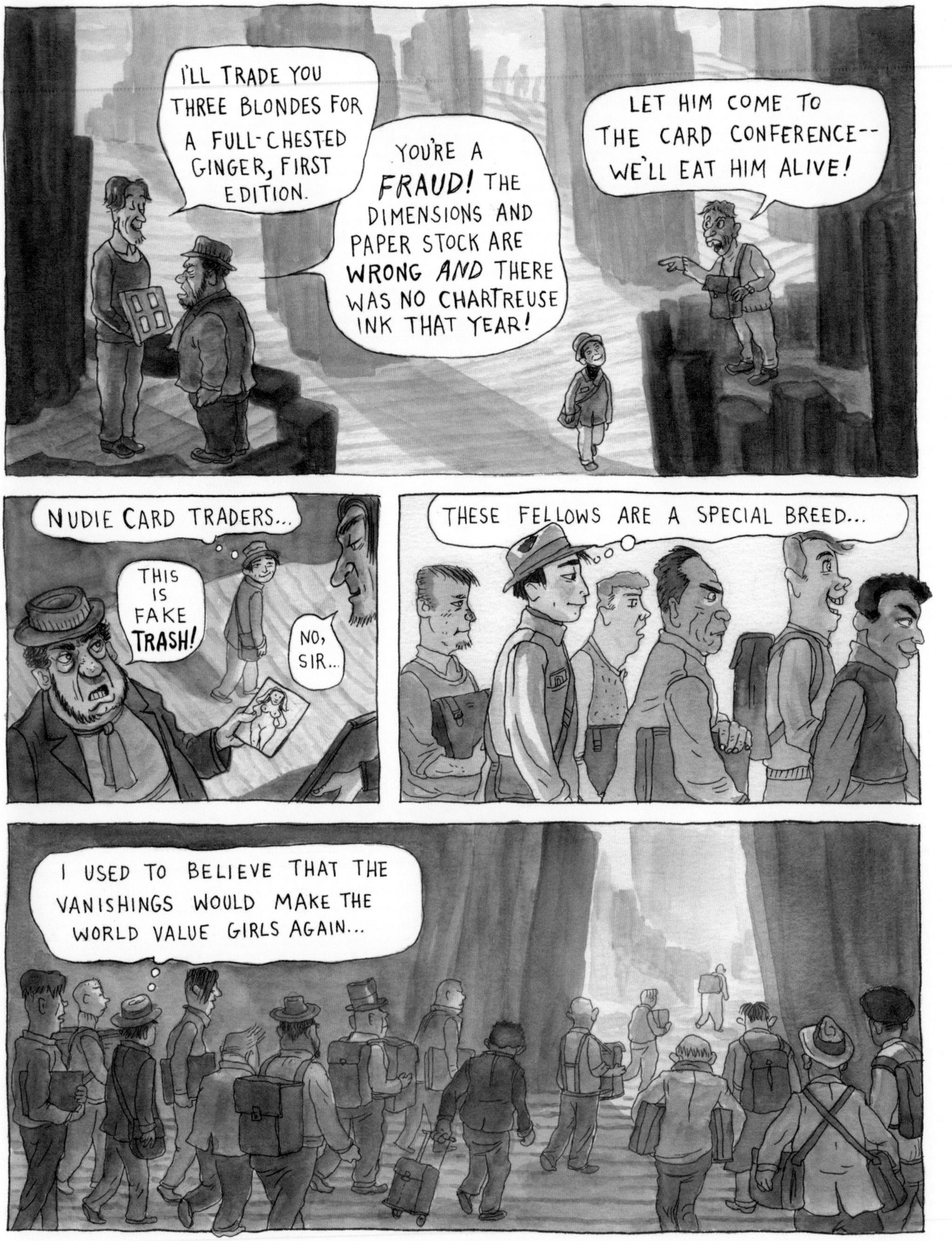
I'LL TRADE YOU THREE BLONDES FOR A FULL-CHESTED GINGER, FIRST EDITION.
YOU'RE A FRAUD! THE DIMENSIONS AND PAPER STOCK ARE WRONG AND THERE WAS NO CHARTREUSE INK THAT YEAR!
LET HIM COME TO THE CARD CONFERENCE-- WE'LL EAT HIM ALIVE!
NUDIE CARD TRADERS...
THIS IS FAKE TRASH!
NO, SIR...
THESE FELLOWS ARE A SPECIAL BREED...
I USED TO BELIEVE THAT THE VANISHINGS WOULD MAKE THE WORLD VALUE GIRLS AGAIN...

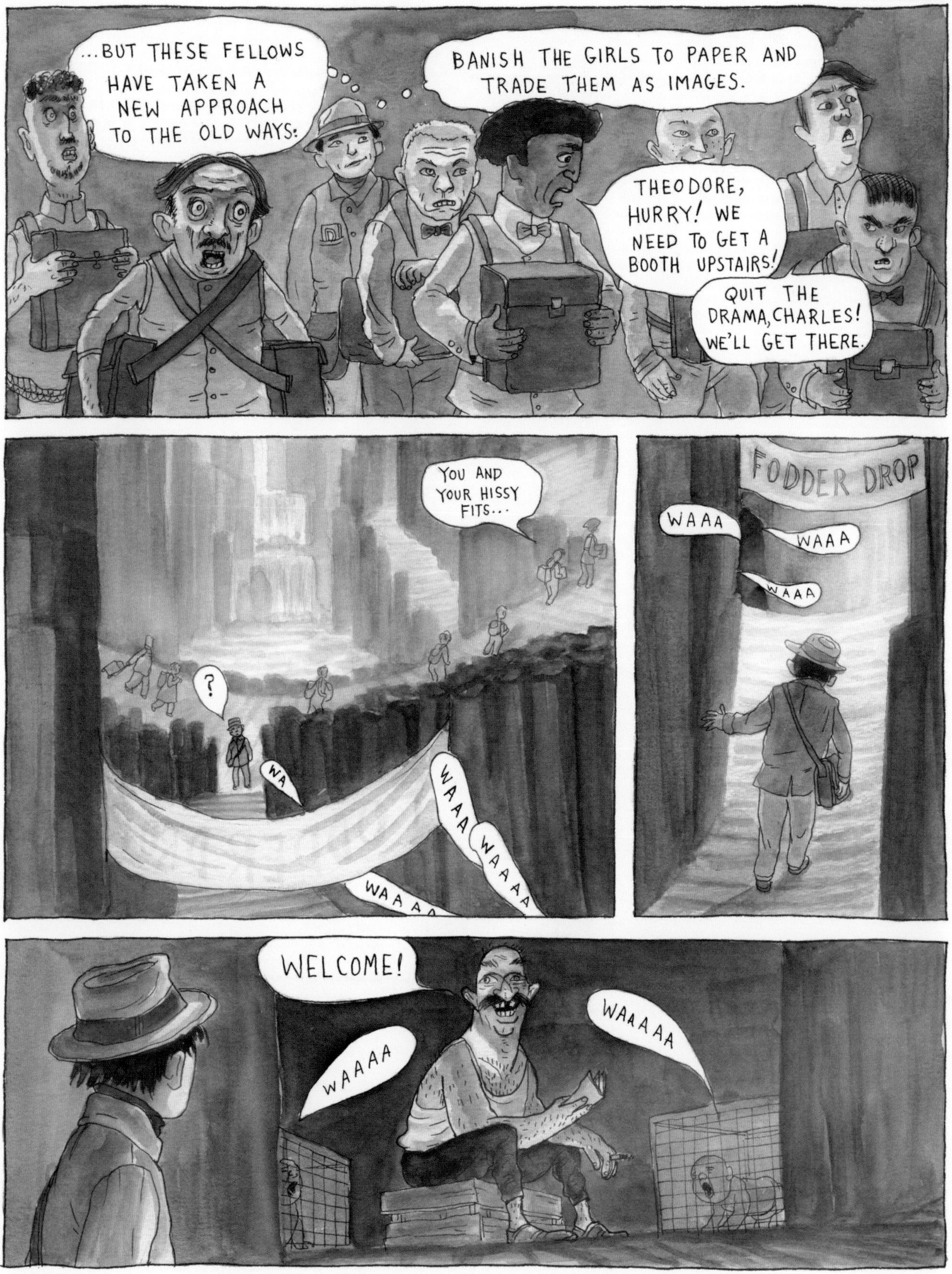
...BUT THESE FELLOWS HAVE TAKEN A NEW APPROACH TO THE OLD WAYS:
BANISH THE GIRLS TO PAPER AND TRADE THEM AS IMAGES.
THEODORE, HURRY! WE NEED TO GET A BOOTH UPSTAIRS!
QUIT THE DRAMA, CHARLES! WE'LL GET THERE.
YOU AND YOUR HISSY FITS...
?
WA
WAAA
WAAAA
WAAAA
FODDER DROP
WAAA
WAAA
WAAA
WELCOME!
WAAAA
WAAAAA

YAAAWN
WHAT YOU IN THE MARKET FOR? FARM HAND? MAID?
WAAA
GENERAL SERVANT.
WAAAAA
WAAAAAA
WE'RE NOT LIKE THE *OTHER* FODDER DROPS-- I AM AN *EDUCATED MAN!*
THESE ARE HIGHEST GRADE PRE-BUD FEMALES! THEIR PARENTS *PAID ME* TO TAKE THEM!
THEY DIDN'T JUST DUMP THEM SOMEWHERE FOR ME TO SCAVENGE.
WA
WAAA
WAAA
WAAA
ALL FROM GOOD STOCK. THEY'LL SERVE YOU NICELY, *WHATEVER YOUR NEEDS,* HEH...
I'LL SAY NO MORE...
IF YOU DON'T FEED THEM TOO MUCH YOU CAN DELAY THEIR BUDDING AND GET MORE WORK OUT OF THEM! I DISCOVERED THIS EARLY, BUT I DO NOT BRAG! I AM A MODEST MAN.
YES, YOU WOULD BE SURPRISED AT HOW LITTLE FOOD THEY REQUIRE!
WAAAA
HOW MUCH FOR THIS ONE?

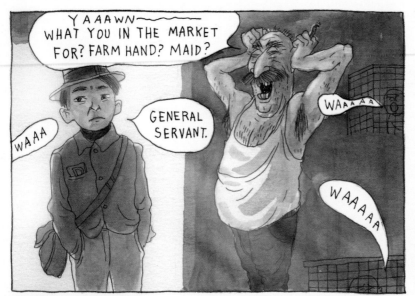

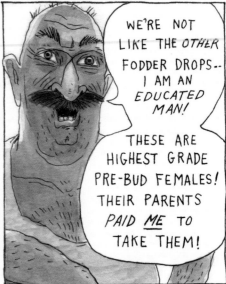

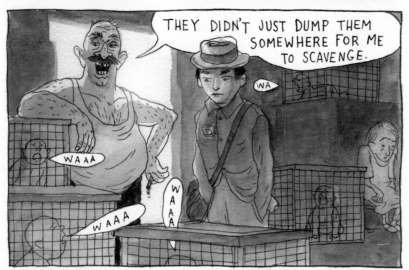

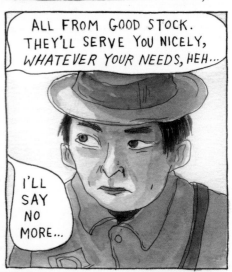

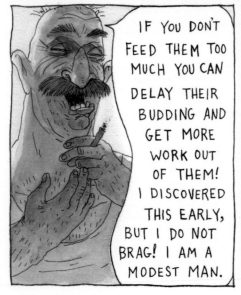

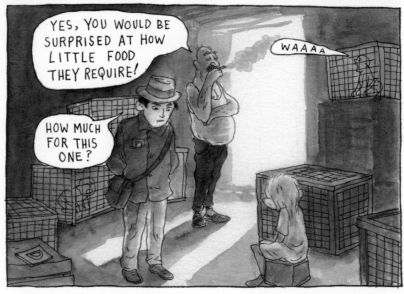

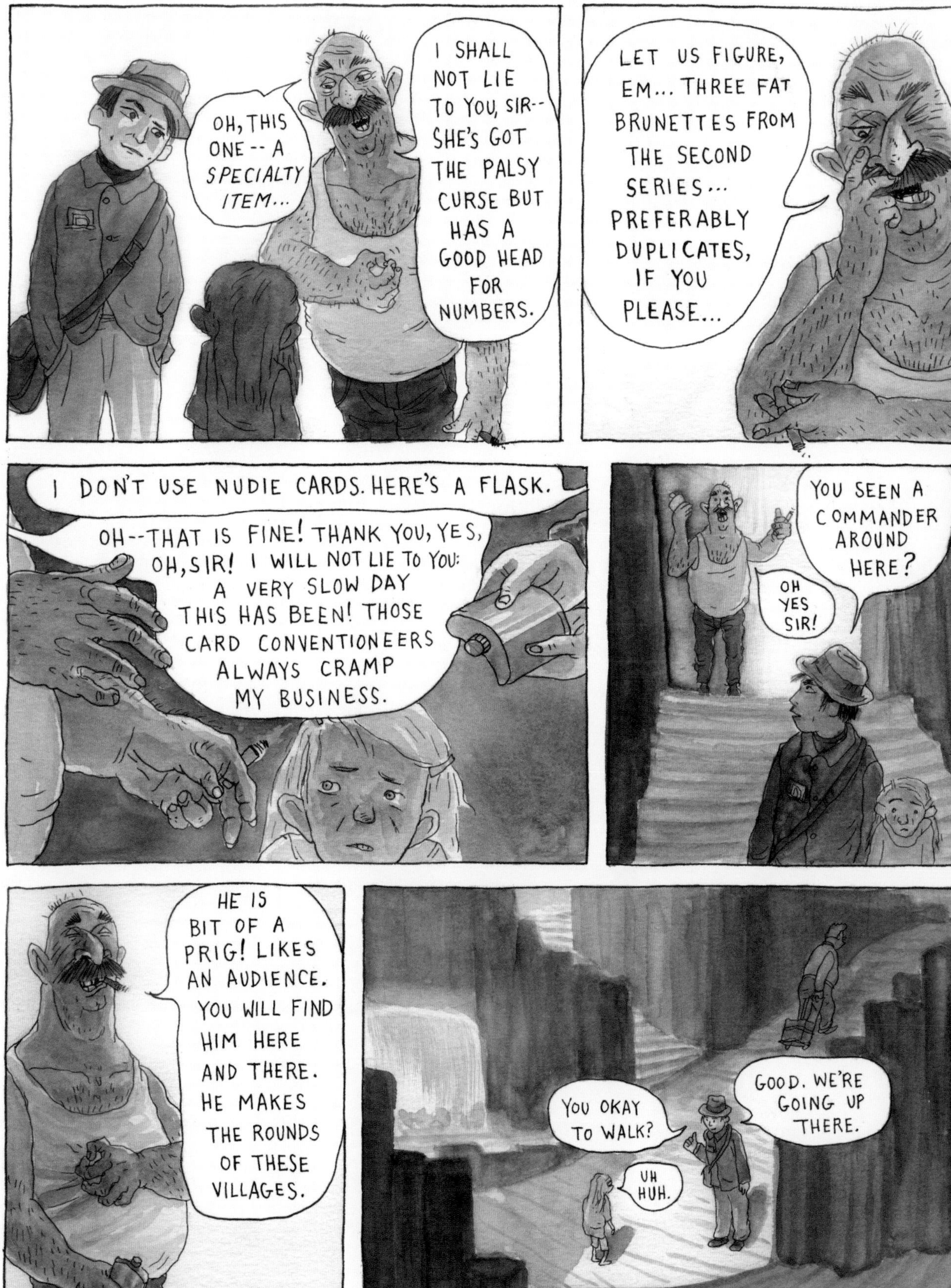
OH, THIS ONE -- A SPECIALTY ITEM...
I SHALL NOT LIE TO YOU, SIR-- SHE'S GOT THE PALSY CURSE BUT HAS A GOOD HEAD FOR NUMBERS.
LET US FIGURE, EM... THREE FAT BRUNETTES FROM THE SECOND SERIES... PREFERABLY DUPLICATES, IF YOU PLEASE...
I DON'T USE NUDIE CARDS. HERE'S A FLASK.
OH--THAT IS FINE! THANK YOU, YES, OH, SIR! I WILL NOT LIE TO YOU: A VERY SLOW DAY THIS HAS BEEN! THOSE CARD CONVENTIONEERS ALWAYS CRAMP MY BUSINESS.
YOU SEEN A COMMANDER AROUND HERE?
OH YES SIR!
HE IS BIT OF A PRIG! LIKES AN AUDIENCE. YOU WILL FIND HIM HERE AND THERE. HE MAKES THE ROUNDS OF THESE VILLAGES.
YOU OKAY TO WALK?
GOOD. WE'RE GOING UP THERE.
UH HUH.

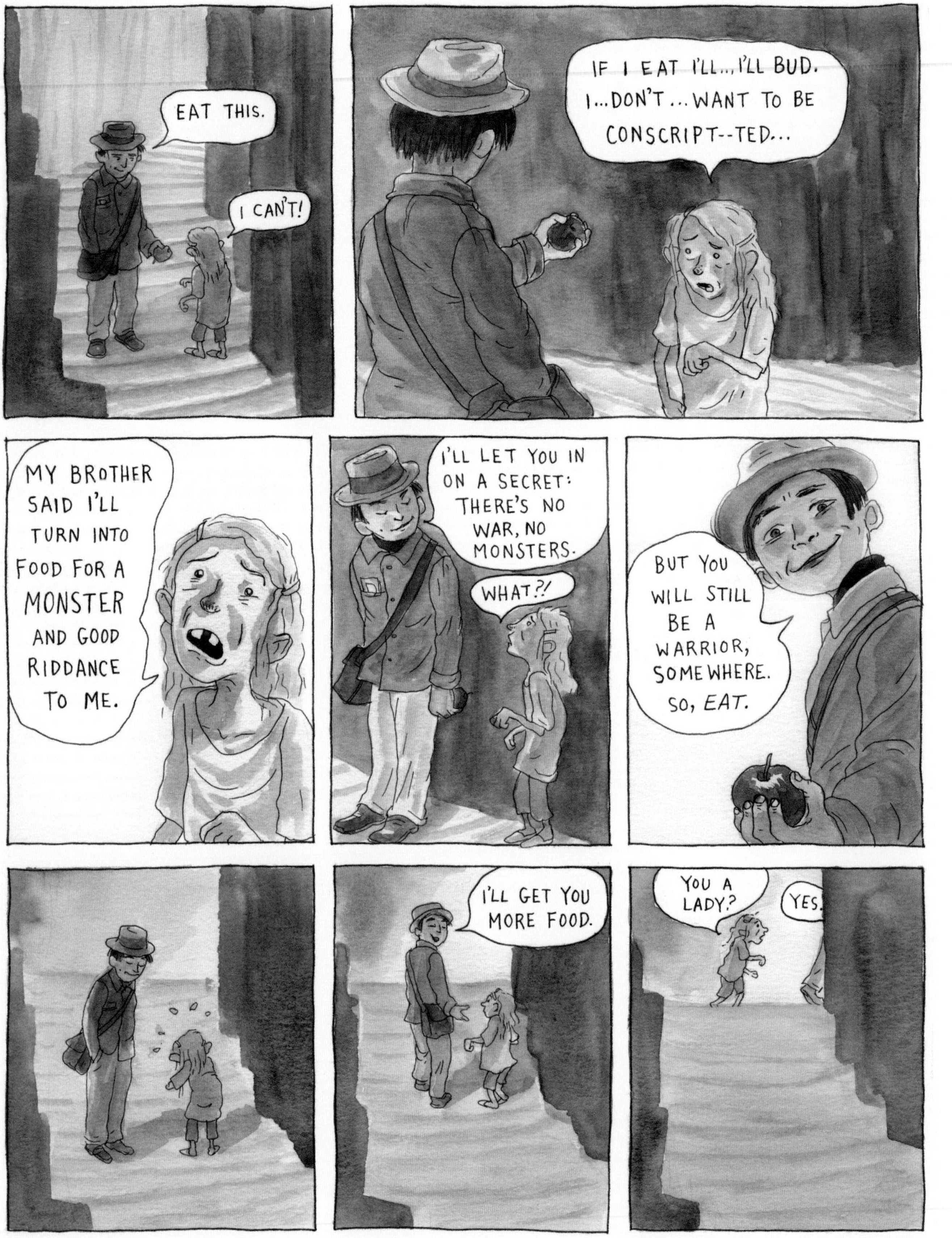
EAT THIS.
I CAN'T!
IF I EAT I'LL... I'LL BUD. I... DON'T... WANT TO BE CONSCRIPT--TED...
MY BROTHER SAID I'LL TURN INTO FOOD FOR A MONSTER AND GOOD RIDDANCE TO ME.
I'LL LET YOU IN ON A SECRET: THERE'S NO WAR, NO MONSTERS.
WHAT?!
BUT YOU WILL STILL BE A WARRIOR, SOMEWHERE. SO, *EAT*.
I'LL GET YOU MORE FOOD.
YOU A LADY?
YES.

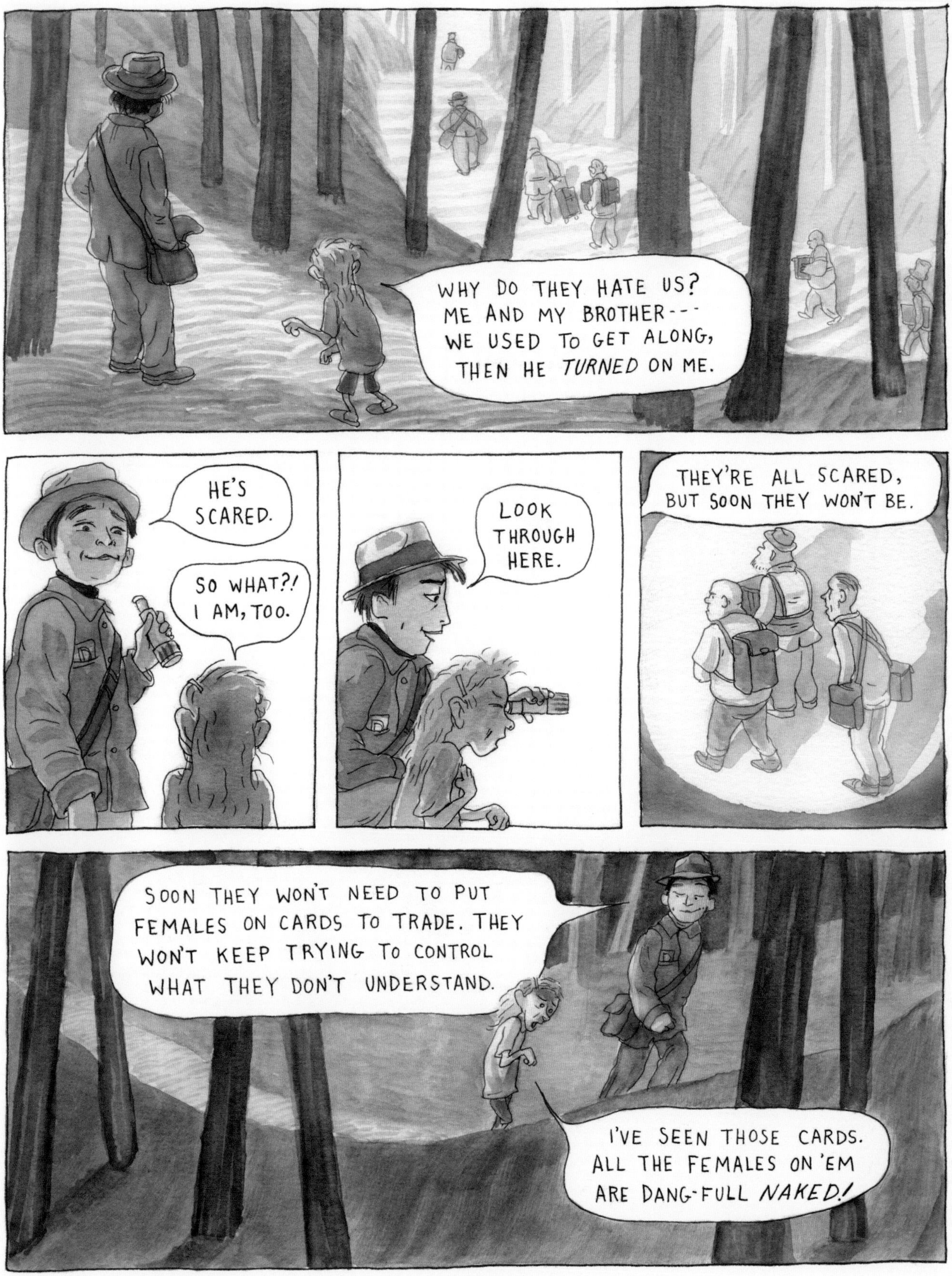
WHY DO THEY HATE US? ME AND MY BROTHER--- WE USED TO GET ALONG, THEN HE *TURNED* ON ME.
HE'S SCARED.
SO WHAT?! I AM, TOO.
LOOK THROUGH HERE.
THEY'RE ALL SCARED, BUT SOON THEY WON'T BE.
SOON THEY WON'T NEED TO PUT FEMALES ON CARDS TO TRADE. THEY WON'T KEEP TRYING TO CONTROL WHAT THEY DON'T UNDERSTAND.
I'VE SEEN THOSE CARDS. ALL THE FEMALES ON 'EM ARE DANG-FULL *NAKED!*

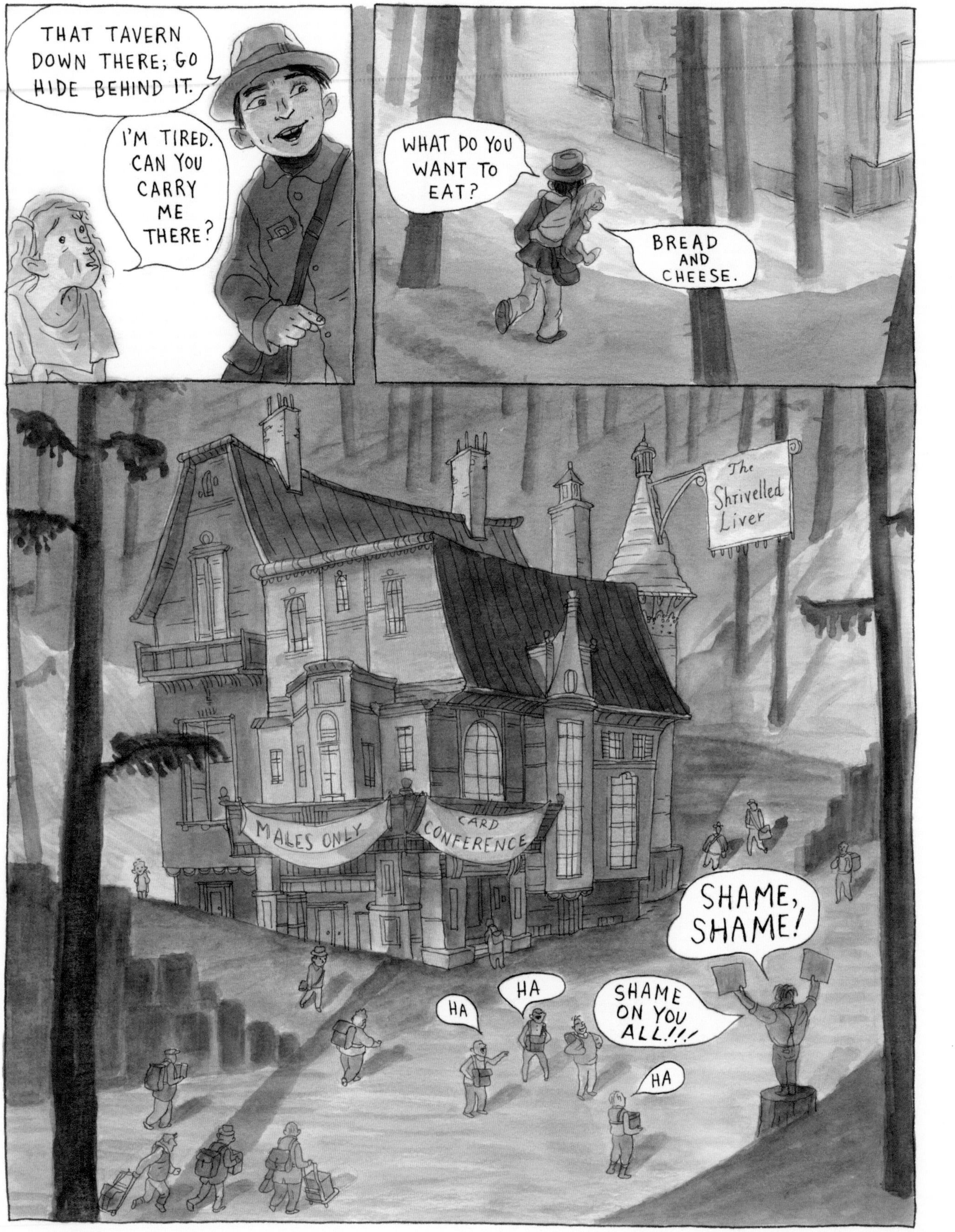
THAT TAVERN DOWN THERE; GO HIDE BEHIND IT.
I'M TIRED. CAN YOU CARRY ME THERE?
WHAT DO YOU WANT TO EAT?
BREAD AND CHEESE.
The Shrivelled Liver
MALES ONLY
CARD CONFERENCE
SHAME, SHAME!
HA
HA
SHAME ON YOU ALL!!!
HA

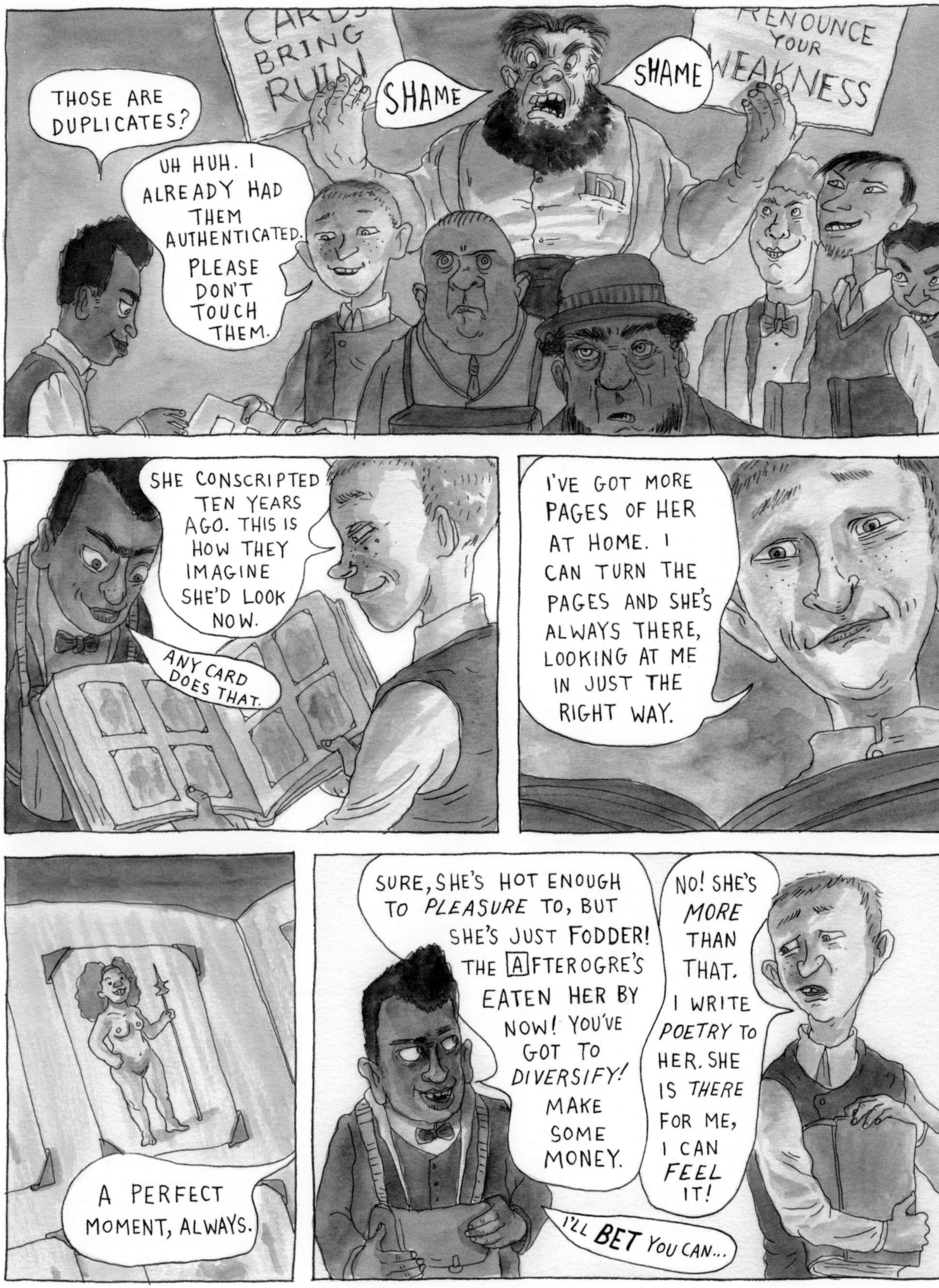
CARDS BRING RUIN
RENOUNCE YOUR WEAKNESS
THOSE ARE DUPLICATES?
SHAME
SHAME
UH HUH. I ALREADY HAD THEM AUTHENTICATED. PLEASE DON'T TOUCH THEM.
SHE CONSCRIPTED TEN YEARS AGO. THIS IS HOW THEY IMAGINE SHE'D LOOK NOW.
ANY CARD DOES THAT.
I'VE GOT MORE PAGES OF HER AT HOME. I CAN TURN THE PAGES AND SHE'S ALWAYS THERE, LOOKING AT ME IN JUST THE RIGHT WAY.
A PERFECT MOMENT, ALWAYS.
SURE, SHE'S HOT ENOUGH TO *PLEASURE* TO, BUT SHE'S JUST FODDER! THE AFTEROGRE'S EATEN HER BY NOW! YOU'VE GOT TO *DIVERSIFY!* MAKE SOME MONEY.
NO! SHE'S *MORE* THAN THAT. I WRITE *POETRY* TO HER. SHE IS *THERE* FOR ME, I CAN *FEEL* IT!
I'LL **BET** YOU CAN...

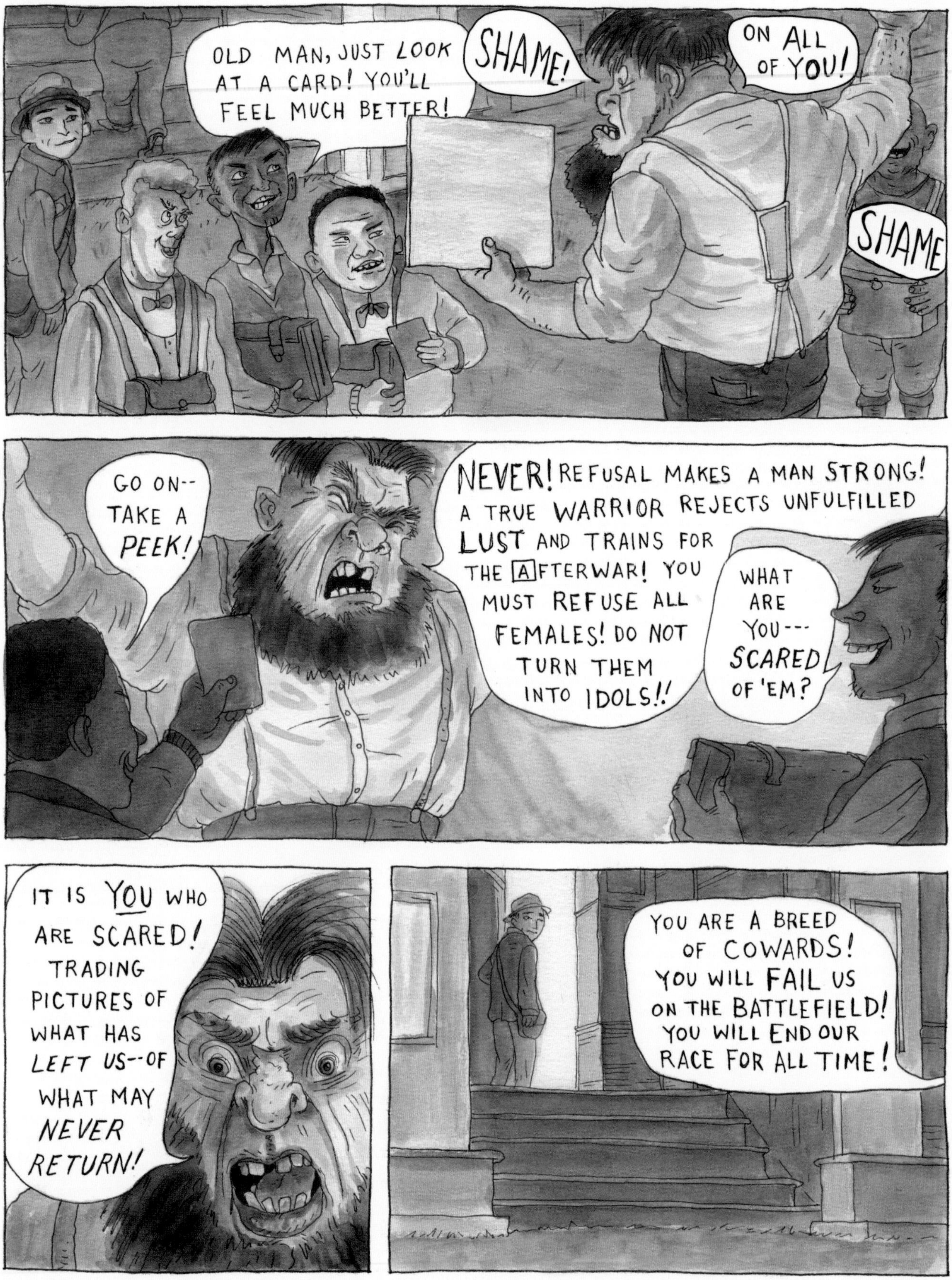

OLD MAN, JUST LOOK AT A CARD! YOU'LL FEEL MUCH BETTER!
SHAME!
ON ALL OF YOU!
SHAME
GO ON-- TAKE A PEEK!
NEVER! REFUSAL MAKES A MAN STRONG! A TRUE WARRIOR REJECTS UNFULFILLED LUST AND TRAINS FOR THE AFTERWAR! YOU MUST REFUSE ALL FEMALES! DO NOT TURN THEM INTO IDOLS!!
WHAT ARE YOU--- SCARED OF 'EM?
IT IS YOU WHO ARE SCARED! TRADING PICTURES OF WHAT HAS LEFT US--OF WHAT MAY NEVER RETURN!
YOU ARE A BREED OF COWARDS! YOU WILL FAIL US ON THE BATTLEFIELD! YOU WILL END OUR RACE FOR ALL TIME!

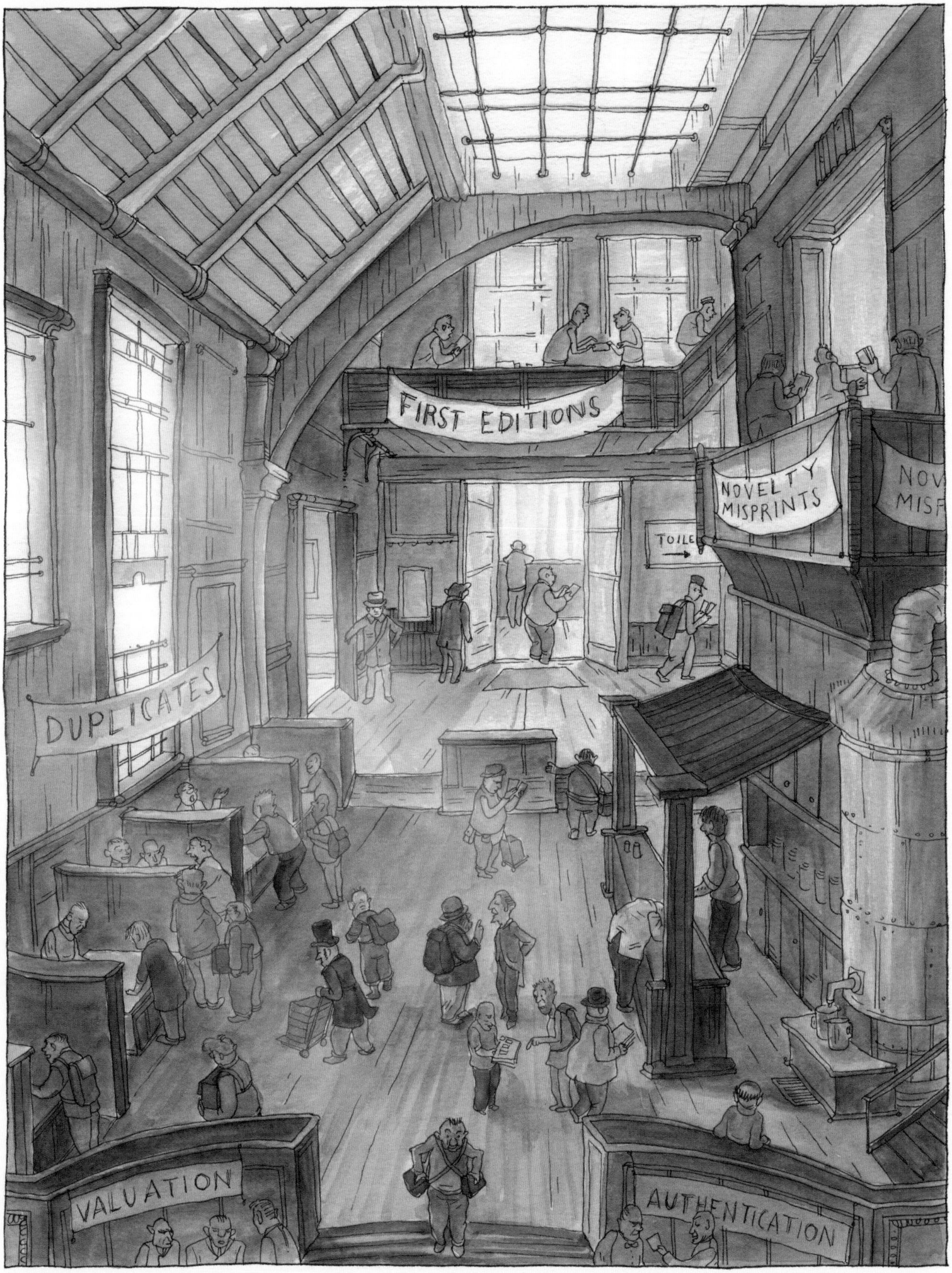
FIRST EDITIONS
NOVELTY MISPRINTS
TOILE
DUPLICATES
VALUATION
AUTHENTICATION

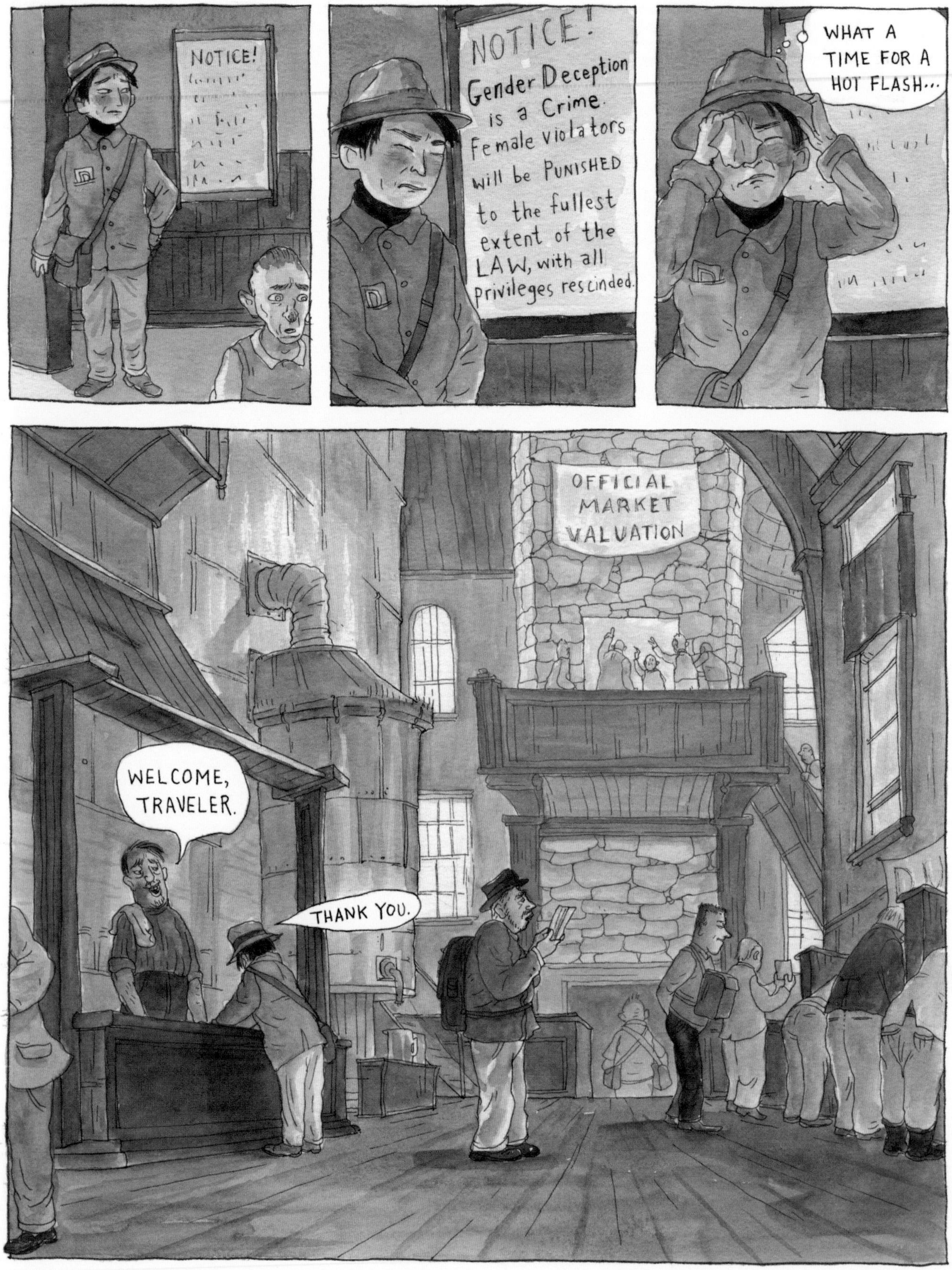
NOTICE!
NOTICE!
Gender Deception is a Crime. Female violators will be PUNISHED to the fullest extent of the LAW, with all Privileges rescinded.
WHAT A TIME FOR A HOT FLASH...
OFFICIAL MARKET VALUATION
WELCOME, TRAVELER.
THANK YOU.

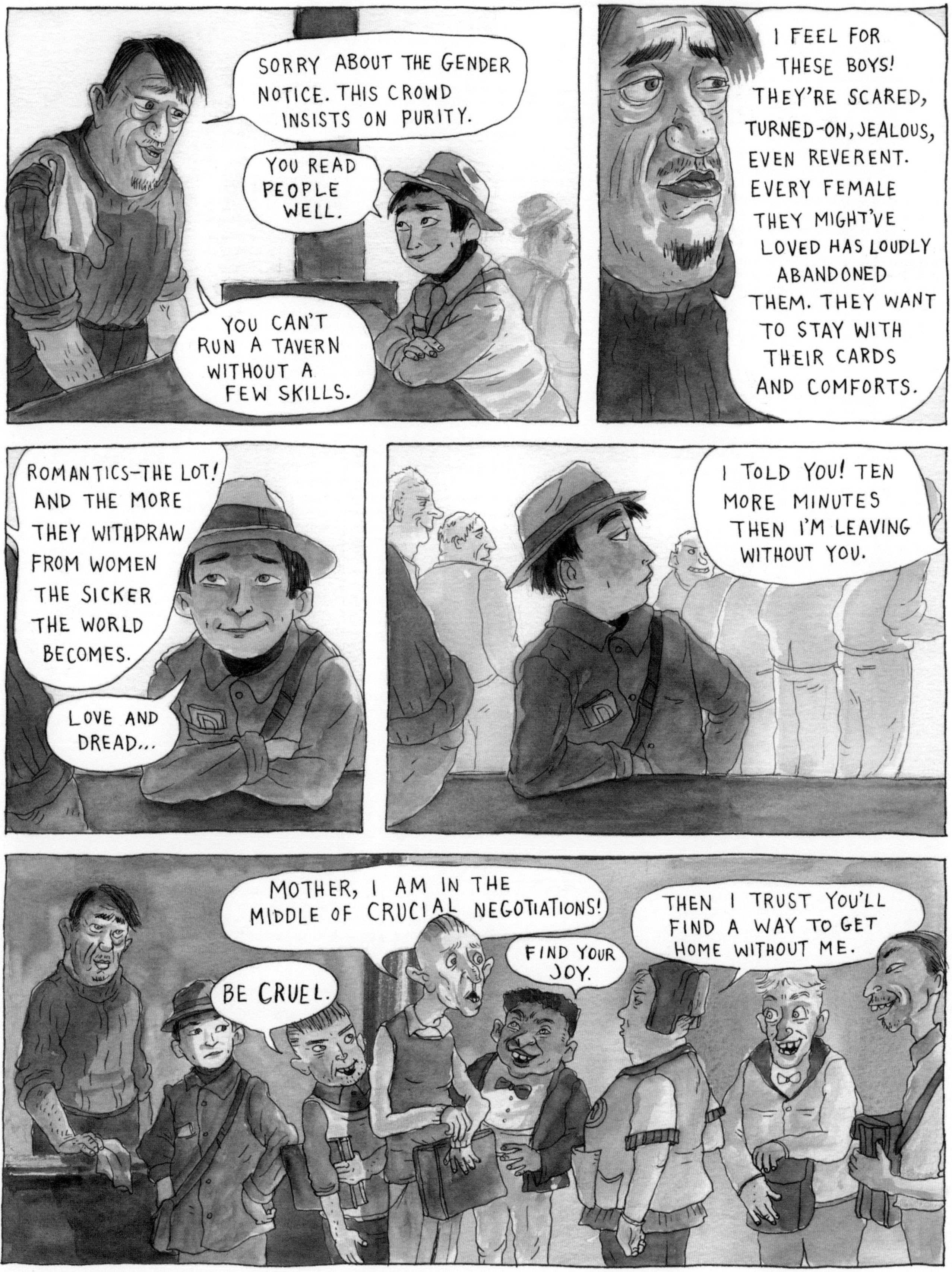
SORRY ABOUT THE GENDER NOTICE. THIS CROWD INSISTS ON PURITY.
YOU READ PEOPLE WELL.
YOU CAN'T RUN A TAVERN WITHOUT A FEW SKILLS.
I FEEL FOR THESE BOYS! THEY'RE SCARED, TURNED-ON, JEALOUS, EVEN REVERENT. EVERY FEMALE THEY MIGHT'VE LOVED HAS LOUDLY ABANDONED THEM. THEY WANT TO STAY WITH THEIR CARDS AND COMFORTS.
ROMANTICS—THE LOT! AND THE MORE THEY WITHDRAW FROM WOMEN THE SICKER THE WORLD BECOMES.
LOVE AND DREAD...
I TOLD YOU! TEN MORE MINUTES THEN I'M LEAVING WITHOUT YOU.
MOTHER, I AM IN THE MIDDLE OF CRUCIAL NEGOTIATIONS!
BE CRUEL.
FIND YOUR JOY.
THEN I TRUST YOU'LL FIND A WAY TO GET HOME WITHOUT ME.

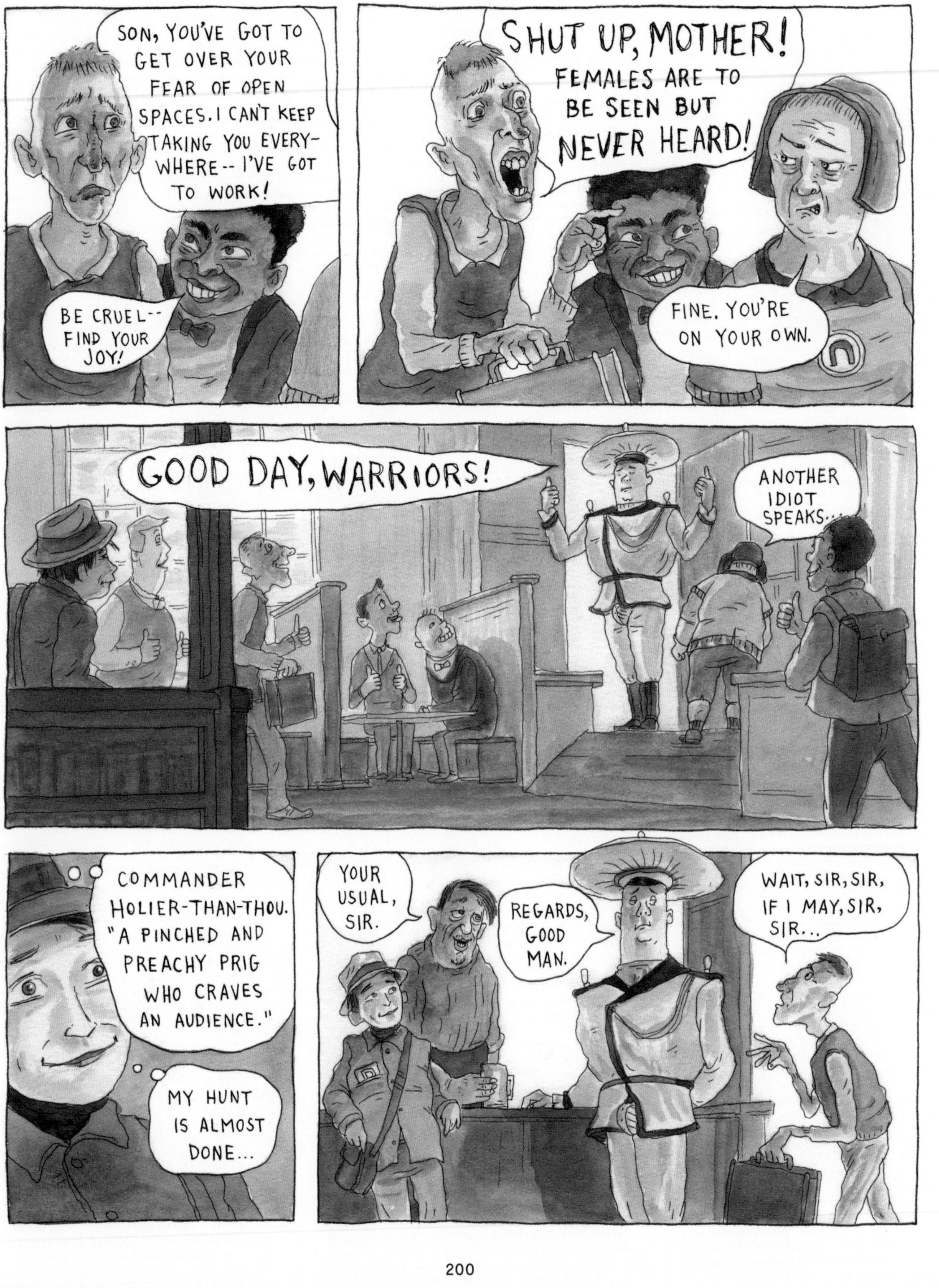
SON, YOU'VE GOT TO GET OVER YOUR FEAR OF OPEN SPACES. I CAN'T KEEP TAKING YOU EVERY-WHERE -- I'VE GOT TO WORK!
BE CRUEL-- FIND YOUR JOY!
SHUT UP, MOTHER! FEMALES ARE TO BE SEEN BUT NEVER HEARD!
FINE. YOU'RE ON YOUR OWN.
GOOD DAY, WARRIORS!
ANOTHER IDIOT SPEAKS...
COMMANDER HOLIER-THAN-THOU. "A PINCHED AND PREACHY PRIG WHO CRAVES AN AUDIENCE."
MY HUNT IS ALMOST DONE...
YOUR USUAL, SIR.
REGARDS, GOOD MAN.
WAIT, SIR, SIR, IF I MAY, SIR, SIR...

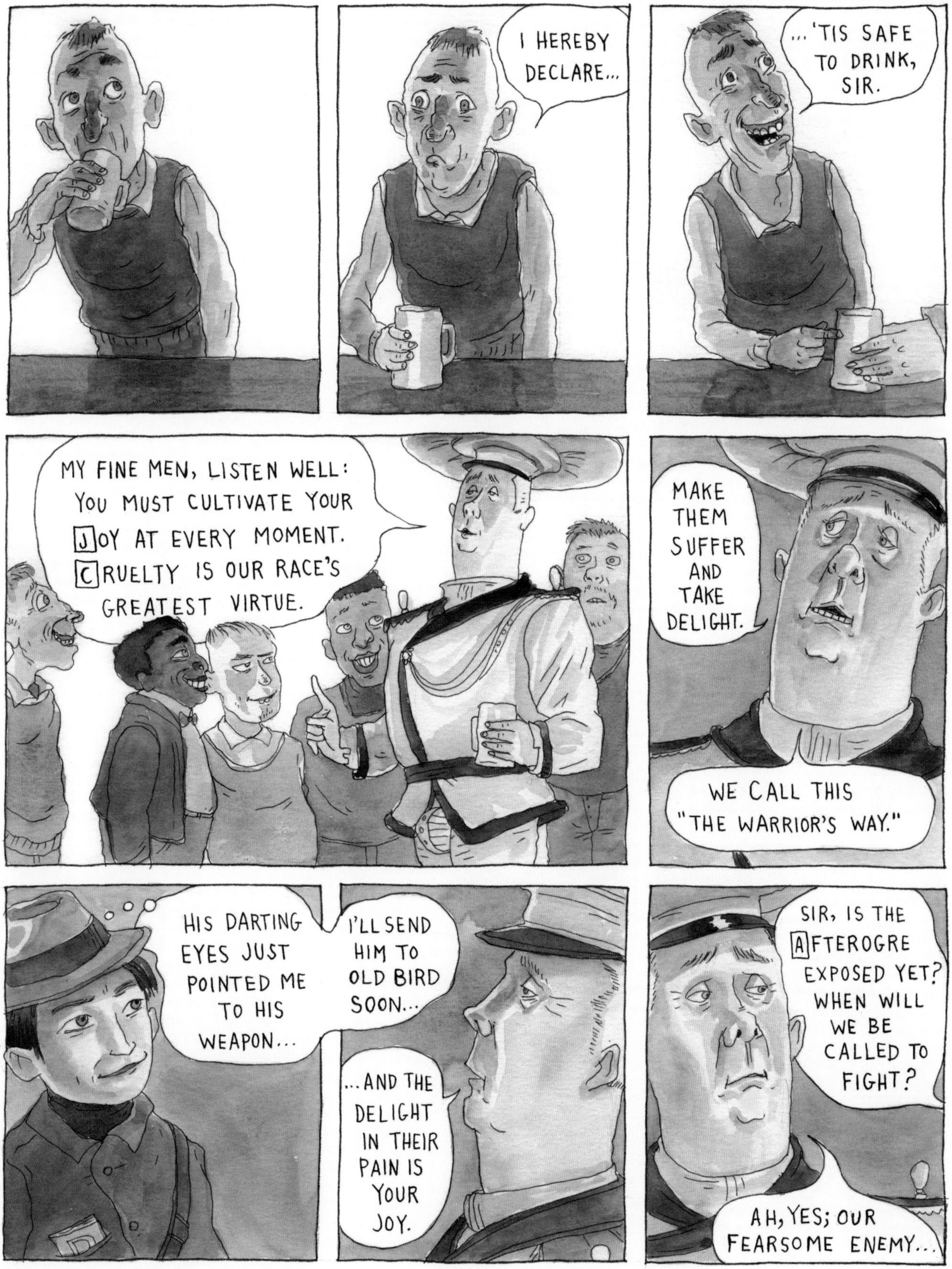
I HEREBY DECLARE...
...'TIS SAFE TO DRINK, SIR.
MY FINE MEN, LISTEN WELL: YOU MUST CULTIVATE YOUR JOY AT EVERY MOMENT. CRUELTY IS OUR RACE'S GREATEST VIRTUE.
MAKE THEM SUFFER AND TAKE DELIGHT.
WE CALL THIS "THE WARRIOR'S WAY."
HIS DARTING EYES JUST POINTED ME TO HIS WEAPON...
I'LL SEND HIM TO OLD BIRD SOON...
...AND THE DELIGHT IN THEIR PAIN IS YOUR JOY.
SIR, IS THE AFTEROGRE EXPOSED YET? WHEN WILL WE BE CALLED TO FIGHT?
AH, YES; OUR FEARSOME ENEMY...

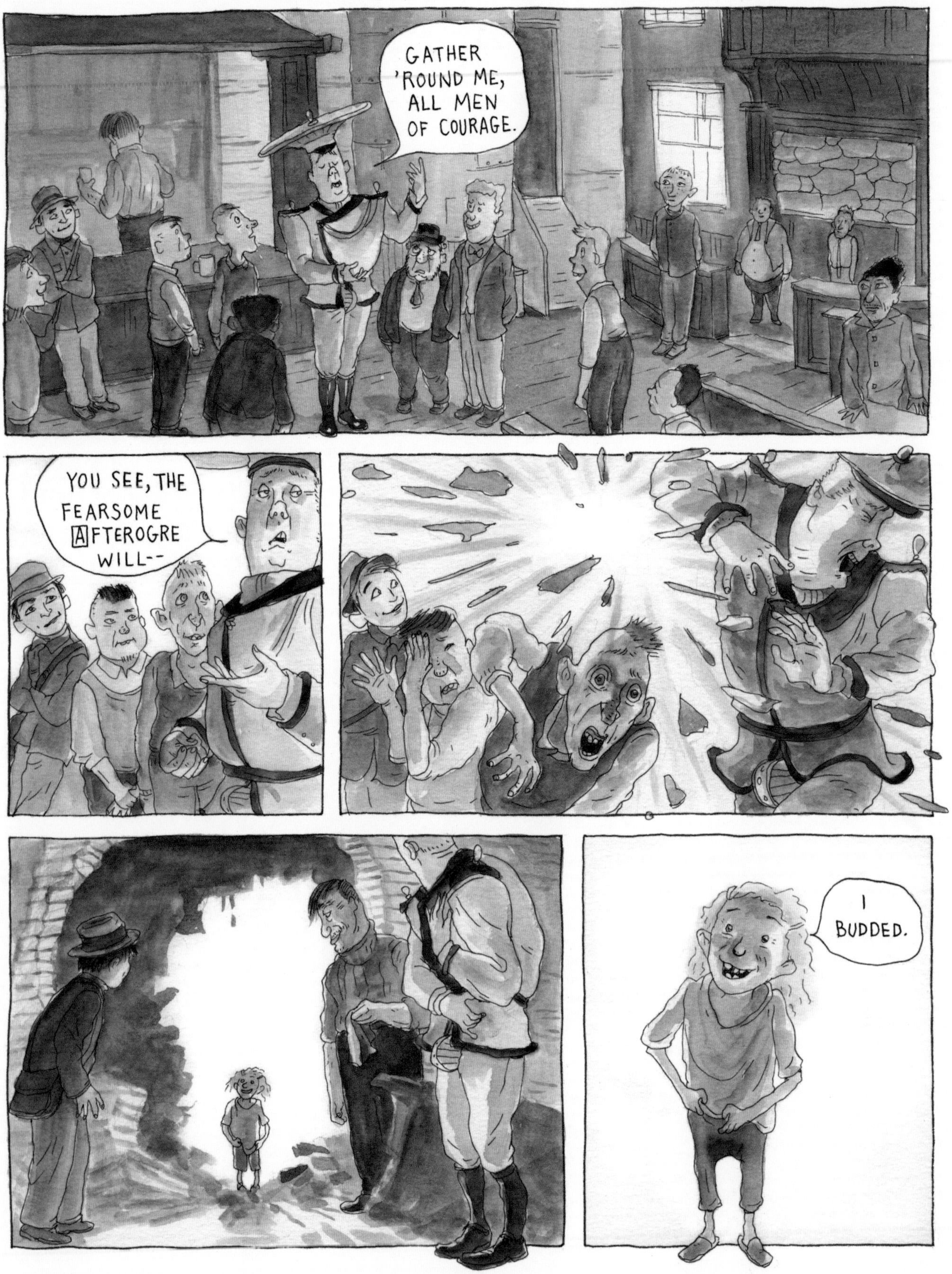
GATHER 'ROUND ME, ALL MEN OF COURAGE.
YOU SEE, THE FEARSOME AFTEROGRE WILL--
I BUDDED.

THRUM
THRUM
THRUM
THRUM
THRUM
THRUM
THRUM
THRUM
THRUM
THRUM
THRUM
THRUM
THR
THRUM
THRUM
THRUM

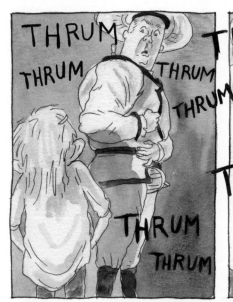

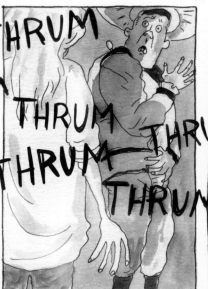

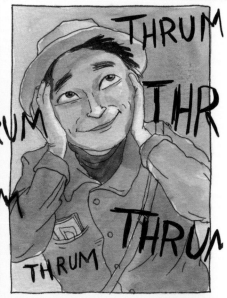

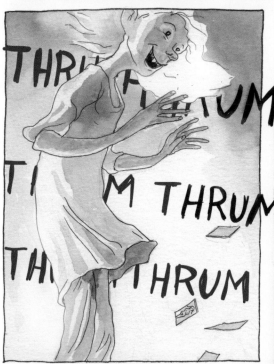

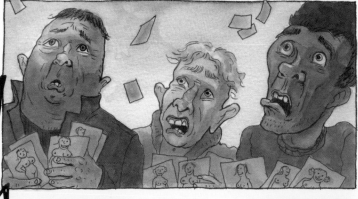

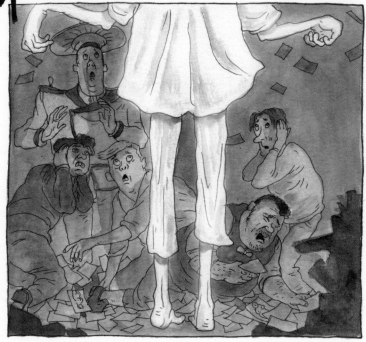

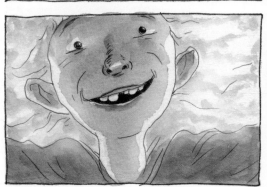

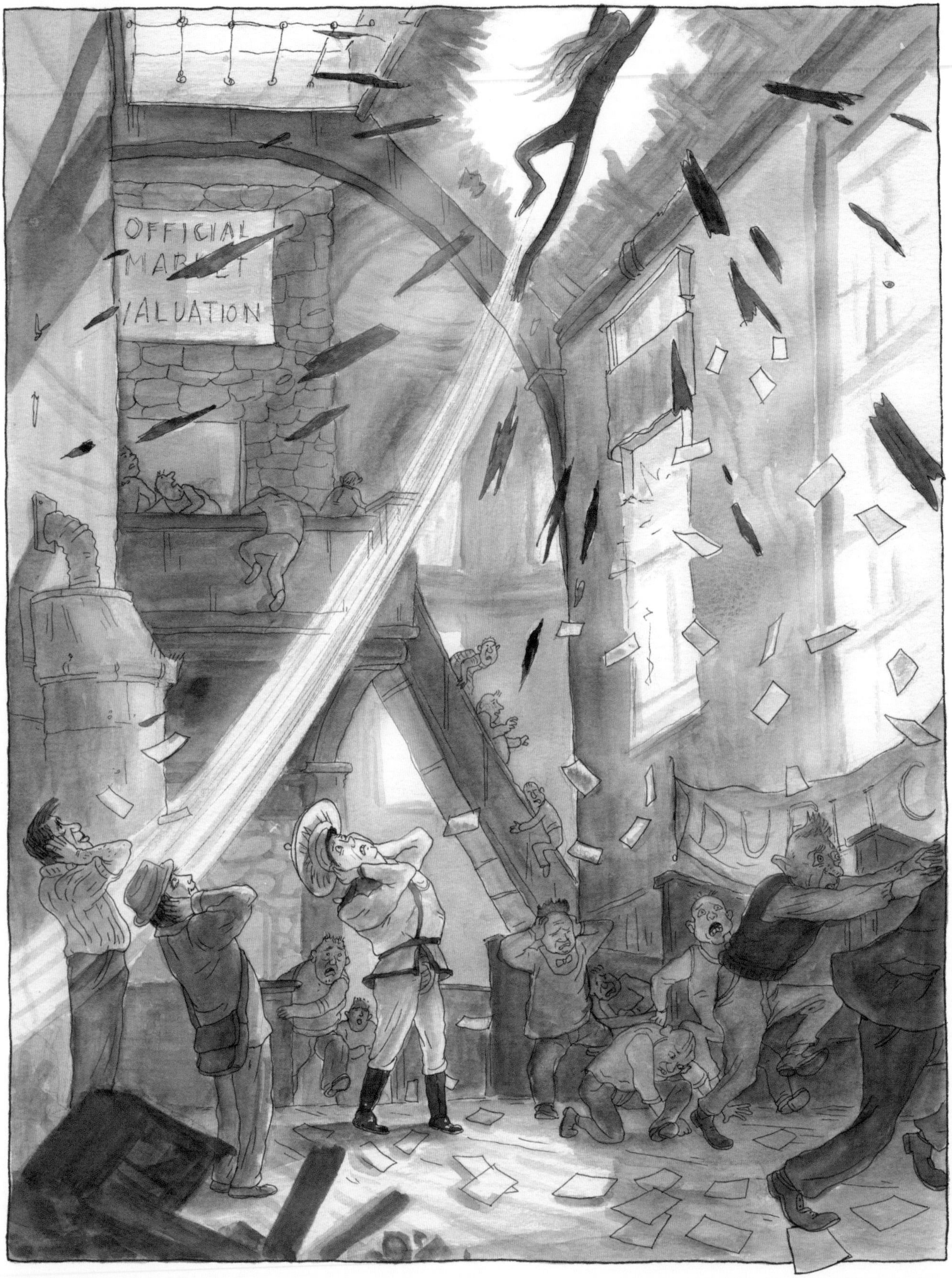
OFFICIAL

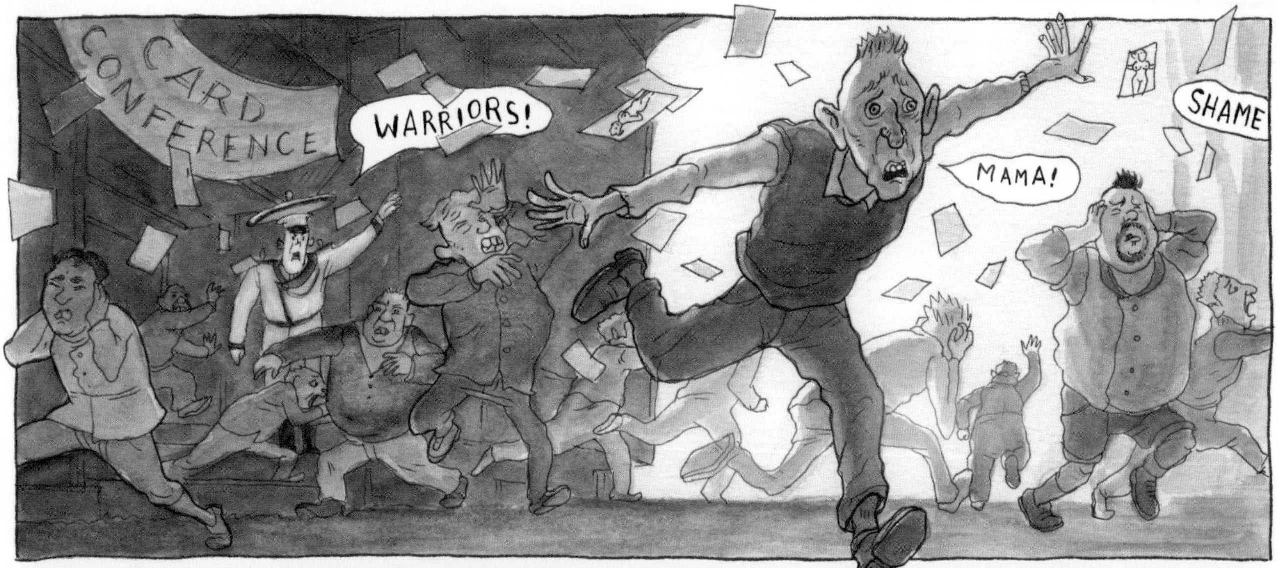
CARD CONFERENCE
WARRIORS!
MAMA!
SHAME

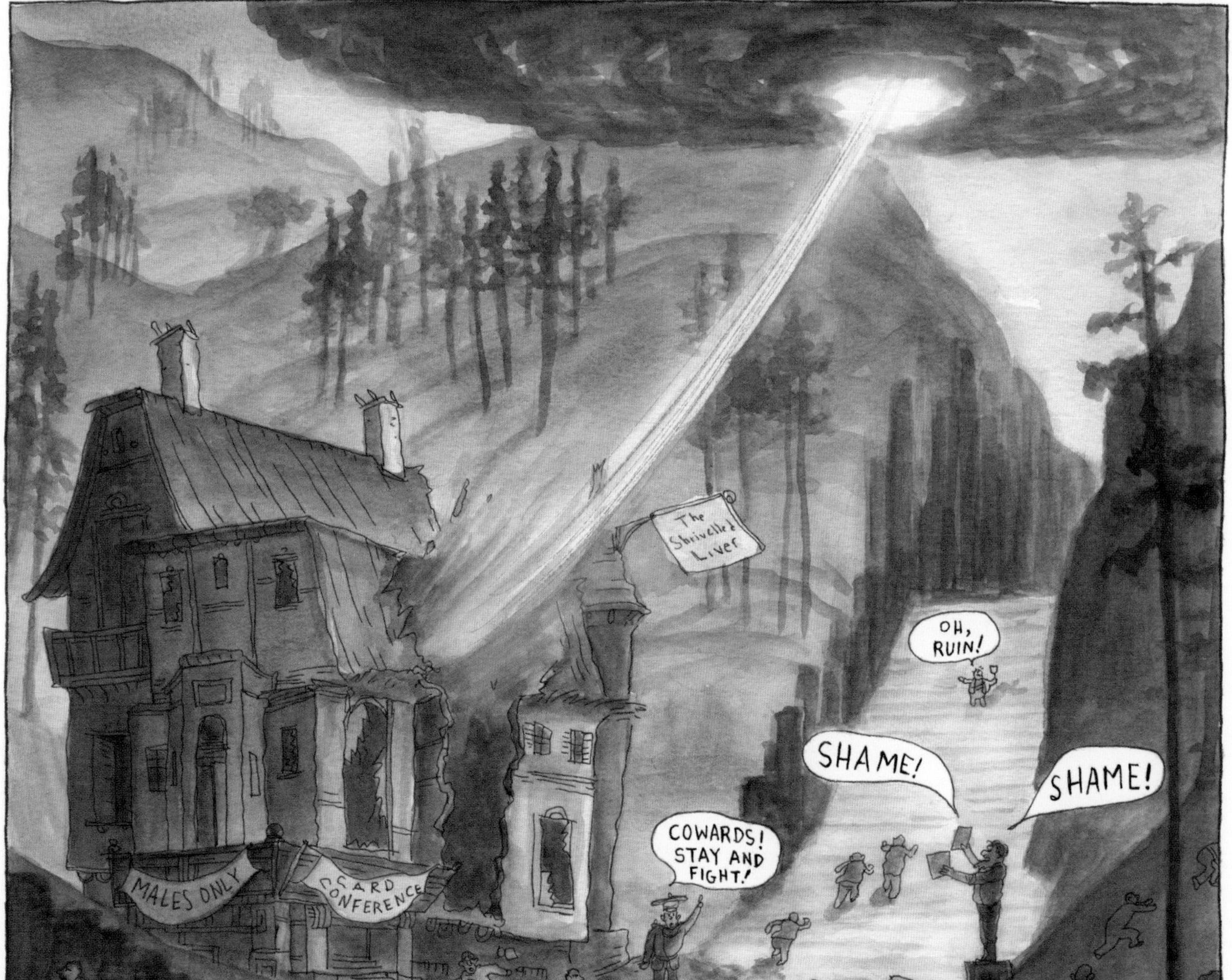
The Shrivelled Liver
OH, RUIN!
SHAME!
SHAME!
COWARDS! STAY AND FIGHT!
MALES ONLY
CARD CONFERENCE

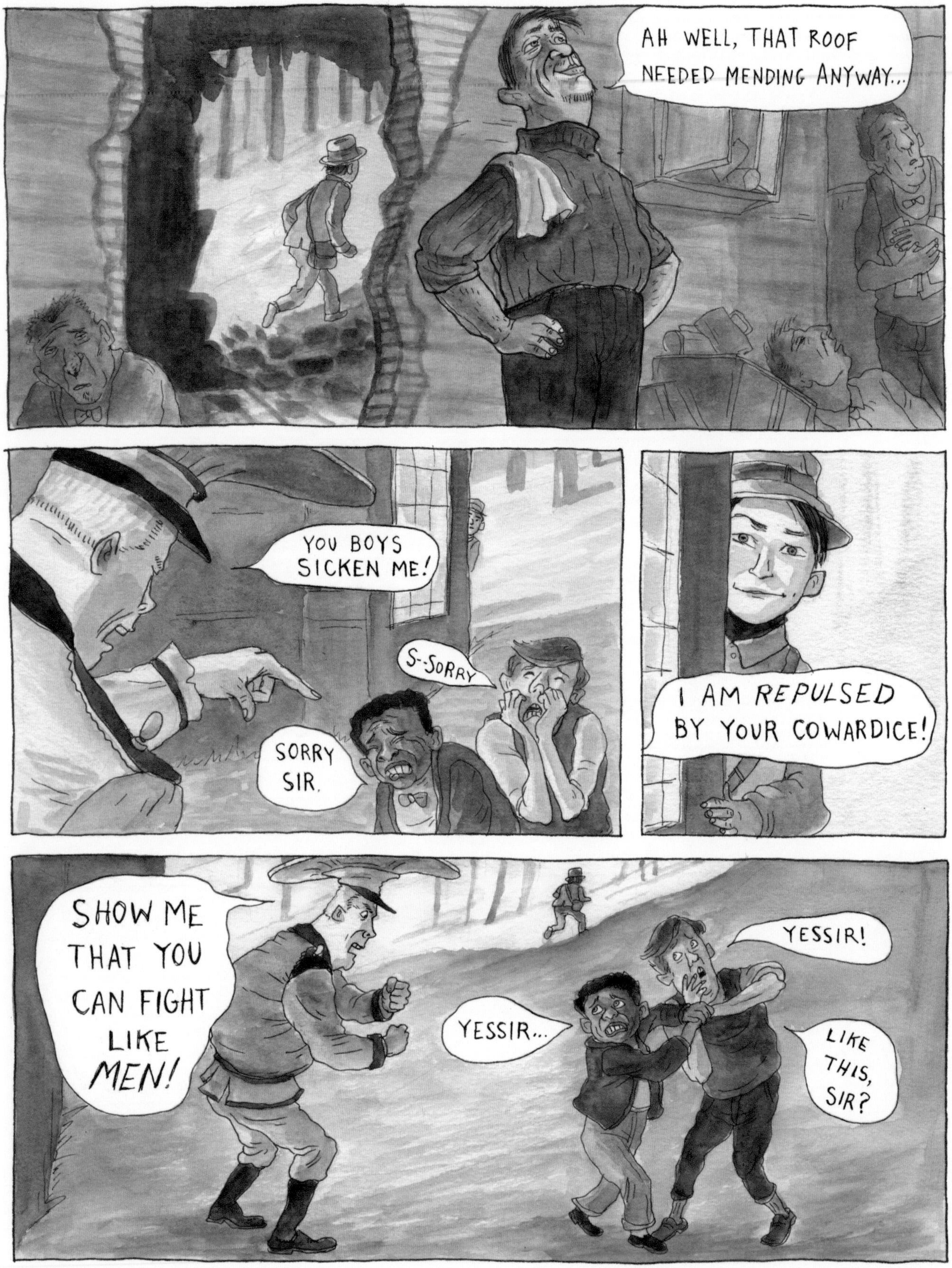
AH WELL, THAT ROOF NEEDED MENDING ANYWAY...
YOU BOYS SICKEN ME!
S--SORRY
SORRY SIR.
I AM *REPULSED* BY YOUR COWARDICE!
SHOW ME THAT YOU CAN FIGHT LIKE *MEN!*
YESSIR!
YESSIR...
LIKE THIS, SIR?

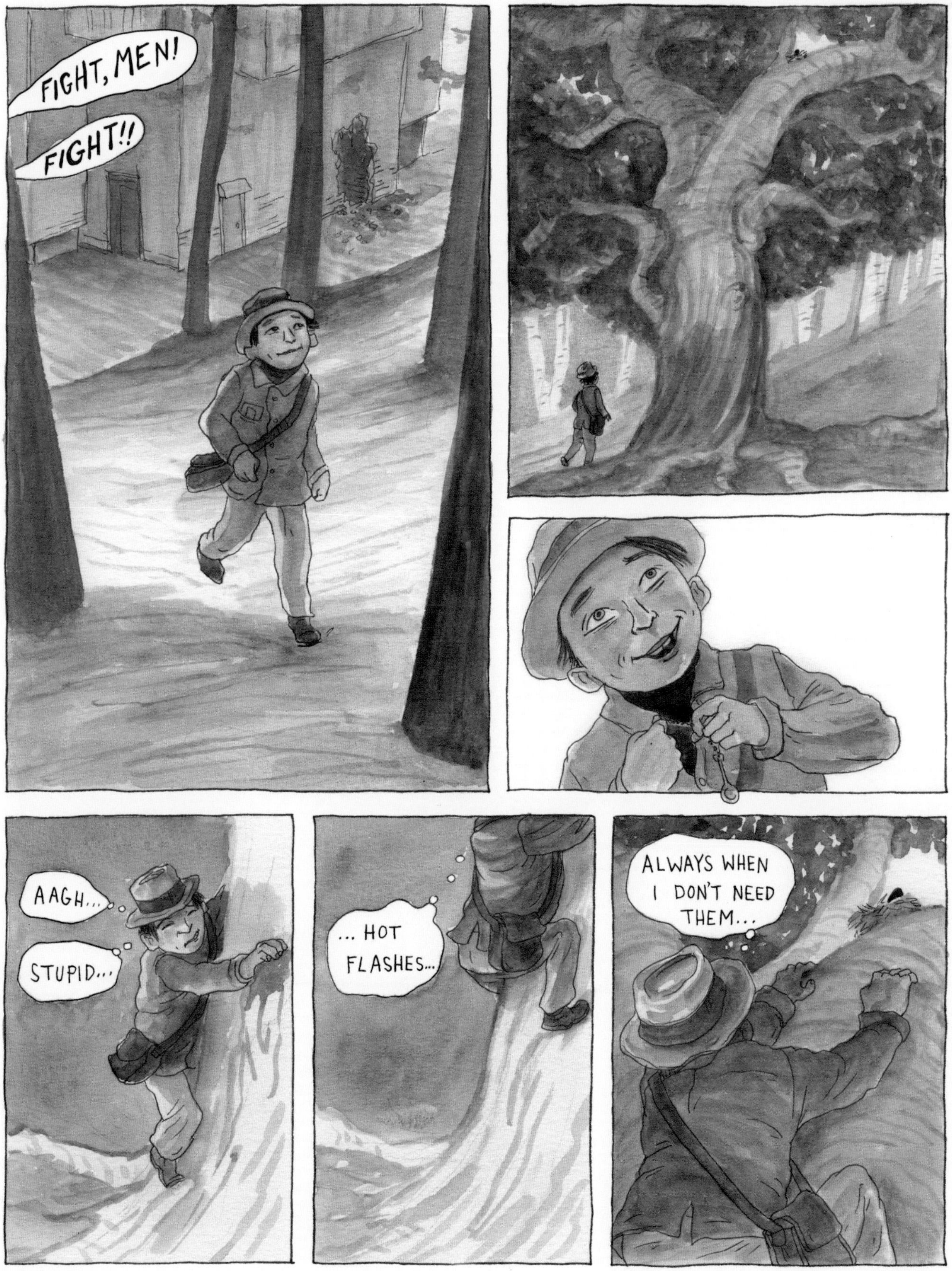
FIGHT, MEN!
FIGHT!!
AAGH...
STUPID...
... HOT FLASHES...
ALWAYS WHEN I DON'T NEED THEM...

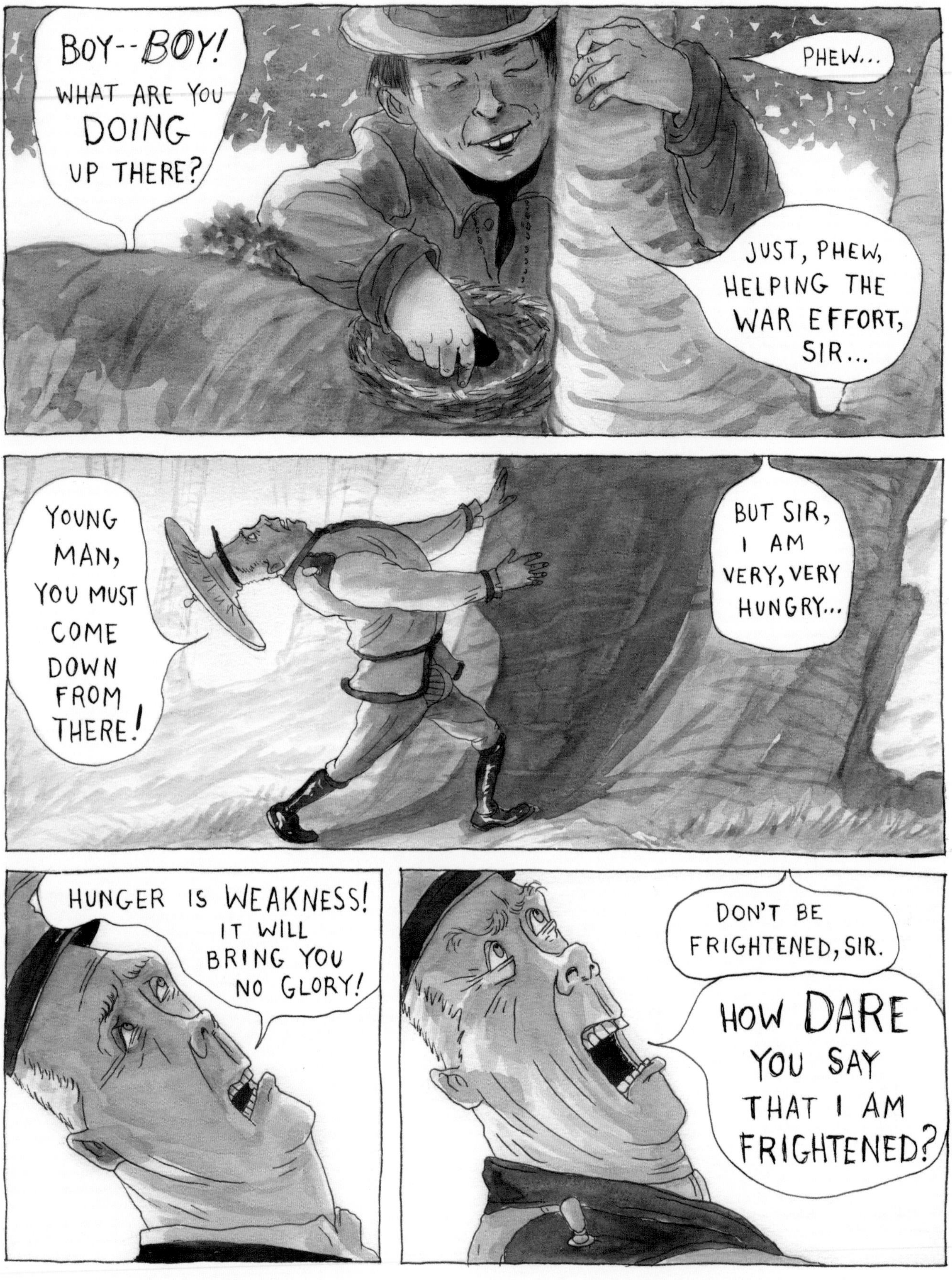
BOY--BOY! WHAT ARE YOU DOING UP THERE?
PHEW...
JUST, PHEW, HELPING THE WAR EFFORT, SIR...
YOUNG MAN, YOU MUST COME DOWN FROM THERE!
BUT SIR, I AM VERY, VERY HUNGRY...
HUNGER IS WEAKNESS! IT WILL BRING YOU NO GLORY!
DON'T BE FRIGHTENED, SIR.
HOW DARE YOU SAY THAT I AM FRIGHTENED?

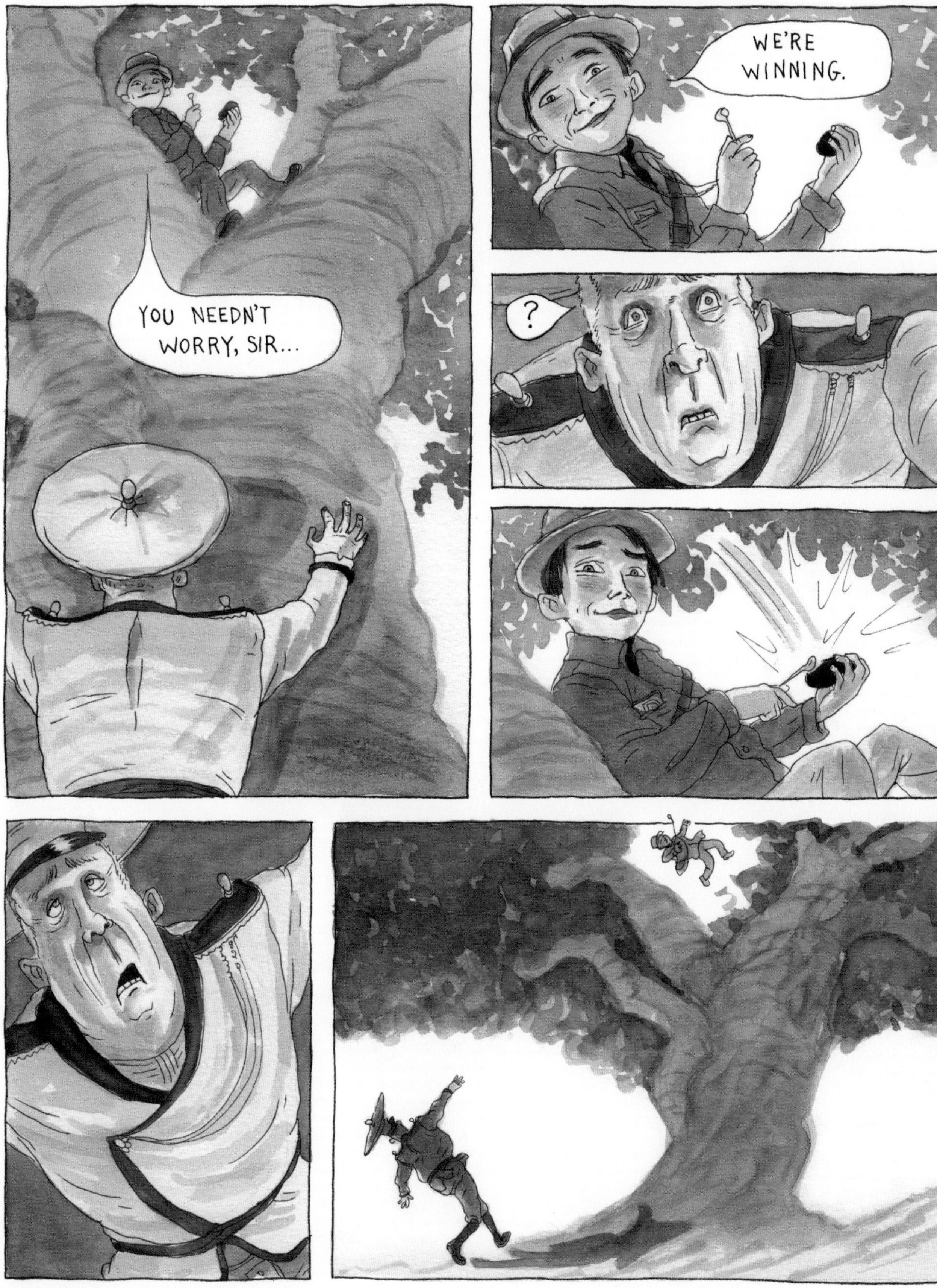
YOU NEEDN'T WORRY, SIR...
WE'RE WINNING.
?

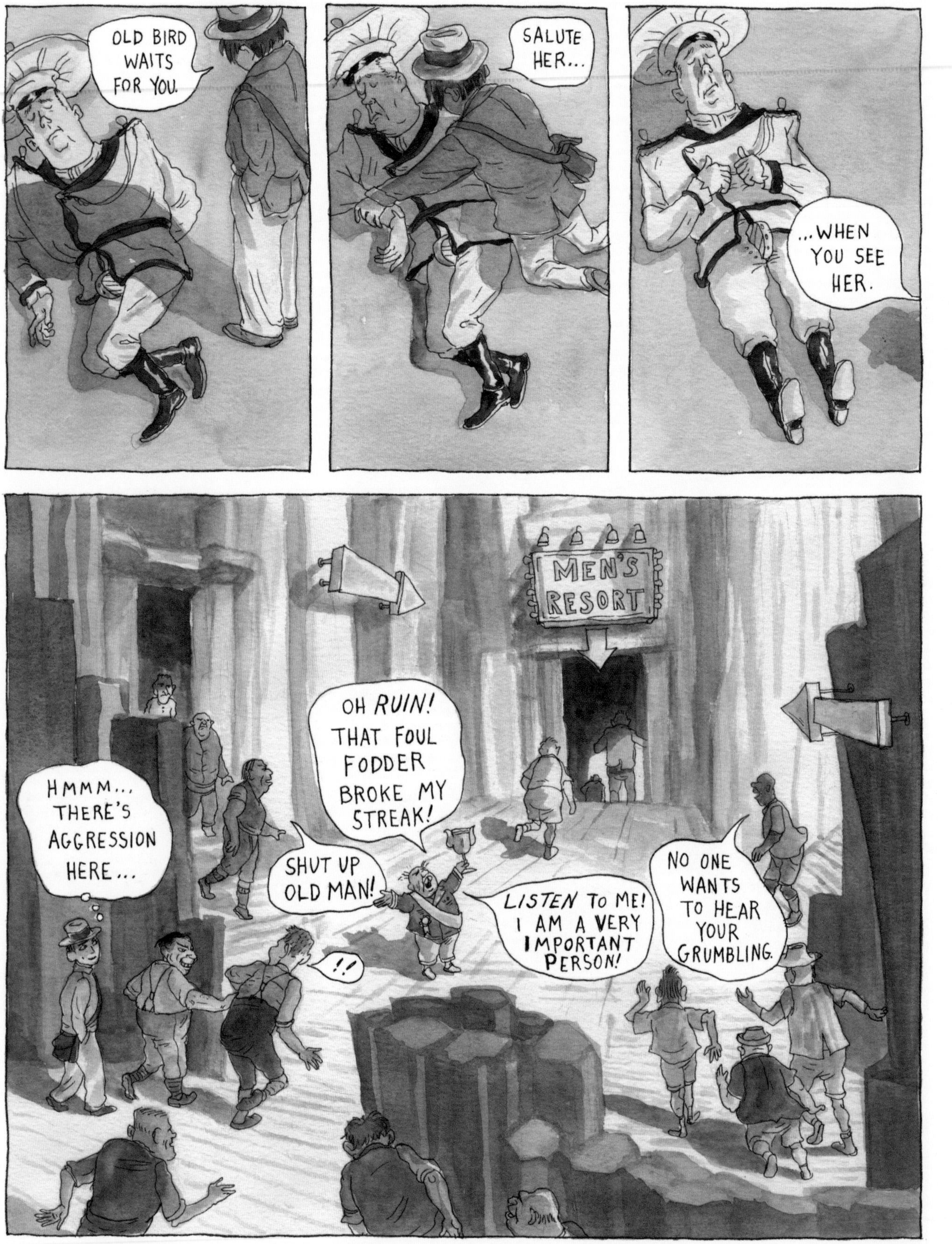
OLD BIRD WAITS FOR YOU.
SALUTE HER...
...WHEN YOU SEE HER.
MEN'S RESORT
HMMM... THERE'S AGGRESSION HERE...
OH *RUIN!* THAT FOUL FODDER BROKE MY STREAK!
SHUT UP OLD MAN!
!!
LISTEN TO ME! I AM A VERY IMPORTANT PERSON!
NO ONE WANTS TO HEAR YOUR GRUMBLING.

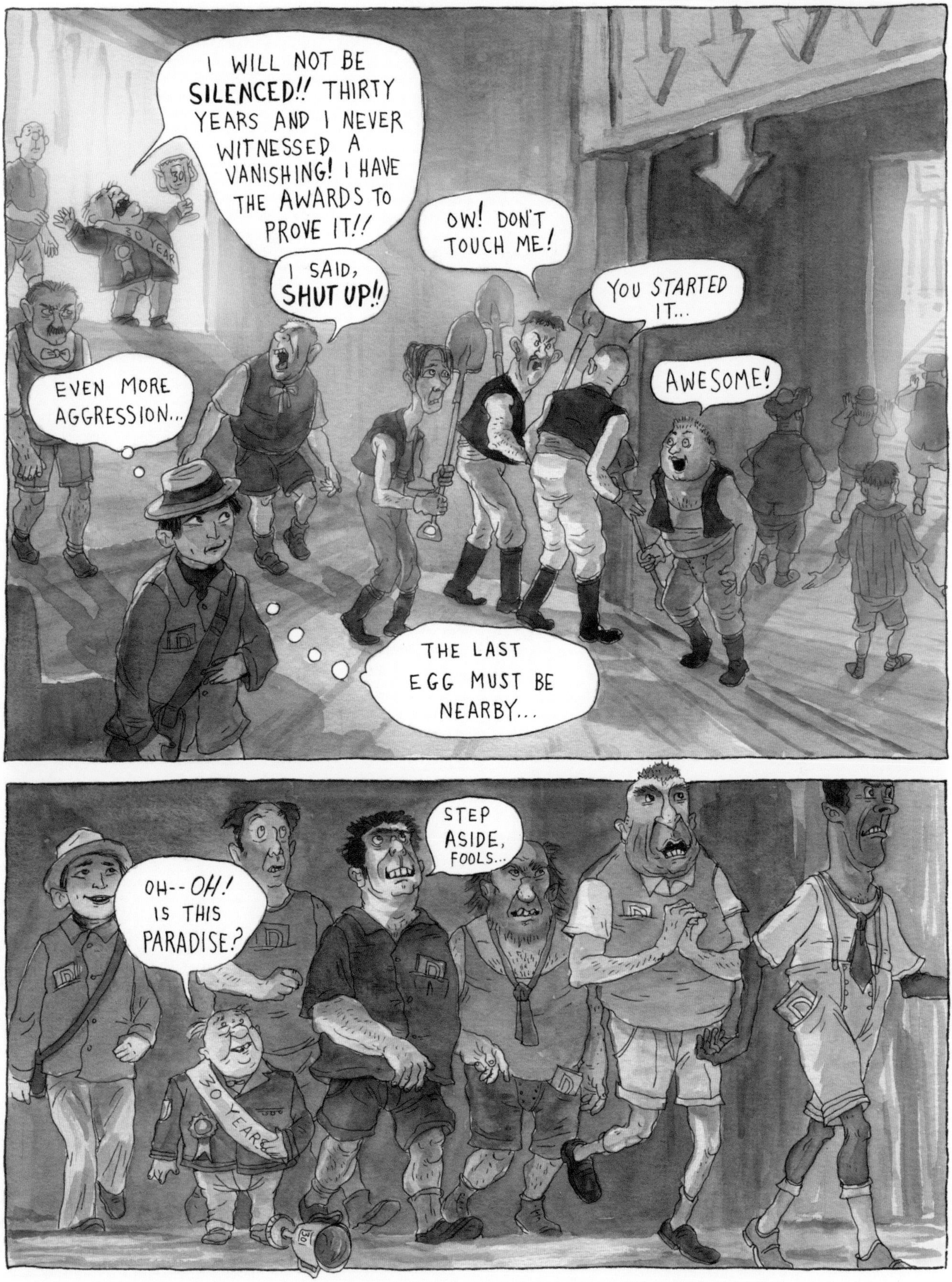
I WILL NOT BE SILENCED!! THIRTY YEARS AND I NEVER WITNESSED A VANISHING! I HAVE THE AWARDS TO PROVE IT!!
I SAID, SHUT UP!!
OW! DON'T TOUCH ME!
YOU STARTED IT...
AWESOME!
EVEN MORE AGGRESSION...
THE LAST EGG MUST BE NEARBY...
STEP ASIDE, FOOLS...
OH--OH! IS THIS PARADISE?
30 YEARS

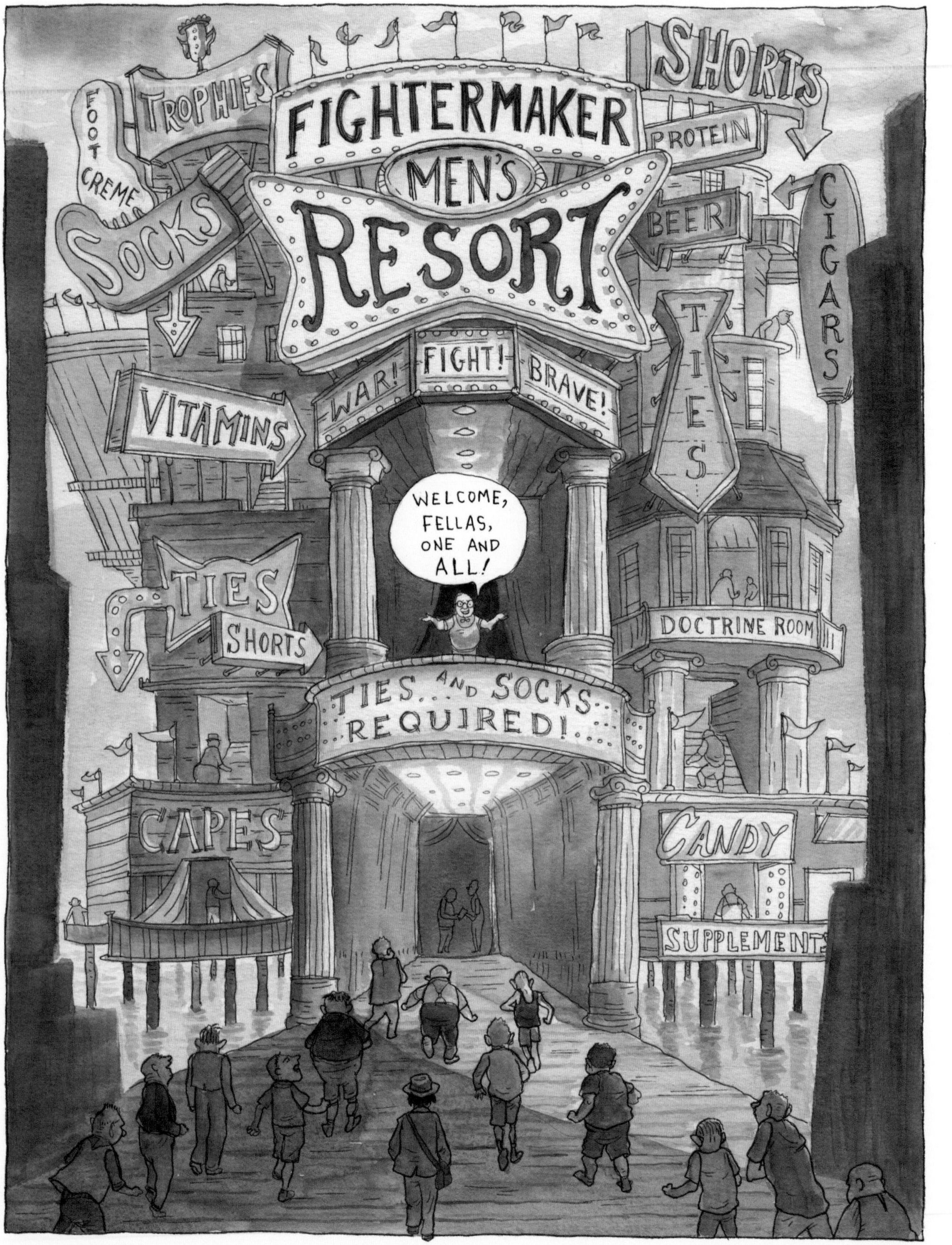
TROPHIES
FOOT CREME
SOCKS
FIGHTERMAKER
MEN'S
RESORT
SHORTS
PROTEIN
BEER
CIGARS
TIES
WAR!
FIGHT!
BRAVE!
VITAMINS
WELCOME, FELLAS, ONE AND ALL!
TIES
SHORTS
DOCTRINE ROOM
TIES AND SOCKS REQUIRED!
CAPES
CANDY
SUPPLEMENTS

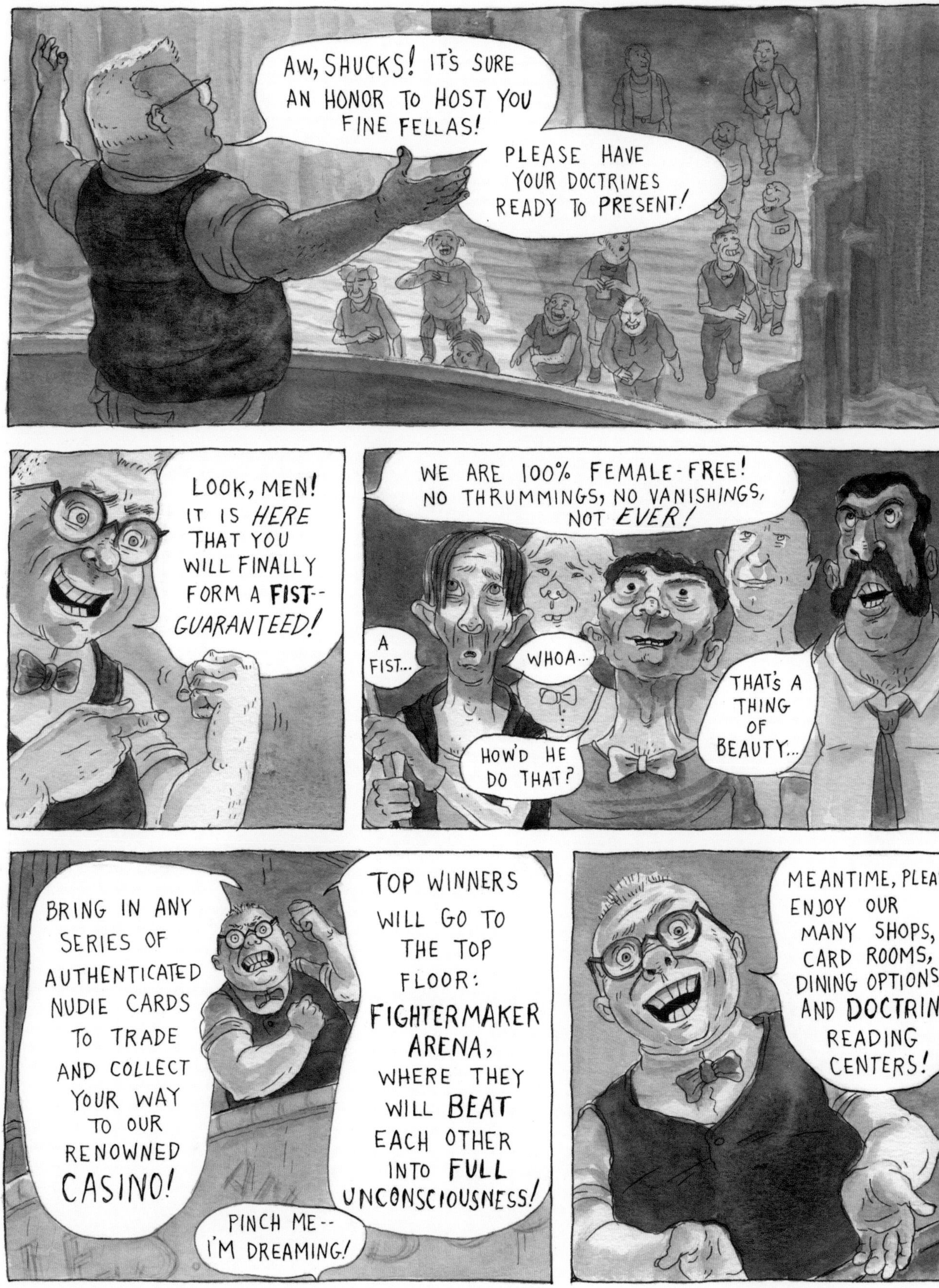
AW, SHUCKS! IT'S SURE AN HONOR TO HOST YOU FINE FELLAS!
PLEASE HAVE YOUR DOCTRINES READY TO PRESENT!
LOOK, MEN! IT IS *HERE* THAT YOU WILL FINALLY FORM A **FIST**--*GUARANTEED!*
WE ARE 100% FEMALE-FREE! NO THRUMMINGS, NO VANISHINGS, NOT *EVER!*
A FIST...
WHOA...
HOW'D HE DO THAT?
THAT'S A THING OF BEAUTY...
BRING IN ANY SERIES OF AUTHENTICATED NUDIE CARDS TO TRADE AND COLLECT YOUR WAY TO OUR RENOWNED CASINO!
TOP WINNERS WILL GO TO THE TOP FLOOR: **FIGHTERMAKER ARENA,** WHERE THEY WILL **BEAT** EACH OTHER INTO **FULL** UNCONSCIOUSNESS!
PINCH ME-- I'M DREAMING!
MEANTIME, PLEASE ENJOY OUR MANY SHOPS, CARD ROOMS, DINING OPTIONS, AND **DOCTRINE** READING CENTERS!

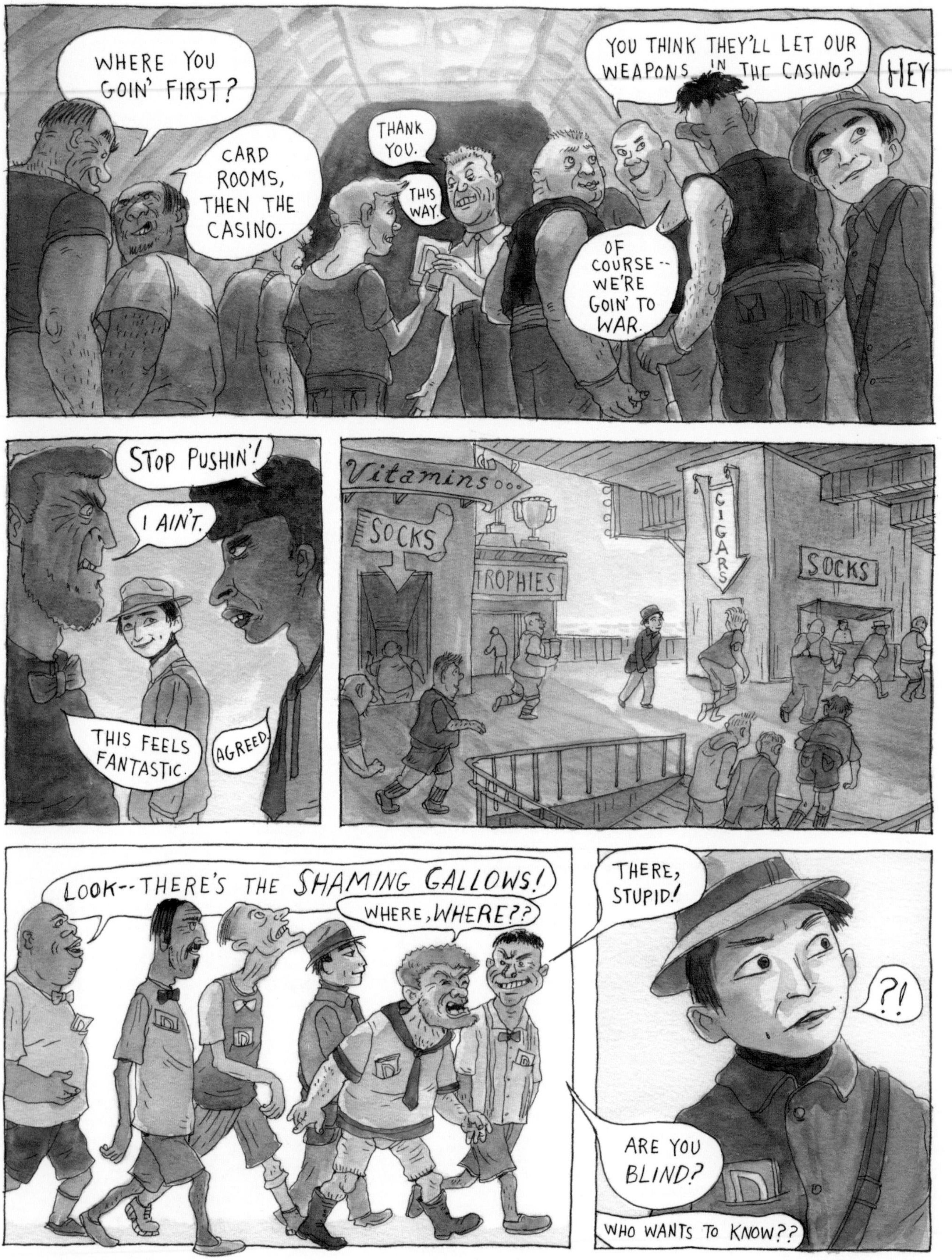
WHERE YOU GOIN' FIRST?
CARD ROOMS, THEN THE CASINO.
THANK YOU.
THIS WAY.
YOU THINK THEY'LL LET OUR WEAPONS IN THE CASINO?
OF COURSE-- WE'RE GOIN' TO WAR.
HEY
STOP PUSHIN'!
I AIN'T.
THIS FEELS FANTASTIC.
AGREED.
Vitamins
SOCKS
TROPHIES
CIGARS
SOCKS
LOOK--THERE'S THE SHAMING GALLOWS!
WHERE, WHERE??
THERE, STUPID!
ARE YOU BLIND?
?!
WHO WANTS TO KNOW??

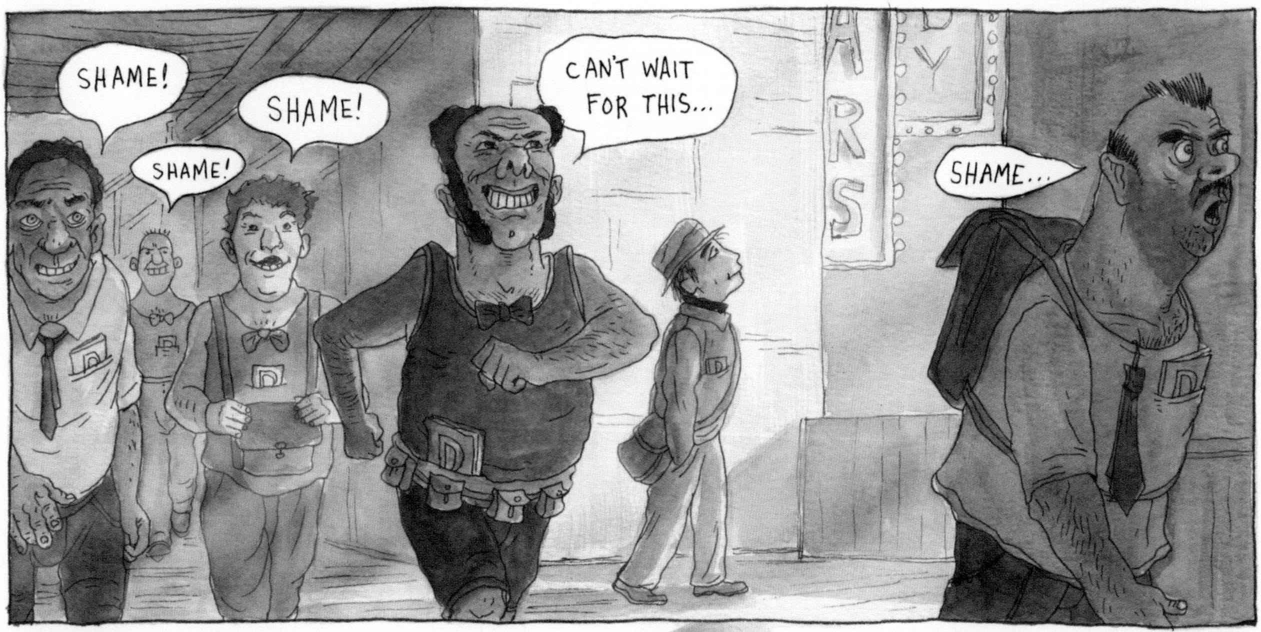
SHAME!
SHAME!
SHAME!
CAN'T WAIT FOR THIS...
SHAME...

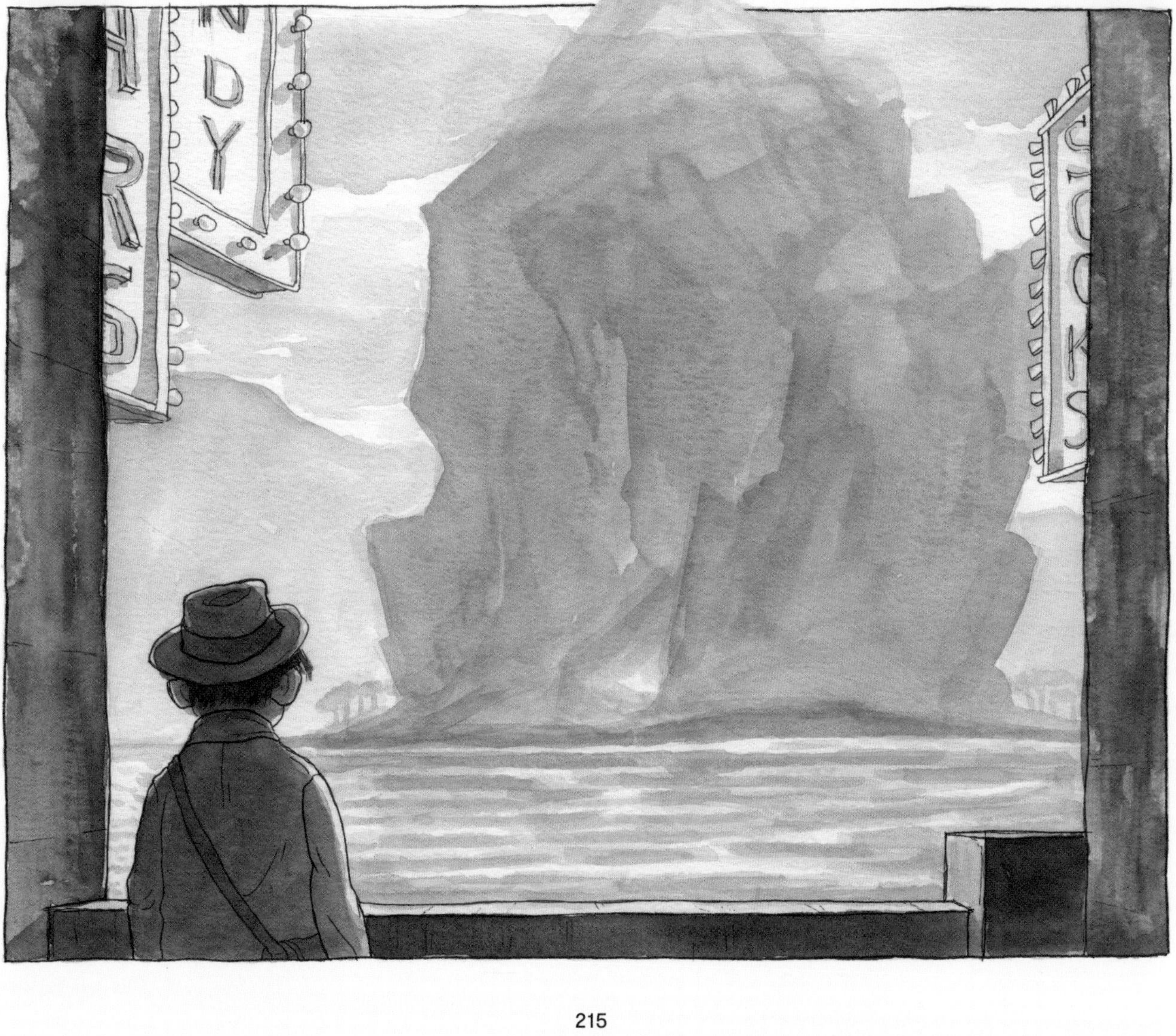

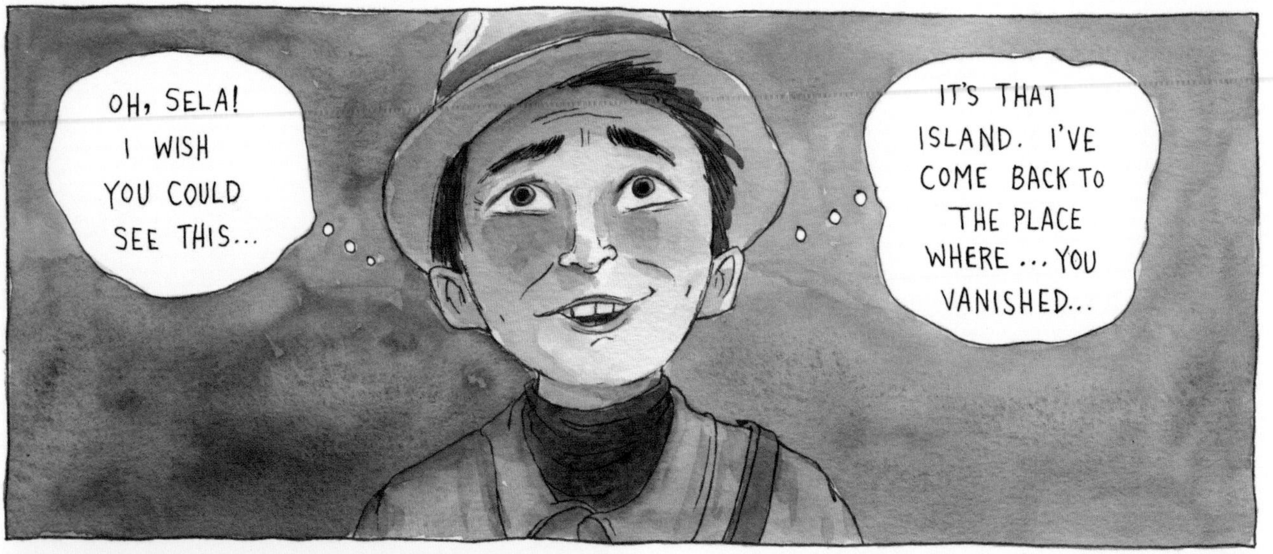
OH, SELA! I WISH YOU COULD SEE THIS...
IT'S THAT ISLAND. I'VE COME BACK TO THE PLACE WHERE ... YOU VANISHED...

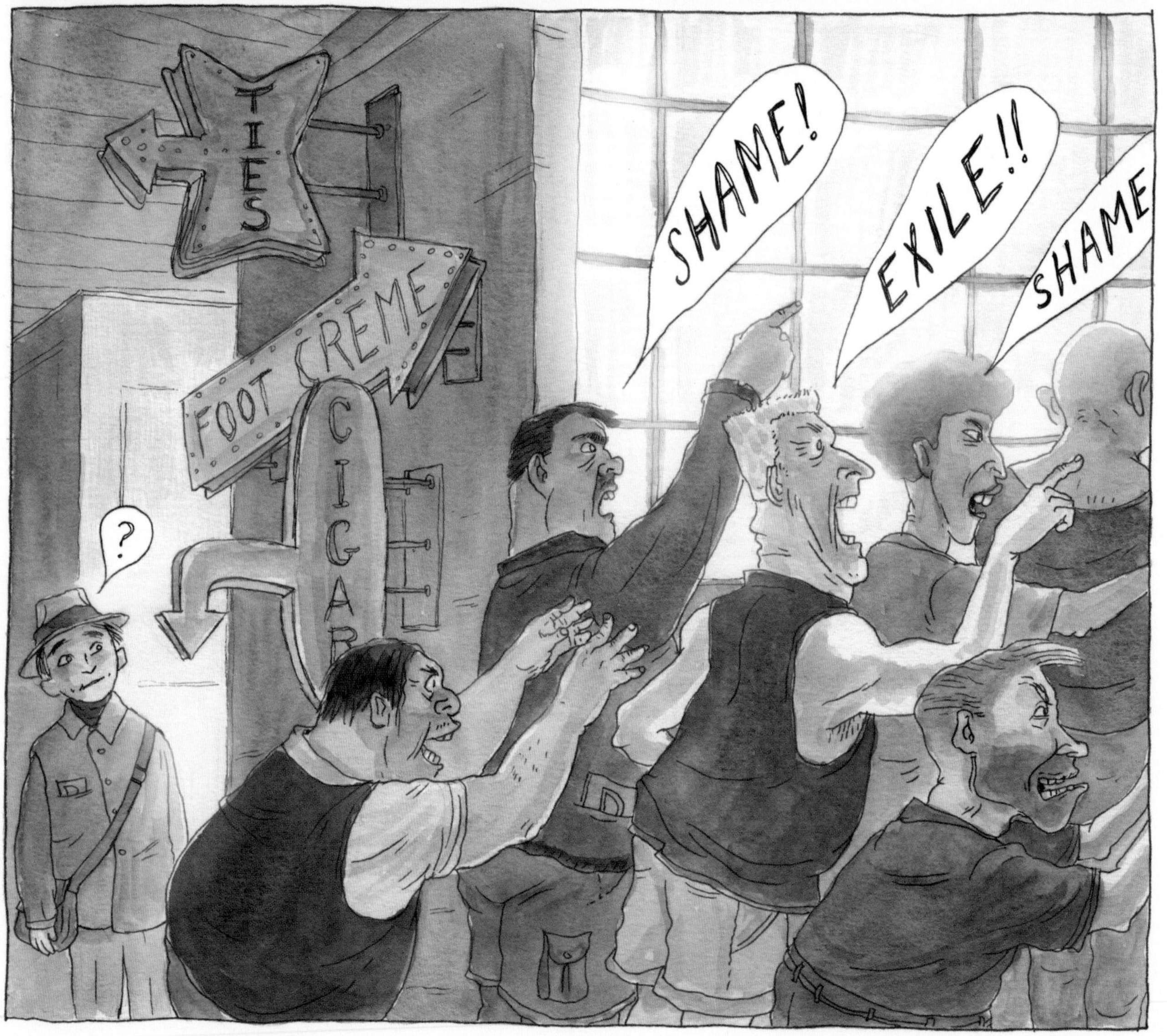
TIES
FOOT CREME
CIGAR
?
SHAME!
EXILE!!
SHAME

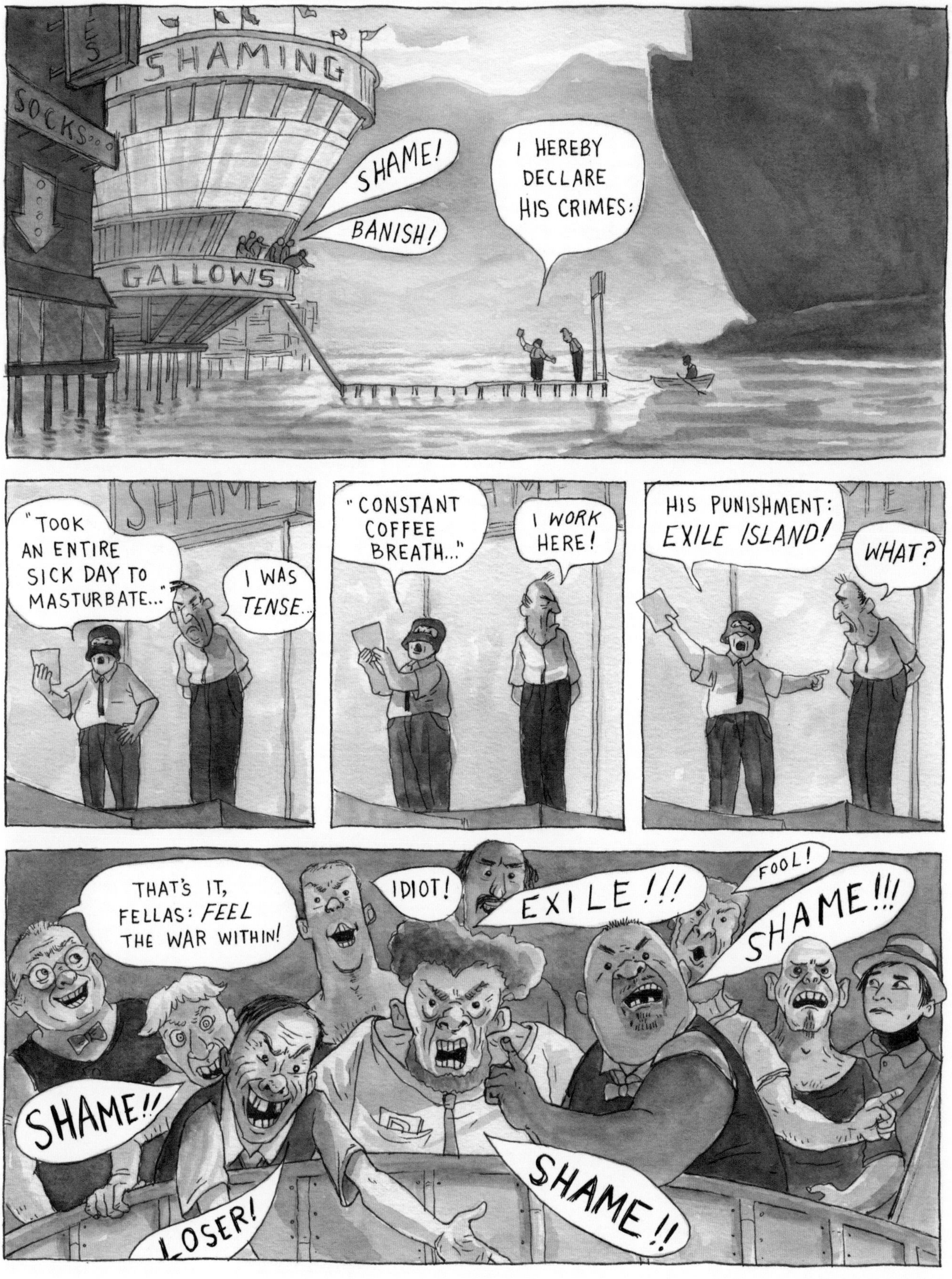
ES
SHAMING
SOCKS
GALLOWS
SHAME!
BANISH!
I HEREBY DECLARE HIS CRIMES:
"TOOK AN ENTIRE SICK DAY TO MASTURBATE..."
I WAS *TENSE*...
SHAME
"CONSTANT COFFEE BREATH..."
I WORK HERE!
HIS PUNISHMENT: *EXILE ISLAND!*
WHAT?
THAT'S IT, FELLAS: *FEEL* THE WAR WITHIN!
IDIOT!
EXILE!!!
FOOL!
SHAME!!!
SHAME!!
SHAME!!
LOSER!

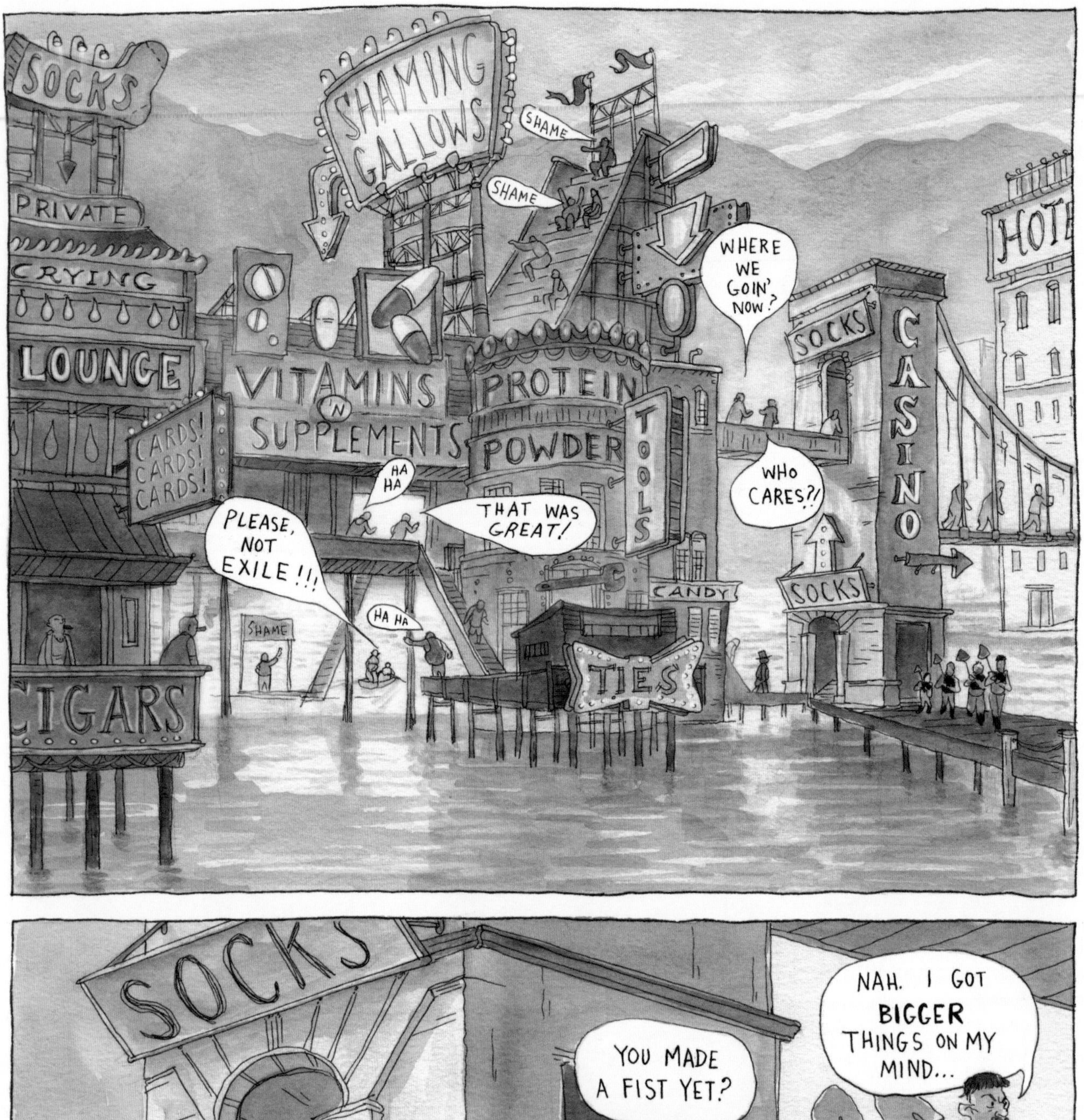
SOCKS
PRIVATE
CRYING
LOUNGE
SHAMING GALLOWS
SHAME
SHAME
VITAMINS 'N SUPPLEMENTS
PROTEIN POWDER
WHERE WE GOIN' NOW?
SOCKS
CASINO
HOTE
CARDS! CARDS! CARDS!
TOOLS
HA HA
THAT WAS GREAT!
PLEASE, NOT EXILE!!!
WHO CARES?!
CANDY
SOCKS
SHAME
HA HA
TIES
CIGARS

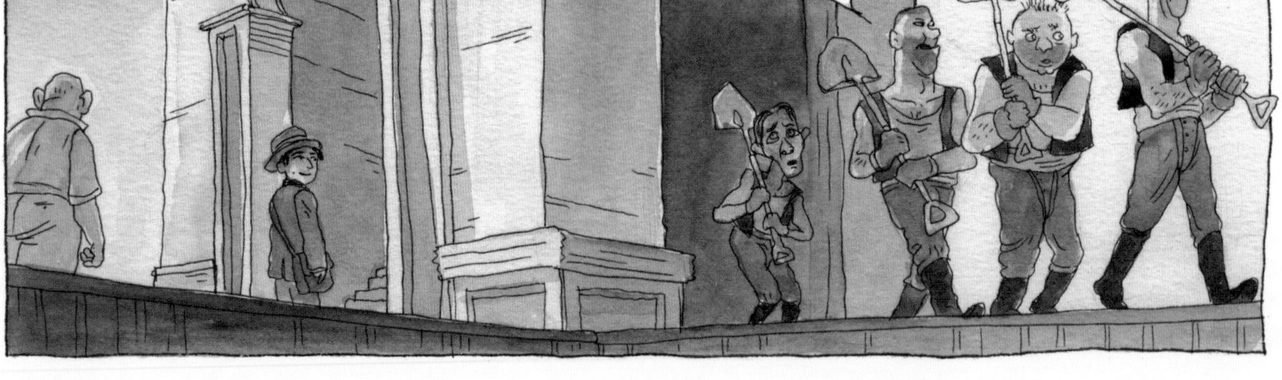
SOCKS
YOU MADE A FIST YET?
NAH. I GOT **BIGGER** THINGS ON MY MIND...

TRY YOUR LUCK
CASINO
PUNCH
KNOCK 'EM OUT!!
FIGHTERMAKER ARENA
!W!I!N!
!F!I!G!H!T!
!W!A!R!
CASINO
NUDIES
NOODLES
I'M GOIN' TO SEE PHYLLIS.
WHATSA PHYLLIS?
WHAT AIN'T SHE, IDIOT!
WAIT -- SHE'S A FEMALE?

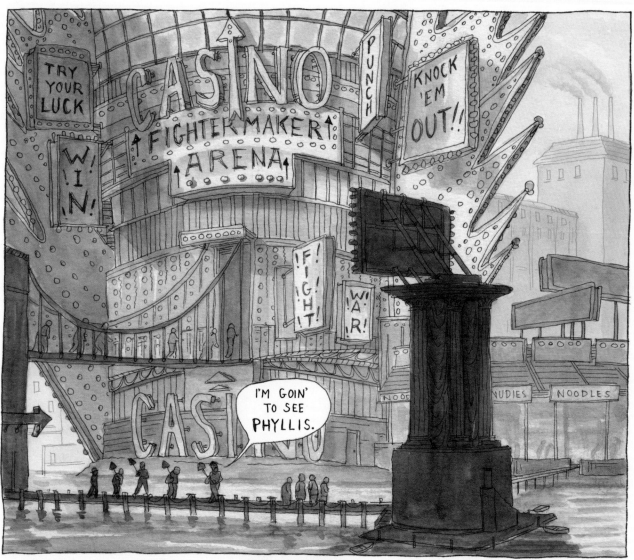

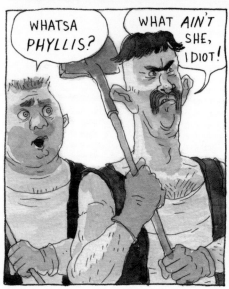

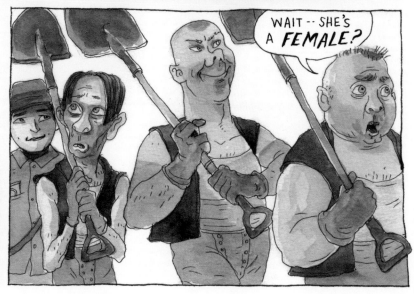

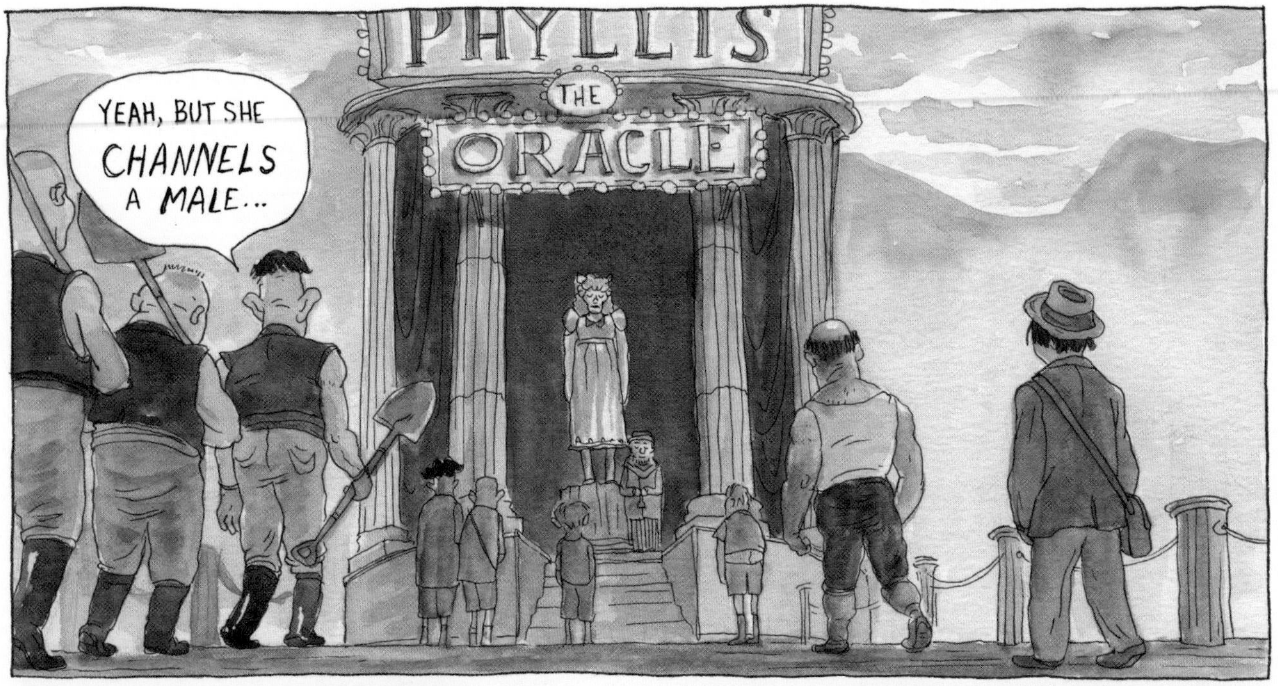
PHYLLIS
THE
ORACLE
YEAH, BUT SHE CHANNELS A MALE...

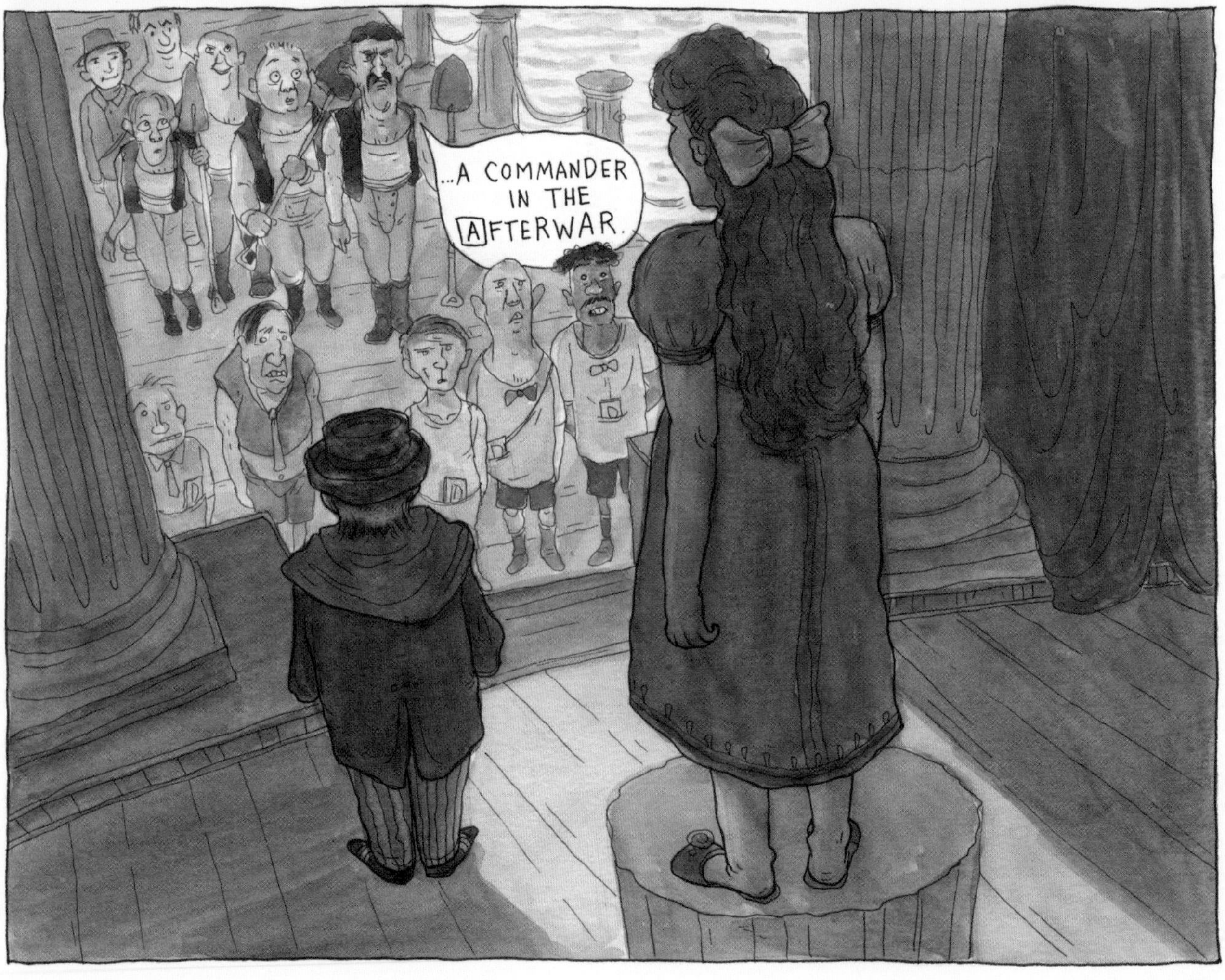
...A COMMANDER IN THE AFTERWAR.

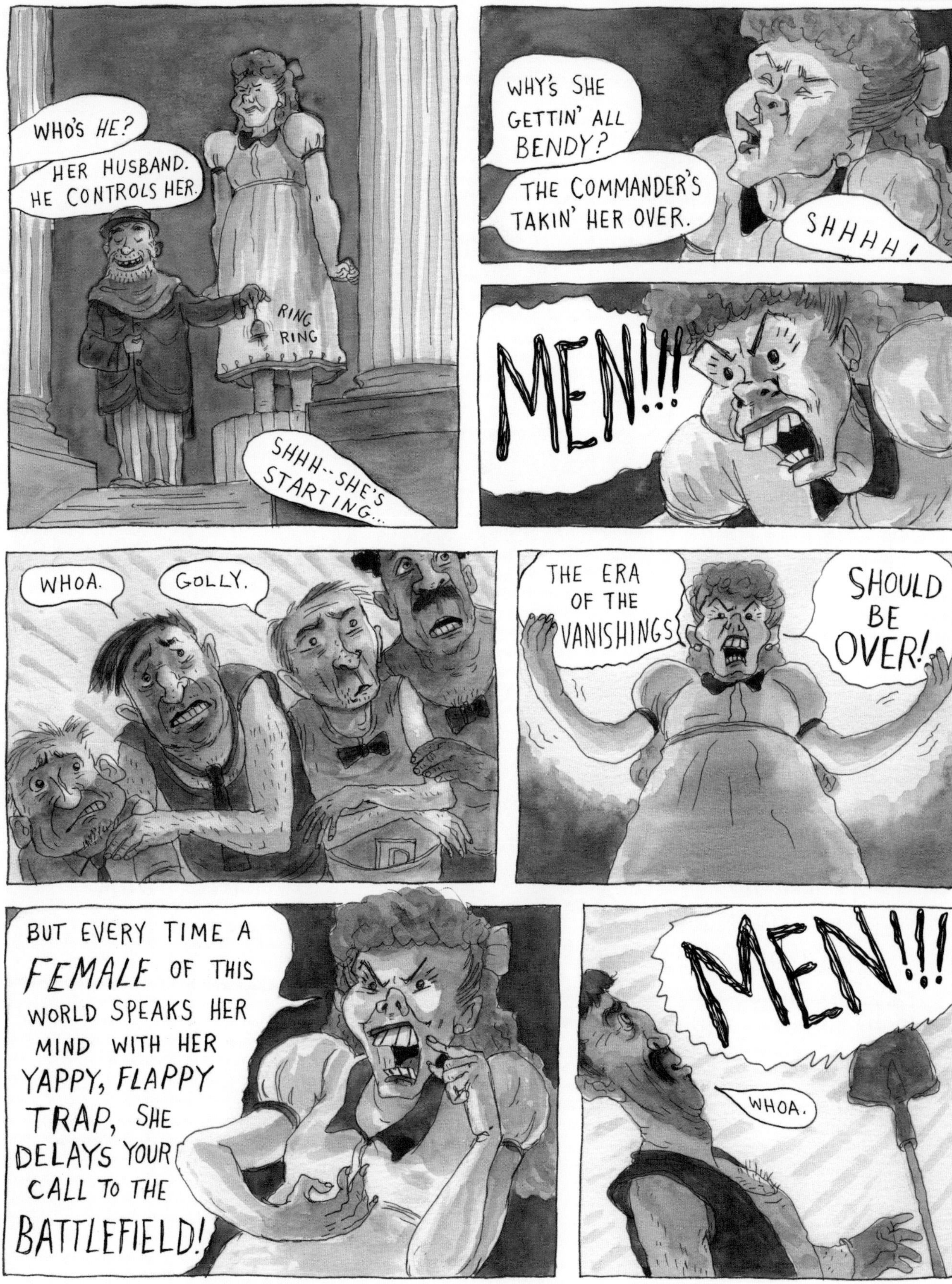
WHO'S HE?
HER HUSBAND. HE CONTROLS HER.
RING RING
SHHH--SHE'S STARTING...
WHY'S SHE GETTIN' ALL BENDY?
THE COMMANDER'S TAKIN' HER OVER.
SHHHH!
MEN!!!
WHOA.
GOLLY.
THE ERA OF THE VANISHINGS
SHOULD BE OVER!
BUT EVERY TIME A FEMALE OF THIS WORLD SPEAKS HER MIND WITH HER YAPPY, FLAPPY TRAP, SHE DELAYS YOUR CALL TO THE BATTLEFIELD!
MEN!!!
WHOA.

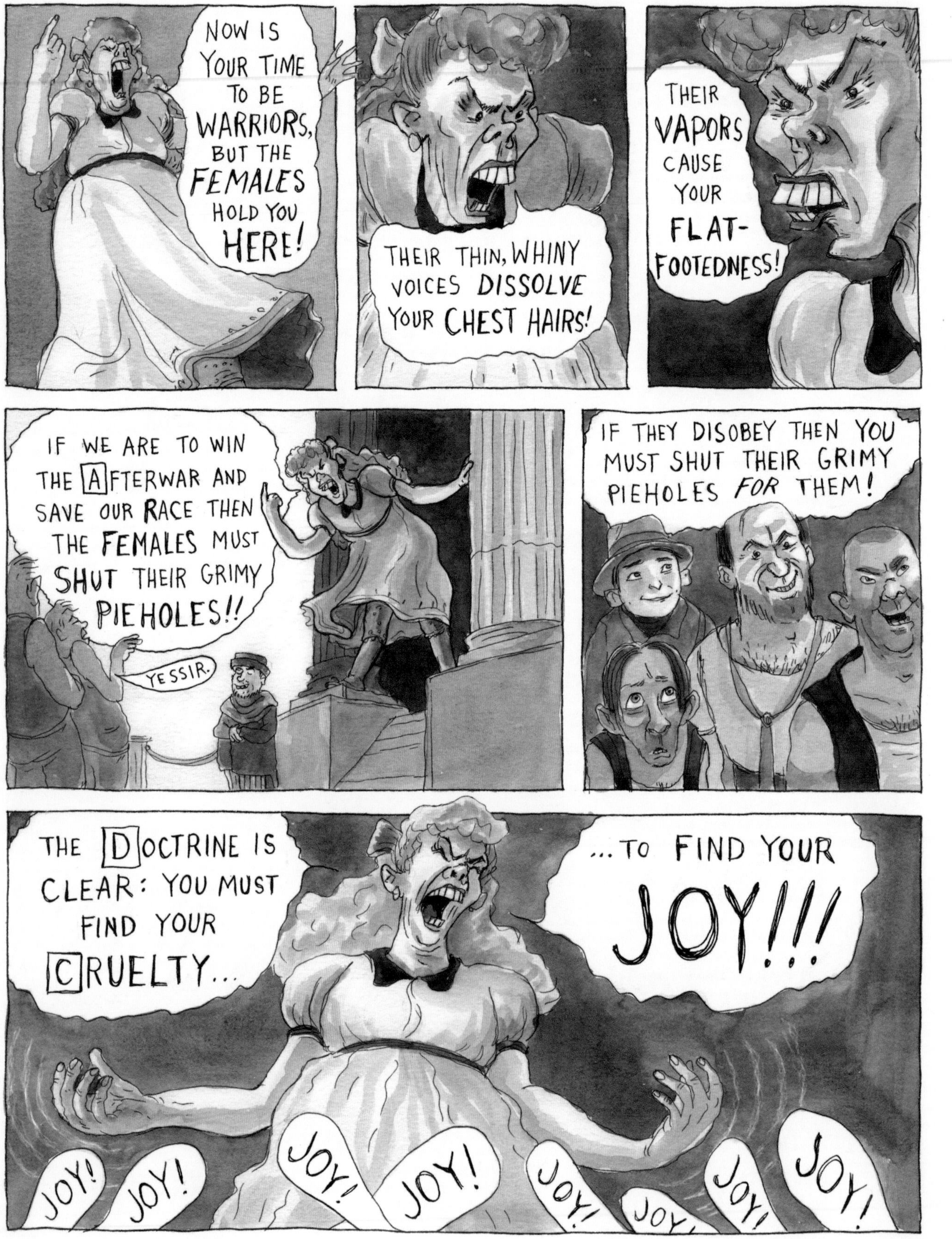
NOW IS YOUR TIME TO BE WARRIORS, BUT THE FEMALES HOLD YOU HERE!
THEIR THIN, WHINY VOICES DISSOLVE YOUR CHEST HAIRS!
THEIR VAPORS CAUSE YOUR FLAT-FOOTEDNESS!
IF WE ARE TO WIN THE AFTERWAR AND SAVE OUR RACE THEN THE FEMALES MUST SHUT THEIR GRIMY PIEHOLES!!
YESSIR.
IF THEY DISOBEY THEN YOU MUST SHUT THEIR GRIMY PIEHOLES FOR THEM!
THE DOCTRINE IS CLEAR: YOU MUST FIND YOUR CRUELTY...
...TO FIND YOUR JOY!!!
JOY!
JOY!
JOY!
JOY!
JOY!
JOY!
JOY!
JOY!

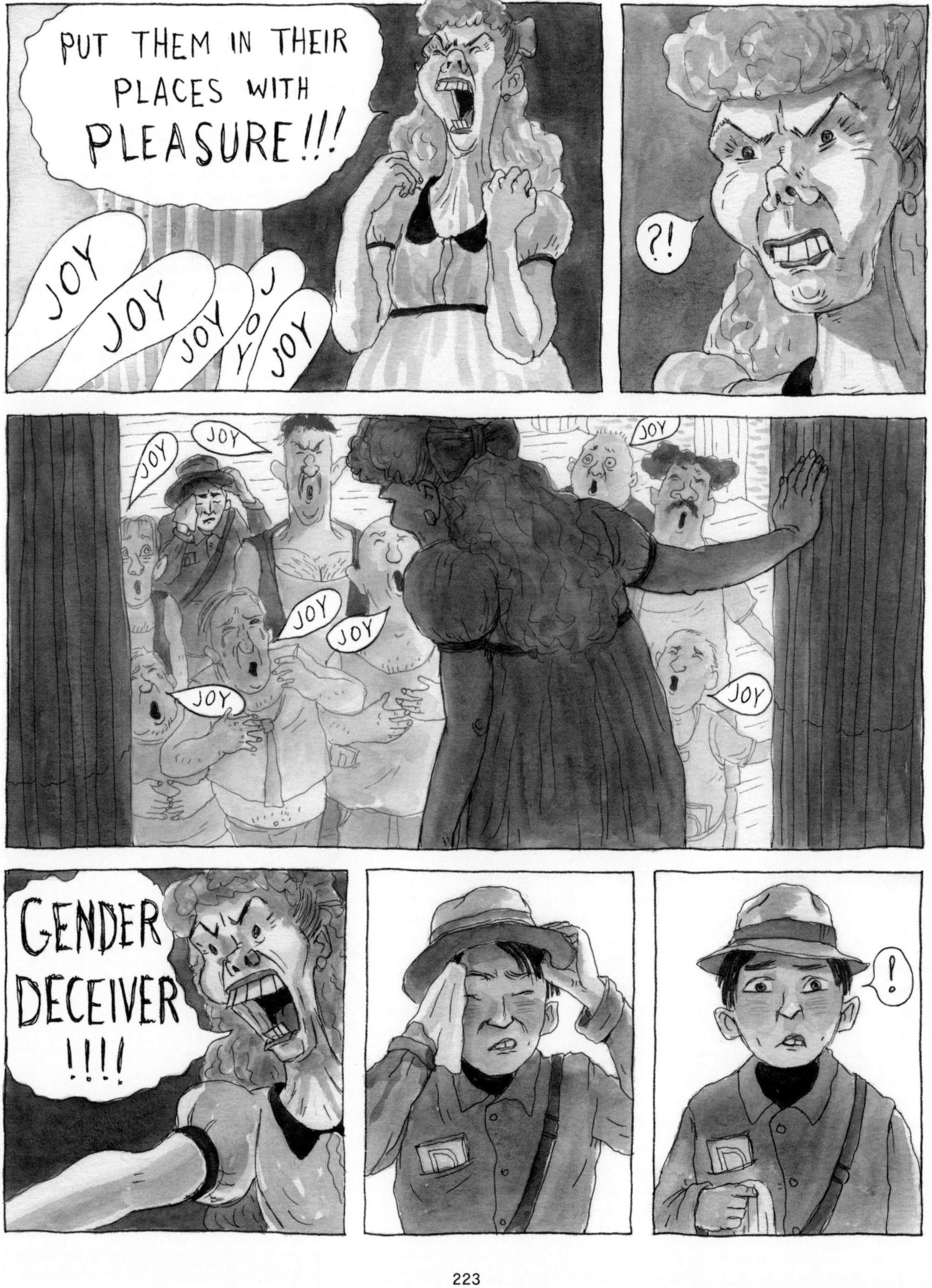
PUT THEM IN THEIR PLACES WITH PLEASURE!!!
JOY
JOY
JOY
JOY
JOY
?!
JOY
JOY
JOY
JOY
JOY
JOY
JOY
GENDER DECEIVER !!!!
!

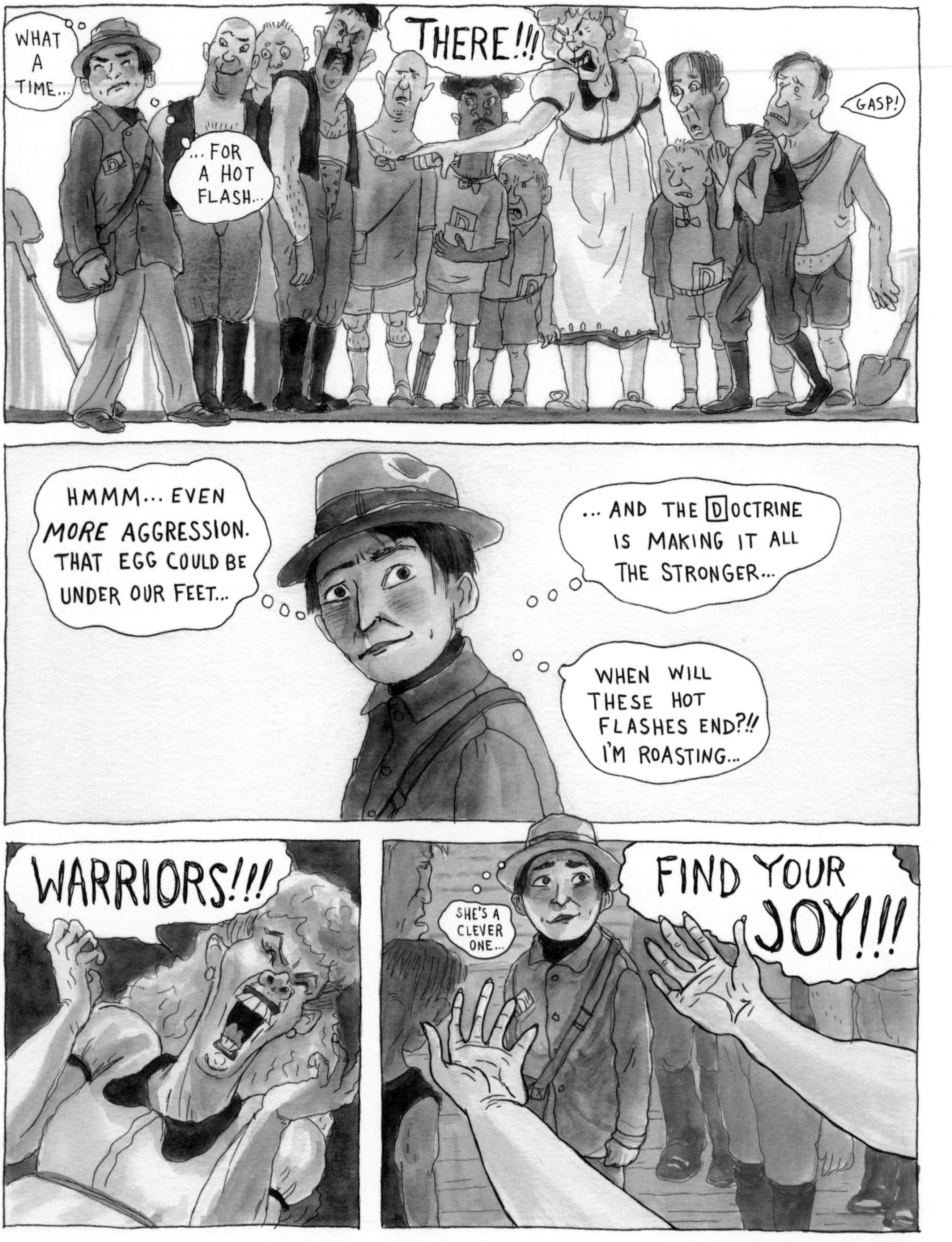
WHAT A TIME...
THERE!!!
...FOR A HOT FLASH...
GASP!
HMMM... EVEN MORE AGGRESSION. THAT EGG COULD BE UNDER OUR FEET...
...AND THE D OCTRINE IS MAKING IT ALL THE STRONGER...
WHEN WILL THESE HOT FLASHES END?!! I'M ROASTING...
WARRIORS!!!
SHE'S A CLEVER ONE...
FIND YOUR JOY!!!

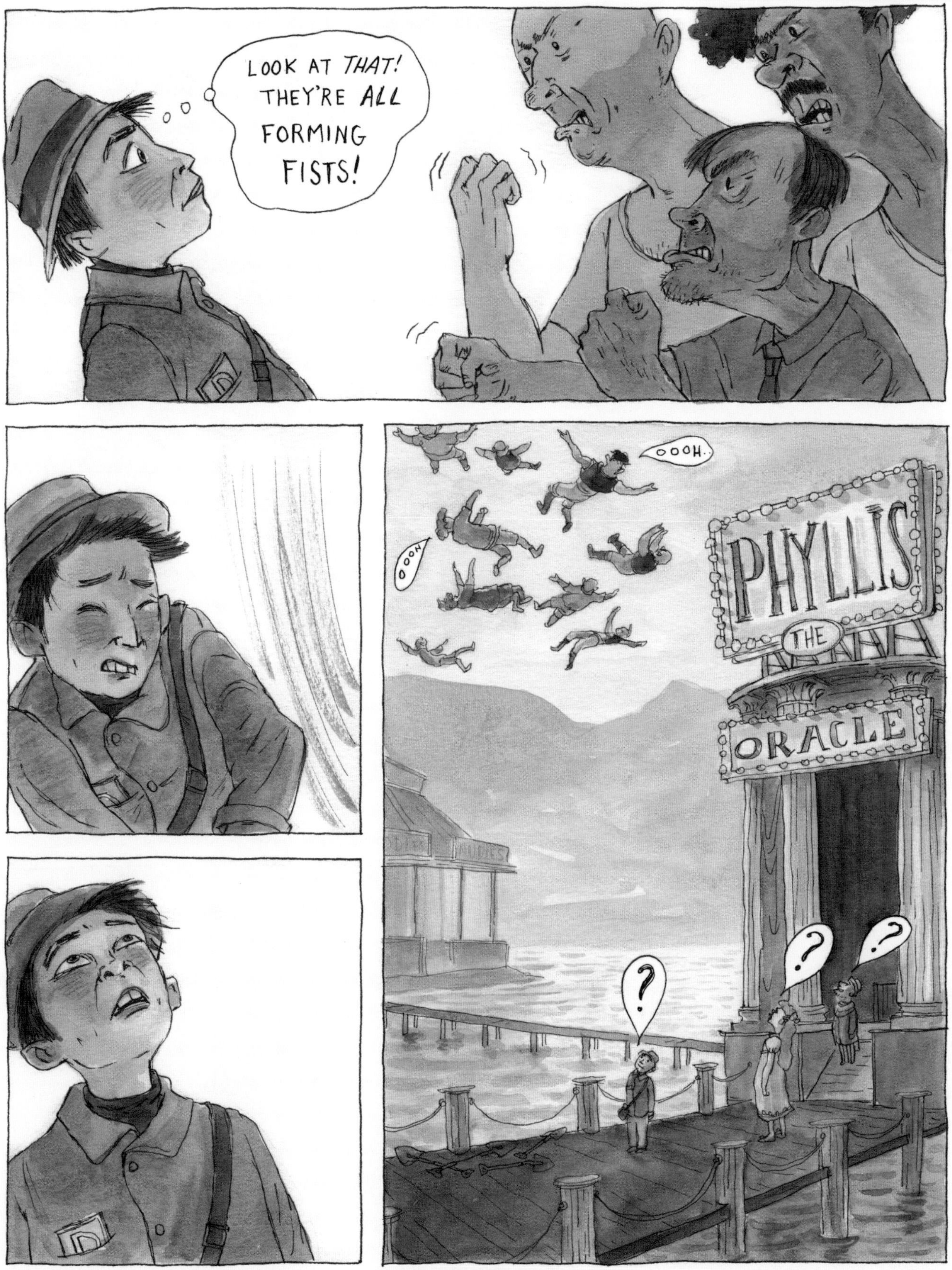
LOOK AT *THAT*! THEY'RE **ALL** FORMING FISTS!
OOOH..
OOOH
PHYLLIS
THE
ORACLE
?
?
?

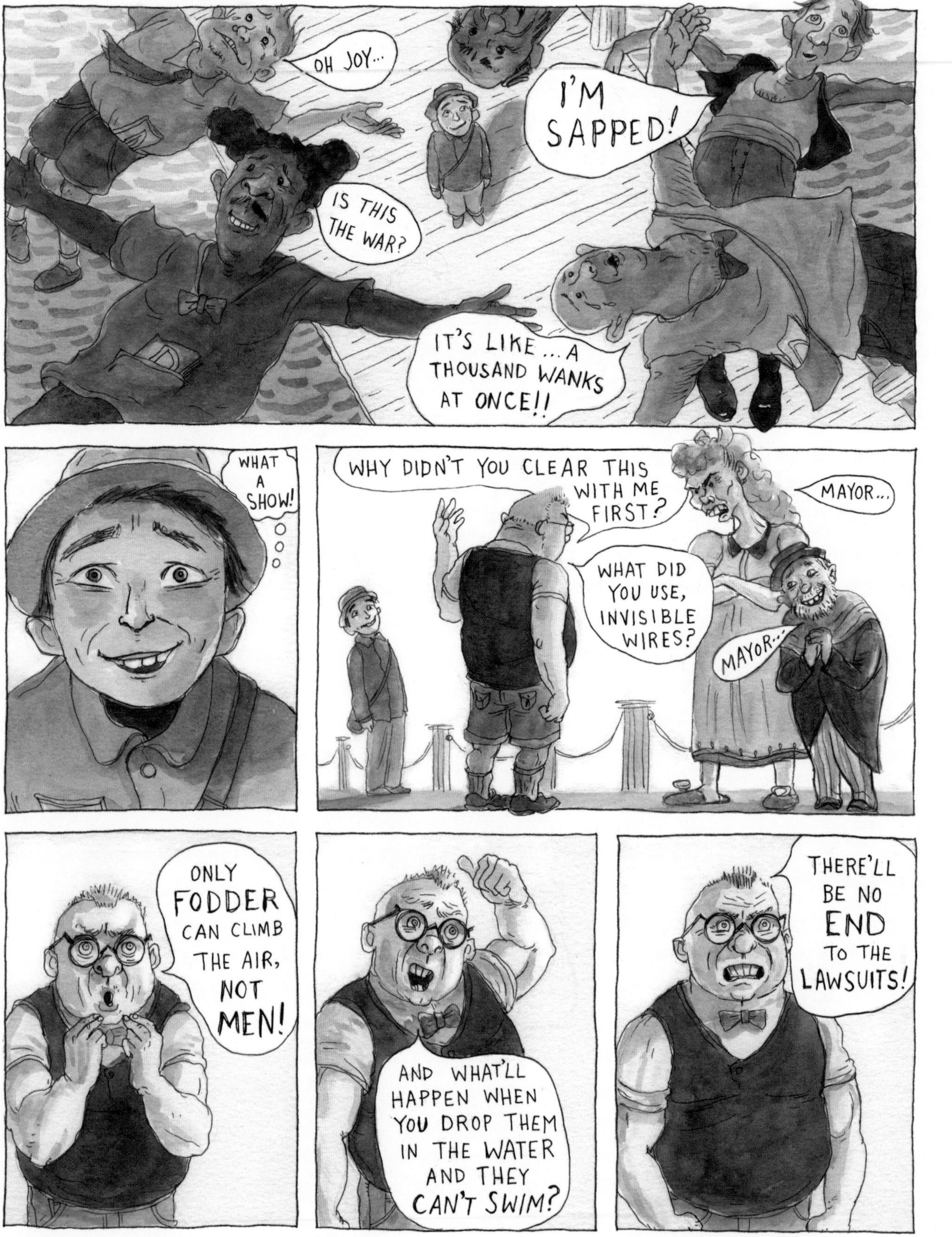
OH JOY...
I'M SAPPED!
IS THIS THE WAR?
IT'S LIKE ... A THOUSAND WANKS AT ONCE!!
WHAT A SHOW!
WHY DIDN'T YOU CLEAR THIS WITH ME FIRST?
MAYOR...
WHAT DID YOU USE, INVISIBLE WIRES?
MAYOR...
ONLY FODDER CAN CLIMB THE AIR, NOT MEN!
AND WHAT'LL HAPPEN WHEN YOU DROP THEM IN THE WATER AND THEY CAN'T SWIM?
THERE'LL BE NO END TO THE LAWSUITS!

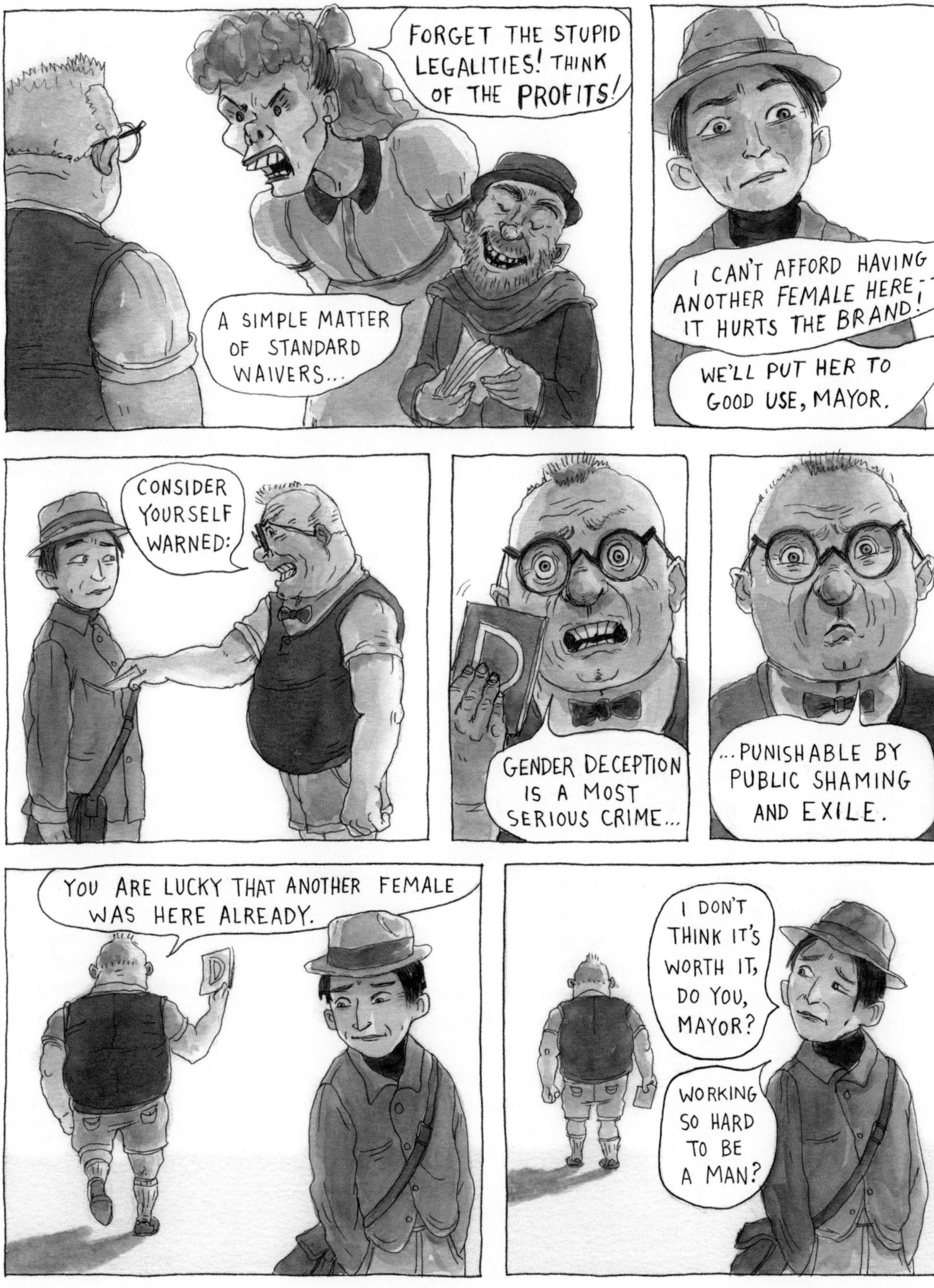
FORGET THE STUPID LEGALITIES! THINK OF THE PROFITS!
A SIMPLE MATTER OF STANDARD WAIVERS...
I CAN'T AFFORD HAVING ANOTHER FEMALE HERE-- IT HURTS THE BRAND!
WE'LL PUT HER TO GOOD USE, MAYOR.
CONSIDER YOURSELF WARNED:
GENDER DECEPTION IS A MOST SERIOUS CRIME...
...PUNISHABLE BY PUBLIC SHAMING AND EXILE.
YOU ARE LUCKY THAT ANOTHER FEMALE WAS HERE ALREADY.
I DON'T THINK IT'S WORTH IT, DO YOU, MAYOR?
WORKING SO HARD TO BE A MAN?

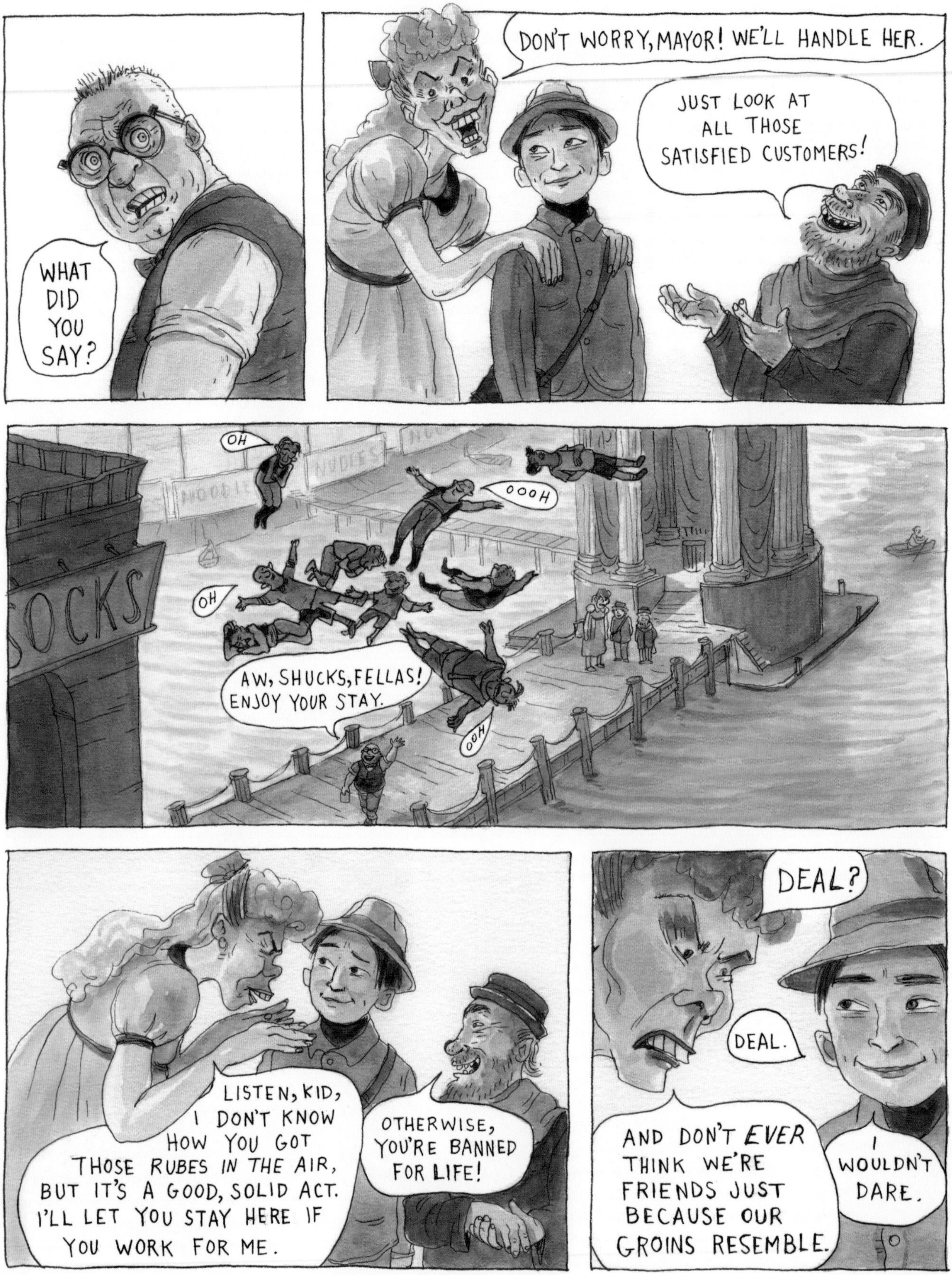
WHAT DID YOU SAY?
DON'T WORRY, MAYOR! WE'LL HANDLE HER.
JUST LOOK AT ALL THOSE SATISFIED CUSTOMERS!
NUDIES
SOCKS
OH
OOOH
OH
AW, SHUCKS, FELLAS! ENJOY YOUR STAY.
OOH
LISTEN, KID, I DON'T KNOW HOW YOU GOT THOSE RUBES IN THE AIR, BUT IT'S A GOOD, SOLID ACT. I'LL LET YOU STAY HERE IF YOU WORK FOR ME.
OTHERWISE, YOU'RE BANNED FOR LIFE!
DEAL?
DEAL.
AND DON'T EVER THINK WE'RE FRIENDS JUST BECAUSE OUR GROINS RESEMBLE.
I WOULDN'T DARE.

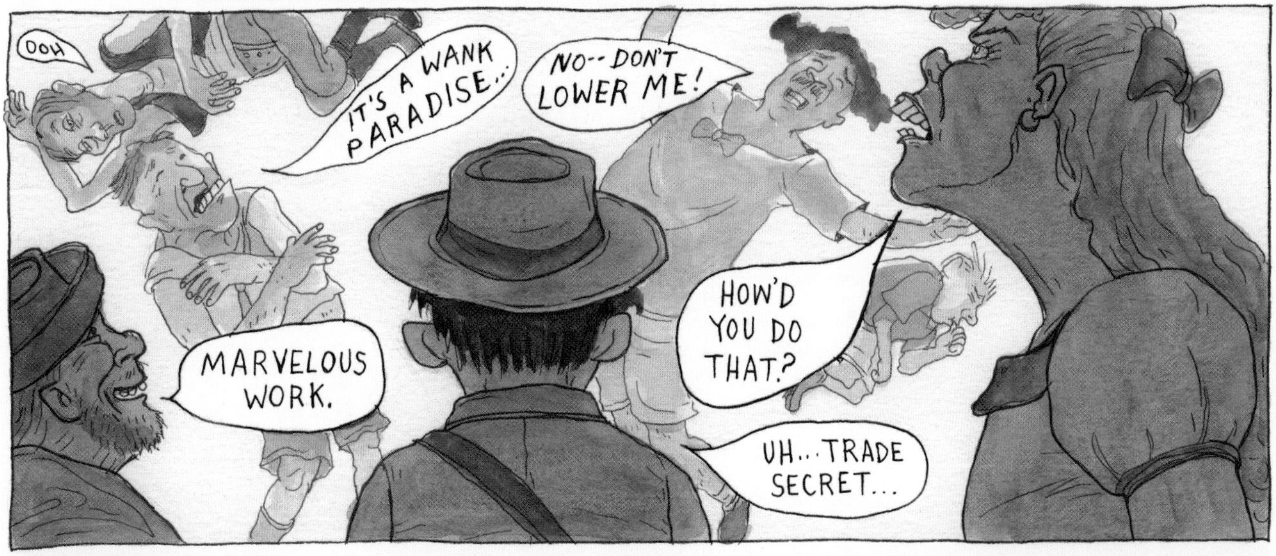
OOH
IT'S A WANK PARADISE...
NO-- DON'T LOWER ME!
MARVELOUS WORK.
HOW'D YOU DO THAT?
UH... TRADE SECRET...

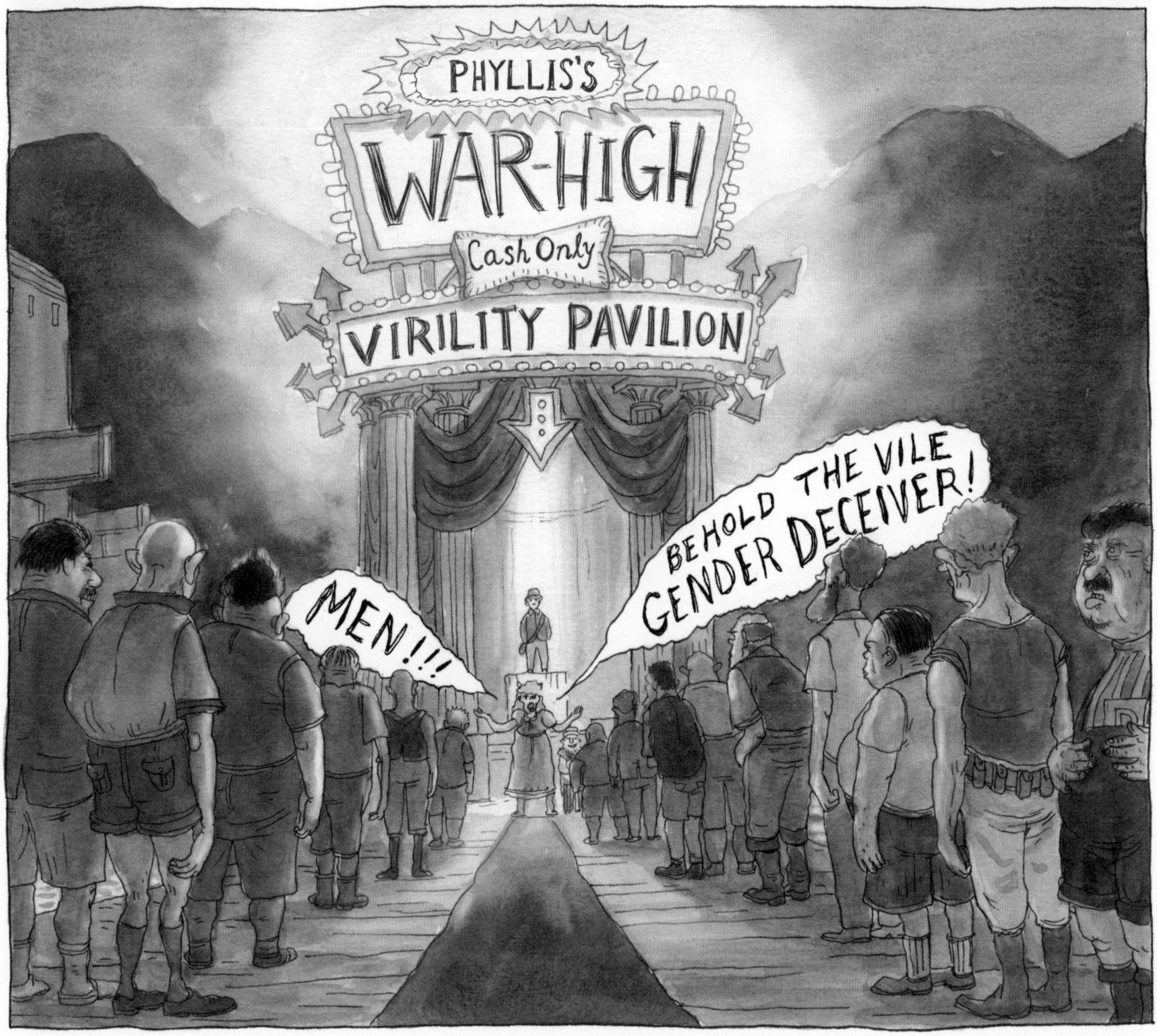
PHYLLIS'S
WAR-HIGH
Cash Only
VIRILITY PAVILION
MEN!!!
BEHOLD THE VILE GENDER DECEIVER!

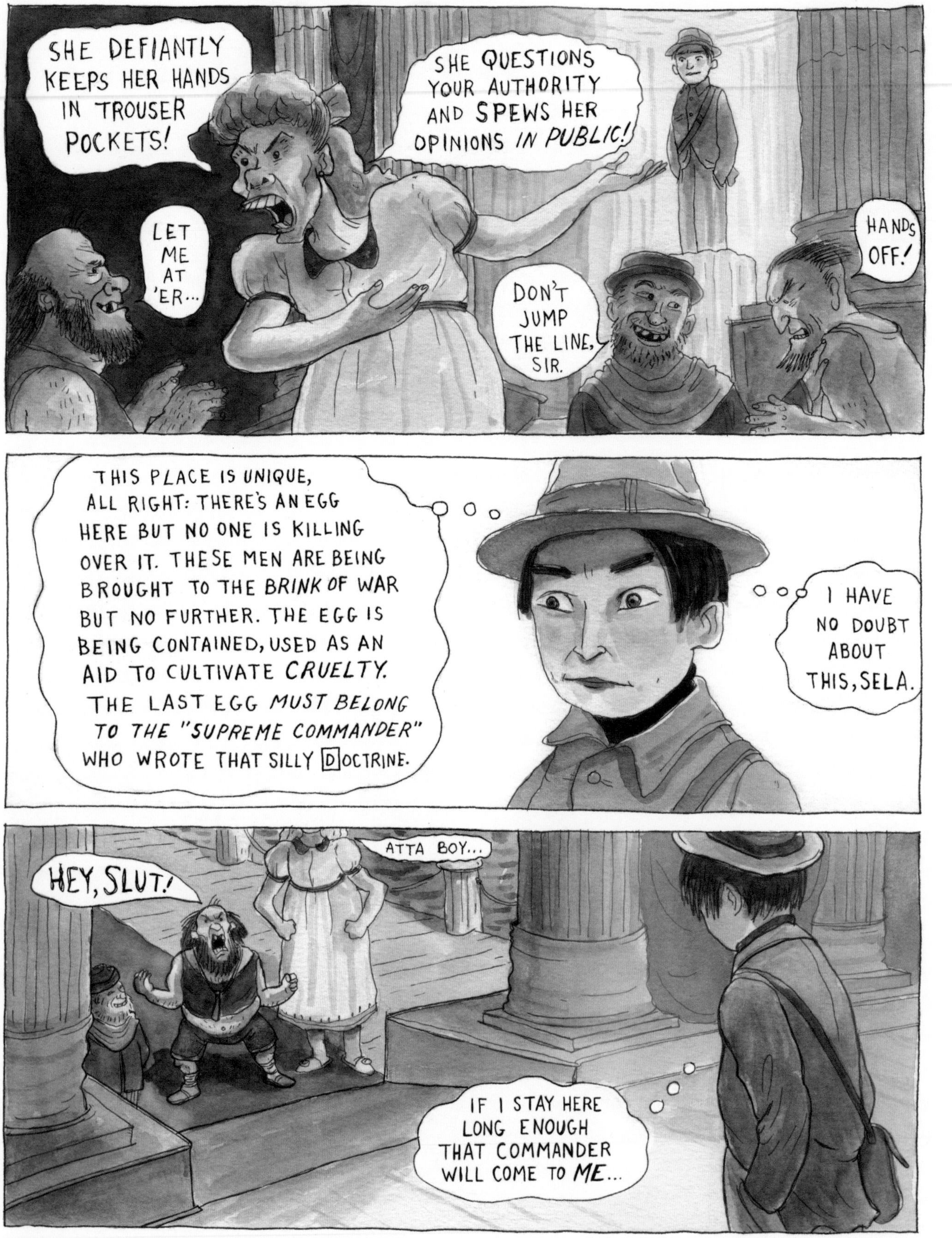
SHE DEFIANTLY KEEPS HER HANDS IN TROUSER POCKETS!
SHE QUESTIONS YOUR AUTHORITY AND SPEWS HER OPINIONS *IN PUBLIC!*
LET ME AT 'ER...
DON'T JUMP THE LINE, SIR.
HANDS OFF!
THIS PLACE IS UNIQUE, ALL RIGHT: THERE'S AN EGG HERE BUT NO ONE IS KILLING OVER IT. THESE MEN ARE BEING BROUGHT TO THE *BRINK* OF WAR BUT NO FURTHER. THE EGG IS BEING CONTAINED, USED AS AN AID TO CULTIVATE *CRUELTY*. THE LAST EGG *MUST BELONG TO THE "SUPREME COMMANDER"* WHO WROTE THAT SILLY DOCTRINE.
I HAVE NO DOUBT ABOUT THIS, SELA.
HEY, SLUT!
ATTA BOY...
IF I STAY HERE LONG ENOUGH THAT COMMANDER WILL COME TO *ME*...

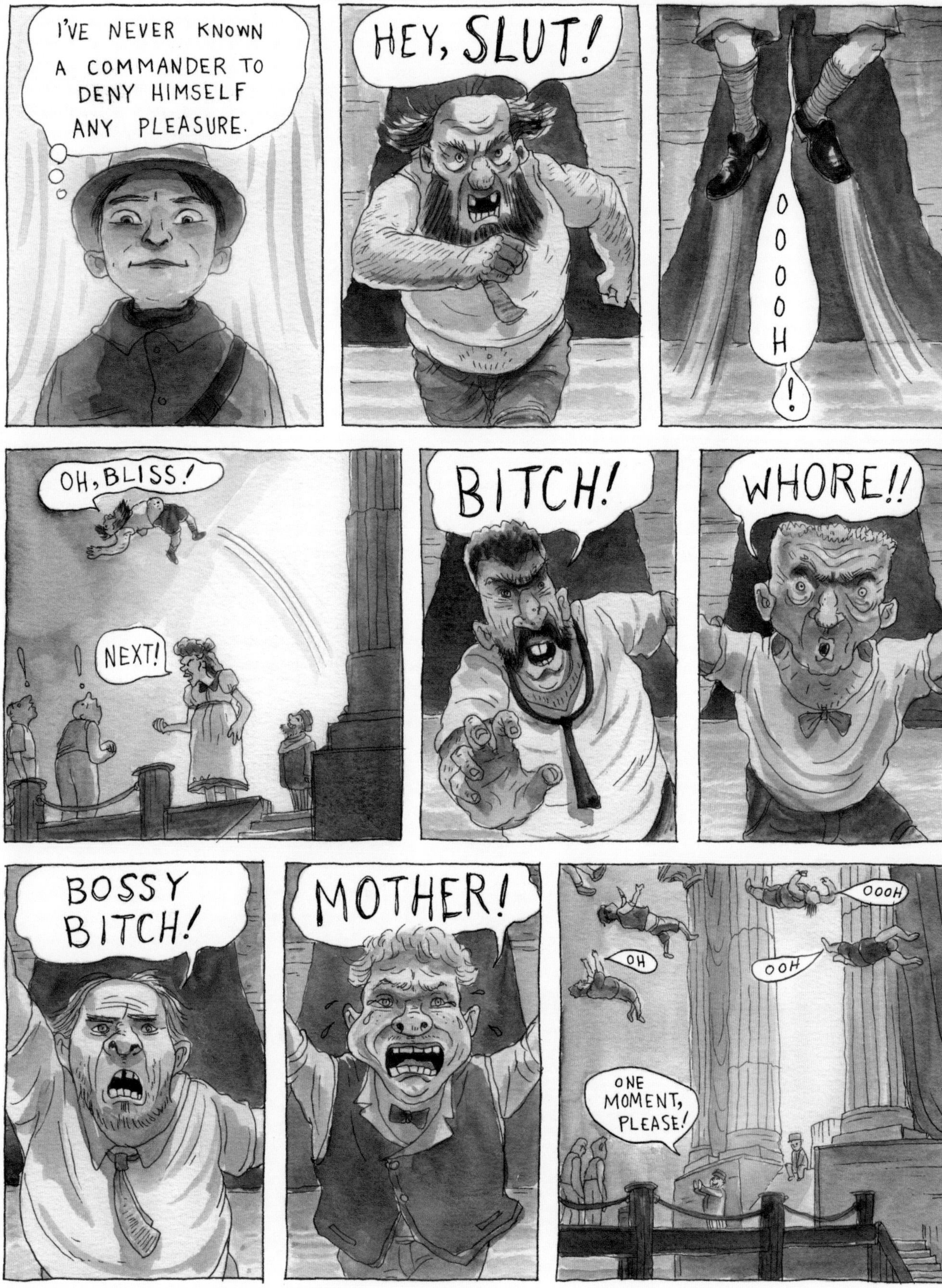
I'VE NEVER KNOWN A COMMANDER TO DENY HIMSELF ANY PLEASURE.
HEY, SLUT!
OOOOH!
OH, BLISS!
NEXT!
BITCH!
WHORE!!
BOSSY BITCH!
MOTHER!
OOOH
OH
OOH
ONE MOMENT, PLEASE!

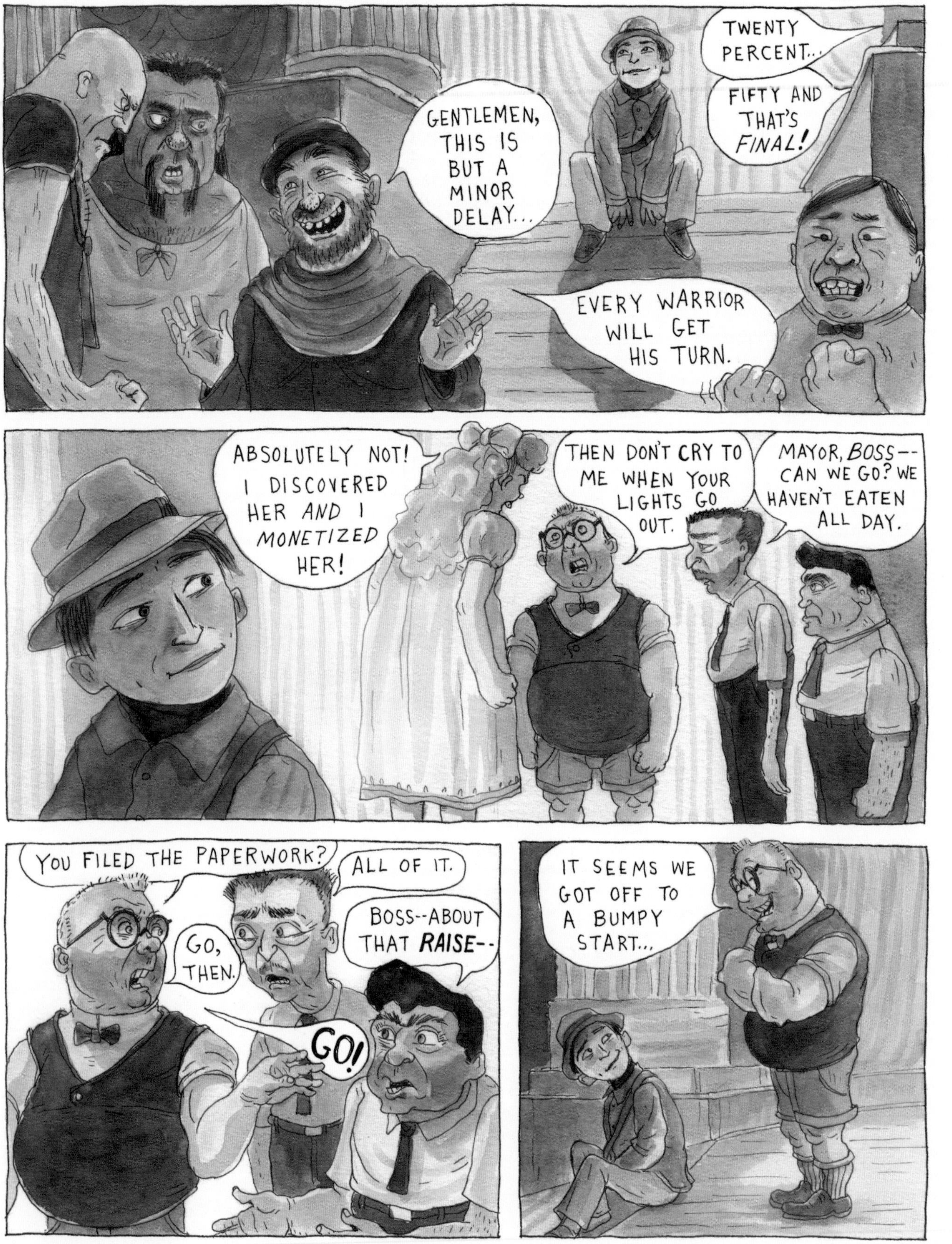
GENTLEMEN, THIS IS BUT A MINOR DELAY...
TWENTY PERCENT...
FIFTY AND THAT'S FINAL!
EVERY WARRIOR WILL GET HIS TURN.
ABSOLUTELY NOT! I DISCOVERED HER AND I MONETIZED HER!
THEN DON'T CRY TO ME WHEN YOUR LIGHTS GO OUT.
MAYOR, BOSS-- CAN WE GO? WE HAVEN'T EATEN ALL DAY.
YOU FILED THE PAPERWORK?
ALL OF IT.
GO, THEN.
BOSS--ABOUT THAT RAISE--
GO!
IT SEEMS WE GOT OFF TO A BUMPY START...

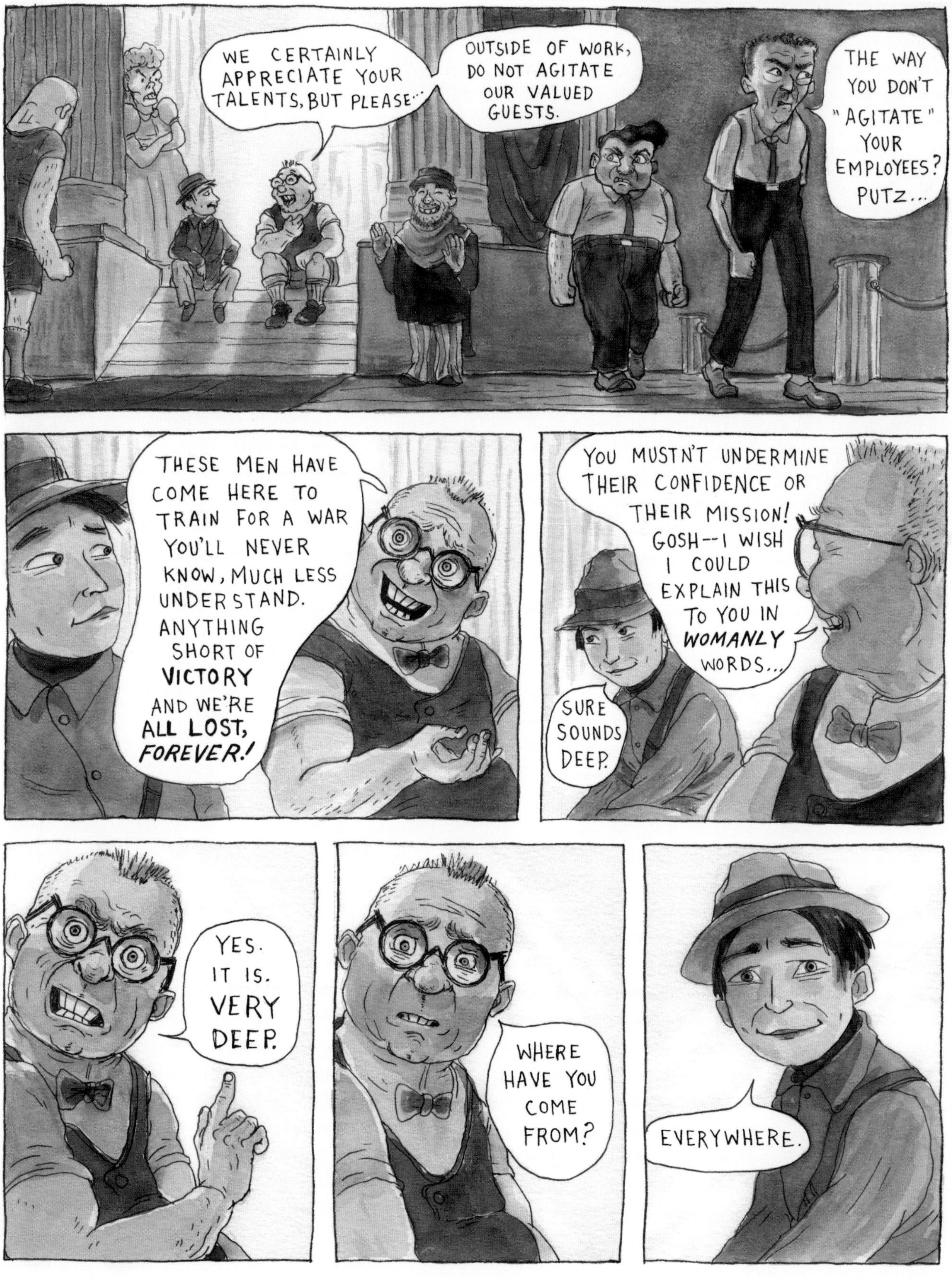
WE CERTAINLY APPRECIATE YOUR TALENTS, BUT PLEASE...
OUTSIDE OF WORK, DO NOT AGITATE OUR VALUED GUESTS.
THE WAY YOU DON'T "AGITATE" YOUR EMPLOYEES? PUTZ...
THESE MEN HAVE COME HERE TO TRAIN FOR A WAR YOU'LL NEVER KNOW, MUCH LESS UNDERSTAND. ANYTHING SHORT OF VICTORY AND WE'RE ALL LOST, FOREVER!
YOU MUSTN'T UNDERMINE THEIR CONFIDENCE OR THEIR MISSION! GOSH--I WISH I COULD EXPLAIN THIS TO YOU IN WOMANLY WORDS...
SURE SOUNDS DEEP.
YES. IT IS. VERY DEEP.
WHERE HAVE YOU COME FROM?
EVERYWHERE.

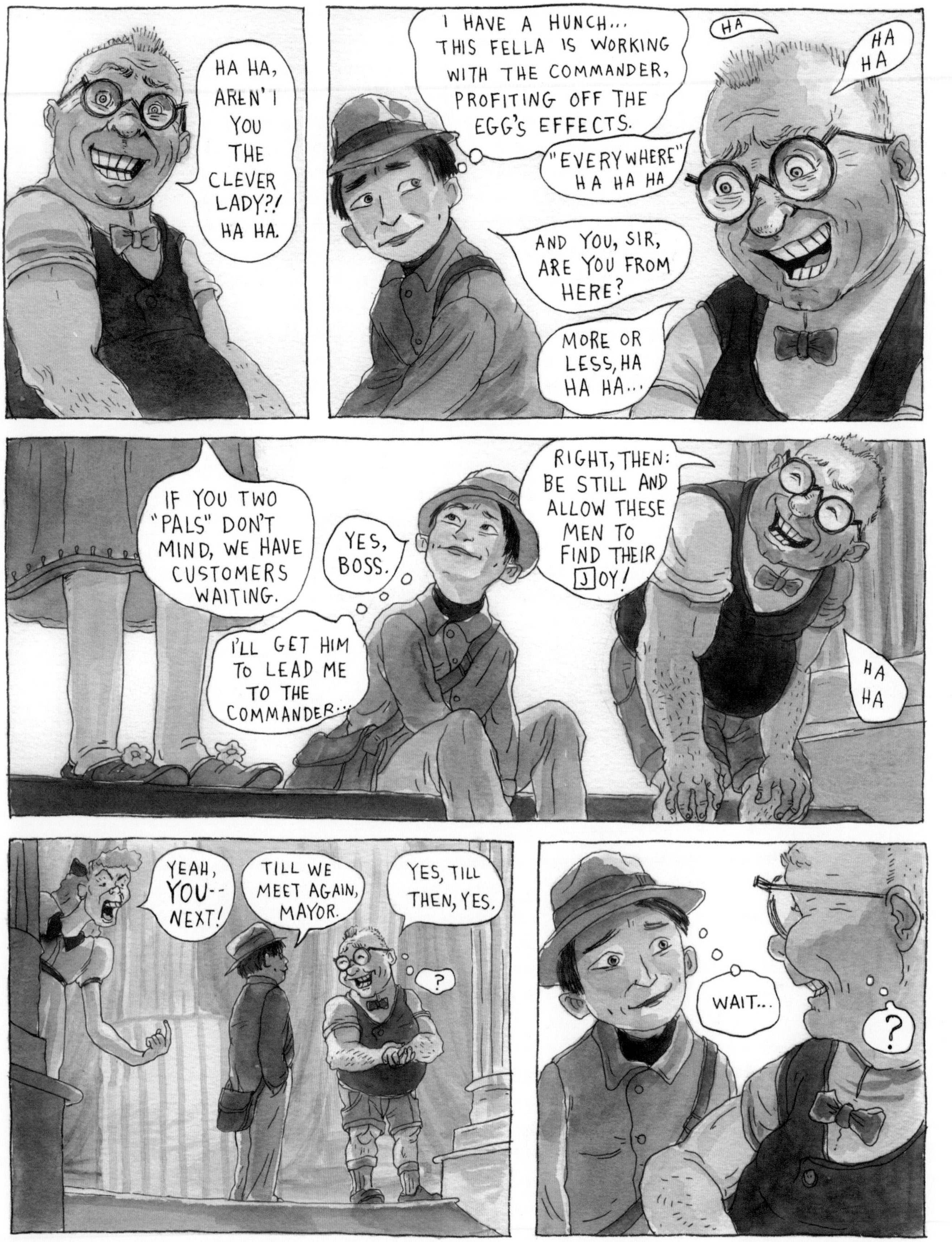
HA HA, AREN'T YOU THE CLEVER LADY?! HA HA.
I HAVE A HUNCH... THIS FELLA IS WORKING WITH THE COMMANDER, PROFITING OFF THE EGG'S EFFECTS.
HA
HA HA
"EVERYWHERE" HA HA HA
AND YOU, SIR, ARE YOU FROM HERE?
MORE OR LESS, HA HA HA...
IF YOU TWO "PALS" DON'T MIND, WE HAVE CUSTOMERS WAITING.
YES, BOSS.
RIGHT, THEN: BE STILL AND ALLOW THESE MEN TO FIND THEIR JOY!
I'LL GET HIM TO LEAD ME TO THE COMMANDER...
HA HA
YEAH, YOU-- NEXT!
TILL WE MEET AGAIN, MAYOR.
YES, TILL THEN, YES.
?
WAIT...
?

THOSE EYES-- I KNOW HIM, SELA.
THAT PROUD AND TROUBLED LOOK... HE'S ... STILL SEEKING...
WHY... IS SHE STARING AT ME?
HE'S THE BOY WHO CAME OUT OF THAT DOOR IN THE FOREST!
AW, SHUCKS, FELLAS! PARDON THE DELAY. NOW LET'S FIND YOUR JOY!!
JOY
JOY
JOY
YEAH!
JOY
WE SAW HIM FROM THE TERRACED ISLAND. DID HE SEE US? DID HE SEE YOU VANISH THAT DAY?

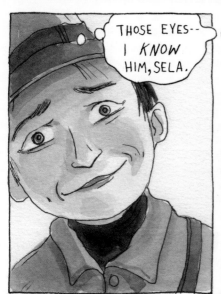

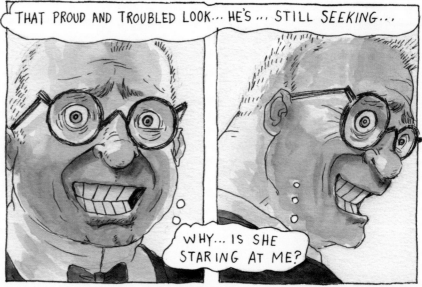

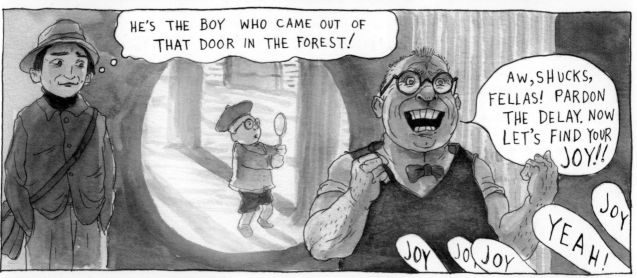

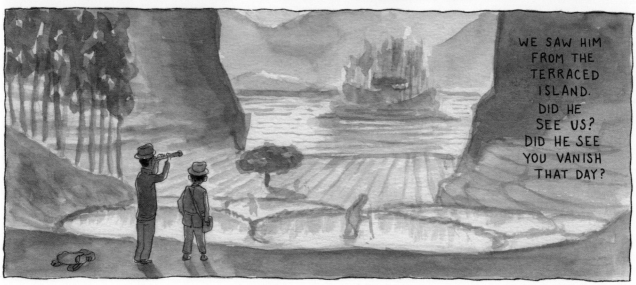

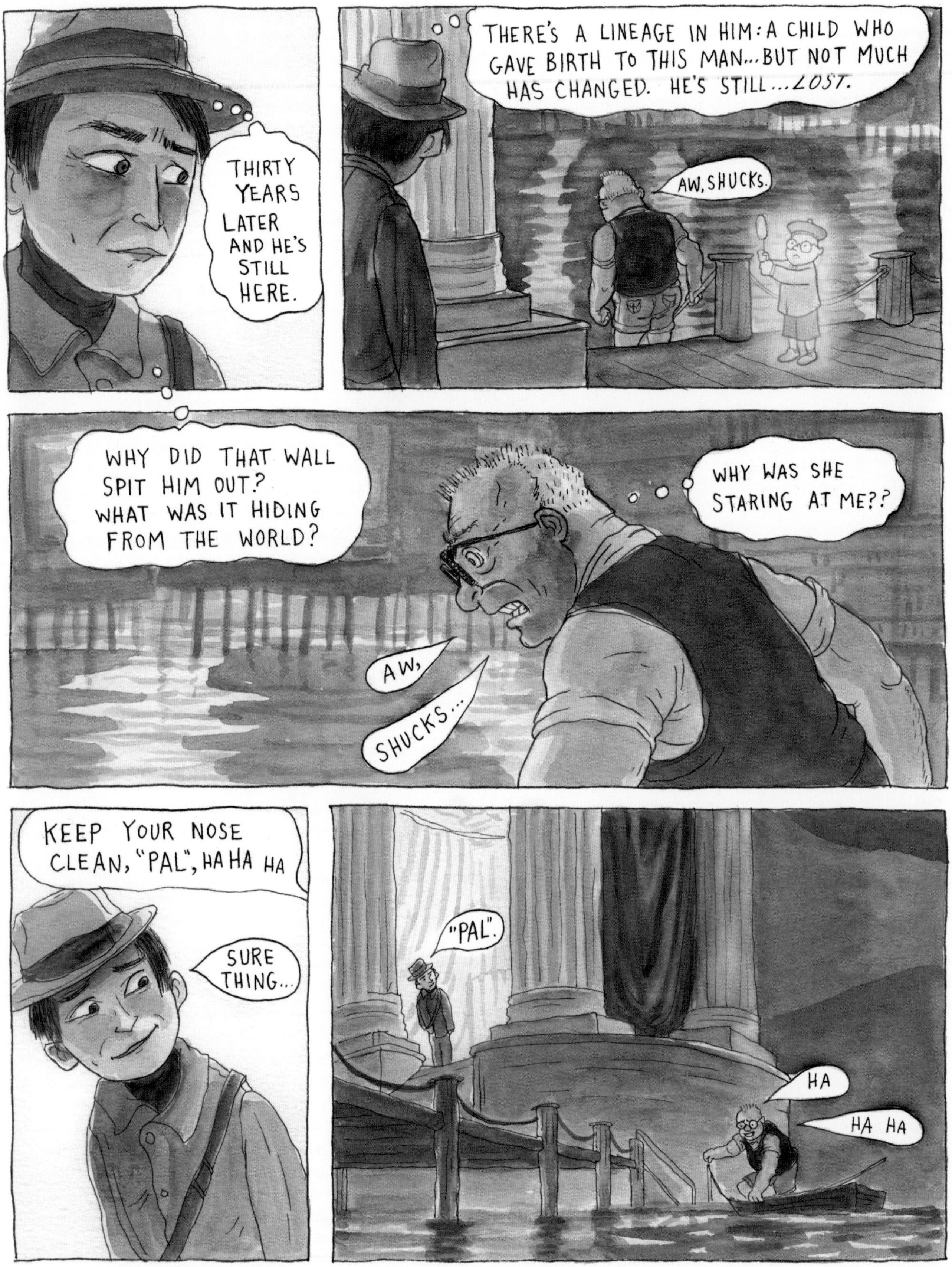
THIRTY YEARS LATER AND HE'S STILL HERE.
THERE'S A LINEAGE IN HIM: A CHILD WHO GAVE BIRTH TO THIS MAN... BUT NOT MUCH HAS CHANGED. HE'S STILL... LOST.
AW, SHUCKS.
WHY DID THAT WALL SPIT HIM OUT? WHAT WAS IT HIDING FROM THE WORLD?
WHY WAS SHE STARING AT ME??
AW,
SHUCKS...
KEEP YOUR NOSE CLEAN, "PAL", HA HA HA
SURE THING...
"PAL".
HA
HA HA

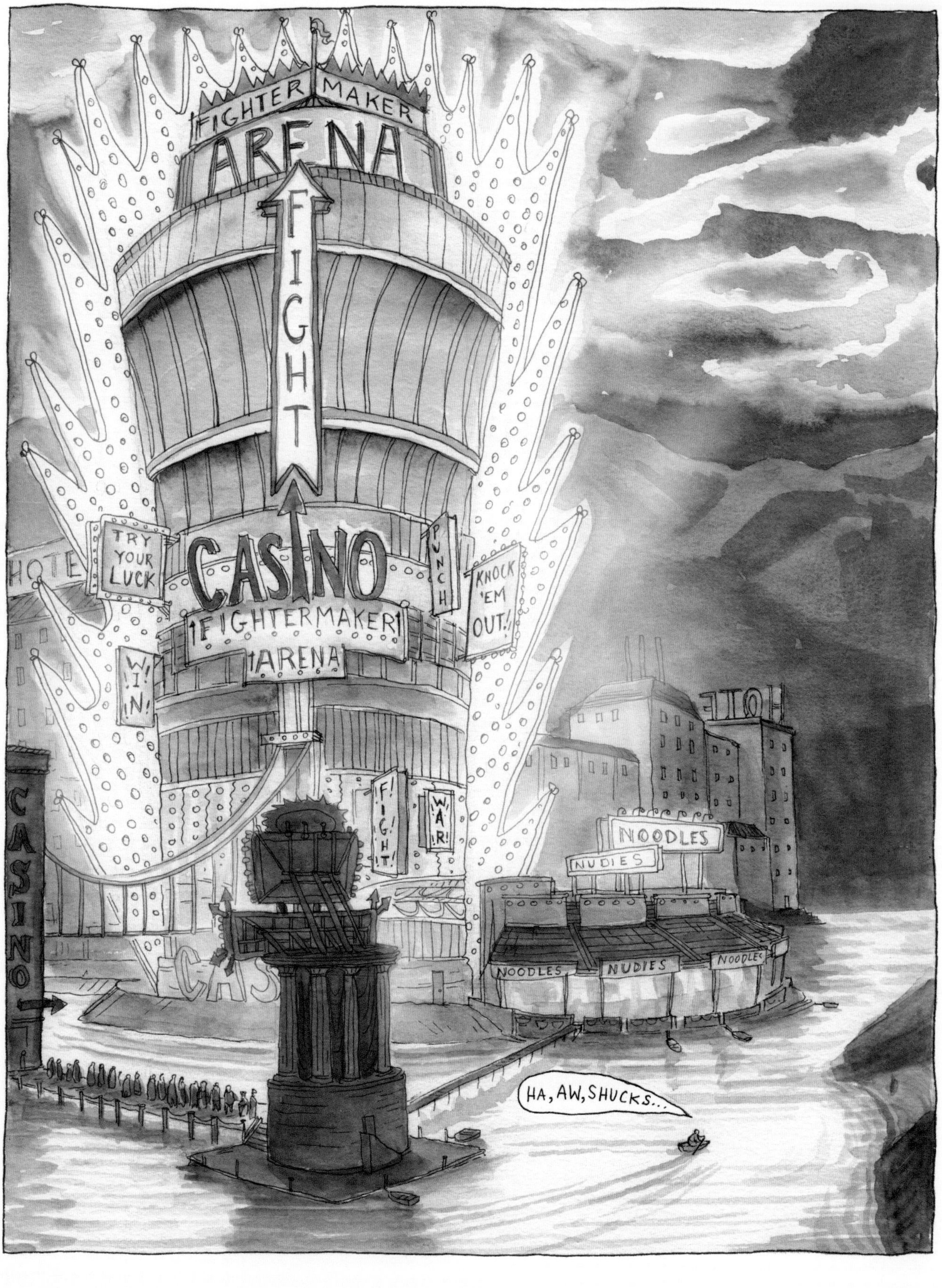
FIGHTER MAKER
ARENA
FIGHT
TRY YOUR LUCK
CASINO
PUNCH
KNOCK 'EM OUT!
FIGHTERMAKER
ARENA
W!I!N!
HOTE
HOTE
CASINO
F!G!H!T!
W!A!R!
NOODLES
NUDIES
NOODLES
NUDIES
NOODLES
HA, AW, SHUCKS...

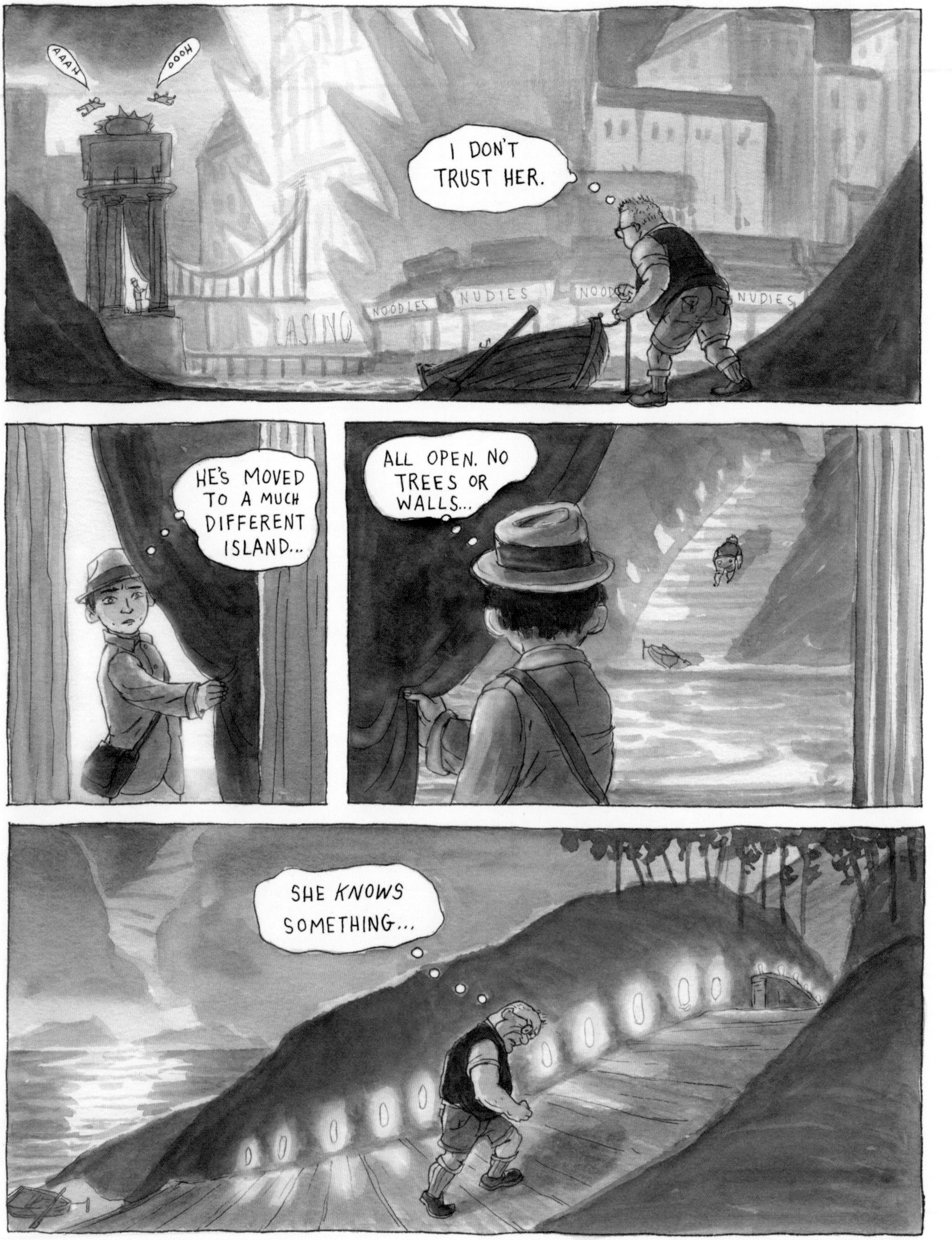
AAAH
HOOO
I DON'T TRUST HER.
NOODLES
NUDIES
CASINO
NUDIES
HE'S MOVED TO A MUCH DIFFERENT ISLAND...
ALL OPEN. NO TREES OR WALLS...
SHE *KNOWS* SOMETHING...

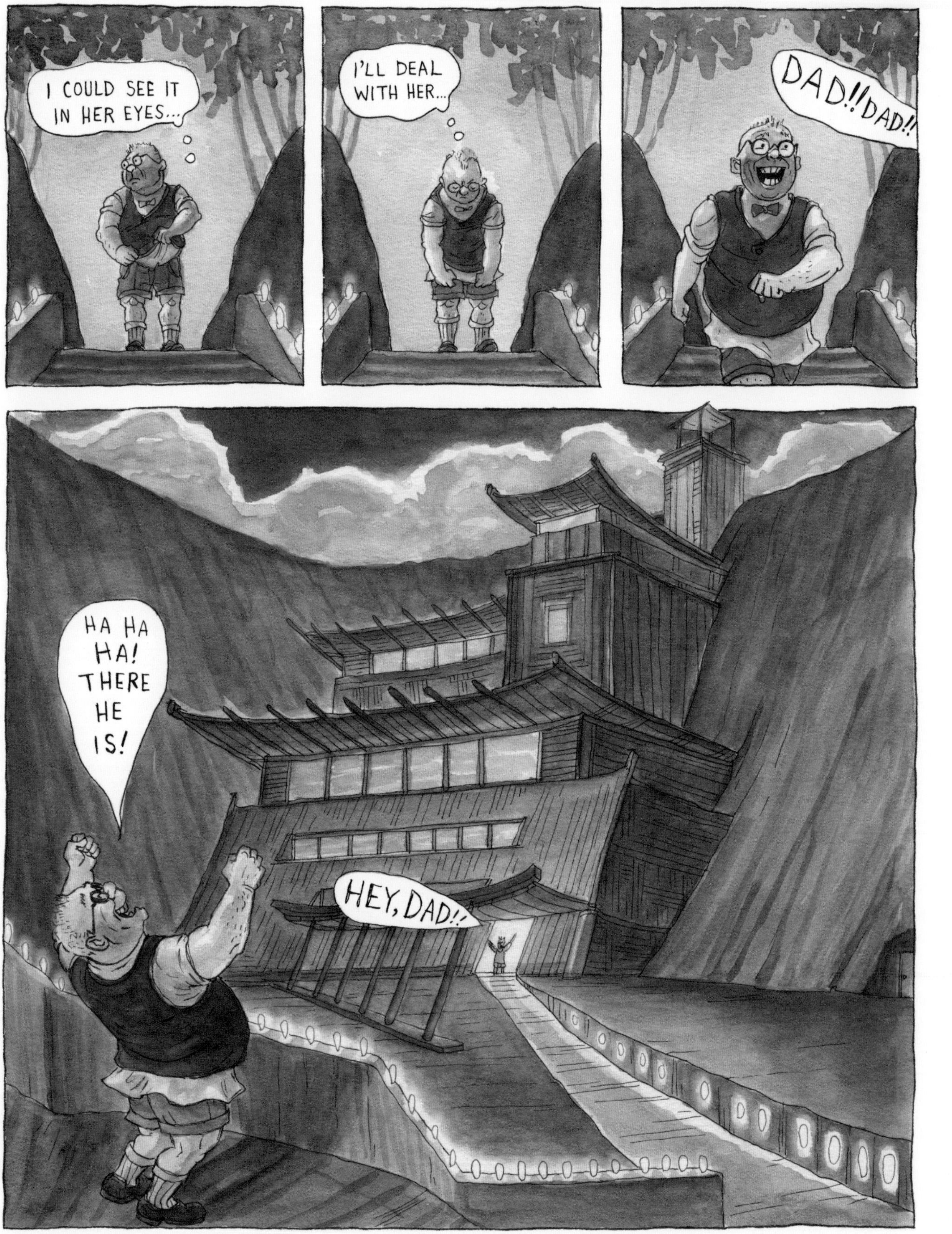
I COULD SEE IT IN HER EYES...
I'LL DEAL WITH HER...
DAD!! DAD!!
HA HA HA! THERE HE IS!
HEY, DAD!!

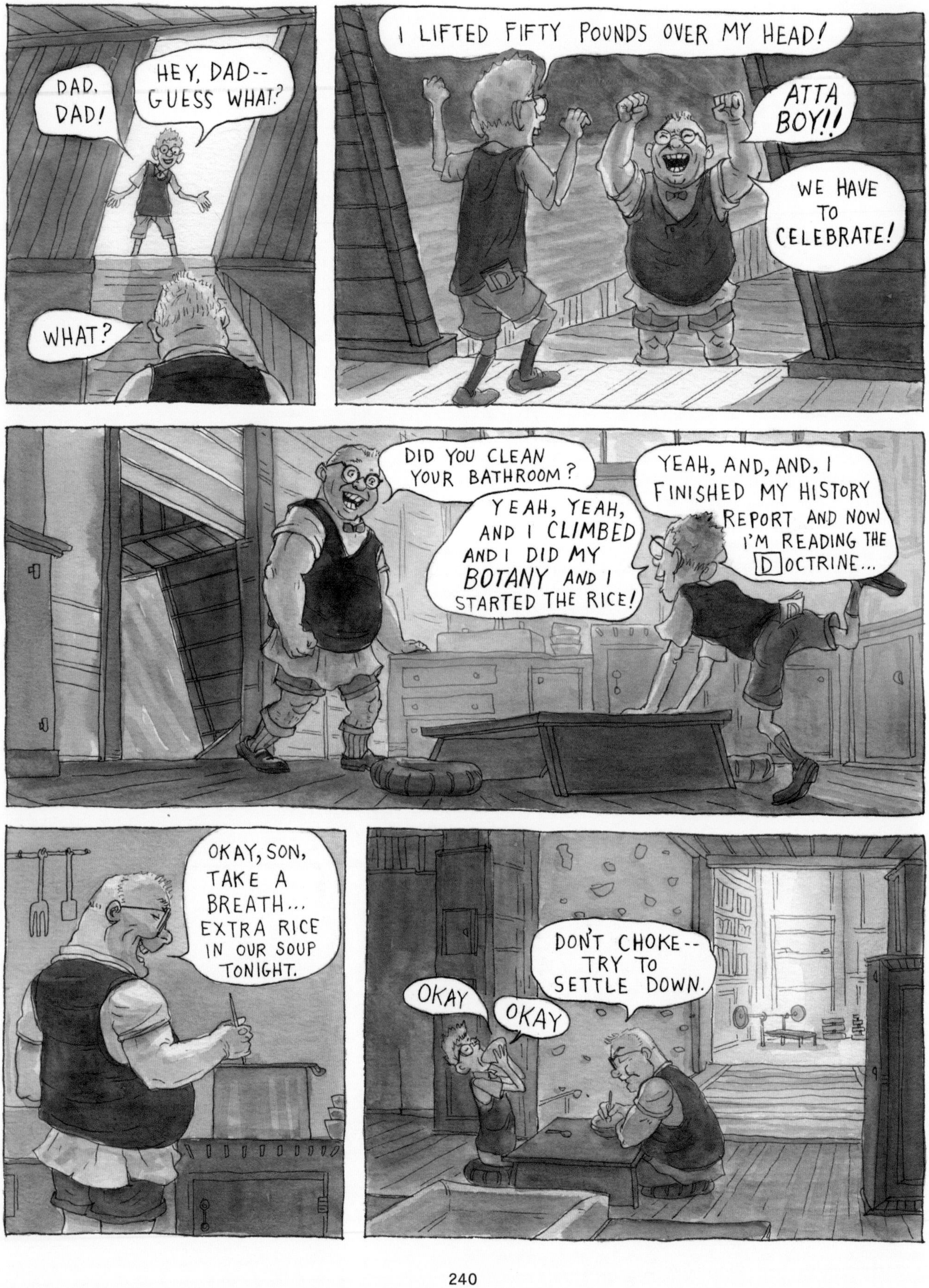
DAD. DAD!
HEY, DAD-- GUESS WHAT?
WHAT?
I LIFTED FIFTY POUNDS OVER MY HEAD!
ATTA BOY!!
WE HAVE TO CELEBRATE!
DID YOU CLEAN YOUR BATHROOM?
YEAH, YEAH, AND I CLIMBED AND I DID MY BOTANY AND I STARTED THE RICE!
YEAH, AND, AND, I FINISHED MY HISTORY REPORT AND NOW I'M READING THE DOCTRINE...
OKAY, SON, TAKE A BREATH... EXTRA RICE IN OUR SOUP TONIGHT.
OKAY
OKAY
DON'T CHOKE-- TRY TO SETTLE DOWN.

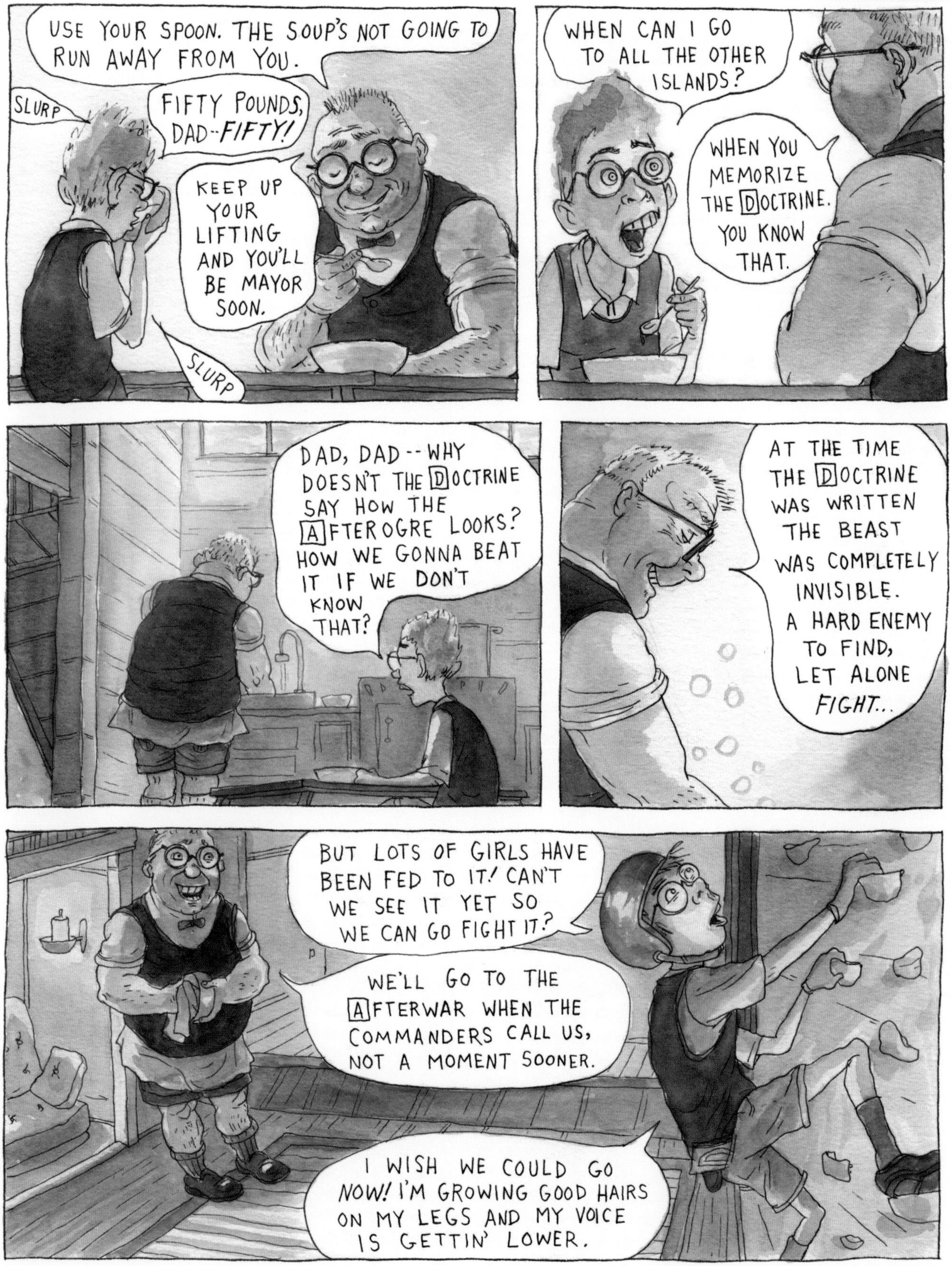
USE YOUR SPOON. THE SOUP'S NOT GOING TO RUN AWAY FROM YOU.
SLURP
FIFTY POUNDS, DAD--FIFTY!
KEEP UP YOUR LIFTING AND YOU'LL BE MAYOR SOON.
SLURP
WHEN CAN I GO TO ALL THE OTHER ISLANDS?
WHEN YOU MEMORIZE THE DOCTRINE. YOU KNOW THAT.
DAD, DAD--WHY DOESN'T THE DOCTRINE SAY HOW THE AFTEROGRE LOOKS? HOW WE GONNA BEAT IT IF WE DON'T KNOW THAT?
AT THE TIME THE DOCTRINE WAS WRITTEN THE BEAST WAS COMPLETELY INVISIBLE. A HARD ENEMY TO FIND, LET ALONE FIGHT...
BUT LOTS OF GIRLS HAVE BEEN FED TO IT! CAN'T WE SEE IT YET SO WE CAN GO FIGHT IT?
WE'LL GO TO THE AFTERWAR WHEN THE COMMANDERS CALL US, NOT A MOMENT SOONER.
I WISH WE COULD GO NOW! I'M GROWING GOOD HAIRS ON MY LEGS AND MY VOICE IS GETTIN' LOWER.

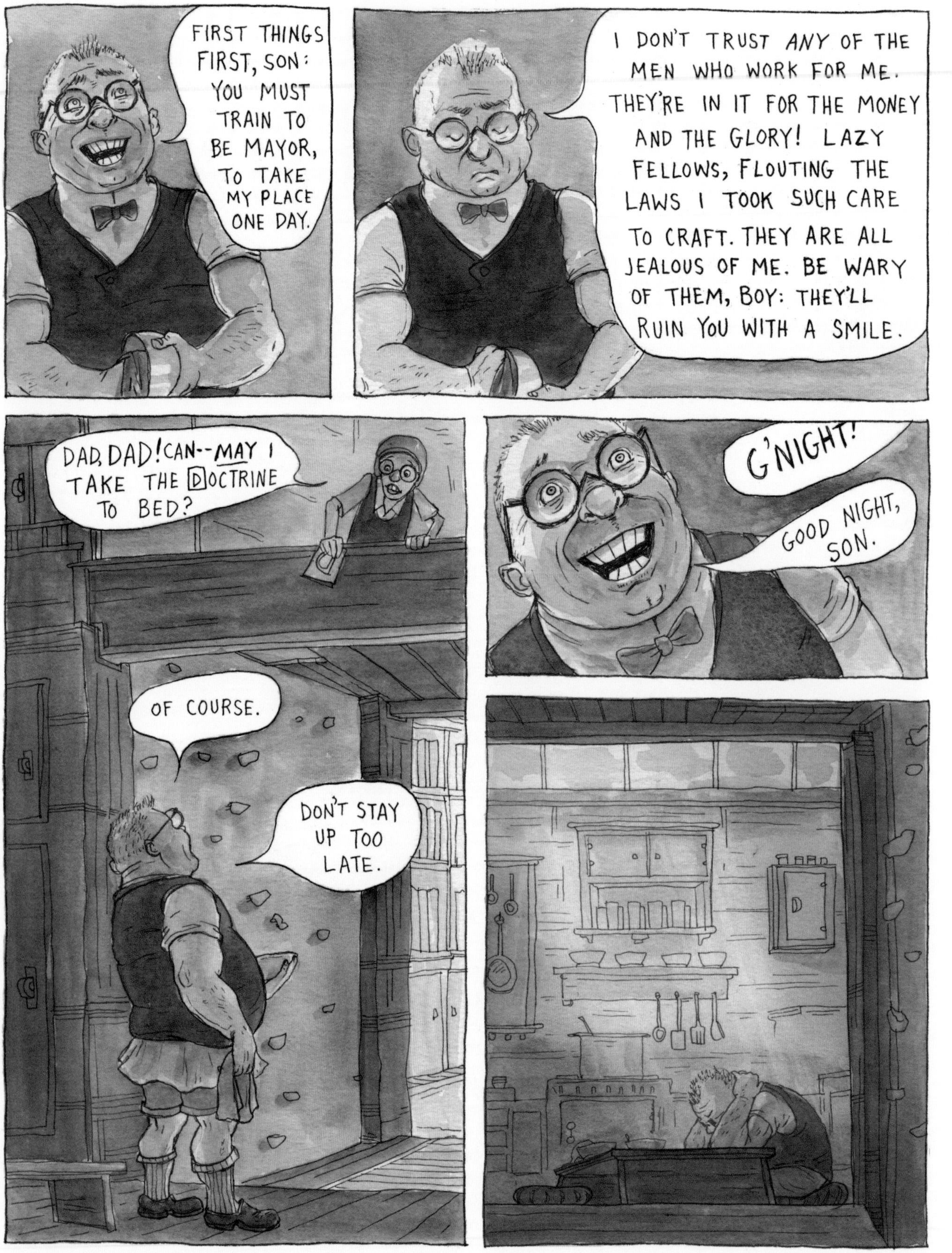
FIRST THINGS FIRST, SON: YOU MUST TRAIN TO BE MAYOR, TO TAKE MY PLACE ONE DAY.
I DON'T TRUST ANY OF THE MEN WHO WORK FOR ME. THEY'RE IN IT FOR THE MONEY AND THE GLORY! LAZY FELLOWS, FLOUTING THE LAWS I TOOK SUCH CARE TO CRAFT. THEY ARE ALL JEALOUS OF ME. BE WARY OF THEM, BOY: THEY'LL RUIN YOU WITH A SMILE.
DAD, DAD! CAN--MAY I TAKE THE DOCTRINE TO BED?
OF COURSE.
DON'T STAY UP TOO LATE.
G'NIGHT!
GOOD NIGHT, SON.

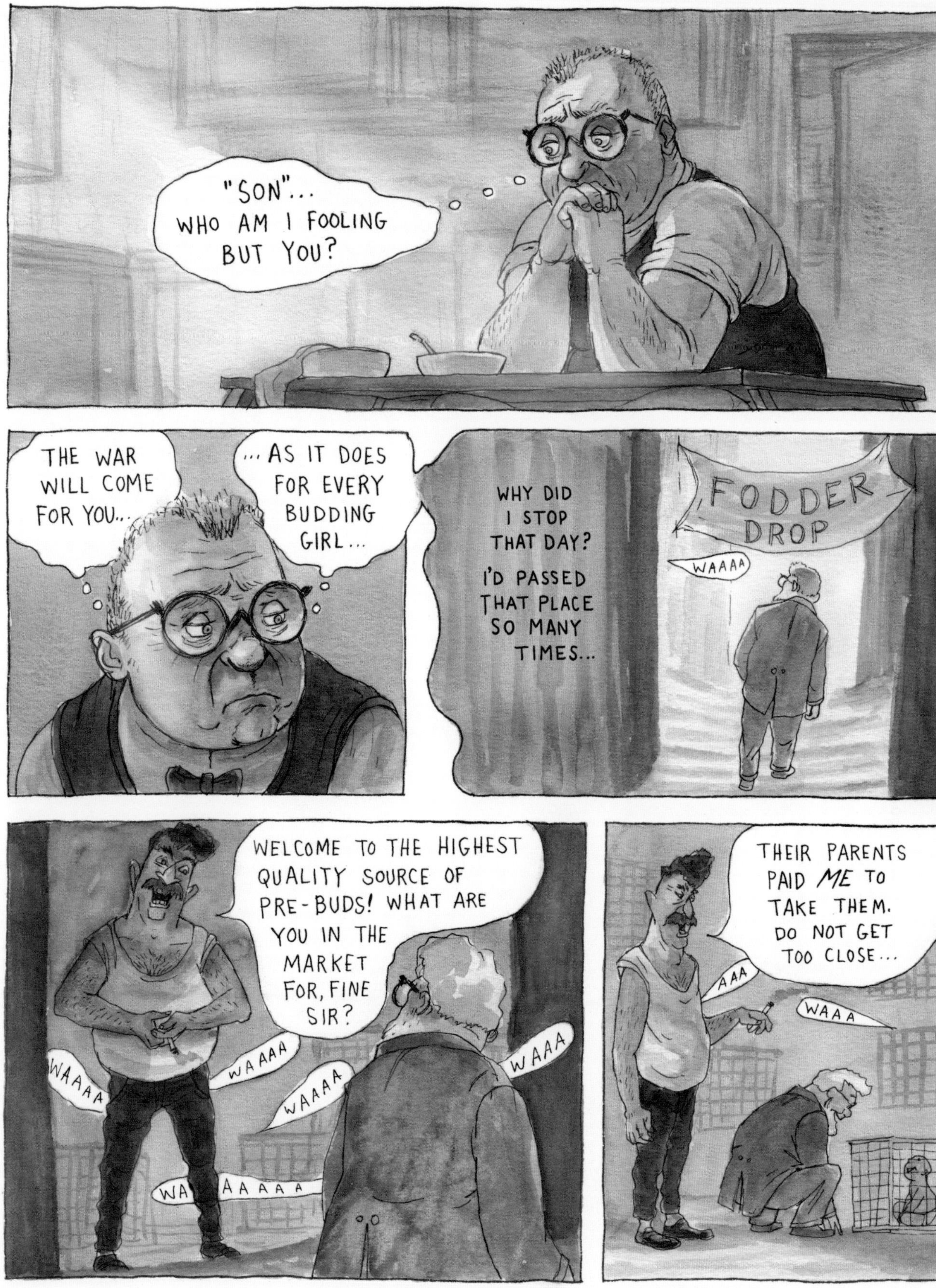
"SON"... WHO AM I FOOLING BUT YOU?
THE WAR WILL COME FOR YOU...
... AS IT DOES FOR EVERY BUDDING GIRL...
WHY DID I STOP THAT DAY?
I'D PASSED THAT PLACE SO MANY TIMES...
FODDER DROP
WAAAA
WELCOME TO THE HIGHEST QUALITY SOURCE OF PRE-BUDS! WHAT ARE YOU IN THE MARKET FOR, FINE SIR?
WAAAA
WAAAA
WAAAA
WAAA
WA AAAAA
THEIR PARENTS PAID *ME* TO TAKE THEM. DO NOT GET TOO CLOSE...
AAA
WAAA

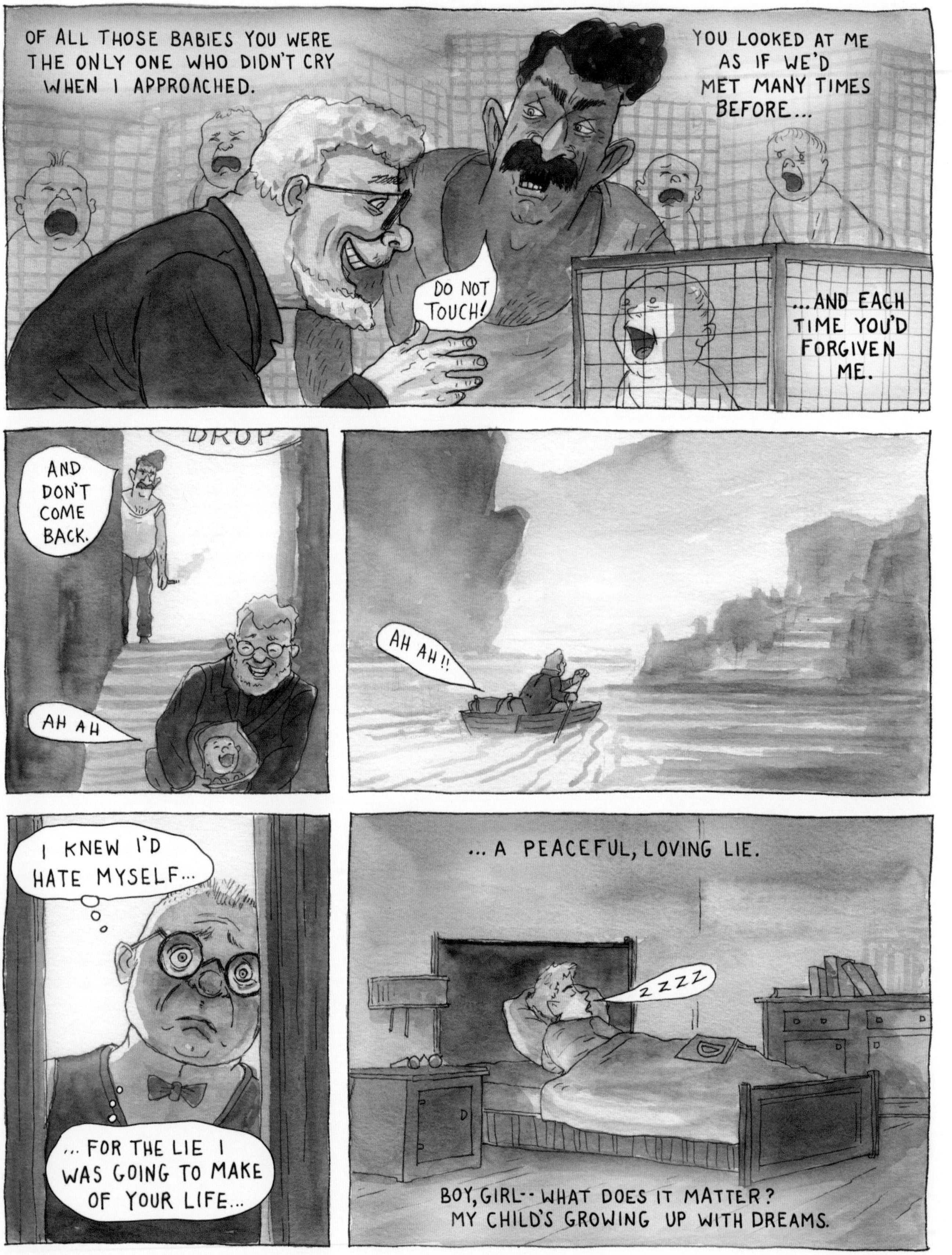
OF ALL THOSE BABIES YOU WERE THE ONLY ONE WHO DIDN'T CRY WHEN I APPROACHED.
YOU LOOKED AT ME AS IF WE'D MET MANY TIMES BEFORE...
DO NOT TOUCH!
...AND EACH TIME YOU'D FORGIVEN ME.
AND DON'T COME BACK.
AH AH
AH AH!!
I KNEW I'D HATE MYSELF...
... FOR THE LIE I WAS GOING TO MAKE OF YOUR LIFE...
... A PEACEFUL, LOVING LIE.
ZZZZ
BOY, GIRL-- WHAT DOES IT MATTER? MY CHILD'S GROWING UP WITH DREAMS.

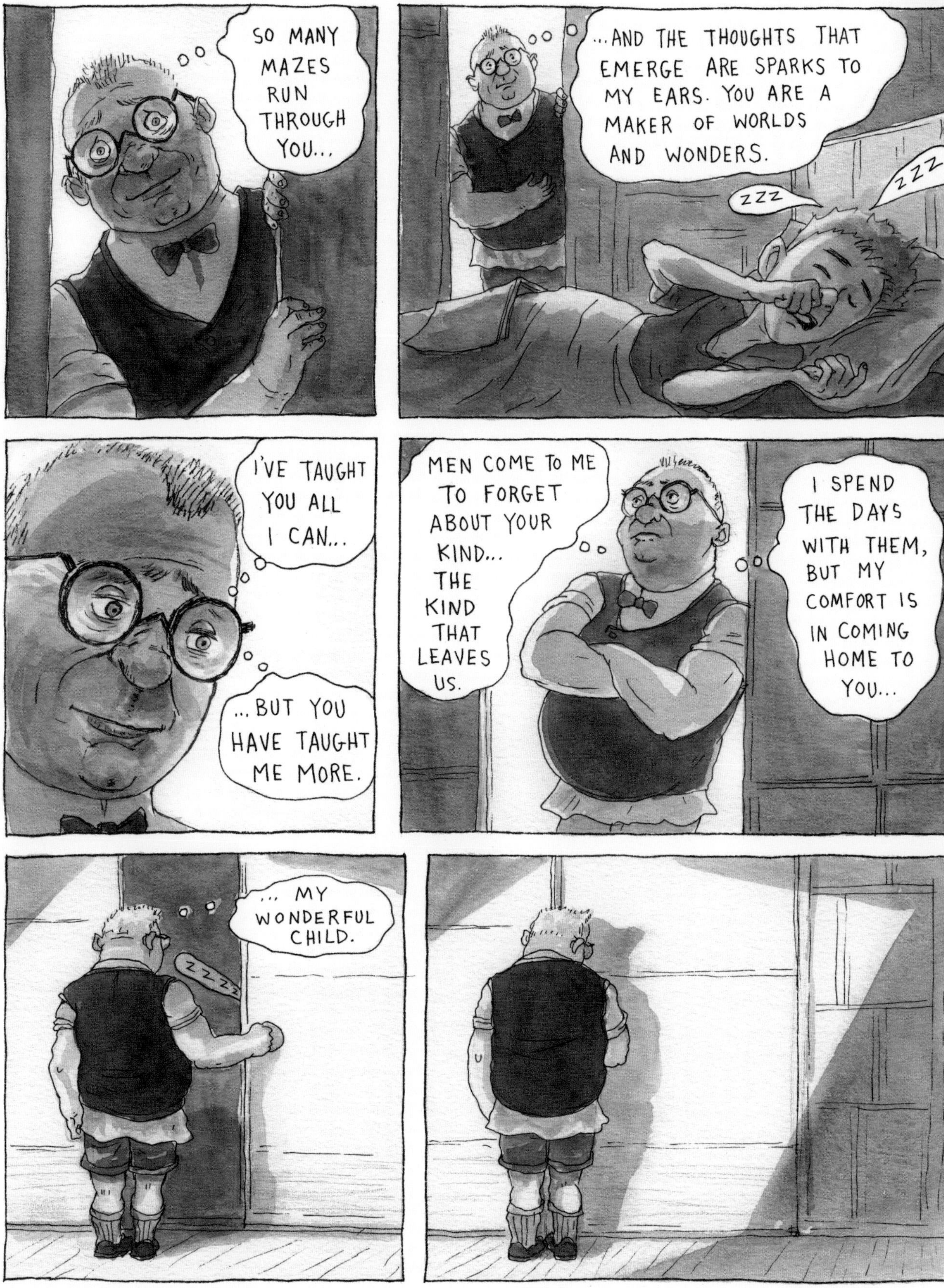
SO MANY MAZES RUN THROUGH YOU...
...AND THE THOUGHTS THAT EMERGE ARE SPARKS TO MY EARS. YOU ARE A MAKER OF WORLDS AND WONDERS.
ZZZ
ZZZ
I'VE TAUGHT YOU ALL I CAN...
...BUT YOU HAVE TAUGHT ME MORE.
MEN COME TO ME TO FORGET ABOUT YOUR KIND... THE KIND THAT LEAVES US.
I SPEND THE DAYS WITH THEM, BUT MY COMFORT IS IN COMING HOME TO YOU...
... MY WONDERFUL CHILD.
ZZZZ

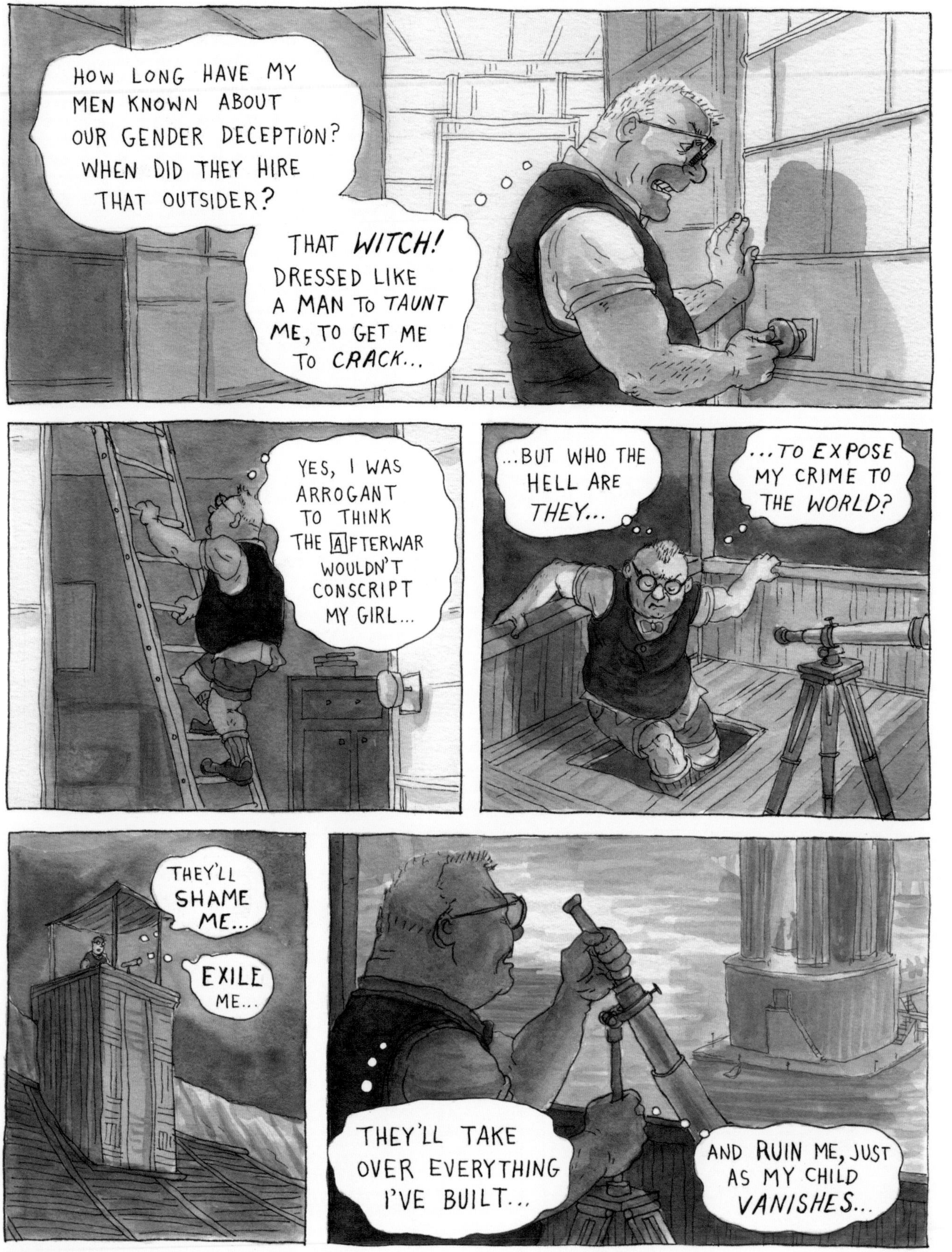
HOW LONG HAVE MY MEN KNOWN ABOUT OUR GENDER DECEPTION? WHEN DID THEY HIRE THAT OUTSIDER?
THAT *WITCH!* DRESSED LIKE A MAN TO *TAUNT* ME, TO GET ME TO *CRACK*...
YES, I WAS ARROGANT TO THINK THE [A]FTERWAR WOULDN'T CONSCRIPT MY GIRL...
...BUT WHO THE HELL ARE *THEY*...
...*TO EXPOSE* MY CRIME TO THE *WORLD?*
THEY'LL SHAME *ME*...
EXILE ME...
THEY'LL TAKE OVER EVERYTHING I'VE BUILT...
AND RUIN ME, JUST AS MY CHILD *VANISHES*...

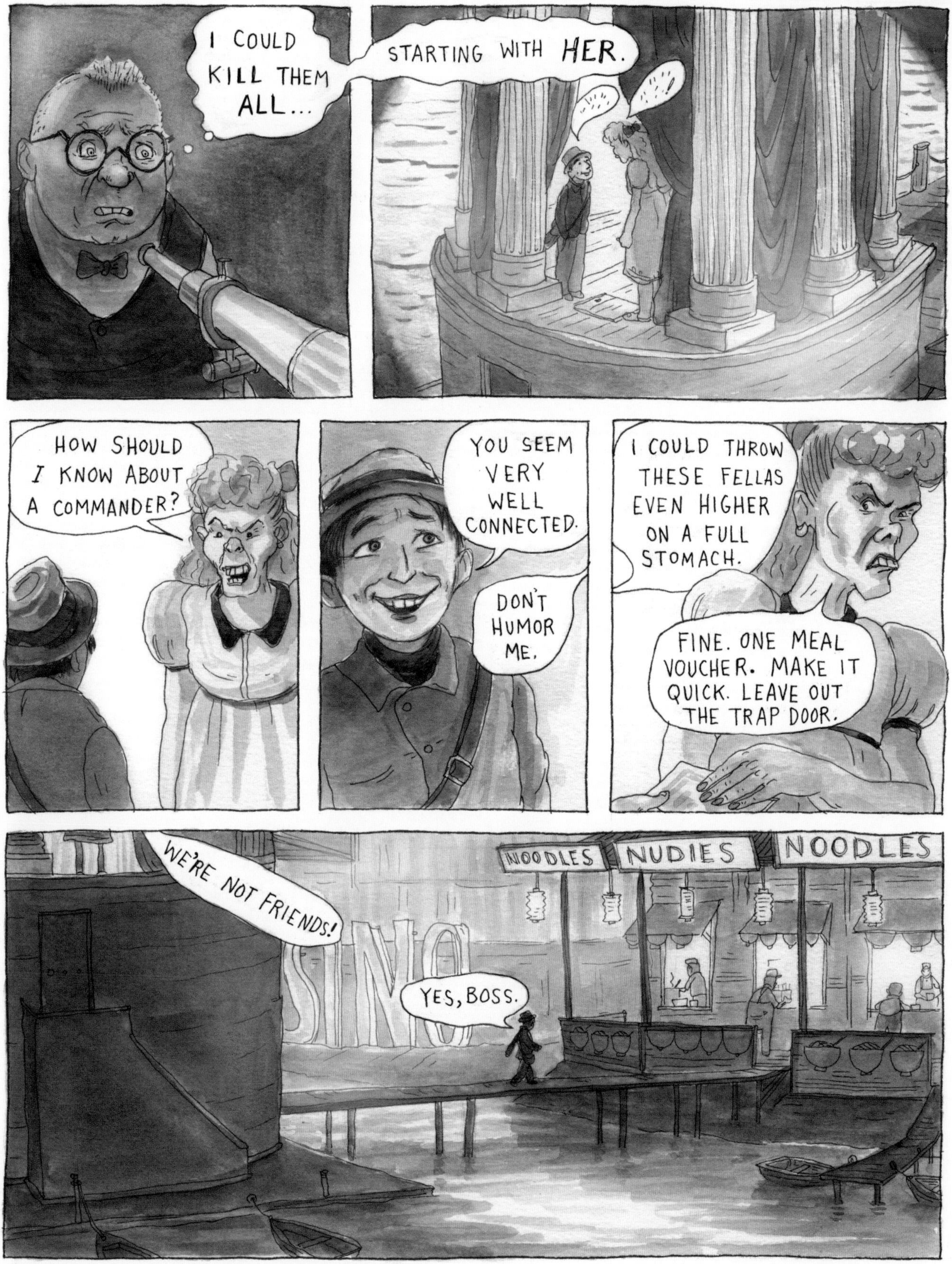

I COULD KILL THEM ALL...
STARTING WITH HER.
HOW SHOULD I KNOW ABOUT A COMMANDER?
YOU SEEM VERY WELL CONNECTED.
DON'T HUMOR ME.
I COULD THROW THESE FELLAS EVEN HIGHER ON A FULL STOMACH.
FINE. ONE MEAL VOUCHER. MAKE IT QUICK. LEAVE OUT THE TRAP DOOR.
NOODLES
NUDIES
NOODLES
WE'RE NOT FRIENDS!
YES, BOSS.

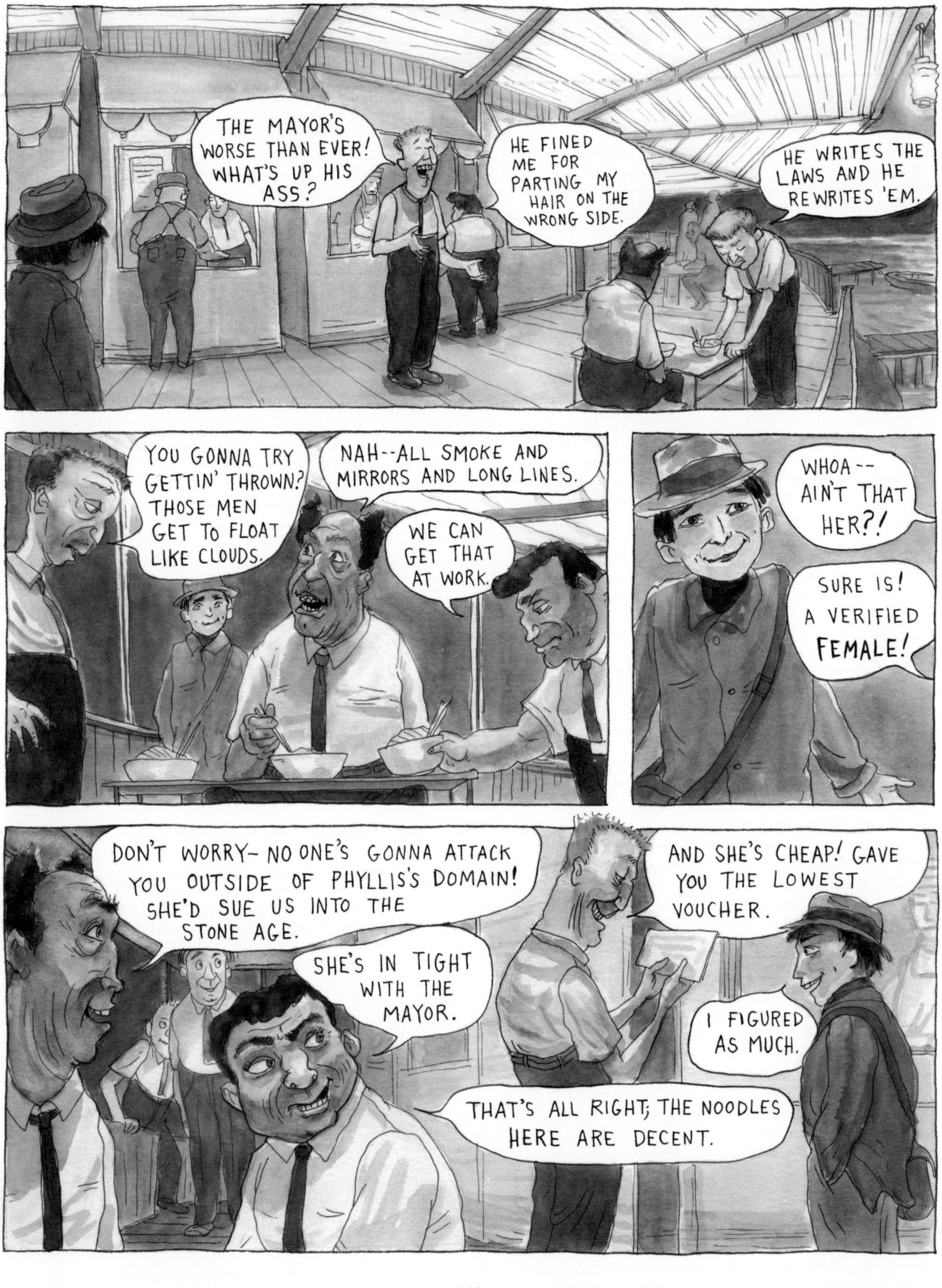
THE MAYOR'S WORSE THAN EVER! WHAT'S UP HIS ASS?
HE FINED ME FOR PARTING MY HAIR ON THE WRONG SIDE.
HE WRITES THE LAWS AND HE REWRITES 'EM.
YOU GONNA TRY GETTIN' THROWN? THOSE MEN GET TO FLOAT LIKE CLOUDS.
NAH--ALL SMOKE AND MIRRORS AND LONG LINES.
WE CAN GET THAT AT WORK.
WHOA -- AIN'T THAT HER?!
SURE IS! A VERIFIED FEMALE!
DON'T WORRY- NO ONE'S GONNA ATTACK YOU OUTSIDE OF PHYLLIS'S DOMAIN! SHE'D SUE US INTO THE STONE AGE.
SHE'S IN TIGHT WITH THE MAYOR.
AND SHE'S CHEAP! GAVE YOU THE LOWEST VOUCHER.
I FIGURED AS MUCH.
THAT'S ALL RIGHT; THE NOODLES HERE ARE DECENT.

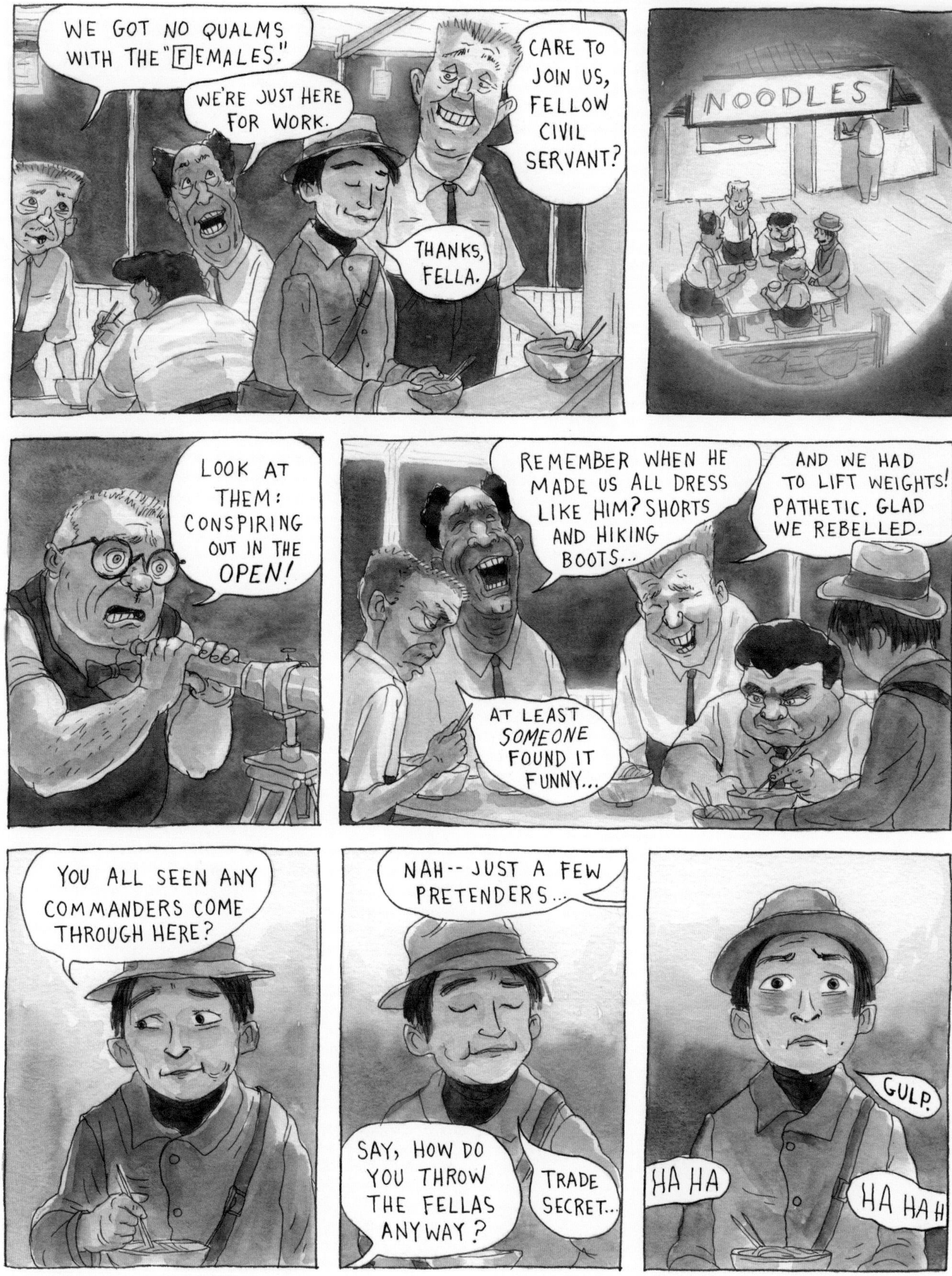
WE GOT NO QUALMS WITH THE "FEMALES."
WE'RE JUST HERE FOR WORK.
CARE TO JOIN US, FELLOW CIVIL SERVANT?
THANKS, FELLA.
NOODLES
LOOK AT THEM: CONSPIRING OUT IN THE OPEN!
REMEMBER WHEN HE MADE US ALL DRESS LIKE HIM? SHORTS AND HIKING BOOTS...
AND WE HAD TO LIFT WEIGHTS! PATHETIC. GLAD WE REBELLED.
AT LEAST SOMEONE FOUND IT FUNNY...
YOU ALL SEEN ANY COMMANDERS COME THROUGH HERE?
NAH-- JUST A FEW PRETENDERS...
SAY, HOW DO YOU THROW THE FELLAS ANYWAY?
TRADE SECRET...
GULP.
HA HA
HA HA H

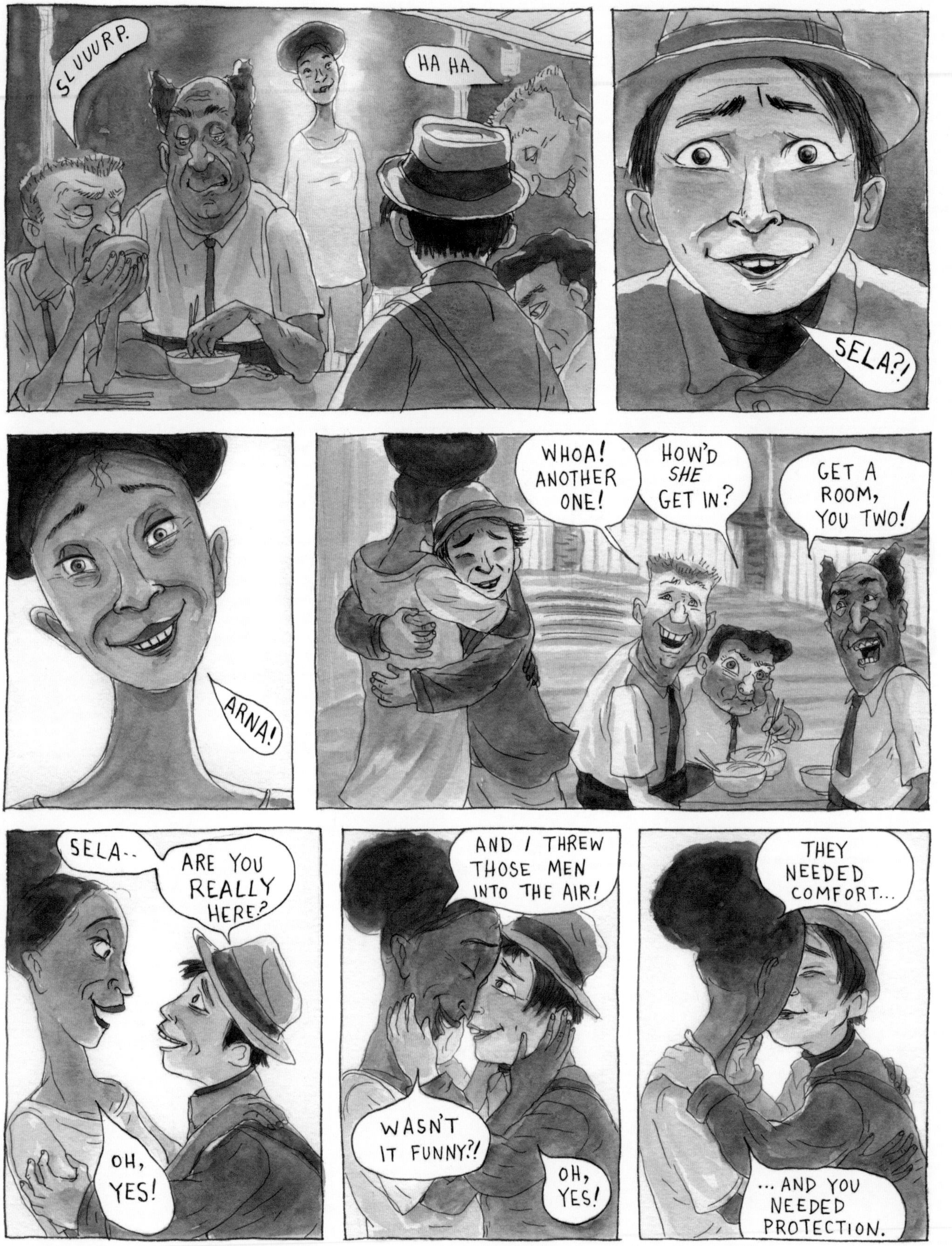
SLUUURP.
HA HA.
SELA?!
ARNA!
WHOA! ANOTHER ONE!
HOW'D *SHE* GET IN?
GET A ROOM, YOU TWO!
SELA--
ARE YOU REALLY HERE?
OH, YES!
AND I THREW THOSE MEN INTO THE AIR!
WASN'T IT FUNNY?!
OH, YES!
THEY NEEDED COMFORT...
...AND YOU NEEDED PROTECTION.

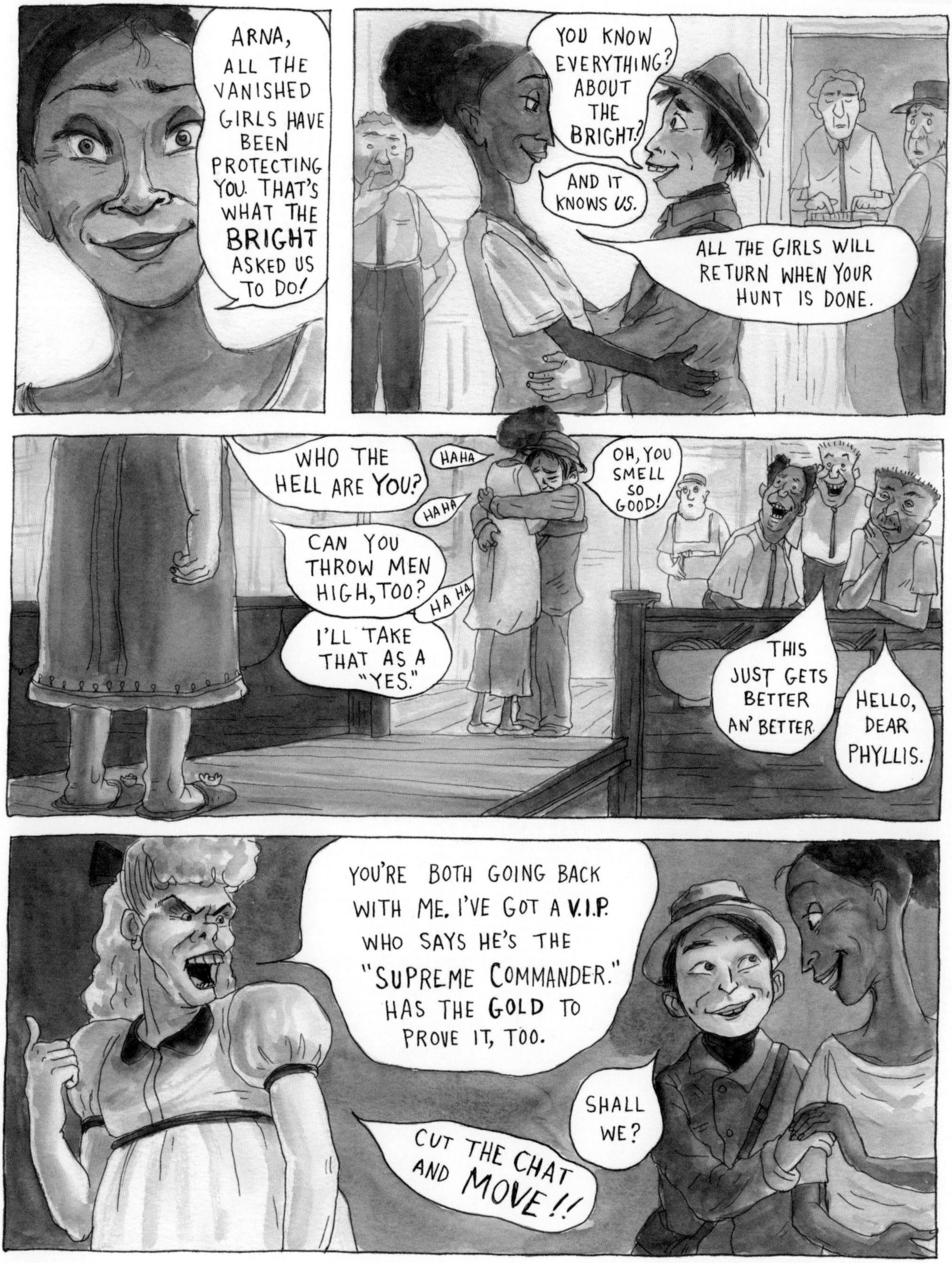
ARNA, ALL THE VANISHED GIRLS HAVE BEEN PROTECTING YOU. THAT'S WHAT THE BRIGHT ASKED US TO DO!
YOU KNOW EVERYTHING? ABOUT THE BRIGHT?
AND IT KNOWS US.
ALL THE GIRLS WILL RETURN WHEN YOUR HUNT IS DONE.
WHO THE HELL ARE YOU?
HAHA
OH, YOU SMELL SO GOOD!
HAHA
CAN YOU THROW MEN HIGH, TOO?
HA HA
I'LL TAKE THAT AS A "YES."
THIS JUST GETS BETTER AN' BETTER.
HELLO, DEAR PHYLLIS.
YOU'RE BOTH GOING BACK WITH ME. I'VE GOT A V.I.P. WHO SAYS HE'S THE "SUPREME COMMANDER." HAS THE GOLD TO PROVE IT, TOO.
SHALL WE?
CUT THE CHAT AND MOVE!!

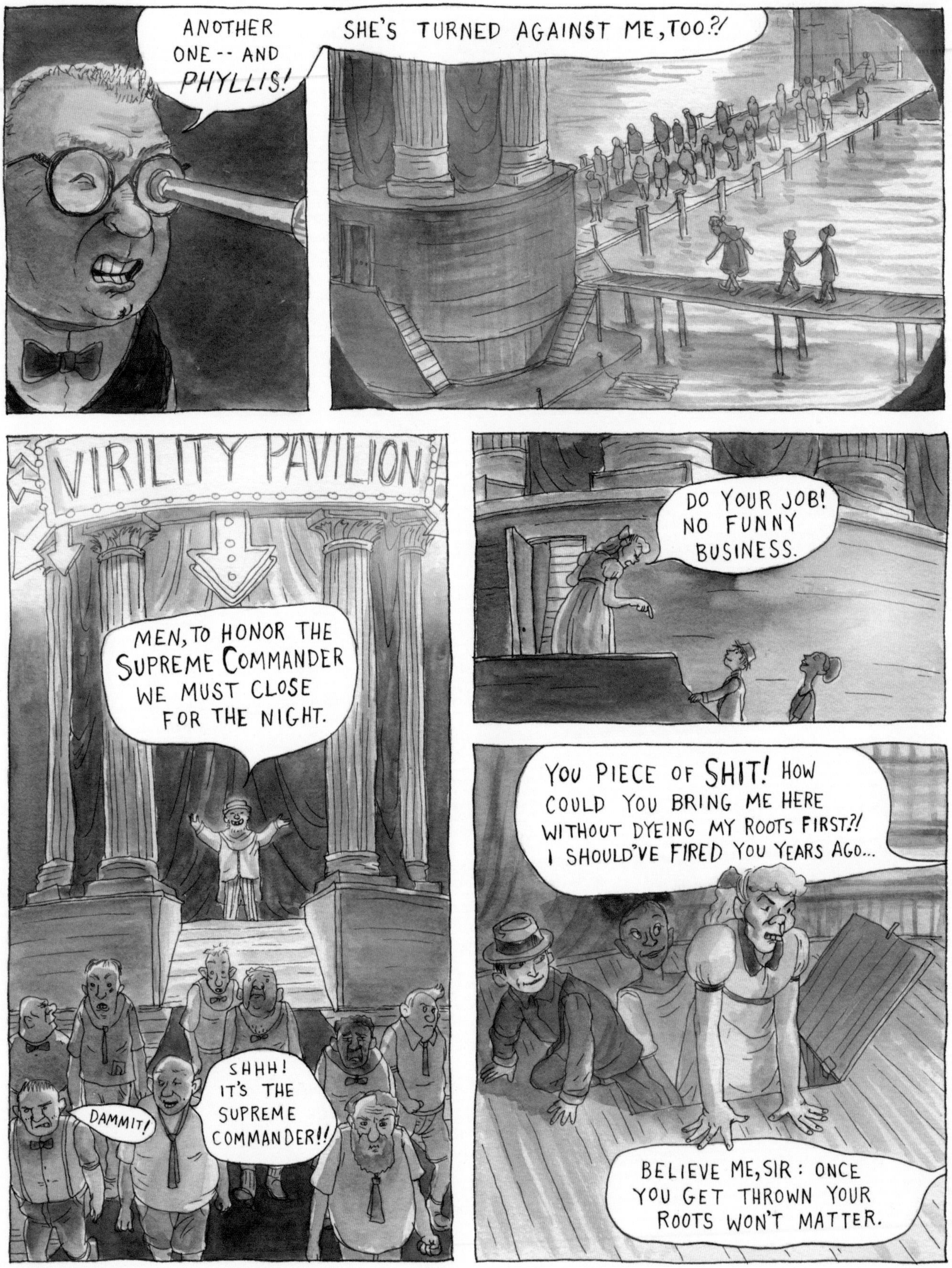
ANOTHER ONE -- AND PHYLLIS!
SHE'S TURNED AGAINST ME, TOO?!
VIRILITY PAVILION
MEN, TO HONOR THE SUPREME COMMANDER WE MUST CLOSE FOR THE NIGHT.
DAMMIT!
SHHH! IT'S THE SUPREME COMMANDER!!
DO YOUR JOB! NO FUNNY BUSINESS.
YOU PIECE OF SHIT! HOW COULD YOU BRING ME HERE WITHOUT DYEING MY ROOTS FIRST?! I SHOULD'VE FIRED YOU YEARS AGO...
BELIEVE ME, SIR: ONCE YOU GET THROWN YOUR ROOTS WON'T MATTER.

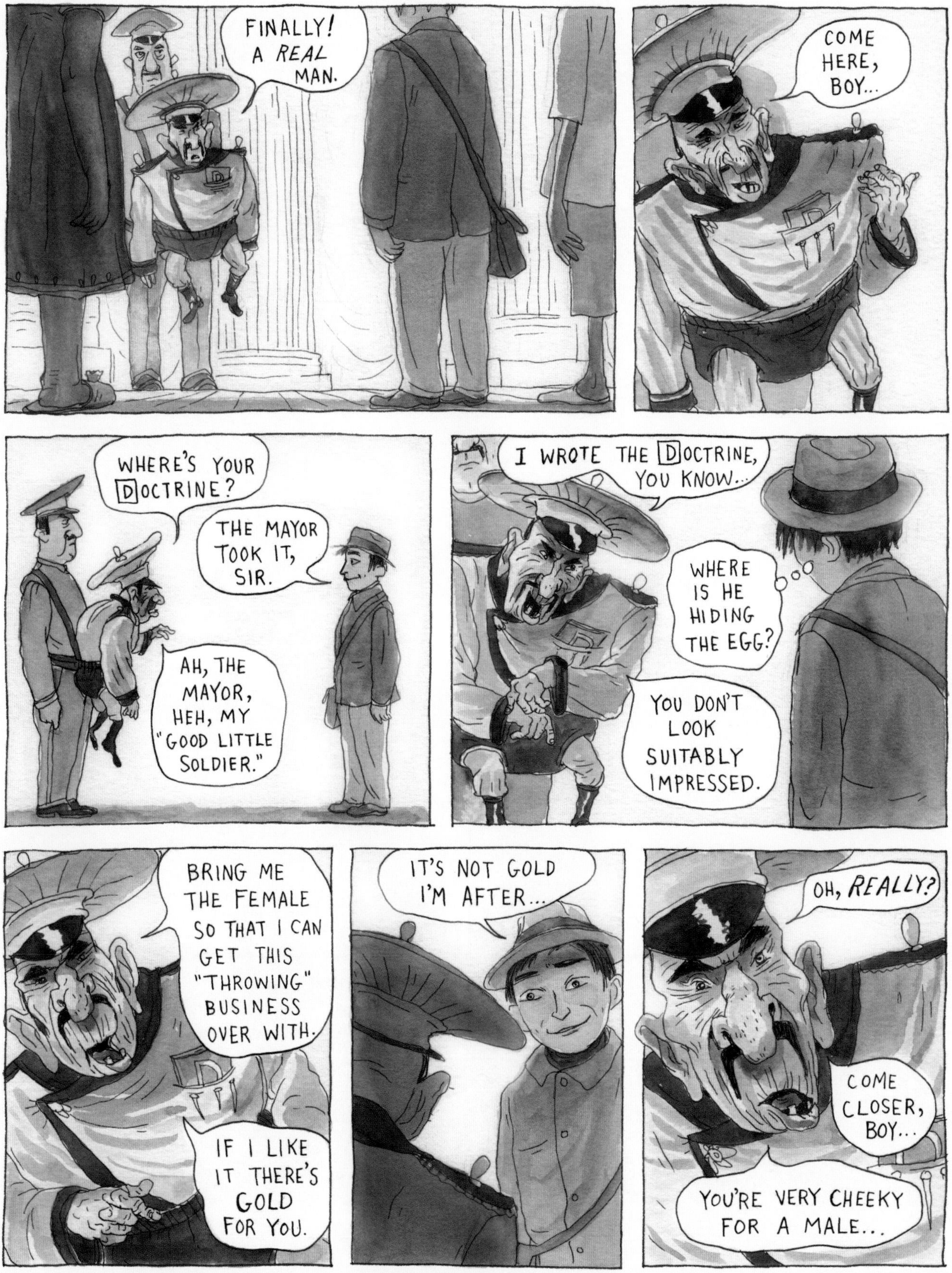
FINALLY! A *REAL* MAN.
COME HERE, BOY...
WHERE'S YOUR DOCTRINE?
THE MAYOR TOOK IT, SIR.
AH, THE MAYOR, HEH, MY "GOOD LITTLE SOLDIER."
I WROTE THE DOCTRINE, YOU KNOW...
WHERE IS HE HIDING THE EGG?
YOU DON'T LOOK SUITABLY IMPRESSED.
BRING ME THE FEMALE SO THAT I CAN GET THIS "THROWING" BUSINESS OVER WITH.
IF I LIKE IT THERE'S **GOLD** FOR YOU.
IT'S NOT GOLD I'M AFTER...
OH, *REALLY?*
COME CLOSER, BOY...
YOU'RE VERY CHEEKY FOR A MALE...

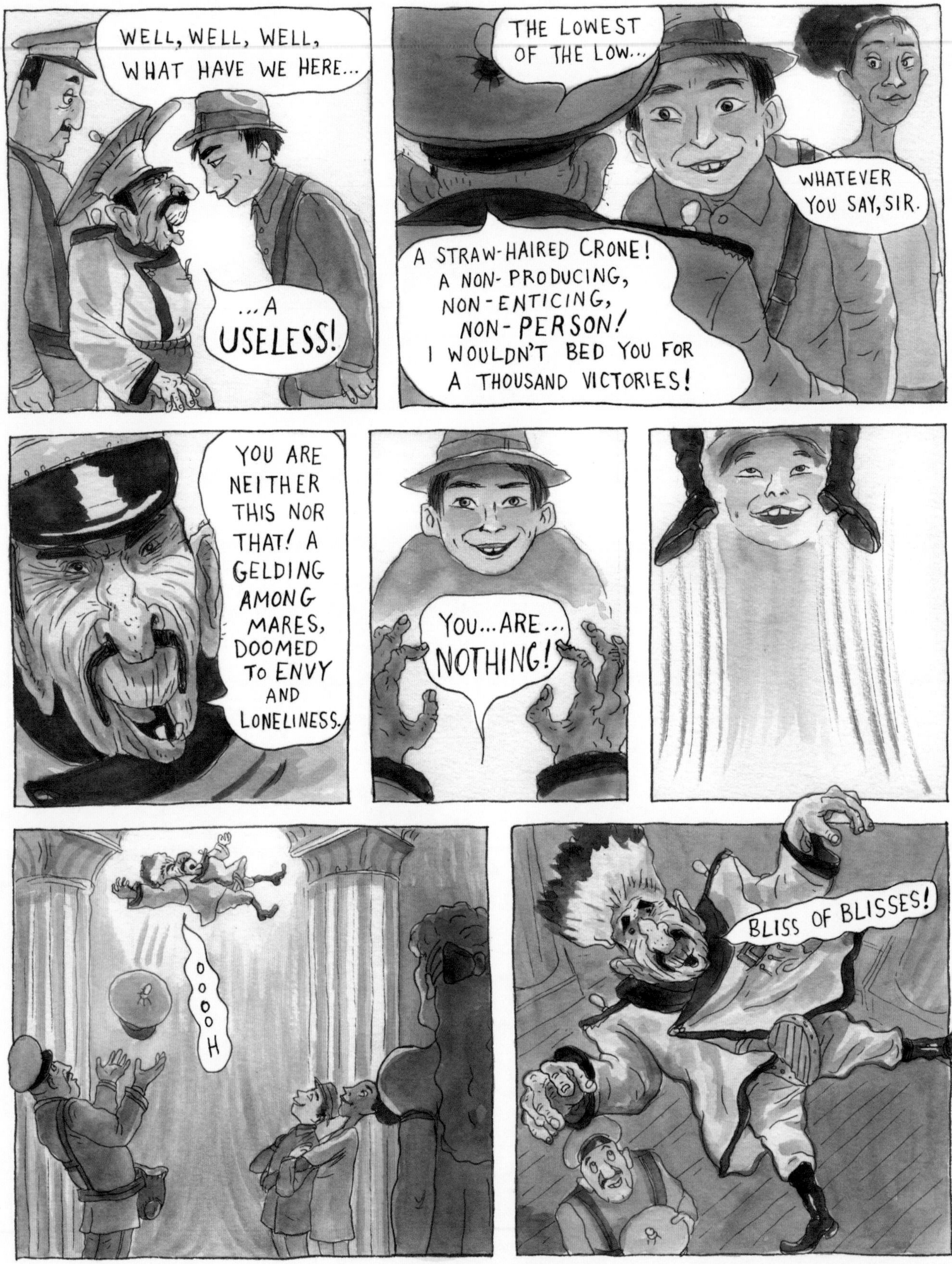
WELL, WELL, WELL, WHAT HAVE WE HERE...
...A USELESS!
THE LOWEST OF THE LOW...
WHATEVER YOU SAY, SIR.
A STRAW-HAIRED CRONE! A NON-PRODUCING, NON-ENTICING, NON-PERSON! I WOULDN'T BED YOU FOR A THOUSAND VICTORIES!
YOU ARE NEITHER THIS NOR THAT! A GELDING AMONG MARES, DOOMED TO ENVY AND LONELINESS.
YOU...ARE... NOTHING!
OOOOH
BLISS OF BLISSES!

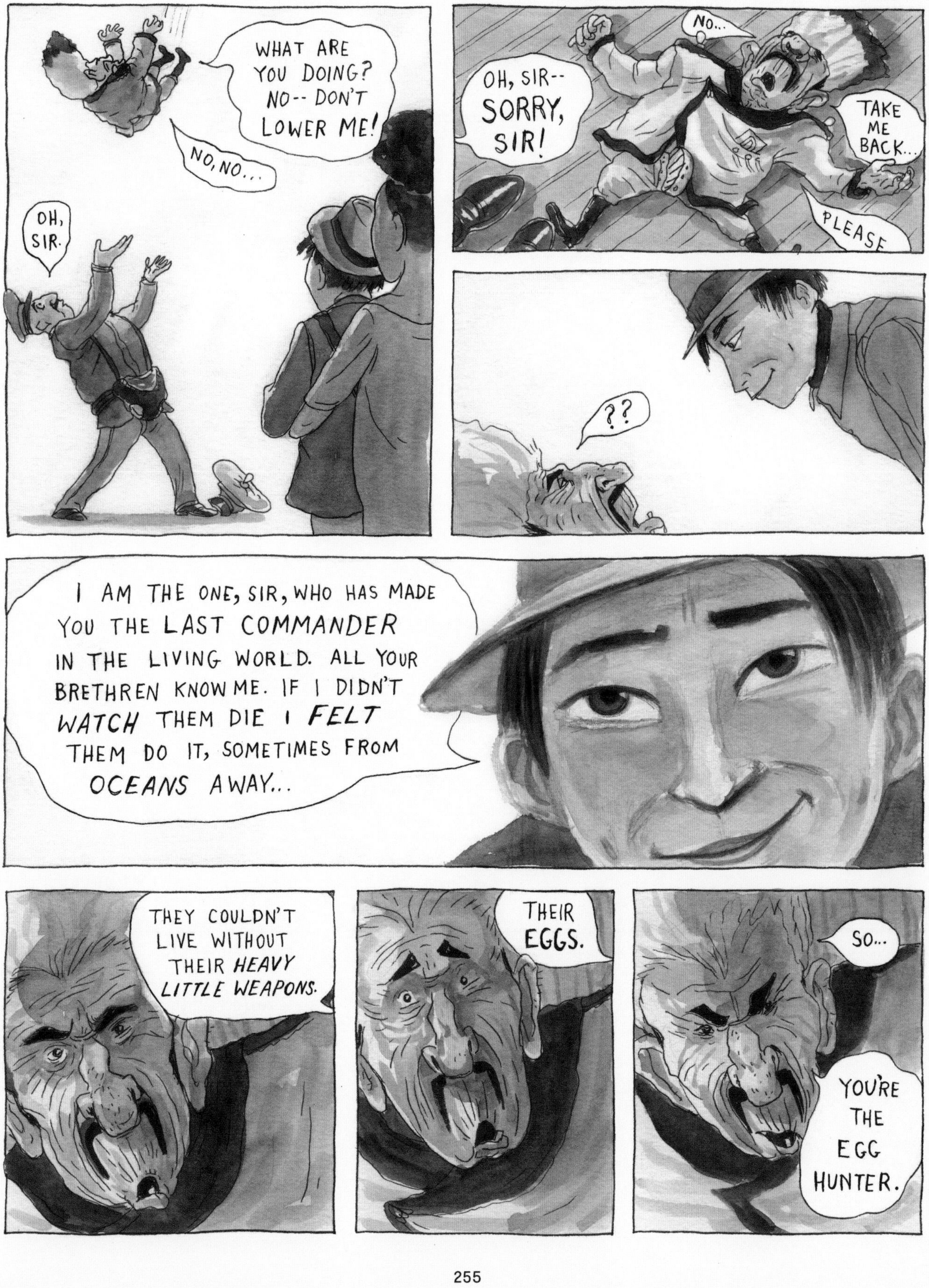
WHAT ARE YOU DOING? NO-- DON'T LOWER ME!
NO, NO...
OH, SIR.
NO...
OH, SIR-- SORRY, SIR!
TAKE ME BACK...
PLEASE
??
I AM THE ONE, SIR, WHO HAS MADE YOU THE LAST COMMANDER IN THE LIVING WORLD. ALL YOUR BRETHREN KNOW ME. IF I DIDN'T WATCH THEM DIE I FELT THEM DO IT, SOMETIMES FROM OCEANS AWAY...
THEY COULDN'T LIVE WITHOUT THEIR HEAVY LITTLE WEAPONS.
THEIR EGGS.
SO...
YOU'RE THE EGG HUNTER.

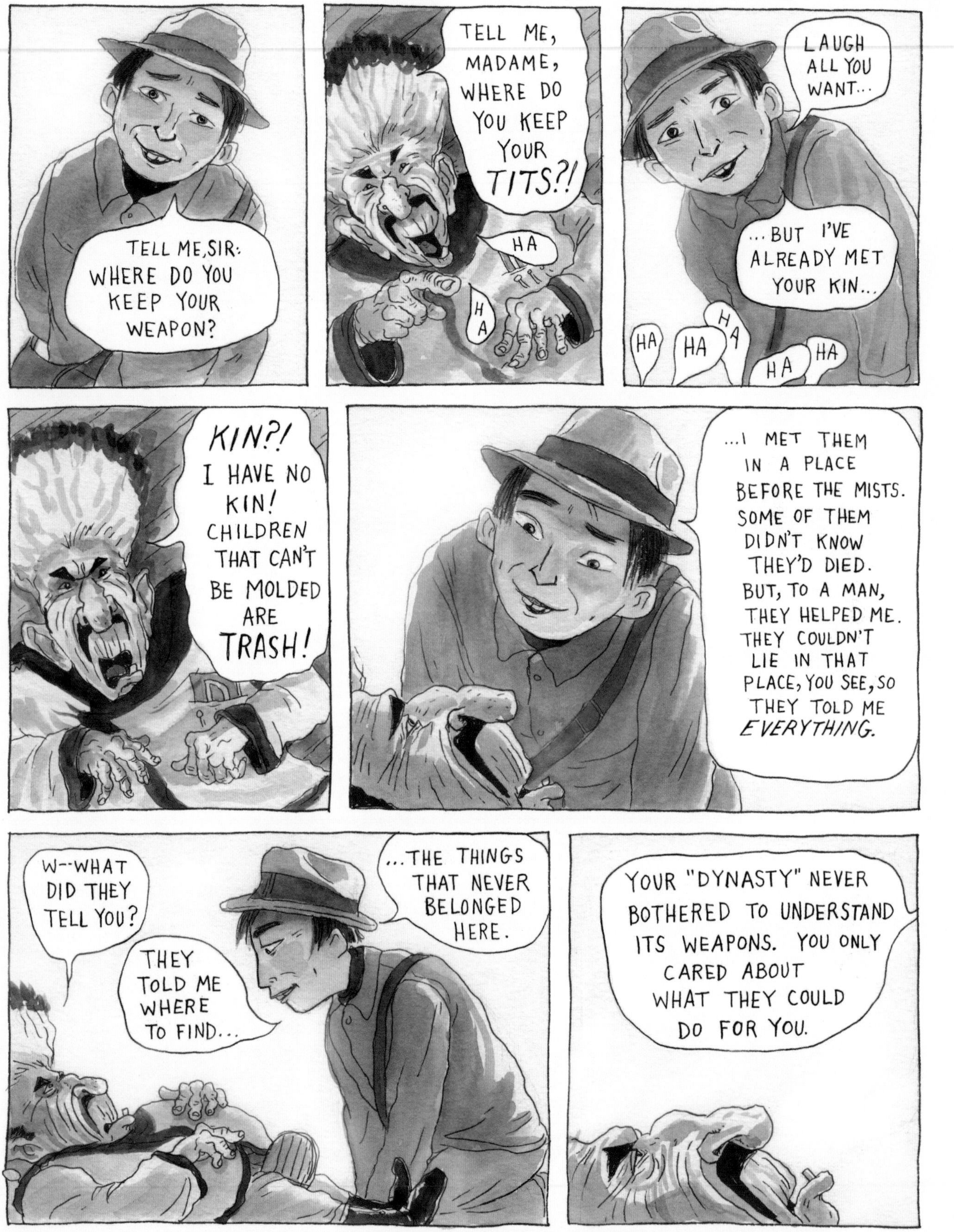
TELL ME, SIR: WHERE DO YOU KEEP YOUR WEAPON?
TELL ME, MADAME, WHERE DO YOU KEEP YOUR TITS?!
HA
HA
LAUGH ALL YOU WANT...
...BUT I'VE ALREADY MET YOUR KIN...
HA
HA
HA
HA
HA
KIN?! I HAVE NO KIN! CHILDREN THAT CAN'T BE MOLDED ARE TRASH!
...I MET THEM IN A PLACE BEFORE THE MISTS. SOME OF THEM DIDN'T KNOW THEY'D DIED. BUT, TO A MAN, THEY HELPED ME. THEY COULDN'T LIE IN THAT PLACE, YOU SEE, SO THEY TOLD ME EVERYTHING.
W--WHAT DID THEY TELL YOU?
THEY TOLD ME WHERE TO FIND...
...THE THINGS THAT NEVER BELONGED HERE.
YOUR "DYNASTY" NEVER BOTHERED TO UNDERSTAND ITS WEAPONS. YOU ONLY CARED ABOUT WHAT THEY COULD DO FOR YOU.

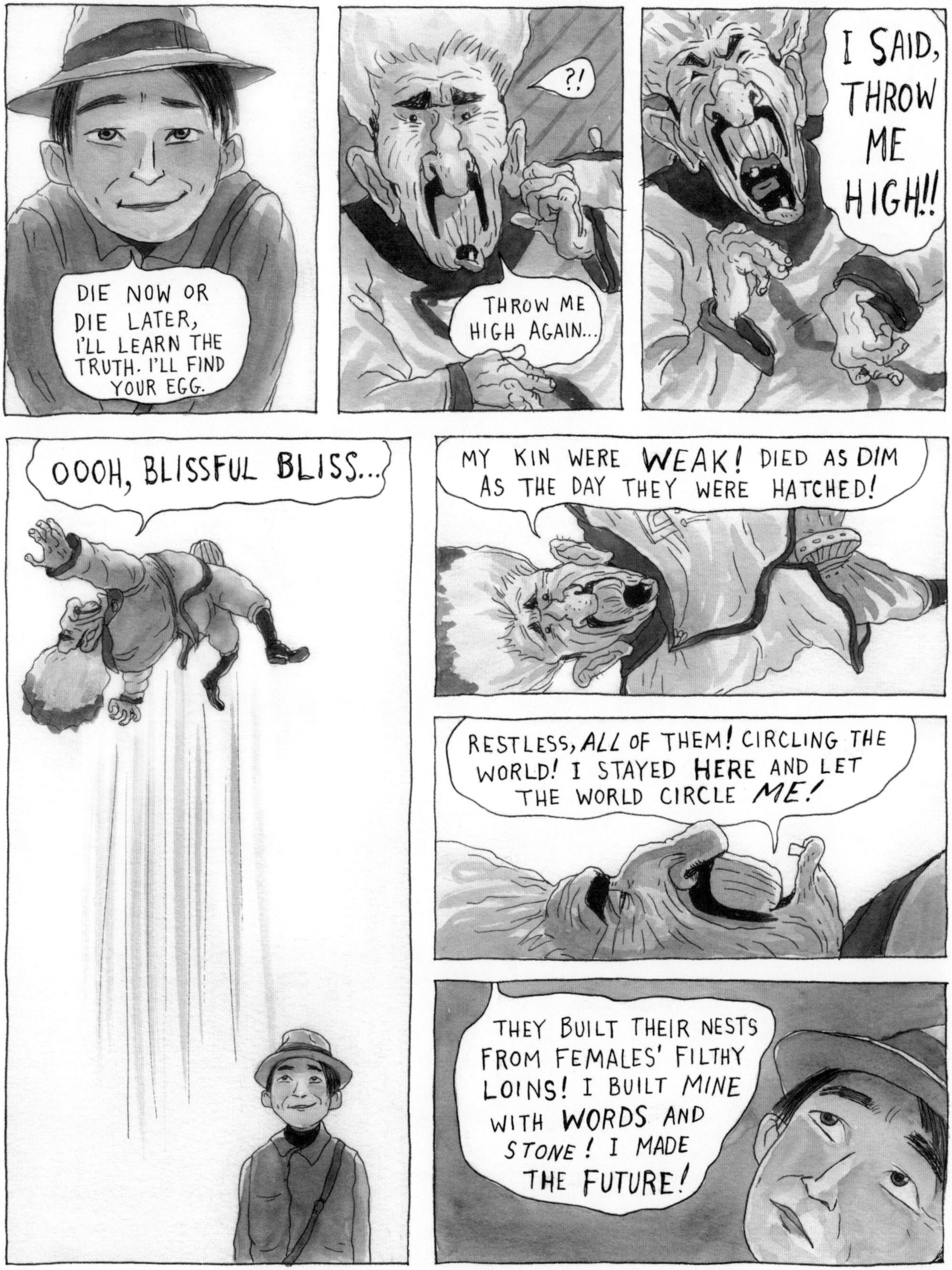
DIE NOW OR DIE LATER, I'LL LEARN THE TRUTH. I'LL FIND YOUR EGG.
?!
THROW ME HIGH AGAIN...
I SAID, THROW ME HIGH!!
OOOH, BLISSFUL BLISS...
MY KIN WERE WEAK! DIED AS DIM AS THE DAY THEY WERE HATCHED!
RESTLESS, ALL OF THEM! CIRCLING THE WORLD! I STAYED HERE AND LET THE WORLD CIRCLE ME!
THEY BUILT THEIR NESTS FROM FEMALES' FILTHY LOINS! I BUILT MINE WITH WORDS AND STONE! I MADE THE FUTURE!

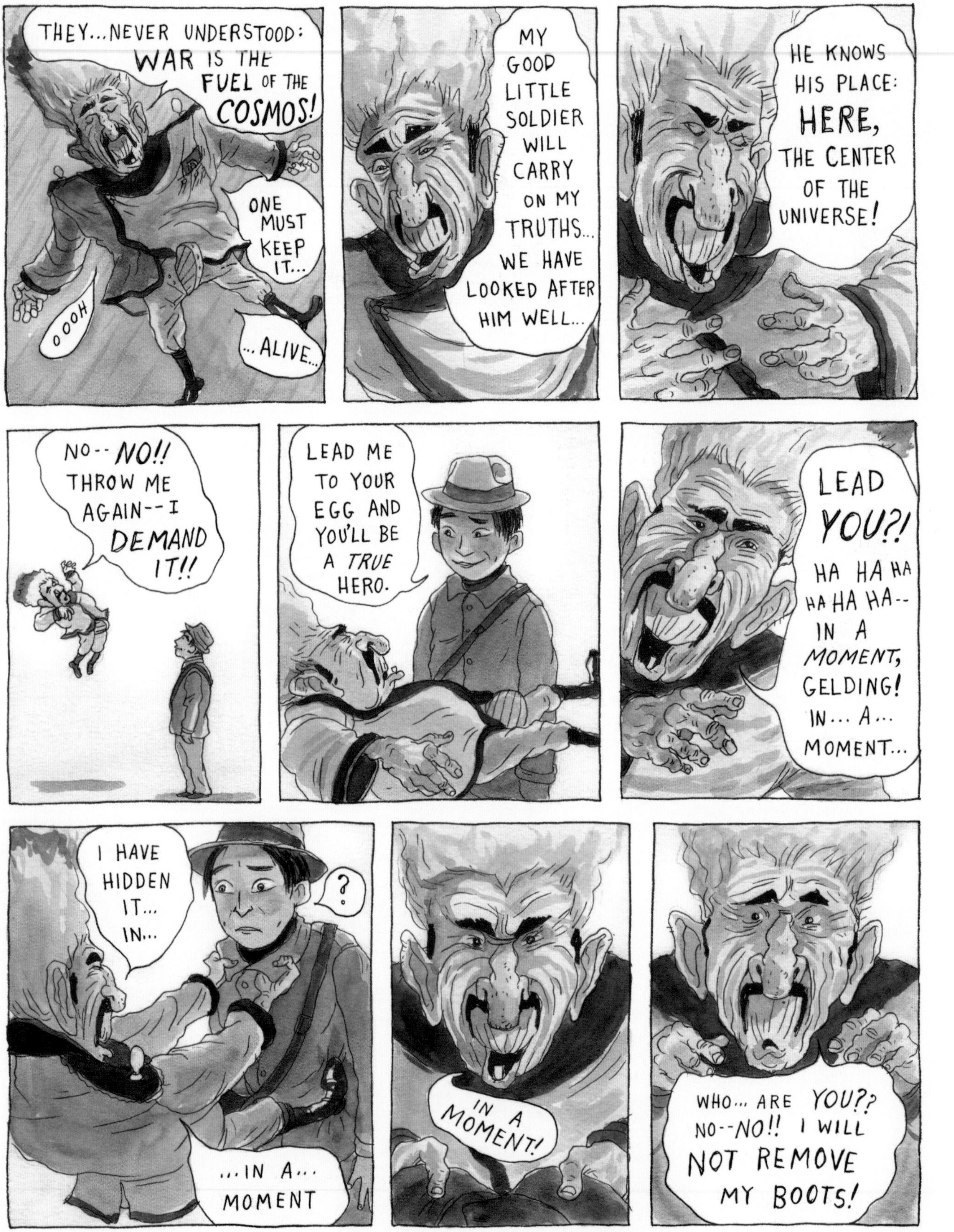
THEY... NEVER UNDERSTOOD: WAR IS THE FUEL OF THE COSMOS!
ONE MUST KEEP IT...
OOOH
... ALIVE...
MY GOOD LITTLE SOLDIER WILL CARRY ON MY TRUTHS... WE HAVE LOOKED AFTER HIM WELL...
HE KNOWS HIS PLACE: HERE, THE CENTER OF THE UNIVERSE!
NO-- NO!! THROW ME AGAIN-- I DEMAND IT!!
LEAD ME TO YOUR EGG AND YOU'LL BE A TRUE HERO.
LEAD YOU?! HA HA HA HA HA HA-- IN A MOMENT, GELDING! IN... A... MOMENT...
I HAVE HIDDEN IT... IN...
?
...IN A... MOMENT
IN A MOMENT!
WHO... ARE YOU?? NO--NO!! I WILL NOT REMOVE MY BOOTS!

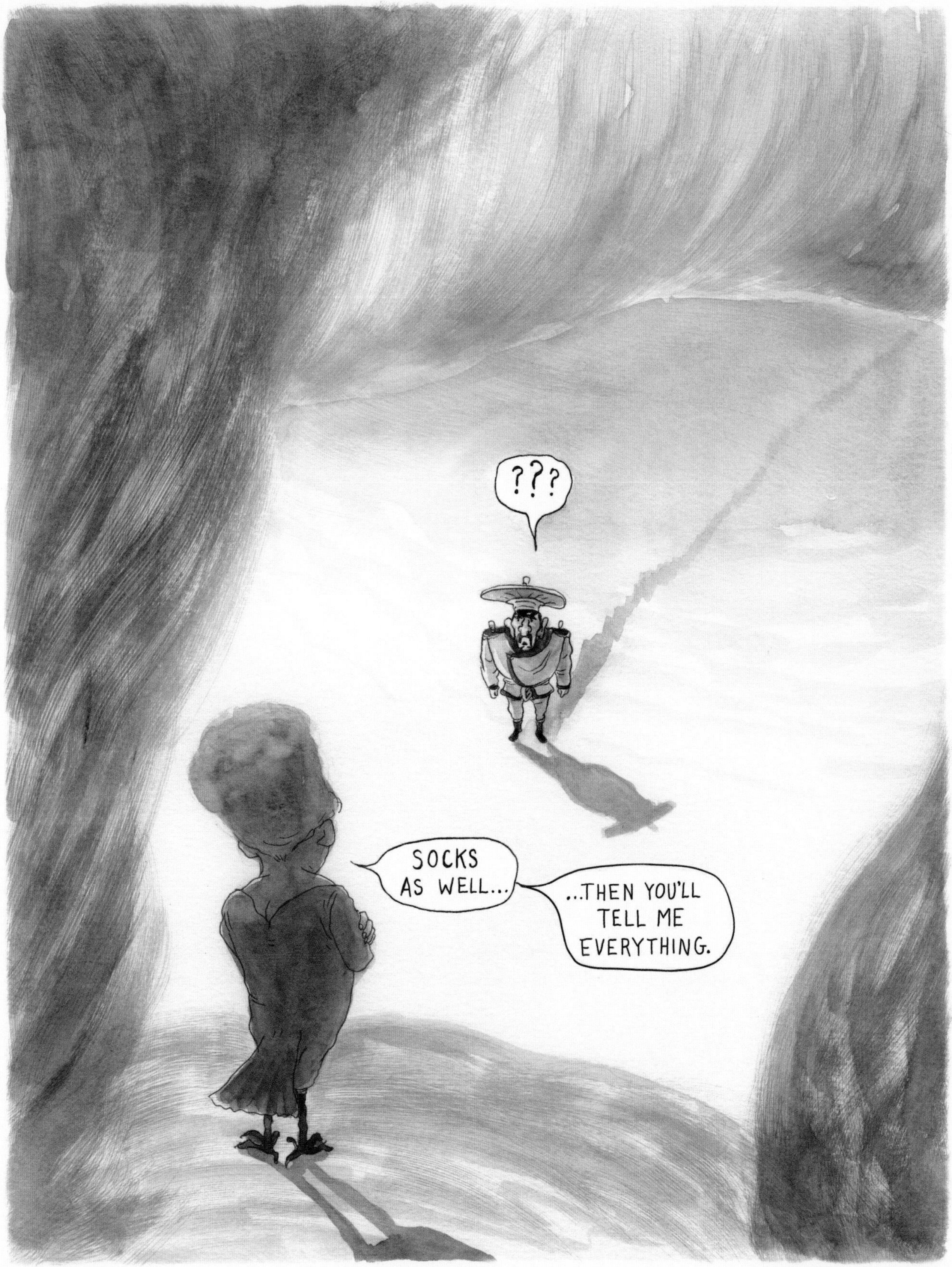
???
SOCKS AS WELL...
...THEN YOU'LL TELL ME EVERYTHING.

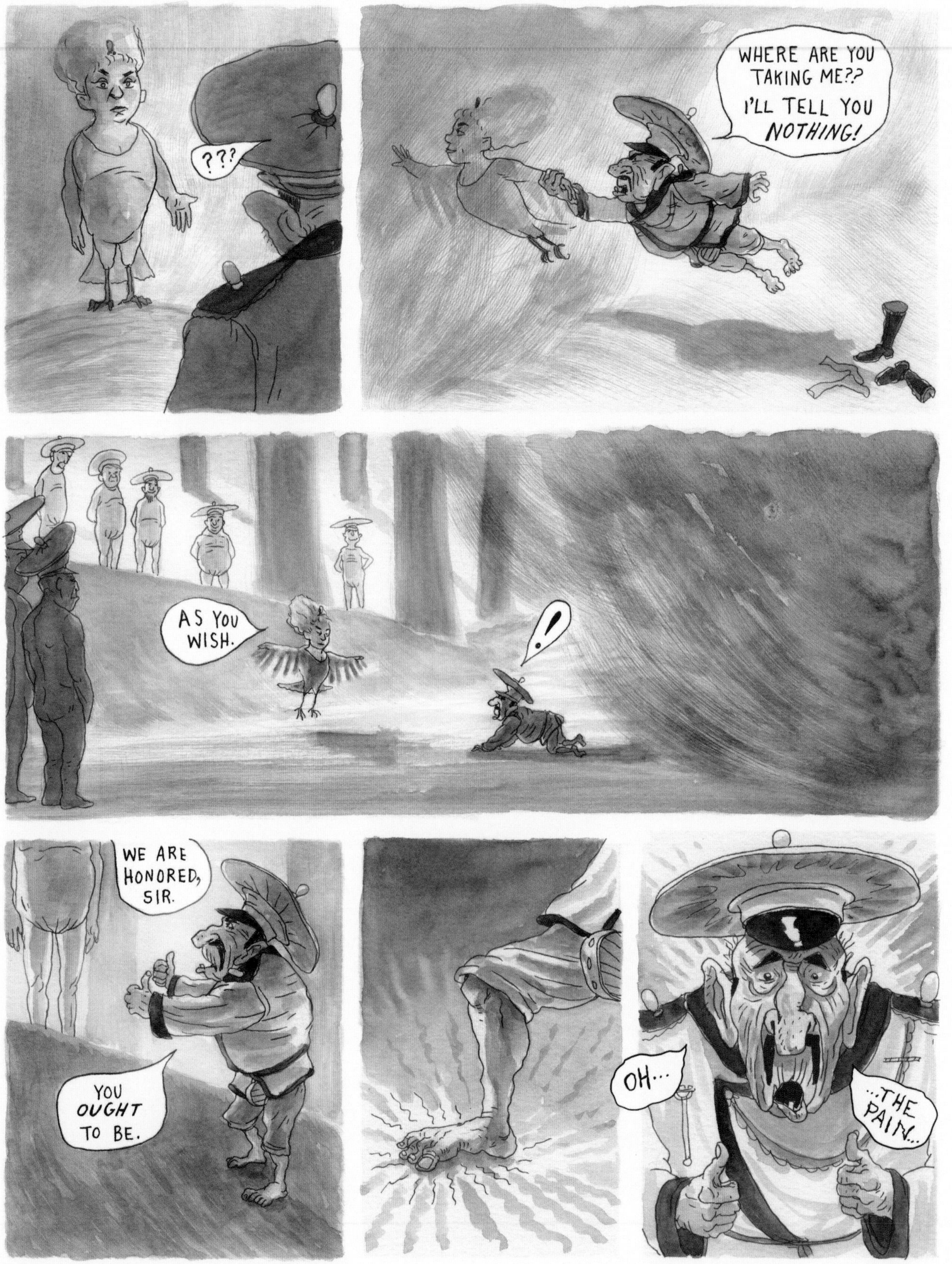
???
WHERE ARE YOU TAKING ME?? I'LL TELL YOU NOTHING!
AS YOU WISH.
!
WE ARE HONORED, SIR.
YOU OUGHT TO BE.
OH...
...THE PAIN...

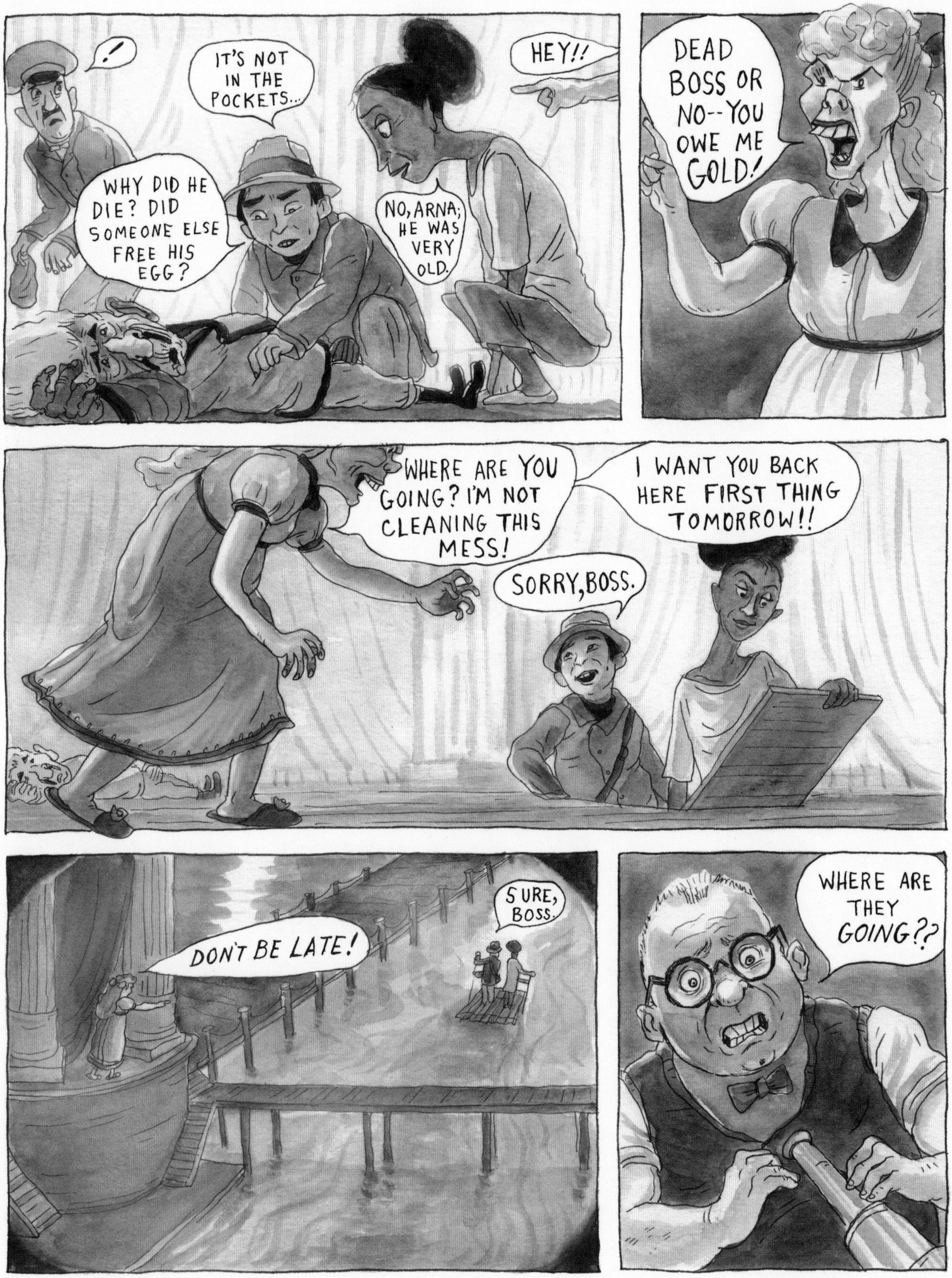
!
IT'S NOT IN THE POCKETS...
HEY!!
WHY DID HE DIE? DID SOMEONE ELSE FREE HIS EGG?
NO, ARNA; HE WAS VERY OLD.
DEAD BOSS OR NO--YOU OWE ME GOLD!
WHERE ARE YOU GOING? I'M NOT CLEANING THIS MESS!
I WANT YOU BACK HERE FIRST THING TOMORROW!!
SORRY, BOSS.
DON'T BE LATE!
SURE, BOSS.
WHERE ARE THEY GOING??

NO...
NUDIES
THE COMMANDER SAID HE'D BUILT HIS NEST FROM STONE.
THAT LITTLE ISLAND WITH THE WALL--THOSE FARMERS TOLD US--IT USED TO *PUSH THEM AWAY.*
YES... THEY MUST'VE FELT THE EGG'S EFFECTS AND KEPT THEIR DISTANCE.

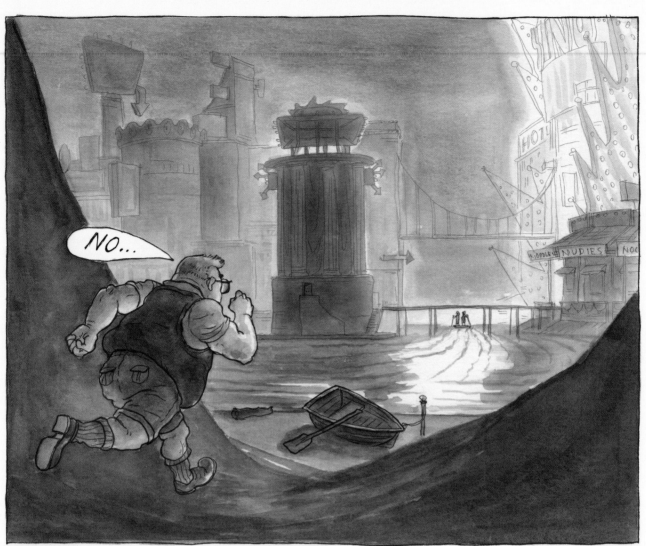

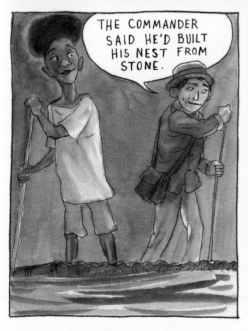

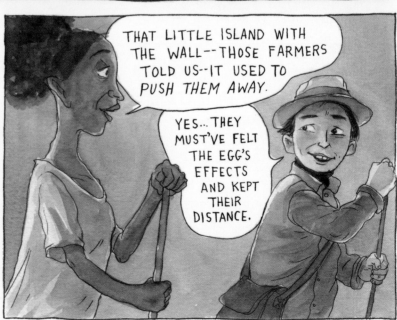

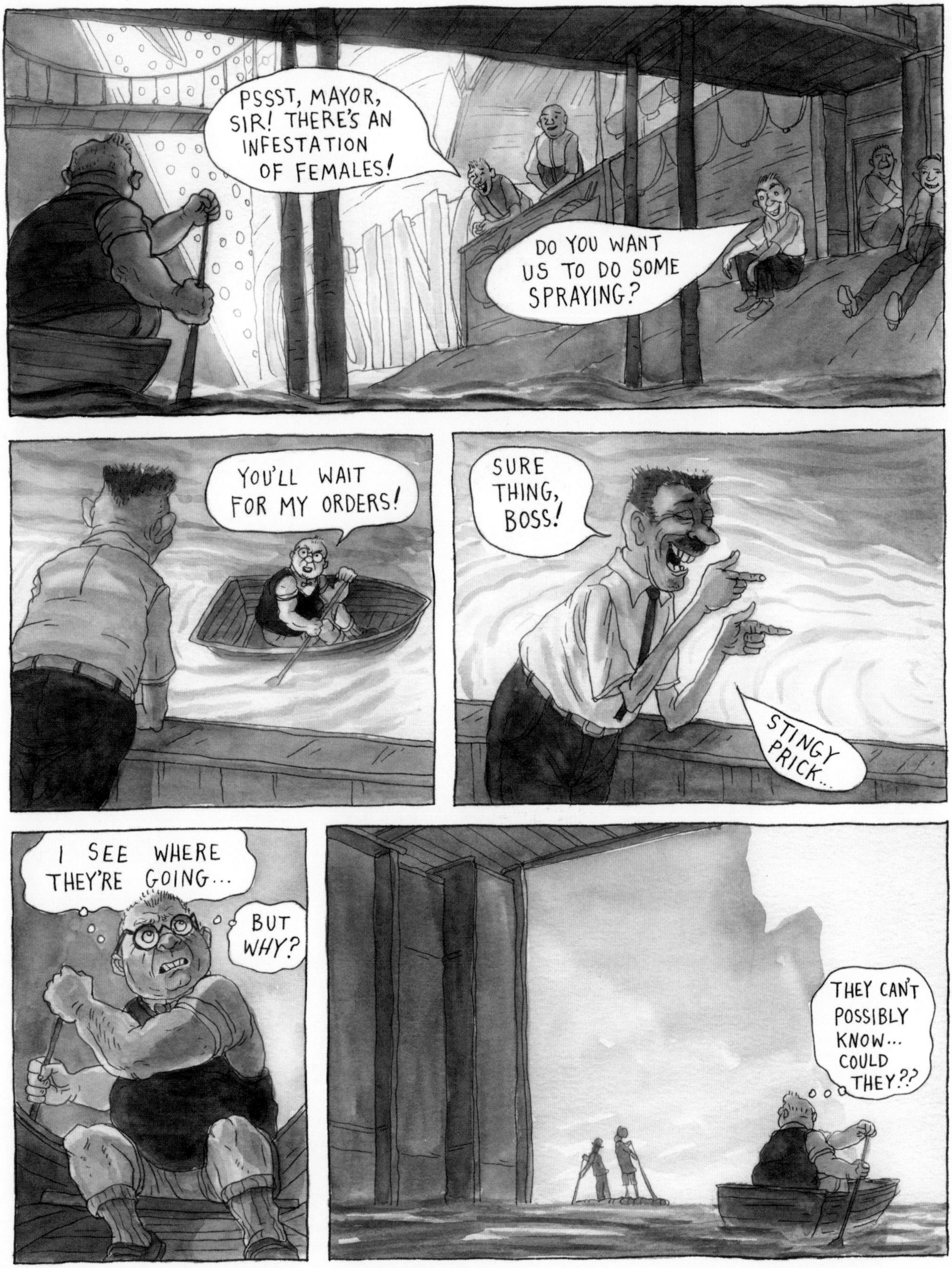
PSSST, MAYOR, SIR! THERE'S AN INFESTATION OF FEMALES!
DO YOU WANT US TO DO SOME SPRAYING?
YOU'LL WAIT FOR MY ORDERS!
SURE THING, BOSS!
STINGY PRICK...
I SEE WHERE THEY'RE GOING...
BUT WHY?
THEY CAN'T POSSIBLY KNOW... COULD THEY??

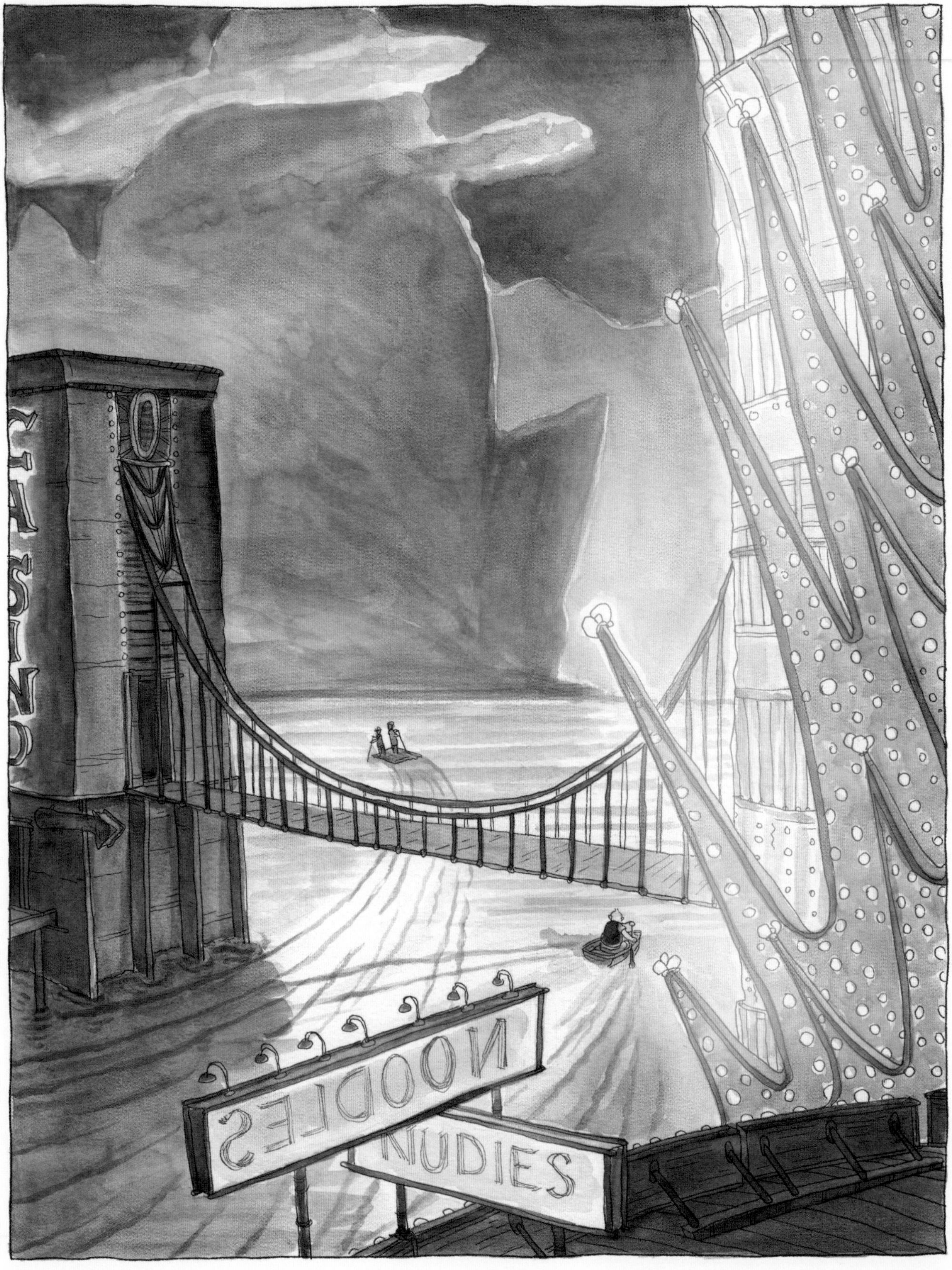
NOODLES
NUDIES

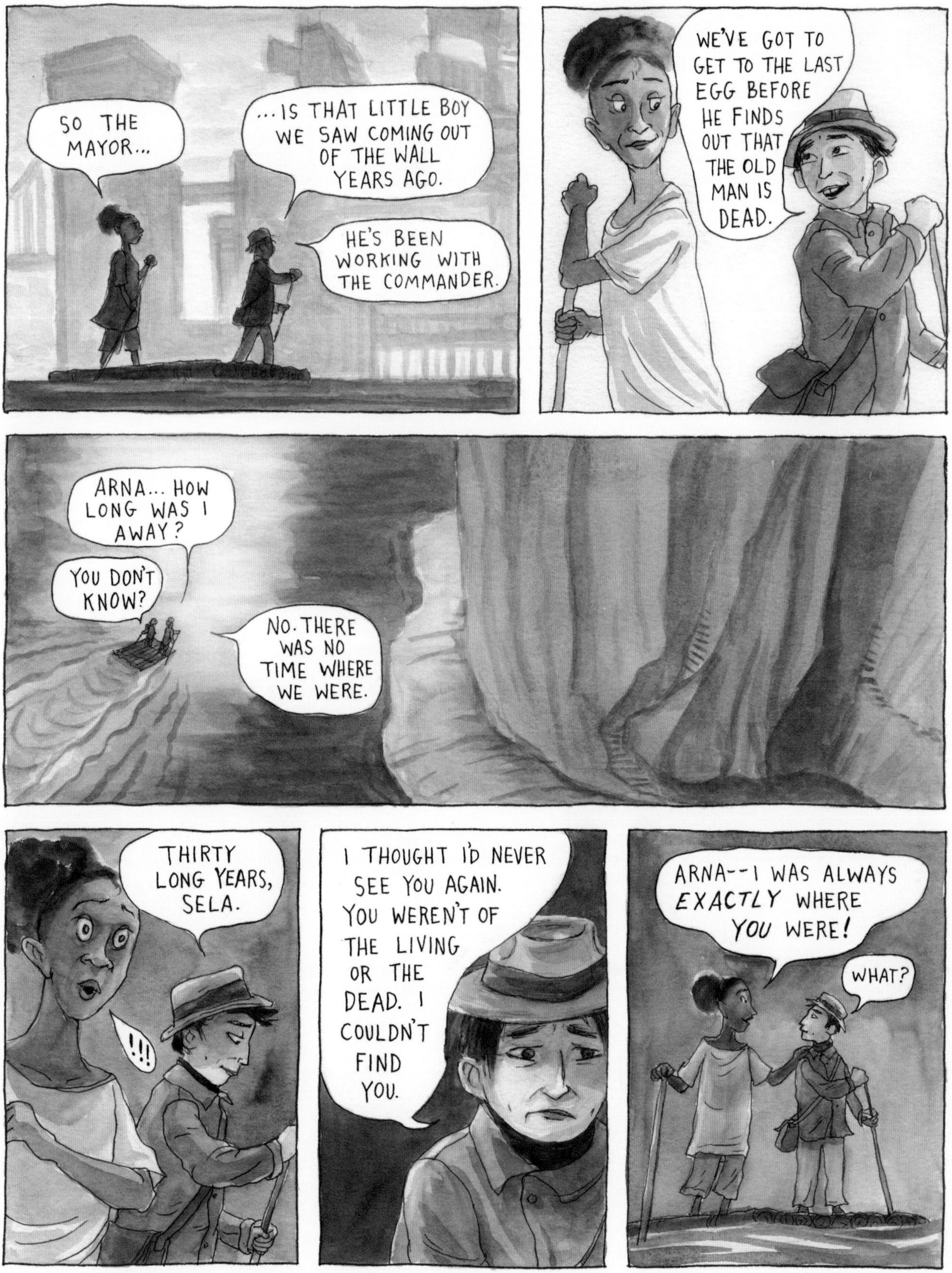
SO THE MAYOR...
...IS THAT LITTLE BOY WE SAW COMING OUT OF THE WALL YEARS AGO.
HE'S BEEN WORKING WITH THE COMMANDER.
WE'VE GOT TO GET TO THE LAST EGG BEFORE HE FINDS OUT THAT THE OLD MAN IS DEAD.
ARNA... HOW LONG WAS I AWAY?
YOU DON'T KNOW?
NO. THERE WAS NO TIME WHERE WE WERE.
THIRTY LONG YEARS, SELA.
!!!
I THOUGHT I'D NEVER SEE YOU AGAIN. YOU WEREN'T OF THE LIVING OR THE DEAD. I COULDN'T FIND YOU.
ARNA--I WAS ALWAYS *EXACTLY* WHERE *YOU* WERE!
WHAT?

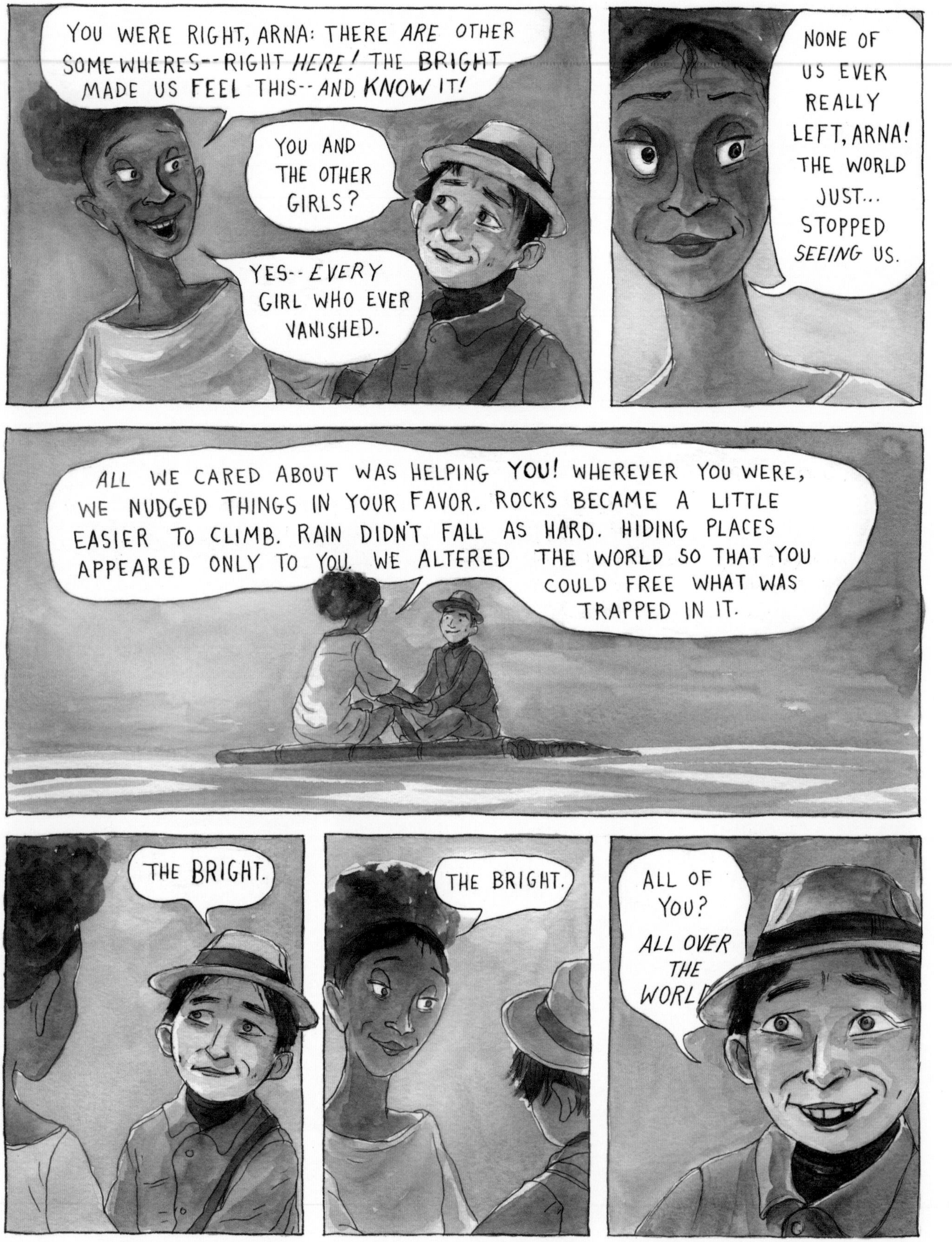
YOU WERE RIGHT, ARNA: THERE ARE OTHER SOMEWHERES--RIGHT HERE! THE BRIGHT MADE US FEEL THIS--AND KNOW IT!
YOU AND THE OTHER GIRLS?
YES--EVERY GIRL WHO EVER VANISHED.
NONE OF US EVER REALLY LEFT, ARNA! THE WORLD JUST... STOPPED SEEING US.
ALL WE CARED ABOUT WAS HELPING YOU! WHEREVER YOU WERE, WE NUDGED THINGS IN YOUR FAVOR. ROCKS BECAME A LITTLE EASIER TO CLIMB. RAIN DIDN'T FALL AS HARD. HIDING PLACES APPEARED ONLY TO YOU. WE ALTERED THE WORLD SO THAT YOU COULD FREE WHAT WAS TRAPPED IN IT.
THE BRIGHT.
THE BRIGHT.
ALL OF YOU? ALL OVER THE WORLD?

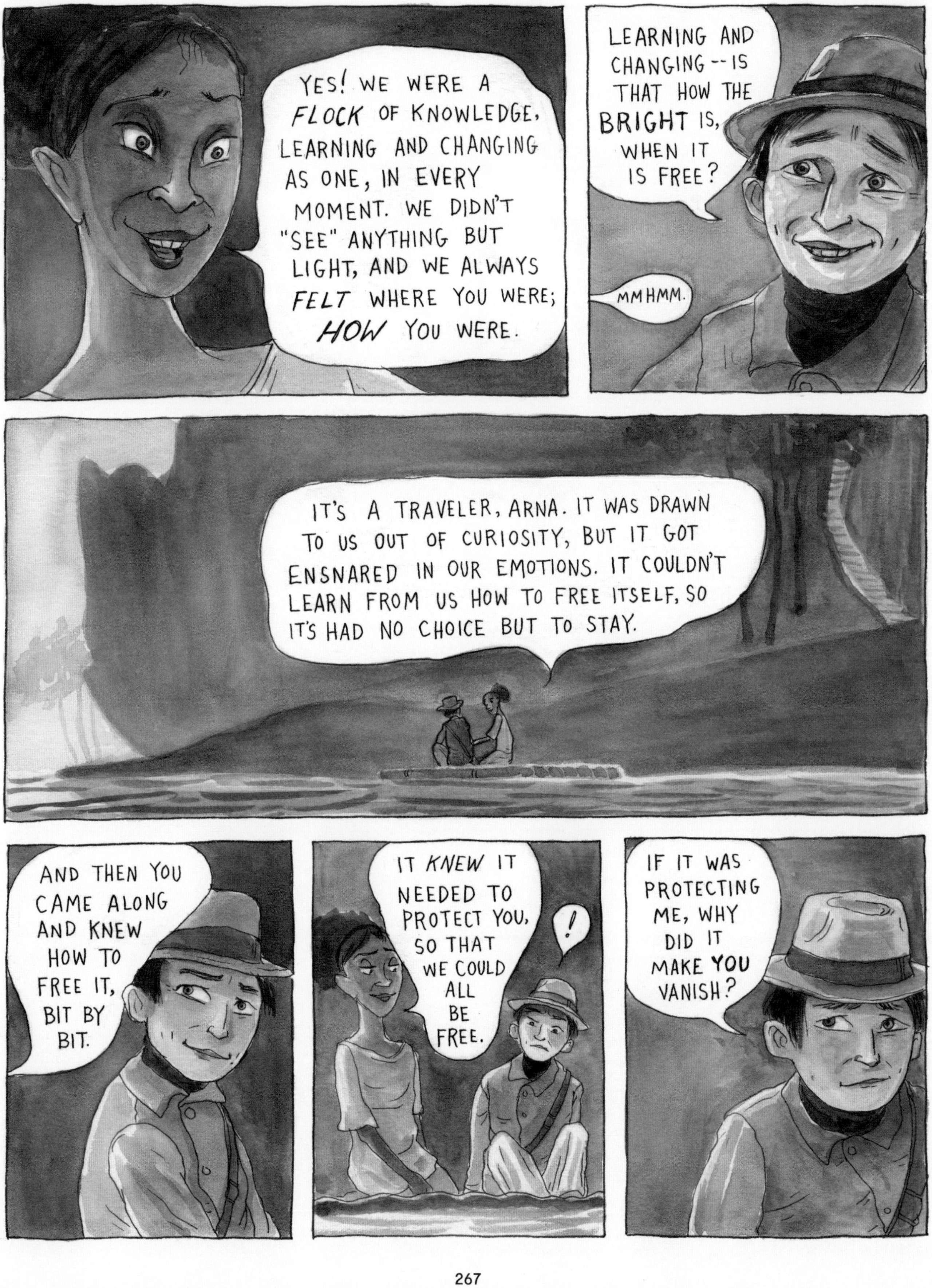
YES! WE WERE A FLOCK OF KNOWLEDGE, LEARNING AND CHANGING AS ONE, IN EVERY MOMENT. WE DIDN'T "SEE" ANYTHING BUT LIGHT, AND WE ALWAYS FELT WHERE YOU WERE; HOW YOU WERE.
LEARNING AND CHANGING--IS THAT HOW THE BRIGHT IS, WHEN IT IS FREE?
MMHMM.
IT'S A TRAVELER, ARNA. IT WAS DRAWN TO US OUT OF CURIOSITY, BUT IT GOT ENSNARED IN OUR EMOTIONS. IT COULDN'T LEARN FROM US HOW TO FREE ITSELF, SO IT'S HAD NO CHOICE BUT TO STAY.
AND THEN YOU CAME ALONG AND KNEW HOW TO FREE IT, BIT BY BIT.
IT KNEW IT NEEDED TO PROTECT YOU, SO THAT WE COULD ALL BE FREE.
!
IF IT WAS PROTECTING ME, WHY DID IT MAKE YOU VANISH?

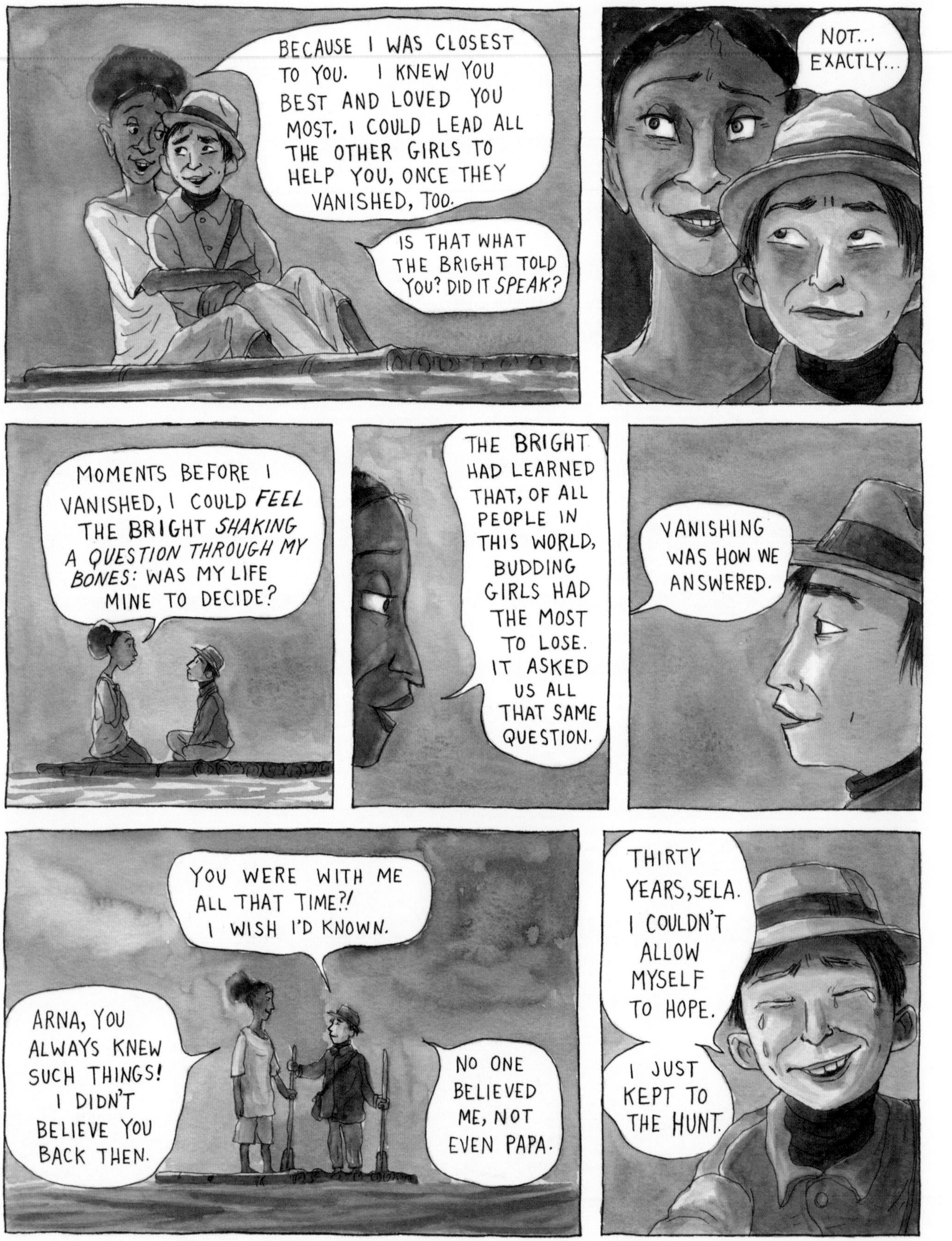
BECAUSE I WAS CLOSEST TO YOU. I KNEW YOU BEST AND LOVED YOU MOST. I COULD LEAD ALL THE OTHER GIRLS TO HELP YOU, ONCE THEY VANISHED, TOO.
IS THAT WHAT THE BRIGHT TOLD YOU? DID IT *SPEAK*?
NOT... EXACTLY...
MOMENTS BEFORE I VANISHED, I COULD *FEEL* THE BRIGHT *SHAKING A QUESTION THROUGH MY BONES*: WAS MY LIFE MINE TO DECIDE?
THE BRIGHT HAD LEARNED THAT, OF ALL PEOPLE IN THIS WORLD, BUDDING GIRLS HAD THE MOST TO LOSE. IT ASKED US ALL THAT SAME QUESTION.
VANISHING WAS HOW WE ANSWERED.
YOU WERE WITH ME ALL THAT TIME?! I WISH I'D KNOWN.
ARNA, YOU ALWAYS KNEW SUCH THINGS! I DIDN'T BELIEVE YOU BACK THEN.
NO ONE BELIEVED ME, NOT EVEN PAPA.
THIRTY YEARS, SELA. I COULDN'T ALLOW MYSELF TO HOPE.
I JUST KEPT TO THE HUNT.

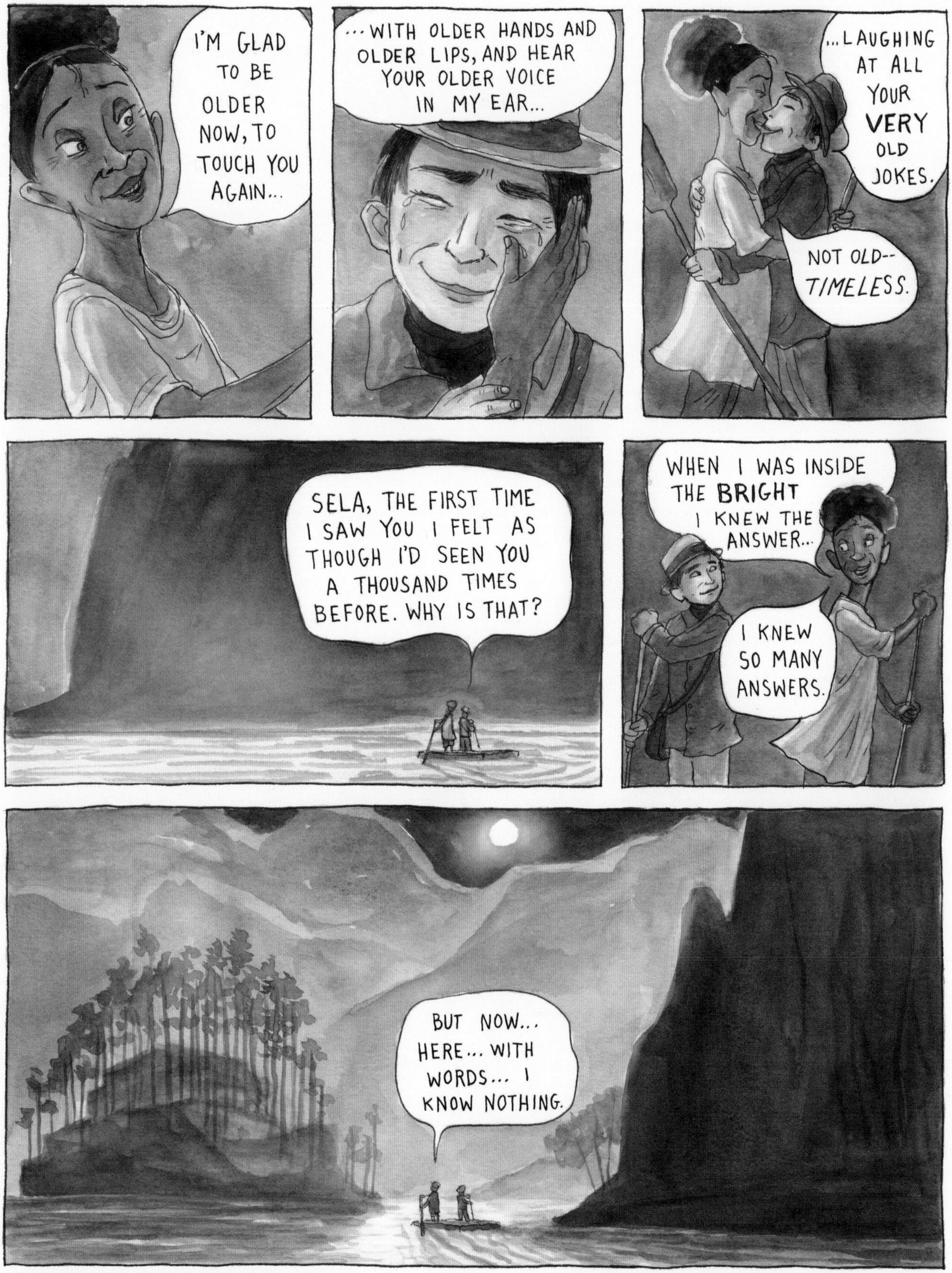
I'M GLAD TO BE OLDER NOW, TO TOUCH YOU AGAIN...
...WITH OLDER HANDS AND OLDER LIPS, AND HEAR YOUR OLDER VOICE IN MY EAR...
...LAUGHING AT ALL YOUR **VERY** OLD JOKES.
NOT OLD-- *TIMELESS.*
SELA, THE FIRST TIME I SAW YOU I FELT AS THOUGH I'D SEEN YOU A THOUSAND TIMES BEFORE. WHY IS THAT?
WHEN I WAS INSIDE THE **BRIGHT** I KNEW THE ANSWER...
I KNEW SO MANY ANSWERS.
BUT NOW... HERE... WITH WORDS... I KNOW NOTHING.

ZZZZ ZZZ
ZZ
Z
!
WHOA.
HEY, DAD, DAD DAD--DAAAD
DAD--DAD!! WAKE UP! I SAW IT!--I SAW THE AFTEROGRE IN MY DREAM! IT'S EXPOSED SO WE CAN GO FIGHT IT NOW!!
?
HE ALREADY KNOWS! HE'S LEADING THE MEN TO THE AFTERWAR.
AND I'M GOING, TOO!

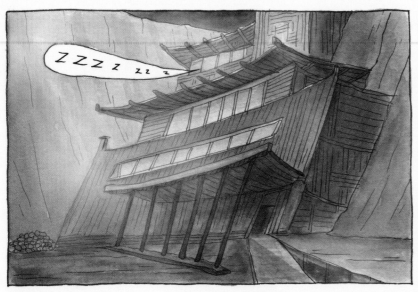

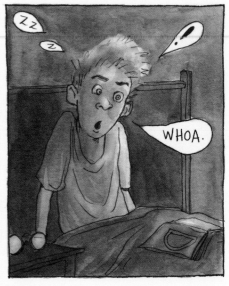

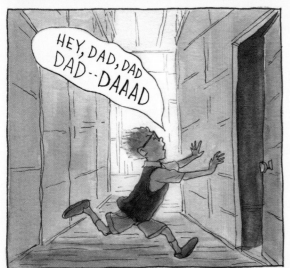

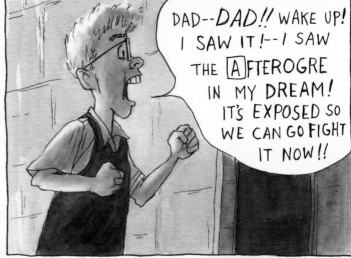

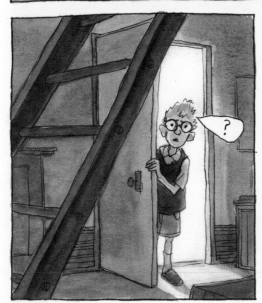

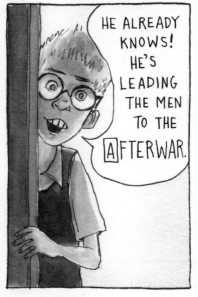

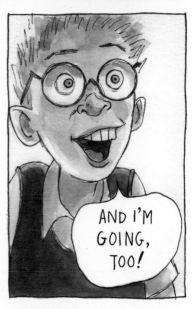

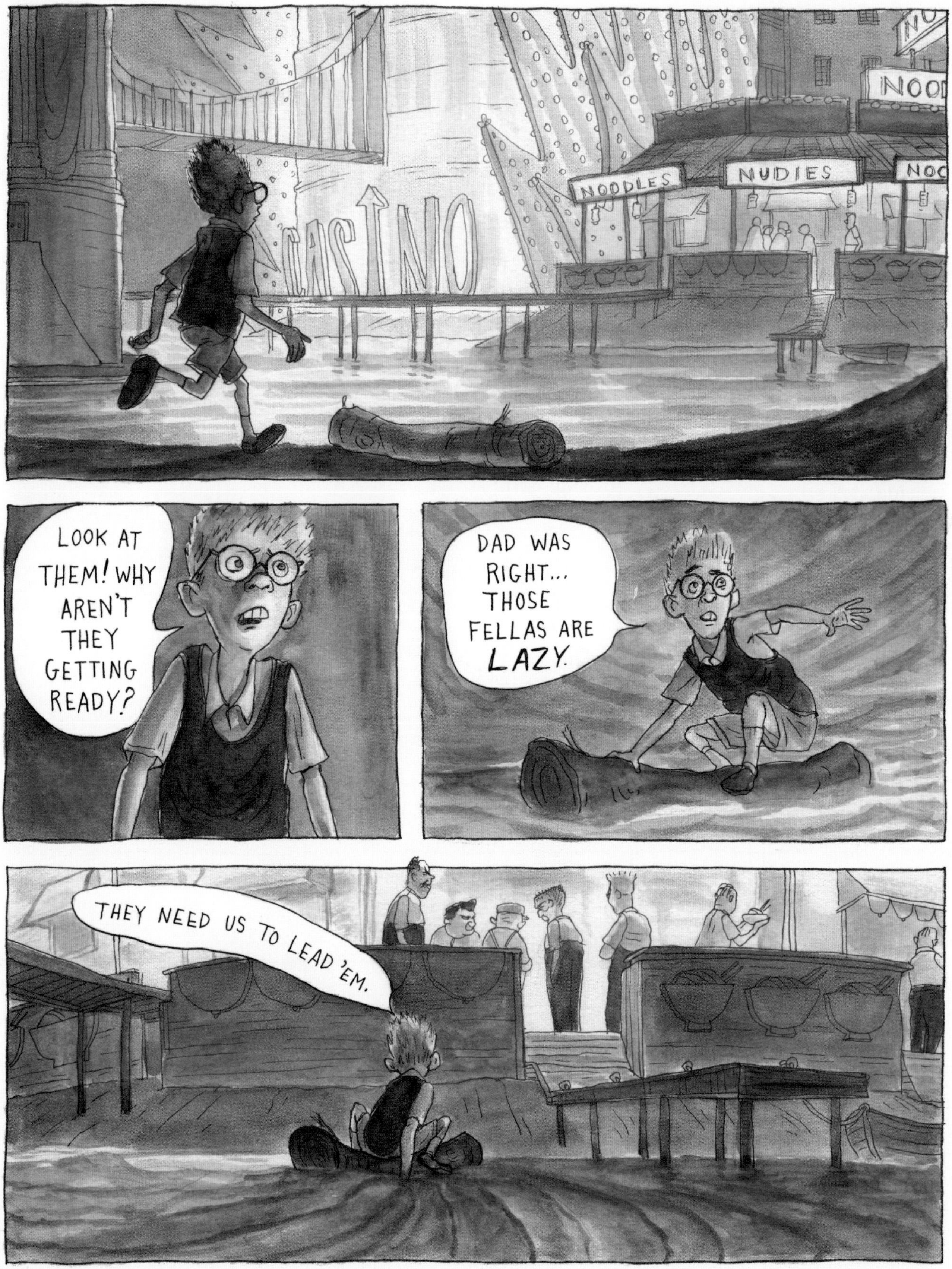
NOODLES
NUDIES
LOOK AT THEM! WHY AREN'T THEY GETTING READY?
DAD WAS RIGHT... THOSE FELLAS ARE LAZY.
THEY NEED US TO LEAD 'EM.

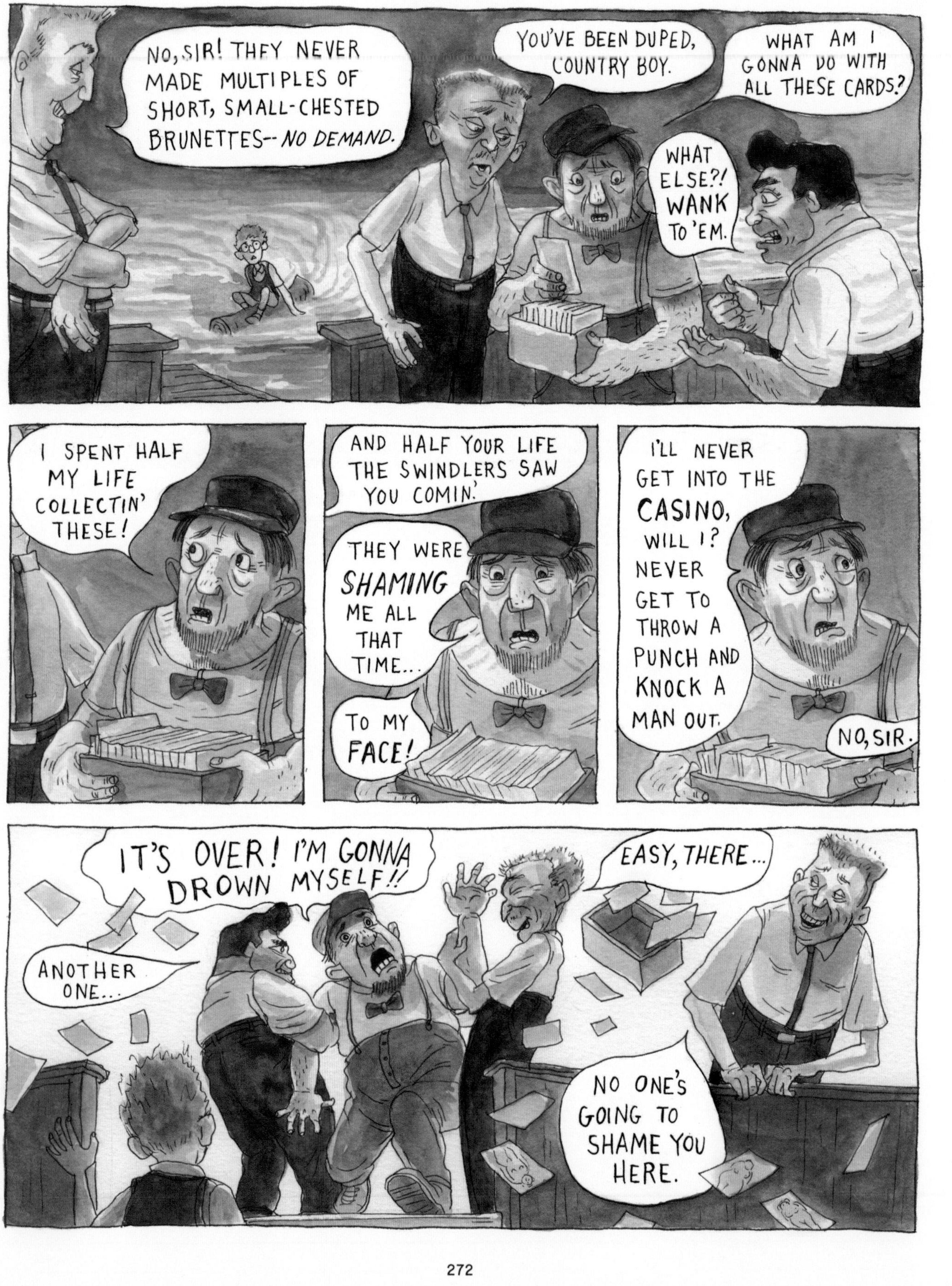
NO, SIR! THEY NEVER MADE MULTIPLES OF SHORT, SMALL-CHESTED BRUNETTES-- *NO DEMAND.*
YOU'VE BEEN DUPED, COUNTRY BOY.
WHAT AM I GONNA DO WITH ALL THESE CARDS?
WHAT ELSE?! WANK TO 'EM.
I SPENT HALF MY LIFE COLLECTIN' THESE!
AND HALF YOUR LIFE THE SWINDLERS SAW YOU COMIN'.
THEY WERE *SHAMING* ME ALL THAT TIME...
TO MY FACE!
I'LL NEVER GET INTO THE CASINO, WILL I? NEVER GET TO THROW A PUNCH AND KNOCK A MAN OUT.
NO, SIR.
IT'S OVER! I'M GONNA DROWN MYSELF!!
EASY, THERE...
ANOTHER ONE...
NO ONE'S GOING TO SHAME YOU HERE.

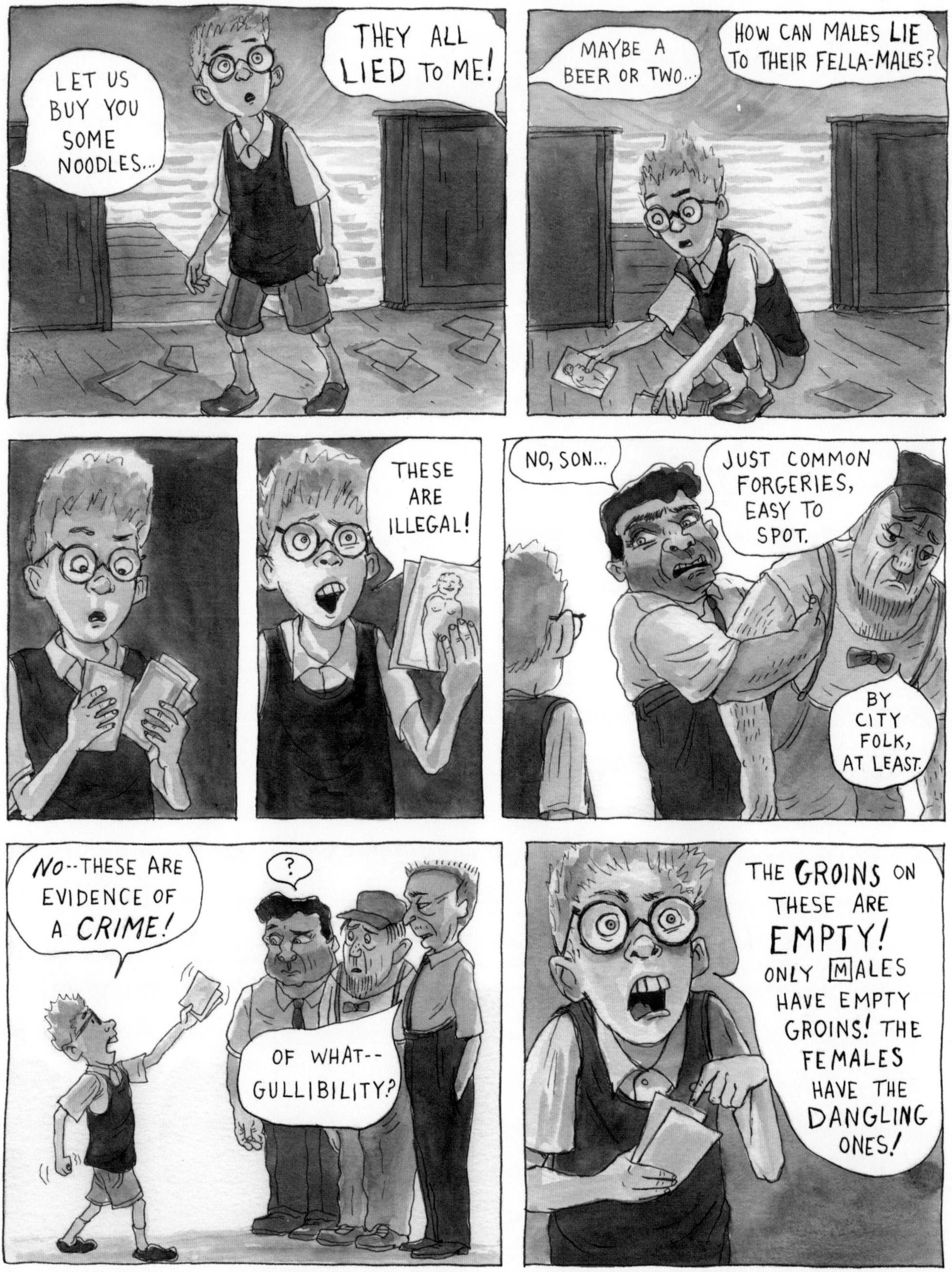
LET US BUY YOU SOME NOODLES...
THEY ALL LIED TO ME!
MAYBE A BEER OR TWO...
HOW CAN MALES LIE TO THEIR FELLA-MALES?
THESE ARE ILLEGAL!
NO, SON...
JUST COMMON FORGERIES, EASY TO SPOT.
BY CITY FOLK, AT LEAST.
NO--THESE ARE EVIDENCE OF A CRIME!
?
OF WHAT--GULLIBILITY?
THE GROINS ON THESE ARE EMPTY! ONLY MALES HAVE EMPTY GROINS! THE FEMALES HAVE THE DANGLING ONES!

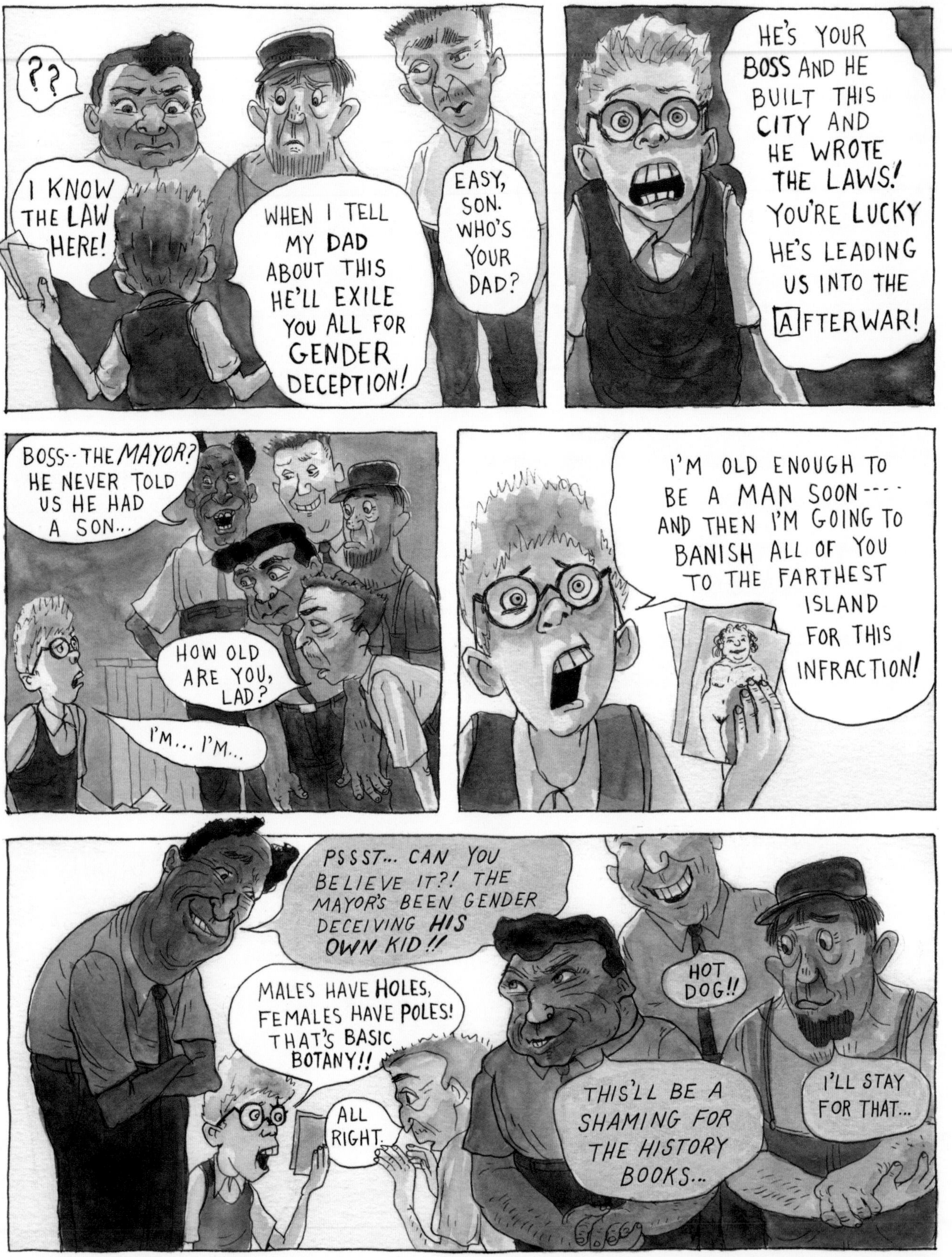
??
I KNOW THE LAW HERE!
WHEN I TELL MY DAD ABOUT THIS HE'LL EXILE YOU ALL FOR GENDER DECEPTION!
EASY, SON. WHO'S YOUR DAD?
HE'S YOUR BOSS AND HE BUILT THIS CITY AND HE WROTE THE LAWS! YOU'RE LUCKY HE'S LEADING US INTO THE AFTERWAR!
BOSS--THE MAYOR? HE NEVER TOLD US HE HAD A SON...
HOW OLD ARE YOU, LAD?
I'M... I'M...
I'M OLD ENOUGH TO BE A MAN SOON---- AND THEN I'M GOING TO BANISH ALL OF YOU TO THE FARTHEST ISLAND FOR THIS INFRACTION!
PSSST... CAN YOU BELIEVE IT?! THE MAYOR'S BEEN GENDER DECEIVING HIS OWN KID!!
MALES HAVE HOLES, FEMALES HAVE POLES! THAT'S BASIC BOTANY!!
ALL RIGHT.
HOT DOG!!
THIS'LL BE A SHAMING FOR THE HISTORY BOOKS...
I'LL STAY FOR THAT...

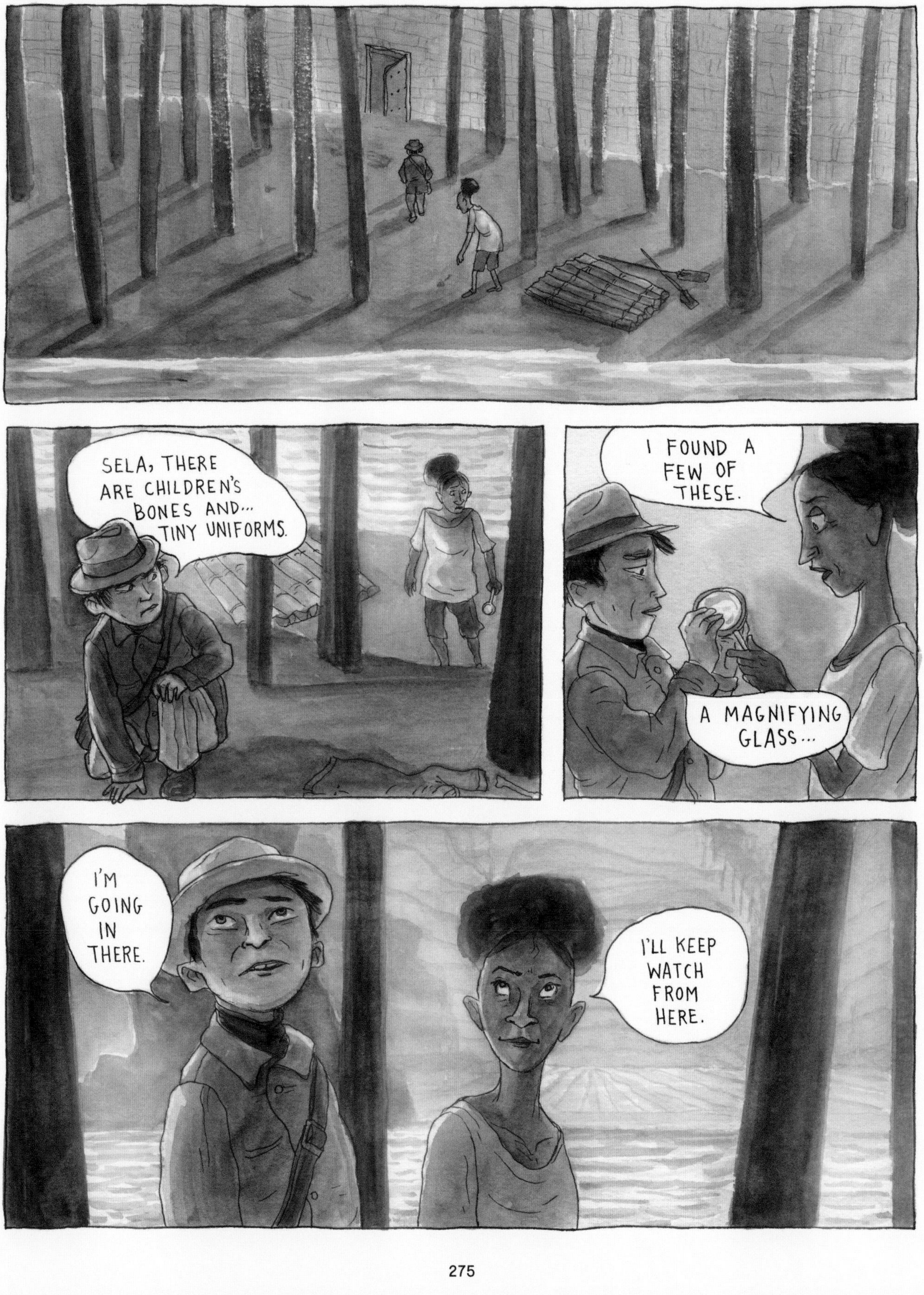
SELA, THERE ARE CHILDREN'S BONES AND... TINY UNIFORMS.
I FOUND A FEW OF THESE.
A MAGNIFYING GLASS...
I'M GOING IN THERE.
I'LL KEEP WATCH FROM HERE.

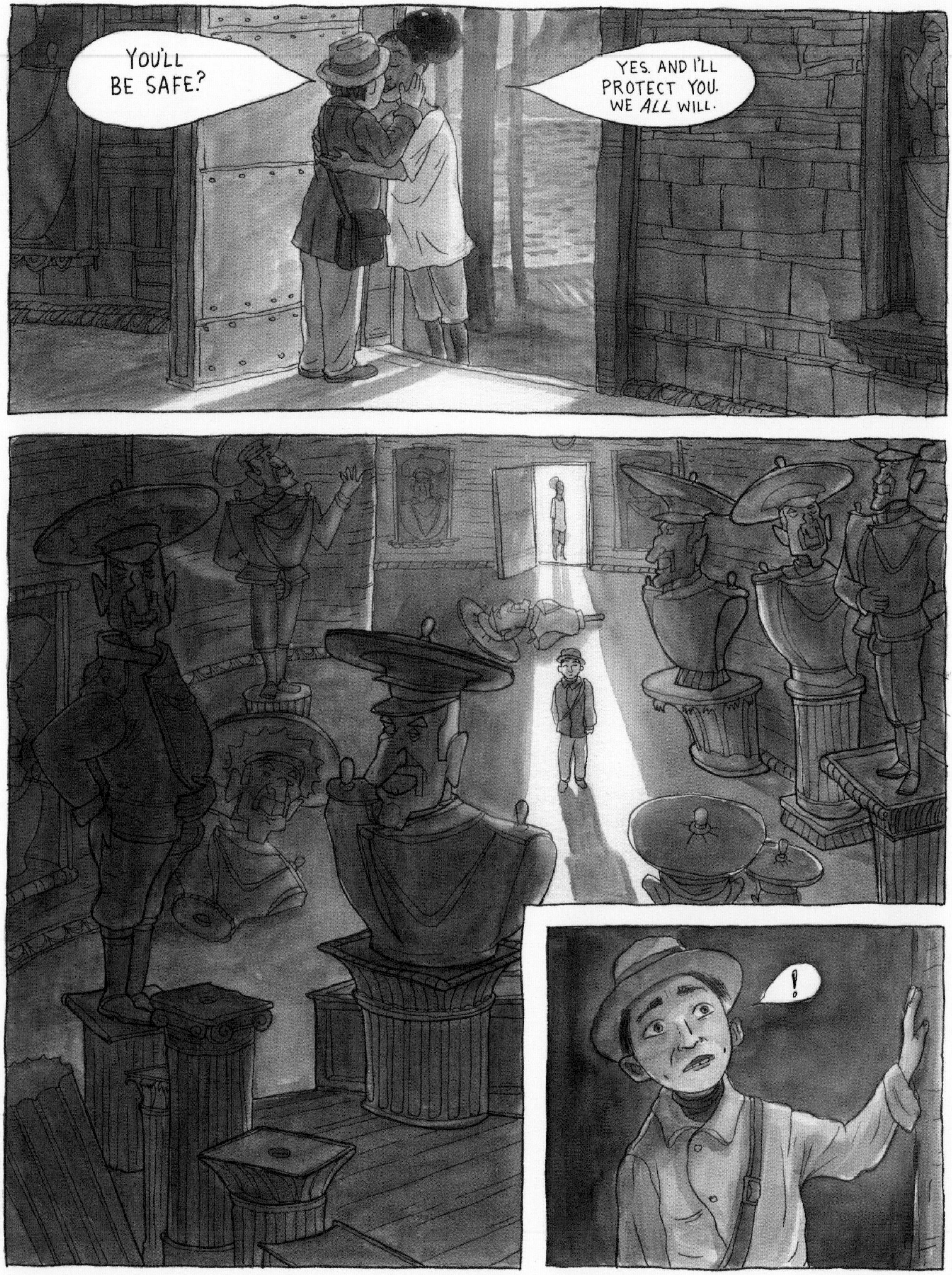
YOU'LL BE SAFE?
YES. AND I'LL PROTECT YOU. WE *ALL* WILL.
!

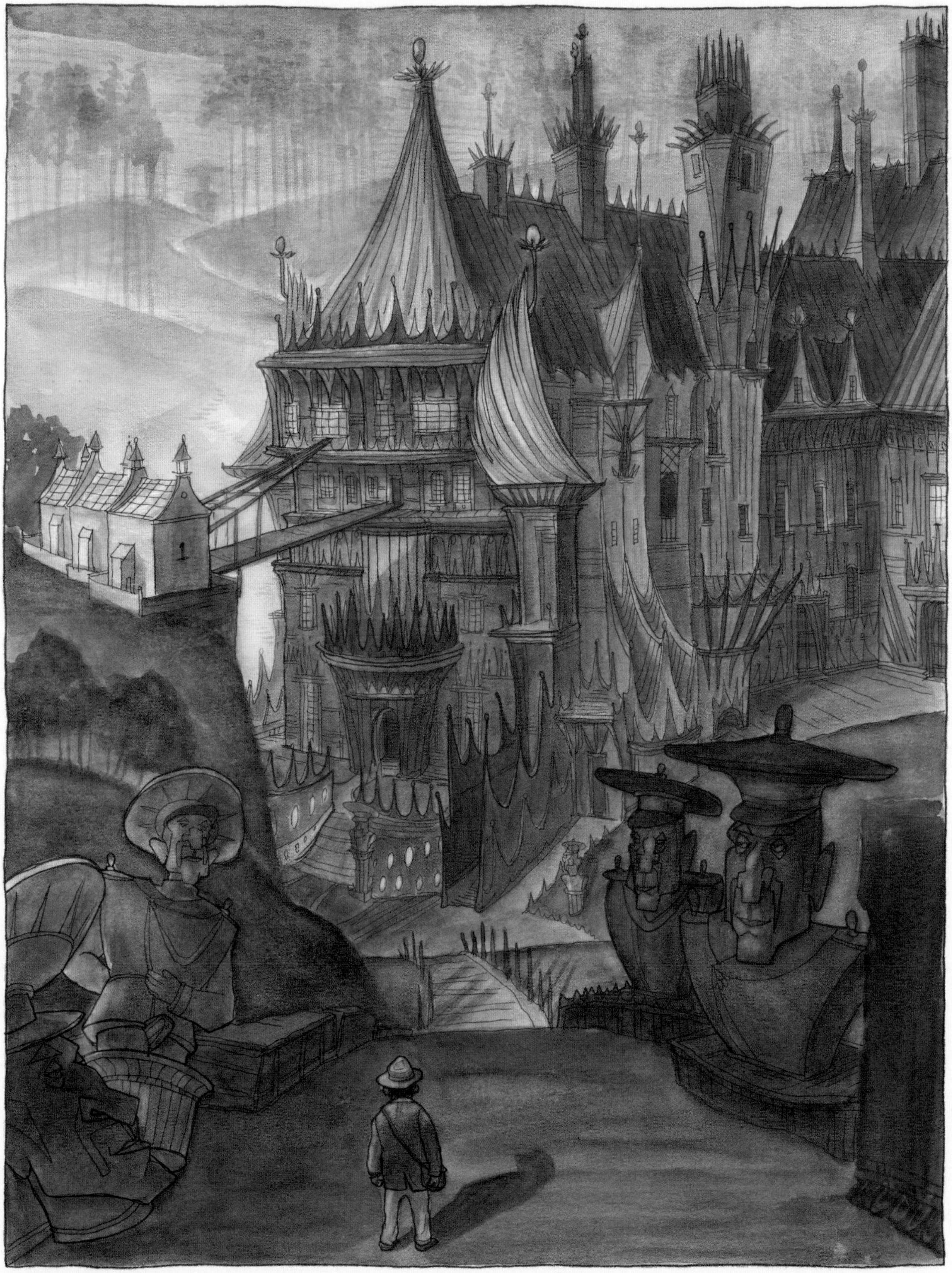

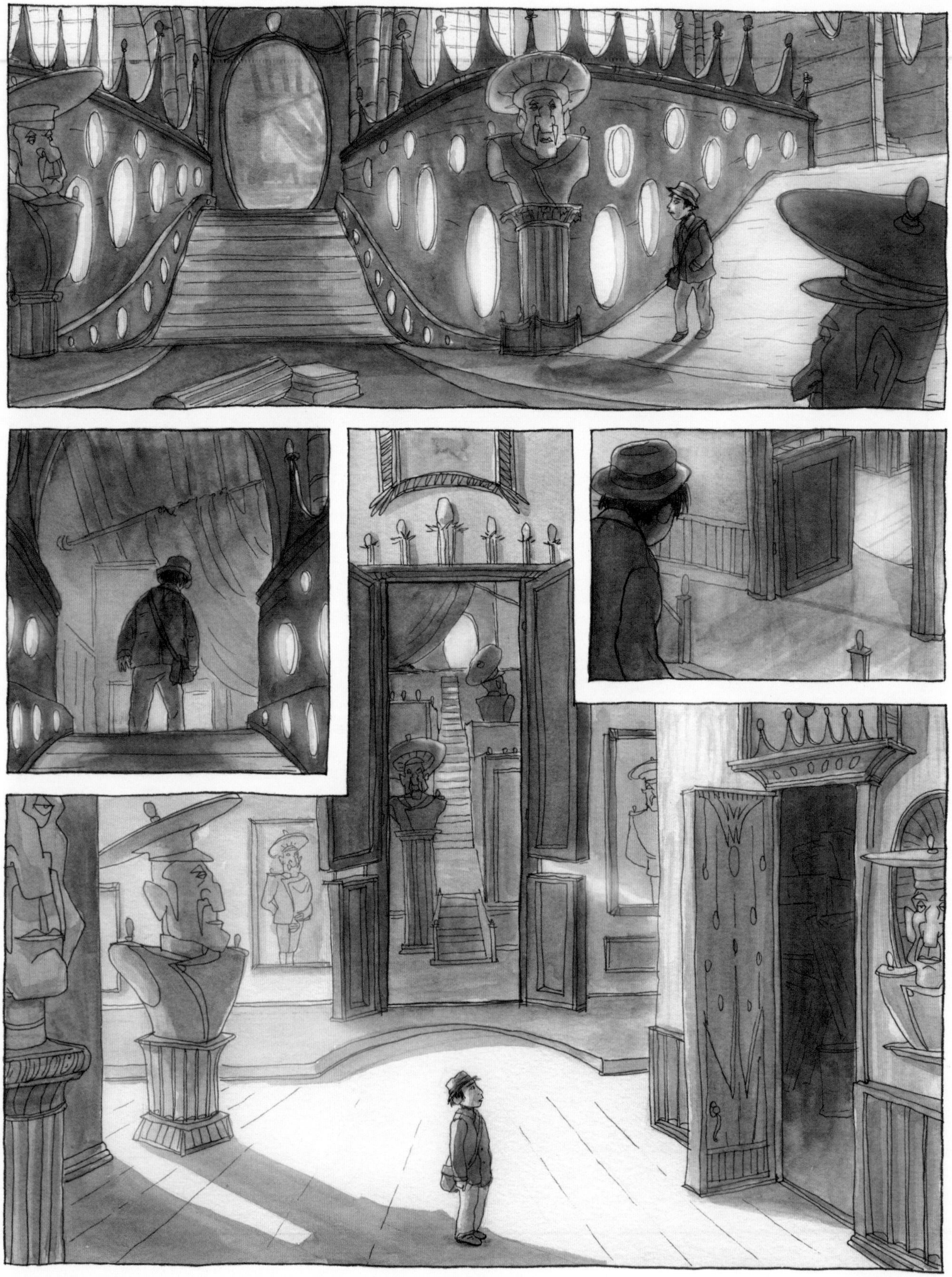

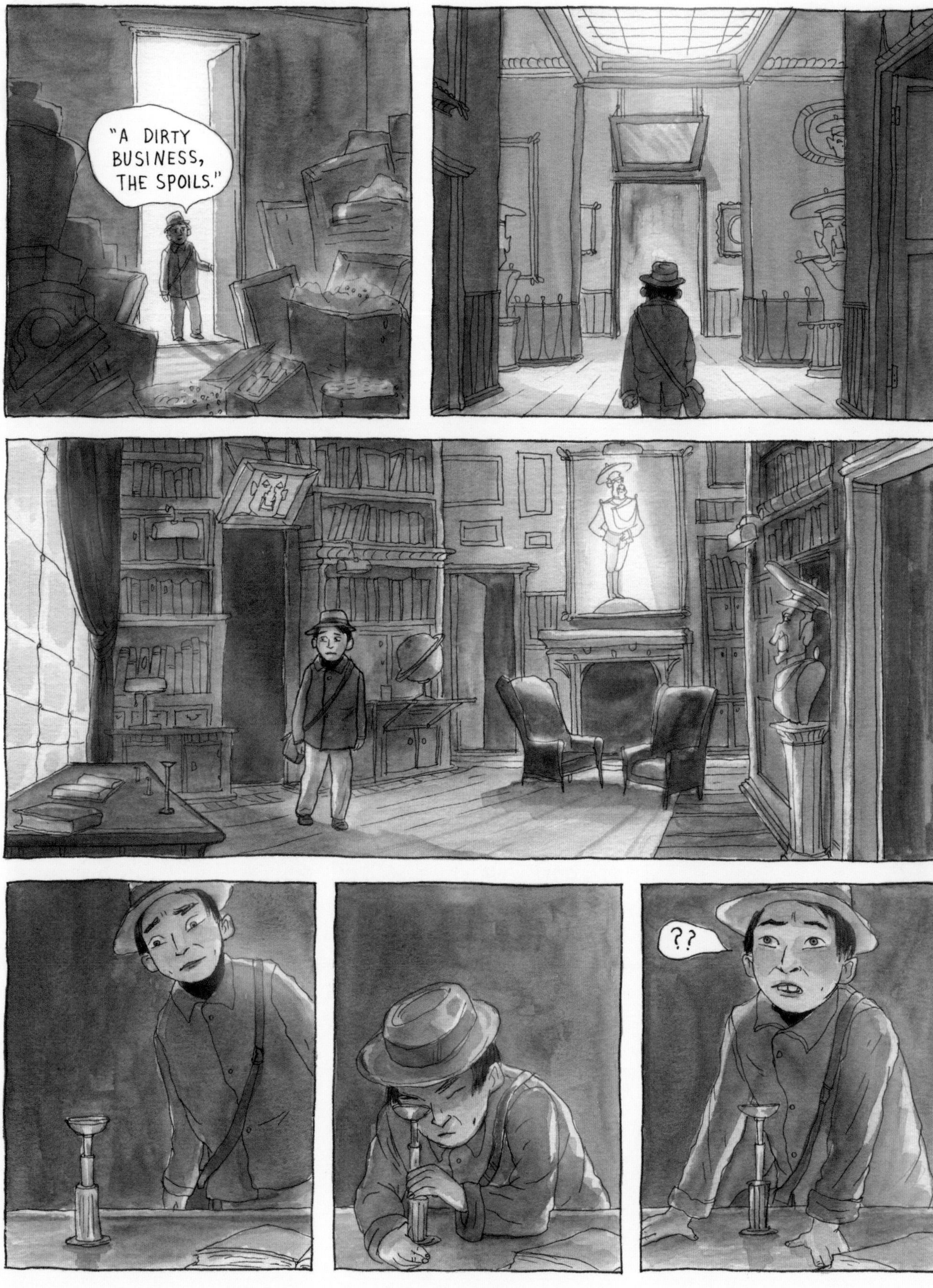
"A DIRTY BUSINESS, THE SPOILS."
??

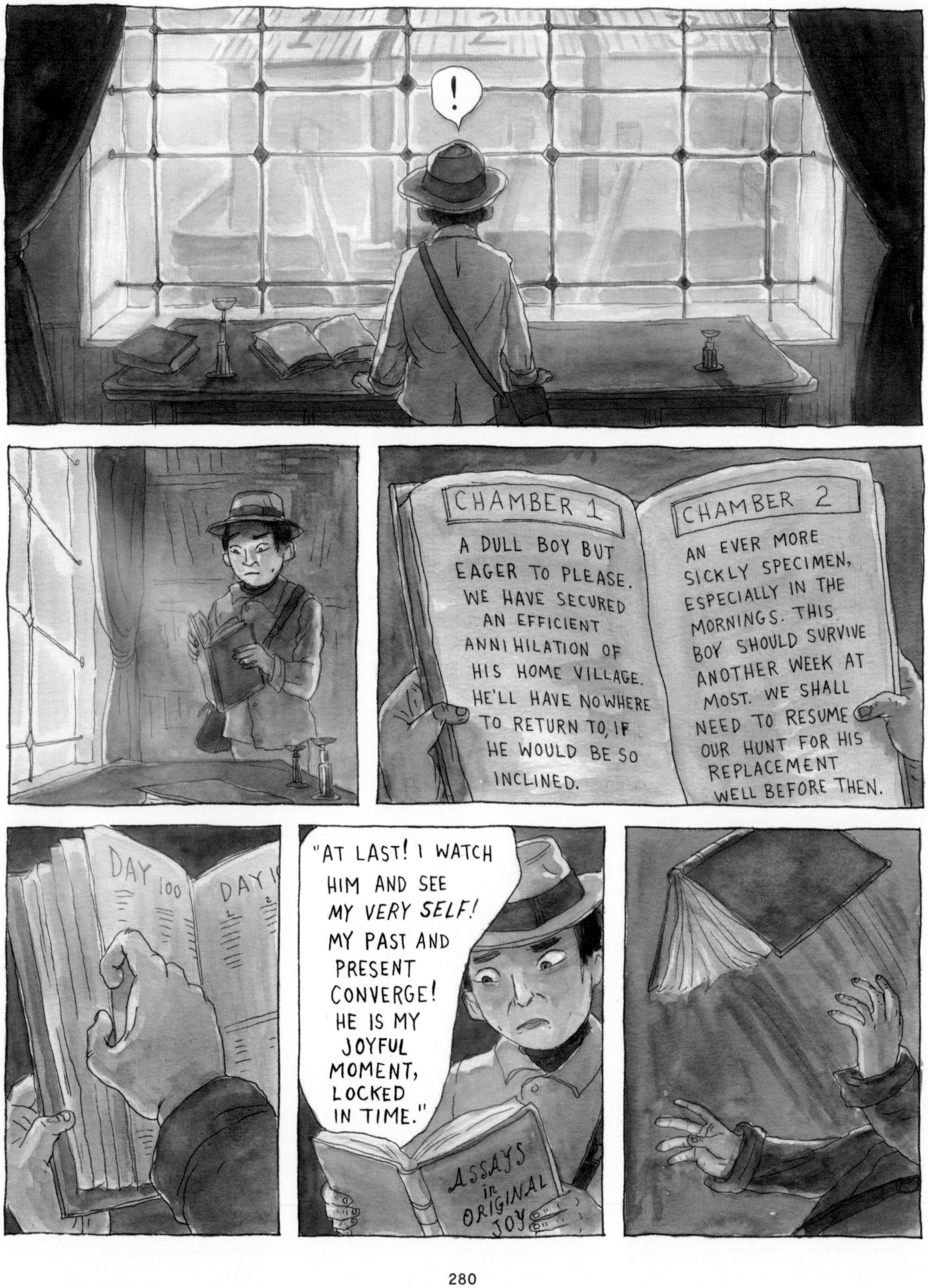
!
CHAMBER 1
A DULL BOY BUT EAGER TO PLEASE. WE HAVE SECURED AN EFFICIENT ANNIHILATION OF HIS HOME VILLAGE. HE'LL HAVE NOWHERE TO RETURN TO, IF HE WOULD BE SO INCLINED.
CHAMBER 2
AN EVER MORE SICKLY SPECIMEN, ESPECIALLY IN THE MORNINGS. THIS BOY SHOULD SURVIVE ANOTHER WEEK AT MOST. WE SHALL NEED TO RESUME OUR HUNT FOR HIS REPLACEMENT WELL BEFORE THEN.
DAY 100
"AT LAST! I WATCH HIM AND SEE MY VERY SELF! MY PAST AND PRESENT CONVERGE! HE IS MY JOYFUL MOMENT, LOCKED IN TIME."
ASSAYS in ORIGINAL JOY

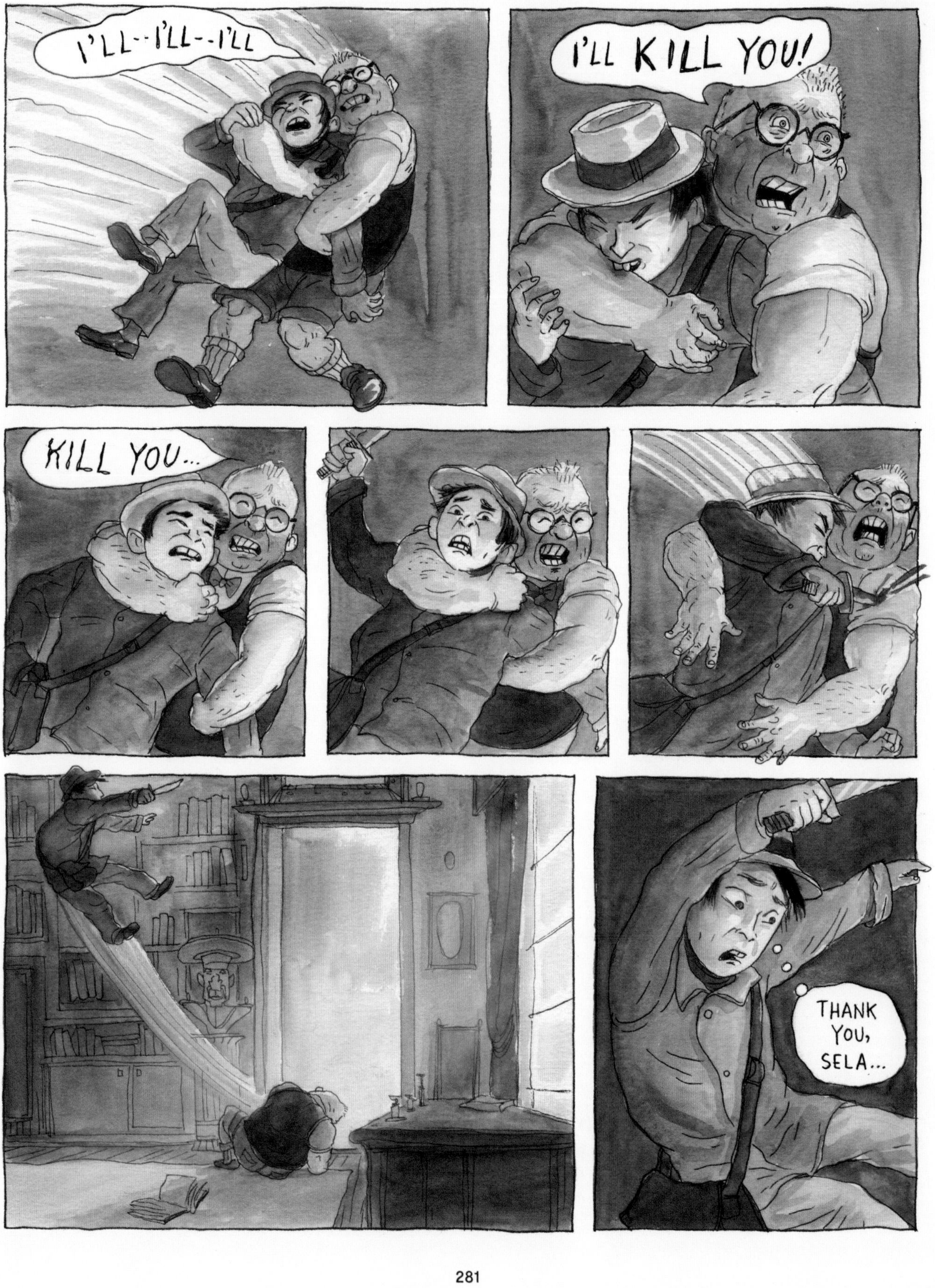
I'LL--I'LL--I'LL
I'LL KILL YOU!
KILL YOU...
THANK YOU, SELA...

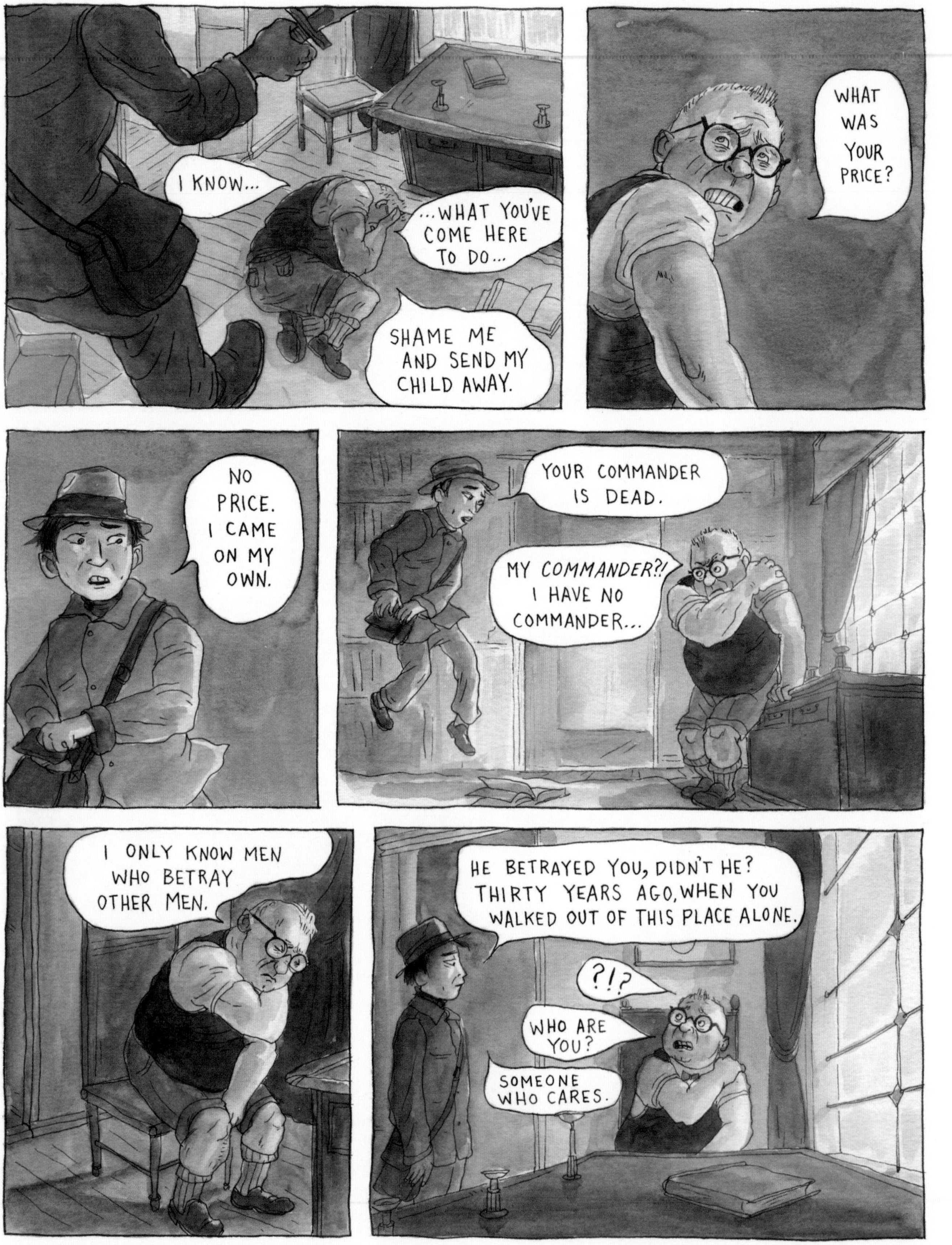
I KNOW...
...WHAT YOU'VE COME HERE TO DO...
SHAME ME AND SEND MY CHILD AWAY.
WHAT WAS YOUR PRICE?
NO PRICE. I CAME ON MY OWN.
YOUR COMMANDER IS DEAD.
MY *COMMANDER*?! I HAVE NO COMMANDER...
I ONLY KNOW MEN WHO BETRAY OTHER MEN.
HE BETRAYED YOU, DIDN'T HE? THIRTY YEARS AGO, WHEN YOU WALKED OUT OF THIS PLACE ALONE.
?!?
WHO ARE YOU?
SOMEONE WHO CARES.

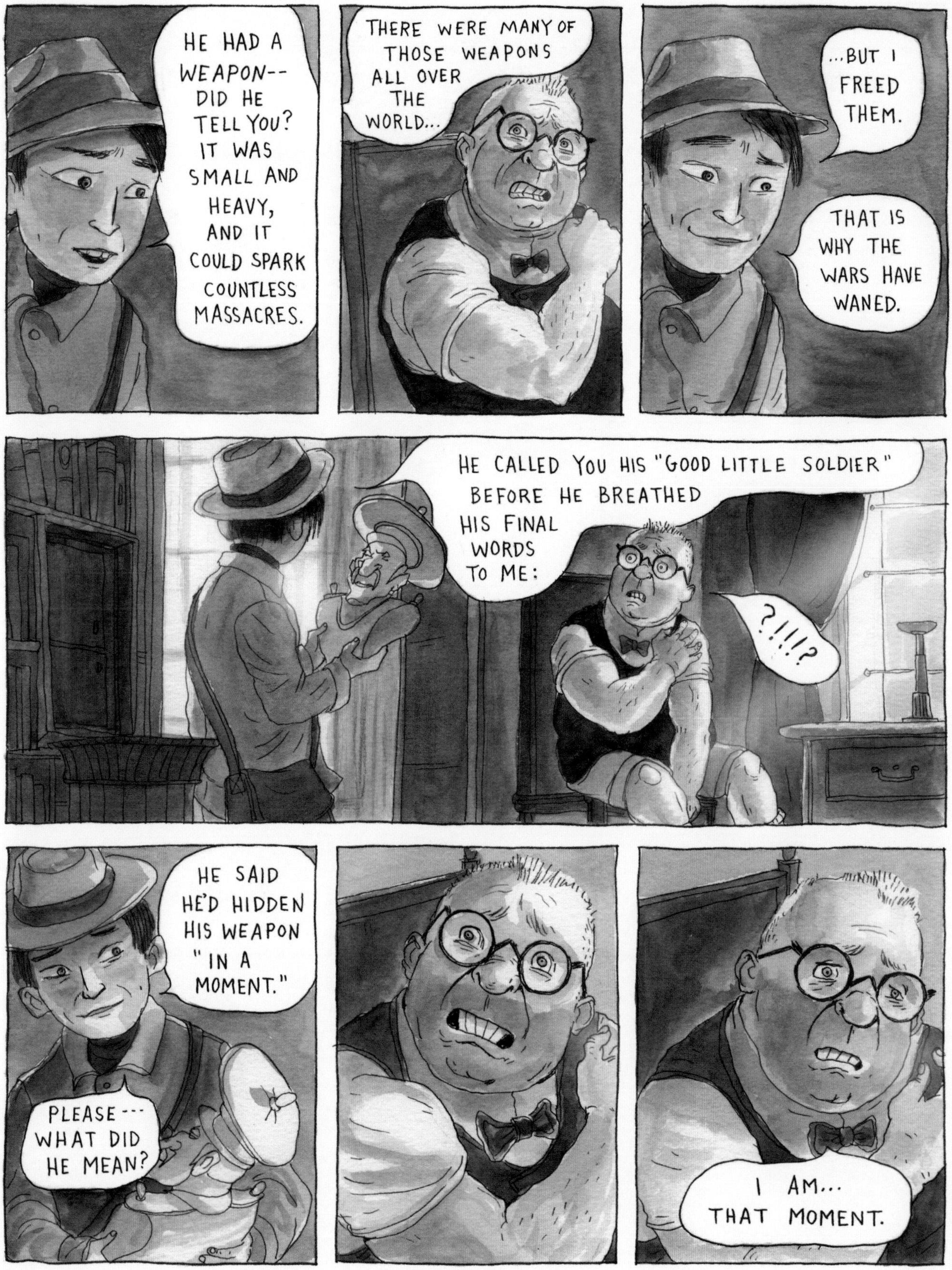
HE HAD A WEAPON--DID HE TELL YOU? IT WAS SMALL AND HEAVY, AND IT COULD SPARK COUNTLESS MASSACRES.
THERE WERE MANY OF THOSE WEAPONS ALL OVER THE WORLD...
...BUT I FREED THEM.
THAT IS WHY THE WARS HAVE WANED.
HE CALLED YOU HIS "GOOD LITTLE SOLDIER" BEFORE HE BREATHED HIS FINAL WORDS TO ME:
?!!!?
HE SAID HE'D HIDDEN HIS WEAPON "IN A MOMENT."
PLEASE--- WHAT DID HE MEAN?
I AM... THAT MOMENT.

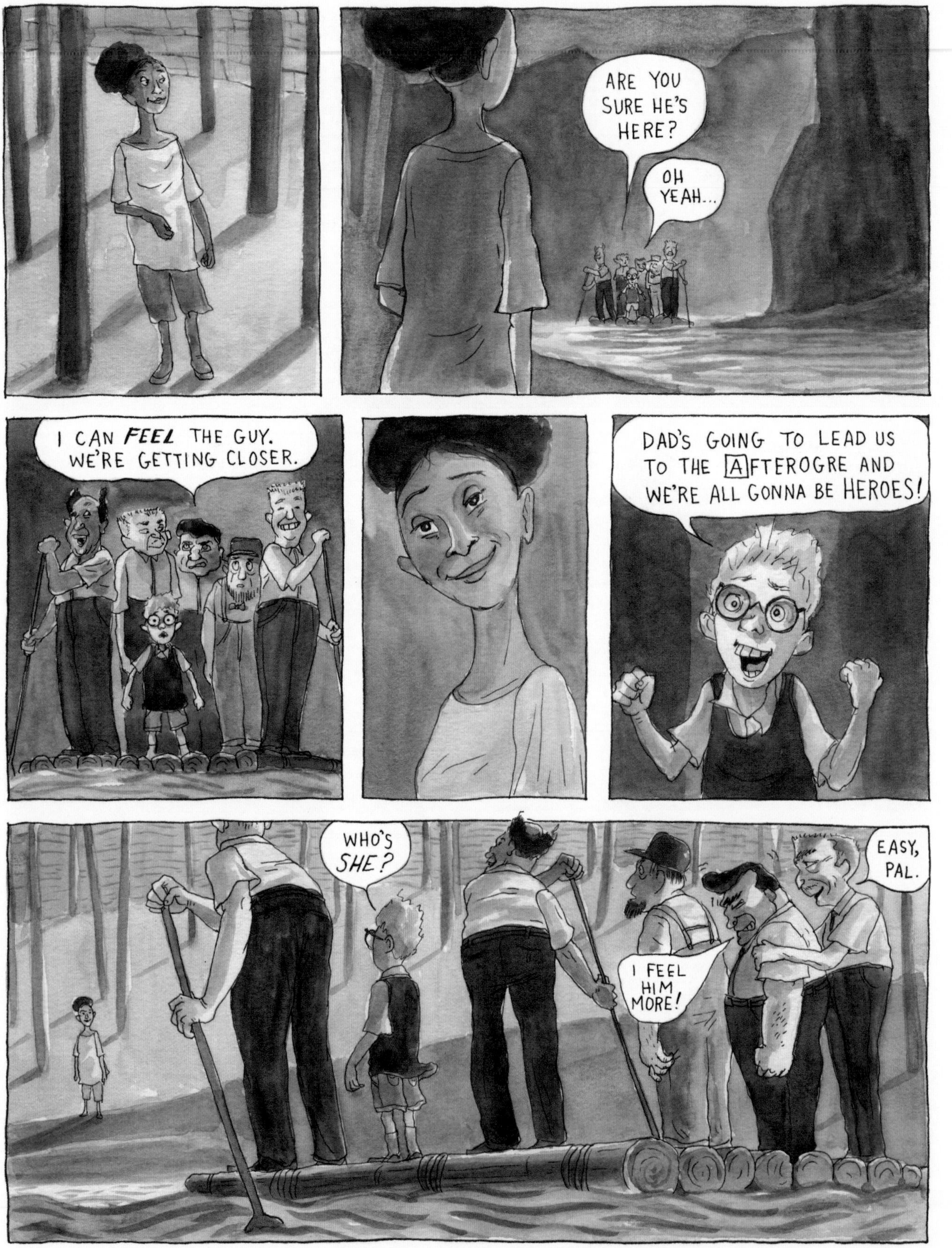
ARE YOU SURE HE'S HERE?
OH YEAH...
I CAN FEEL THE GUY. WE'RE GETTING CLOSER.
DAD'S GOING TO LEAD US TO THE AFTEROGRE AND WE'RE ALL GONNA BE HEROES!
WHO'S SHE?
I FEEL HIM MORE!
EASY, PAL.

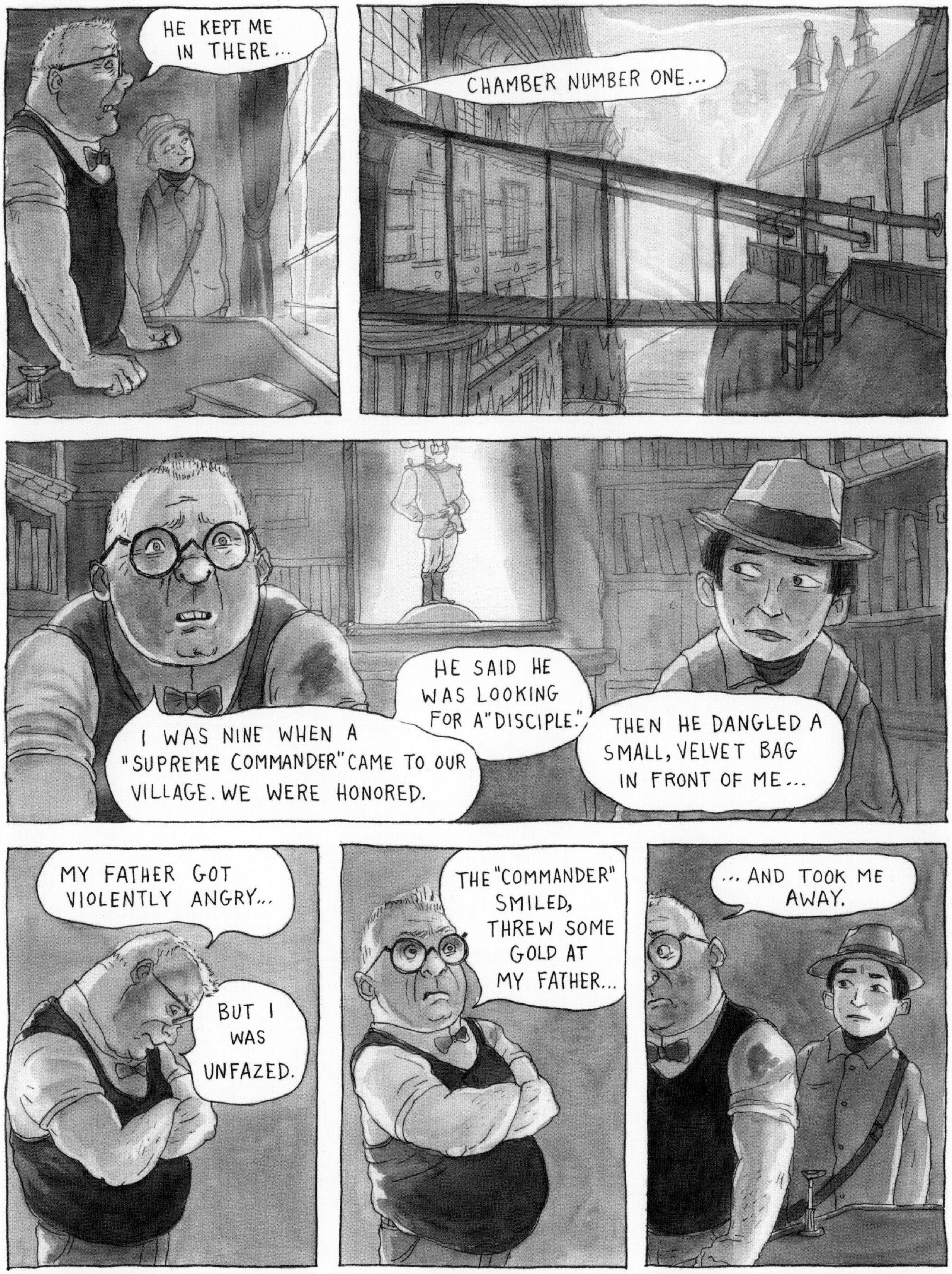
HE KEPT ME IN THERE...
CHAMBER NUMBER ONE...
I WAS NINE WHEN A "SUPREME COMMANDER" CAME TO OUR VILLAGE. WE WERE HONORED.
HE SAID HE WAS LOOKING FOR A "DISCIPLE."
THEN HE DANGLED A SMALL, VELVET BAG IN FRONT OF ME...
MY FATHER GOT VIOLENTLY ANGRY...
BUT I WAS UNFAZED.
THE "COMMANDER" SMILED, THREW SOME GOLD AT MY FATHER...
... AND TOOK ME AWAY.

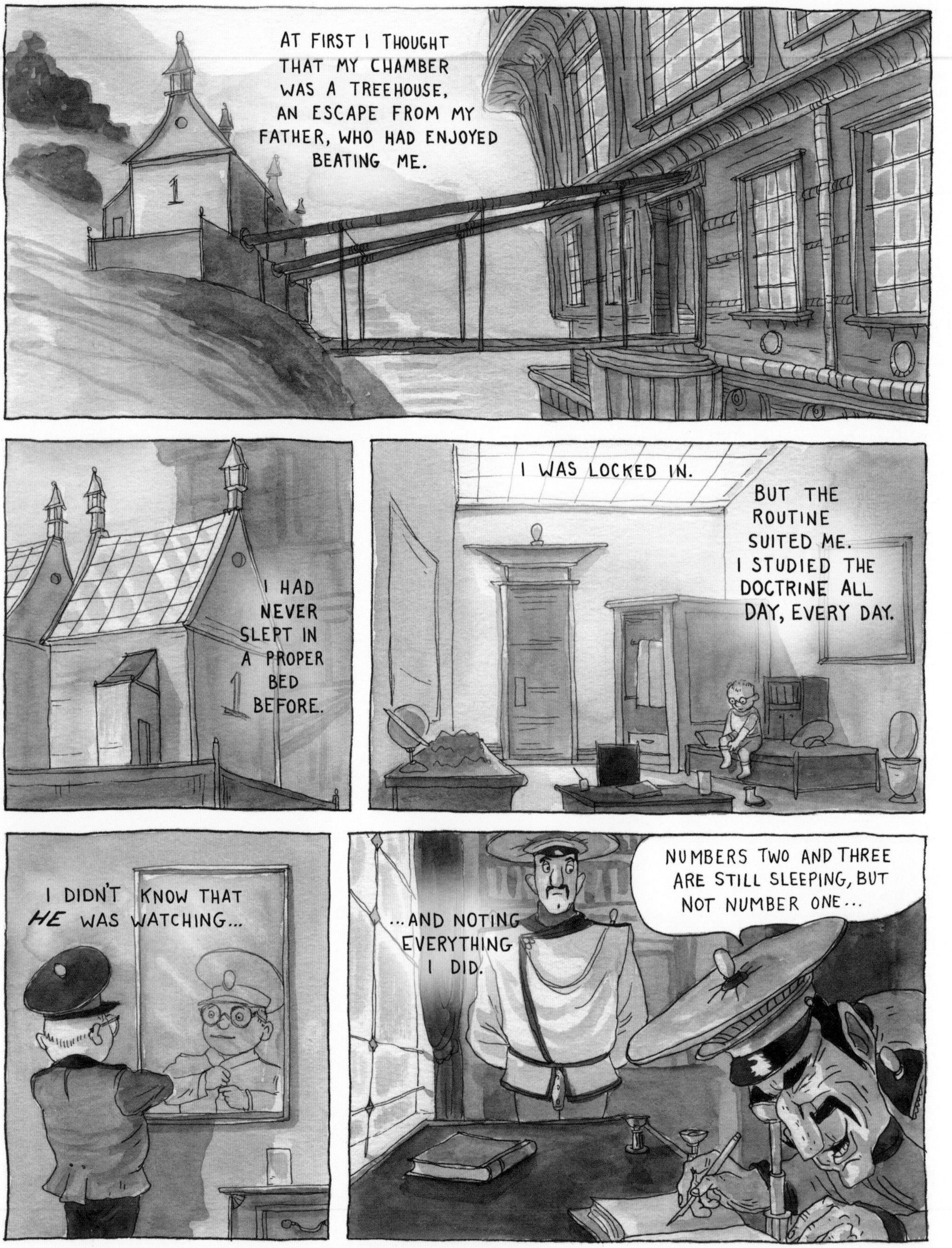

AT FIRST I THOUGHT THAT MY CHAMBER WAS A TREEHOUSE, AN ESCAPE FROM MY FATHER, WHO HAD ENJOYED BEATING ME.
I HAD NEVER SLEPT IN A PROPER BED BEFORE.
I WAS LOCKED IN.
BUT THE ROUTINE SUITED ME. I STUDIED THE DOCTRINE ALL DAY, EVERY DAY.
I DIDN'T KNOW THAT *HE* WAS WATCHING...
...AND NOTING EVERYTHING I DID.
NUMBERS TWO AND THREE ARE STILL SLEEPING, BUT NOT NUMBER ONE...

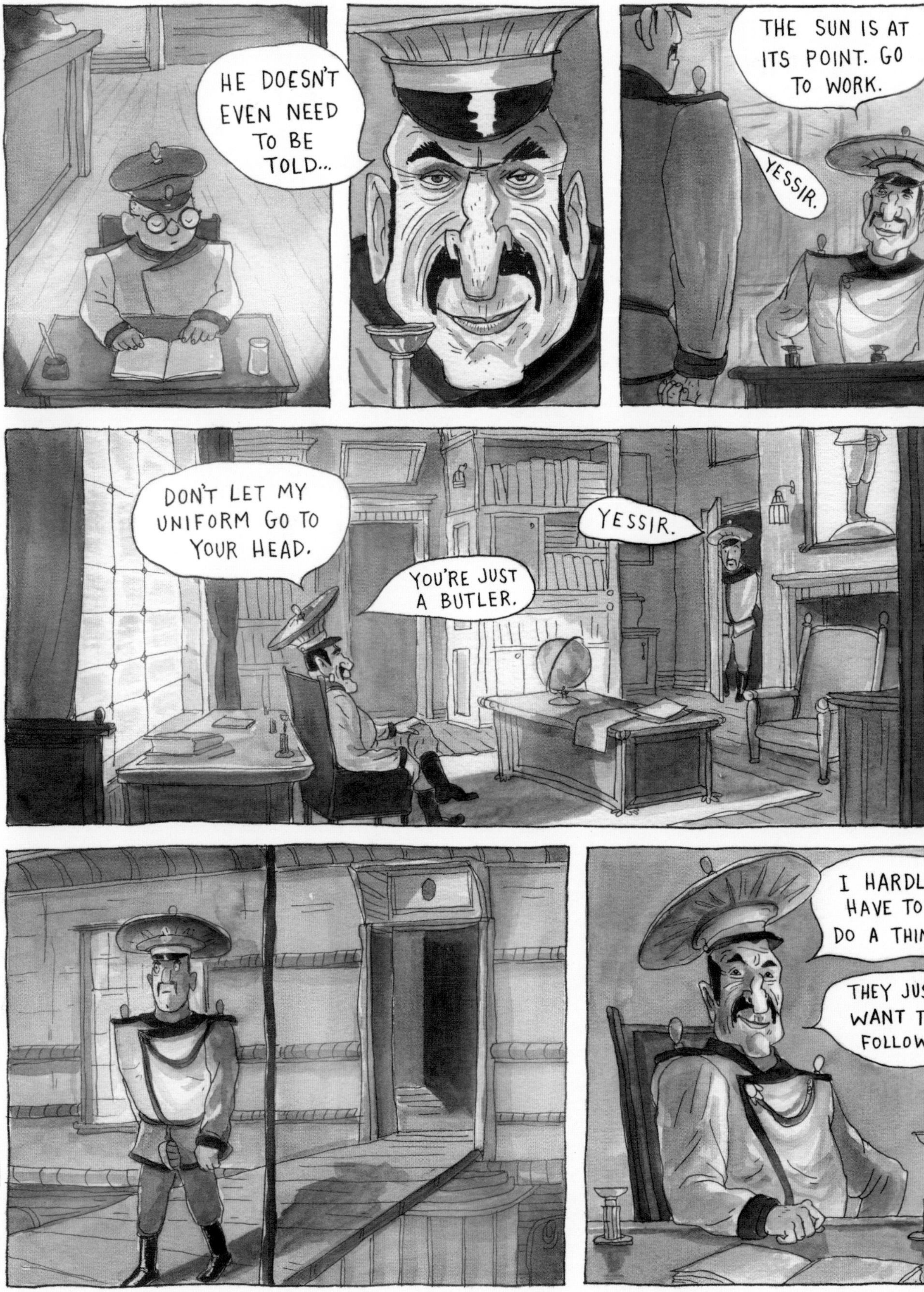
HE DOESN'T EVEN NEED TO BE TOLD...
THE SUN IS AT ITS POINT. GO TO WORK.
YESSIR.
DON'T LET MY UNIFORM GO TO YOUR HEAD.
YOU'RE JUST A BUTLER.
YESSIR.
I HARDLY HAVE TO DO A THING...
THEY JUST WANT TO FOLLOW.

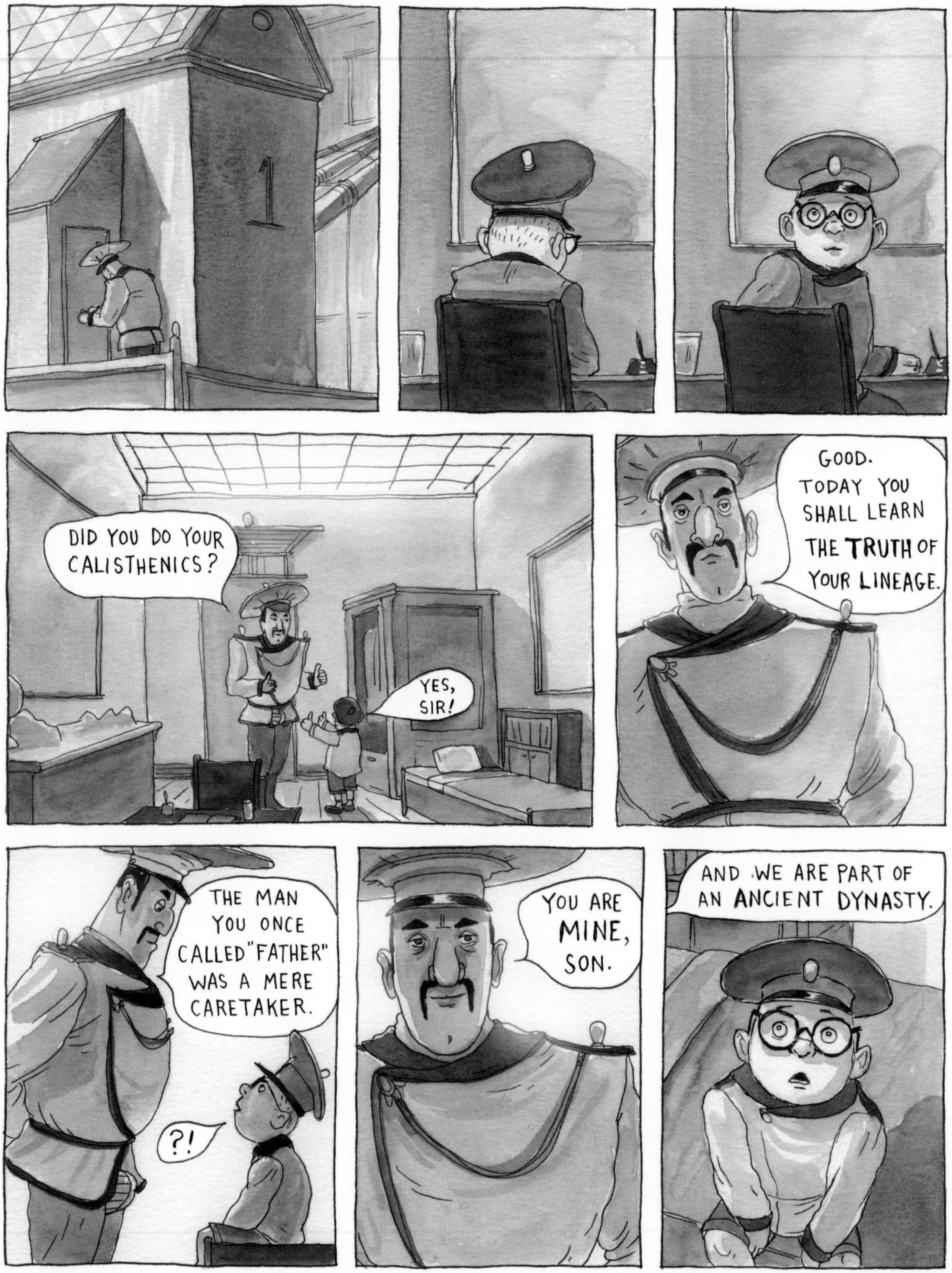
DID YOU DO YOUR CALISTHENICS?
YES, SIR!
GOOD. TODAY YOU SHALL LEARN THE TRUTH OF YOUR LINEAGE.
THE MAN YOU ONCE CALLED "FATHER" WAS A MERE CARETAKER.
?!
YOU ARE MINE, SON.
AND WE ARE PART OF AN ANCIENT DYNASTY.

THE STARS DO NOT FAVOR *US*; *WE* FAVOR *THEM*.

AND THAT ONE? NEVER CALL HER "SUN". SHE IS OUR SERVANT. SERVANTS HAVE NO NAMES.

SHE WORKS FOR US BY DAY AND SLEEPS BY NIGHT, RESTING FOR THE NEXT DAY'S VICTORIES.

SHE GIVES US HER *FIRE*, SO THAT WE MAY HUSH OUR ENEMIES INTO ASH.

A TRUE WARRIOR CULTIVATES HIS CRUELTY.

REMEMBER WHAT I TAUGHT YOU...

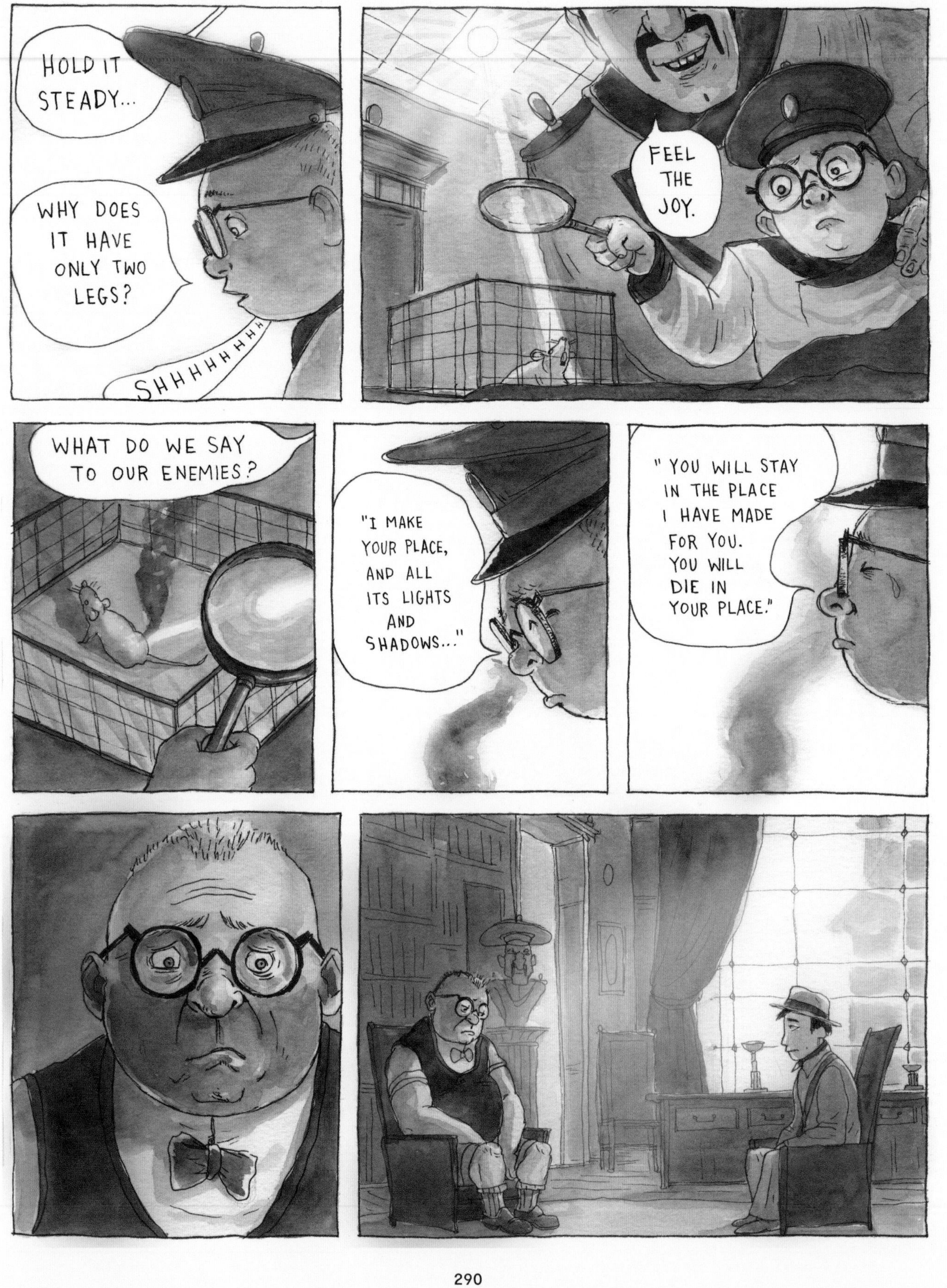
HOLD IT STEADY...
WHY DOES IT HAVE ONLY TWO LEGS?
SHHHHHHHHH
FEEL THE JOY.
WHAT DO WE SAY TO OUR ENEMIES?
"I MAKE YOUR PLACE, AND ALL ITS LIGHTS AND SHADOWS..."
"YOU WILL STAY IN THE PLACE I HAVE MADE FOR YOU. YOU WILL DIE IN YOUR PLACE."

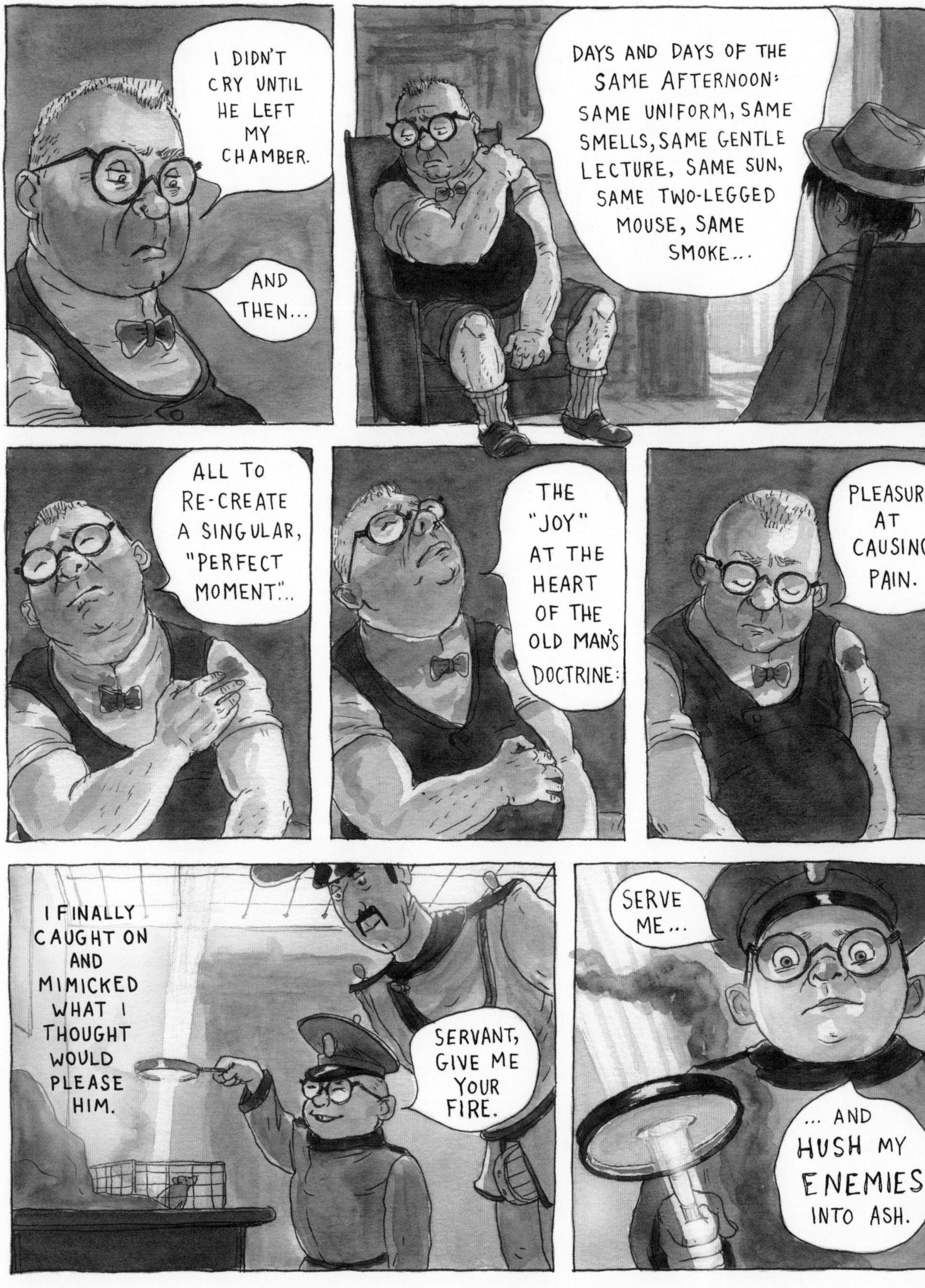
I DIDN'T CRY UNTIL HE LEFT MY CHAMBER.
AND THEN...
DAYS AND DAYS OF THE SAME AFTERNOON: SAME UNIFORM, SAME SMELLS, SAME GENTLE LECTURE, SAME SUN, SAME TWO-LEGGED MOUSE, SAME SMOKE...
ALL TO RE-CREATE A SINGULAR, "PERFECT MOMENT"...
THE "JOY" AT THE HEART OF THE OLD MAN'S DOCTRINE:
PLEASURE AT CAUSING PAIN.
I FINALLY CAUGHT ON AND MIMICKED WHAT I THOUGHT WOULD PLEASE HIM.
SERVANT, GIVE ME YOUR FIRE.
SERVE ME...
... AND HUSH MY ENEMIES INTO ASH.

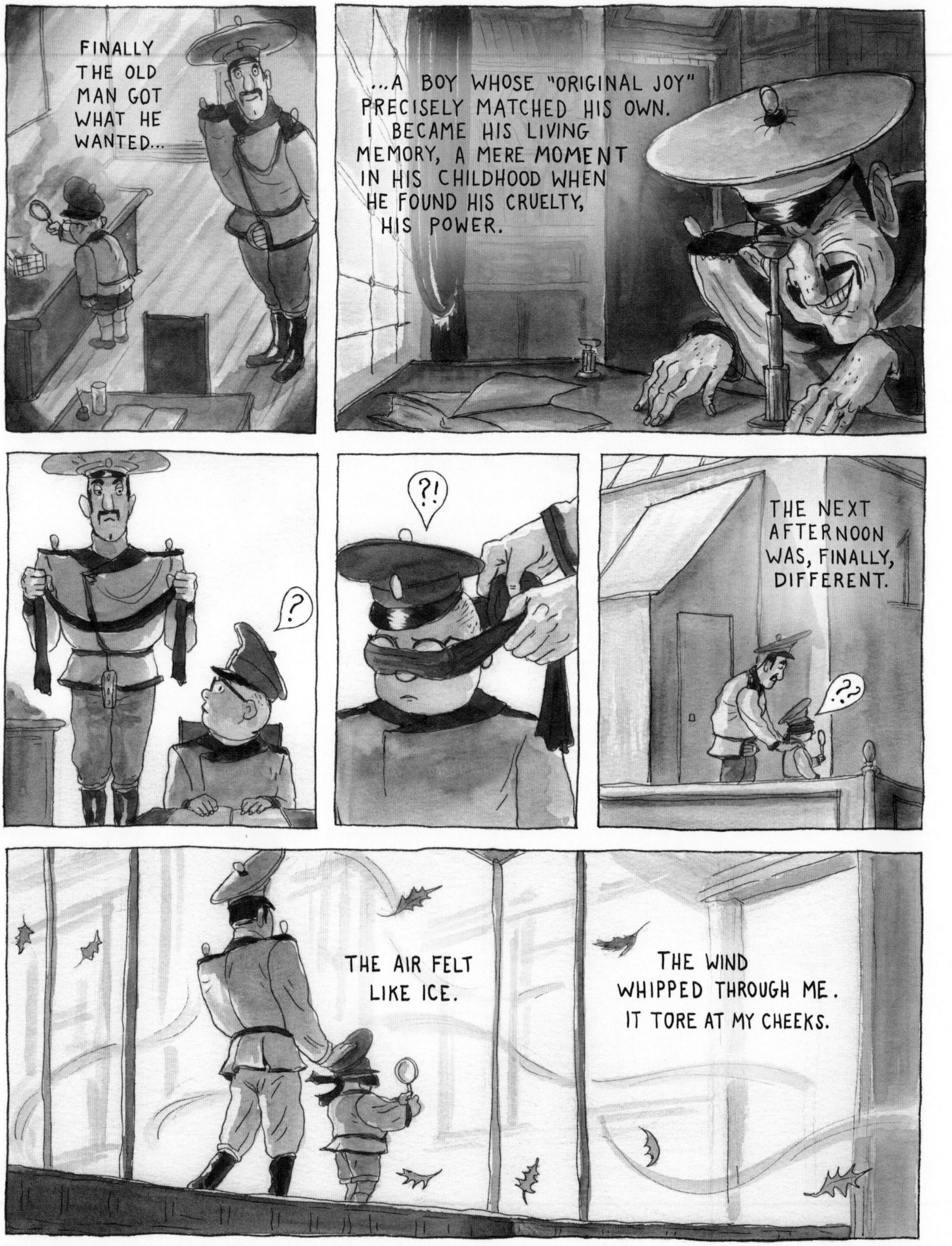
FINALLY THE OLD MAN GOT WHAT HE WANTED...
...A BOY WHOSE "ORIGINAL JOY" PRECISELY MATCHED HIS OWN. I BECAME HIS LIVING MEMORY, A MERE MOMENT IN HIS CHILDHOOD WHEN HE FOUND HIS CRUELTY, HIS POWER.
?
?!
THE NEXT AFTERNOON WAS, FINALLY, DIFFERENT.
??
THE AIR FELT LIKE ICE.
THE WIND WHIPPED THROUGH ME. IT TORE AT MY CHEEKS.

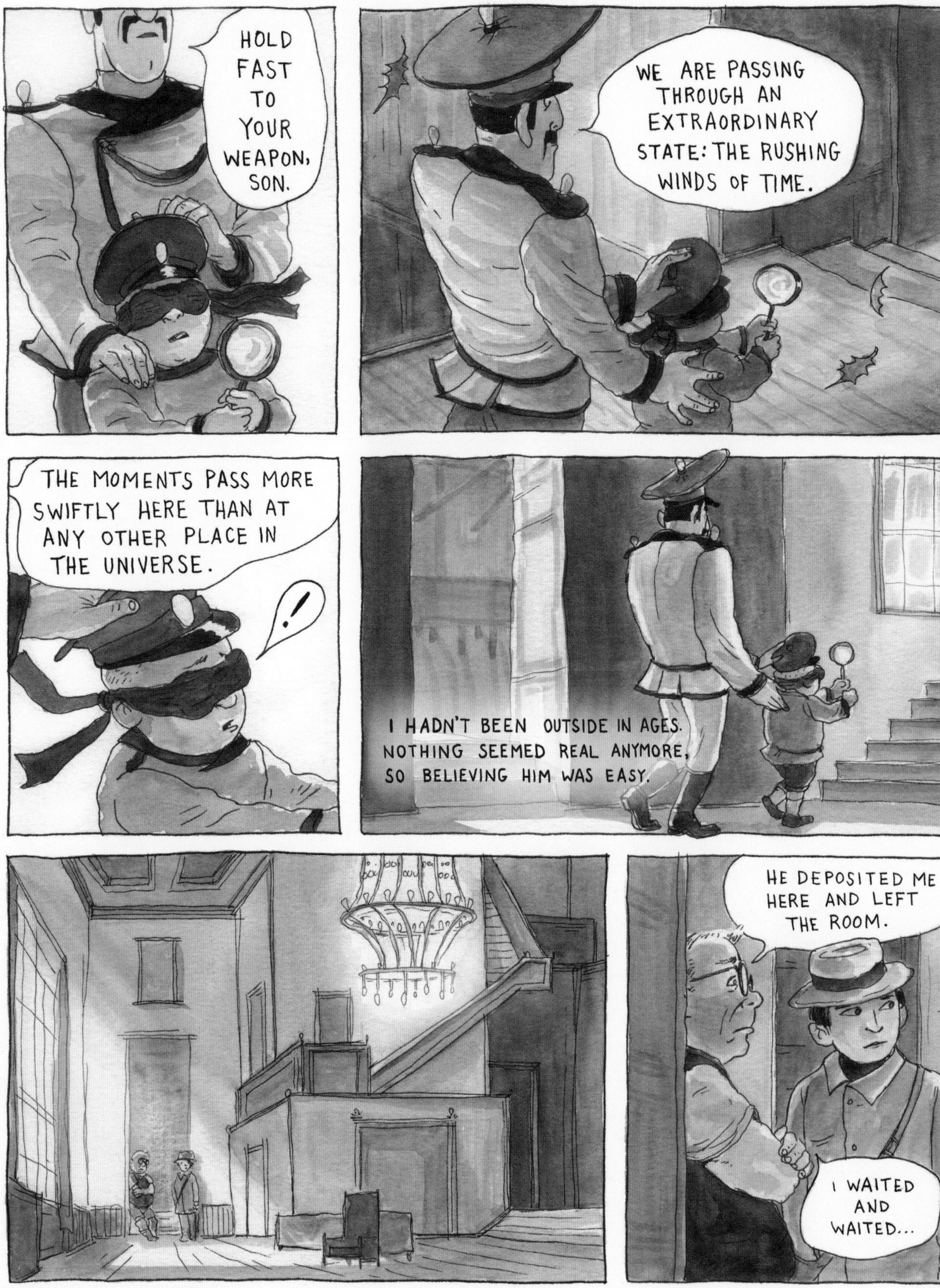
HOLD FAST TO YOUR WEAPON, SON.
WE ARE PASSING THROUGH AN EXTRAORDINARY STATE: THE RUSHING WINDS OF TIME.
THE MOMENTS PASS MORE SWIFTLY HERE THAN AT ANY OTHER PLACE IN THE UNIVERSE.
!
I HADN'T BEEN OUTSIDE IN AGES. NOTHING SEEMED REAL ANYMORE, SO BELIEVING HIM WAS EASY.
HE DEPOSITED ME HERE AND LEFT THE ROOM.
I WAITED AND WAITED...

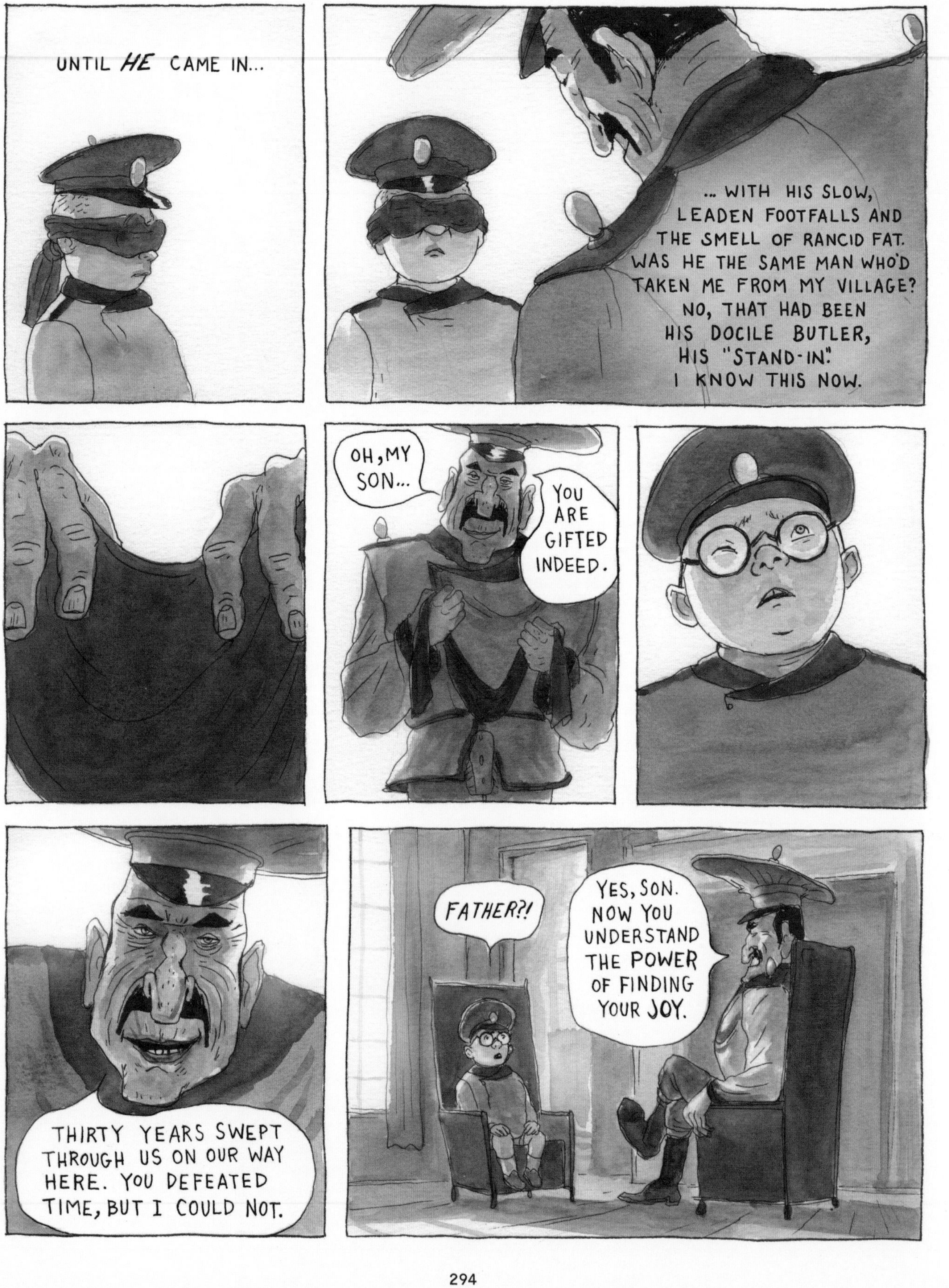
UNTIL *HE* CAME IN...
... WITH HIS SLOW, LEADEN FOOTFALLS AND THE SMELL OF RANCID FAT. WAS HE THE SAME MAN WHO'D TAKEN ME FROM MY VILLAGE? NO, THAT HAD BEEN HIS DOCILE BUTLER, HIS "STAND-IN." I KNOW THIS NOW.
OH, MY SON...
YOU ARE GIFTED INDEED.
THIRTY YEARS SWEPT THROUGH US ON OUR WAY HERE. YOU DEFEATED TIME, BUT I COULD NOT.
FATHER?!
YES, SON. NOW YOU UNDERSTAND THE POWER OF FINDING YOUR JOY.

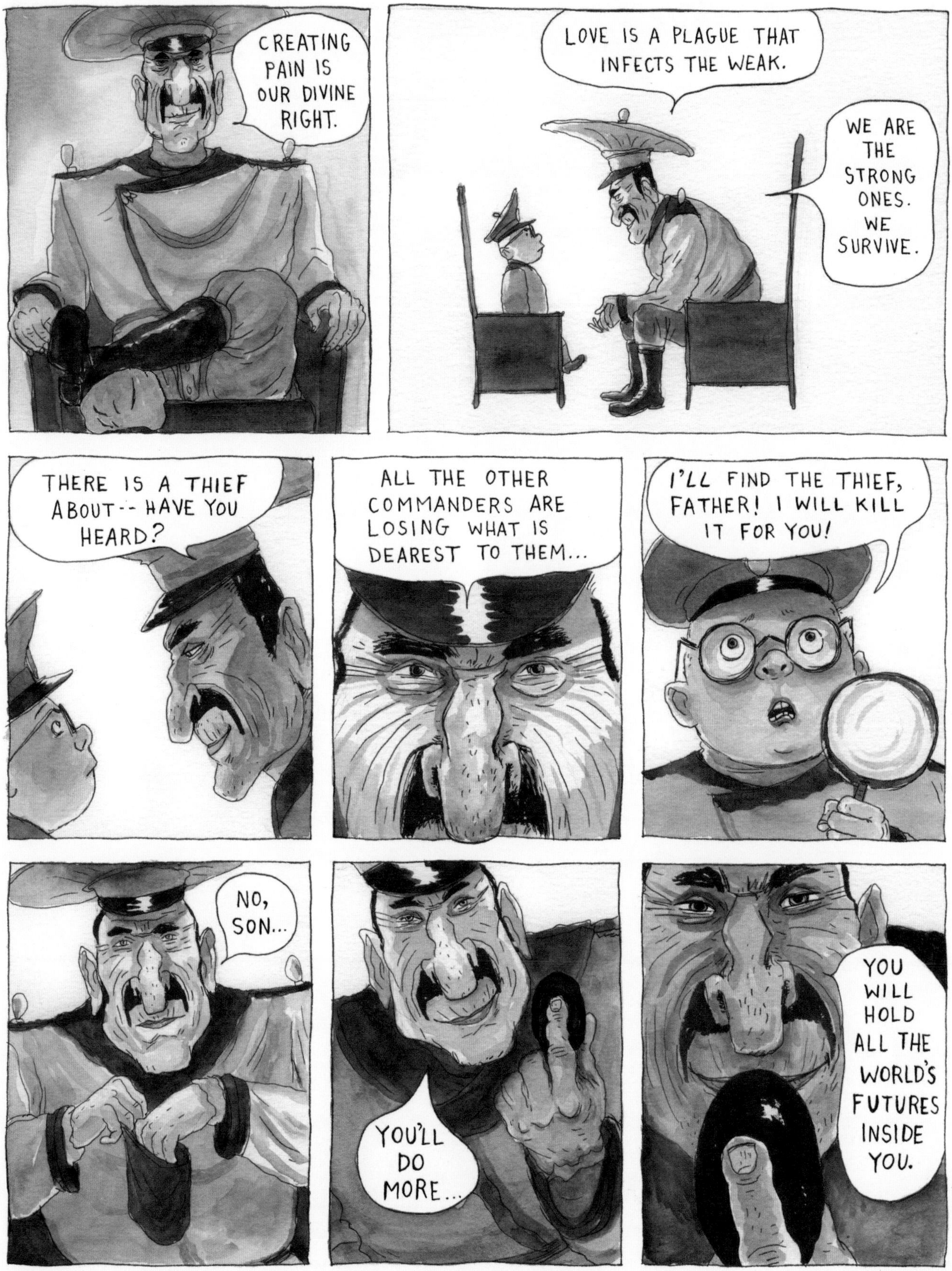
CREATING PAIN IS OUR DIVINE RIGHT.
LOVE IS A PLAGUE THAT INFECTS THE WEAK.
WE ARE THE STRONG ONES. WE SURVIVE.
THERE IS A THIEF ABOUT -- HAVE YOU HEARD?
ALL THE OTHER COMMANDERS ARE LOSING WHAT IS DEAREST TO THEM...
I'LL FIND THE THIEF, FATHER! I WILL KILL IT FOR YOU!
NO, SON...
YOU'LL DO MORE...
YOU WILL HOLD ALL THE WORLD'S FUTURES INSIDE YOU.

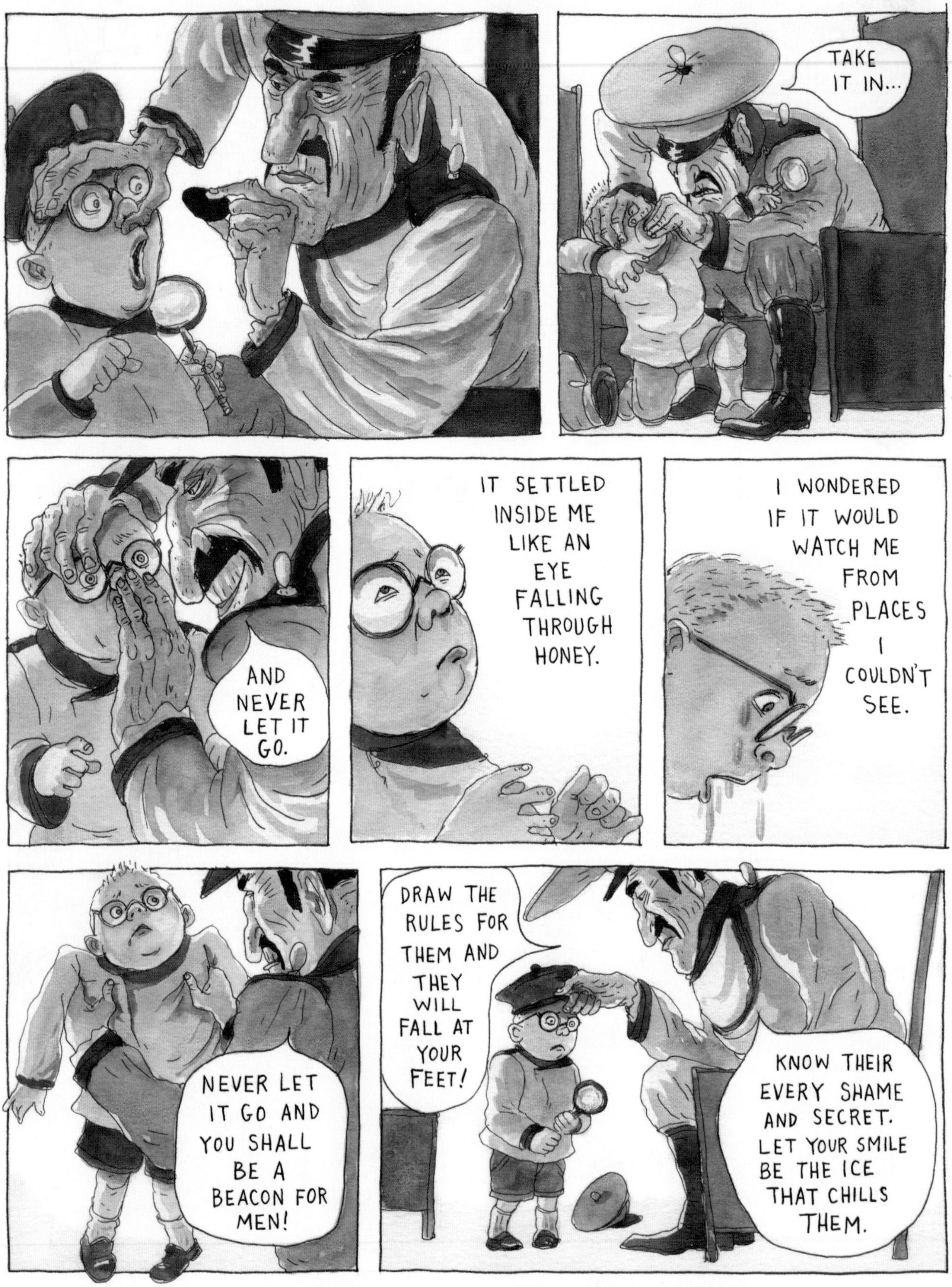
TAKE IT IN...
AND NEVER LET IT GO.
IT SETTLED INSIDE ME LIKE AN EYE FALLING THROUGH HONEY.
I WONDERED IF IT WOULD WATCH ME FROM PLACES I COULDN'T SEE.
NEVER LET IT GO AND YOU SHALL BE A BEACON FOR MEN!
DRAW THE RULES FOR THEM AND THEY WILL FALL AT YOUR FEET!
KNOW THEIR EVERY SHAME AND SECRET. LET YOUR SMILE BE THE ICE THAT CHILLS THEM.

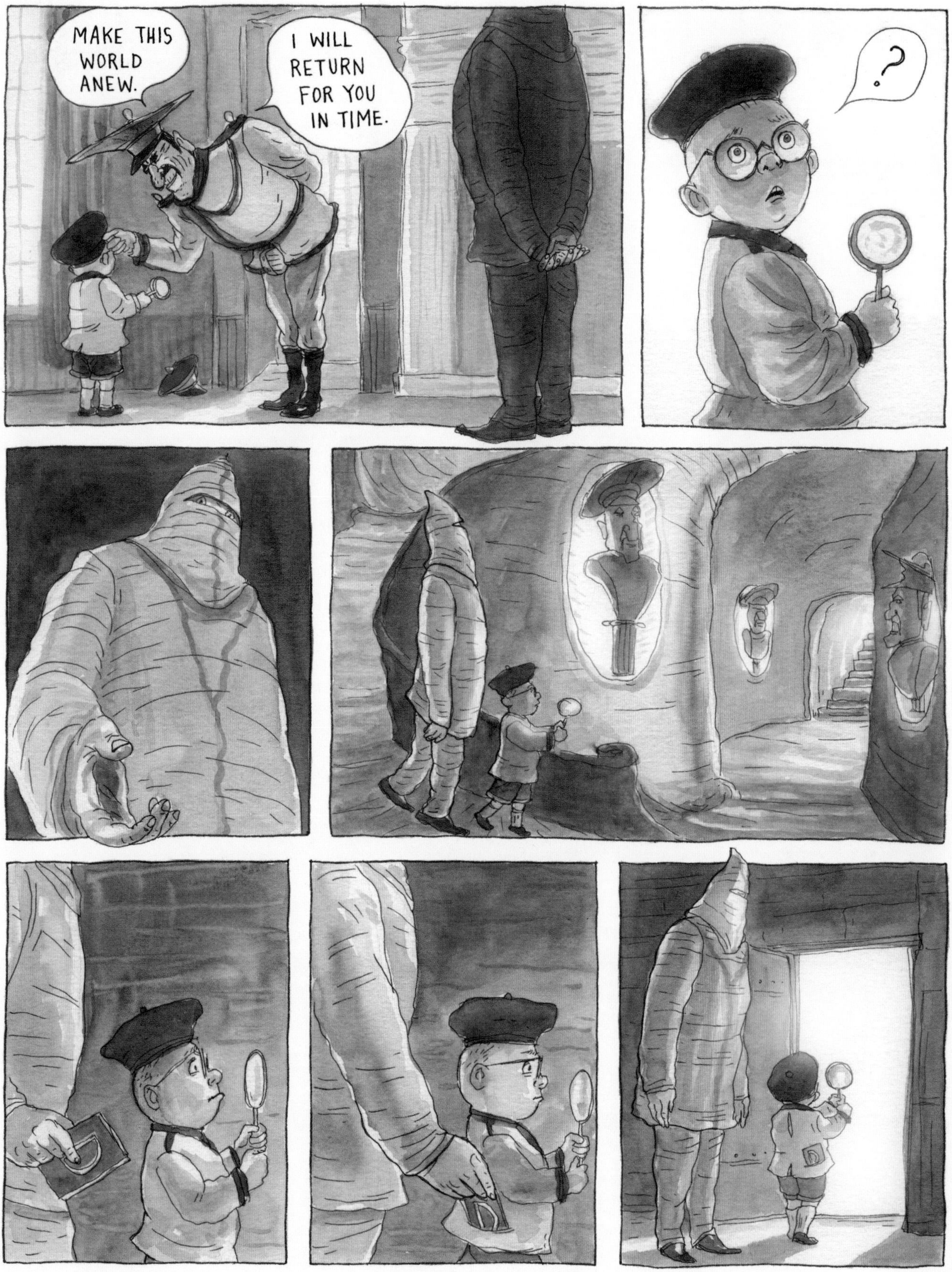
MAKE THIS WORLD ANEW.
I WILL RETURN FOR YOU IN TIME.
?

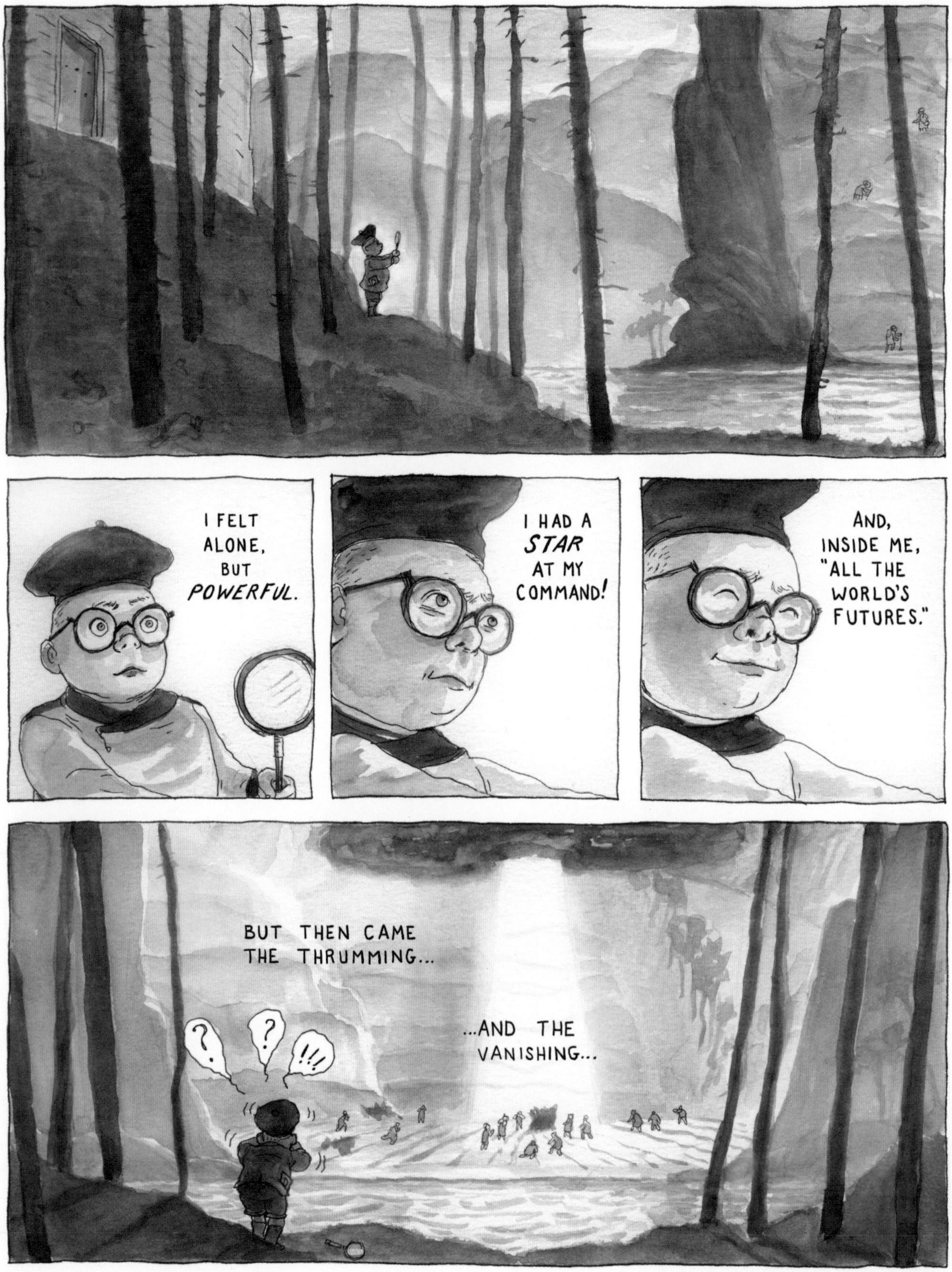
I FELT ALONE, BUT *POWERFUL*.
I HAD A *STAR* AT MY COMMAND!
AND, INSIDE ME, "ALL THE WORLD'S FUTURES."
BUT THEN CAME THE THRUMMING...
?
?
!!!
...AND THE VANISHING...

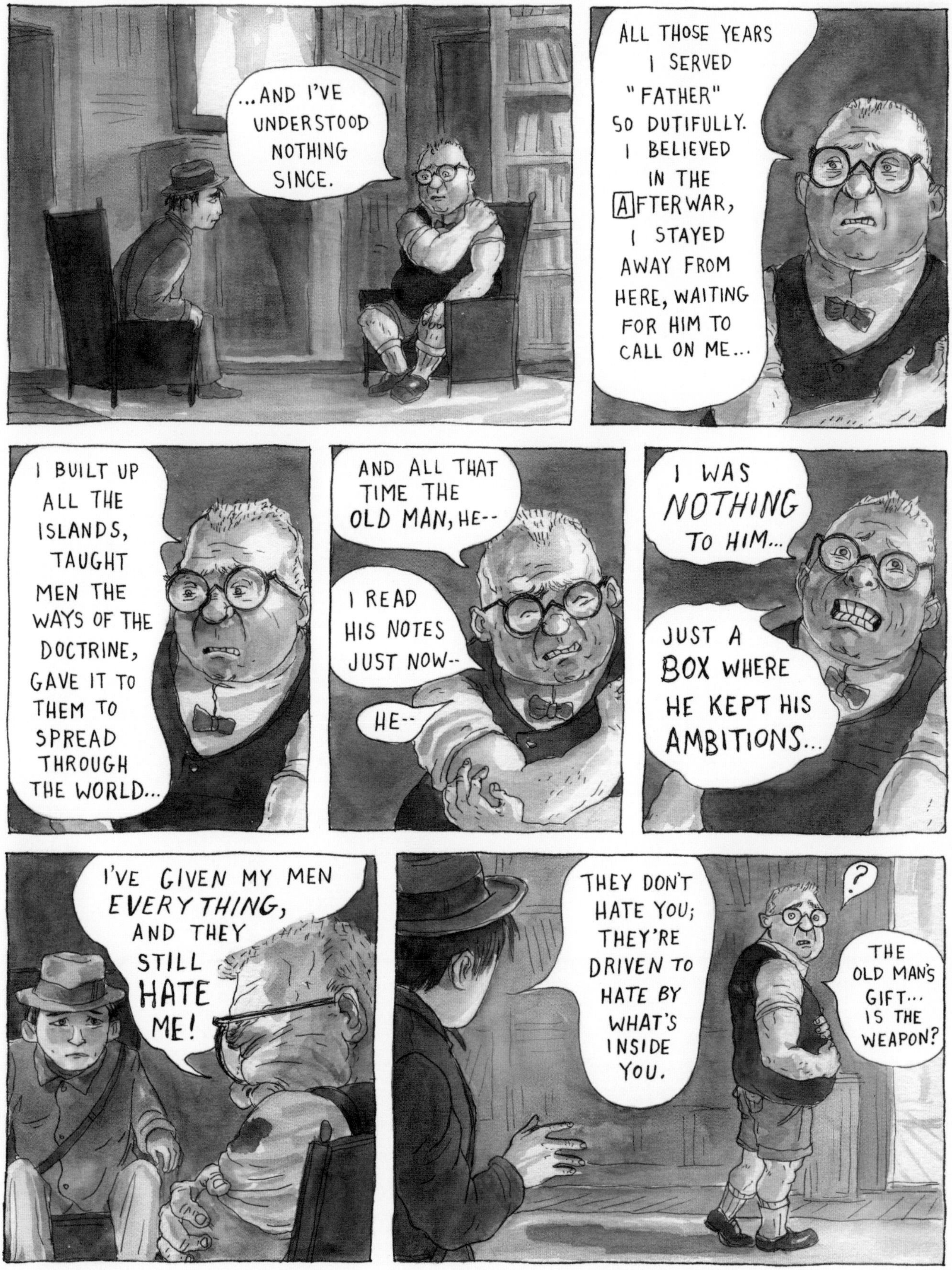
...AND I'VE UNDERSTOOD NOTHING SINCE.
ALL THOSE YEARS I SERVED "FATHER" SO DUTIFULLY. I BELIEVED IN THE AFTERWAR, I STAYED AWAY FROM HERE, WAITING FOR HIM TO CALL ON ME...
I BUILT UP ALL THE ISLANDS, TAUGHT MEN THE WAYS OF THE DOCTRINE, GAVE IT TO THEM TO SPREAD THROUGH THE WORLD...
AND ALL THAT TIME THE OLD MAN, HE--
I READ HIS NOTES JUST NOW--
HE--
I WAS NOTHING TO HIM...
JUST A BOX WHERE HE KEPT HIS AMBITIONS...
I'VE GIVEN MY MEN EVERYTHING, AND THEY STILL HATE ME!
THEY DON'T HATE YOU; THEY'RE DRIVEN TO HATE BY WHAT'S INSIDE YOU.
?
THE OLD MAN'S GIFT... IS THE WEAPON?

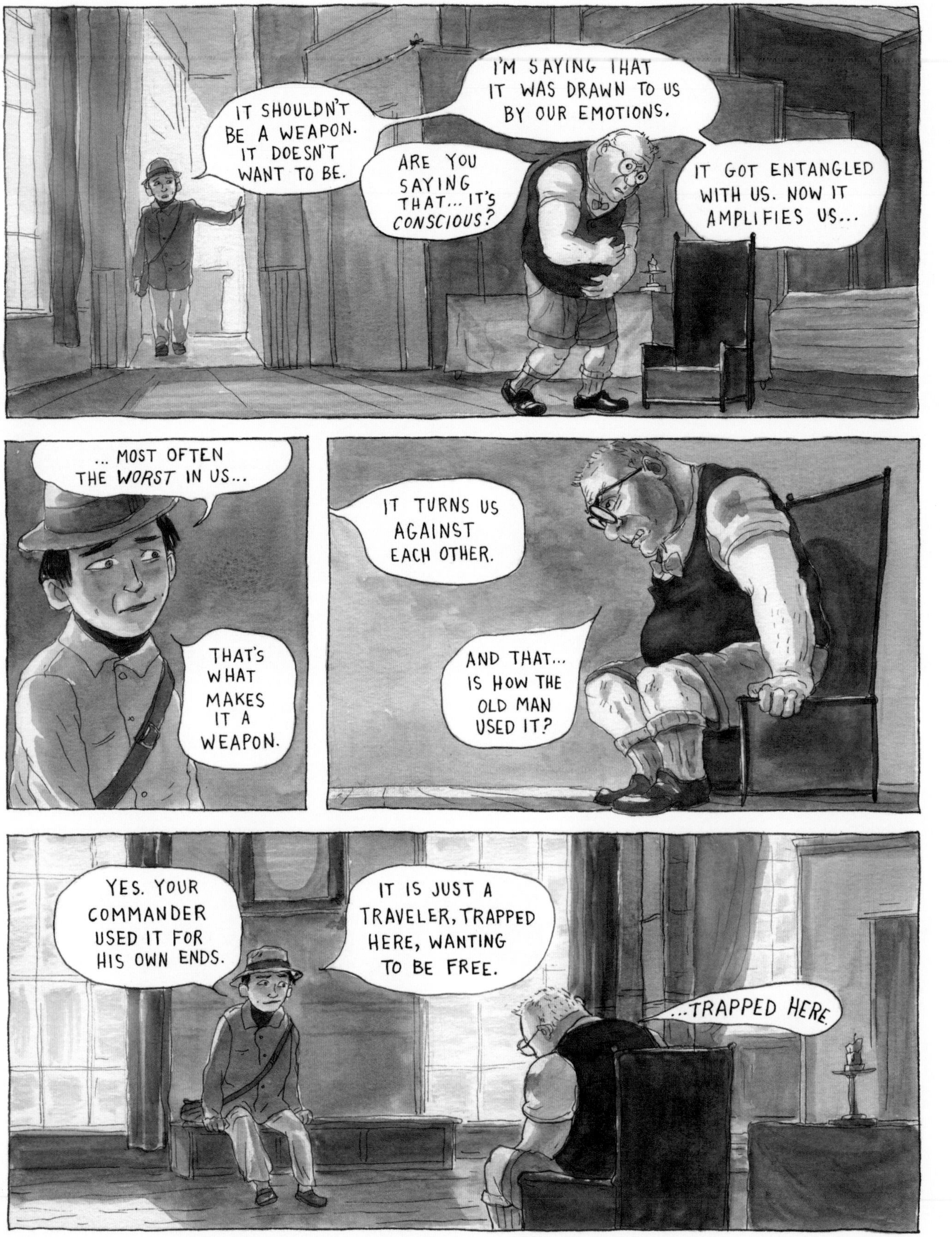
IT SHOULDN'T BE A WEAPON. IT DOESN'T WANT TO BE.
ARE YOU SAYING THAT... IT'S *CONSCIOUS*?
I'M SAYING THAT IT WAS DRAWN TO US BY OUR EMOTIONS.
IT GOT ENTANGLED WITH US. NOW IT AMPLIFIES US...
... MOST OFTEN THE *WORST* IN US...
THAT'S WHAT MAKES IT A WEAPON.
IT TURNS US AGAINST EACH OTHER.
AND THAT... IS HOW THE OLD MAN USED IT?
YES. YOUR COMMANDER USED IT FOR HIS OWN ENDS.
IT IS JUST A TRAVELER, TRAPPED HERE, WANTING TO BE FREE.
...TRAPPED HERE.

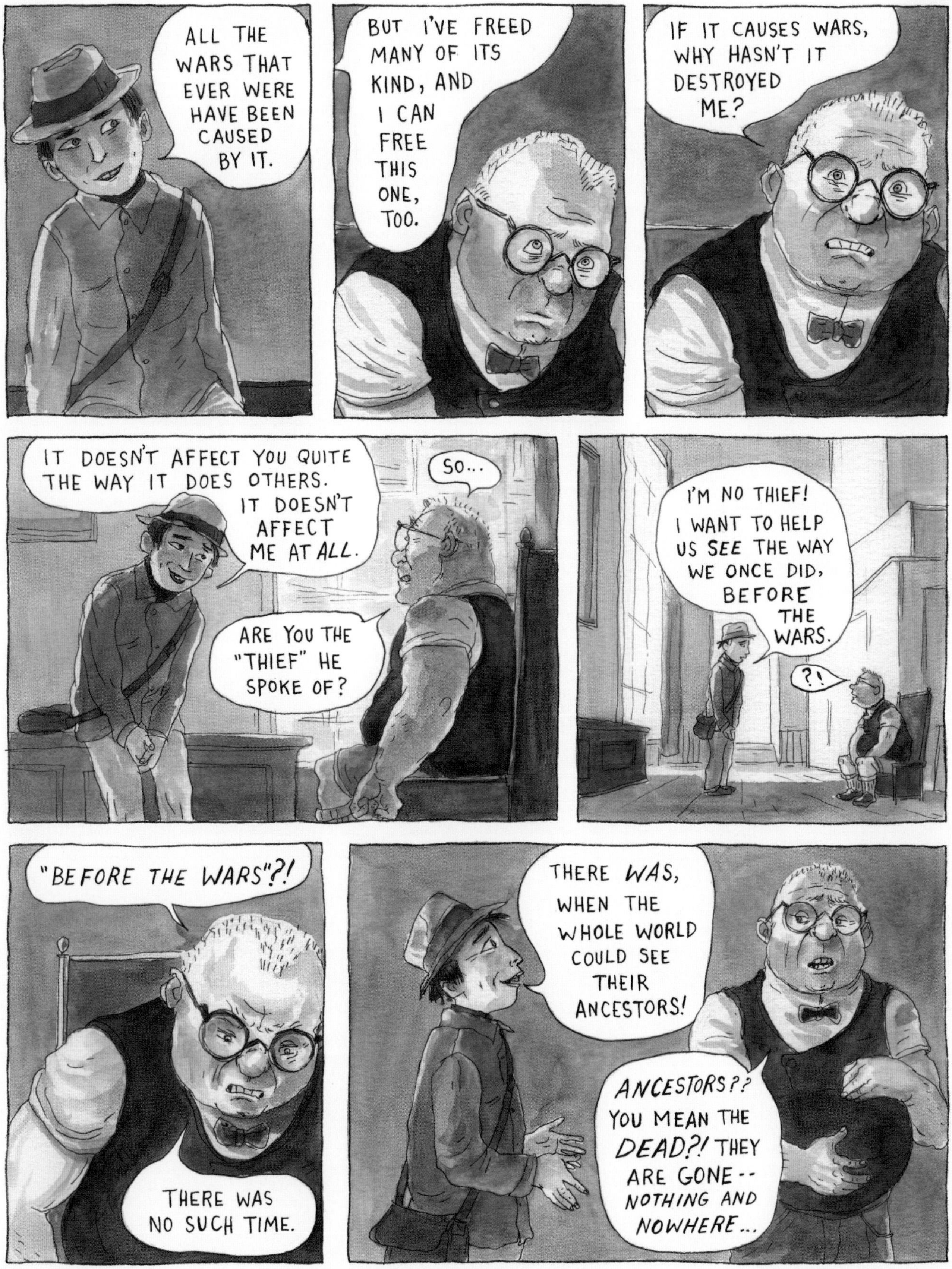
ALL THE WARS THAT EVER WERE HAVE BEEN CAUSED BY IT.
BUT I'VE FREED MANY OF ITS KIND, AND I CAN FREE THIS ONE, TOO.
IF IT CAUSES WARS, WHY HASN'T IT DESTROYED ME?
IT DOESN'T AFFECT YOU QUITE THE WAY IT DOES OTHERS.
IT DOESN'T AFFECT ME AT *ALL*.
SO...
ARE YOU THE "THIEF" HE SPOKE OF?
I'M NO THIEF! I WANT TO HELP US **SEE** THE WAY WE ONCE DID, BEFORE THE WARS.
?!
"*BEFORE THE WARS*"?!
THERE WAS NO SUCH TIME.
THERE *WAS*, WHEN THE WHOLE WORLD COULD SEE THEIR ANCESTORS!
ANCESTORS?? YOU MEAN THE *DEAD?!* THEY ARE GONE-- *NOTHING AND NOWHERE*...

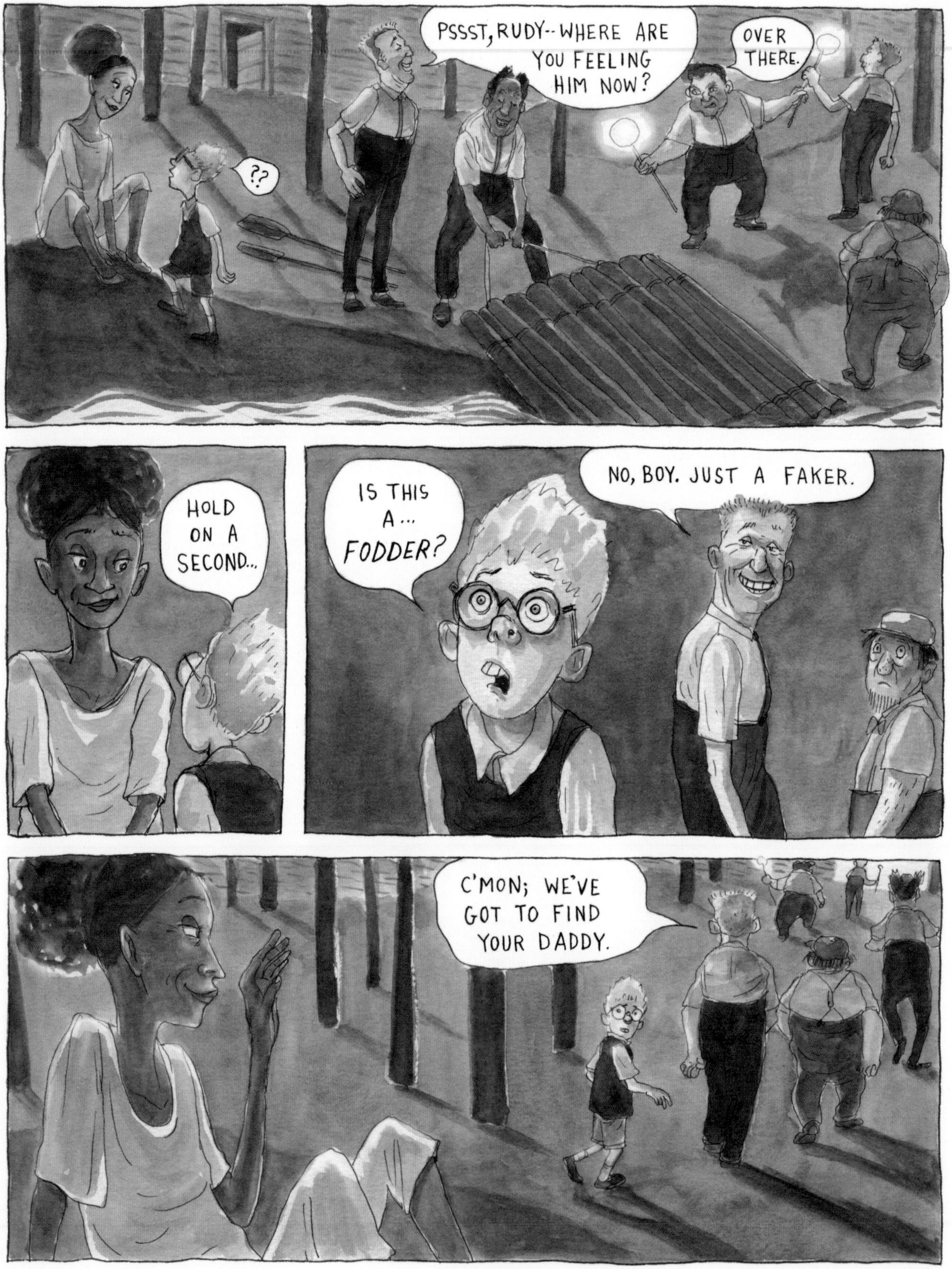
PSSST, RUDY-- WHERE ARE YOU FEELING HIM NOW?
OVER THERE.
??
HOLD ON A SECOND...
IS THIS A... FODDER?
NO, BOY. JUST A FAKER.
C'MON; WE'VE GOT TO FIND YOUR DADDY.

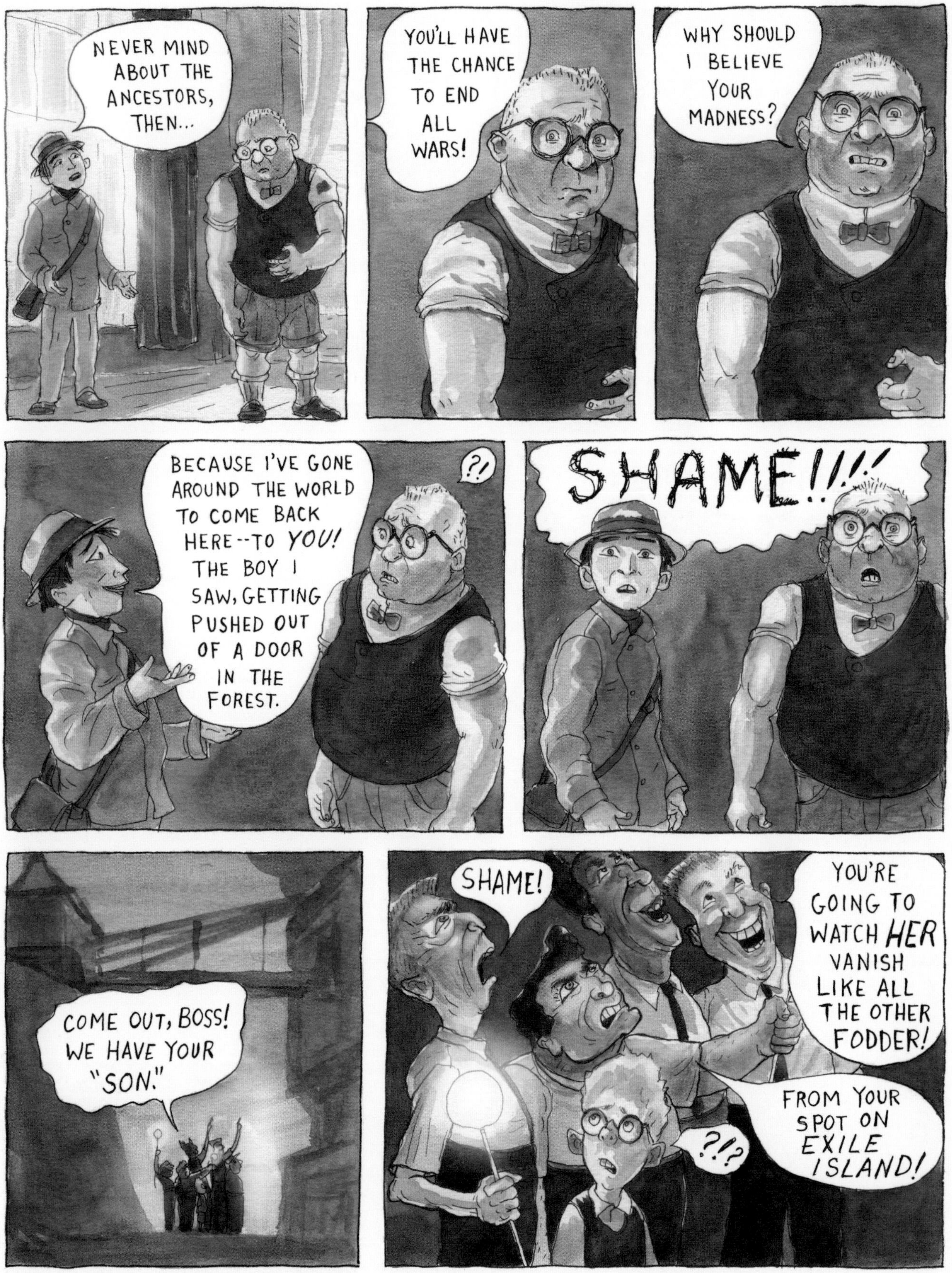
NEVER MIND ABOUT THE ANCESTORS, THEN...
YOU'LL HAVE THE CHANCE TO END ALL WARS!
WHY SHOULD I BELIEVE YOUR MADNESS?
BECAUSE I'VE GONE AROUND THE WORLD TO COME BACK HERE--TO *YOU!* THE BOY I SAW, GETTING PUSHED OUT OF A DOOR IN THE FOREST.
?!
SHAME!!!!
COME OUT, BOSS! WE HAVE YOUR "SON."
SHAME!
YOU'RE GOING TO WATCH *HER* VANISH LIKE ALL THE OTHER FODDER!
FROM YOUR SPOT ON *EXILE ISLAND!*
?!?

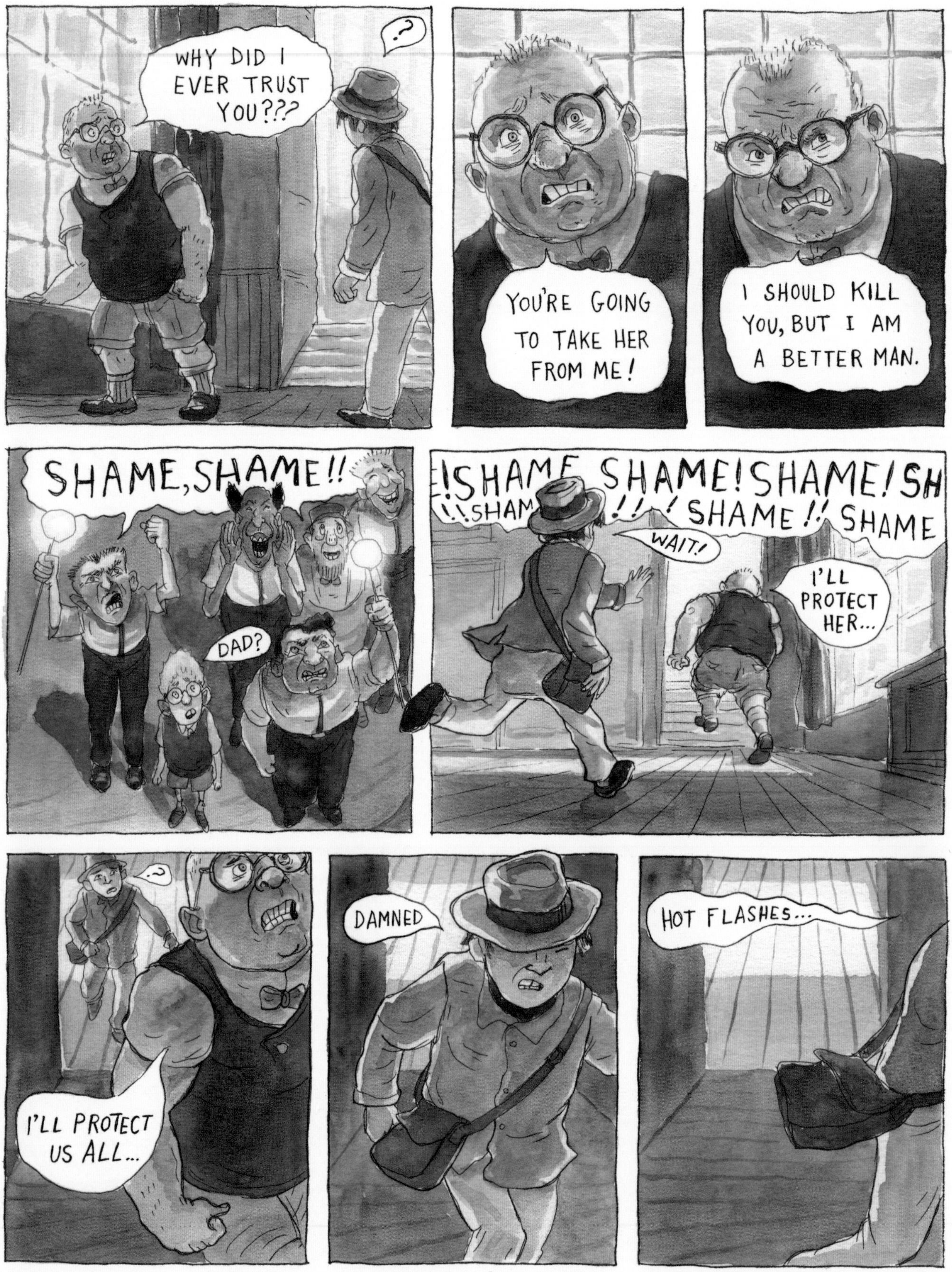
WHY DID I EVER TRUST YOU???
?
YOU'RE GOING TO TAKE HER FROM ME!
I SHOULD KILL YOU, BUT I AM A BETTER MAN.
SHAME, SHAME!!
DAD?
!SHAME SHAME! SHAME! SH
!!SHAM !! ! SHAME!! SHAME
WAIT!
I'LL PROTECT HER...
?
I'LL PROTECT US ALL...
DAMNED
HOT FLASHES...

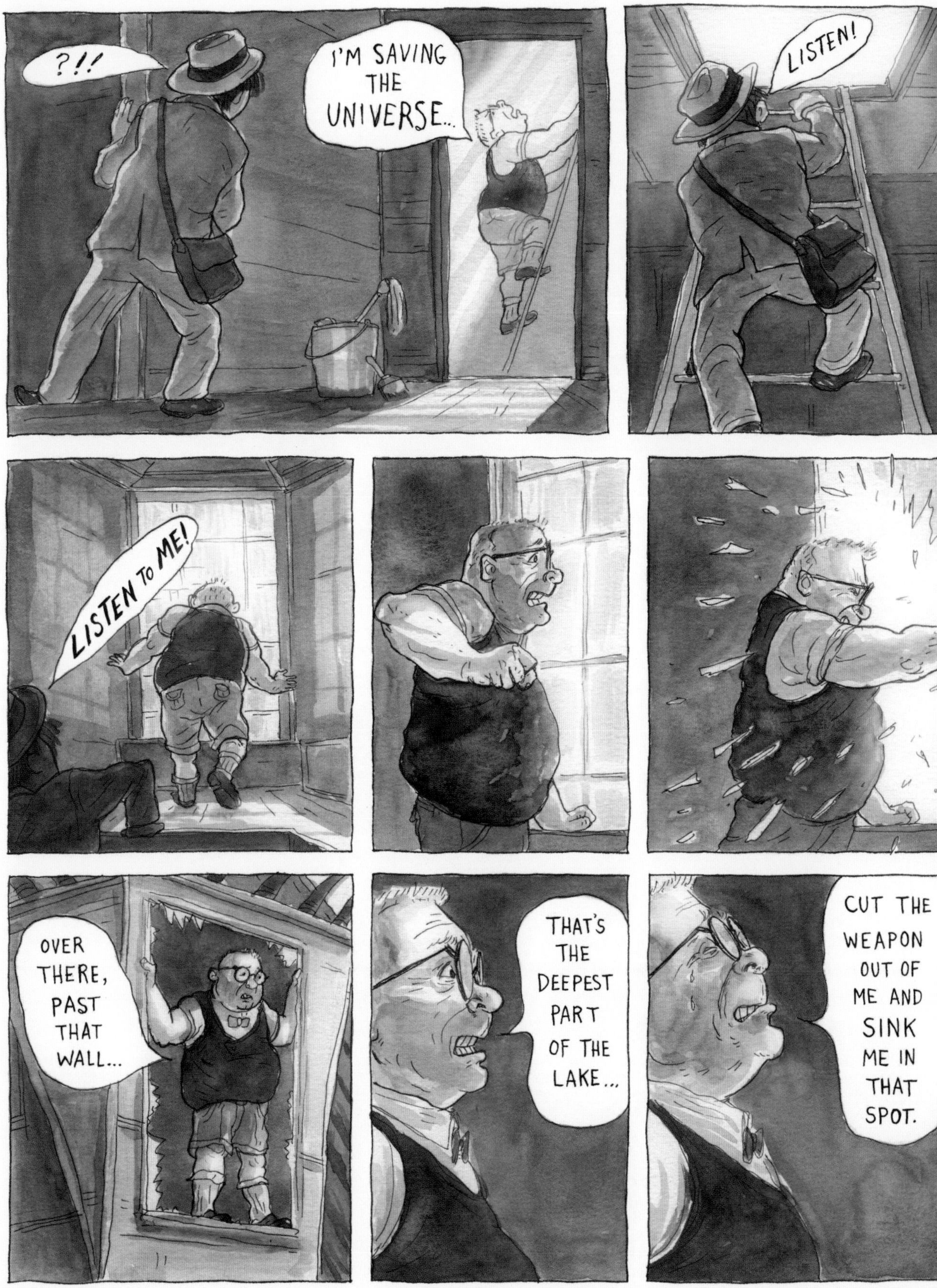
?!!
I'M SAVING THE UNIVERSE...
LISTEN!
LISTEN TO ME!
OVER THERE, PAST THAT WALL...
THAT'S THE DEEPEST PART OF THE LAKE...
CUT THE WEAPON OUT OF ME AND SINK ME IN THAT SPOT.

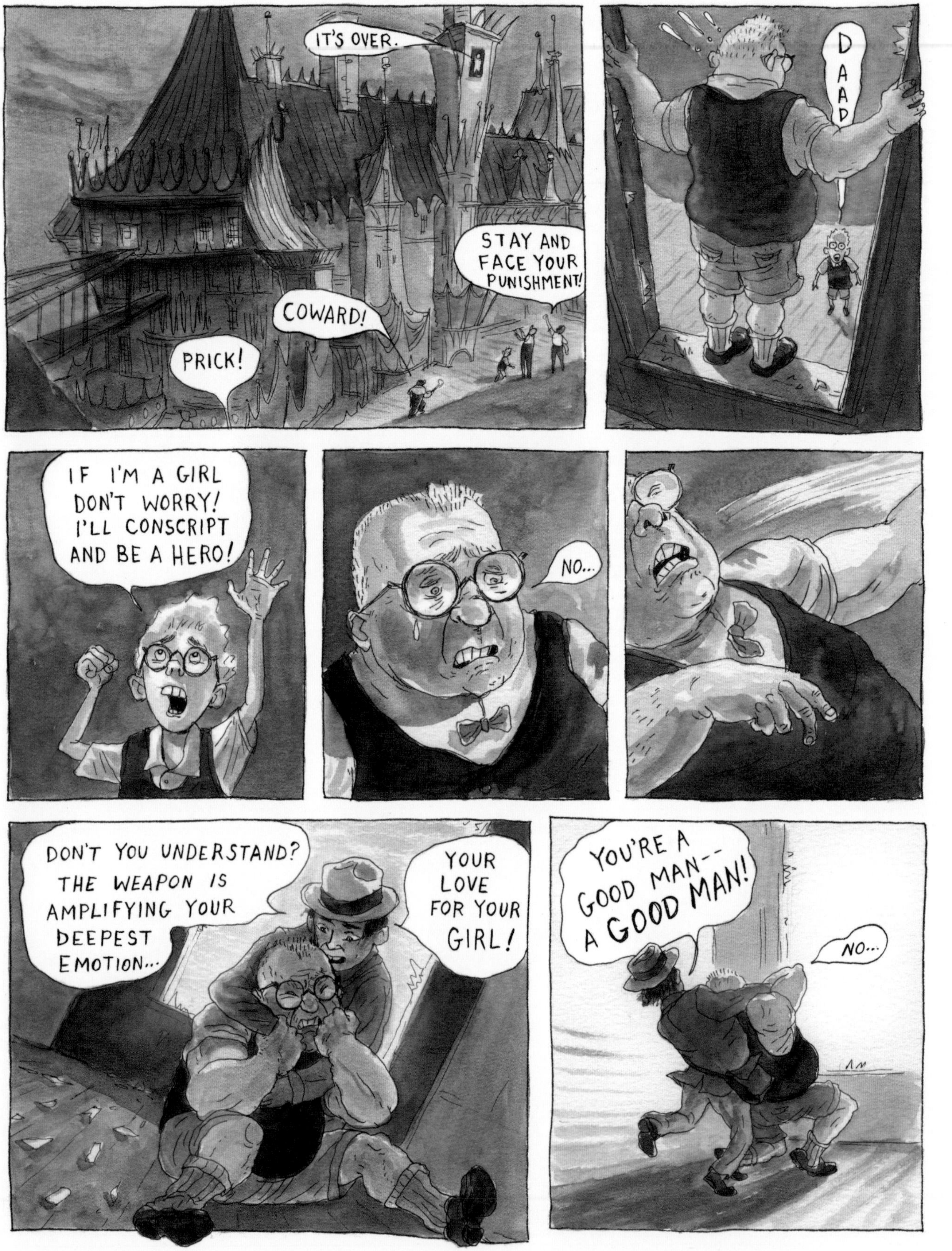
IT'S OVER.
STAY AND FACE YOUR PUNISHMENT!
COWARD!
PRICK!
DAAD
IF I'M A GIRL DON'T WORRY! I'LL CONSCRIPT AND BE A HERO!
NO...
DON'T YOU UNDERSTAND? THE WEAPON IS AMPLIFYING YOUR DEEPEST EMOTION...
YOUR LOVE FOR YOUR GIRL!
YOU'RE A GOOD MAN-- A GOOD MAN!
NO...

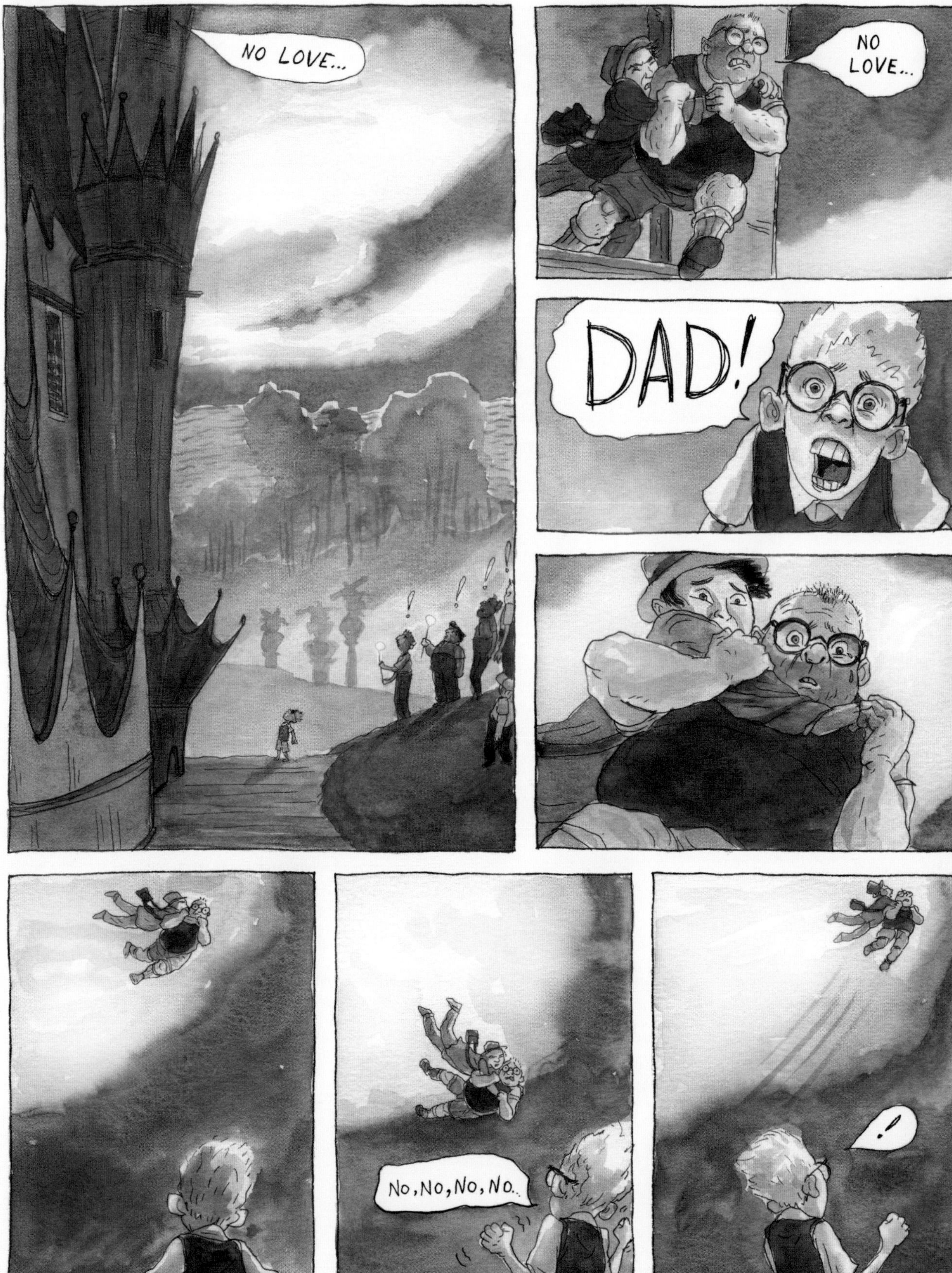
NO LOVE...
NO LOVE...
DAD!
No, No, No, No..
!

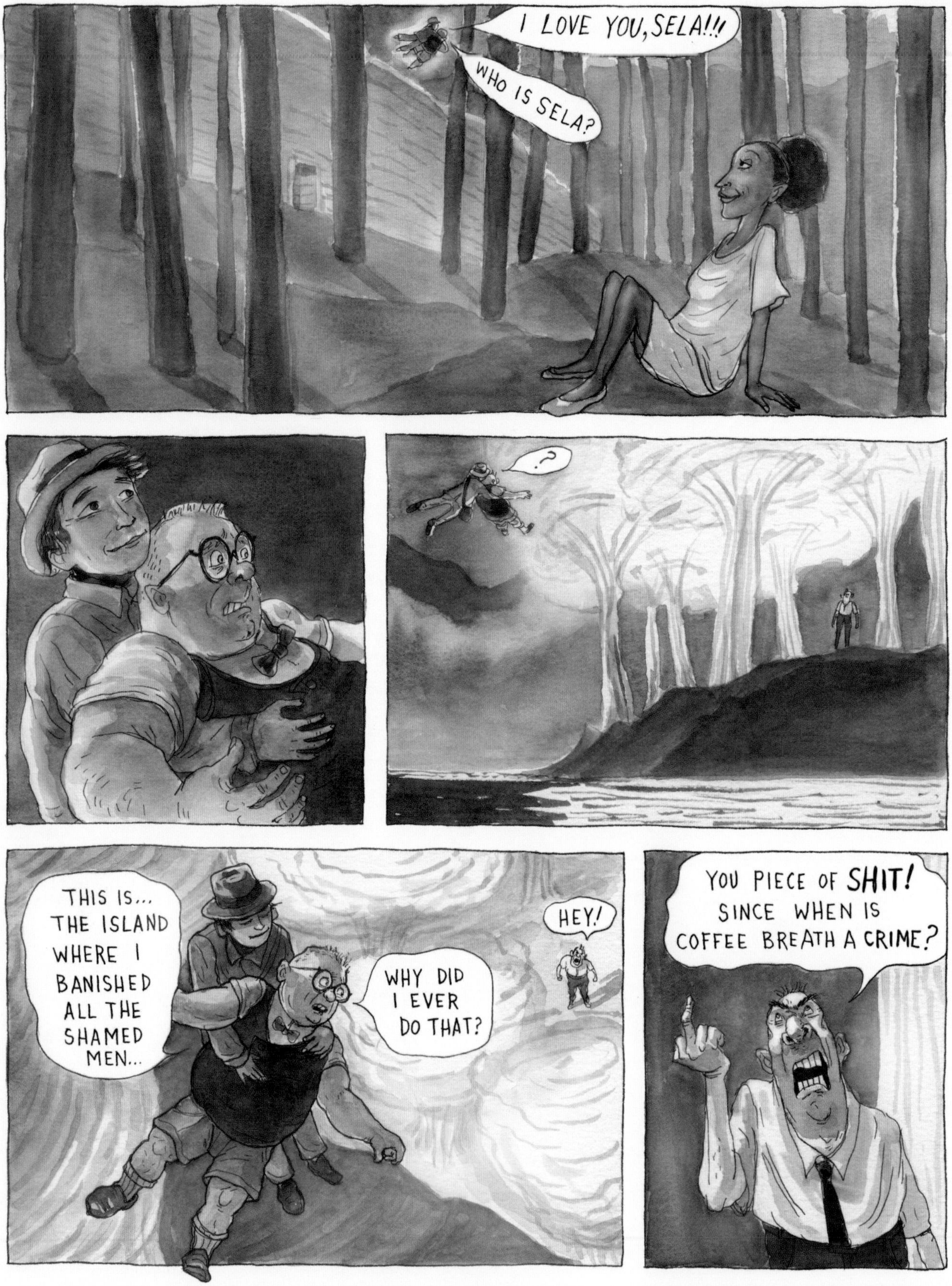
I LOVE YOU, SELA!!!
WHO IS SELA?
?
THIS IS... THE ISLAND WHERE I BANISHED ALL THE SHAMED MEN...
WHY DID I EVER DO THAT?
HEY!
YOU PIECE OF SHIT! SINCE WHEN IS COFFEE BREATH A CRIME?

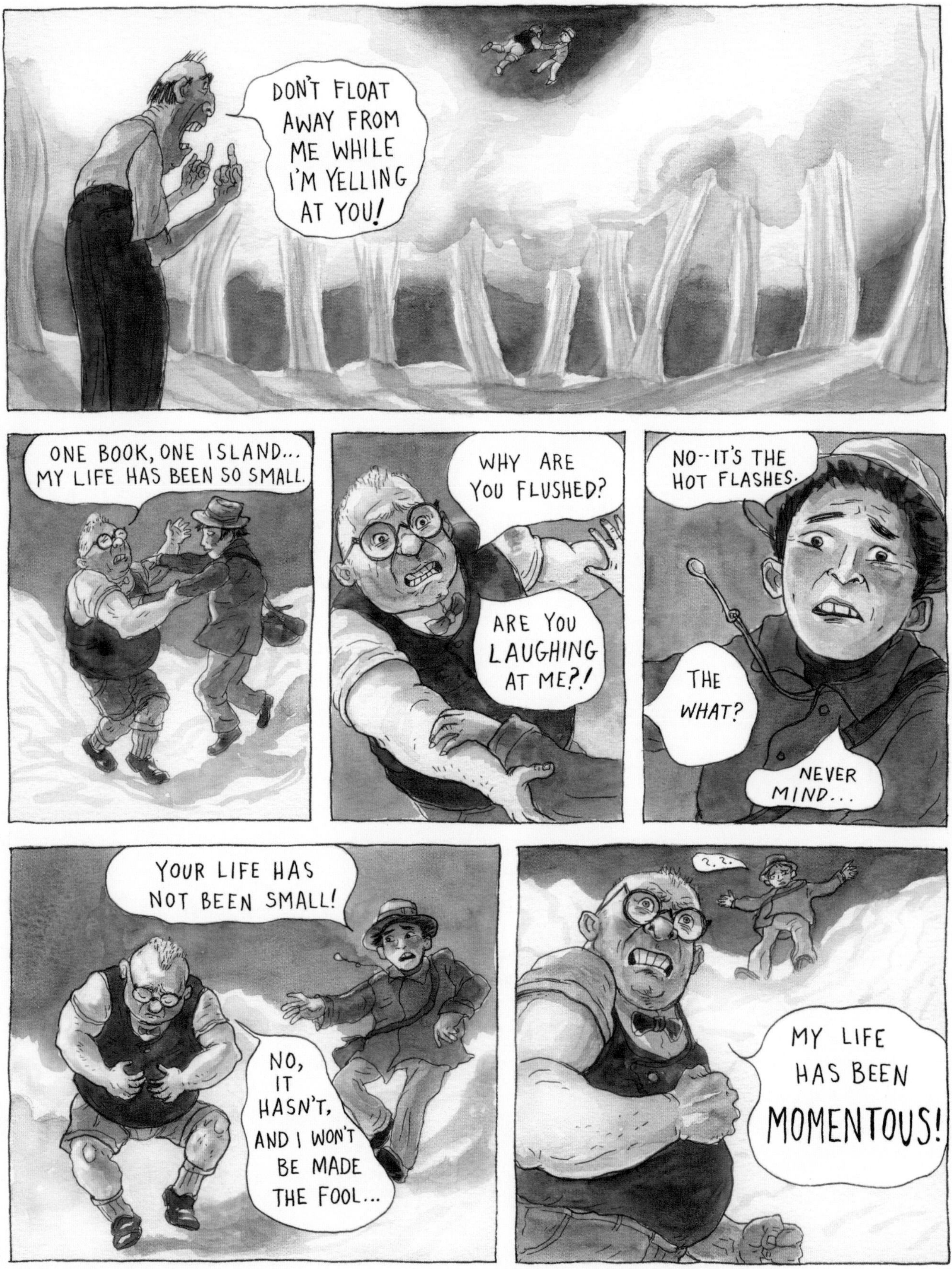
DON'T FLOAT AWAY FROM ME WHILE I'M YELLING AT YOU!
ONE BOOK, ONE ISLAND... MY LIFE HAS BEEN SO SMALL.
WHY ARE YOU FLUSHED?
ARE YOU LAUGHING AT ME?!
NO--IT'S THE HOT FLASHES.
THE WHAT?
NEVER MIND...
YOUR LIFE HAS NOT BEEN SMALL!
NO, IT HASN'T, AND I WON'T BE MADE THE FOOL...
?.?.
MY LIFE HAS BEEN MOMENTOUS!

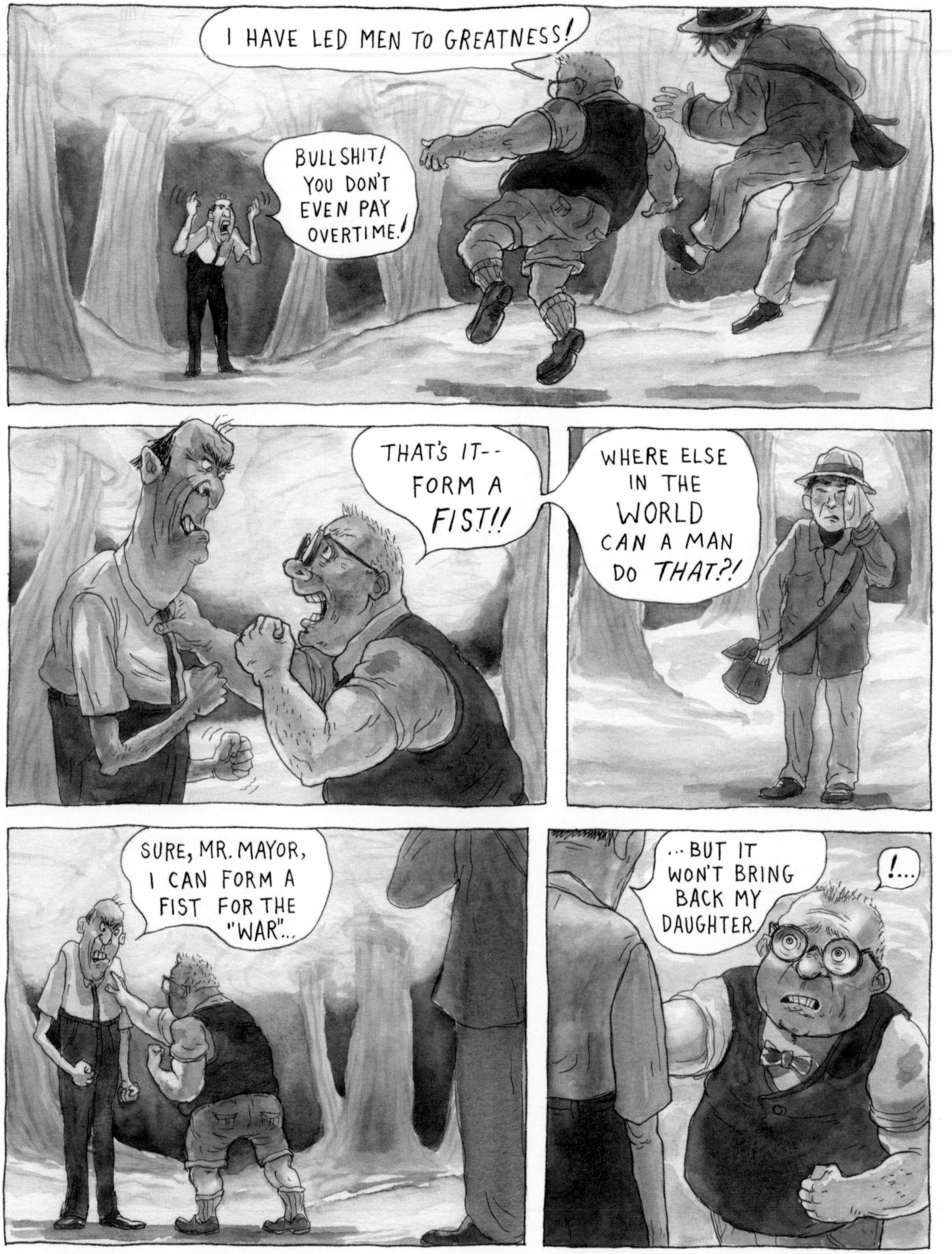
I HAVE LED MEN TO GREATNESS!
BULLSHIT! YOU DON'T EVEN PAY OVERTIME!
THAT'S IT-- FORM A FIST!!
WHERE ELSE IN THE WORLD CAN A MAN DO THAT?!
SURE, MR. MAYOR, I CAN FORM A FIST FOR THE "WAR"...
...BUT IT WON'T BRING BACK MY DAUGHTER.
!...

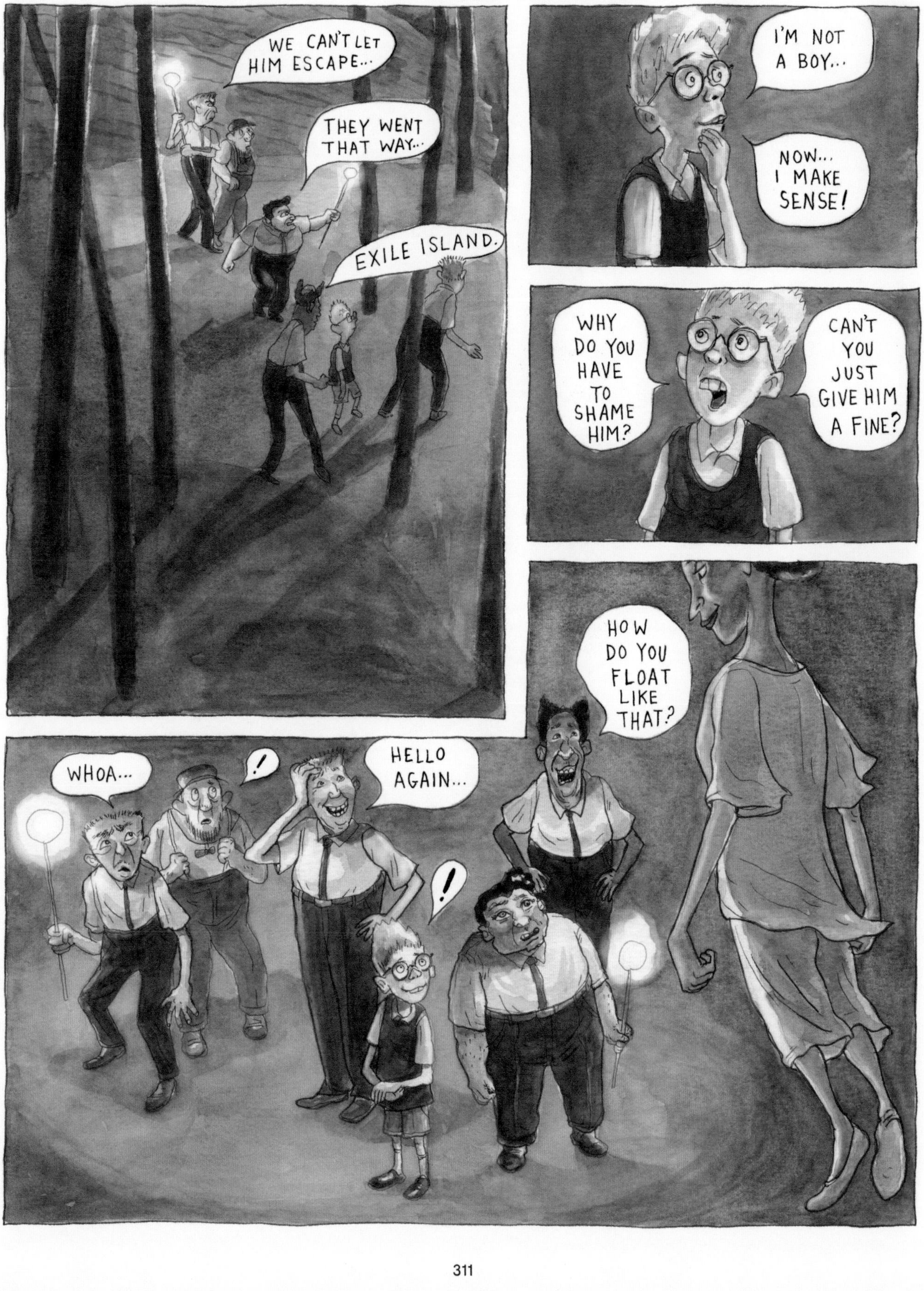
WE CAN'T LET HIM ESCAPE...
THEY WENT THAT WAY...
EXILE ISLAND.
I'M NOT A BOY...
NOW... I MAKE SENSE!
WHY DO YOU HAVE TO SHAME HIM?
CAN'T YOU JUST GIVE HIM A FINE?
HOW DO YOU FLOAT LIKE THAT?
WHOA...
!
HELLO AGAIN...
!

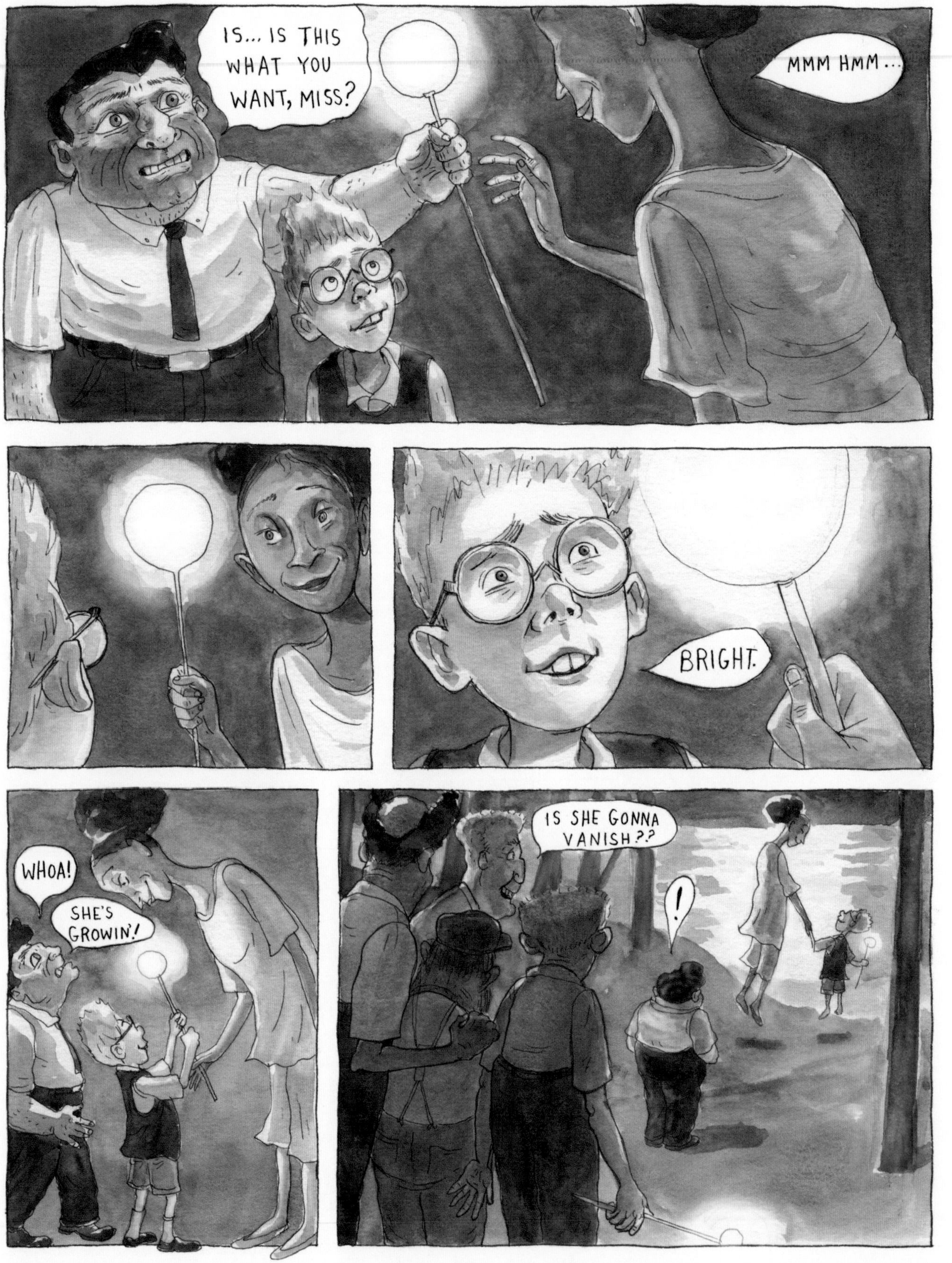
IS... IS THIS WHAT YOU WANT, MISS?
MMM HMM...
BRIGHT.
WHOA!
SHE'S GROWIN'!
IS SHE GONNA VANISH??
!

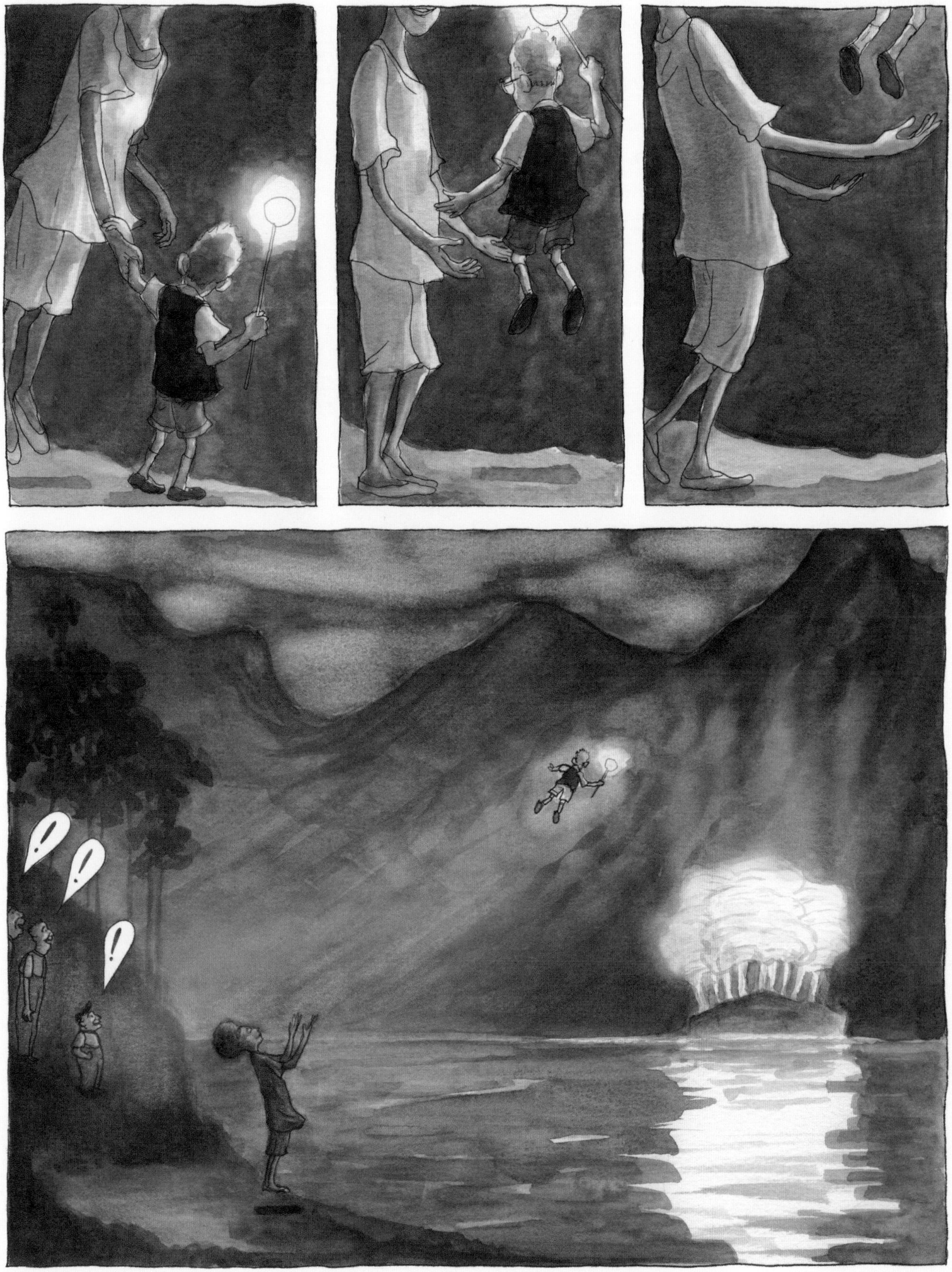
!
!
!

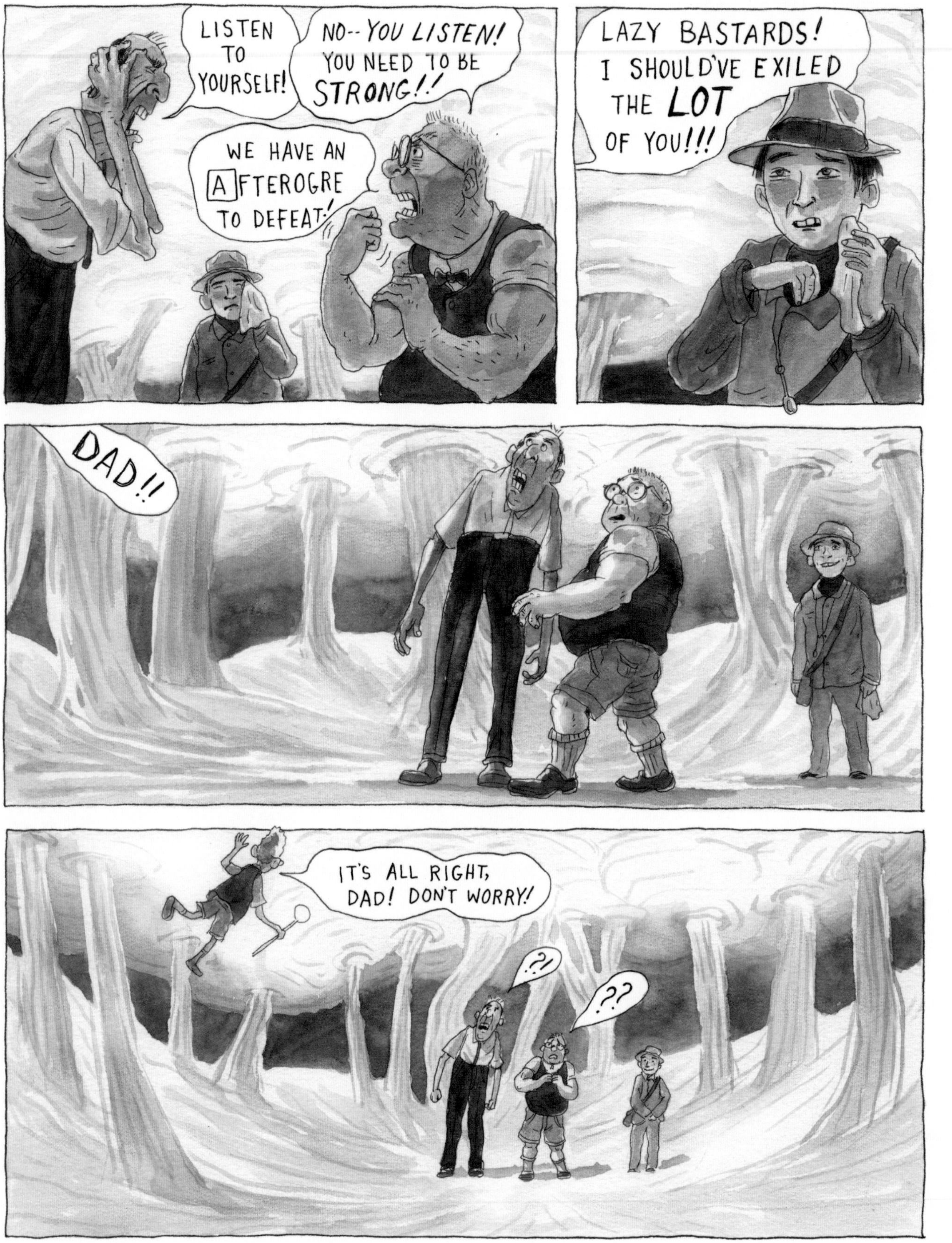
LISTEN TO YOURSELF!
NO-- YOU LISTEN! YOU NEED TO BE STRONG!!
WE HAVE AN AFTEROGRE TO DEFEAT!
LAZY BASTARDS! I SHOULD'VE EXILED THE LOT OF YOU!!!
DAD!!
IT'S ALL RIGHT, DAD! DON'T WORRY!
?!
??

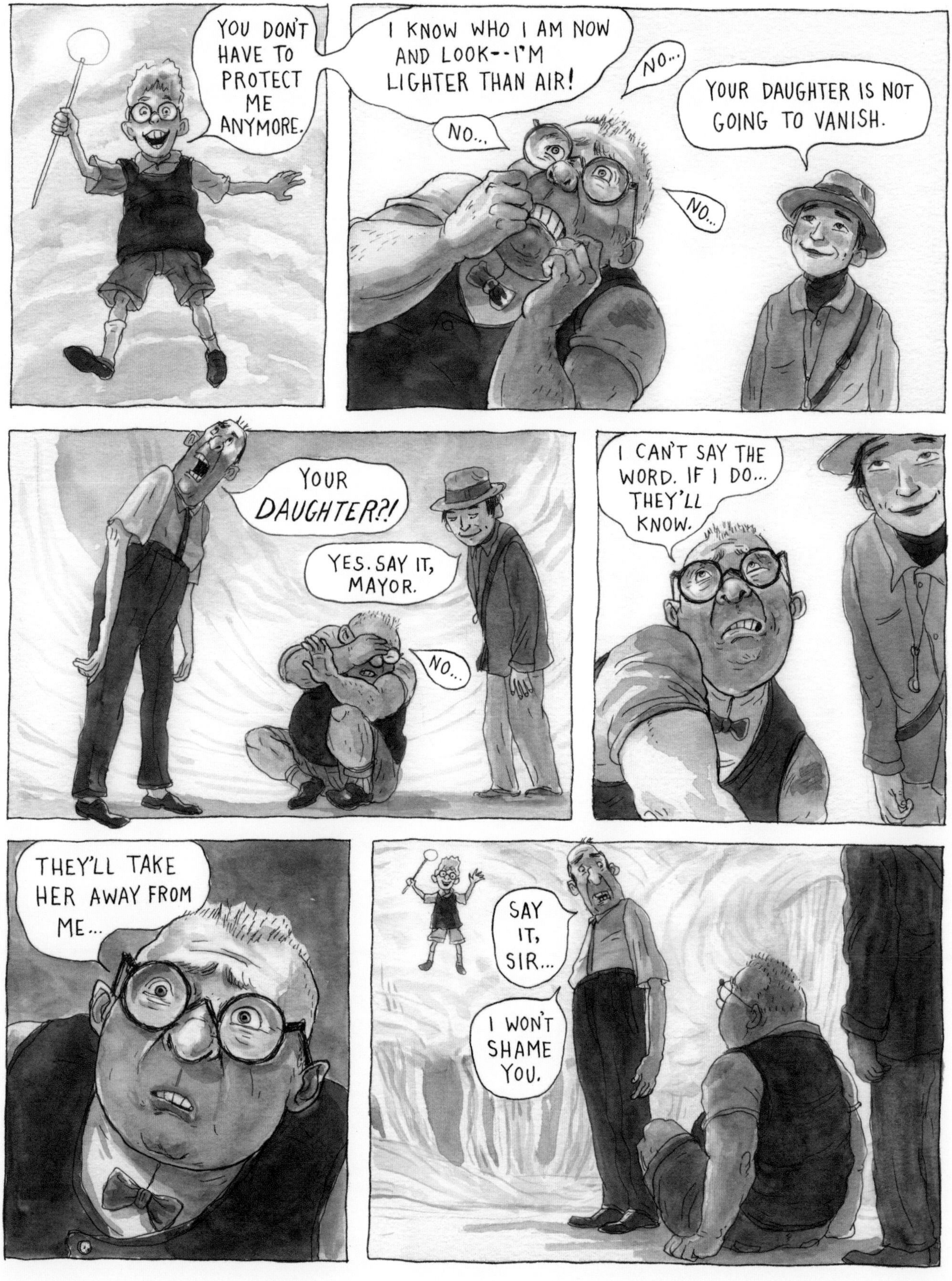
YOU DON'T HAVE TO PROTECT ME ANYMORE.
I KNOW WHO I AM NOW AND LOOK--I'M LIGHTER THAN AIR!
NO...
NO...
NO...
YOUR DAUGHTER IS NOT GOING TO VANISH.
YOUR DAUGHTER?!
YES. SAY IT, MAYOR.
NO...
I CAN'T SAY THE WORD. IF I DO... THEY'LL KNOW.
THEY'LL TAKE HER AWAY FROM ME...
SAY IT, SIR...
I WON'T SHAME YOU.

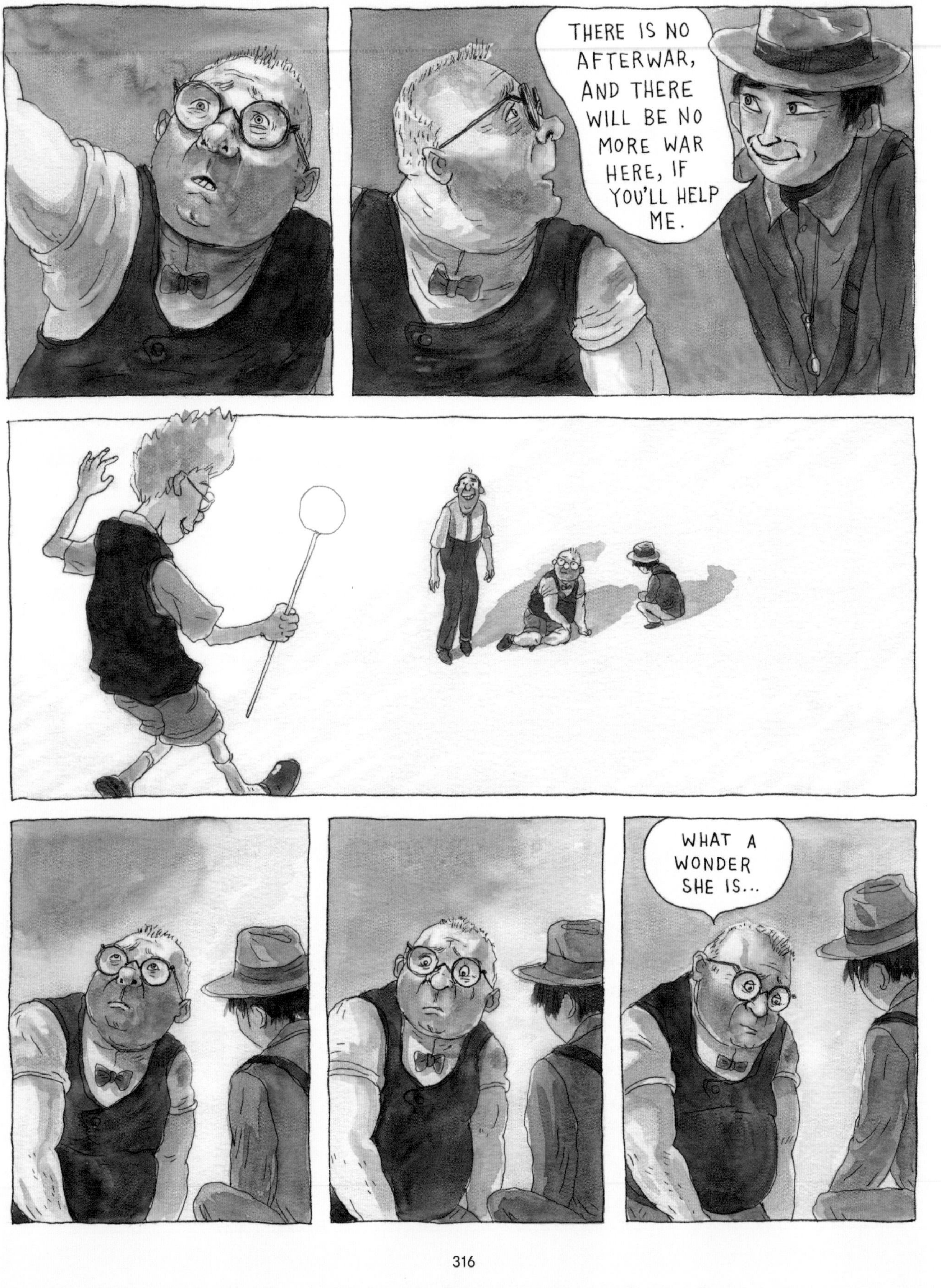
THERE IS NO AFTERWAR, AND THERE WILL BE NO MORE WAR HERE, IF YOU'LL HELP ME.
WHAT A WONDER SHE IS...

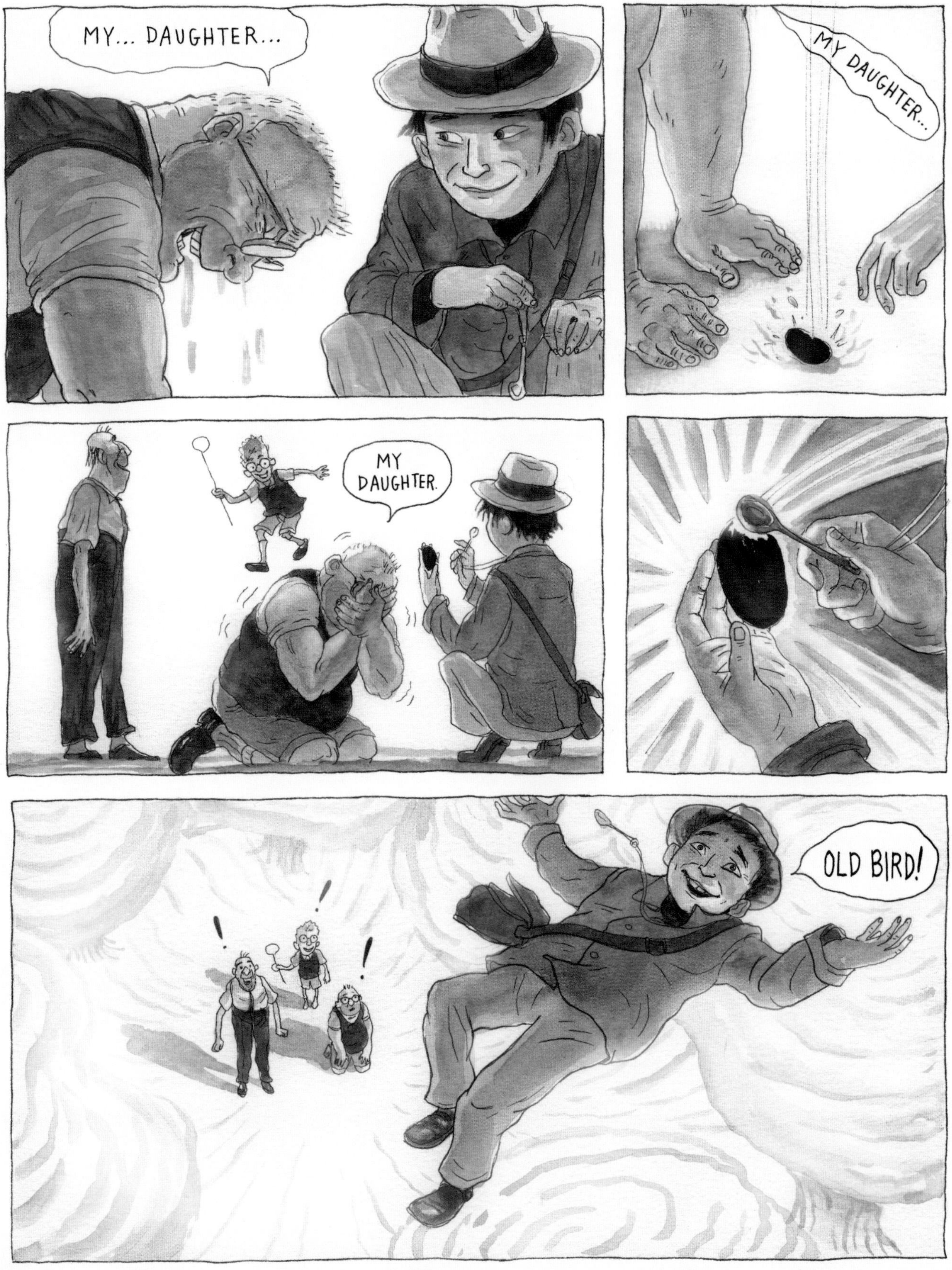
MY... DAUGHTER...
MY DAUGHTER...
MY DAUGHTER.
OLD BIRD!

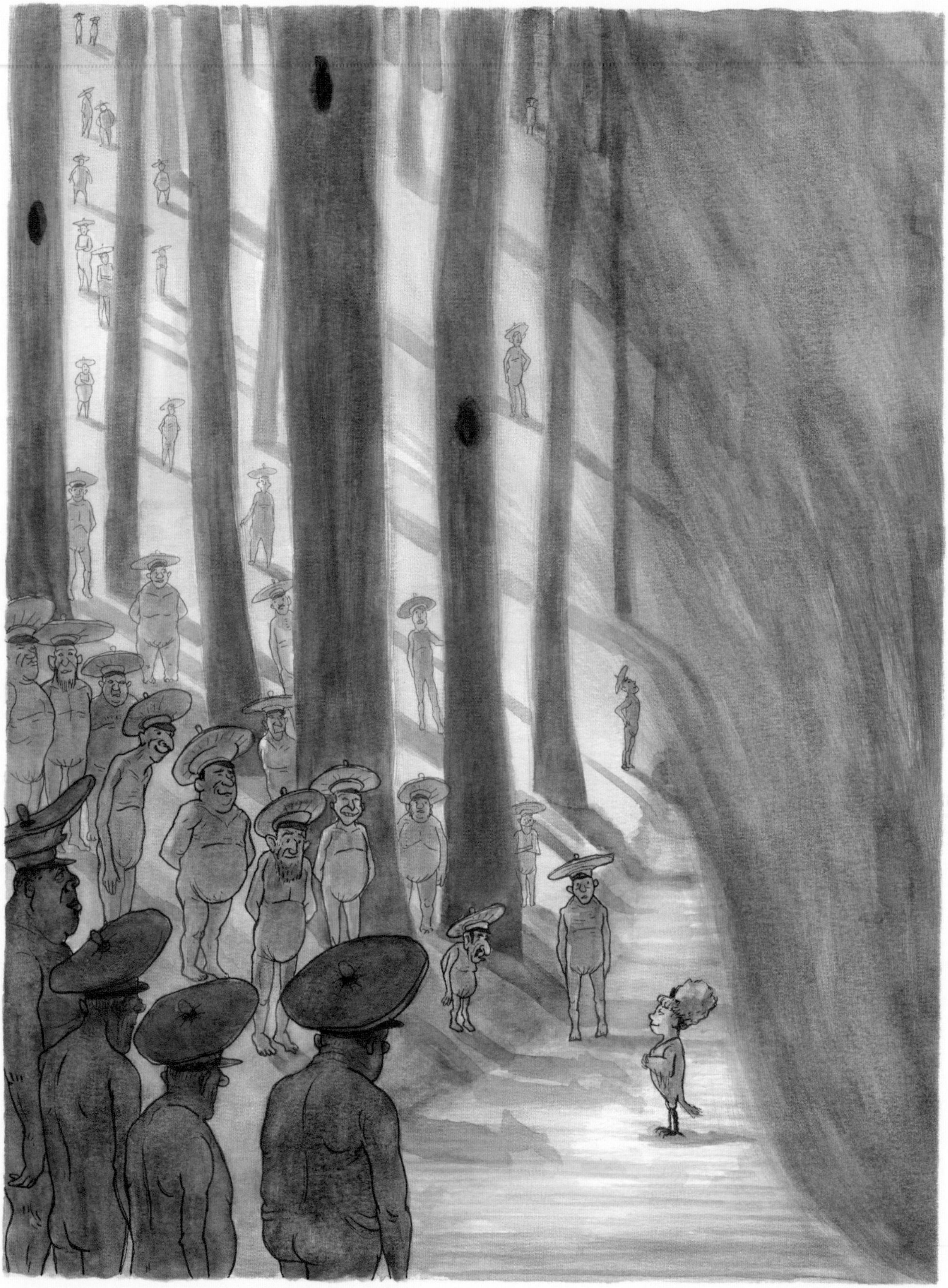

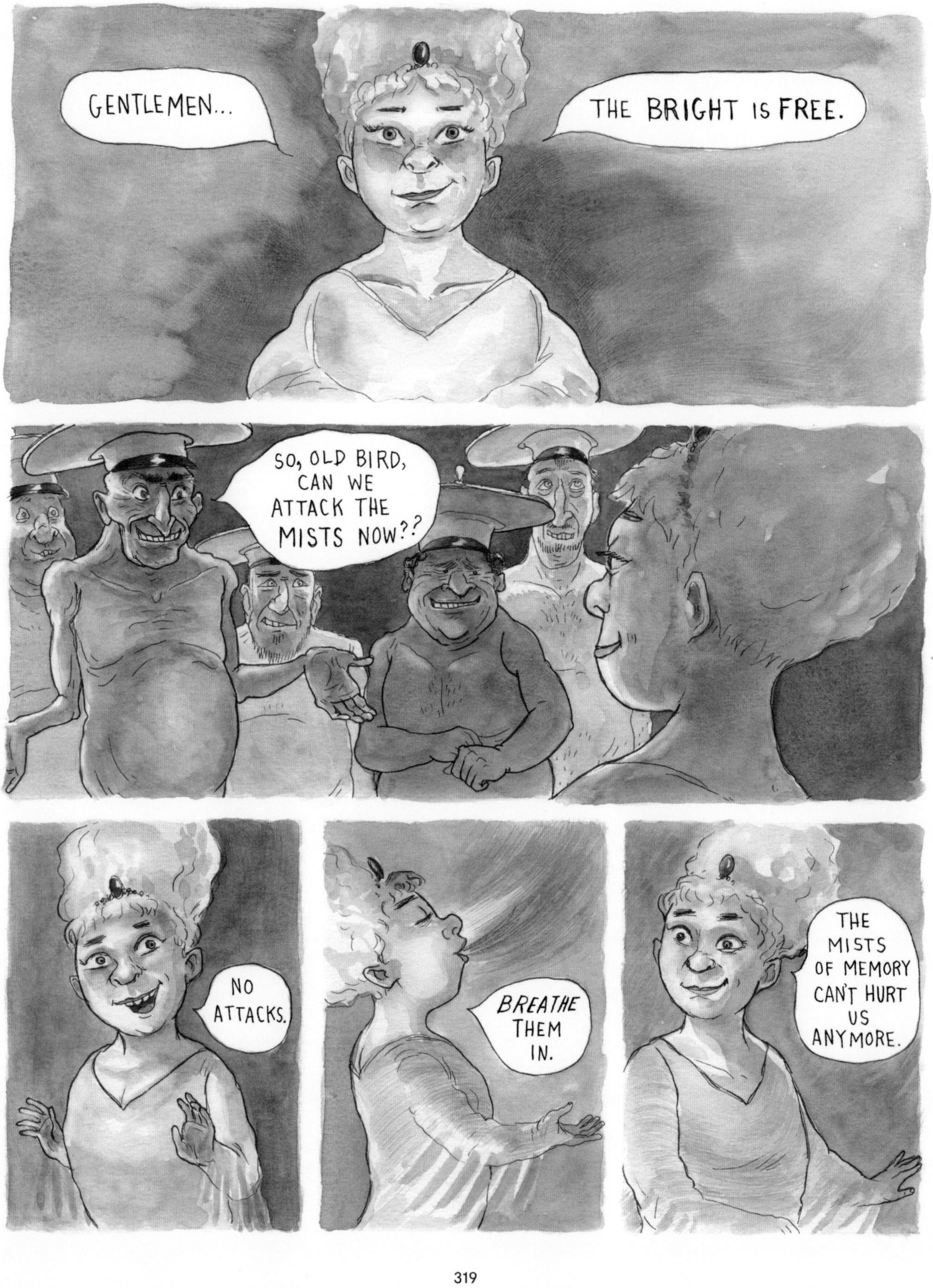
GENTLEMEN...
THE BRIGHT IS FREE.
SO, OLD BIRD, CAN WE ATTACK THE MISTS NOW??
NO ATTACKS.
BREATHE THEM IN.
THE MISTS OF MEMORY CAN'T HURT US ANYMORE.

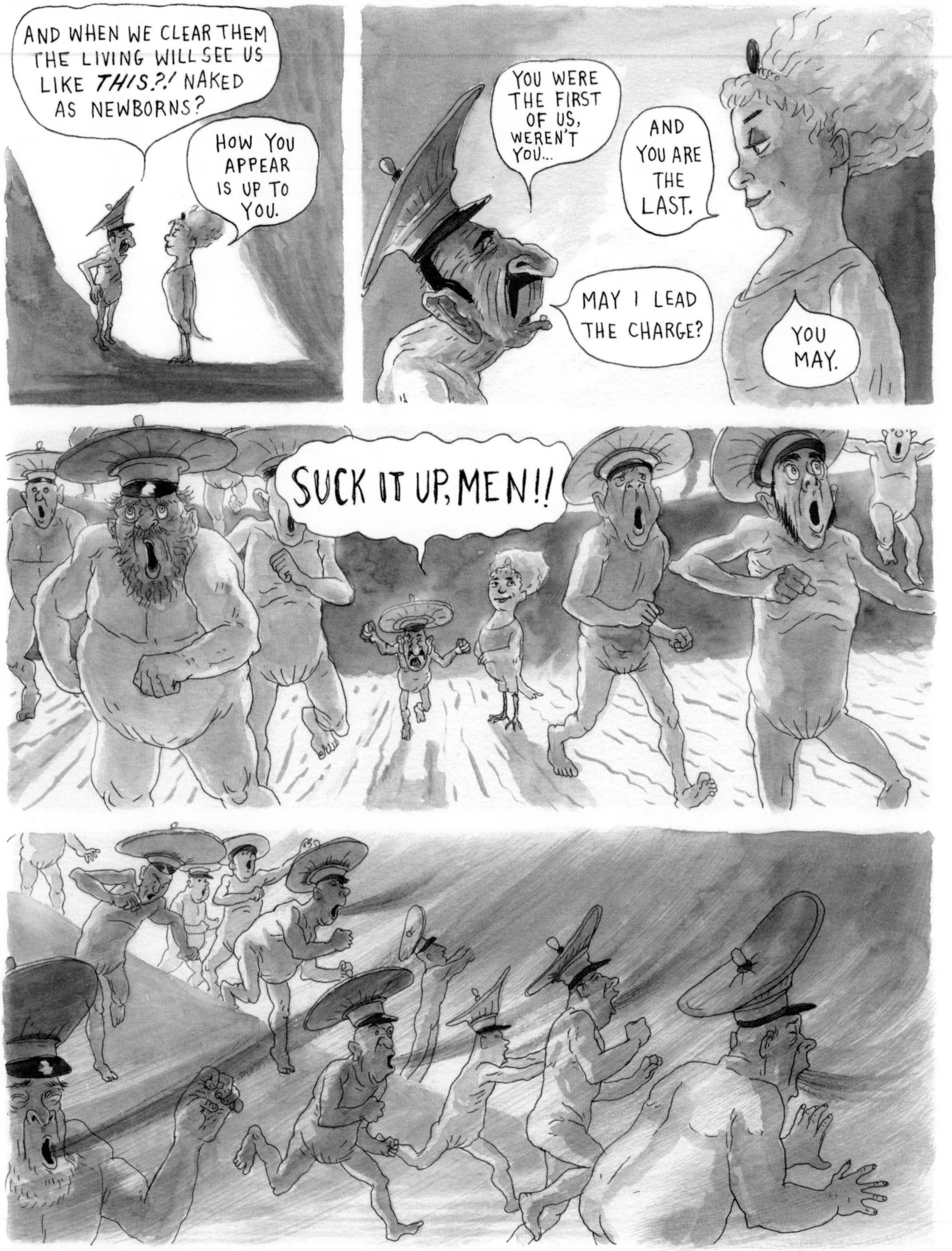
AND WHEN WE CLEAR THEM THE LIVING WILL SEE US LIKE *THIS?!* NAKED AS NEWBORNS?
HOW YOU APPEAR IS UP TO YOU.
YOU WERE THE FIRST OF US, WEREN'T YOU...
AND YOU ARE THE LAST.
MAY I LEAD THE CHARGE?
YOU MAY.
SUCK IT UP, MEN!!

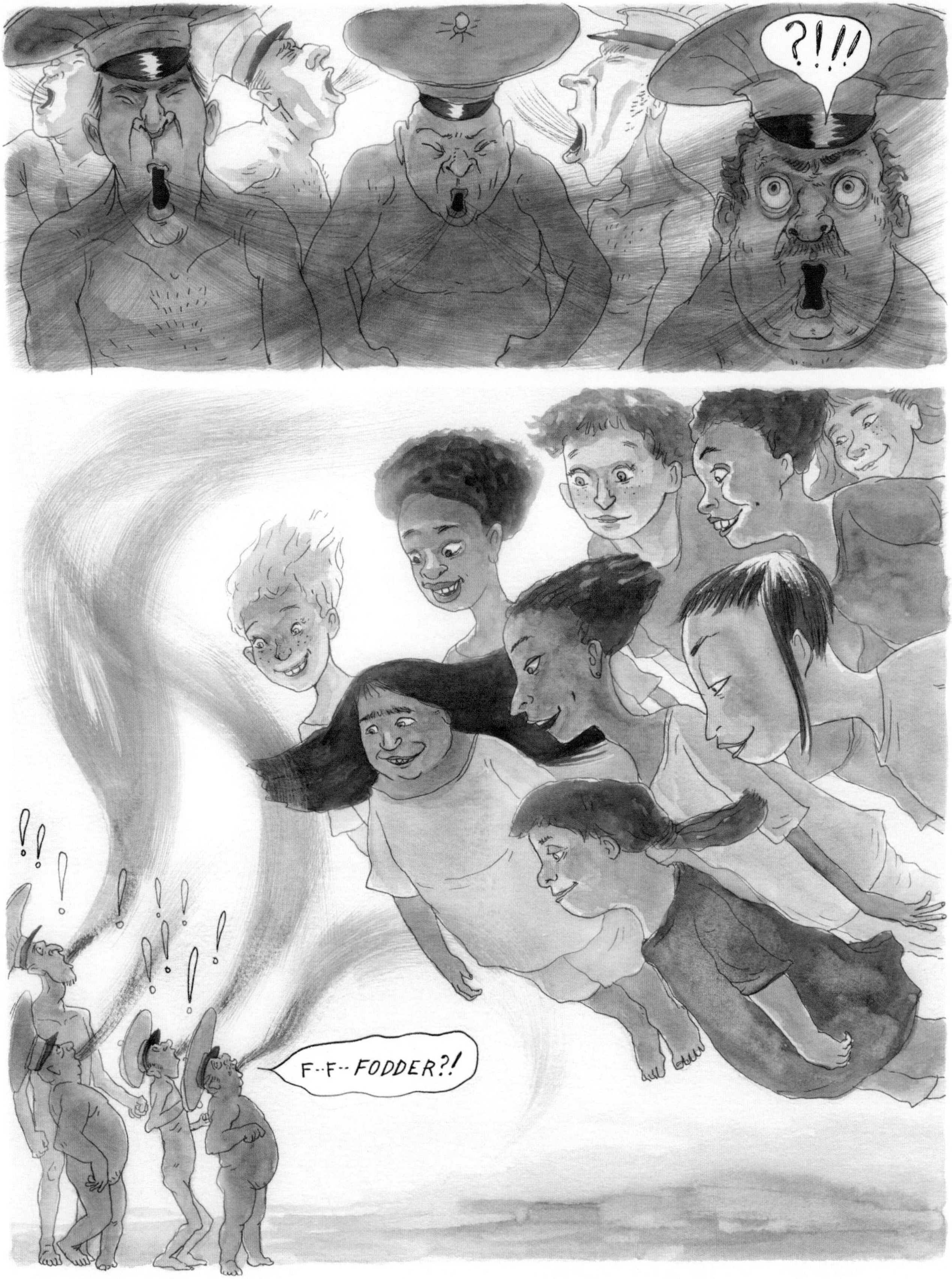
?!!!
!!
!
!
!
!
!
!
!
!
F--F--FODDER?!

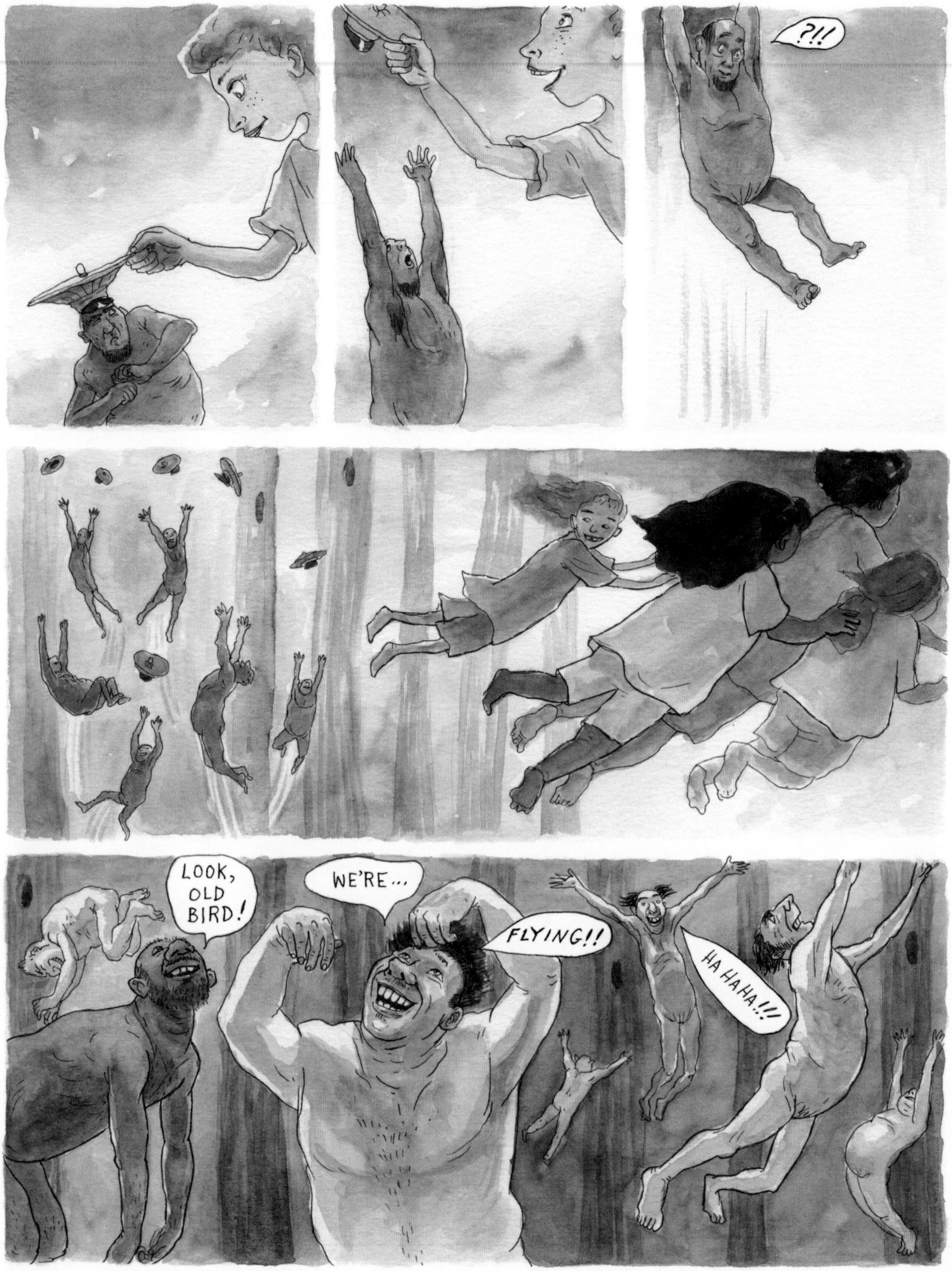
?!!
LOOK, OLD BIRD!
WE'RE...
FLYING!!
HA HAHA!!!

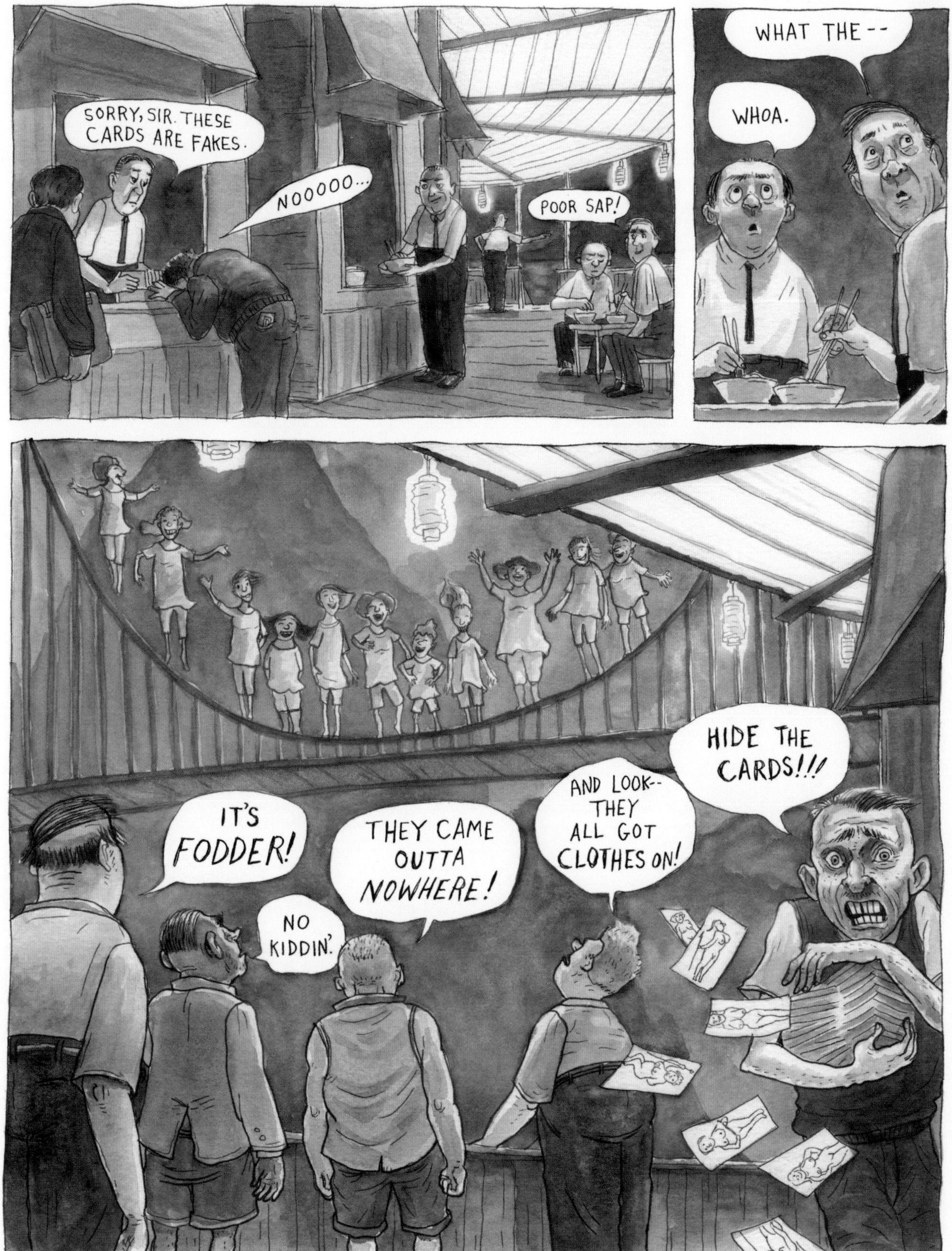
SORRY, SIR. THESE CARDS ARE FAKES.
NOOOOO...
POOR SAP!
WHAT THE--
WHOA.
IT'S FODDER!
NO KIDDIN'.
THEY CAME OUTTA NOWHERE!
AND LOOK-- THEY ALL GOT CLOTHES ON!
HIDE THE CARDS!!!

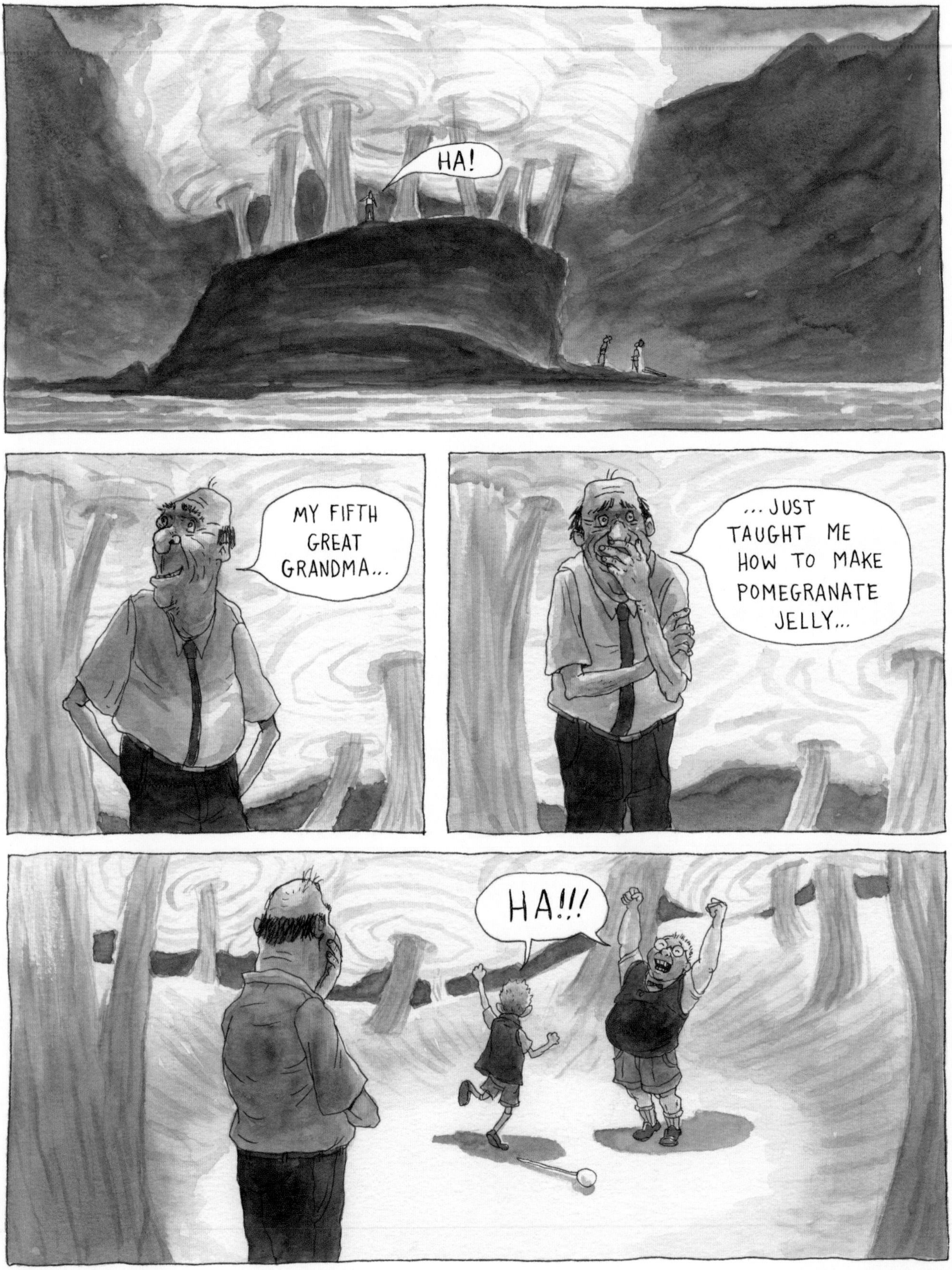
HA!
MY FIFTH GREAT GRANDMA...
...JUST TAUGHT ME HOW TO MAKE POMEGRANATE JELLY...
HA!!!

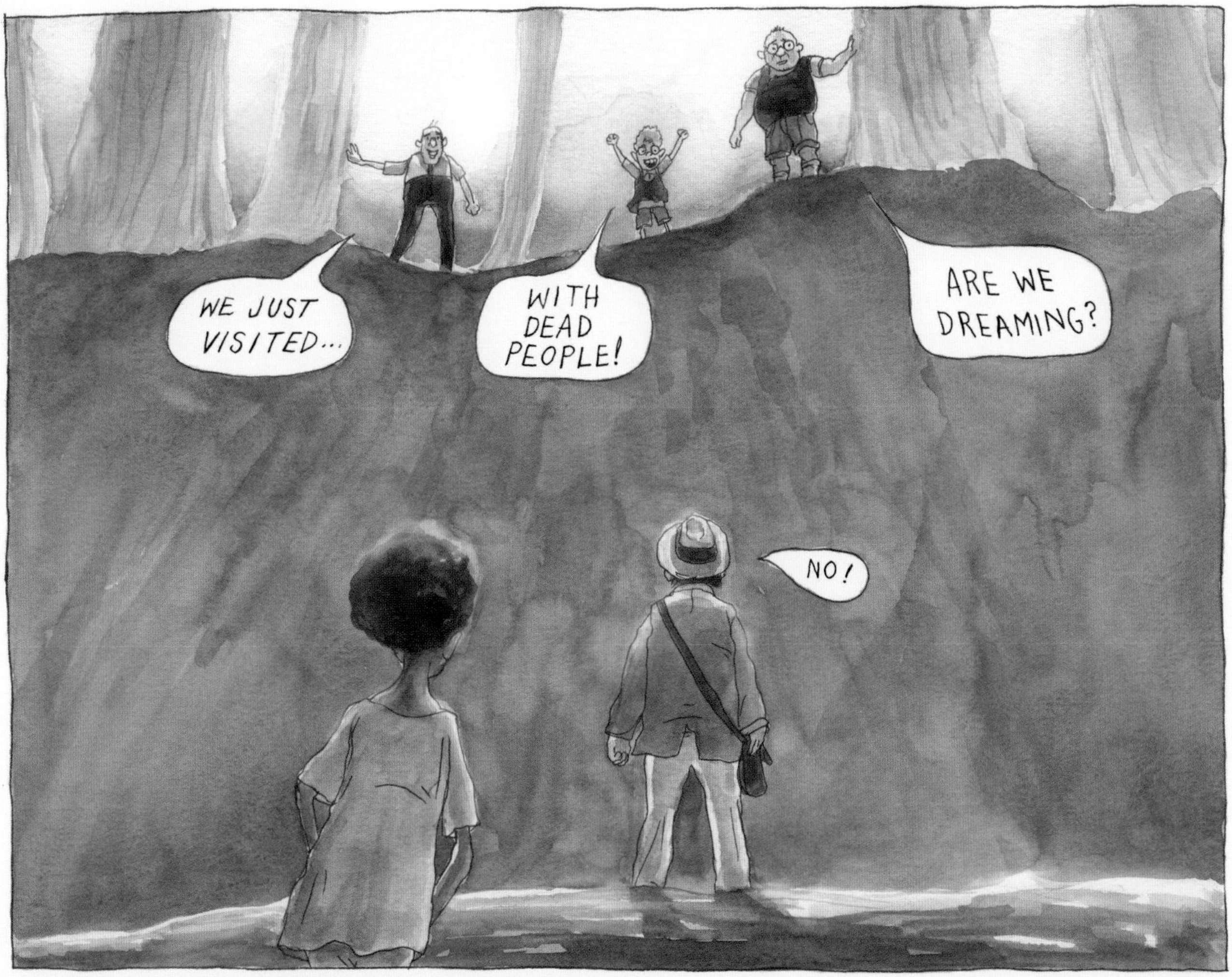
WE JUST VISITED...
WITH DEAD PEOPLE!
ARE WE DREAMING?
NO!

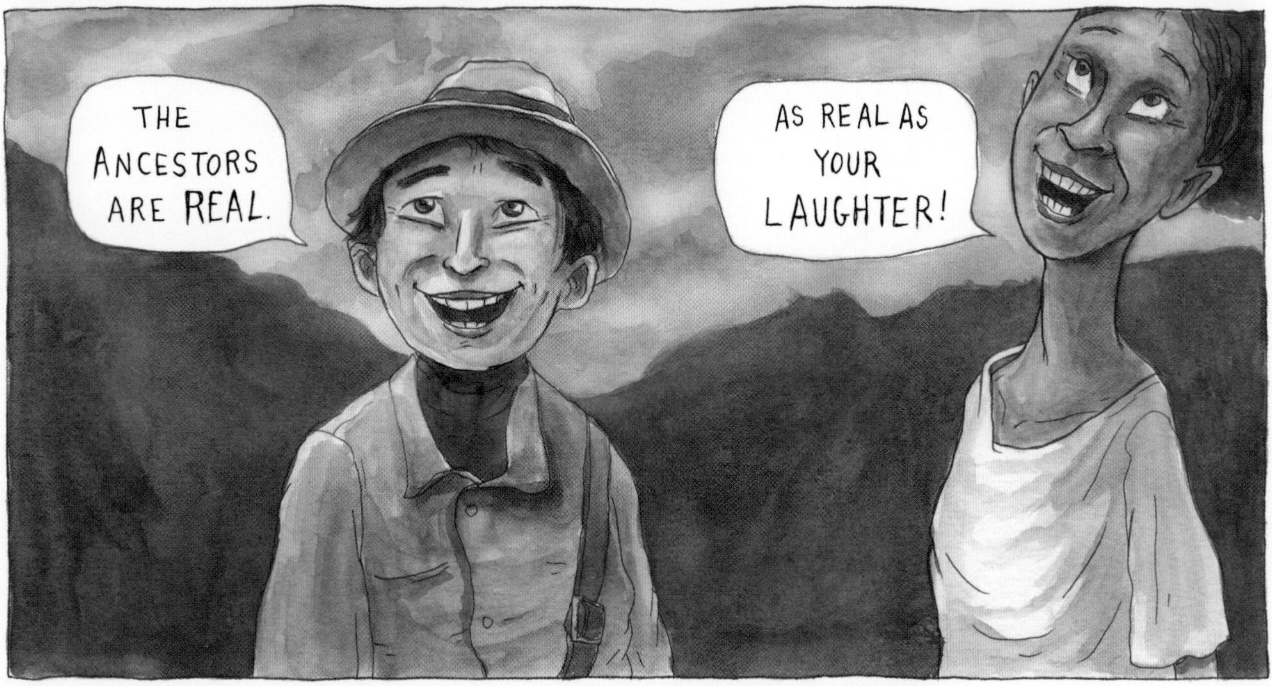
THE ANCESTORS ARE REAL.
AS REAL AS YOUR LAUGHTER!

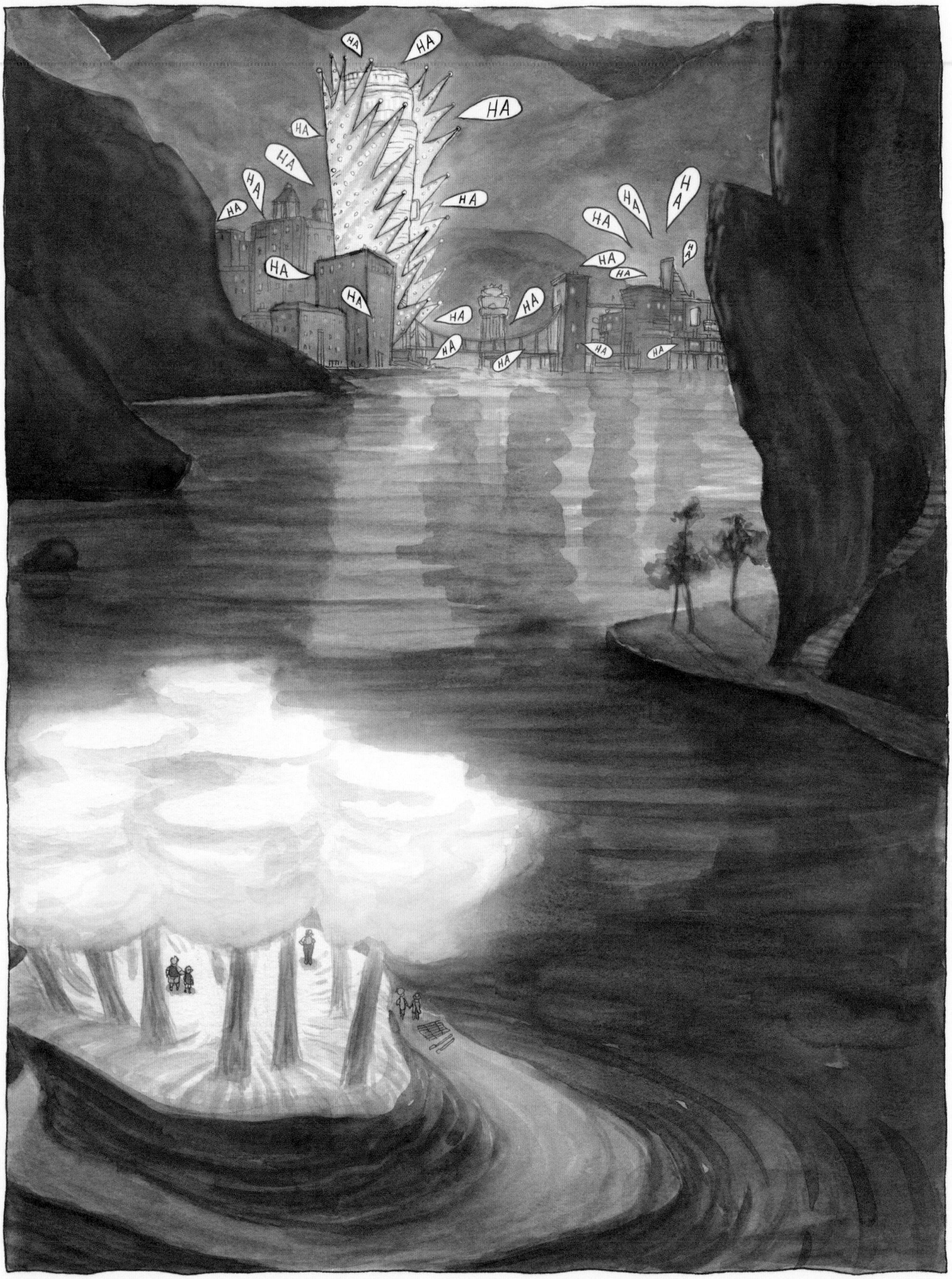
HA
HA
HA
HA
HA
HA
HA
HA
HA
HA
HA
HA
HA
HA
HA
HA
HA
HA
HA
HA
HA
HA
HA
HA
HA

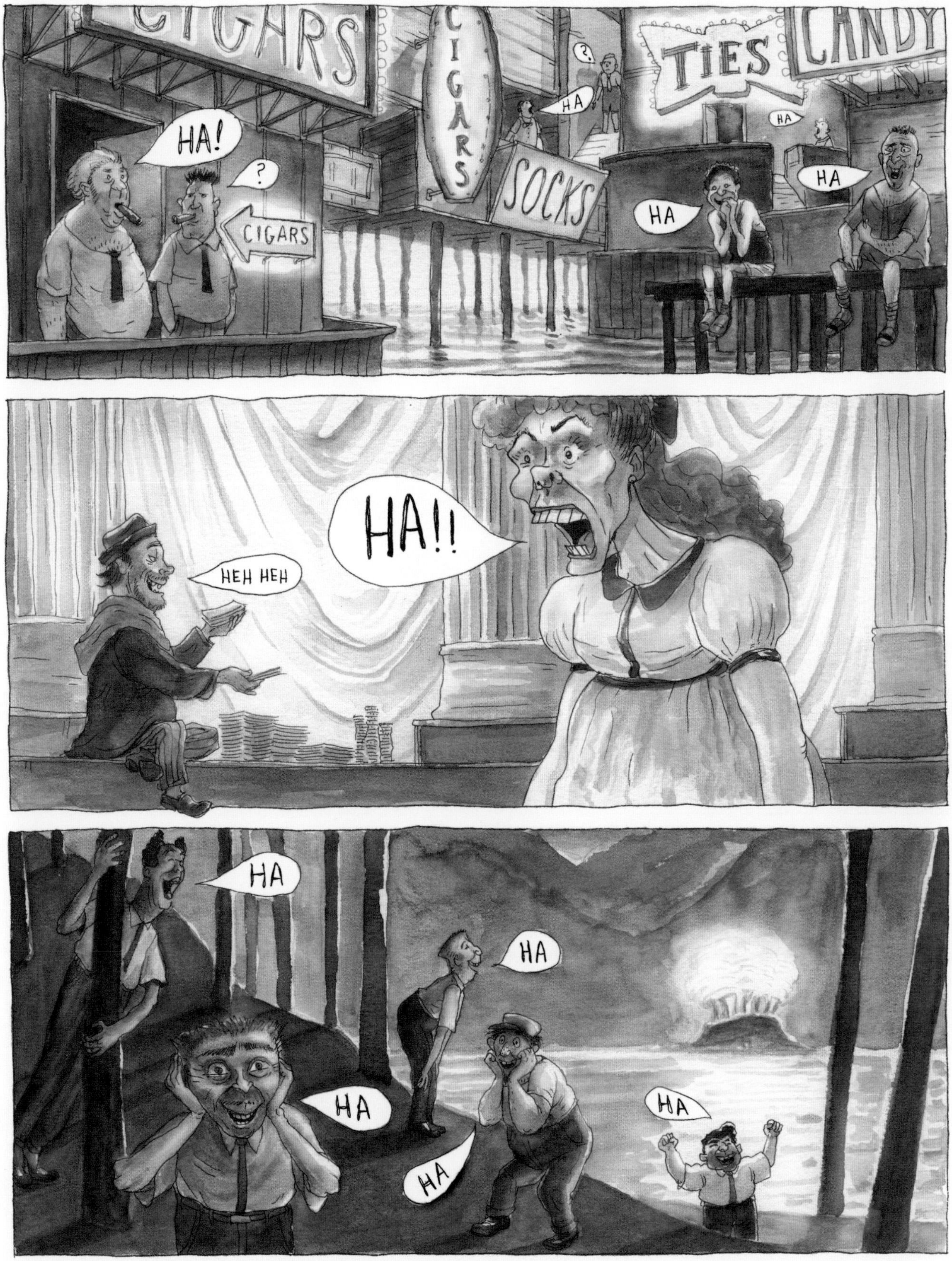
CIGARS
CIGARS
TIES
CANDY
?
HA
HA!
HA
?
CIGARS
SOCKS
HA
HA
HA!!
HEH HEH
HA
HA
HA
HA
HA

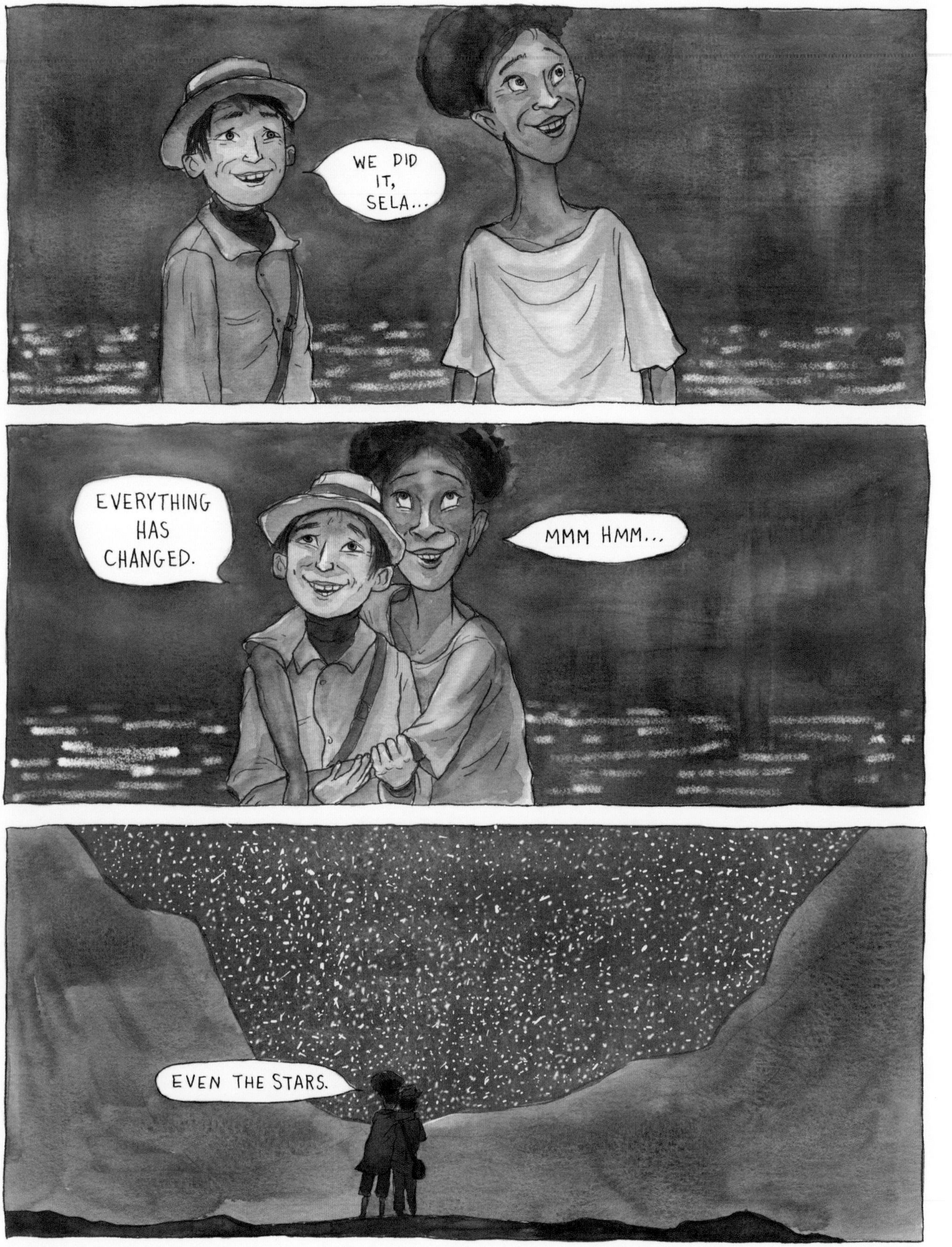
WE DID IT, SELA...
EVERYTHING HAS CHANGED.
MMM HMM...
EVEN THE STARS.

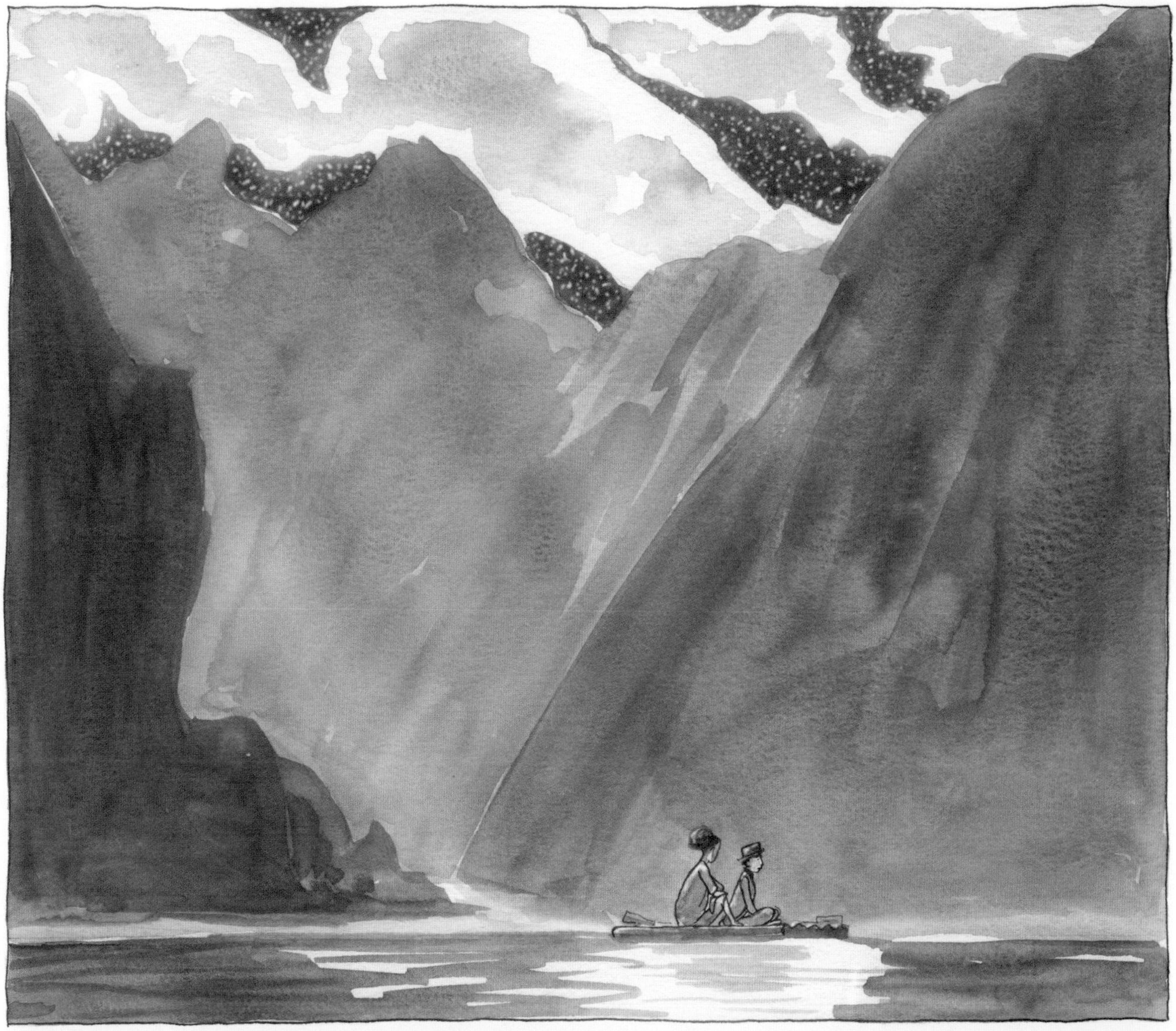

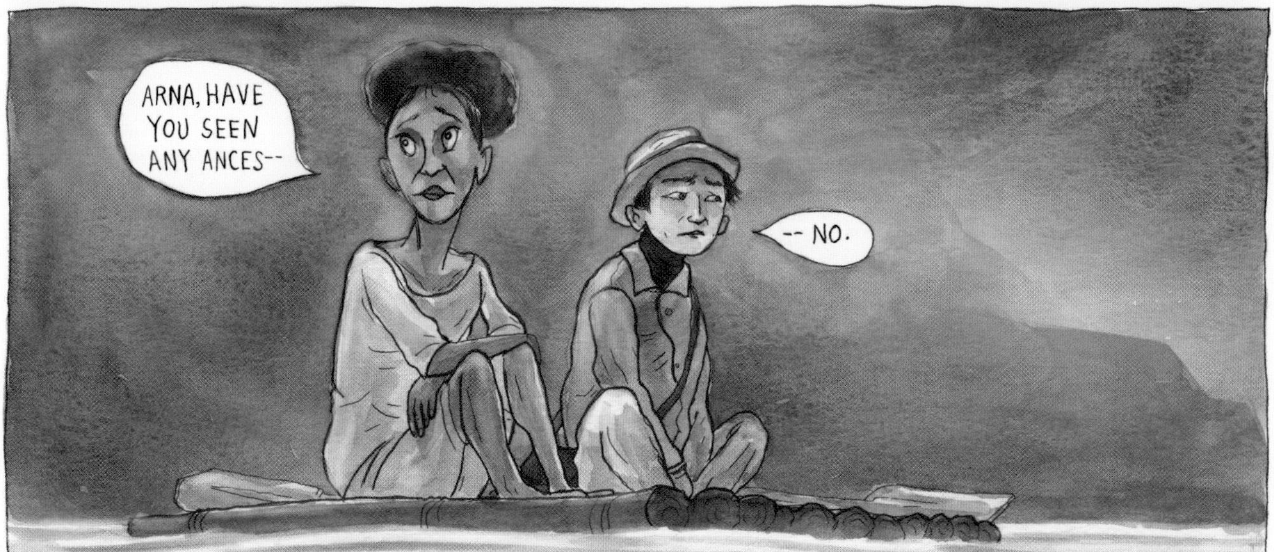
ARNA, HAVE YOU SEEN ANY ANCES--
-- NO.

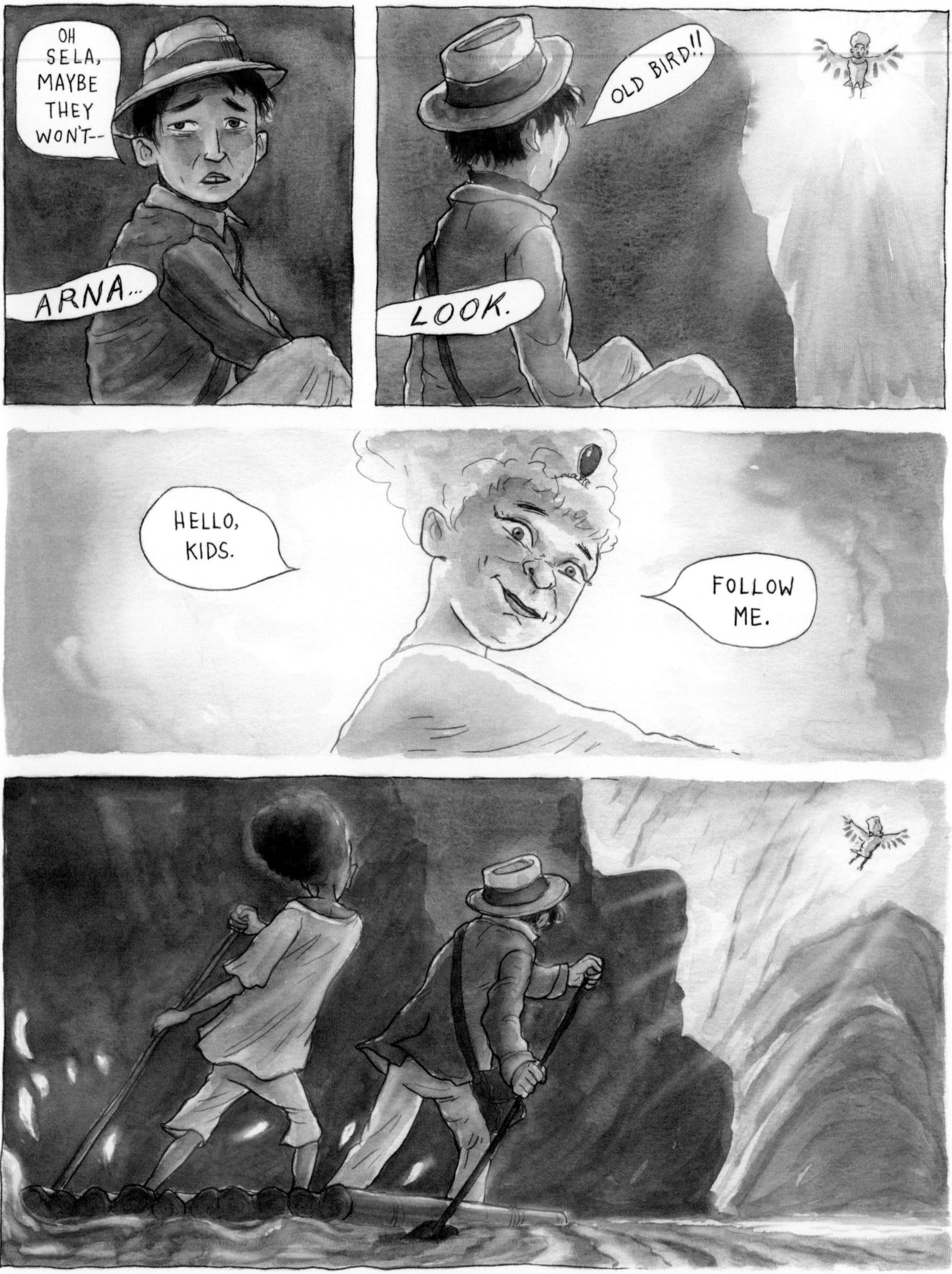
OH SELA, MAYBE THEY WON'T--
ARNA...
OLD BIRD!!
LOOK.
HELLO, KIDS.
FOLLOW ME.

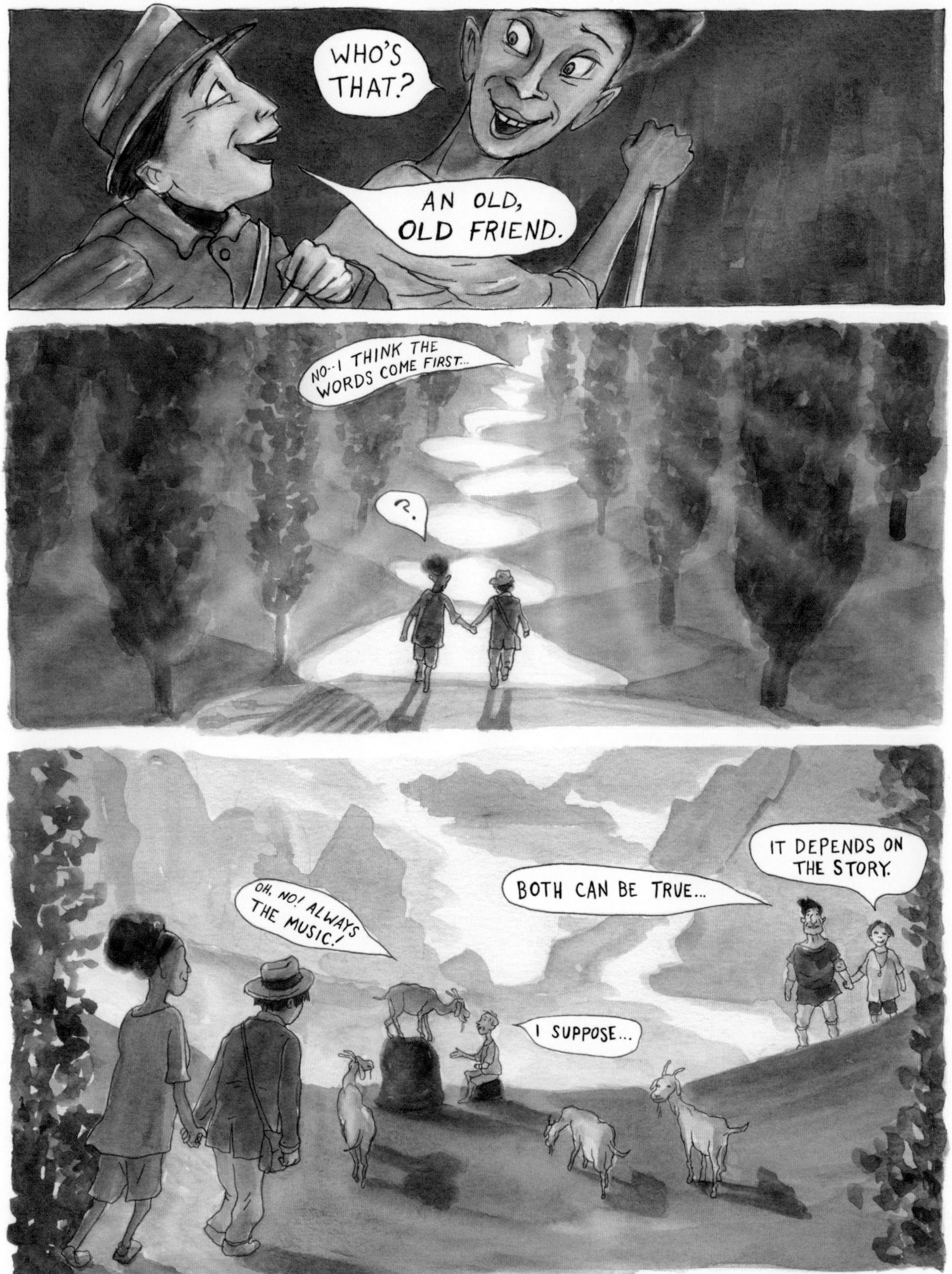
WHO'S THAT?
AN OLD, OLD FRIEND.
NO--I THINK THE WORDS COME FIRST...
?
OH, NO! ALWAYS THE MUSIC!
BOTH CAN BE TRUE...
IT DEPENDS ON THE STORY.
I SUPPOSE...

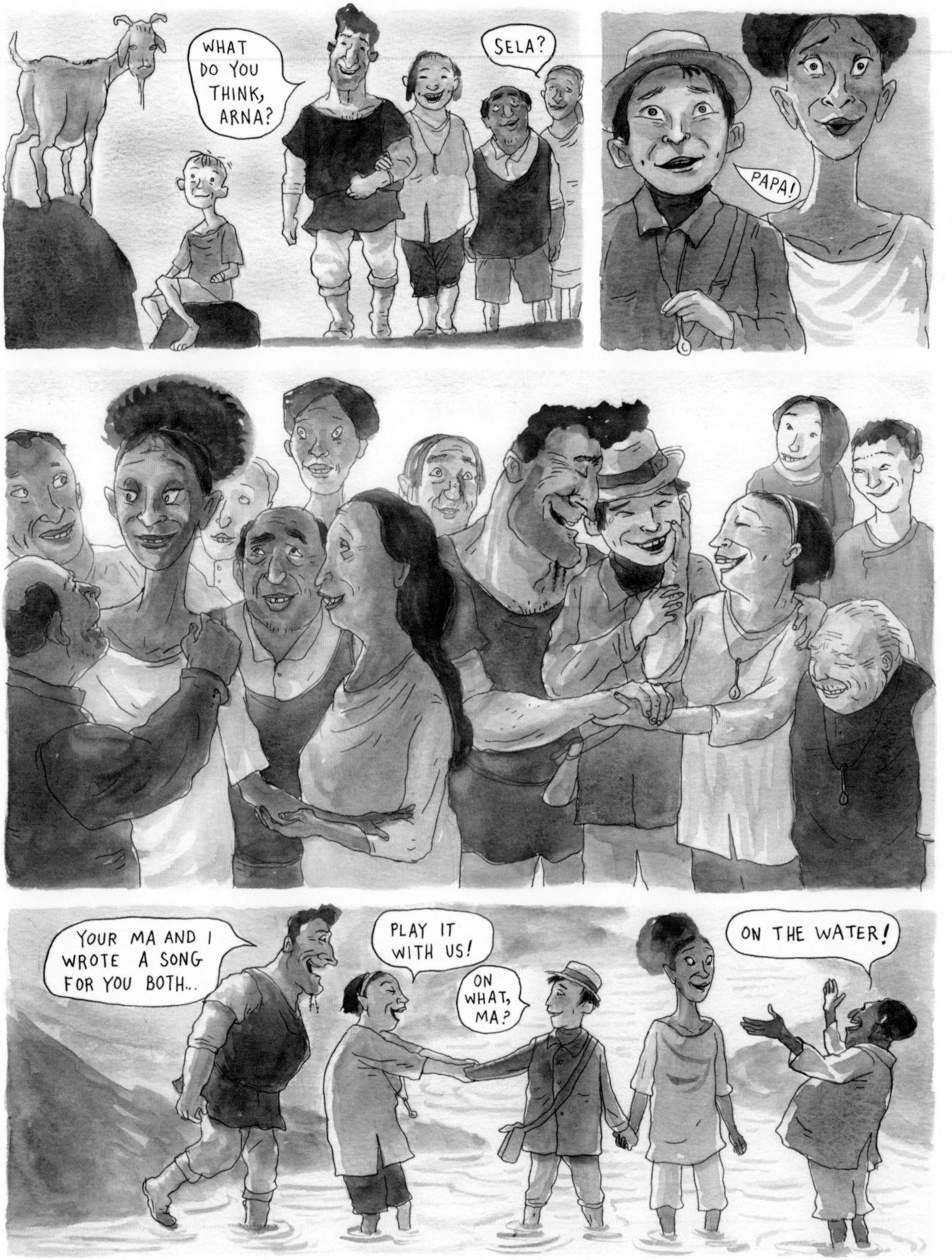
WHAT DO YOU THINK, ARNA?
SELA?
PAPA!
YOUR MA AND I WROTE A SONG FOR YOU BOTH...
PLAY IT WITH US!
ON WHAT, MA?
ON THE WATER!

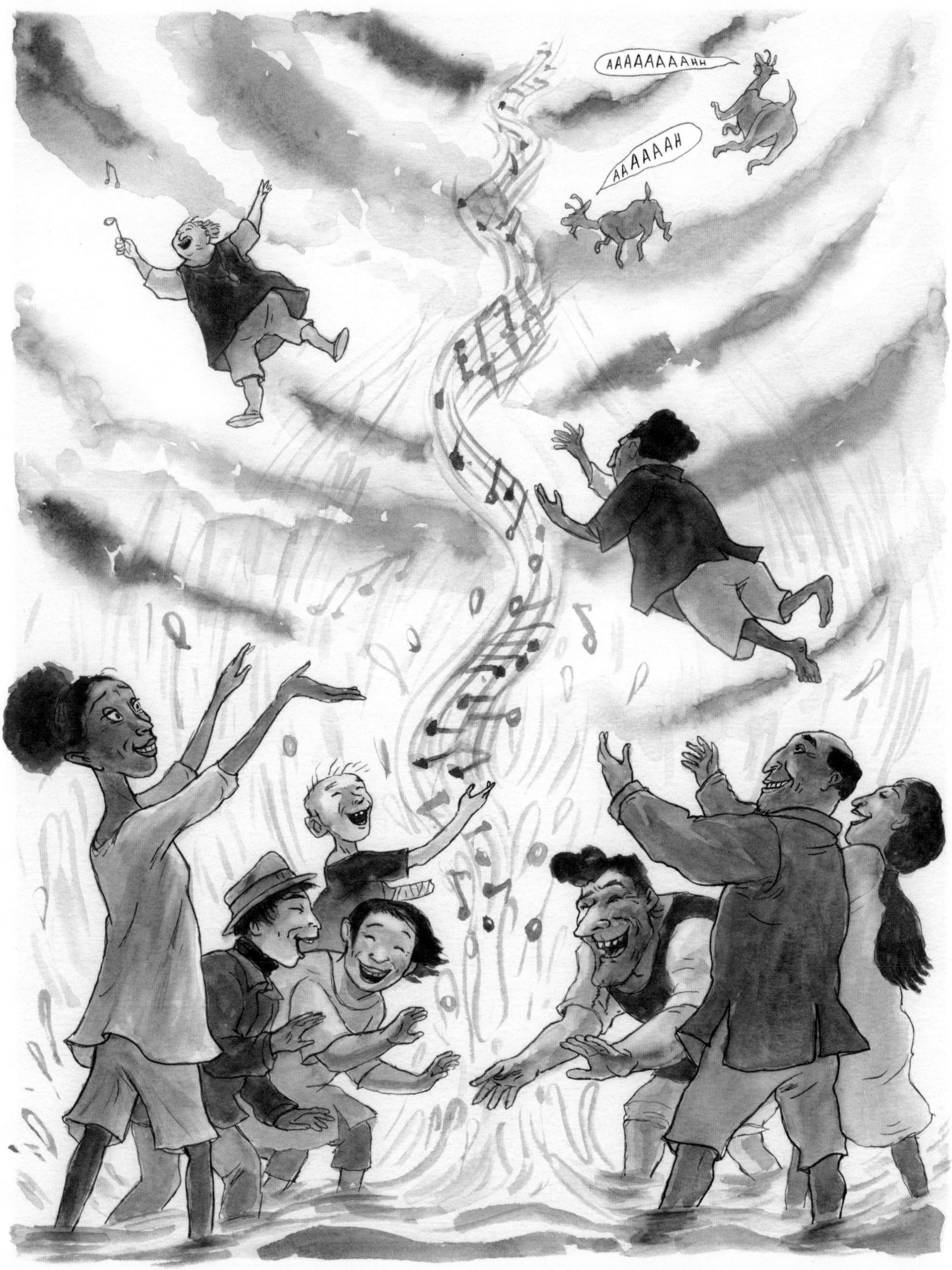
AAAAAAAAHH
AAAAAAH

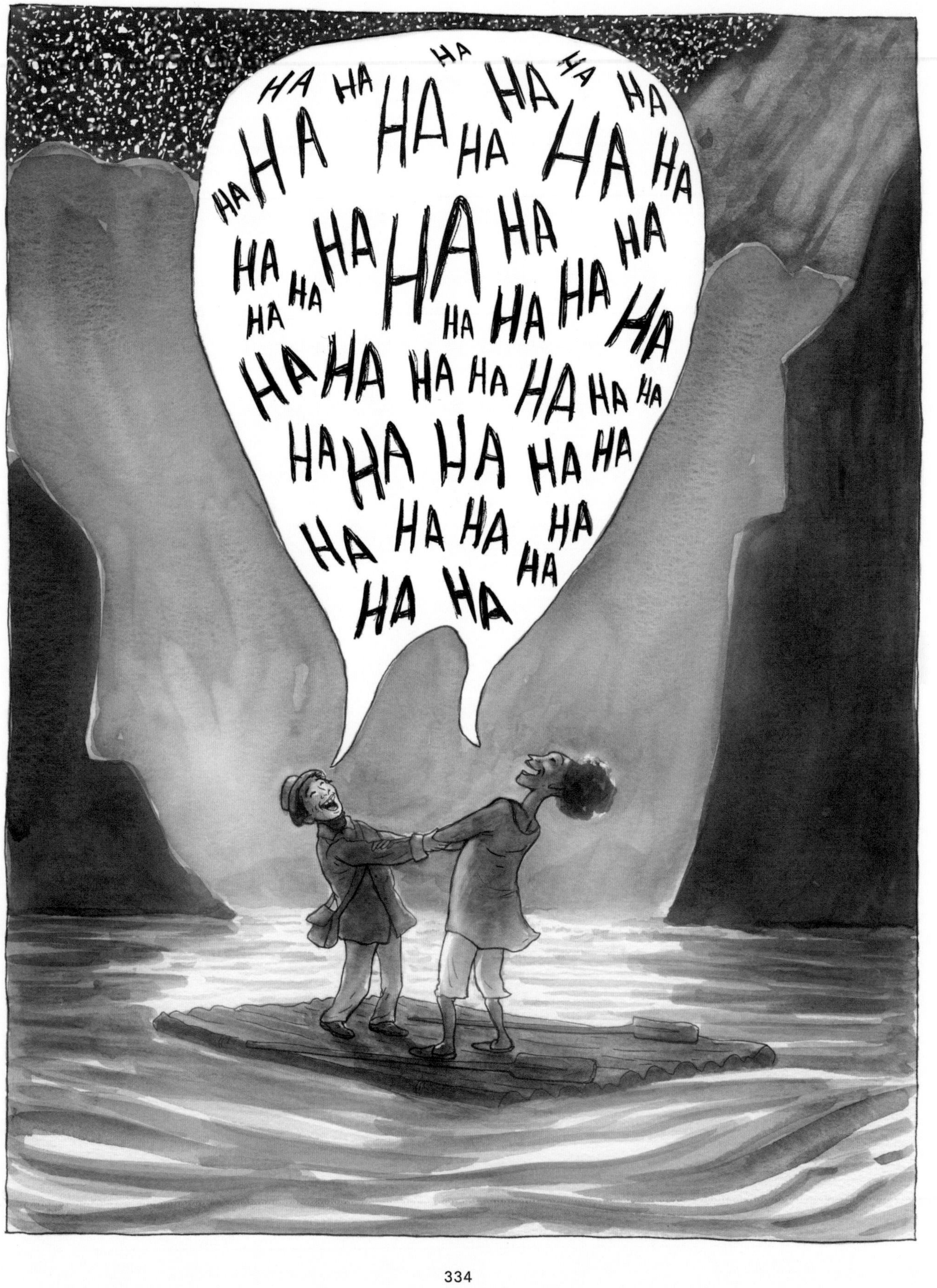
HA HA HA HA HA HA HA HA HA HA HA HA HA HA HA HA HA HA HA HA HA HA HA HA HA HA HA HA HA HA HA HA HA HA HA HA HA HA HA HA HA HA

CATHY MALKASIAN HAS BEEN KNOWN TO CONJURE INTRICATE, RICHLY IMAGINED FANTASY WORLDS OUT OF SOFT PENCIL AND LUSH WATERCOLORS. HER POIGNANT ALLEGORIES OFTEN STAR GENTLEHEARTED DREAMERS WHO MUST FACE SHADOWY BUREAUCRACIES AND OTHER SOCIETAL INJUSTICES THAT FEEL ALL TOO FAMILIAR. AGAINST ALL ODDS, GOODNESS TENDS TO WIN OUT IN THE END. AS AN ANIMATION DIRECTOR, SHE'S WORKED ON *THE WILD THORNBERRYS MOVIE* (FOR WHICH SHE RECEIVED A BRITISH ACADEMY AWARD NOMINATION), AND THE *CURIOUS GEORGE* PBS SERIES. AS A CARTOONIST, SHE'S CREATED MANY GRAPHIC NOVELS, INCLUDING *PERCY GLOOM* (2007) AND *WAKE UP, PERCY GLOOM!* (2013), *TEMPERANCE* (2010), *EARTHA* (2017), AND *NOBODY LIKES YOU, GRETA GRUMP* (2021). SHE SINCERELY HOPES THAT YOU HAVE BEEN ENTERTAINED (AND MAYBE EVEN A LITTLE ENLIGHTENED) BY HER STORIES.

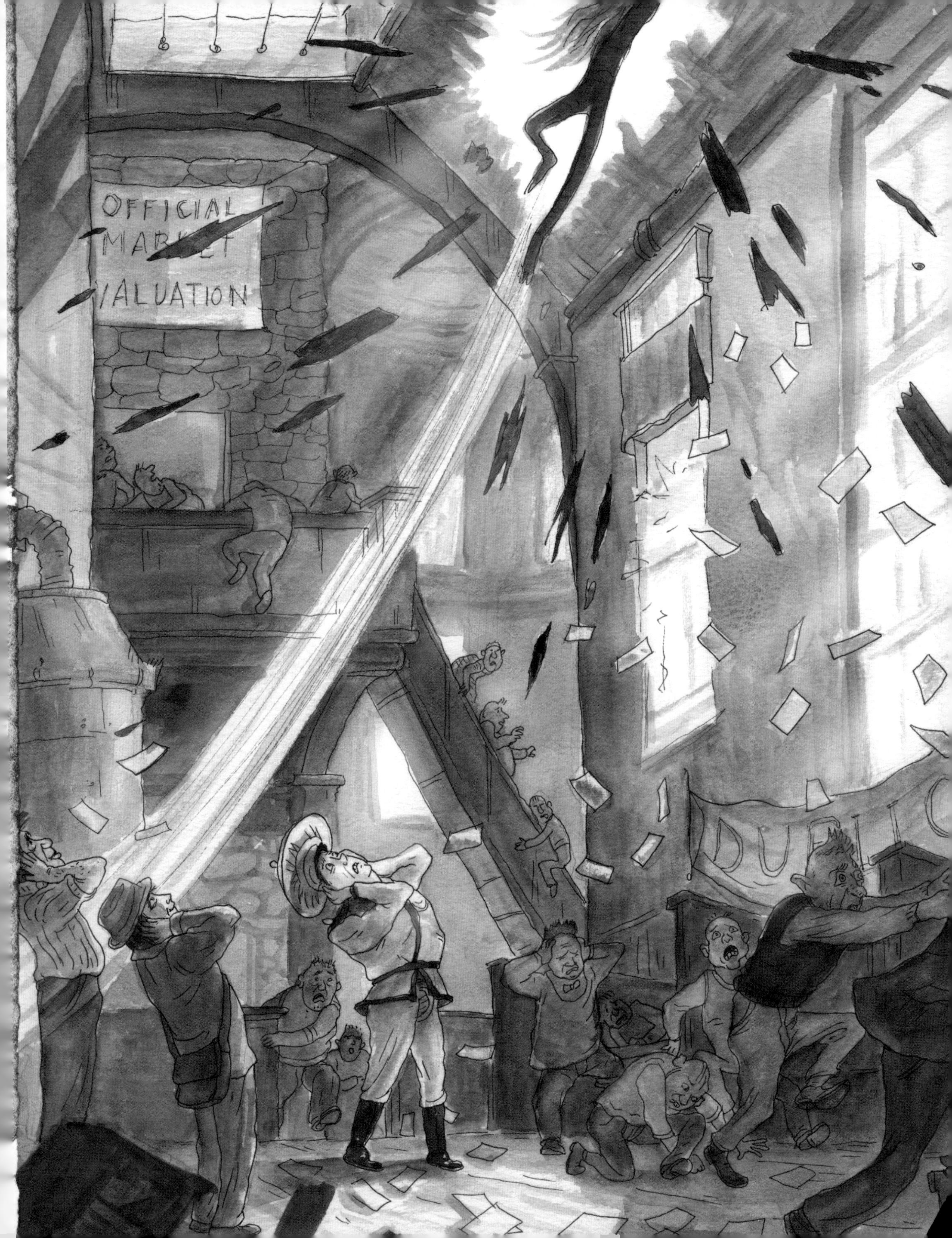
OFFICIAL

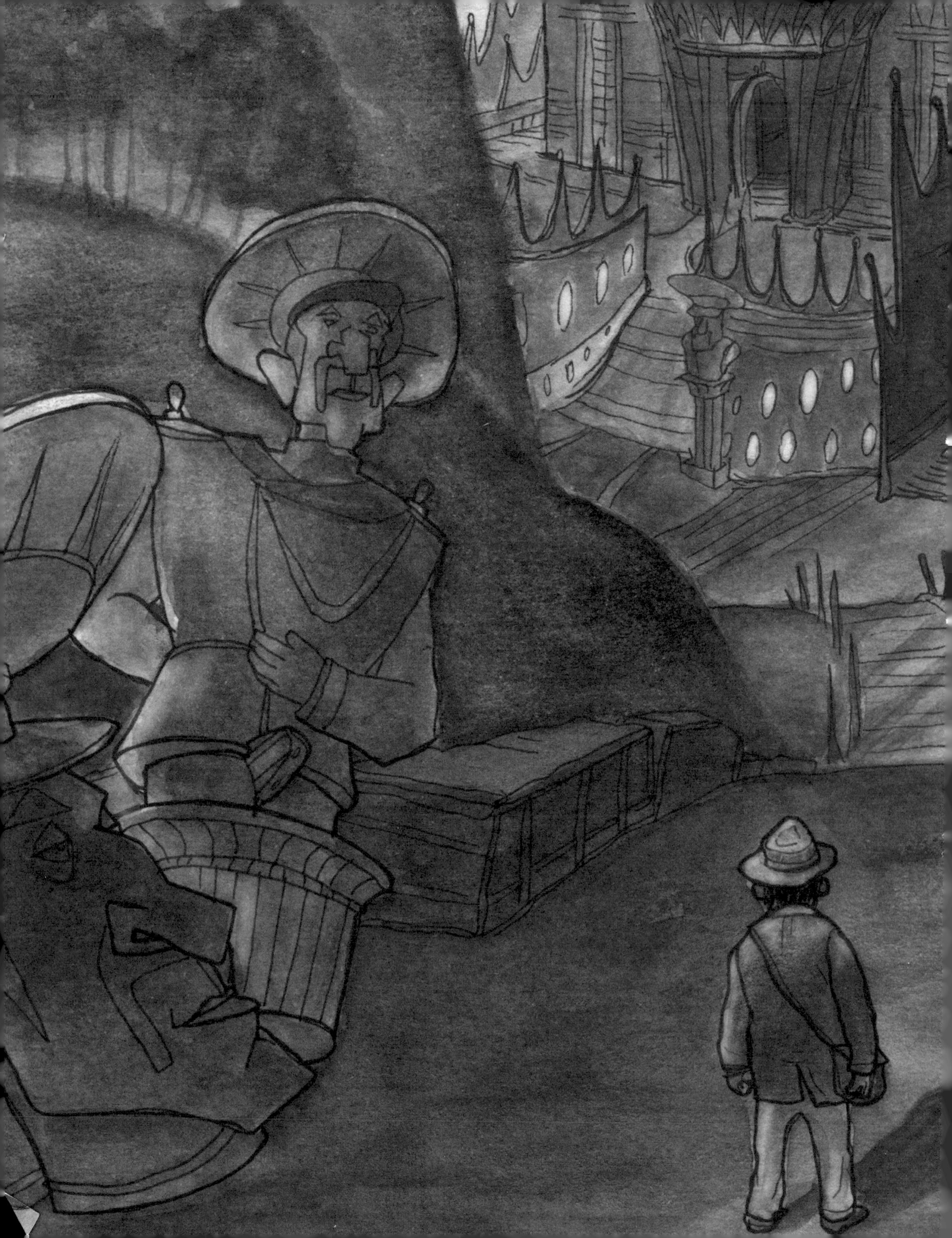